WEB SITES FOR ACCOUNTANTS

Standard Setting:

Financial Accounting Standards Board, http://www.fasb.org

Governmental Finance Officers Association, http://www.gfoa.org

International Accounting Standards Board, http://www.iasb.org

Regulatory:

Internal Revenue Service, http://www.irs.gov

Public Company Accounting Oversight Board, http://www.pcaobus.org

Securities and Exchange Commission, http://www.sec.gov

Other:

American Accounting Association, http://www.aaahq.org

American Institute of Certified Public Accountants, http://www.aicpa.org

Association of Certified Fraud Examiners, http://www.cfenet.com

Association of Governmental Accountants, http://www.agacgfm.org

Center for Corporate Financial Leadership, http://www.ccflinfo.org

Financial Executives International, http://www.fei.org

Financial Planning Interactive, http://www.financial-planning.com

Information Systems Audit and Control Association, http://www.isaca.org

Institute of Internal Auditors, http://www.theiia.org

Institute of Management Accountants, http://www.imanet.org

International Federation of Accountants, http://www.ifac.org

National Association of Corporate Directors, http://www.nacdonline.org

Rutgers Accounting Web, http://www.accounting.rutgers.edu

Securities and Exchange Commission, http://www.sec.gov

Tax Web, http://www.taxweb.com

Yahoo Finance, http://www.finance.yahoo.com

Fundamentals of
Advanced Accounting

Paul Marcus Fischer, PhD, CPA
Jerry Leer Professor of Accounting
University of Wisconsin, Milwaukee

William James Taylor, PhD, CPA, CVA
Professor Emeritus of Accounting
University of Wisconsin, Milwaukee

Rita Hartung Cheng, PhD, CPA
Professor of Accounting
University of Wisconsin, Milwaukee

SOUTH-WESTERN
CENGAGE Learning

Australia · Brazil · Canada · Mexico · Singapore · Spain · United Kingdom · United States

SOUTH-WESTERN
CENGAGE Learning

Fundamentals of Advanced Accounting
Paul M. Fischer, William J. Taylor, Rita H. Cheng

VP/Editorial Director
Jack W. Calhoun

Publisher
Rob Dewey

Acquisitions Editor
Matthew Filimonov

Associate Developmental Editor
Jessica Kempf

Marketing Manager
Kristen Hurd

Senior Content Project Manager
Tim Bailey

Manager, Editorial Media
John Barans

Technology Project Manager
Scott Hamilton

Web Site Project Manager
Brian Courter

Manufacturing Frontlist Buyer
Doug Wilke

Production House
LEAP Publishing Services, Inc.

Compositor
Cadmus Communications

Art Director
Linda Helcher

Cover and Internal Designer
Stratton Design

Cover Image
Stone/Robin Smith

Printer
Transcontinental Gagné
Louiseville, Quebec

Library of Congress Control Number:
2007920847

For more information about our
products, contact us at:
Cengage Learning
Customer & Sales Support,
1-800-354-9706

South-Western
5191 Natorp Boulevard
Mason, OH 45040
USA

Brief Contents

Preface   viii

Acknowledgments   xv

About the Authors   xvi

Part 1
Combined Corporate Entities and Consolidations

Chapter 1
Business Combinations: America's Most Popular Business Activity, Bringing an End to the Controversy   1

Chapter 2
Consolidated Statements: Date of Acquisition   57

Chapter 3
Consolidated Statements: Subsequent to Acquisition   109

Chapter 4
Intercompany Transactions: Merchandise, Plant Assets, and Notes   181

Chapter 5
Intercompany Bonds, Cash Flow, EPS, and Unconsolidated Investments   227

Special Appendix
Analysis of FASB Exposure Drafts for Business Combinations by Impact on Chapters 1–5   293

Part 2
Multinational Accounting and Other Reporting Concerns

Chapter 6
Foreign Currency Transactions   325

Chapter 7
Translation of Foreign Financial Statements   369

Part 3
Partnerships

Chapter 8
Partnerships: Characteristics, Formation, and Accounting for Activities   431

Chapter 9
Partnerships: Ownership Changes and Liquidations   455

Part 4
Governmental and Not-for-Profit Accounting

Chapter 10
Governmental Accounting: The General Fund and the Account Groups (including Other Governmental Funds, Proprietary Funds, and Fiduciary Funds)   497

Chapter 11
Financial Reporting Issues   555

Chapter 12
Accounting for Private Not-for-Profit Organizations (including Colleges and Universities and Health Care Organizations)   589

Index of APB and FASB Pronouncements   643

City of Milwaukee, Wisconsin Comprehensive Annual Financial Report For the Year Ended December 31, 2004   651

Index   670

Contents

Preface   viii
Acknowledgments   xv
About the Authors   xvi

Part 1
Combined Corporate Entities and Consolidations

Chapter 1
Business Combinations: America's Most Popular Business Activity, Bringing an End to the Controversy   1

Economic Advantages of Combinations   3

Tax Advantages of Combinations 3

Obtaining Control   4

Accounting Ramifications of Control 5

Purchase versus Pooling   6
Valuation under the Purchase Method   7

Assigning Value to Assets and Liabilities 8   Recording Goodwill 8

Recording a Purchase with Goodwill   10

Entry to Record the Purchase 11   Required Disclosure 12   Accounting for the Purchase by the Selling Company 18

Accounting for the Acquired Assets and Liabilities after the Purchase   19

Tangible Assets and All Liabilities 19   Separately Identified Intangible Assets 20   Example of Future Effects 20   Goodwill Impairment 21

Recording a Bargain Purchase   26

Priority Accounts 26   Applying the Priorities 26   FASB Exposure Draft 28

Purchase Accounting: Added Considerations   29

Expenditures to Accomplish Business Combination 29   Revaluation of Long-Term Liabilities 29   Lease Agreements 30   Nontaxable Exchanges 31   Contingent Consideration Included in the Purchase Agreement 32

Transition Issues   35
Appendix: Calculating and Recording Goodwill   36

Chapter 2
Consolidated Statements: Date of Acquisition   57

Levels of Investment   58

The Function of Consolidated Statements   59

Traditional Criteria for Consolidated Statements 60   Consolidation Based on Control 60

Techniques of Consolidation   61

Reviewing an Asset Acquisition 61   Consolidating a Stock Acquisition 63

Adjustment of Subsidiary Accounts   64

Analysis of Complicated Purchases—100% Interest 65   Bargain Purchases—100% Interest 70   Extraordinary Gain—100% Interest 72

Consolidating a Less than 100% Interest   75

Analysis of Complicated Purchase—Less than 100% Interest 75

Preexisting Goodwill   81

Existing Goodwill in a Bargain 83

Push-Down Accounting   84

Chapter 3
Consolidated Statements: Subsequent to Acquisition   109

Accounting for the Investment in a Subsidiary   109

Equity Method 110   Cost Method 110   Example of the Equity and Cost Methods 111

Elimination Procedures   112

Effect of Simple Equity Method on Consolidation 112   Effect of Cost Method on Consolidation 117   Effect of Sophisticated Equity Method on Consolidation 119   Determination of the Method Being Used 120

Complicated Purchase, Several Distributions of Excess   121
Intraperiod Purchase under the Simple Equity Method   128

Intraperiod Purchase under the Cost Method 131

Summary: Worksheet Technique   132
Goodwill Impairment Losses   132
Appendix: Tax-Related Adjustments   134

Chapter 4
Intercompany Transactions: Merchandise, Plant Assets, and Notes   181

Intercompany Merchandise Sales   181

No Intercompany Goods in Purchasing Company's Inventories 183   Intercompany Goods in Purchasing Company's Ending Inventory 185   Intercompany Goods in Purchasing Company's Beginning and Ending Inventories 187   Eliminations for Periodic Inventories 188   Effect of Lower-of-Cost-or-Market

Method on Inventory Profit 189   Losses on
Intercompany Sales 189

Intercompany Plant Asset Sales   190

Intercompany Sale of a Nondepreciable
Asset 190   Intercompany Sale of a Depreciable
Asset 192

Intercompany Debt   194

Chapter 5
Intercompany Bonds, Cash Flow,
EPS, and Unconsolidated
Investments   227

Intercompany Investment in Bonds   227

Bonds Originally Issued at Face Value 228   Bonds
Not Originally Issued at Face Value 231   Purchase
of Only a Portion of the Bonds 232   Interest Method
of Amortization 233

Consolidated Statement of Cash Flows   235

Cash Acquisition of Controlling Interest 235   Noncash
Acquisition of Controlling Interest 236   Adjustments
Resulting from Business Combinations 237
Preparation of Consolidated Statement of
Cash Flows 238

Consolidated Earnings Per Share   242
Equity Method for Unconsolidated
Investments   246

Calculation of Equity Income 246   Unusual Equity
Adjustments 249   Disclosure Requirements 251

Appendix: The Vertical Worksheet   251

Special Appendix
Analysis of FASB Exposure Drafts for
Business Combinations by Impact
on Chapters 1–5   293

Summary of Major Changes   293
Changes As They Impact Each Chapter   294
Chapter 1   294
Chapter 1 Exercises and Problems   297
Chapter 2   298

Determination and Distribution of Excess
Schedule 299   Formal Balance Sheet 301   Adjustment
of Goodwill Applicable to NCI 301   Gain on
Purchase of Subsidiary 303   Valuation Schedule
Strategy 305   Gain on Parent Asset Transferred to
Subsidiary to Acquire Interest 306

Chapter 2 Exercises and Problems   309
Chapter 3   311
Chapter 3 Problems   319
Chapter 4   321
Chapter 5   322

Part 2
Multinational Accounting and
Other Reporting Concerns

Chapter 6
Foreign Currency Transactions   325

The International Monetary System   326

Alternative International Monetary Systems 326
The Mechanics of Exchange Rates 327

Accounting for Foreign Currency
Transactions   330

Unsettled Foreign Currency Transactions 331

The Exposure to Foreign Currency
Exchange Risk and the Use
of Derivatives   333

Derivatives: Characteristics and Types 334

Characteristics of Derivatives   335
Common Types of Derivatives   335
Accounting for Derivatives that are
Designated as a Hedge   338

Special Accounting for Fair Value Hedges 338
Special Accounting for Cash Flow Hedges 340

Examples of the Accounting for
Fair Value Hedges   340

Hedging an Existing Foreign Currency Denominated
Asset or Liability 340   Special Hedging
Complications 345   Hedging an Identifiable
Foreign Currency Firm Commitment 346

Examples of the Accounting
for Cash Flow Hedges   351

Hedging a Foreign Currency Forecasted
Transaction 351   Summary of Hedging
Transactions 358   Disclosures Regarding Hedges
of Foreign Currency Exposure 360

Chapter 7
Translation of Foreign Financial
Statements   369

Statement of Financial Accounting
Standards No. 52   371

Functional Currency Identification 372   Objectives
of the Translation Process 374

Basic Translation Process: Functional
Currency to Reporting Currency   382

Demonstrating the Current Rate/Functional
Method 383   Consolidating the Foreign
Subsidiary 387   Gains and Losses Excluded from
Income 389   Unconsolidated Investments: Translation
for the Cost or Equity Method 391

Advanced Leadership

INNOVATION

Fundamentals of Advanced Accounting by Paul Fischer, William Taylor, and Rita Cheng continues the tradition of excellence maintained by the nine editions of *Advanced Accounting* by the same author team. This text maintains the innovative coverage of advanced topics essential for the practice of accounting and for the CPA Exam. The end result is a valuable and useful resource for both the present and the future. Fischer/Taylor/Cheng's *Fundamentals of Advanced Accounting* offers the learner the ability to understand and apply new knowledge like The Advanced Text has, but for a narrower set of topics. Leading the way are these unique, innovative and helpful features:

- ◆ **Excelling with ease—An easy-to-follow Excel tutorial and convenient electronic working papers on the companion web site academic.cengage.com/accounting/fischer:**

  - ◆ This unique tutorial teaches a step-by-step process for completing consolidations worksheets in an Excel-based environment. The tutorial makes it possible to master consolidations worksheets more quickly.
  - ◆ The tutorial guides the student through the creation of Excel worksheets. Each chapter of the tutorial adds the consolidations processes to parallel those presented in Chapters 2–5 and Chapter 7 of the text.
  - ◆ The electronic working papers in Excel format provide students with the basic worksheet structure for selected assignments throughout the text. These assignments are identified in the text by the icon shown here.

- ◆ **Comprehending through consistency—Common coding for the worksheets:**

  - ◆ All consolidations worksheets use a common coding for the eliminations and adjustments. A complete listing of the codes is presented on the inside of the front cover. Students are now able to quickly recall worksheet adjustments as they move from one chapter to the next.
  - ◆ Within the chapter narrative, the worksheet eliminations and adjustments are shown in journal entry form and are referenced using the same coding. This provides consistent reinforcement of the consolidations process and aids students in their understanding of the worksheet procedures. An example of the coding follows:

(CY1)	Eliminate current-year equity income:		
	Subsidiary Income..	60,000	
	Investment in Company S..............................		60,000
(EL)	Eliminate 80% of subsidiary equity against investment in subsidiary account:		
	Common Stock ($10 par), Company S...................	80,000	
	Retained Earnings, January 1, 20X1, Company S..........	56,000	
	Investment in Company S..............................		136,000
(IS)	Eliminate intercompany merchandise sales:		
	Sales..	100,000	
	Cost of Goods Sold..................................		100,000

- ◆ The same codes are continued in the Excel tutorial and the worksheet solutions.

- **Preparing for new consolidations rules—A new appendix to explain the FASB Exposure Drafts issued June 30, 2005, that will impact accounting for business combinations:**

  - The FASB issued two new exposure drafts on business combinations in June 2005, and a new standard is expected in 2007.
  - Major changes may include the recognition of full fair values for assets even for bargain purchases, recognizing 100% of fair values for all accounts in less than 100% purchases, new rules for block purchases, and changes in ownership interest.
  - All major expected changes are explained and demonstrated in a new appendix, Special Appendix, that encompasses all of the business combination chapters.
  - The text web site at academic.cengage.com/accounting/fischer will keep adopters posted on the progress of the Exposure Draft.

- **Concise Coverage of Governmental and Not-for-Profit Accounting**

  - Comprehensive coverage of governmental standards through GASB Statement No. 49, including the historic changes to the reporting model.
  - Government and not-for-profit chapters include material for CPA exam preparation.
  - Chapters are designed for use in advanced accounting courses or in standalone governmental and not-for-profit courses.

- **Measuring student mastery—Learning Objectives:**

  - Each chapter begins with a list of measurable learning objectives, which are repeated as "Objective" in the margin near the related coverage.
  - The exercises and problems at the end of the chapter indicate the specific learning objectives that they reinforce. This helpful indicator, along with the assignment titles, provides a quick reference for both student and instructor.

- **Communicating the core content—Reflection:**

  - Concluding every main section is a reflection on the core information contained in that section.

1

OBJECTIVE

Explain why transactions between members of a consolidated firm should not be reflected in the consolidated financial statements.

REFLECTION

- Merchandise sales between affiliated companies are eliminated; only the purchase and sale to the "outside world" should remain in the statements.

- The profit must be removed from beginning inventory by reducing the cost of goods sold and the retained earnings.

  - These reflections provide students with a clear picture of the key points they should grasp and give them a helpful tool for quick review.

- **Thinking it through—Understanding the Issues:**

  - These questions at the end of the chapter emphasize and reinforce the core main issues of the chapter.

UNDERSTANDING THE ISSUES

5. Company P had internally generated net income of $200,000 (excludes share of subsidiary income). Company P has 100,000 shares of outstanding common stock. Subsidiary Company S has a net income of $60,000 and 40,000 shares of outstanding common stock. Company P owns 100% of the Company S shares. What is consolidated diluted EPS, if:

   a. Company S has outstanding stock options for Company S shares, which cause a dilutive effect of 2,000 additional shares of Company S shares?
   b. Company S has outstanding stock options for Company P shares, which cause a dilutive effect of 2,000 additional shares of Company P shares?
   c. Company P has outstanding stock options for Company P shares, which cause a dilutive effect of 2,000 additional shares of Company P shares?

6. Company S is an 80%-owned subsidiary of Company P. For 20X1, Company P reports internally generated income before tax of $100,000. Company S reports an income before tax of $40,000. A 30% tax rate applies to both companies. Calculate consolidated net income (after taxes) and the distribution of income to the controlling and noncontrolling interests, if:

   a. The consolidated firm meets the requirements of an affiliated firm and files a consolidated tax return.
   b. The consolidated firm does not meet the requirements of an affiliated firm and files separate tax returns. Assume an 80% dividend exclusion rate.

- ◆ They encourage students to think in greater depth about the topics and expand their reasoning skills. Discussion skills are also developed through use of the questions as springboards for class interaction.

THEORY BLENDED WITH APPLICATION

With a strong tradition of combining sound theoretical foundations with a hands-on, learn-by-example approach, *Fundamentals of Advanced Accounting* continues its prominent leadership position in advanced accounting classrooms across the country. The authors build on *Advanced Accounting's* clear writing style, comprehensive coverage, and focus on conceptual understanding.

Realizing that students reap the greatest benefits when they can visualize the application of theories, this text closely links theory and practice by providing examples through relevant exhibits and tables that are common to real-world accounting. When students can visualize the concept being discussed and apply it directly to an example, their understanding greatly improves. This focus on conceptual understanding makes even the most complex topics approachable.

Assignments are clearly defined. Questions are used to reinforce theory, and exercises are short, focused applications of specific topics in the chapter. These exercises are very helpful when students use them as preparations for class presentation. The book's problems—more comprehensive than the exercises—often combine topics and are designed to work well as after-class assignments. For group projects, the cases found in the business combinations chapters provide an innovative way to blend theoretical and numerical analysis.

ENHANCED COVERAGE

Fundamentals of Advanced Accounting reflects changes in accounting procedures and standards while maintaining the features that aid in student comprehension.

- **Comprehensive coverage of the impact of the latest FASB statements, including:**

  - Included in this text is the Special Appendix, Analysis of FASB Exposure Drafts for Business Combinations. This new appendix is based on the Exposure Drafts: Consolidated Financial Statements, Including Accounting and Reporting of Noncontrolling Interests in Subsidiaries—a replacement of ARB No. 51, and Business Combinations—a replacement of FASB No. 141. The appendix summarizes the major changes of these new accounting procedures and demonstrates how these changes impact the accounting procedures taught in the text. Exercises and problems that utilize the new accounting procedures are included.

- **Up-to-date coverage of governmental and not-for-profit accounting:**

  - Chapter 10 incorporates the latest guidance on accounting for revenues of nonexchange transactions, post-retirement benefits other than pensions, and investments.
  - The authors have included a chapter (Chapter 11) to focus on the reporting model for state and local governments.
  - Chapters 12 presents the challenging area of not-for-profit accounting. Since many of the not-for-profit organizations also have government counterparts and GASB standards are at times different from applying the FASB not-for-profit standards, the text separates the discussion of college and university, health-care organizations, voluntary health and welfare, and other not-for-profit organizations.

- **Comprehensive coverage of the impact of the latest GASB statements, including**:

  - A complete explanation and presentation of the comprehensive annual financial report (CAFR) provides students with a strong basis for understanding the reporting requirements as set forth in GASB Statement Nos. 34, 35, and 37.
  - The authors have provided a comprehensive presentation of revenue recognition requirements for nonexchange transactions, found in GASB Statement Nos. 33 and 36. The note disclosure requirements in GASB Statement No. 38 are described.
  - Coverage of additional guidance on post-retirement benefits other than pensions (GASB Statement Nos. 43 and 45) and content on the statistical section (GASB Statement No. 44) are included.

FLEXIBILITY

The book's flexible coverage of topics allows for professors to teach their course at their own pace and in their preferred order. There are no dependencies between major sections of the text except that coverage of consolidations should precede multinational accounting if one is to understand accounting for foreign subsidiaries.

The text is divided into the following major topics:

Business Combinations (Chapters 1–5)

Chapter 1 demonstrates the FASB rules, under Statement Nos. 141 and 142, for allocating the cost of a purchased company to its assets and liabilities. Goodwill impairment replaces amortization and is fully explained.

Chapters 2 through 4 cover the basics of preparing a consolidated income statement and balance sheet. In 1977, we introduced two schedules in *Advanced Accounting* that have been much appreciated by students and faculty alike for nearly 30 years—the Determination and Distribution of Excess Schedule and Income Distribution Schedule. The determination and distribution schedule (quickly termed the D&D schedule by students) analyzes the difference between the price paid in a purchase and the underlying equity of the subsidiary. It provides a check figure for all subsequent years' worksheets, details all information for the distribution of differences between book and market values, and reveals all data for the amortization of the differences. The schedule provides rules for all types of purchase situations and for alternative consolidation theories. The income distribution schedule (known as the IDS) is a set of T accounts that distributes income between the noncontrolling and controlling interests. It also provides a useful check function to ensure that all intercompany eliminations are properly accounted for. These chapters give the student all topics needed for the CPA Exam. (For easy reference, the text contains an icon in the margin, as shown here, that ties the narrative to the worksheets. All demonstration worksheets appear in the text, just before the assignment material. In addition, the related narrative pages are indicated in the upper right side of each worksheet. This allows the reader to quickly locate important explanations.)

With regard to the alternative worksheet methods and why we follow the approaches we do, consider the method used to record the investment in the subsidiary's and the parent's books. There are two key points of general agreement. The first is that it doesn't really matter which method is used, since the investment account is eliminated. Second, when the course is over, a student should know how to handle each method: simple equity, full (we call it sophisticated) equity, and cost. The real issue is which method is the easiest one to learn first. We believe the winner is simple equity, since it is totally symmetric with the equity accounts of the subsidiary. It simplifies elimination of subsidiary equity against the investment account. Every change in subsidiary equity is reflected, on a pro rata basis, in the parent's investment account. Thus, the simple equity method becomes the mainline method of the text. We teach the student to convert investments maintained under the cost method to the simple equity method. In practice, most firms and the majority of the problems in the text use the cost method. This means that the simple equity method is employed to solve problems that begin as either simple equity or cost method problems.

We also cover the sophisticated equity method, which amortizes the excess of cost or book value through the investment account. This method should also adjust for intercompany profits through the investment account. The method is cumbersome because it requires the student to deal with amortizations of excess and intercompany profits in the investment account before getting to the consolidated worksheet, which is designed to handle these topics. This means teaching consolidating procedures without the benefit of a worksheet. We cover the method after the student is proficient with a worksheet and the other methods. Thorough understanding of the sophisticated method is important so that it can be applied to influential investments that are not consolidated.

Another major concern among advanced text professors has to do with the worksheet style used. There are three choices: the horizontal (trial balance) format, the vertical (stacked) method, and the balance sheet only. Again, we do cover all three, but the horizontal format is our main method. Horizontal is by far the most appealing to students. They have used it in both introductory and intermediate accounting. It is also the most likely method to be found in practice. On this basis, we use it initially to develop all topics. We cover the vertical format but not until the student is proficient with the horizontal format. There is no difference in the elimination entries; only the worksheet logistics differ. It takes only one problem assignment to teach the students this approach so they are prepared for its possible appearance on the CPA Exam. The balance-sheet-only format has no reason to exist other than its use as a CPA Exam testing shortcut. We cover it in an appendix.

Chapter 5 may be more essential for those entering practice than it is for the CPA Exam. It contains inter-company bond holdings, cash flow for consolidated firms, consolidated EPS and the use of the sophisticated equity method for influential investments. The equity method for influential investments can be quickly learned using elements of the consolidation procedures from the prior chapters.

A special appendix follows the consolidations chapters explains and demonstrates the changes that may occur as a result of the new FASB Exposure Drafts issued June 30, 2005. The changes would include:

- Expensing direct acquisition costs.
- Eliminating allocation to nonpriority accounting in a bargain purchase. A gain would be recorded when the price paid is less than the amount assigned to net identifiable assets.
- Adjusting subsidiary assets to 100% of fair value no matter what the size of the controlling interest.

Multinational Accounting (Chapters 6 and 7)

As business has developed beyond national boundaries, the discipline of accounting also has evolved to measure and report various international business activities. Chapter 6 discusses the mechanics of foreign currency exchange rates and accounting for foreign currency transactions. When a transaction is denominated or settled in a currency different than the currency in which it is measured or recorded special accounting is necessary to reflect changes in exchange rates over time. When business is conducted between parties with different currencies, one of the transacting parties will be exposed to the exchange rate risk associated with having a transaction denominated in a foreign currency. Derivative financial instruments are commonly used to hedge against the risks associated with changes in currency rates. Chapter 6 discusses the characteristics of derivatives and the accounting implications as it relates directly to foreign currency transactions. Primary focus is on how forward contracts and options may be used as hedging instruments in both fair value and cash flow hedges. More specifically, the use of a derivative to hedge a recognized transaction (asset or liability), an unrecognized firm commitment, or a forecasted transaction is discussed and illustrated. Throughout the chapter, illustrative entries and graphics are used to improve the students' understanding of this topic.

Chapter 7 discusses the processes involved when a foreign entity's financial statements which are measured in a foreign currency must now be expressed or translated into a different currency such as that of a parent entity. The objectives of translation are clearly discussed and illustrated. Both translation and remeasurement proceeds are demonstrated and related to the objectives of translation. Relating the material in this chapter to the earlier discussion of business combinations, the chapter incorporates worksheets that demonstrate the consolidation of a foreign subsidiary and a domestic parent and the preparation of consolidated financial statements.

Accounting for Partnerships (Chapters 8 and 9)

Chapters 8 and 9 take students through the entire life cycle of a partnership, beginning with formation and ending in liquidation. Although new forms of organization such as the limited liability corporation are available, partnerships continue to be a common form of organization. Practicing accountants must be aware of the characteristics of this form of organization and the unique accounting principles. The accounting aspects of profit and loss agreements, changes in the composition of partners (admissions and withdrawals), and partnership liquidations are fully illustrated. The end-of-chapter material in this area focuses on evaluating various alternative strategies available to partners, for example, deciding whether it would be better to liquidate a partnership or admit a new partner.

Governmental and Not-for-Profit Accounting (Chapters 10–12)

Chapters 10–12 provide comprehensive coverage of accounting and financial reporting of state and local governments, colleges and universities, health-care entities, and not-for-profit organizations. Since the ninth edition of this text was released, standards-setting bodies have issued several accounting, auditing, and financial reporting standards that impact topics covered in these chapters. This new edition discusses recent developments in state and local government accounting and financial reporting, emphasizing the details in the Governmental Accounting Standards Board's (GASB's) financial reporting model (GASB Statement Nos. 34 and 35).

Chapter 10 covers the unique accounting and financial reporting issues of state and local governments. This chapter has been updated to cover the basics of accounting and financial reporting of the general fund and account groups. The chapter incorporates GASB guidance on accounting for revenues and expenditures using a financial resources measurement focus and a modified accrual basis of accounting. The unique ways of accounting for capital assets and long-term debt are detailed.

Chapter 10 also details accounting for the specialized funds of government, e.g., those established to account for restricted operating resources, long-term construction projects or acquisition of major fixed assets, and servicing of principal and interest on long-term debt. The chapter covers the unique accounting for various trust funds, including permanent funds and proprietary (business-type) funds. Accounting for pensions, post-retirement benefits other than pensions, recognition of assets and liabilities and related disclosures arising from securities lending transactions, accounting for certain investments at fair value, and accounting for landfill operations are illustrated.

Chapter 11 presents the government's basic financial statements required in the reporting model. The unique features of the *funds-based statements*, which maintain the traditional measurement focus and basis of accounting for both governmental and proprietary funds, and *the government-wide statements*, which use the flow of economic resources measurement focus and full accrual basis of accounting for both the government and proprietary activities, are detailed.

The chapter includes a discussion of the requirement for governments to report all capital assets, including retroactive reporting of infrastructure assets. Detailed illustrations help to clarify the requirements to report depreciation or use the modified approach. The chapter contains a sample government-wide statement of net assets that reports governmental and proprietary activities in separate columns and a program- or function-oriented statement of activities. The requirements for the *management's discussion and analysis* (MD&A) are high lighted. Additional coverage surrounds key issues in governmental audit, including the single audit requirements, from AICPA, OMB, and GAO authoritative sources.

Chapter 12 begins with an overall summary of the accounting and financial reporting standards as they apply to all not-for-profit organizations. Coverage of FASB Statement Nos. 116, 117, 124, and 136 is included. Expanded illustrations enable the student to better grasp the unique requirements for revenue and expense recognition of not-for-profit organizations. Chapter 12 offers a complete description of accounting for voluntary health and welfare organizations, universities and health-care organizations. Comparisons of the governmental and nongovernmental reporting requirements and/or practices are highlighted to enable the student to gain a better understanding of differences between them.

UNPARALLELED SUPPORT

Supplementary Materials for the Instructor:

Instructor's Resource CD (0-324-37893-9). The IRCD provides instructors with a convenient and complete source of support materials. It contains all of the solutions manual files, the test bank files (in Word and ExamView®), the Excel solutions to the Excel tutorial, and the PowerPoint slides.

Solutions Manual (0-324-37892-0). This manual provides answers to all end-of-chapter "Understanding the Issues" questions and solutions to all exercises, problems, and cases, as well as the problems in the Special Appendix. The electronic files for this ancillary can be found on the Instructor's Resource CD.

Test Bank (0-324-37895-5). Consisting of a variety of multiple-choice questions and short problems and the related solutions, this test bank had been newly updated and revised by Deb Kiss of Davenport University). The test bank is available electronically in Word and ExamView on the Instructor's Resource CD.

Dedicated Product Web Site (academic.cengage.com/accounting/fischer). The Instructor Resources section contains:

- ◆ **PowerPoint® Presentations.** Author-developed electronic slides are available to enrich classroom teaching of concepts and practice.
- ◆ **Check Figures.** A list of helpful check figures to the end-of-chapter problems is provided. Instructors may share these with their students, if desired.
- ◆ **Updates for new FASB and GASB statements.**
- ◆ **See below for the content of the Student Resources section.**

Valuable Supplementary Materials for the Student:

Dedicated Product Web Site (academic.cengage.com/accounting/fischer). The Student Resources section contains:

- ◆ **City of Milwaukee Financial Statements.** These statements provide a helpful reference for coverage in the governmental chapters.
- ◆ **Learning Objectives and Reflections.** These are repeated here to serve as a study aid.
- ◆ **Chapter Quizzes.**
- ◆ **Glossary.**
- ◆ **Content Updates relevant to changes in FASB standards.**

Acknowledgments

In preparation for the new edition, over one hundred Advanced Accounting instructors provided helpful responses to our survey. We thank them all for their timely information. In addition, the following individuals shared detailed ideas and suggestions for changes and improvements, of which many have been implemented in this text and supplements.

Earl H. Godfrey, Jr., Gardner-Webb University
Paul D. Hutchison, University of North Texas
Cynthia Jeffrey, Iowa State University
Thomas D. Klein, University of Arizona
Heibatollah Sami, Temple University
Wesley A. Tucker, Austin Community College
Scott Whisenant, University of Houston

We thank the following ancillary writers and verifiers for their conscientious effort to make sure the support materials are accurate and tie closely to the text's up-to-date content.

Writers:
Test Bank: Deb Kiss (Davenport University)

Web Quizzes: Sara Wilson

PowerPoint: Michele Etzold (Johnson & Wales University)

Verifiers:
Solutions Manual: Dianne Feldman

Test Bank: Sara Wilson

Their patience in the revision process is greatly appreciated.

Finally, a special thank you goes to Carol Fischer (University of Wisconsin—Waukesha) for her many hours of extensive, creative work on developing the Excel tutorial materials. This product provides easy-to-follow assistance to students as they learn the worksheet process.

Paul Fischer
William Taylor
Rita Cheng

About the Authors

Paul M. Fischer is the Jerry Leer Professor of Accounting and Accounting Area Chair at the University of Wisconsin, Milwaukee. He teaches intermediate, advanced financial and management accounting at the undergraduate and graduate levels. He has received the AMOCO Outstanding Professor Award, the Outstanding Executive MBA Professor Award, and the School of Business Administration Advisory Council Teaching Award. He also teaches continuing education classes and provides executive training courses for several large corporations. He earned his undergraduate accounting degree at Milwaukee and earned an MBA and Ph.D. at the University of Wisconsin, Madison. Dr. Fischer is a CPA and is a member of the American Institute of CPAs, the Wisconsin Institute of CPAs, and the American Accounting Association. Dr. Fischer has previously authored *Cost Accounting: Theory and Applications* (with Frank), *Advanced Accounting* (with Taylor and Cheng), *Financial Dimensions of Marketing Management* (with Crissy and Mossman), journal articles, and computer software. He actively pursues research and consulting interests in the areas of leasing, pension accounting, and business combinations.

William James Taylor primarily teaches financial accounting and auditing at both the undergraduate and graduate levels. In addition, he is involved in providing executive training courses for several large corporations and through an executive MBA program. He has been recognized for his teaching excellence and has received both the AMOCO Outstanding Professor Award and the School of Business Administration Advisory Council Teaching Award. He earned his Ph.D. from Georgia State University and is a CPA and a CVA (Certified Valuation Analyst). His professional experience includes working for Deloitte and Touche and Arthur Andersen & Co. in their audit practices. His private consulting activities include business valuations, litigation services, and issues affecting closely held businesses. Dr. Taylor is a member of the American Institute of CPAs, the Wisconsin Institute of CPAs, and the National Association of Certified Valuation Analysts. He serves as a director and officer for a number of organizations.

Rita H. Cheng is a Professor of Accounting at the University of Wisconsin, Milwaukee. She teaches government and not-for-profit accounting and advanced financial accounting. She has published numerous journal articles and technical reports and is often asked to speak on government and not-for-profit accounting topics. She has been recognized for her teaching excellence and is a recipient of the School of Business Administration Advisory Council Outstanding Teaching Award. She earned her Ph.D. in Accounting from Temple University. She is a CPA and a Certified Government Financial Manager. Dr. Cheng is actively involved in research focusing on the quality of accounting and financial reporting by state and local governments and the influence of accounting regulation on corporate business competitiveness. She is a member of the Government and Nonprofit Section of the American Accounting Association and has served as the section's president. She has also testified before the Governmental Accounting Standards Board and coordinated the academic response to several proposed standards.

Combined Corporate Entities and Consolidations

Chapter 1: *Business Combinations: America's Most Popular Business Activity, Bringing an End to the Controversy*

Chapter 2: *Consolidated Statements: Date of Acquisition*

Chapter 3: *Consolidated Statements: Subsequent to Acquisition*

Chapter 4: *Intercompany Transactions: Merchandise, Plant Assets, and Notes*

Chapter 5: *Intercompany Bonds, Cash Flow, EPS, and Unconsolidated Investments*

Special Appendix: *Analysis of FASB Exposure Drafts for Business Combinations by Impact on Chapters 1–5*

The acquisition of one company by another is a commonplace business activity. Frequently, a company is groomed for sale. Also, the recent proliferation of new technology businesses and financial services firms that merge into larger companies is an expected, and often planned for, occurrence. For three decades, prior to 2001, accounting standards for business combinations had remained stable. Two models of recording combinations had coexisted. The pooling-of-interests method brought over the assets and liabilities of the acquired company at existing book values. The purchase method brought the acquired company's assets and liabilities to the acquiring firm's books at fair market value. FASB Statement No. 141, issued in July of 2001, ended the use of the pooling method and gave new guidance for recording business combinations under purchase accounting principles.

There are two types of accounting transactions to accomplish a combination. The first is to acquire the assets and liabilities of a company directly from the company itself by paying cash or by issuing bonds or stock. This is called a *direct asset acquisition* and is studied in Chapter 1. All of the theory involving combinations is first explained in this context.

The more common way to achieve control is to acquire a controlling interest, usually over 50%, in the voting common stock of another company. When two companies are under common control, a single set of *consolidated statements* must be prepared. Chapters 2 through 5 provide the methods for consolidating the separate statements of the affiliated firms into a consolidated set of financial statements. The consolidation process becomes a continuous activity, which is further complicated by continuing transactions between the affiliated companies.

On June 30, 2005, the FASB published two exposure drafts: "Consolidated Financial Statements, Including Accounting and Reporting of Noncontrolling Interests in Subsidiaries – A Replacement of ARB No. 51" and "Business Combinations – A Replacement of FASB No. 141." Special Appendix analyzes and applies the provisions of these exposure drafts to Chapters 1–3 and 6–8.

Business Combinations: America's Most Popular Business Activity, Bringing an End to the Controversy

"There are few areas of accounting that need improvement more than the accounting for business combinations. The current accounting literature allows two economically similar business combinations to be accounted for using different accounting methods that produce dramatically different financial results, which is confusing to investors."

Edmund L. Jenkins, Chairman of the Financial Accounting Standards Board
Testimony before the U.S. House of Representative, May 4, 2000

Learning Objectives

When you have completed this chapter, you should be able to

1. Describe the major economic advantages of business combinations.

2. Understand the basic accounting differences between an acquisition accomplished by purchasing the assets of a company versus purchasing a controlling interest in the voting common stock of a company.

3. Demonstrate an understanding of the major difference between purchase and pooling-of-interests accounting.

4. Allocate the purchase cost to the assets and liabilities of the acquired company.

5. Account for assets and liabilities included in a business combination that involves goodwill.

6. Account for acquired assets and liabilities subsequent to a purchase, and apply impairment testing to goodwill.

7. Use zone analysis to account for purchases made at a price below the fair value of the company's net assets.

8. Explain the special issues that may arise in a purchase, and show how to account for them.

9. Be aware of transition rules for the use of pooling of interests and the procedures for existing goodwill.

10. (Appendix) Estimate the value of goodwill.

Business combinations have been a common business transaction since the start of commercial activity. The concept is simple: A business combination is the group acquisition of all of a company's assets at a single price. *Business combinations* is a comprehensive term covering all acquisitions of one firm by another. Business combinations can be further categorized as either mergers or consolidations. The term *merger* applies when an existing company acquires another company and combines that company's operations with its own. The term *consolidation* applies when two or more previously separate firms merge into one new, continuing company. Business combinations make headlines not only in the business press but also in the local newspapers of the communities where the participating companies are located. While investors may delight in the price received for their interest, employees become concerned about continued employment, and local citizens worry about a possible relocation of the business.

The popularity of business combinations grew exponentially during the 1990s but peaked in the late 90's. From then until 2002, activity slowed considerably, with the dollar amount of deals falling even more than the number of deals. Activity has resumed after the low of 2002. Exhibit 1-1 includes the Merger Completion Record covering 1996 through 2005. The drastic change in business combinations can be attributed to several causes.

- The growth period prior to 1999 reflects, in part, the boom economy of that period, especially in high-tech industries. There was also a motivation to complete acquisitions prior to July 1, 2001, when FASB Statement 141, Business Combinations, became effective. FASB Statement 141 eliminated the pooling-of-interests method. Pooling allowed companies to record the acquired assets at existing book value. This meant less depreciation and amortization charges in later periods. When the alternative purchase method was used prior to 2001, goodwill that was recorded could be amortized over four years. After 2001, FASB Statement 141 required goodwill impairment testing, which meant there was a risk of a major goodwill impairment loss in a future period.
- The decline in acquisition activity could also be attributed to the soft economy during the post-2000 period. The high-tech sector of the economy, which had been a hotbed of combinations, was especially weak. Add to it the increased scrutiny of companies being acquired, as caused by the accounting and business scandals of the period, and the motivation to acquire was lessened.
- Aside from broad-based accounting infractions, there arose specific allegations of "*precombination beautification.*" It became clear that adjustments were made to the books of the company being acquired to make it look more valuable as a takeover candidate. This included arranging in advance to meet the pooling-of-interests criteria and making substantial write-offs to enhance postacquisition income. In the fall of 1999, it was alleged that Tyco International arranged to have acquired companies take major write-downs before being acquired by Tyco. This concern caused a major decline in the value of Tyco shares and led to stockholder suits against the company.

Exhibit 1-1
Merger Completion Record 1996–2005

10-Year Merger Completion Record 1996 to 2005				
Year	No. of Deals	% Change	Value ($bil.)	% Change
1996	7,347	–	$663.0	–
1997	8,479	16.4%	771.5	97.0%
1998	10,193	20.2	1,373.8	78.1
1999	9,173	–10.0	1,422.9	3.6
2000	8,853	–3.5	1,781.6	25.2
2001	6,296	–28.9	1,155.8	–36.1
2002	5,497	–12.7	625.0	–46.9
2003	5,969	6.4	621.5	–16.6
2004	7,031	18.0	657.1	64.4
2005	7,298	3.8	980.8	14.4

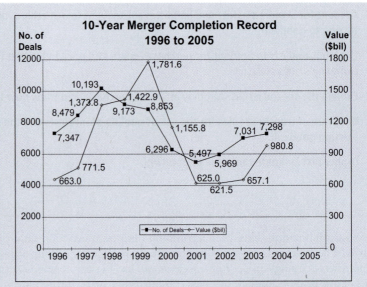

Source: Mergers and Acquisitions Alamanac, February 2006, p. 31.

ECONOMIC ADVANTAGES OF COMBINATIONS

1

OBJECTIVE

Describe the major economic advantages of business combinations.

Business combinations are typically viewed as a way to jump-start economies of scale. Savings may result from the elimination of duplicative assets. Perhaps both companies will utilize common facilities and share fixed costs. There may be further economies as one management team replaces two separate sets of managers. It may be possible to better coordinate production, marketing, and administrative actions.

Horizontal combinations involve those where competitors serving similar functions hope to economize by combining those functions, such as the SBC acquisition of Ameritech Corporation. The following comments from the 1999 Annual Report of SBC Communications Inc. refer to its acquisition of Ameritech Corporation:

> *We grew our customer base significantly through the acquisition of Ameritech Corporation, which made us the local communications provider to about 53 million American homes and businesses. Being the incumbent provider is a huge advantage in a marketplace where customers increasingly look to one company to provide all their communications needs. This much larger customer base gives us the scope to achieve significant merger synergies and expand to 30 new major U.S. markets within the next two years.*[1]

Vertical combinations are the combinations of companies that were at different levels within the marketing chain. An example would be the acquisition of a food distribution company by a restaurant chain. The intended benefit of the vertical combination is the closer coordination of different levels of activity in a given industry. Recently, manufacturers have purchased retail dealers to control the distribution of their products. For example, the major automakers have been actively acquiring auto dealerships.

Conglomerates are combinations of dissimilar businesses. A company may want to diversify by entering a new industry. The purchase of Nabisco Holdings Corporation, a food product company, by Philip Morris, a tobacco company, was just such a diversification.

Tax Advantages of Combinations

Perhaps the most universal economic benefit in business combinations is a possible tax advantage. The owners of a small business, whether sole proprietors, partners, or shareholders, may wish to retire from active management of the company. If they were to sell their interest for cash or accept debt instruments, they would have an immediate taxable gain. If, however, they accept the common stock of another corporation in exchange for their interest and carefully craft the transaction as a "tax-free reorganization," they may account for the transaction as a tax-free exchange. No taxes are paid until the shareholders sell the shares received in the business combination. The shareholder records the new shares received (for tax purposes) at the book value of the exchanged shares.

In early 2005, SBC proposed to acquire AT&T. The following information was proposed to shareholders:

> *AT&T shareholders will receive .7792 shares of SBC common stock for each share of AT&T. Based on SBC's closing stock price on January 28, 2005, this exchange ratio equals $18.41 per share. In addition, at the time of closing, AT&T will pay its shareholders a special dividend of $1.30 per share. The stock consideration in the transaction is expected to be tax free to AT&T shareholders.*

Further tax advantages exist when the target company has reported losses on its tax returns in prior periods. Section 172 (b) of the Internal Revenue Code provides that operating losses can be carried back two years to obtain a refund of taxes paid in previous years. Should the loss not be offset by income in the two prior years, the loss may be carried forward up to 20 years to offset future taxable income, thus eliminating or reducing income taxes that would otherwise be payable. These loss maneuvers have little or no value to a target company that has not had income in the two prior years and does not expect profitable operations in the near future. However, tax

---

1 SBC Communications Inc. Annual Report 1999, p. 2, San Antonio, Texas, 2000.

losses are transferable in a business combination. To an acquiring company that has a profit in the current year and/or expects profitable periods in the future, the tax losses of a target company may have real value. That value, viewed as an asset by the acquiring company, will be reflected in the price paid. However, the acquiring company must exercise caution in anticipating the benefits of tax loss carryovers. The realization of the tax benefits may be denied if it can be shown that the primary motivation for the combination was the transfer of the tax loss benefit.

A tax benefit may also be available in a subsequent period as a single consolidated tax return is filed by the single remaining corporation. The losses of one of the affiliated companies can be used to offset the net income of another affiliated company to lessen the taxes that would otherwise be paid by the profitable company. In some cases, it may be disadvantageous to file as a consolidated company. Companies with low incomes may fare better by being taxed separately due to the progressive income tax rate structure. The marginal tax rate of each company may be lower than that resulting when the incomes of the two companies are combined.[2]

REFLECTION

- Business combinations may have economic advantages for a firm desiring to expand horizontally or vertically or may be a means of diversifying risk by purchasing dissimilar businesses.

- Potential sellers may be motivated by the tax advantages available to them in a business combination.

2
OBJECTIVE

Understand the basic accounting differences between an acquisition accomplished by purchasing the assets of a company versus purchasing a controlling interest in the voting common stock of a company.

OBTAINING CONTROL

Control of another company may be achieved by either acquiring the assets of the target company or purchasing a controlling interest (typically over 50%) in the target company's voting common stock. In an acquisition of assets, *all* of the company's assets are acquired *directly* from the company. In most cases, existing liabilities of the acquired company also are assumed. When assets are acquired and liabilities are assumed, we refer to the transaction as an acquisition of "net assets." Payment could be made in cash, exchanged property, or issuance of either debt or equity securities. It is common to issue securities, since this avoids depleting cash or other assets that may be needed in future operations. Legally, a *statutory consolidation* refers to the combining of two or more previously independent legal entities into one new legal entity. The previous companies are dissolved and are then replaced by a single continuing company. A *statutory merger* refers to the absorption of one or more former legal entities by another company that continues as the sole surviving legal entity. The absorbed company ceases to exist as a legal entity but may continue as a division of the surviving company.

In a *stock acquisition*, a controlling interest (typically, more than 50%) of another company's voting common stock is acquired. The company making the acquisition is termed the *parent*, and the company acquired is termed a *subsidiary*. Both the parent and the subsidiary remain separate legal entities and maintain their own financial records and statements. However, for external financial reporting purposes, the companies usually will combine their individual financial statements into a single set of consolidated statements. Thus, a consolidation may refer to a statutory combination or, more commonly, to the consolidated statements of a parent and its subsidiary.

There may be several advantages to obtaining control by purchasing a controlling interest in stock. Most obvious is that the total cost is lower, since only a controlling interest in the assets, and not the total assets, must be acquired. In addition, control through stock ownership may be simpler to achieve, since no formal negotiations or transactions with the acquired company's management are necessary. Further advantages may result from maintaining the separate legal identity of the former company. First of all, risk is lowered because the legal liability of each corporation is limited to its own assets. Secondly, separate legal entities may be desirable when only

---

2 See Chapter 5, "Intercompany Bonds, Cash Flow, EPS, and Unconsolidated Investments," pp. 227 to 291.

one of the companies is subject to government control. Lastly, there may be tax advantages resulting from the preservation of the legal entities.

Stock acquisitions are said to be "friendly" when the stockholders of the target corporation, as a group, decide to sell or exchange their shares. In such a case, an offer may be made to the board of directors by the acquiring company. If the directors approve, they will recommend acceptance of the offer to the shareholders, who are likely to approve the transaction. Often, a two-thirds vote is required. Once approval is gained, the exchange of shares will be made with the individual shareholders. If the officers decline the offer, or if no offer is made, the acquiring company may deal directly with individual shareholders in an attempt to secure a controlling interest. Frequently, the acquiring company may make a formal *tender offer*. The tender offer typically will be published in newspapers and will offer a greater-than-market price for shares made available by a stated date. The acquiring company may reserve the right to withdraw the offer if an insufficient number of shares are made available to it. Where management and/or a significant number of shareholders oppose the purchase of the company by the intended buyer, the acquisition is viewed as hostile. Unfriendly offers are so common that several standard defensive mechanisms have evolved. These include purchasing treasury shares, locating a different buyer, selling key assets, or an attempt by management to purchase the company.

Some protection against takeovers is offered by federal and state law. The Clayton Act of 1914 (section 7) is a federal law that prohibits business combinations in which "the effect of such acquisition may be substantially to lessen competition or to tend to create a monopoly." The Williams Act of 1968 is a federal law that regulates tender offers; it is enforced by the SEC. Several states also have enacted laws to discourage hostile takeovers. These laws are motivated, in part, by the fear of losing employment and taxes.

Accounting Ramifications of Control

When control is achieved through an asset acquisition, the acquiring company records the assets and assumed liabilities of the acquired company on its own books. From the acquisition date on, all transactions of both the acquiring and acquired company are recorded in one combined set of accounts. The only new skill one needs to master is the proper recording of the acquisition when it occurs. **Once the initial acquisition is properly recorded, subsequent accounting procedures are the same as for any single accounting entity.** Combined statements of the new, larger company for periods following the combination are automatic.

Accounting procedures are more involved when control is achieved through a stock acquisition. The controlling company, the parent, will record only an investment account to reflect its interest in the controlled company, the subsidiary. Both the parent and the subsidiary remain separate legal entities with their own separate sets of accounts and separate financial statements. Accounting theory holds that where one company has effective control over another, there is only one economic entity, and there should be only one set of financial statements that combines the activities of the entities under common control. The accountant will prepare a worksheet, referred to as the *consolidated worksheet*, that starts with the separate accounts of the parent and the subsidiary. Various adjustments and eliminations will be made on this worksheet to merge the separate accounts of the two companies into a single set of financial statements, which are called *consolidated statements*.

This chapter discusses business combinations resulting from asset acquisitions, since the accounting principles are more easily understood in this context. The principles developed are applied directly to stock acquisitions that are presented in the chapters that follow.

REFLECTION

- Control of another company is gained by either acquiring all of that firm's assets (and usually its liabilities) or by purchasing a controlling interest in that company's voting common stock.

- Control through an acquisition of assets requires the correct initial recording of the purchase. Combined statements for future periods are automatically produced.

3

O B J E C T I V E

Demonstrate an understanding of the major difference between purchase and pooling-of-interests accounting.

PURCHASE VERSUS POOLING

Prior to the issuance of FASB Statement No. 141,[3] in 2001, there were two methods available to record the acquisition of a company. The primary method, applicable to most acquisitions, was the purchase method. Purchase accounting recorded all assets and liabilities at their estimated fair values. When the price exceeded the sum of the fair values for individual, identifiable assets, the excess was attributed to goodwill. Prior to July 2001, goodwill was amortized up to 40 years. With the issuance of FASB Statement No. 142,[4] goodwill is no longer amortized. It is now tested for, and, if necessary, adjusted for impairment. Under the pooling method, all assets and liabilities were transferred to the acquiring company at existing book values, and no new goodwill could be created (existing goodwill on the books of the acquired company was recorded).

Purchase and pooling were not meant to be alternative methods available for any acquisition. It was intended that pooling would apply only to a "merger of equals." Toward this objective, in 1970, *APB Opinion No. 16*[5] restricted the use of pooling to transactions that met a strict set of criteria. The most important of the criteria required that 90% of the acquired firm's common stock shares be received in exchange for the acquiring company's common stock. All shareholders had to be treated equally in the distribution of shares. Over time, many business combinations were "managed" so that they would meet the pooling criteria. This meant that the acquiring company would receive the more favorable accounting treatment. Several perceived advantages led firms to try to use the pooling method. Below is a summary of the major differences between pooling and purchases.

Differences in Accounting	Pooling Advantage
Asset valuation: Under purchase accounting, assets are recorded at fair value, and goodwill may be recorded. Under pooling, assets were recorded at existing book value (which is generally lower than fair value), and no new goodwill was created.	◆ Reported income is higher because depreciation expense is lower (based on book values) and there was no new goodwill amortization. (Goodwill was amortized over 40 years or less prior to FASB Statement No. 142.) ◆ Return on assets is greater as a higher income is divided by a lower asset base.
Current-year income: Under purchase accounting, the acquired firm's income is added to the acquiring firm's income statement starting on the purchase date. Under pooling, the acquired firm's income was added as of the first day of the reporting period (no matter when the acquisition occurs).	◆ Assuming that the acquired firm is profitable, the acquiring firm was able to include the acquired firm's income, along with its own, for the entire year even if the pooling occurred on the last day of the reporting period.
Retained earnings: In a purchase, the acquired firm's retained earnings cannot be added to that of the purchasing company. Under pooling, the retained earnings of the acquired firm were added to that of the acquiring firm (with some rare exceptions).	◆ There was an instant increase in retained earnings, which made prior periods look more profitable. ◆ Prior-year income statements were retroactively combined; thus, the acquiring firm "pulled in" the income of the acquired firm in its prior-year statements.

---

3 FASB Statement No. 141, *Business Combinations* (Norwalk, CT: Financial Accounting Standards Board, June 2001).

4 FASB Statement No. 142, *Goodwill and Other Intangible Assets* (Norwalk, CT: Financial Accounting Standards Board, June 2001).

5 Accounting Principles Board Opinion No. 16, *Business Combinations* (New York: American Institute of Certified Public Accountants, 1970).

Direct acquisition costs: In a purchase, these costs are added to the cost of the company purchased. This increases the amount assigned to the assets of the purchased company. In a pooling, these costs were expensed in the period of the purchase.

Total equity: In a purchase, the fair value of the shares issued to pay for the purchase must be added to the equity of the acquiring firm. In a pooling, the book value of the acquired firm's equity was assigned to the shares issued by the acquiring firm.

◆ Income could have been higher in later periods, since there was no added amortization of these costs. However, pooling income was decreased in the period of the acquisition, since these costs were expensed in the period of acquisition.

◆ Total equity was usually lower. Return on equity was greater, since a higher income was divided by a lower equity amount.

The financial statement advantages incurred by the pooling method and the increased "gaming" to use the pooling method led to its elimination in July 2001 with the issuance of FASB Statement No. 141. The FASB held that fair values should be used in all combinations. The lack of comparability due to financial statement distortions, which resulted from companies using alternative methods, could no longer be tolerated. Even before the statement was issued, companies were reluctant to use pooling.

Some foreign countries still allow the use of the pooling method when similar-size firms combine; it is difficult to determine the buyer versus the seller in such cases. There were, of course, many combinations in the United States, prior to July 2001, which used the pooling method.

REFLECTION

- Purchase and pooling created very different account values and caused significant differences in income.

- Pooling generally resulted in more favorable income statements in periods following the combination.

- Pooling accounting will no longer be allowed in the future.

VALUATION UNDER THE PURCHASE METHOD

4

OBJECTIVE

Allocate the purchase cost to the assets and liabilities of the acquired company.

The purchase of another business is viewed as a group purchase of assets. In most cases, the purchasing firm assumes the liabilities of the acquired company. This means that the purchaser will record the liabilities on its books and pay them as they become due. Where liabilities are assumed, the purchase is termed a *purchase of net assets*.

All assets acquired and liabilities assumed are to be recorded at individually determined fair values. *Fair value* is the amount that the asset or liability could be bought or sold for in a current, normal (nonforced) sale between willing parties. The preferred measure is quoted market value, where an active market for the item exists. When there is not an active market, independent appraisals, discounted cash flow analysis, and other types of valuations are used to determine fair values. The list of assets includes intangible assets that may or may not be recorded on the selling company's books. If the price paid for the entire company exceeds the values assigned to individually identifiable net assets, the remaining balance is recorded as goodwill.

Assigning Value to Assets and Liabilities

The allocation of value begins by determining the fair value of tangible assets, including accounts such as receivables, inventory, investments, and fixed assets. Fair values are also established for liabilities. Typically, current liabilities are recorded at book value, since this tends to approximate fair value. However, long-term liabilities may have fair values that are different than recorded book value due to changes in market interest rates.

The next step is to identify and value intangible assets. In order to record an intangible asset, the intangible must meet the general requirements to be recognized as an asset under FASB Conceptual Statements Nos. 5 and 6. An asset must have "probable future economic benefits defined or controlled by a particular entity as a result of past transactions and events."[6] In addition, the attributes must be able to be reliably measured.[7] FASB Statement No. 141 further requires that an intangible asset meet one of the two following criteria:[8]

- Contractual or other legal rights assure control over future economic benefits. This includes rights that cannot be separated or transferred individually apart from other assets. For example, the Pepsi trademark could have a separate value even though, in reality, it could not be separated from the recipe and production process.
- The asset can be separated or divided so that it can be sold, exchanged, licensed, rented, or transferred. This does not require that a market for the asset currently exists. An intangible asset meets this test even if it could only be sold, exchanged, licensed, rented, or transferred with a group of other related assets or liabilities. For example, a client list of a service firm might have little value without the transfer of the company name in the same transaction.

Exhibit 1-2 contains examples of intangible assets that meet the criteria for recognition apart from goodwill.[9]

One of the intangible assets identified may be research and development (R&D). Value is assigned to R&D as though it was an asset, but the amount is usually expensed in the period of the purchase. The only case in which R&D can be treated as an asset and not immediately expensed is when there are R&D assets with multiple future uses.[10] Multiple-use R&D is later allocated to benefiting projects. A major purchase of R&D occurred in 1995 when IBM purchased Lotus Development Corporation for $2.9 billion. A $1.84 billion amount was assigned to R&D, which was immediately expensed. Imagine telling stockholders that it was prudent to buy this expense!

Recording Goodwill

When the price paid for a business exceeds the sum of the values assigned to net identifiable assets, including intangible assets, the excess price is recorded as goodwill. Goodwill cannot be recorded unless the price paid for a company exceeds the total fair values assigned to all identifiable assets, net of liabilities assumed. Goodwill reflects intangible assets that could not be measured separately. It also includes the future benefits from other factors, such as excess earnings ability, achieving economies of scale, and creating synergies with existing businesses. In this sense, goodwill is a residual value used to account for the price paid that cannot be assigned to other assets.

Prior to establishing the final price to be paid for a company, the buyer may want to estimate the value of goodwill attributable to anticipated excess earnings. Estimating the amount by which future income exceeds the amount considered normal for the industry can provide a reasonable value. The expected excess future income may be valued by multiplying it by the number of years it is expected to occur or by discounting the excess incomes to their present value. The appendix at the end of this chapter includes the use of a discounted cash flow model to estimate goodwill.

---

6 Statement of Financial Accounting Concepts No. 6, *Elements of Financial Statements* (Stamford, CT: Financial Accounting Standards Board, December 1985), par. 25.

7 Statement of Financial Accounting Concepts No. 5, *Recognition and Measurement in Financial Statements of Business Enterprises* (Stamford, CT: Financial Accounting Standards Board, December 1984), par. 63.

8 FASB Statement No. 141, *Business Combinations* (Norwalk, CT: Financial Accounting Standards Board, June 2001), par. 39.

9 Ibid., par. A14.

10 Financial Accounting Standards Board Interpretation No. 4, *Applicability of FASB Statement No. 2 to Business Combinations* (Stamford, CT: Financial Accounting Standards Board, 1975).

Exhibit 1-2
Examples of Intangibles

Examples of Intangibles	Meet the Contractual-Legal Criterion*	Meet the Separability Criterion
Marketing-related intangible assets:		
Trademarks, tradenames	X	
Service marks, collective marks, certification marks	X	
Trade dress (unique color, shape, or package design)	X	
Newspaper mastheads	X	
Internet domain names	X	
Noncompetition agreements	X	
Customer-related intangible assets:		
Customer lists		X
Order or production backlog	X	
Customer contracts and related customer relationships	X	
Noncontractual customer relationships		X
Artistic-related intangible assets:		
Plays, operas, ballets	X	
Books, magazines, newspapers, other literary works	X	
Musical works such as compositions, song lyrics, advertising jingles	X	
Pictures, photographs	X	
Video and audiovisual material, including motion pictures, music videos, television programs	X	
Contract-based intangible assets:		
Licensing, royalty, standstill agreements	X	
Advertising, construction, management, service or supply contracts	X	
Lease agreements	X	
Construction permits	X	
Franchise agreements	X	
Operating and broadcast rights	X	
Use rights such as drilling, water, air, mineral, timber cutting, and route authorities	X	
Servicing contracts, such as mortgage servicing contracts	X	
Employment contracts	X	
Technology-based intangible assets:		
Patented technology	X	
Computer software and mask work	X	
Unpatented technology		X
Databases, including title plants		X
Trade secrets, such as formulas, processes, and recipes	X	

*Some intangibles listed may also meet the separability criterion.

REFLECTION

- Under the purchase method, assets and liabilities generally are recorded at fair value.

- Identifiable intangible assets are included in the assets recorded at fair value.

- Goodwill is the excess of the price paid over the amount assigned to identifiable net assets.

5
OBJECTIVE

Account for assets and liabilities included in a business combination that involves goodwill.

RECORDING A PURCHASE WITH GOODWILL

When the purchase of an existing company is being considered, a thorough appraisal should be made to determine the fair value of the company's assets and liabilities. A complete appraisal will usually precede negotiations over the price to be paid. Generally, the prospective purchaser will seek the seller's permission to conduct a preacquisition audit. The audit will determine whether all assets and liabilities are properly recorded. The purchaser knows that, while book values may be indicative of the fair values of most current assets, they seldom represent a reasonable fair value for fixed and intangible assets. Even among current assets, an inventory valued on a LIFO basis has value unrelated to fair value. Fixed and intangible assets are recorded at historical cost less an arbitrary estimate of accumulated depreciation or amortization, which has little to do with fair value. Intangible assets, such as customer lists, brand names, and favorable lease agreements, may exist yet not be recorded. Some liabilities may not be recorded at an amount that represents fair value because the fair value of liabilities changes as interest rates change.

The company being purchased may have goodwill on its books (arising from a prior purchase of another company). **Existing goodwill is ignored.** The only goodwill recorded is that caused by the current purchase.

Acknowledging the limitations of (and for some assets, the absence of) recorded book values, the purchaser will typically engage an independent consultant to estimate the fair value of the individual assets to be acquired and the liabilities to be assumed. These estimates of fair value are of primary consideration when determining the price to be paid for the entire company.

To illustrate, assume that Acquisitions Inc. is considering the purchase of Johnson Company. The audited balance sheet on the date of purchase, December 31, 20X1, and a comparison of fair and book values follows:

Johnson Company
Balance Sheet
December 31, 20X1

Assets			Liabilities and Equity		
Current assets:					
Accounts receivable...........	$28,000		Current liabilities	$ 5,000	
Inventory	40,000		Bonds payable................	20,000	
Total current assets..........		$ 68,000	Total liabilities		$ 25,000
Long-term assets:					
Land.......................	$10,000				
Buildings (net)	40,000		Stockholders' equity:		
Equipment (net)	20,000		Common stock, $1 par	$ 1,000	
Patent (net)..................	15,000		Paid-in capital in excess of par ..	59,000	
Goodwill (existing)	20,000		Retained earnings	88,000	
Total long-term assets........		105,000	Total stockholders' equity.....		148,000
Total assets		$173,000	Total liabilities and equity		$173,000

Johnson Company
Fair Values
December 31, 20X1

Assets	Book Value	Fair Value	Liabilities and Equity	Book Value	Fair Value
Current assets:					
Accounts receivable..........	$ 28,000	$ 28,000	Current liabilities..............	$ 5,000	$ 5,000
Inventory	40,000	45,000	Bonds payable	20,000	21,000
Total current assets........	$ 68,000	$ 73,000	Total liabilities..............	$ 25,000	$ 26,000
Long-lived assets:					
Land...................	$ 10,000	$ 50,000			
Buildings (net)	40,000	80,000			
Equipment (net)	20,000	50,000			
Patent (net).................	15,000	30,000			
Brand-name copyright*...	—	**40,000**			
Goodwill (preexisting)........	20,000				
Total long-lived assets	$105,000	$250,000	Value of net assets		
Total assets	$173,000	$323,000	(assets − liabilities)	$148,000	$297,000

*Previously unrecorded assets.

Let us assume that the price to be paid to the seller for the net (of liabilities) assets is $350,000. Direct acquisition costs of $10,000 are added to the purchase price (see below). The total price paid is $360,000. Under FASB Statement No. 141, goodwill exists only to the extent that the price paid exceeds the fair values assigned to all identifiable net assets including intangible assets that may not have existed on the books of the selling company. Notice that the sum of the fair values assigned to identifiable net assets is **$297,000** ($323,000 assets − $26,000 liabilities). Thus, at a price of $360,000, **goodwill would be recorded at $63,000**, the excess of the $360,000 total price over the $297,000 assigned to all net assets, including identifiable intangible assets, at fair value.

Entry to Record the Purchase

Assume that Acquisitions Inc. has agreed to pay $350,000 to Johnson Company for its net assets. Payment could be made in cash or by issuing bonds or stocks to Johnson's shareholders. For our initial analysis, we will assume that $350,000 cash is paid to Johnson Company and that another $10,000 is paid to independent attorneys and accountants for direct acquisition costs. The journal entry to record the purchase would be as follows:

Accounts Receivable	28,000	
Inventory	45,000	
Land...	50,000	
Building	80,000	
Equipment	50,000	
Patent..	30,000	
Brand-Name Copyright..................................	40,000	
Goodwill (based on current purchase)	**63,000**	
Current Liabilities......................................		5,000
Bonds Payable...		20,000
Premium on Bonds Payable		1,000
Cash (for direct acquisition costs)		10,000
Cash (payment to Johnson Company)		350,000
Dr. = Cr. Check Totals	*386,000*	*386,000*

Note that all fixed and intangible assets are recorded at their estimated fair value, with no allowance for accumulated depreciation or amortization. Any adjustment of bonds payable is accomplished using a premium (in this case) or discount account. This is done to maintain a record of the legal face value.

The more common method of payment is for the purchaser to issue additional shares of its common stock. This preserves both cash and future borrowing ability. Let us assume that Acquisitions Inc. will issue $1 par value shares with a fair value of $50 per share. Acquisitions Inc. would issue 7,000 shares ($350,000/$50 per share). The journal entry to record the purchase follows. Note that the only difference between this and the preceding entry is the replacement of the credit to cash (for the payment to Johnson) with a credit to the buyers' paid-in equity accounts.

Accounts Receivable	28,000	
Inventory	45,000	
Land	50,000	
Building	80,000	
Equipment	50,000	
Patent	30,000	
Brand-Name Copyright	40,000	
Goodwill	**63,000**	
Current Liabilities		5,000
Bonds Payable		20,000
Premium on Bonds Payable		1,000
Cash (for direct acquisition costs)		10,000
Common Stock ($1 par, 7,000 shares)		7,000
Paid-In Capital in Excess of Par ($350,000 – $7,000 par)		343,000
Dr. = Cr. Check Totals	*386,000*	*386,000*

Issue costs resulting from the issuance of stock are not included in the cost of the company purchased. Instead, issue costs are subtracted from the amount assigned to the stock issued. Issue costs could always be recorded in a separate entry so that there is no opportunity to confuse them with the price paid for the company purchased. If the issue costs were $5,000 in the above example, the added entry would be as follows:

Paid-In Capital in Excess of Par (reduced for issue costs)	5,000	
Cash (for payment of issue costs)		5,000

Required Disclosure

For the period in which a purchase occurs, a schedule must be presented in the notes to the statements that discloses the fair value to the accounts of the company purchased. The schedule would be prepared as follows for the purchase of Johnson Company:

Schedule of Assigned Values
Johnson Company Purchase
December 31, 20X1

Accounts	Assigned Value
Accounts Receivable	$ 28,000
Inventory	45,000
Land	50,000
	(continued)

Accounts	Assigned Value
Building..	80,000
Equipment......................................	50,000
Patent...	30,000
Brand-Name Copyright........................	40,000
Goodwill..	63,000
Current Liabilities.............................	(5,000)
Bonds Payable.................................	(20,000)
Premium on Bonds Payable...................	(1,000)
Net assets acquired......................	**$360,000**

The following additional information must be included in the notes to the financial statements of the acquiring company in the period the purchase occurs:

1. Name and description of the firm purchased and the percentage of voting shares purchased.
2. The primary reason for the purchase and the factors that led to the price if goodwill is recorded.
3. The portion of the financial reporting period for which the results of the purchased firm are included.
4. The cost of the company purchased and, if stock was issued as payment, the value assigned to the shares including a description of how the value per share was determined.
5. Disclosure of contingent payment agreements, options, or commitments included in the purchase agreement and the accounting methods that would be used if the contingency occurs.
6. The amount of in-process R&D purchased and written off during the period.
7. Disclosures as to any purchase price allocation that has not been finalized and an explanation as to why it has not been completed. In subsequent periods, any adjustment to the allocation is to be disclosed.

When the amount of goodwill recorded is significant with respect to other assets acquired, disclosure is also required as to:

1. The amount of goodwill related to each reporting segment (under FASB Statement No. 131).
2. The amount of acquired goodwill that is tax deductible.

Pro Forma Income Disclosures. Pro forma income disclosure is also required in the period in which the purchase occurs. The disclosure seeks to provide consistency over the current and prior periods by showing what the income would have been had the purchase occurred at the start of the prior accounting period. The following pro forma disclosures are made:

1. Results of operations for the current period as if the purchase occurred at the beginning of the period (unless the purchase was at or near the beginning of the period).
2. Results of operations for the immediately prior period if comparative statements are issued.

The statements themselves are not adjusted. The footnote must include, at a minimum, revenue, income before extraordinary items and cumulative effect of accounting changes, net income and earnings per share. This disclosure would include the impact of the values assigned to accounts in the purchase transaction. Exhibit 1-3 presents the disclosure for business combinations from the 2004 Annual Report of Quest Diagnostics Inc.

Exhibit 1-3
Quest Diagnostics Incorporated and Subsidiaries
Notes to Consolidated Financial Statements
(dollars in thousands unless otherwise indicated)

3. Business Acquisitions

Acquisition of Unilab Corporation

On February 28, 2003, the Company completed the acquisition of Unilab Corporation ("Unilab"), the leading commercial clinical laboratory in California. In connection with the acquisition, the Company paid $297 million in cash and issued 7.1 million shares of Quest Diagnostics common stock to acquire all of the outstanding capital stock of Unilab. In addition, the Company reserved approximately 0.3 million shares of Quest Diagnostics common stock for outstanding stock options of Unilab which were converted upon the completion of the acquisition into options to acquire shares of Quest Diagnostics common stock (the "converted options").

The aggregate purchase price of $698 million included the cash portion of the purchase price of $297 million and transaction costs of approximately $20 million, with the remaining portion of the purchase price paid through the issuance of 7.1 million shares of Quest Diagnostics common stock (valued at $372 million or $52.80 per share, based on the average closing stock price of Quest Diagnostics common stock for the five trading days ended March 4, 2003) and the issuance of approximately 0.3 million converted options (valued at approximately $9 million, based on the Black Scholes option-pricing model). Of the total transaction costs incurred, approximately $8 million was paid during fiscal 2002.

In conjunction with the acquisition of Unilab, the Company repaid $220 million of debt, representing substantially all of Unilab's then existing outstanding debt, and related accrued interest. Of the $220 million, $124 million represents payments related to the Company's cash tender offer, which was completed on March 7, 2003, for all of the outstanding $101 million principal amount and related accrued interest of Unilab's $12\frac{3}{4}$% Senior Subordinated Notes due 2009 and $23 million of related tender premium and associated tender offer costs.

The Company financed the cash portion of the purchase price and related transaction costs, and the repayment of substantially all of Unilab's outstanding debt and related accrued interest, with the proceeds from a new $450 million amortizing term loan due June 2007 and cash on-hand. During 2003, the Company repaid $145 million of principal outstanding under the term loan due June 2007. During 2004, the Company refinanced the remaining $305 million of principal outstanding under the term loan due June 2007 (see Note 10).

As part of the Unilab acquisition, Quest Diagnostics acquired all of Unilab's operations, including its primary testing facilities in Los Angeles, San Jose and Sacramento, California, and approximately 365 patient service centers and 35 rapid response laboratories and approximately 4,100 employees. As the leading commercial clinical laboratory in California, the acquisition of Unilab further solidified the Company's leading position within the clinical laboratory testing industry, and further enhanced its national network and access to its comprehensive range of services for physicians, hospitals, patients, and healthcare insurers.

In connection with the acquisition of Unilab, as part of a settlement agreement with the United States Federal Trade Commission, the Company entered into an agreement to sell to Laboratory Corporation of America Holdings, Inc., ("LabCorp"), certain assets in northern California for $4.5 million, including the assignment of agreements with four independent physician associations ("IPA") and leases for 46 patient service centers [five of which also serve as rapid response laboratories (the "Divestiture")]. Approximately $27 million in annual net revenues were generated by capitated fees under the IPA agreements and associated fee-for-service testing for physicians whose patients use these patient service centers, as well as from specimens received directly from the IPA physicians. The Company completed the transfer of assets and assignment of the IPA agreements to LabCorp and recorded a $1.5 million gain in the third quarter of 2003 in connection with the Divestiture, which is included in "other operating expense (income), net" within the consolidated statements of operations.

The acquisition of Unilab was accounted for under the purchase method of accounting. As such, the cost to acquire Unilab has been allocated to the assets and liabilities acquired based on estimated fair values as of the closing date. The consolidated financial statements include the results of operations of Unilab subsequent to the closing of the acquisition.

(continued)

Exhibit 1-3 *(Continued)*

The following table summarizes the Company's purchase price allocation related to the acquisition of Unilab based on the estimated fair value of the assets acquired and liabilities assumed on the acquisition date.

	Fair Values as of February 28, 2003
Current assets	$193,798
Property, plant and equipment	10,855
Goodwill	735,853
Other assets	47,777
Total assets acquired	988,283
Current liabilities	62,002
Long-term liabilities	7,369
Long-term debt	221,291
Total liabilities assumed	290,662
Net assets acquired	$697,621

Based on management's review of the net assets acquired and consultations with third-party valuation specialists, no intangible assets meeting the criteria under SFAS No. 141, "Business Combinations," were identified. Of the $736 million allocated to goodwill, approximately $85 million is expected to be deductible for tax purposes.

Acquisition of American Medical Laboratories, Incorporated

On April 1, 2002, the Company completed its acquisition of all of the outstanding voting stock of American Medical Laboratories, Incorporated ("AML"), and an affiliated company of AML, LabPortal, Inc. ("LabPortal") provider of electronic connectivity products, in an all-cash transaction with a combined value of approximately $500 million, which included the assumption of approximately $160 million in debt.

Through the acquisition of AML, Quest Diagnostics acquired all of AML's operations, including two full-service laboratories, 51 patient service centers, and hospital sales, service, and logistics capabilities. The all-cash purchase price of approximately $335 million and related transaction costs, together with the repayment of approximately $150 million of principal and related accrued interest, representing substantially all of AML's debt, was financed by Quest Diagnostics with cash on-hand, $300 million of borrowings under its secured receivables credit facility, and $175 million of borrowings under its unsecured revolving credit facility. During 2002, Quest Diagnostics repaid all of the $475 million in borrowings related to the acquisition of AML.

The acquisition of AML was accounted for under the purchase method of accounting. As such, the cost to acquire AML has been allocated to the assets and liabilities acquired based on estimated fair values as of the closing date. The consolidated financial statements include the results of operations of AML subsequent to the closing of the acquisition.

The following table summarizes the Company's purchase price allocation related to the acquisition of AML based on the estimated fair value of the assets acquired and liabilities assumed on the acquisition date.

	Fair Values as of April 1, 2002
Current assets	$ 83,403
Property, plant and equipment	31,475
Goodwill	426,314
Other assets	8,211
Total assets acquired	549,403

(continued)

Exhibit 1-3 *(Continued)*

	Fair Values as of April 1, 2002
Current portion of long-term debt	$ 11,834
Other current liabilities	51,403
Long-term debt	139,465
Other liabilities	4,925
Total liabilities assumed	207,627
Net assets acquired	$341,776

Based on management's review of the net assets acquired and consultations with valuation specialists, no intangible assets meeting the criteria under SFAS No. 141, "Business Combinations," were identified. Of the $426 million allocated to goodwill, approximately $17 million is expected to be deductible for tax purposes.

Acquisition of LabPortal

The all-cash purchase price for LabPortal of approximately $4 million and related transaction costs, together with the repayment of all of LabPortal's outstanding debt of approximately $7 million and related accrued interest, was financed by Quest Diagnostics with cash on-hand. The acquisition of LabPortal was accounted for under the purchase method of accounting. As such, the cost to acquire LabPortal has been allocated to the assets and liabilities acquired based on estimated fair values as of the closing date, including approximately $8 million of goodwill. The consolidated financial statements include the results of operations of LabPortal subsequent to the closing of the acquisition.

Pro Forma Combined Financial Information

The following unaudited pro forma combined financial information for the years ended December 31, 2003 and 2002 assumes that the Unilab and AML acquisitions and the Divestiture were completed on January 1, 2002 (in thousands, except per share data):

	2003	2002
Net revenues	$4,803,875	$4,607,242
Net income	444,944	365,448
Basic earnings per common share:		
Net income	$ 4.26	$ 3.53
Weighted averaged common shares outstanding—basic	104,552	103,522
Diluted earnings per common share:		
Net income	$ 4.08	$ 3.36
Weighted average common shares outstanding—diluted	109,936	109,783

The pro forma combined financial information presented above reflects certain reclassifications to the historical financial statements of Unilab and AML to conform the acquired companies' accounting policies and classification of certain costs and expenses to that of Quest Diagnostics. These adjustments had no impact on pro forma net income. Pro forma results for the year ended December 31, 2003, exclude $14.5 million of direct transaction costs, which were incurred and expensed by Unilab in conjunction with its acquisition by Quest Diagnostics. Pro forma results for the year ended December 31, 2002, exclude $14.5 million and $6.3 million, respectively, of direct transaction costs, which were incurred and expensed by AML and Unilab, respectively, in conjunction with their acquisitions by Quest Diagnostics.

4. Integration of Acquired Businesses

In July 2002, the FASB issued SFAS No. 146, "Accounting for Costs Associated with Exit or Disposal Activities" ("SFAS 146"). SFAS 146, which the Company adopted effective January 1,

(continued)

Exhibit 1-3 *(Continued)*

2003, requires that a liability for a cost associated with an exit activity, including those related to employee termination benefits and contractual obligations, be recognized when the liability is incurred, and not necessarily the date of an entity's commitment to an exit plan, as under previous accounting guidance. The provisions of SFAS 146 apply to integration costs associated with actions that impact the employees and operations of Quest Diagnostics. Costs associated with actions that impact the employees and operations of an acquired company, such as Unilab, are accounted for as a cost of the acquisition and included in goodwill in accordance with EITF No. 953, "Recognition of Liabilities in Connection with a Purchase Business Combination."

Integration of Unilab Corporation

During the fourth quarter of 2003, the Company finalized its plan related to the integration of Unilab into Quest Diagnostics' laboratory network. As part of the plan, following the sale of certain assets to LabCorp as part of the Divestiture, the Company closed its previously owned clinical laboratory in the San Francisco Bay area and completed the integration of remaining customers in the northern California area to Unilab's laboratories in San Jose and Sacramento. The Company currently operates two laboratories in the Los Angeles metropolitan area. As part of the integration plan, the Company plans to open a new regional laboratory in the Los Angeles metropolitan area into which it will integrate all of its business in the area.

During 2003, the company recorded $9 million of costs associated with executing the Unilab integration plan. The majority of these integration costs related to employee severance and contractual obligations associated with leased facilities and equipment. Employee groups affected as a result of this plan include those involved in the collection and testing of specimens, as well as administrative and other support functions. Of the $9 million in costs, $7.9 million, which was recorded in the fourth quarter of 2003 and related to actions that impact the employees and operations of Unilab, was accounted for as a cost of the Unilab acquisition and included in goodwill. Of the $7.9 million, $6.8 million related to employee severance benefits for approximately 150 employees, with the reminder primarily related to contractual obligations. In addition, $1.1 million of integration costs, related to actions that impact Quest Diagnostics' employees and operations and comprised principally of employee severance benefits for approximately 30 employees, was accounted for as a charge to earnings in the third quarter of 2003 and included in "other operating expense (income), net" within the consolidated statements of operations. As of December 31, 2004 and 2003, accruals related to the Unilab integration plan totaled $3.0 million and $6.6 million, respectively. The remaining accruals at December 31, 2004, substantially all of which represented severance costs, are expected to be paid in 2005.

Integration of American Medical Laboratories, Incorporated

During the third quarter of 2002, the Company finalized its plan related to the integration of AML into Quest Diagnostics' laboratory network. The plan focused principally on improving customer service by enabling the Company to perform esoteric testing on the east and west coasts of the United States, and redirecting certain physician testing volumes within its national network to provide more local testing. As part of the plan, the Company's Chantilly, Virginia laboratory, acquired as part of the AML acquisition, has become the primary esoteric testing laboratory and hospital service center for the eastern United States, complementing the Company's Nichols Institute esoteric testing facility in San Juan Capistrano, California. Esoteric testing volumes have been redirected within the Company's national network to provide customers with improved turnaround time and customer service. The Company has completed the transition of certain routine clinical laboratory testing previously performed in the Chantilly, Virginia laboratory to other testing facilities within the Company's regional laboratory network. A reduction in staffing occurred as the Company executed the integration plan and consolidated duplicate or overlapping functions and facilities. Employee groups affected as a result of this plan included those involved in the collection and testing of specimens, as well as administrative and other support functions.

In connection with the AML integration plan, the Company recorded $11 million of costs associated with executing the plan. The majority of these integration costs related to employee severance and contractual obligations associated with leased facilities and equipment. Of the total costs indicated above, $9.5 million, related to actions that impact the employees and operations of AML, was accounted for as a cost of the AML acquisition and included in goodwill. Of the $9.5 million, $5.9 million related to employee severance benefits for approximately 200 employees,

(continued)

Exhibit 1-3 *(Continued)*

with the remainder primarily related to contractual obligations associated with leased facilities and equipment. In addition, $1.5 million of integration costs, related to actions that impact Quest Diagnostics' employees and operations and comprised principally of employee severance benefits for approximately 100 employees, were accounted for as a charge to earnings in the third quarter of 2002 and included in "other operating expense (income), net" within the consolidated statements of operations. As of December 31, 2003, accruals related to the AML integration plan totaled $4.1 million. The actions associated with the AML integration plan, including those related to severed employees, were completed in 2003. The remaining accruals associated with the AML integration were not material at December 31, 2004.

Integration of Clinical Diagnostic Services, Inc.

During 2001, the Company acquired Clinical Diagnostics Services, Inc. ("CDS"), which operated a diagnostic testing laboratory and more than 50 patient service centers in New York and New Jersey. During the fourth quarter of 2002, the Company finalized its plan related to the integration of CDS into Quest Diagnostics' laboratory network in the New York metropolitan area. Of the $13.3 million of costs recorded in the fourth quarter of 2002 in connection with the execution of the CDS integration plan, all of which were associated with actions impacting the employees and operations of CDS, $3 million related to employee severance benefits for approximately 150 employees with the remainder primarily associated with remaining contractual obligations under facility and equipment leases. The costs outlined above were recorded as a cost of the acquisition and included in goodwill. As of December 31, 2004 and 2003, accruals related to the CDS integration plan totaled $4.0 million and $5.3 million, respectively. The actions associated with the CDS integration plan, including those related to severed employees, were completed in 2003. The remaining accruals at December 31, 2004, substantially all of which represented remaining contractual obligations under facility leases, have terms extending beyond 2005.

Source: Quest Diagnostics Inc. 10-K 2004-12-31.

Accounting for the Purchase by the Selling Company

The goodwill recorded by the buyer is not tied to the gain (or loss) recorded by the seller. The seller records the removal of net assets at their book values. The excess of the price received by the seller ($350,000[11]) over the sum of the net asset book values ($173,000 assets − $25,000 liabilities) is recorded as a gain on the sale. In this case, the gain is $202,000. The entry on Johnson's books would be as follows:

Investment in Acquisitions Inc. Stock	350,000	
Current Liabilities	5,000	
Bonds Payable	20,000	
Accounts Receivable		28,000
Inventory		40,000
Land		10,000
Buildings (net)		40,000
Equipment (net)		20,000
Patent (net)		15,000
Goodwill (preexisting)		20,000
Gain on Sale of Business		202,000
Dr. = Cr. Check Totals	*375,000*	*375,000*

---

11 Remember that the $10,000 in direct acquisition costs is paid by the purchaser to a third party, not to the seller.

The only remaining asset of Johnson Company is cash. Johnson would typically distribute the stock received to its shareholders and cease operations.

REFLECTION

- The buyer records all accounts, including identifiable assets, at fair value.

- Existing book values, including existing goodwill, do not affect the amount assigned to accounts.

- In the period of the purchase, the amounts assigned to accounts must be disclosed.

- The entry of the seller is based on book values and records a gain for the excess of the price over the net book value of the assets transferred.

ACCOUNTING FOR THE ACQUIRED ASSETS AND LIABILITIES AFTER THE PURCHASE

6

OBJECTIVE

Account for acquired assets and liabilities subsequent to a purchase, and apply impairment testing to goodwill.

Normal depreciation and amortization procedures are applied to the newly acquired identifiable tangible assets and to the liabilities. FASB Statement No. 142 requires special amortization and impairment procedures for intangible assets. Goodwill is not subject to amortization but has unique impairment testing procedures.

Tangible Assets and All Liabilities

All tangible asset accounts are considered newly acquired and are accounted for based on their assigned values and, when applicable, anticipated lives. The accounting procedures for the acquired tangible accounts are as follows:

Inventory—Maintained at assigned fair value until sold. Upon sale, the fair value is assigned to the cost of goods sold.

Receivables—Accounts and notes receivable may be adjusted to a lower amount by using an allowance for bad debts. Once created, the allowance is accounted for in the normal manner. Adjustments to notes receivable and other debt investments may be necessary due to a change in interest rates. An adjustment to reflect a change in interest rates is amortized as a premium or discount over the remaining term of the investment.

Equity Investments—They are adjusted to a new fair value that will be their cost for all subsequent fair value adjustments and sales.

Fixed Assets—These are fixed assets used by the business, such as land, buildings, and equipment. Except for land, depreciation will be calculated on the newly assigned value, using the newly estimated salvage value and remaining life. Any appropriate depreciation method may be used. Long-lived assets are also subject to impairment testing under FASB Statement No. 121. Impairment testing requires that assets, or groups of assets, be tested for future cash flows upon the occurrence of certain events that could suggest a decline in value. When the anticipated, undiscounted, future cash flows are less than carrying value, the assets are adjusted down to their fair value.[12]

Liabilities—Current liabilities are recorded at the amounts that are expected to be paid. Long-term liabilities are recorded at their legal face value, and a premium or discount is recorded and then amortized over the life of the liability.

---

12 FASB Statement No. 121, *Impairment Testing of Long-Lived Assets and for Long-lived Assets to Be Disposed Of* (Norwalk, CT: Financial Accounting Standards Board, 1995), pars. 4–11.

Separately Identified Intangible Assets

Intangible assets with a determinable life are to be amortized over their useful economic lives. Where a residual value at the end of the economic life can be estimated, it is subtracted from the amount to be amortized. There is no maximum amortization period. The amortization method should reflect the pattern of benefits conveyed by the asset, but if the pattern cannot be reliably determined, the straight-line method is to be used. As with other long-lived assets, intangible assets are subject to normal asset impairment testing under FASB Statement No. 121.

In the period that the purchase occurs, there must be a footnote disclosure of the following information if intangible assets were a material amount of the price paid:

◆ For intangible assets subject to amortization, disclose the following:
  1. The total amount assigned to intangible assets and the amounts assigned to each major class of intangible assets.
  2. The amount of any significant residual values in total and by major classes of intangible assets.
  3. The weighted average amortization period applicable to all intangible assets and to major classes of intangible assets.
◆ For intangible assets not subject to amortization, disclose the total amount assigned to these assets and to each major class of such intangible assets.

FASB Statement No. 142 states that "If no legal, regulatory, contractual, competitive, economic, or other factors limit the useful life of the intangible asset to the reporting entity, the useful life of the asset shall be considered to be indefinite."[13]

Intangible assets with indefinite economic lives are not amortized until a determinable life can be established. An indefinite economic life is not synonymous with an infinite life; rather, it means that the life extends beyond the foreseeable horizon. Intangible assets not subject to amortization are subject to separate impairment testing on an annual basis or on an interim basis if it appears that impairment has occurred. An impairment loss is recorded if the fair value of the intangible asset is less than the book value.

The notes to each period's financial statements must include total carrying amounts and cumulative amortization for each major class of identifiable intangible asset subject to amortization. Amortization expense must also be disclosed for the period. The notes must also include the estimated annual amortization expense for each of the next five fiscal periods.

Example of Future Effects

At the time of the purchase, amortization procedures will be determined for all assets and liabilities acquired. Let us assume that Acquisitions Inc. adopted the following amortization policies for the assets and liabilities acquired in the purchase of Johnson Company. [The asterisk (*) identifies an adjustment that applies only to the year following the purchase.]

Accounts	Assigned Value	Amortization Procedure	Amortization Amount
Accounts receivable	$ 28,000	None	
Inventory	45,000	Sold during the first year	$45,000*
Land	50,000	Not amortized; realized when sold	
Building	80,000	$0 salvage, 20 years, straight-line	4,000
Equipment	50,000	$10,000 salvage, 5 years, straight-line	8,000
Patent	30,000	No salvage, 4-year estimated useful life, straight-line	7,500

13 FASB Statement No. 142, *Goodwill and Other Intangible Assets,* par. 11.

Accounts	Assigned Value	Amortization Procedure	Amortization Amount
Brand-name copyright......	40,000	No salvage, 10-year estimated useful life, straight-line...................	4,000
Goodwill...............	63,000	No amortization (will be subject to impairment procedures)	
Current liabilities..........	(5,000)	None	
Notes payable............	(21,000)	$1,000 premium amortized over 5 years straight-line, reduces interest expense..	(200)
Net assets acquired.....	**$360,000**		

Acquisitions Inc. might also do a pro forma analysis of what the impact of the purchase will be on future income. Future financial statements will be based on the combined transactions of both companies. There will no longer be separate accounts maintained for each of the former companies. Thus, all of the above adjustments will be included in the accounts of Acquisitions Inc.

Acquisitions Inc.
Pro Forma Income Statement
For the Year Ending December 31, 20X2

Adjustments Necessary Due to
Purchase of Johnson Company

Sales revenue		$350,000
Less: Cost of goods sold (includes $45,000 Johnson inventory)........		130,000
Gross profit		$220,000
Selling expenses (includes $4,000, copyright amortization)	$44,000	
Administrative expenses	63,000	
Depreciation—building (includes $4,000, Johnson building)..........	25,000	
Depreciation—equipment (includes $8,000, Johnson equipment)	18,000	
Patent amortization (for Johnson patents)	7,500	
Total operating expenses..		157,500
Operating income		$ 62,500
Less: Interest expense (minus $200 premium amortization)		9,800
Income before taxes...		$ 52,700
Provision for income tax (40%)		(21,080)
Net income		$ 31,620

Goodwill Impairment

Goodwill is not amortized but is subject to separate and distinct impairment procedures. Five specific concerns need to be addressed:

1. Goodwill must be allocated to reporting units if the purchased company contains more than one reporting unit.
2. A reporting unit valuation plan must be established within one year of a purchase. This sets forth the procedures that will be used to measure the fair value of reporting units in future periods.
3. Impairment testing is normally done on an annual basis. There are, however, exceptions to annual testing and some cases where testing may be required between annual testing dates.
4. The procedure for determining if impairment has occurred must be established.
5. The procedure for determining the amount of the impairment loss, which is also the decrease in the goodwill amount recorded, must be established.

Allocating Goodwill to Reporting Units. In most cases, the company purchased will be made up of more than one reporting unit. For purposes of segment reporting, under FASB Statement No. 131,[14] a reporting unit is either the same level or one level lower than an operating segment. To be a reporting unit, one level below an operating unit, both of the following criteria must be met:

◆ Segment managers measure and review performance at this level.
◆ The unit has separate financial information available and has economic characteristics that distinguish it from other units of the operating segment.

All assets and liabilities are to be allocated to the underlying reporting units. Goodwill is allocated to the reporting segments by subtracting the identifiable net assets of the unit from the estimated fair value of the entire reporting unit. The method of estimating the fair value of the reporting unit should be documented. In essence, an estimate must be made of the price that would have been paid for only the specific reporting unit. In only limited cases would a reporting unit have its own equity issues that would allow fair value to be inferred from the fair value of the shares. Even if a unit had its own stock, this would not have to be the sole determinant of its fair value.

Reporting Unit Valuation Procedures. The steps in the reporting unit measurement process will be illustrated with the following example of the purchase of Johnson Company, which is a purchase of a single operating unit.

A.   Determine the valuation method and estimated fair value of the identifiable assets, goodwill, and all liabilities of the reporting unit.

At the time of purchase, the valuations of Johnson Company's identifiable assets, liabilities, and goodwill were as shown below. [The asterisk (*) indicates numbers have been rounded for presentation purposes.]

Assets	Comments	Valuation Method	Fair Value
Inventory	Replacement cost available	Market replacement cost for similar items	$ 45,000
Accounts receivable	Recorded amount is adjusted for estimated bad debts	Aging schedule used for valuation	28,000
Land	Per-acre value well established	Five acres at $10,000 per acre	50,000
Building	Most reliable measure is rent potential	Rent estimated at $20,000 per year for 20 years, discounted at 14% return for similar properties; present value of $132,463 reduced for $50,000 land value	80,000*
Equipment	Cost of replacement capacity can be estimated	Estimated purchase cost of equipment with similar capacity	50,000

(continued)

---

14 FASB Statement No. 131, *Disclosure about Segments of an Enterprise and Related Information* (Norwalk, CT: Financial Accounting Standards Board,1997). See Chapter 12 for detailed coverage of accounting for segments of a business.

Assets	Comments	Valuation Method	Fair Value
Patent	Recorded by seller at only legal cost; has significant future value	Added profit made possible by patent is $11,600 per year for four years; discounted at risk adjusted rate for similar investments of 20% per year; PV equals $30,029	$ 30,000*
Brand-name copyright	Not recorded by seller value	Estimated sales value	40,000
Current liabilities	Recorded amounts are accurate	Recorded value	(5,000)
Bonds payable	Specified interest rate is above market rate	Discount at market interest rate	(21,000)
Net identifiable assets at fair value			297,000
Price paid for reporting unit			360,000
Goodwill	Believed to exist based on reputation and customer list	Implied by price paid	63,000

B. Measure the fair value of the reporting unit and document assumptions and models used to make the measurement.

If the stock of the reporting unit is publicly traded, the market capitalization of the reporting unit may be indicative of its fair value, but it need not be the only measure considered. The price paid to acquire all of the shares or a controlling interest could exceed the product of the fair value per share times the number of shares outstanding. A common method used to estimate fair value is to determine the present value of the unit's future cash flows. The following is an example of that approach.

Assumptions:

1. The reporting unit will provide operating cash flows, net of tax, of $40,000 during the next reporting period.
2. Operating cash flows will increase at the rate of 10% per year for the next four reporting periods and then will remain steady for 15 more years.
3. Forecast cash flows will be adjusted for capital expenditures needed to maintain market position and productive capacity.
4. Cash flows defined as net of cash from operations less capital expenditures will be discounted at an after-tax discount rate of 12%. An annual rate of 12% is a reasonable risk-adjusted rate of return for investments of this type.
5. An estimate of salvage value (net of tax effect of gains or losses) of the assets at the end of 20 years will be used to approximate salvage value. This is a conservative assumption, since the unit may be operated after that period.

Schedule of net of tax cash flows:

Year	Net of Tax Operating Flow	Capital Expenditure	Salvage Value	Net Cash Flow
1	$40,000			$ 40,000
2	44,000			44,000
3	48,400			48,400
4	53,240			53,240
5	58,564	$(25,000)		33,564
6	58,564			58,564
7	58,564			58,564
8	58,564			58,564
9	58,564			58,564
10	58,564	(30,000)		28,564
11	58,564			58,564
12	58,564			58,564
13	58,564			58,564
14	58,564			58,564
15	58,564	(35,000)		23,564
16	58,564			58,564
17	58,564			58,564
18	58,564			58,564
19	58,564			58,564
20	58,564		$75,000	133,564
	Net present value at 12% annual rate			376,173

C.   Compare fair value of reporting unit with amounts assigned to identifiable net assets.

Estimated fair value of reporting unit $376,173

Estimated fair value of identifiable net assets. 297,000

Excess of fair value of reporting unit over net assets. **$79,173**

The $79,173 excess is an estimate of what would be a reasonable amount to pay for goodwill. In this case, the actual payment for goodwill was less. If the goodwill implied by the purchase price ($63,000) exceeded the above excess of ($73,173), the model used to determine the fair value of the reporting unit should be reassessed. If the reestimation of the values assigned to the net assets and the reporting unit still indicate that the implied goodwill based on the purchase price exceeds the estimated excess of fair value, goodwill would be reduced to the lesser amount and a loss recorded at the time of purchase.

The procedure outlined above would be used in subsequent periods for the two-part goodwill impairment procedure.

Frequency of Impairment Testing. The normal procedure is to do impairment testing of goodwill on an annual basis. Testing need not be at period end; it can be done on a consistent, scheduled, annual basis during the reporting period.

The annual impairment test is not needed if all the following criteria are met:

- The assets and liabilities of the unit have not significantly changed since the last valuation;
- The last calculation of the unit's fair value far exceeded book value, thus making it unlikely that the unit's fair value could now be less than book value; and
- No adverse events have occurred since the last valuation, indicating that the fair value of the unit has fallen below book value.

There may also be instances when goodwill must be impairment tested sooner than the normal annual measurement date. These situations include the occurrence of an adverse event that could diminish the unit's fair value, the likelihood that the unit will be disposed of, the impairment of a group of the unit's assets (under FASB Statement No. 121), or a goodwill impairment loss that is recorded in a higher level organization of which the unit is a part.

Impairment Testing. **Goodwill is considered to be impaired if the implied fair value of the reporting unit is less than the book value of the reporting unit's net assets** (including goodwill). Let us revisit the Johnson Company example. Assume that the following new estimates were made at the end of the first year:

Estimated implied fair value of reporting unit, based on analysis of projected cash
   flow using the model previously illustrated (discounted at 12% annual rate)............ $320,000
Existing net book value of reporting unit (including goodwill)........................ 345,000

The cash flow projections are not shown; they would be based on new projections made on the date of the impairment test. The book values of the net assets would have changed since the purchase date due to the addition of new assets and sale of some assets that existed on the purchase date.

Since the recorded net book value of the reporting unit exceeds its implied fair value, goodwill is considered to be impaired. If the estimated fair value exceeds the existing book value, there would be no impairment.

Goodwill Impairment Loss. If the above test indicates impairment, the impairment loss must be estimated. **The impairment loss for goodwill is the excess of the recorded goodwill over the estimated value of goodwill on the impairment date.** The estimated goodwill on the impairment date is the excess of the fair value of the reporting unit ($320,000) over the estimated fair value of the net assets on the impairment date.

For our example, the following calculation is made for the impairment loss:

Estimated implied fair value of reporting unit, based on cash flow
   analysis discounted at a 12% annual rate.................................... $320,000
Less: Fair value of net assets on the date of measurement,
exclusive of goodwill.. 285,000
Implied fair value of goodwill .... $ 35,000
Existing recorded goodwill 63,000
Estimated impairment loss.. $ (28,000)

The following journal entry would be made:

Goodwill Impairment Loss...................................... 28,000
   Goodwill   28,000

The impairment loss will be shown as a separate line item within the operating section unless it is identified with a discontinued operation, in which case, it is part of the gain or loss on disposal. **Once goodwill is written down, it cannot be adjusted to a higher amount.**

Two important issues must be understood at this point:

1. The **impairment test** compares the implied fair value of the reporting unit to the unit's **book value (including goodwill)**. The **impairment loss calculation** compares the implied fair value of the reporting unit to the unit's estimated **fair values (excluding goodwill)** on the impairment date.

2. While fair values of net assets are used to measure the impairment loss, they are not recorded. The existing book values on the impairment date remain in place (unless they are adjusted for their own impairment loss).

Significant disclosure requirements for goodwill exist in any period in which goodwill changes. A note must accompany the balance sheet in any period that has a change in goodwill. The note would explain the goodwill acquired, the goodwill impairment losses, and the goodwill written off as part of a disposal of a reporting unit. It is further required that information be included that provides the details of any impairment loss recorded during the period. The information would include the reporting unit involved, the circumstances leading to the impairment, and the possibility of further adjustments.

REFLECTION

- Tangible assets and liabilities are expensed, depreciated, or amortized based on their fair values recorded on the purchase date.

- Identifiable intangible assets are amortized unless they can be shown to have an indefinite life.

- Goodwill is not amortized but is subject to precise impairment testing procedures.

RECORDING A BARGAIN PURCHASE

7

OBJECTIVE

Use zone analysis to account for purchases made at a price below the fair value of the company's net assets.

A bargain purchase occurs when the price paid for the company is less than the total estimated fair value of the net assets purchased. In the preceding example for the purchase of Johnson Company, a **price below $297,000** ($323,000 assets − $26,000 liabilities assumed) would be a bargain. Obviously, no goodwill is recorded in a bargain purchase. Certain *priority accounts* are *always* recorded at fair value, no matter what the price. The remaining *nonpriority accounts* are discounted below their fair values in a bargain purchase. In an extreme case, the price paid for a company could be less than the sum of its net priority accounts. Should this occur, the excess of the fair value of the net priority accounts over the price paid is recorded as an extraordinary gain.

Priority Accounts

Priority accounts are recorded at full fair value, no matter how low the price paid for the company is. These accounts include **all current assets and all liabilities plus the following assets that would not otherwise qualify as current assets:**

- All investments, except for influential investments accounted for under the equity method.
- Assets to be disposed of by sale (excess assets included in the purchase).
- Deferred tax assets (as well as deferred tax liabilities).
- Prepaid assets relating to pension plans and other postretirement benefit plans.

Typically, priority accounts should have readily determinable fair values and will be recorded at full fair value, no matter what price is paid. Should the price paid be less than the sum of the values assigned to the priority accounts, the excess of their fair value over the price is recorded as an **extraordinary gain.**

Applying the Priorities

Zone analysis is used to guide the assignment of the price paid to purchase a company. The zones and their application to the Johnson Company example are as follows:

Account Groups	Accounts Included	Fair Value	Group Total	Cumulative Group Totals
Priority	Accounts receivable	$ 28,000		
	Inventory	45,000		
	Current liabilities	(5,000)		
	Bonds payable	(21,000)	$ 47,000	$ 47,000
Nonpriority	Land.	$ 50,000		
	Buildings (net)	80,000		
	Equipment (net)	50,000		
	Patent (net).	30,000		
	Brand-name copyright.	40,000	$250,000	$297,000

Notice that existing goodwill is not considered. Now, consider alternative prices and the assignment of value that would occur. For each price, the number of $50 fair value shares will be adjusted to equal the price tested.

Premium Price (over $297,000). All accounts are at full fair value, and the amount above $297,000 is recorded as goodwill. That is the case in the example given earlier at a price of $360,000, where goodwill is $63,000.

Bargain (greater than $47,000, but less than $297,000). Priority accounts are recorded at full fair value. The nonpriority accounts receive the amount by which the price exceeds $47,000. For example, assume that 4,000 shares of common stock, with a fair value of $50 each, were issued as consideration. The total price paid would be $210,000, which is $200,000 (4,000 shares × $50) of stock plus $10,000 of direct acquisition costs. This leaves $163,000 ($210,000 − $47,000) available for the nonpriority accounts. The $163,000 would be allocated as follows:

Nonpriority Accounts	Fair Value	Percent of Nonpriority Total	Amount to Allocate	Allocated Value
Land.	**$ 50,000**	**20%**	**$163,000**	**$ 32,600**
Buildings (net)	**80,000**	**32**	**163,000**	**52,160**
Equipment (net)	**50,000**	**20**	**163,000**	**32,600**
Patent (net)	**30,000**	**12**	**163,000**	**19,560**
Brand-name copyright.	**40,000**	**16**	**163,000**	**26,080**
Total.	$250,000	100%		$163,000

The journal entry to record the purchase would be as follows:

Accounts Receivable (book and fair value)	28,000	
Inventory (fair value)	45,000	
Land (allocation)	**32,600**	
Building (allocation)	**52,160**	
Equipment (allocation)	**32,600**	
Patent (allocation)	**19,560**	
Brand-Name Copyright (allocation).	**26,080**	
Current Liabilities (book and fair value)		5,000
Bond Payable (face value)		20,000
Premium on Bond Payable (adjust bonds to fair value)		1,000
Common Stock ($1 par, 4,000 shares)		4,000
Paid-In Capital in Excess of Par ($200,000 − $4,000 par)		196,000
Cash (for direct acquisition costs)		10,000
Dr. = Cr. Check Totals	236,000	236,000

Notice that when the price is a bargain, no amount is recorded for goodwill, because the price paid does not exceed the fair value of the net assets acquired. Existing goodwill on the books of the seller is ignored in all computations and entries.

Extraordinary Gain (price less than $47,000). Priority accounts are still recorded at full fair value. No amount is available for nonpriority accounts or for goodwill. The excess value of the priority accounts over the price paid will be recorded as an extraordinary gain. This situation is rare, but it did occur in 2005 when Briggs and Stratton purchased the financially distressed Murray Corporation.

For example, assume that 600 shares of common stock, with a fair value of $50 each, were issued as consideration. The total price paid would be $40,000, which is $30,000 (600 shares ×$50) of stock plus $10,000 of direct acquisition costs. The $40,000 is $7,000 less than the amount assigned to priority accounts, resulting in an extraordinary gain of $7,000. No allocations are needed, and the following entry is recorded:

Accounts Receivable (book and fair value)	28,000	
Inventory	45,000	
Current Liabilities (book and fair value)		5,000
Bond Payable (face value)		20,000
Premium on Bond Payable (adjust bonds to fair value)		1,000
Extraordinary Gain		**7,000**
Common Stock ($1 par, 600 shares)		600
Paid-In Capital in Excess of Par ($30,000 − $600 par)		29,400
Cash (for direct acquisition costs)		10,000
Dr. = Cr. Check Totals	73,000	73,000

No amounts are recorded for nonpriority accounts or for goodwill.

The **Excel tutorial, provided on a CD with this text,** assists you in building an Excel template to allocate price to accounts under all possible price scenarios. An example of its application is included in the Summary Problem at the end of this chapter.

FASB Exposure Draft

In June of 2005, the FASB issued two exposure drafts that impact business combinations. Under the proposed procedures, all identifiable assets would be recorded at fair value, no matter what the price paid for the business was. Using the above example where the net identifiable assets totaled $297,000:

♦ A price above $297,000 would result in goodwill as is the current case, and
♦ Any price below $297,000 would result in an ordinary gain.

The special appendix at the end of the business combination chapters provides details on the exposure drafts. The text Web site (academic.cengage.com/accounting/fischer) will update you on the status of this proposal.

REFLECTION

• If a price paid is less than the net assets at fair value, there is no goodwill. The nonpriority accounts are discounted. Current assets, all liabilities, investments (other than investments under the equity method), deferred taxes, and prepaid pension assets are priority accounts and are not discounted.

• If the price paid is less than the sum of the net priority accounts, there is an extraordinary gain.

PURCHASE ACCOUNTING: ADDED CONSIDERATIONS

8

OBJECTIVE

Explain the special issues that may arise in a purchase, and show how to account for them.

Several complications may arise in a purchase, such as the following:

1. Substantial expenditures may be incurred to accomplish the business combination. These expenditures must be recorded properly.
2. Debt issuances outstanding may need to be recorded at fair value. This will require the application of present value analysis.
3. The acquired company may be a lessee or a lessor. This requires a consideration of the classification of the leases and the resulting assets and/or liabilities that need to be recorded.
4. Frequently, purchases are structured as tax-free exchanges for the seller. This means that the seller may, for tax purposes, assign the book value of the net assets sold to the stock received from the buyer. No tax is due until the shares are sold.
5. Finally, there may be contingent consideration. This is an agreement to pay additional consideration (pay more cash or issue additional securities) at a later date if certain future events occur.

Expenditures to Accomplish Business Combination

Three categories of expenditures may be involved in negotiating and consummating the purchase of another company. These categories and their recording are as follows:

Category	Examples	Accounting
Direct costs	Paid to outside parties such as lawyers, consultants, brokers, and CPAs. Could include preaudit, broker's fees, and legal fees.	Included in the price paid for the company purchased and, therefore, is included in amounts assigned to assets and, possibly, goodwill.
Indirect costs	Allocation of existing expenses of the acquiring firm connected to negotiating and consummating the purchase. Could include salaries for employees who worked on the acquisition and related overhead expenses.	They remain an expense of the period and are not included in the price paid.
Issue costs	Costs connected with issuing the stock or bonds used as payment for the acquisition.	Recorded as a separate asset or deducted from the value of the issued stock or bonds, since they relate to the method of payment. Not included in the price paid.

Direct costs may also include the costs of integrating the operating activities of the acquired company with those of the purchasing company. These costs could include expenses related to revising information systems, terminating employees, and closing duplicative facilities. A liability may be established for these costs at the time of the purchase. Subsequent payments for these costs would reduce the estimated liability account.

The 2005 FASB exposure drafts would expense all of the above acquisition costs.

Revaluation of Long-Term Liabilities

Liabilities that are assumed by the buyer in a purchase transaction must always be recorded at their current fair value. When interest rates have increased since the original issue of the debt, the fair value of the debt will be less than the book value, and a discount will be recorded. If interest rates have decreased since issuance of the debt, the debt will have a value in excess of book value and a premium will be recorded. For large corporations with publicly traded debt securities, the fair value of the debt is easily secured. In those cases where quoted market prices are not available, the current value of the debt instrument is imputed using the market rate of interest for similar debt instruments. Consider the following example of imputing the current value of an existing bond. The company being acquired has outstanding a $100,000, 8% bond with five years remaining to maturity. Interest is paid annually each December 31. The acquisition date is January 1, 20X1. The current interest rate for a similar bond is 6%. The current value of the debt would be imputed as follows:

Present value of interest payments at 6%	
($8,000 annual interest × 5-year, 6% present value of annuity factor of 4.2124)	$ 33,699
Present value of principal ($100,000 × 5-year present value factor of 0.7473)	74,730
Imputed market value of liability	$108,429

The purchase entry would include the following credits:

Bonds payable	$100,000
Premium on bonds payable	8,429

The premium will be amortized over the remaining five-year term using either the effective interest or straight-line amortization methods. Had the current interest rate exceeded the original face rate of 8%, the bonds would have a fair value below $100,000, and a discount would result.

Lease Agreements

Special analysis of the purchase price in a business combination is necessary when the company acquired in a purchase transaction is bound contractually by existing leases as either a lessee or lessor. Sometimes, the terms of the lease may be modified as a result of the combination. These modifications would require the consent of the third party (lessee or lessor). When the terms of the lease are modified to the extent that a new lease is created, the new lease is classified and recorded according to the requirements of FASB Statement No. 13.[15] It is more common, however, to find that the contractual terms of a lease are not altered as a result of the purchase. In such cases, it is necessary to record only the fair value of the acquired firm's existing rights and obligations under the lease.

    When the company acquired is a lessee under an operating lease, it has recorded rent as an expense but has not recorded any asset or long-term liability. Thus, there is no existing recorded asset or liability to adjust. At acquisition, if the contractual rent under the remaining lease term is materially below fair rental value, an asset should be recorded equal to the value of the rent savings. The asset should be amortized over the lease term as an adjustment to rent expense. If the contractual rent exceeds the fair rental value, a liability should be credited, equal to the value of the excess rent, using an appropriate market interest rate. The liability should be amortized as a reduction of rent expense in future periods. Under both situations, future rent expense would reflect fair rental value as of the date of the combination.[16]

    When the acquired company is a lessee under a capital lease, it has recorded the asset as well as the liability under that lease. At the time of the purchase, both the asset and the liability should be analyzed independently and recorded at their separate fair values.

    When the acquired company is a lessor under an operating lease, it has recorded the cost of the leased asset less accumulated depreciation. In the purchase transaction, the asset should be recorded at its current fair value. However, the fair value may be based partly on the present value of the rents due under existing leases.

    When the acquired company is a lessor under a capital lease, it has recorded only a receivable due for future rents and perhaps an unguaranteed residual value. In the purchase transaction, the receivable should be recorded at its fair value based on prevailing current interest rates. The unguaranteed residual value should be estimated and discounted to its present value, using the same current interest rate.

---

15 FASB Statement No. 13, *Accounting for Leases* (Stamford, CT: Financial Accounting Standards Board, 1976), par. 9.

16 Accounting Principles Board Opinion No. 16, *Business Combinations* (New York: American Institute of Certified Public Accountants, 1970), par. 88.

Nontaxable Exchanges

The selling company may wish to structure the purchase so as to avoid a taxable gain at the time of the combination. Section 368(a)(1) of the Tax Code authorizes seven types of reorganizations that qualify as tax-free exchanges. For asset acquisitions, the tax-free exchange status is accomplished by exchanging the common stock of the purchasing company for substantially all the assets of the acquired company. After the exchange, the acquired corporation liquidates by distributing the shares received to its shareholders. The shareholders of the acquired company do not record a gain for tax purposes until the shares received are sold. The purchasing company in a nontaxable exchange inherits the book values of the assets purchased for use in future tax calculations. This means that only the net book value on the books of the acquired company are used as the tax basis of the assets acquired when they are later sold or depreciated. This results in the recording of a deferred tax liability because the depreciation and amortization expense recorded on the financial statements will be higher than what is recorded on the tax return.

As an example, assume that in a nontaxable exchange the tax basis of a given fixed asset is $50,000, and its fair value at acquisition is $150,000. Depreciation on the $100,000 difference will be deducted in the financial statements but not in the tax return. If the purchasing company is in a 35% tax bracket, the future tax payments will be $35,000 greater than the recorded tax expense. This added tax burden is recognized by recording a deferred tax liability to be amortized over the life of the asset.

The goodwill arising in a tax-free exchange is also not deductible. This means that a deferred tax liability also arises applicable to the goodwill. Suppose that after recording all other assets and liabilities at fair value, $65,000 of unallocated cost remains. This represents the "net value" of goodwill. The gross amount of goodwill (GG) is calculated as follows:

$$\$65,000 = GG - (0.35 \times GG)$$
$$\$65,000 = 0.65 \times GG$$
$$\$65,000 \div 0.65 = \$100,000$$

Thus, the goodwill is recorded at a gross value of $100,000 ($65,000 ÷ 0.65), and a deferred tax liability of $35,000 is recorded.

Consider an example of a purchase that qualifies as a nontaxable exchange. Farlow Inc. is purchasing Granada Company, which has the following balance sheet on the purchase date:

Assets		Liabilities and Equity	
Inventory	$ 50,000	Liabilities	$ 80,000
Land	100,000	Common stock ($10 par)	100,000
Building	270,000	Retained earnings	170,000
Accumulated depreciation	(70,000)		
Total assets	$350,000	Total liabilities and equity	$350,000

The fair values of the land and building are $100,000 and $300,000, respectively. Farlow Inc. issued 8,500, $10 par value common shares with a fair value of $50 each for the net assets of Granada in a transaction structured as a tax-free exchange. Farlow also paid $6,000 in direct acquisition costs. Farlow has a 30% tax. The following zone analysis is prepared:

Account Groups	Accounts Included	Fair Value	Group Total	Cumulative Group Totals
Priority	Inventory	$ 50,000		
	Liabilities	(80,000)	$ (30,000)	$ (30,000)
Nonpriority	Land	$100,000		
	Building (net)	300,000		
	Deferred tax liability—building, 30% × ($300,000 fair value − $200,000 book value)	(30,000)	$370,000	$340,000

Theoretically, deferred tax assets and liabilities are priority accounts. However, in this case, the *deferred tax liability (DTL)* only exists to the extent that the building is valued in excess of its existing book value. Since it is proportionate to the amount of value assigned in excess of existing book value, it has the same priority as the asset itself.

The price paid exceeds the cumulative sum of all identifiable assets, less liabilities. The amount assigned to goodwill is determined as follows:

Market value of shares issued ($50 × 8,500 shares)	$425,000
Direct acquisition costs	6,000
Total cost	$431,000
Total amount assigned to identifiable assets, less liabilities.	340,000
Excess remaining for goodwill, net of tax	$ 91,000
Goodwill, divide by (1 − tax rate) (1.0 − 0.3) = 0.7	130,000
Deferred tax liability applicable to goodwill (30% × $130,000).	$ (39,000)

The journal entry to record the purchase is as follows:

Inventory	50,000	
Land.	100,000	
Building	300,000	
Goodwill	130,000	
Liabilities		80,000
Deferred Tax Liability ($30,000 building + $39,000 goodwill)		69,000
Common Stock ($10 par, 8,500 shares).		85,000
Paid-In Capital in Excess of Par (8,500 shares × $40)		340,000
Cash (for direct acquisition costs)		6,000
Dr. = Cr. Check Totals	580,000	580,000

Contingent Consideration Included in the Purchase Agreement

A purchase agreement may provide that the purchaser will transfer additional consideration to the seller, contingent upon the occurrence of specified future events or transactions. This consideration could involve the transfer of cash or other assets or the issuance of additional securities. During the period preceding the date on which the contingency is resolved, the purchaser has a contingent liability that is disclosed in a footnote to the financial statements but is not recorded.[17] On the date that the contingency is resolved, the contingent liability ceases, and the purchaser records any additional consideration as an adjustment to the original purchase transaction. The method used to make the adjustment is dependent upon the nature of the contingency.

Contingent Consideration Based on Earnings. A purchaser may agree to make a final payment contingent upon the earnings of the acquired company during a specified future time period. If, during this period, the earnings of the acquired company reach or exceed an agreed-upon amount, further payment will be made at the end of the contingency period. In essence, the value of all or part of the goodwill is to be confirmed before full payment is made. Clearly, when an earnings contingency exists, the total price to be paid for the acquired company is not known until the end of the contingency period. As is the case for the initial payment, the purchaser must record the fair value of the consideration given, including the fair value of additional securities issued. Normally, the amount of the additional payment will result in an increased

---

17 APB Opinion No. 16 (par. 78) provides that a liability is to be recorded if the amount of the contingent liability is determinable at the date of the acquisition. Of course, doing so would increase the price paid for the firm and would impact values assigned to the assets.

amount of goodwill.[18] Adjustments to other assets would be made only if the contingency was based on their value.

To illustrate, assume that Company A acquires the assets of Company B on January 1, 20X2, in exchange for Company A's common stock. Also, Company A agrees to issue 10,000 additional common shares to the former stockholders of Company B on January 1, 20X5, if the acquired company's average annual income before taxes for the three years, 20X2 through 20X4, reaches or exceeds $50,000. During the contingency period, Company A will disclose the contingent liability in the footnotes to its financial statements. If the earnings condition is met, Company A will record the final payment on January 1, 20X5, by increasing the goodwill account. Assuming the 10,000 shares have a par value of $1 and a fair value of $8 per share on January 1, 20X5, the following entry would be made:

Goodwill ($8 fair value × 10,000 shares)	80,000	
Common Stock ($1 par × 10,000 shares)		10,000
Paid-In Capital in Excess of Par		70,000

The additional goodwill is added to existing goodwill, and the resulting total is subject to impairment testing.

Special procedures are needed when there is contingent consideration, based on performance, in a purchase that is at a price (before the contingent consideration) below the fair value of net identifiable assets. For example, the price paid on the purchase date is $600,000, the net priority assets total $100,000, and the nonpriority assets total $700,000. If the contingent consideration is less than the price deficiency of $200,000, the amount of possible contingent consideration is recorded as a liability. If the possible contingent consideration was $150,000, the following summary entry would record the purchase:

Net Priority Assets	100,000	
Nonpriority Assets ($700,000 less $50,000 bargain)	650,000	
Estimated Liability (for contingent consideration)		150,000
Cash (for original payment)		600,000

If the amount is paid, the liability is debited. If the amount is not paid, nonpriority accounts gain is credited as follows:

Estimated Liability (for contingent consideration)	150,000	
Nonpriority Accounts		150,000

If the possible contingent payment exceeds the price deficiency, the liability recorded is limited to the deficiency. Thus, if the possible contingent payment was $300,000, only a $200,000 liability would be recorded as follows:

Net Priority Assets	100,000	
Nonpriority Assets	700,000	
Estimated Liability (for contingent consideration)		200,000
Cash (for original payment)		600,000

If the $300,000 contingent payment was made, the summary entry would be:

Estimated Liability (for contingent consideration)	200,000	
Goodwill	100,000	
Cash		300,000

---

18 When the contingency involves the value of an asset other than goodwill, that asset's value is to be adjusted as a result of the contingent payment. For example, with a contingency involving the value of a building, the value would be adjusted at the time the contingency was resolved and the added payment made.

If the contingent payment were not made, the liability would be removed, and the nonpriority accounts would be recorded as follows:

Estimated Liability (for contingent consideration)	200,000	
Nonpriority Accounts.		200,000

Contingent Consideration Based on Issuer's Security Prices. In exchange for its assets, a seller may be reluctant to accept the securities of the purchasing company. This reluctance is caused by the seller's fear of a possible future decline in the fair value of the securities. When a stock issuance is involved, the concern may be based, in part, on the dilutive effect of a significant increase in the number of shares outstanding. To combat this apprehension, the purchaser may guarantee the total value of the securities on a given future date. The purchaser agrees to transfer additional assets or issue additional securities on that date, for the amount by which the guaranteed value exceeds the fair value on the date selected. For example, on January 1, 20X2, Company C issues 100,000 shares of its common stock, which has a $1 par value and a $12 fair value per share, in exchange for the assets of Company D. The following summarized entry would be recorded:

Net Assets ($12 fair value × 100,000 shares)	1,200,000	
Common Stock ($1 par × 100,000 shares)		100,000
Paid-In Capital in Excess of Par		1,100,000

Company C guarantees the value of the stock at $12 per share as of January 1, 20X3. If necessary, additional consideration will be paid in cash. During the contingency period, Company C must disclose the contingent liability in a footnote. Should the market price of the common stock be less than $12 per share on January 1, 20X3, additional consideration will be recorded.

Assume that on January 1, 20X3, the fair value is $10 per share. Then, $200,000 (100,000 shares × $2 per share deficiency) is the amount by which the guaranteed value of the shares exceeds the total fair value. Company C will have to pay an additional $200,000 in cash. How should the payment be recorded? The payment is not based on a revaluation of the purchase price, as is the case with an earnings contingency. Instead, the payment reflects the fact that the value assigned to the original security issuance was only an estimate, with the final amount to be determined later. To record the adjustment of the estimate, the original credit to Paid-In Capital in Excess of Par should be decreased as shown by the following entry:

Paid-In Capital in Excess of Par	200,000	
Cash		200,000

In the preceding example, the value guaranteed was satisfied in cash. More often, the satisfaction will involve the issuance of additional securities. In that case, Company C would issue 20,000 additional shares ($200,000 fair value deficiency, $10 current fair value per share). Company C will now need 120,000 shares to equal the $1,200,000 original consideration, rather than the 100,000 shares previously issued. Accordingly, the $1,200,000 originally assigned to the 100,000 shares must be reassigned to 120,000 shares. The following entry will accomplish the reassignment:

Paid-In Capital in Excess of Par	20,000	
Common Stock ($1 par × 20,000 shares)		20,000

The 2005 FASB exposure draft on business combinations would require that contingent consideration be estimated and included in the original recording of the purchase. Any later adjustment would impact income in the later period.

REFLECTION

- The direct costs of a purchase are included in the price allocated to accounts. Indirect costs are expensed. Issue costs are either separately capitalized or subtracted from the amount assigned to the securities issued.

- Leases retain their classification unless terms are changed. Fair value is used for all existing, lease-related accounts.

- Assets acquired in a nontaxable exchange are recorded at full fair value, and a separate deferred tax liability is recorded equal to the dollar value of the forfeited depreciation or amortization deductions.

- Contingent consideration that arises from an earnings contingency results in more goodwill. Contingent consideration caused by a price guarantee applicable to stock issued as payment is an adjustment of the amount previously assigned to the stock issued.

TRANSITION ISSUES

9

OBJECTIVE

Be aware of transition rules for the use of pooling of interests and the procedures for existing goodwill.

The pooling-of-interests method continues to be applied to business combinations that occurred before July 1, 2001, if they met the pooling criteria at the time of the transaction. The pooling method may also be used for transactions that were initiated prior to July 1, 2001, but were not competed until after that date. APB Opinion No. 16 (par. 46) defines the initiation date for a business combination. If, however, the terms of the combination were altered after June 30, 2001, the pooling method is not allowed.

For transactions initiated prior to July 1, 2001, that did not then qualify as a pooling of interests, the new purchase accounting procedures are applied if the transaction was completed on or after July 1, 2001.

The most universal transition concern applies to purchase transactions completed prior to July 1, 2001, that resulted in the recording of intangible assets and/or goodwill. The following rules apply to fiscal years starting after December 15, 2001 (with some exceptions for early adoption):

1. The remaining book value of an existing intangible asset that no longer meets the criteria for a separately identifiable intangible asset is added to goodwill.
2. If a portion of a purchase price assigned to an intangible asset that now meets the test for separate recording was included in goodwill, the carrying value of such an asset is to be removed from goodwill and recorded as a separate intangible asset.
3. Prior to FASB Statement No. 141, a price below the sum of the priority accounts resulted in recording a "deferred credit." This credit was amortized as an addition to income over a period not to exceed 40 years. Any balance of such a deferred credit is recorded as income from a change in accounting principle.
4. The remaining book value of existing goodwill and the goodwill created by a transfer of an intangible asset balance must be assigned to reporting units.
5. The first step of the goodwill impairment test that compares the fair value of the reporting unit with its book value must be completed within six months of adoption of the statement. The measurement uses values on the first day of the reporting period. If impairment is indicated, the impairment loss is measured as of the first day of the period and is included in that year's financial statements. The loss is recorded as a change in accounting principle and included in the first interim period reports. If an event occurs during the initial period that would lead to impairment, that loss is separately measured and is reported as a loss on impairement.
6. Annual goodwill impairment testing is applied in addition to the transitional impairment test applied on the adoption date.
7. Intangible assets that are subject to amortization should have their remaining lives reconsidered. Existing intangible assets that are no longer subject to amortization remain at their existing book values.

8. Statements included in comparative results covering periods prior to the adoption of FASB Statement Nos. 141 and 142 shall include footnote disclosure of the impact of applying the new statements to those periods. The disclosure should include income before extraordinary items, net income, and earnings per share.

REFLECTION

- Poolings initiated prior to July 2001 remain in effect.
- Goodwill existing on July 1, 2001, will no longer be amortized but will be impairment tested.

10

OBJECTIVE

(Appendix) Estimate the value of goodwill.

APPENDIX: CALCULATING AND RECORDING GOODWILL

A purchaser may attempt to forecast the future income of a target company in order to arrive at a logical purchase price. Goodwill is often, at least in part, a payment for above-normal expected future earnings. A forecast of future income may start by projecting recent years' incomes into the future. When this is done, it is important to factor out "one-time" occurrences that will not likely recur in the near future. Examples would include the cumulative effect of changes in accounting principles, extraordinary items, discontinued operations, or any other unusual event. Expected future income is compared to "normal" income. Normal income is the product of the appropriate industry rate of return on assets times the fair value of the gross assets (no deduction for liabilities) of the acquired company. Gross assets include specifically identifiable intangible assets such as patents and copyrights but do not include existing goodwill. The following calculation of earnings in excess of normal might be made for the Johnson Company example on page 11:

Expected average future income		$40,000
Less normal return on assets:		
Fair value of total identifiable assets	$345,000	
Industry normal rate of return	×10%	
Normal return on assets		34,500
Expected annual earnings in excess of normal		$ 5,500

There are several methods that use the expected annual earnings in excess of normal to estimate goodwill. A common approach is to pay for a given number of years' excess earnings. For instance, Acquisitions Inc. might offer to pay for four years of excess earnings, which would total $22,000. Alternatively, the excess earnings could be viewed as an annuity. The most optimistic purchaser might expect the excess earnings to continue forever. If so, the buyer might capitalize the excess earnings as a perpetuity at the normal industry rate of return according to the following formula:

$$\text{Goodwill} = \frac{\text{Annual excess earnings}}{\text{Industry normal rate of return}}$$

$$= \frac{\$5,500}{0.10}$$

$$= \$55,000$$

Another estimation method views the factors that produce excess earnings to be of limited duration, such as 10 years, for example. This purchaser would calculate goodwill as follows:

Goodwill = Discounted present value of a $5,500-per-year annuity for 10 years at 10%

= $5,500 × 10-year, 10% present value of annuity factor

= $5,500 × 6.145

= $33,798

Other analysts view the normal industry earning rate to be appropriate only for identifiable assets and not goodwill. Thus, they might capitalize excess earnings at a higher rate of return to reflect the higher risk inherent in goodwill.

All calculations of goodwill are only estimates used to assist in the determination of the price to be paid for a company. For example, Acquisitions might add the $33,798 estimate of goodwill to the $319,000 fair value of Johnson's other net assets to arrive at a tentative maximum price of $352,798. However, estimates of goodwill may differ from actual negotiated goodwill. If the final agreed-upon price for Johnson's assets was $350,000, the actual negotiated goodwill would be $31,000, which is the price paid less the fair value of the net assets acquired.

REFLECTION

- Goodwill valuation is often based on an estimation of the future earnings of the target company.

UNDERSTANDING THE ISSUES

1. Identify each of the following business combinations as being vertical, horizontal, or conglomerate:
   a. An inboard marine engine company is acquired by an outboard engine manufacturer.
   b. A cosmetics manufacturer purchases a drug store chain.
   c. A medical clinic purchases an apartment complex.

2. Abrams Company is a sole proprietorship. The book value of its identifiable net assets is $400,000, and the fair value of the same net assets is $600,000. It is agreed that the business is worth $850,000. What advantage might there be for the seller if the company were exchanged for the common stock of another corporation as opposed to receiving cash? Consider both the immediate and future impact.

3. Major Corporation is acquiring Abrams Company by issuing its common stock in a tax-free exchange. Major is issuing common stock with a fair value of $850,000 for net identifiable assets with book and fair values of $400,000 and $600,000, respectively. What values will Major assign to the identifiable assets, to goodwill, and to the deferred tax liability? Assume a 40% tax rate.

4. Panther Company is about to acquire a 100% interest in Snake Company. Snake has identifiable net assets with book and fair values of $300,000 and $500,000, respectively. Panther will issue common stock as payment with a fair value of $750,000. When and how would the fair value of the net assets and goodwill be recorded if the acquisition is:
   a. A purchase of net assets.
   b. A purchase of Snake's common stock and Snake remains a separate legal entity.

5. Puncho Company is acquiring Semos Company in exchange for common stock valued at $900,000. Semos' identifiable net assets have book and fair values of $400,000 and $800,000, respectively. Compare accounting for the purchase (including assignment of the price paid) by Puncho with accounting for the sale by Semos.

6. Pallos Company is purchasing the net assets of Shrilly Company. The book and fair values of Shrilly's accounts are as follows:

Accounts	Book	Fair
Current assets	$100,000	$120,000
Land	50,000	80,000
Building and equipment	300,000	400,000
Customer list	0	20,000
Liabilities	100,000	100,000

What values will be assigned to current assets, land, buildings and equipment, the customer list, liabilities, goodwill, and extraordinary gain under each of the following purchase price scenarios?
a. $800,000
b. $450,000
c. $15,000

7. Pablo Company incurred the following expenses to consummate the purchase of a subsidiary:
a. $30,000 paid to a legal firm to structure and record the transaction.
b. $35,000 preacquisition audit of subsidiary company accounts prior to purchase to determine purchase price.
c. $10,000 paid to American Appraisal Company to determine fair values of assets acquired.
d. $20,000 paid to All States Investment Company to issue common stock used as consideration to pay for subsidiary.
e. Pablo Company's controller has allocated $56,000 of Pablo payroll costs to the purchase. How would Pablo account for each of the above costs?

8. What are the accounting ramifications of each of the two following situations involving the payment of contingent consideration in a purchase?
a. P Company issued 100,000 shares of its $50 fair value common stock as payment to buy S Company on January 1, 20X1. P agreed to issue 10,000 additional shares of its stock two years later if S income exceeded an income target. The target was exceeded.
b. P Company issued 100,000 shares of its $50 fair value common stock as payment to buy S Company on January 1, 20X1. P agreed to issue additional shares two years later if the fair value of P shares fell below $50 per share. Two years later, the stock had a value far below $50, and added shares were issued to S.

EXERCISES

Exercise 1-1 *(LO 3)* **Historical comparison—income effect of purchase versus pooling.** World Corporation acquired the net assets of Globe Company on July 1, 1998. In exchange for Globe's net assets, World issued 10,000 shares of its $5 par common stock, which had a $40 fair value on the date of acquisition. Globe Company had the following balance sheet on the date of acquisition:

Globe Company
Balance Sheet
July 1, 1998

Assets		Liabilities and Equity	
Accounts receivable	$ 50,000	Total liabilities	$450,000
Inventory	100,000	Common stock ($5 par).........	125,000
Buildings (net)	300,000	Paid-in capital in excess of par....	25,000
Equipment (net)	200,000	Retained earnings	50,000
Total assets..............	$650,000	Total liabilities and equity	$650,000

Appraisals have determined that fair values agree with the book values of the net assets.

Reported income amounts for both World and Globe for the year ended December 31, 1998, are as follows:

Income Statement
For the Year Ended December 31, 1998

	World	Globe
Sales	$ 800,000	$ 500,000
Less: Cost of goods sold.......................................	(400,000)	(300,000)
Operating expenses	(150,000)	(75,000)
Other expenses	(50,000)	(25,000)
Net income	$ 200,000	$ 100,000

No goodwill is reflected in the above income statement. At this point in time, goodwill was amortized. World amortized goodwill over 10 years. Assuming that income is earned evenly throughout the year, compare combined current-year income using the purchase method and the pooling method.

Exercise 1-2 *(LO 4, 5)* **Asset versus stock purchase.** Benz Company is contemplating the purchase of the net assets of Cardinal Company for $800,000 cash. To complete the transaction, direct acquisition costs are $15,000. The balance sheet of Cardinal Company on the purchase date is as follows:

Cardinal Company
Balance Sheet
December 31, 20X1

Assets		Liabilities and Equity	
Current assets	$ 80,000	Liabilities	$100,000
Land.......................................	50,000	Common stock ($10 par)...................	100,000
Building....................................	450,000	Paid-in capital in excess of par	150,000
Accumulated depreciation, building...........	(200,000)	Retained earnings	230,000
Equipment	300,000		
Accumulated depreciation, equipment.........	(100,000)		
Total assets............................	$ 580,000	Total liabilities and equity	$580,000

The following fair values have been obtained for Cardinal's assets and liabilities:

Current assets	$100,000
Land.......................................	75,000
Building....................................	300,000
Equipment	275,000
Liabilities	102,000

1. Record the purchase of the net assets of Cardinal Company on Benz Company's books.
2. Record the sale of the net assets on the books of Cardinal Company.
3. Record the purchase of 100% of the common stock of Cardinal Company on Benz's books. Cardinal Company will remain a separate legal entity.

Exercise 1-3 *(LO 5)* **Purchase with goodwill.** Smith Company was acquired by Rogers Corporation on July 1, 20X1. Rogers exchanged 60,000 shares of its $5 par stock, with a fair value of $20 per share, for the net assets of Smith Company.

Rogers incurred the following costs as a result of this transaction:

Direct acquisition costs	$25,000
Indirect acquisition costs	30,000
Stock registration and issuance costs	10,000
Total costs	$65,000

The balance sheet of Smith Company, on the day of the acquisition, was as follows:

Smith Company
Balance Sheet
July 1, 20X1

Assets			Liabilities and Equity		
Cash		$ 100,000	Current liabilities		$ 80,000
Inventory		300,000	Bonds payable		550,000
Property, plant, and equipment:			Stockholders' equity:		
Land	$200,000		Common stock	$200,000	
Buildings (net)	250,000		Paid-in capital in excess of par	100,000	
Equipment (net)	200,000	650,000	Retained earnings	120,000	420,000
Total assets		$1,050,000	Total liabilities and equity		$1,050,000

The appraised fair values as of July 1, 20X1, are as follows:

Inventory	$250,000
Equipment	220,000
Land	180,000
Buildings	300,000
Current liabilities	80,000
Bonds payable	410,000

Record the purchase of Smith Company on the books of Rogers Corporation.

Exercise 1-4 *(LO 6)* **Income after a purchase.** On December 31, 20X1, Panama Corporation acquired the net assets of Keyes Corporation. On the date of acquisition, book values agreed with fair values of the net assets, with the following exceptions:

	Book Value	Fair Value
Inventory	$100,000	$125,000
Land	200,000	250,000
Equipment (net)	350,000	380,000
Buildings (net)	400,000	475,000

Despite these markups, there was still an excess of purchase price over fair values, and goodwill of $75,000 was recorded by Panama Corporation. The following pro forma income statement for 20X2 was prepared just prior to the acquisition:

	Panama	Keyes
Sales	$ 400,000	$ 300,000
Less: Cost of goods sold	(200,000)	(140,000)
Operating expenses	(100,000)	(85,000)
Other expenses	(30,000)	(20,000)
Net income	$ 70,000	$ 55,000

Prepare an adjusted 20X2 pro forma income statement for the combined company. Fixed assets are depreciated using the straight-line method over a 20-year life.

Exercise 1-5 *(LO 7)* **Bargain purchase.** Nectar Corporation has agreed to purchase the net assets of Pyramid Corporation. Just prior to the purchase, Pyramid's balance sheet was as follows:

Pyramid Corporation
Balance Sheet
January 1, 20X1

Assets		Liabilities and Equity		
Accounts receivable	$200,000	Current liabilities	$ 80,000	
Inventory	270,000	Mortgage payable	250,000	$330,000
Equipment (net)	100,000	Stockholders' equity:		
		Common stock ($10 par)	$100,000	
		Retained earnings	140,000	240,000
Total assets	$570,000	Total liabilities and equity		$570,000

Fair values agree with book values except for the equipment, which has an estimated fair value of $40,000. Also, it has been determined that brand-name copyrights have an estimated value of $15,000. Nectar Corporation paid $10,000 in direct acquisition costs and $15,000 in indirect acquisition costs to consummate the transaction.

Record the purchase on the books of Nectar Corporation assuming the cash paid to Pyramid Corporation was $180,000.

Suggestion: Use zone analysis to guide your calculations and entries.

Exercise 1-6 *(LO 7)* **Purchase below value of priority accounts.** Use the facts of Exercise 1-5 for the acquisition of Pyramid Corporation by Nectar Corporation. Record the purchase on the books of Nectar Corporation assuming the cash paid to Pyramid Corporation was $125,000. Use zone analysis to guide your calculations and entries.

Exercise 1-7 *(LO 7)* **Bargain purchase with allocation.** Carp Corporation is purchasing the net assets of Bass Company on December 31, 20X6, when Bass Company has the following balance sheet:

Assets		Liabilities and Equity	
Current assets	$100,000	Liabilities	$ 90,000
Land	50,000	Common stock ($10 par)	200,000
Buildings (net)	200,000	Retained earnings	140,000
Equipment (net)	60,000		
Patents	20,000		
Total assets	$430,000	Total liabilities and equity	$430,000

Carp has obtained the following fair values for Bass Company accounts:

Current assets	$120,000
Land	80,000
Buildings	250,000
Equipment	150,000
Liabilities	92,000
Patents	20,000

Direct acquisition costs are $18,000, and indirect acquisition costs are $5,000.

Prepare the entries to record the purchase of Bass Company assuming the cash payment by Carp Corporation to Bass Company is $400,000. Carp Corporation will assume the liabilities of Bass Company. Zone analysis is recommended.

Exercise 1-8 *(LO 7)* **Bargain purchase, extraordinary gain.** Use the facts of Exercise 1-7 for the acquisition of Bass Company by Carp Corporation. Prepare the entries to record the purchase of Bass Company assuming the cash paid by Carp Corporation to Bass Company is $5,000. Use zone analysis to guide your calculations and entries.

Exercise 1-9 *(LO 6, 7)* **Goodwill impairment.** Anton Company purchased the net assets of Hair Company on January 1, 20X1, for $600,000. Using a business valuation model, the estimated value of Anton Company was $650,000 immediately after the purchase. The fair value of Anton's net assets was $400,000.

1. What amount of goodwill was recorded by Anton Company when it purchased Hair Company?
2. Using the information above, answer the questions posed in the following two independent situations:

   a. On December 31, 20X2, there were indications that goodwill might have been impaired. At that time, the existing recorded book value of Anton Company's net assets, including goodwill, was $500,000. The fair value of the net assets, exclusive of goodwill, was estimated to be $340,000. The value of the business was estimated to be $520,000. Is goodwill impaired? If so, what adjustment is needed?

   b. On December 31, 20X4, there were indications that goodwill might have been impaired. At that time, the existing recorded book value of Anton Company's net assets, including goodwill, was $450,000. The fair value of the net assets, exclusive of goodwill, was estimated to be $340,000. The value of the business was estimated to be $400,000. Is goodwill impaired? If so, what adjustment is needed?

Exercise 1-10 *(LO 8)* **Deferred tax liability.** Your client, Lewison International, has informed you that it has reached an agreement with Herro Company for the purchase of all of Herro's assets. This transaction will be accomplished through the issue of Lewison's common stock.

After your examination of the financial statements and the purchase agreement, you have discovered the following important facts.

The Lewison common stock issued has a fair value of $800,000. The fair value of Herro's assets, net of all liabilities, is $700,000. All asset book values equaled their fair values except for one machine valued at $200,000. This machine was originally purchased two years ago by Herro for $180,000. This machine has been depreciated using the straight-line method with an assumed useful life of 10 years and no salvage value. The acquisition is to be considered a tax-free exchange for tax purposes.

Assuming a 30% tax rate, what amounts will be recorded for the machine, deferred tax liability, and goodwill?

APPENDIX EXERCISE

Exercise 1A-1 *(LO 10)* **Estimating goodwill.** Green Company is considering acquiring the assets of Gold Corporation by assuming Gold's liabilities and by making a cash payment. Gold Corporation has the following balance sheet on the date negotiations occur:

Gold Corporation
Balance Sheet
December 31, 20X6

Assets		Liabilities and Equity	
Accounts receivable	$100,000	Total liabilities	$200,000
Inventory	100,000	Capital stock ($10 par)	100,000
Land	100,000	Paid-in capital in excess of par	200,000
Buildings (net)	220,000	Retained earnings	300,000
Equipment (net)	280,000		
Total assets.	$800,000	Total liabilities and equity	$800,000

Appraisals indicate that the inventory is undervalued by $25,000, the building is undervalued by $80,000, and the equipment is overstated by $30,000. Past earnings have been considered above average and were as follows:

Year	Net Income
20X1	$ 90,000
20X2	110,000
20X3	120,000
20X4	140,000*
20X5	130,000

*Includes extraordinary gain of $40,000

It is assumed that the average operating income of the past five years will continue. In this industry, the average return on assets is 12% on the fair value of the total identifiable assets.

1. Prepare an estimate of goodwill based on each of the following assumptions:
   a. The purchasing company paid for five years of excess earnings.
   b. Excess earnings will continue indefinitely and are to be capitalized at the industry normal return.
   c. Excess earnings will continue for only five years and should be capitalized at a higher rate of 16%, which reflects the risk applicable to goodwill.
2. Determine the actual goodwill recorded if Green pays $900,000 cash for the net assets of Gold Corporation and assumes all existing liabilities.

PROBLEMS

Problem 1-1 *(LO 3)* **Zone analysis, alternative prices.** Browne Corporation agreed to purchase the net assets of White Corporation on January 1, 20X1. White had the following balance sheet on the date of acquisition:

White Corporation
Balance Sheet
January 1, 20X1

Assets		Liabilities and Equity	
Accounts receivable	$ 79,000	Current liabilities	$145,000
Inventory	112,000	Bonds payable	100,000
Other current assets..........	55,000	Common stock................	200,000
Equipment (net)	294,000	Paid-in capital in excess of par ...	50,000
Trademark.................	30,000	Retained earnings	75,000
Total assets..............	$570,000	Total liabilities and equity	$570,000

An appraiser determines that In-Process R&D exists and has an estimated value of $14,000. The appraisal indicates that the following assets had fair values that differed from their book values:

	Fair Value
Inventory	$120,000
Equipment	307,000
Trademark..............	27,000

Required ▶ ▶ ▶ ▶ ▶ Use zone analysis to prepare the entry on the books of Browne Corporation to purchase the net assets of White Corporation under each of the following purchase price scenarios:

a. $500,000
b. $250,000
c. $5,000

Problem 1-2 *(LO 3)* **Purchase of two companies with goodwill.** Barker Corporation has been looking to expand its operations and has decided to acquire the assets of Verk Company and Kent Company. Barker will issue 30,000 shares of its $10 par common stock to acquire the net assets of Verk Company and will issue 15,000 shares to acquire the net assets of Kent Company.

Verk and Kent have the following balance sheets as of December 31, 20X1:

Assets	Verk	Kent
Accounts receivable	$ 200,000	$ 80,000
Inventory	150,000	85,000
Property, plant, and equipment:		
Land......................................	150,000	50,000
Buildings	500,000	300,000
Accumulated depreciation...........................	(150,000)	(110,000)
Total assets	$ 850,000	$ 405,000

Liabilities and Equity	Verk	Kent
Current liabilities	$160,000	$ 55,000
Bonds payable	100,000	100,000
Stockholders' equity:		
Common stock ($ 10 par)	300,000	100,000
Retained earnings	290,000	150,000
Total liabilities and equity	$850,000	$405,000

The following fair values are agreed upon by the two firms:

Assets	Verk	Kent
Inventory	$200,000	$100,000
Bonds payable	90,000	95,000
Land...	300,000	80,000
Buildings	450,000	400,000

Barker's stock is currently trading at $40 per share. Barker will incur $5,000 of direct acquisition costs in Verk and $4,000 of direct acquisition costs in Kent. Barker also incurred $13,000 of indirect acquisition costs and $15,000 of registration and issuance costs.

Barker stockholders' equity is as follows:

Common stock, $ 10 par......................	$1,200,000
Paid-in capital in excess of par	800,000
Retained earnings	750,000

Record the acquisition on the books of Barker Corporation, using purchase accounting principles. Zone analysis is suggested to guide your work.   ◄ ◄ ◄ ◄ ◄ **Required**

Problem 1-3 *(LO 4, 7)* **Pro forma income after a purchase.** Molitor Company is contemplating the acquisition of Yount Inc. on January 1, 20X1. If Molitor proceeded to acquire Yount, it would pay $730,000 in cash to Yount and direct acquisition costs of $20,000.

The January 1, 20X1, balance sheet of Yount Inc. is anticipated to be as follows:

Yount Inc.
Pro Forma Balance Sheet
January 1, 20X1

Book Values

Assets		Liabilities and Equity	
Cash equivalents	$100,000	Current liabilities	$ 30,000
Accounts receivable	120,000	Long-term liabilities	165,000
Inventory	50,000	Common stock ($10 par)........	80,000
Depreciable fixed assets	200,000	Retained earnings	115,000
Accumulated depreciation	(80,000)		
Total assets...............	$390,000	Total liabilities and equity	$390,000

Fair values agree with book values except for the inventory and the depreciable fixed assets, which have fair values of $70,000 and $400,000, respectively.

Your projections of the combined operations for 20X1 are as follows:

Combined sales...	$200,000
Combined cost of goods sold, including beginning inventory of	
Yount at book value which will be sold in 20X1	120,000
Other expenses not including depreciation of Yount assets	25,000

Depreciation on Yount fixed assets is straight-line using a 20-year life.

1. Prepare a zone analysis for the purchase, and record the purchase.   ◄ ◄ ◄ ◄ ◄ **Required**
2. Prepare a pro forma income statement for the combined firm for 20X1. Show supporting calculations for consolidated income. Ignore tax issues.

Problem 1-4 *(LO 7)* **Alternate consideration, bargain.** Kent Corporation is considering the purchase of Williams Incorporated. Kent has asked you, its accountant, to evaluate the various offers it might make to Williams Incorporated. The December 31, 20X1, balance sheet of Williams is as follows:

Williams Incorporated
Balance Sheet
December 31, 20X1

Assets			Liabilities and Equity			
Current assets:			Accounts payable			$ 40,000
Accounts receivable.	$ 50,000					
Inventory	300,000					
		$350,000	Stockholders' equity:			
			Common stock	$ 40,000		
Noncurrent assets:			Paid-in capital in excess of par . .	110,000		
Land.	$ 20,000		Retained earnings	250,000	400,000	
Building (net)	70,000	90,000				
Total assets		$440,000	Total liabilities and equity			$440,000

The following fair values differ from existing book values:

Inventory	$250,000
Land.	40,000
Building	120,000

Required ▶ ▶ ▶ ▶ ▶   Record the purchase entry for Kent Corporation that would result under each of the alternative offers. Price zone analysis is suggested.

1. Kent Corporation issues 20,000 of its $10 par common stock with a fair value of $25 per share for the net assets of Williams Incorporated.
2. Kent Corporation pays $385,000 in cash.

Problem 1-5 *(LO 4, 7)* **Revaluation of assets.** Jansen Company is a corporation that was organized on July 1, 20X1. The June 30, 20X6, balance sheet for Jansen is as follows:

Assets		
Investments		$ 400,500
Accounts receivable	$1,250,000	
Allowance for doubtful accounts	(300,000)	950,000
Inventory		1,500,000
Prepaid insurance		18,000
Land.		58,000
Machinery and equipment (net)		1,473,500
Goodwill		100,000
Total assets.		$4,500,000

Liabilities and Equity	
Current liabilities	$1,475,000
Common stock, $10 par	1,200,000
Retained earnings	1,825,000
Total liabilities and equity	$4,500,000

   Machinery was purchased in fiscal years 20X2, 20X4, and 20X5 for $500,000, $850,000, and $660,000, respectively. The straight-line method of depreciation and a 10-year estimated life with no salvage value have been used for all machinery, with a half-year of depreciation taken in the year of acquisition. The experience of other companies over the last several years indicates that the machinery can be sold at 125% of its book value.

An analysis of the accounts receivable indicates that the allowance for doubtful accounts should be increased to $337,500. An independent appraisal made in June 20X1 valued the land at $70,000. Using the lower-of-cost-or-market rule, inventory is to be restated at $1,200,000.

To be exchanged are 16,000 shares of Clark Corporation for 120,000 Jansen shares. During June 20X6, the fair value of a share of Clark Corporation was $265. The stockholders' equity account balances of Clark Corporation as of June 30, 20X6, were as follows:

Common stock, $10 par	$2,000,000
Additional paid-in capital	580,000
Retained earnings	2,496,400
Total stockholders' equity	$5,076,400

Direct acquisition costs are $12,000.

Assuming the books of Clark Corporation are to be retained, prepare the necessary journal ◀ ◀ ◀ ◀ ◀ **Required**
entry (or entries) to effect the business combination on July 1, 20X6, as a purchase. Use zone analysis to support the purchase entries.

Problem 1-6 *(LO 7)* **Cash purchase, several of each priority, with goodwill.** Tweedy Corporation is contemplating the purchase of the net assets of Sylvester Corporation in anticipation of expanding its operations. The balance sheet of Sylvester Corporation on December 31, 20X1, is as follows:

Sylvester Corporation
Balance Sheet
December 31, 20X1

Current assets:

			Current liabilities:		
Notes receivable	$ 24,000		Accounts payable	$ 45,000	
Accounts receivable	56,000		Payroll and benefit-related		
Inventory	31,000		liabilities..................	12,500	
Other current assets.........	18,000		Debt maturing in one year.......	10,000	
Total current assets.........		$129,000	Total current liabilities		$ 67,500
Investments		65,000			

Fixed assets:			**Other liabilities:**		
Land........................	$ 32,000		Long-term debt................	$248,000	
Building....................	245,000		Payroll and benefit-related		
Equipment	387,000		liabilities..................	156,000	
Total fixed assets		664,000	Total other liabilities..........		404,000

Intangibles:			**Stockholders' equity:**		
Goodwill	$ 45,000		Common stock................	$100,000	
Patents.....................	23,000		Paid-in capital in excess of par ...	250,000	
Trade names	10,000		Retained earnings	114,500	
Total intangibles		78,000	Total equity ....:...........		464,500
Total assets		$936,000	Total liabilities and equity		$936,000

An appraiser for Tweedy determined the fair values of the assets and liabilities to be as follows:

Assets		Liabilities	
Notes receivable	$ 24,000	Accounts payable	$ 45,000
Accounts receivable	56,000	Payroll and benefit-related	
Inventory	30,000	liabilities	12,500
Other current assets..........	15,000	Debt maturing in one year........	10,000

(continued)

Assets		Liabilities	
Investments	63,000		
Land.........................	55,000	Long-term debt................	248,000
Building	275,000	Payroll and benefit-related	
Equipment	426,000	liabilities—long-term	156,000
Goodwill	—		
Patents......................	20,000		
Trade names	15,000		

The agreed-upon purchase price was $580,000 in cash. Direct acquisition costs paid in cash totaled $20,000.

Required ▶ ▶ ▶ ▶ ▶   Using the above information, do zone analysis, and prepare the entry on the books of Tweedy Corporation to purchase the net assets of Sylvester Corporation on December 31, 20X1.

Problem 1-7 *(LO 5, 7)* **Stock purchase, goodwill.** HT Corporation is contemplating the acquisition of the net assets of Smith Company on December 31, 20X1. It is considering making an offer, which would include a cash payout of $290,000 along with giving 10,000 shares of its $2 par value common stock that is currently selling for $20 per share. The balance sheet of Smith Company is given below, along with estimated fair values of the net assets to be acquired.

Goodwill $3,000

Smith Company
Balance Sheet
December 31, 20X1

	Book Value	Fair Value		Book Value	Fair Value
Current assets:			**Current liabilities:**		
Notes receivable	$ 33,000	$ 33,000	Accounts payable	$ 63,000	$ 63,000
Inventory	89,000	80,000	Taxes payable.................	15,000	15,000
Prepaid expenses	15,000	15,000	Interest payable...............	3,000	3,000
Total current assets...........	$137,000	$128,000	Total current liabilities	$ 81,000	$ 81,000
Investments	$ 36,000	$ 55,000			
Fixed assets:			**Other liabilities:**		
Land.........................	$ 15,000	$ 90,000	Bonds payable	$250,000	$250,000
Buildings	115,000	170,000	Discount on bonds payable......	(18,000)	(30,000)
Equipment	256,000	250,000			
Vehicles.....................	32,000	25,000			
Total fixed assets	$418,000	$535,000	Total other liabilities..........	$232,000	$220,000
Intangibles:			**Stockholders' equity:**		
Franchise....................	$ 56,000	$ 70,000	Common stock................	$ 50,000	
			Paid-in capital in excess of par ...	200,000	
			Retained earnings	84,000	
			Total equity	$334,000	
Total assets	$647,000	$788,000	Total liabilities and equity	$647,000	

Required ▶ ▶ ▶ ▶ ▶   Do zone analysis and prepare the entry on the books of HT Corporation to record the acquisition of Smith Company.

Problem 1-8 *(LO 5, 7)* Cash purchase, extraordinary gain, allocate to nonpriority accounts.

James Company owned by Howard and Jane James has been experiencing financial difficulty for the past several years. Both Howard and Jane have not been in good health and have decided to find a buyer. J&K International, after being approached by Howard and Jane and reviewing the financial statements for the previous three years, has decided to make an offer of $23,000 for the net assets of James Company on January 1, 20X2. The balance sheet as of this date is as follows:

James Company
Balance Sheet
January 1, 20X2

Current assets:		**Current liabilities:**	
Accounts receivable	$ 87,000	Accounts payable	$ 56,000
Inventory	36,000	Accrued liabilities	14,000
Other current assets	14,000		
Total current assets	$137,000	Total current liabilities	$ 70,000
Fixed assets:		**Other liabilities:**	
Equipment	$105,000	Notes payable	$ 30,000
Vehicles	69,000		
Total fixed assets	$174,000	Total liabilities	$100,000
Intangibles:		**Stockholders' equity:**	
Mailing lists	$ 4,000	Common stock	$ 60,000
		Paid-in capital in excess of par . . .	100,000
		Retained earnings	55,000
		Total equity	$215,000
Total assets	$315,000	Total liabilities and equity	$315,000

In reviewing the above balance sheet, J&K's appraiser felt the liabilities were stated at their fair values. He placed the following fair values on the assets of the company.

James Company
Fair Values
January 1, 20X2

Current assets:	
Accounts receivable	$ 87,000
Inventory	30,000
Other current assets	8,000
Total current assets	$125,000
Fixed assets:	
Equipment	$ 80,000
Vehicles	71,000
Total fixed assets	$151,000
Intangibles:	
Mailing lists	$ 0
Total intangibles	$ 0
Total assets	$276,000

Required ▶ ▶ ▶ ▶ ▶
    1. Using this information, do zone analysis, and prepare the entry to record the purchase of the net assets of James Company on the books of J&K International.

    2. Howard and Jane were disappointed in J&K International's offer and initially rejected it. J&K International then offered them $45,000 in cash. Assuming this offer is accepted, do zone analysis, and prepare the entry that should be made on J&K International's books. (Assume that the fair values of the net assets have not changed.)

Problem 1-9 *(LO 6)* **Pro forma income after purchase.** On January 1, 20X1, Arthur Enterprises acquired Ann's Tool Company. Prior to the merger of the two companies, each company had prepared an estimate of its income for the year ended December 31, 20X1. These estimates are as follows:

Income Statement Accounts	Arthur Enterprises		Ann's Tool Company	
Sales revenue		$550,000		$140,000
Cost of goods sold		200,000		50,000
Gross profit		$350,000		$ 90,000
Selling expenses	$125,000		$30,000	
Administrative expenses	150,000		45,000	
Depreciation expense	13,800		7,500	
Amortization expense	5,600		2,000	
Total operating expenses		294,400		84,500
Operating income		$ 55,600		$ 5,500
Nonoperating revenues and expenses:				
Interest expense				4,000
Interest income		7,000		
Dividend income		4,000		
Income before taxes		$ 66,600		$ 1,500
Provision for income taxes (30% rate)		19,980		450
Net income		$ 46,620		$ 1,050

An analysis of the merger agreement revealed that the purchase price exceeded the fair value of all assets by $40,000. The book and fair values of Ann's Tool Company are given in the table below along with an estimate of the useful lives of each of these asset categories.

Asset Account	Book Value	Fair Value	Useful Life
Inventory	$30,000	$ 28,000	Sold during 20X1
Land	50,000	80,000	Unlimited
Buildings	75,000	125,000	25 years
Equipment	32,000	56,000	8 years
Truck	1,000	3,000	2 years
Patent	12,000	18,000	6 years
Computer software	0	10,000	2 years
Copyright	0	20,000	10 years

Management believes the company will be in a combined tax bracket of 30%. The company uses the straight-line method of computing depreciation and amortization and assigns a zero salvage value.

Required ▶ ▶ ▶ ▶ ▶ Using the above information, prepare a pro forma income statement for the combined companies.

Problem 1-10 *(LO 5, 7)* Issue stock, several of each priority account, goodwill, purchase entry and pro forma income.

Part A. Garden International has been looking to expand its operations and has decided to acquire the net assets of Iris Company. Garden will be issuing 10,000 shares of its $5 par value common stock for the net assets of Iris. Garden's stock is currently selling for $27 per share. In addition, Garden paid $10,000 in direct acquisition costs. A balance sheet for Iris Company as of December 31, 20X1, is as follows:

Current assets:			Current liabilities:		
Accounts receivable		$ 15,000	Accounts payable		$ 22,000
Inventory		38,000	Interest payable		2,000
Prepaid expenses		12,000			
Total current assets		$ 65,000	Total current liabilities		$ 24,000
Investments		19,000			
Fixed assets:			**Other liabilities:**		
Land	$30,000		Long-term notes payable		40,000
Building	70,000				
Equipment	56,000				
Total fixed assets		156,000	Total liabilities		$ 64,000
Intangibles:			**Stockholders' equity:**		
Patent	$17,000		Common stock	$ 40,000	
Copyright	22,000		Paid-in capital in excess of par .	120,000	
Goodwill	8,000		Retained earnings	63,000	
Total intangibles		47,000	Total equity		223,000
Total assets		$287,000	Total liabilities and equity		$287,000

In reviewing Iris's balance sheet and in consulting with various appraisers, Garden has determined that the inventory is understated by $2,000, the land is understated by $10,000, the building is understated by $15,000, and the copyrights are understated by $4,000. Garden has also determined that the equipment is overstated by $6,000, and the patent is overstated by $5,000.

The investments have a fair value of $33,000 on December 31, 20X1, and the amount of goodwill (if any) must be determined.

Part A. Using the information above, do zone analysis, and record the acquisition of Iris ◄ ◄ ◄ ◄ ◄ **Required**
Company on Garden International's books.

Part B. Garden International wishes to estimate its net income after the acquisition of Iris. Projected income statements for 20X2 are as follows:

Income Statement Accounts	Garden International	Iris Company
Sales revenue	$(350,000)	$(125,000)
Cost of goods sold	147,000	55,000
Gross profit	$(203,000)	$ (70,000)
Selling expenses*	$ 100,000	$ 20,000
Administrative expenses*	50,000	30,000
Depreciation expense	12,500	8,600
Amortization expense	1,000	3,900
Total operating expenses	$ 163,500	$ 62,500

(continued)

Income Statement Accounts	Garden International	Iris Company
Operating income	$ (39,500)	$ (7,500)
Nonoperating revenues and expenses:		
Interest expense		3,000
Investment income	(12,000)	(4,500)
Income before taxes	$ (51,500)	$ (9,000)
Provision for income taxes (40% rate)	20,600	3,600
Net income	$ (30,900)	$ (5,400)

*Does not include depreciation or amortization expense.

Garden International estimates that the following amount of depreciation and amortization should be taken on the revalued assets of Iris Company.

Building depreciation	$4,000
Equipment depreciation	5,000
Patent amortization	1,200
Copyright amortization	2,600

Required ▶ ▶ ▶ ▶ ▶ **Part B.** Using the above information, prepare a pro forma income statement for Garden International combined with Iris Company for the year ended December 31, 20X2.

Problem 1-11 *(LO 8)* **Tax-free exchange.** Gusty Company issued 10,000 shares of $10 par common stock for the net assets of Marco Incorporated on December 31, 20X2. The stock has a fair value of $60 per share. Direct acquisition costs were $10,000, and the cost of issuing the stock was $3,000. At the time of the purchase, Marco had the following summarized balance sheet:

Assets		Liabilities and Equity	
Current assets	$150,000	Bonds payable	$200,000
Equipment (net)	200,000	Common stock ($10 par).	100,000
Land and buildings (net)	250,000	Retained earnings	300,000
Total assets.	$600,000	Total liabilities and equity	$600,000

The only fair value differing from book value is equipment, which is worth $300,000. The previous asset values are also the tax basis of the assets, which will be the tax basis for Gusty, since the acquisition is a tax-free exchange. The applicable tax rate is 30%.

Required ▶ ▶ ▶ ▶ ▶ Record the purchase of the net assets of Marco Incorporated by Gusty Company. You may assume the price paid will allow goodwill to be recorded.

APPENDIX PROBLEM

Problem 1A-1 *(LO 10)* **Estimate goodwill, record purchase.** Caswell Company is contemplating the purchase of LaBelle Company as of January 1, 20X6. LaBelle Company has provided the following current balance sheet:

Assets		Liabilities and Equity	
Cash and receivables	$ 150,000	Current liabilities	$120,000
Inventory	180,000	9% bonds payable	300,000
Land.	50,000	Common stock ($5 par).	100,000
			(continued)

Assets		Liabilities and Equity	
Building	600,000	Paid-in capital in excess of par	200,000
Accumulated depreciation	(150,000)	Retained earnings	150,000
Goodwill	40,000		
Total assets.	$ 870,000	Total liabilities and equity	$870,000

The following information exists relative to balance sheet accounts:

a. The inventory has a fair value of $200,000.
b. The land is appraised at $100,000 and the building at $600,000.
c. The 9% bonds payable have five years to maturity and pay annual interest each December 31. The current interest rate for similar bonds is 8% per year.
d. It is likely that there will be a payment for goodwill based on projected income in excess of the industry average, which is 10% on total assets. Caswell will project the average past five years' operating income and will pay for excess income based on an assumption of a five-year life and a risk rate of return of 16%. The past five years' net incomes for LaBelle are as follows:

20X1	$120,000
20X2	140,000
20X3	150,000
20X4	200,000 (includes $40,000 extraordinary gain)
20X5	180,000

1. Provide an estimate of fair value for the bonds and for goodwill. ◄ ◄ ◄ ◄ ◄ **Required**
2. Using the values derived in Requirement 1, record the purchase on the Caswell books.

The High Price of Cookies — Case 1-1

Part A. In June of 2000, Philip Morris Companies Inc, the large food and tobacco conglomerate, announced it would purchase Nabisco Holdings Corp. for $55 per share. Philip Morris chairman and chief executive Geoffrey Bible said in a statement that the purchase at $55 per share would greatly expand the firm's food offerings. "The combination of Kraft and Nabisco will create the most dynamic company in the food industry, both in terms of earnings levels and the revenues and earnings growth rates."

Philip Morris purchased the net assets of Nabisco and assumed all of Nabisco's debt. The price of a Nabisco share increased from $30 per share in April 2000 to $51.62, just prior to the purchase announcement.

Exhibit A shows a balance sheet for Nabisco Holding S Corp. as of March 31, 2000. The goodwill shown is from prior purchases made by Nabisco and does not reflect the purchase of the company by Philip Morris. The purchase included all of the Class A and Class B common stock shown on the balance sheet.

Exhibit A

Nabisco Holdings Corp.
Nabisco, Inc.
Consolidated Condensed Balance Sheets
(dollars in millions)

| | March 31, 2000 | | December 31, 1999 | |
	Nabisco Holdings	Nabisco	Nabisco Holdings	Nabisco
ASSETS				
Current assets:				
Cash and cash equivalents	$ 94	$ 94	$ 110	$ 110
Accounts receivable, net	553	553	681	681
Deferred income taxes	100	100	116	116
Inventories	964	964	898	898
Prepaid expenses and other current assets	82	82	79	79
Total current assets	1,793	1,793	1,884	1,884
Property, plant and equipment—at cost	5,087	5,087	5,053	5,053
Less accumulated depreciation	(2,030)	(2,030)	(1,966)	(1,966)
Net property, plant and equipment	3,057	3,057	3,087	3,087
Trademarks, net of accumulated amortization of $1,242 and $1,214, respectively	3,414	3,414	3,443	3,443
Goodwill, net of accumulated amortization of $1,032 and $1,007, respectively	3,151	3,151	3,159	3,159
Other assets and deferred charges	163	163	134	134
	$11,578	$11,578	$11,707	$11,707
LIABILITIES AND STOCKHOLDERS' EQUITY				
Current liabilities:				
Notes payable	$ 72	$ 72	$ 39	$ 39
Accounts payable	403	403	642	642
Accrued liabilities	982	932	1,020	970
Intercompany payable to Nabisco Holdings	—	7	—	7
Current maturities of long-term debt	11	11	158	158
Income taxes accrued	121	121	104	104
Total current liabilities	1,589	1,546	1,963	1,920
Long-term debt (less current maturities)	4,094	4,094	3,892	3,892
Other noncurrent liabilities	770	770	744	744
Deferred income taxes	1,180	1,180	1,176	1,176
Stockholders' equity:				
Class A common stock (51,412,707 shares issued and outstanding at March 31, 2000 and December 31, 1999)	1	—	1	—
Class B common stock (213,250,000 shares issued and outstanding at March 31, 2000 and December 31, 1999)	2	—	2	—
Paid-in capital	4,093	4,141	4,093	4,141
Retained earnings	158	137	148	127
Treasury stock, at cost	(17)	—	(17)	—
Accumulated other comprehensive income (loss)	(290)	(290)	(293)	(293)
Notes receivable on common stock purchases	(2)	—	(2)	—
Total stockholders' equity	3,945	3,988	3,932	3,975
	$11,578	$11,578	$11,707	$11,707

Required (Part A):

Calculate the price paid for the net assets of Nabisco and compare it to book value. By what amount will net assets have to be increased to reflect the price paid for Nabisco?

Part B. For the year ended December 31, 1999, Nabisco reported a net income of $357 million or $1.35 per share. The interesting issue is, will this influx of income have a favorable effect on Philip Morris's reported income? For the year ended December 31, 1999, Philip Morris reported a net income of $7.75 billion on 2,339 billion shares of common stock. Earnings per share, after various adjustments, was $3.91 per share.

   Assume that the excess of the price paid for Nabisco over the book value of its net assets is primarily attributable to goodwill. At the time of the purchase, the amortization period for goodwill was 40 years. Further assume that the added goodwill amortization expense is tax deductible at a rate of 38%.

Required (Part B):

Assuming that Nabisco has the same income (prior to asset adjustments resulting from the purchase) in years after the purchase, how much net income will Nabisco add to Philip Morris using a 40-year amortization period for goodwill? What would the income increment be if goodwill is not amortized?

Structured Example of Goodwill Impairment

Case 1-2

Modern Company purchased the net assets of the Frontier Company for $1,300,000 on January 1, 20X1. A business valuation consultant arrived at the price and deemed it to be a good value.

Part 1. The following list of fair values was provided to you by the consultant:

Assets and Liabilities	Comments	Valuation Method	Fair Value
Cash equivalents	Sellers values are accepted.	Existing book value	$ 80,000
Inventory	Replacement cost is available.	Market replacement cost for similar items is used.	150,000
Accounts receivable	Asset is adjusted for estimated bad debts.	Aging schedule is used for valuation.	180,000
Land	Per-acre value is well established.	Calculation is based on 20 acres at $ 10,000 per acre.	200,000
Building	Most reliable measure is rent potential.	Rent is estimated at $80,000 per year for 20 years, discounted at 14% return for similar properties. Present value is reduced for land value.	329,850
Equipment	Cost of replacement capacity can be estimated.	Estimated purchase cost of equipment with similar capacity is used.	220,000
Patent	Recorded by seller at only legal cost; has significant future value.	Added profit made possible by patent is $40,000 per year for 4 years. Discounted at risk-adjusted rate for similar investments of 20% per year.	103,550
Current liabilities	Recorded amounts are accurate.	Recorded value is used.	(120,000)

(continued)

Assets and Liabilities	Comments	Valuation Method	Fair Value
Mortgage payable	Specified interest rate is below market rate.	Discount the $50,000 annual payments for 5 years at annual market rate of 7%.	(205,010)
Net identifiable assets at fair value			$ 938,390
Price paid for reporting unit			1,300,000
Goodwill	Believed to exist based on reputation and customer list.	Implied by price paid.	$ 361,610

Required:

1. Using the information in the preceding table, confirm the accuracy of the present value calculations made for the building, patent, and mortgage payable.

Part 2. Frontier did not have publicly traded stock. You made an estimate of the value of the company based on the following assumptions that will later be included in the reporting unit valuation procedure:

1. Frontier will provide operating cash flows, net of tax, of $150,000 during the next fiscal year.

2. Operating cash flows will increase at the rate of 10% per year for the next 4 fiscal years and then will remain steady for 15 more years.

3. Cash flows, defined as net of cash from operations less capital expenditures, will be discounted at an after-tax discount rate of 12%. An annual rate of 12% is a reasonable risk-adjusted rate of return for investments of this type.

4. Added capital expenditures will be $100,000 after 5 years, $120,000 for 10 years, and $130,000 after 15 years.

5. An estimate of salvage value (net of the tax effect of gains or losses) of the assets after 20 years is estimated to be $300,000. This is a conservative assumption, since the unit may be operated after that period.

Required:

2. Prepare a schedule of net-of-tax cash flows for Frontier and discount them to present value.

3. Compare the estimated fair value of the reporting unit with amounts assigned to identifiable assets plus goodwill less liabilities.

4. Record the purchase.

Part 3. Revisit the information in Part 1 that illustrates the reporting unit valuation procedure.

Assume that by fiscal year-end, December 31, 20X1, events have occurred suggesting goodwill could be impaired. You have the following information. These new estimates were made at the end of the first year:

Net book value of Frontier Company including goodwill $1,300,000
Estimated implied fair value of the reporting unit,
  based on cash flow analysis discounted at a 12% annual rate   1,200,000
Estimated fair value of identifiable net assets using methods
  excluding goodwill   1,020,000

Required:

5. Has goodwill been impaired? Perform the impairment testing procedure. If goodwill has been impaired, calculate the adjustment to goodwill and make the needed entry.

Consolidated Statements: Date of Acquisition

Learning Objectives

When you have completed this chapter, you should be able to

1. Differentiate among the accounting methods used for investments, based on the level of common stock ownership in another company.

2. State the traditional criteria for presenting consolidated statements, and explain why disclosure of separate subsidiary financial information might be important.

3. Explain when control might exist without majority ownership.

4. Demonstrate the worksheet procedures needed to eliminate the investment account.

5. Demonstrate the worksheet procedures needed to merge subsidiary accounts.

6. Apply zone and price analyses to guide the adjustment process to reflect the price paid for the controlling interest.

7. Create a determination and distribution of excess (D&D) schedule.

8. Explain the impact of a noncontrolling interest on worksheet procedures and financial statement preparation.

9. Show the impact of preexisting goodwill on the consolidation process.

10. Define push-down accounting, and explain when it may be used and its impact.

The preceding chapter dealt with business combinations that are accomplished as asset acquisitions. The net assets of an entire company are purchased and recorded directly on the books of the purchasing company. Consolidation of the two companies is automatic because all subsequent transactions are recorded on a single set of books.

A company will commonly purchase a large enough interest in another company's voting common stock to obtain control of operations. The company owning the controlling interest is termed the *parent*, while the controlled company is termed the *subsidiary*. Legally, the parent company has only an investment in the stock of the subsidiary and will only record an investment account in its accounting records. The subsidiary will continue to prepare its own financial statements. However, accounting principles require that when one company has effective control over another, a single set of *consolidated statements* must be prepared for the companies under common control. The consolidated statements present the financial statements of the parent and its subsidiaries as those of a single economic entity. Worksheets are prepared to merge the separate statements of the parent and its subsidiary(s) into a single set of consolidated statements.

This chapter is the first of several that will show how to combine the separate statements of a parent and its subsidiaries. The theory of purchase accounting, developed in Chapter 1, is applied in the consolidation process. In fact, the consolidated statements of a parent and its 100% owned subsidiary look exactly like they would have had the net assets been purchased. **This chapter contains only the procedures necessary to prepare consolidated statements**

on the day that the controlling investment is acquired. The procedures for consolidating controlling investments in periods subsequent to the purchase date will be developed in Chapter 3. The effect of operating activities between the parent and its subsidiaries, such as intercompany loans, merchandise sales, and fixed asset sales, will be discussed in Chapters 4 and 5. Later chapters deal with taxation issues and changes in the level of ownership.

LEVELS OF INVESTMENT

The purchase of the voting common stock of another company receives different accounting treatments depending on the level of ownership and the amount of influence or control caused by the stock ownership. The ownership levels and accounting methods can be summarized as follows:

Level of Ownership	Initial Recording	Recording of Income
Passive—generally under 20% ownership.	At cost including brokers' fees.	Dividends as declared (except stock dividends).
Influential—generally 20% to 50% ownership.	At cost including brokers' fees.	Ownership share of income (or loss) is reported. Shown as investment income on financial statements. (Dividends declared are distributions of income already recorded; they reduce the investment account.)
Controlling—generally over 50% ownership.	At cost including all direct acquisition costs.	Ownership share of income (or loss). (Some adjustments are explained in later chapters.) Accomplished by merging the subsidiary income statement accounts with those of the parent in the consolidation process.

To illustrate the differences in reporting the income applicable to the common stock shares owned, consider the following example based on the reported income of the investor and investee (company whose shares are owned by investor):

Account	Investor*	Investee
Sales	$500,000	$300,000
Less: Cost of goods sold	250,000	180,000
Gross profit	$250,000	$120,000
Less: Selling and administrative expenses	100,000	80,000
Net income	$150,000	$ 40,000

*Does not include any income from investee.

Assume that the investee company paid $10,000 in cash dividends. The investor would prepare the following income statements, depending on the level of ownership:

Level of Ownership	10% Passive	30% Influential	80% Controlling
Sales	$ 500,000	$ 500,000	$ 800,000
Less: Cost of goods sold	250,000	250,000	430,000
Gross profit	$ 250,000	$ 250,000	$ 370,000
Less: Selling and administrative expenses	100,000	100,000	180,000

(continued)

Level of Ownership	10% Passive	30% Influential	80% Controlling
Operating income	$ 150,000	$ 150,000	
Dividend income (10% × $10,000 dividends)	1,000		
Investment income (30% × $40,000 reported income)		12,000	
Net income	**$151,000**	**$162,000**	$ 190,000
Noncontrolling interest (20% × $40,000 reported income)			$ 8,000
Controlling interest			**$182,000**

With a 10% passive interest, the investor included only its share of the dividends declared by the investee as its income. With a 30% influential ownership interest, the investor reported 30% of the investee income as a separate source of income. With an 80% controlling interest, the investor (now termed the parent) merges the investee's (now a subsidiary) nominal accounts with its own amounts. Dividend and investment income no longer exist. The essence of consolidated reporting is the portrayal of the separate legal entities as a single economic entity. If the parent owned a 100% interest, net income would simply be reported as $190,000. Since this is only an 80% interest, the net income must be shown as allocated between the noncontrolling and controlling interests. The noncontrolling interest is the 20% of the subsidiary not owned by the parent. The controlling interest is the parent income, plus 80% of the subsidiary income.

REFLECTION

- An influential investment (generally over 20% ownership) requires recording the investor's share of income as it is earned as a single line item amount.

- A controlling investment (generally over 50% ownership) requires that subsidiary income statement accounts be combined with those of the parent company.

THE FUNCTION OF CONSOLIDATED STATEMENTS

2

OBJECTIVE

State the traditional criteria for presenting consolidated statements, and explain why disclosure of separate subsidiary financial information might be important.

Consolidated financial statements are designed to present the results of operations, cash flow, and the balance sheet of both the parent and its subsidiaries as if they were a single company. Generally, consolidated statements are the most informative to the stockholders of the controlling company. Yet, consolidated statements do have their shortcomings. The rights of the noncontrolling shareholders are limited to only the company they own, and, therefore, they get little value from consolidated statements. They really need the separate statements of the subsidiary. Similarly, creditors of the subsidiary need its separate statements, because they may look only to the legal entity that is indebted to them for satisfaction of their claims. The parent's creditors should be content with the consolidated statements, since the investment in the subsidiary will produce cash flows that can be used to satisfy their claims.

Consolidated statements have been criticized for being too aggregated. Unprofitable subsidiaries may not be very obvious, because, when consolidated, their performance is combined with that of other affiliates. However, this shortcoming is easily overcome. One option is to prepare separate statements of the subsidiary as supplements to the consolidated statements. The second option, which may be required, is to provide disclosure for major business segments. When subsidiaries are in businesses distinct from the parent, the definition of a segment may parallel that of a subsidiary.

Traditional Criteria for Consolidated Statements

Generally, statements are to be consolidated when a parent firm owns over 50% of the voting common stock of another company. There may be instances where consolidation is appropriate even though less than 51% of the voting common stock is owned by the parent. SEC Regulation S-X defines control in terms of power to direct or cause the direction of management and policies of a person, whether through the ownership of voting securities, by contract, or otherwise. Thus, control has been said to exist when a less than 51% ownership interest exists but where there is no other large ownership interest that can exert influence on management. The exception to consolidating when control exists is if control is only temporary or does not rest with the majority owner. For example, control would be presumed not to reside with the majority owner when the subsidiary is in bankruptcy, in legal reorganization, or when foreign exchange restrictions or foreign government controls cast doubt on the ability of the parent to exercise control over the subsidiary.

Prior to 1988, it was acceptable to exclude subsidiaries from consolidation when their operations were not homogeneous with those of the parent. It was common for a manufacturing-based parent to exclude from consolidations those subsidiaries involved in banking, financing, real estate, or leasing activities, but this exception for "nonhomogeneity" came under criticism. Frequently, firms diversified and excluded some types of subsidiaries from consolidation. This meant that a significant amount of assets, liabilities, and cash flows were not presented. The option of not consolidating selected subsidiaries was often considered a form of "off-balance-sheet" financing. For instance, Ford Motor Company, General Motors, and Chrysler did not consolidate their financing company subsidiaries; this meant that millions of dollars of debt did not appear on the consolidated balance sheets of these firms. Stockholders are interested in the total financial position of the corporation, regardless of how diversified the operations have become. Based on their concerns and the divergence in practice as to consolidation policy, the nonhomogeneity exception was eliminated by FASB Statement No. 94.[1] In addition, the statement eliminated less commonly used exceptions for large noncontrolling interests and foreign locations. There is a concern that the combining of unlike operations will cloud the interpretation of financial statements. In response to this concern, many corporations are preparing classified balance sheets that separate the assets and liabilities of the nonhomogeneous operations. Ford segregates its financial services subsidiaries, which in the past had not been consolidated.

Nonconsolidated subsidiaries now have become a rarity. When they do exist, they are accounted for as an investment under the equity method. The accounting methods for such an investment are discussed in Chapter 5.

<table>
<tr><td>

3

────────────
OBJECTIVE
────────────

Explain when control might exist without majority ownership.

</td><td>

Consolidation Based on Control

The SEC has suggested that consolidation may be appropriate where control exists without majority (over 50%) ownership of controlling shares. A revised FASB exposure draft, issued in 1999, also recommends consolidation where control is achieved with less than majority ownership. Under the latest modification to the exposure draft in 2000, the FASB would presume that control exists, without majority ownership, if one of several possible situations exists:

◆ The parent company has the right to appoint or elect a majority of the members of the governing board. This could occur without owning a majority of the common voting shares because of a voting trust, the controlled corporation's charter or bylaws, or through other similar devices.

◆ The parent company has the ability to elect a majority of the members of the governing board of an entity through a large noncontrolling (less than 50%) voting interest. Again, this can be accomplished by owning a large noncontrolling interest through an agreement, a trust, or a stipulation in the entity's charter or bylaws. A large noncontrolling interest is one that is expected to cast at least 50% of the votes actually cast (not the total that could theoretically be cast) in an election of the governing board. No other party or group may

</td></tr>
</table>

───────────────

1 Statement of Financial Accounting Standards No. 94, *Consolidation of All Majority-Owned Subsidiaries* (Stamford: Financial Accounting Standards Board, 1987).

own a significant interest. An interest is assumed to be significant if it exceeds one-third the size of the parent company interest. For example, if the parent holds a 40% interest, no other party or group may own more than 13%.

♦ The parent has the ability to elect a majority of the members of the governing board of an entity through the ownership of securities that can be exercised or converted to obtain sufficient shares of voting common stock.

♦ The parent company is the only general partner in a limited partnership, and no other partner group may dissolve the partnership or remove the general partner.

♦ The parent has the unilateral ability to assume the role of general partner in a limited partnership through the present ownership of convertible securities or other rights that are currently exercisable.

There has been a common practice of not consolidating a newly acquired subsidiary if control was only temporary. This practice would no longer be allowed under the current FASB proposal.

REFLECTION

• There are many circumstances where control will exist and consolidation will be required without a greater than 50% ownership interest in a subsidiary's voting common stock.

TECHNIQUES OF CONSOLIDATION

4

OBJECTIVE

Demonstrate the worksheet procedures needed to eliminate the investment account.

This chapter builds an understanding of the techniques used to consolidate the separate balance sheets of a parent and its subsidiary immediately subsequent to the acquisition. The consolidated balance sheet as of the acquisition date is discussed first. The impact of consolidations on operations after the acquisition date is discussed in Chapters 3 through 5.

Chapter 1 emphasized that there are two means of achieving control over the assets of another company. A company may directly acquire the assets of another company, or it may acquire a controlling interest in the other company's voting common stock. In an *asset acquisition*, the company whose assets were purchased is dissolved. The assets acquired are recorded directly on the books of the purchaser, and consolidation of balance sheet amounts is automatic. Where control is achieved through a *stock acquisition*, the acquired company (the subsidiary) remains as a separate legal entity with its own financial statements. While the initial accounting for the two types of acquisitions differs significantly, a 100% stock acquisition and an asset acquisition have the same effect of creating one larger single reporting entity and should produce the same consolidated balance sheet. There is, however, a difference if the stock acquisition is less than 100%. Then there will be a noncontrolling interest in the consolidated balance sheet, which is not possible when the assets are purchased directly.

In the following discussion, the recording of an asset acquisition and a 100% stock acquisition are compared, and the balance sheets that result from each type of acquisition are studied. Then the chapter deals with the accounting procedures needed when there is less than a 100% stock ownership and a noncontrolling equity interest exists.

Reviewing an Asset Acquisition

Illustration 2-1 demonstrates an asset acquisition of Company S by Company P for cash. Part A of the illustration presents the balance sheets of the two companies just prior to the acquisition. Part B shows the entry to record Company P's payment of $500,000 in cash for the net assets of

Company S. The book values of the assets and liabilities acquired are assumed to be representative of their fair values, and no goodwill is acknowledged. The assets and liabilities of Company S are added to those of Company P to produce the balance sheet for the combined company, shown in Part C. Since account balances are combined in recording the acquisition, **statements for the single combined reporting entity are produced automatically, and no consolidation process is needed.**

Illustration 2-1
Asset Acquisition

A. Balance sheets of Companies P and S prior to acquisition:

Company P Balance Sheet

Assets		Liabilities and Equity	
Cash	$ 800,000	Current liabilities	$ 150,000
Accounts receivable	300,000	Bonds payable	500,000
Inventory	100,000	Common stock.	100,000
Equipment (net)	150,000	Retained earnings	600,000
Total.	$1,350,000	Total.	$1,350,000

Company S Balance Sheet

Assets		Liabilities and Equity	
Accounts receivable	$ 200,000	Current liabilities	$ 100,000
Inventory	100,000	Common stock.	200,000
Equipment (net)	300,000	Retained earnings	300,000
Total.	$ 600,000	Total.	$ 600,000

B. Entry on Company P's books to record acquisition of the net assets of Company S by Company P:

Accounts Receivable	200,000	
Inventory	100,000	
Equipment	300,000	
Current Liabilities		100,000
Cash		500,000

C. Balance sheet of Company P subsequent to asset acquisition:

Company P Balance Sheet

Assets		Liabilities and Equity	
Cash	$ 300,000	Current liabilities	$ 250,000
Accounts receivable	500,000	Bonds payable	500,000
Inventory	200,000	Common stock.	100,000
Equipment (net)	450,000	Retained earnings	600,000
Total.	$1,450,000	Total.	$1,450,000

Consolidating a Stock Acquisition

In a stock acquisition, the acquiring company deals only with existing shareholders, not the company itself. Assuming the same facts as those used in Illustration 2-1, except that Company P will purchase all the outstanding stock of Company S from its shareholders for $500,000, Company P would make the following entry:

Investment in Subsidiary S	500,000	
Cash		500,000

This entry does not record the individual underlying assets and liabilities over which control is achieved. Instead, the acquisition is recorded in an investment account that represents the controlling interest in the net assets of the subsidiary. If no further action was taken, the investment in the subsidiary account would appear as a long-term investment on Company P's balance sheet. However, such a presentation is permitted only if consolidation were not required.

Assuming consolidated statements are required, the balance sheet of the two companies must be combined into a single consolidated balance sheet. The consolidation process is separate from the existing accounting records of the companies and requires completion of a worksheet. No journal entries are actually made to the parent's or subsidiary's books, so the elimination process starts anew each year.

The first example of a consolidated worksheet, Worksheet 2-1, appears later in the chapter on page 85. (The icon in the margin indicates the location of the worksheet at the end of the chapter. The worksheets are also repeated in the Student Companion Book.) The first two columns of the worksheet include the trial balances (balance sheet only for this chapter) for Companies P and S. The trial balances and the consolidated balance sheet are presented in single columns to save space. Credit balances are shown in parentheses. Obviously, since there are no nominal accounts listed, the income statement accounts have already been closed to retained earnings.

Worksheet 2-1: page 85

The consolidated worksheet requires elimination of the investment account balance because the two companies will be treated as one. (How can a company have an investment in itself?) Similarly, the subsidiary's stockholders' equity accounts are eliminated because its assets and liabilities belong to the parent, not to outside equity owners. In general journal form, the elimination entry is as follows:

(EL)	Common Stock, Company S	200,000	
	Retained Earnings, Company S	300,000	
	Investment in Company S		500,000

— *Eliminating Entries*

Note that the key "EL" will be used in all future worksheets. Keys, once introduced, will be assigned to all similar items throughout the text. A list of all "Keys" used is maintained inside the front cover of this text. The balances in the consolidated balance sheet column (the last column) are exactly the same as in the balance sheet prepared for the preceding asset acquisition example—as they should be.

REFLECTION

- Consolidation is required for any company that is controlled, even in cases where less than 50% of the company's shares is owned by the parent.

- Consolidation produces the same balance sheet that would result in an asset acquisition.

- Consolidated statements are separate but derived from the individual statements of the parent and its subsidiaries.

5

OBJECTIVE

Demonstrate the worksheet
procedures needed to
merge subsidiary accounts.

ADJUSTMENT OF SUBSIDIARY ACCOUNTS

In the last example, the price paid for the investment in the subsidiary was equal to the net book value of the subsidiary (which means the price was also equal to the subsidiary's stockholders' equity). In most purchases, the price will exceed the book value of the subsidiary's net assets. Typically, fair values will exceed the recorded book values of assets. The price may also reflect unrecorded intangible assets including goodwill. Let us revisit the last example and assume that instead of paying $500,000 cash, Company P paid $700,000 cash for all the common stock shares of Company S and made the following entry for the purchase:

Investment in Subsidiary S	700,000	
Cash		700,000

Use the same Company S balance sheet as in Illustration 2-1, with the following additional information on fair values:

Company S Book and Estimated Fair Values
December 31, 20X1

Assets	Book Value	Fair Value	Liabilities and Equity	Book Value	Fair Value
Accounts receivable	$ 200,000	$ 200,000	Current liabilities	$ 100,000	$ 100,000
Inventory	100,000	120,000			
Equipment (net)	300,000	400,000	**Market value of net**		
Total assets	**$600,000**	**$720,000**	**assets (assets – liabilities)**	**$500,000**	**$620,000**

If this were an asset acquisition, the identifiable assets and liabilities would be recorded at fair value and goodwill at $80,000 (price paid of $700,000 minus $620,000 fair value of net assets). Adding fair values to Company P's accounts, the new balance sheet would appear as follows:

Company P
Consolidated Balance Sheet
December 31, 20X1

Assets		Liabilities and Equity		
Current assets:		Current liabilities	$250,000	
Cash	$100,000	Bonds payable	500,000	
Accounts receivable.	500,000	Total liabilities		$ 750,000
Inventory	220,000			
Total		$ 820,000		

(continued)

Assets			Liabilities and Equity		
Long-term assets:			Stockholders' equity:		
Equipment (net)	$550,000		Common stock	$100,000	
Goodwill	80,000		Retained earnings	600,000	
Total		630,000	Total		700,000
Total assets		$1,450,000	Total liabilities and equity . . .		$1,450,000

As before, the consolidated worksheet should produce a consolidated balance sheet that looks exactly the same as the preceding balance sheet for an asset acquisition. Worksheet 2-2 on page 86 shows how this is accomplished.

Worksheet 2-2: page 86

◆ The (EL) entry is the same as before; $500,000 of subsidiary equity is eliminated against the investment account.
◆ Entry (**D**) distributes the remaining cost of $200,000 to the acquired assets to bring them from book to fair value and to record goodwill of $80,000.

In general journal entry form, the elimination entries are as follows:

(EL)	Common Stock, Company S	200,000	
	Retained Earnings, Company S.	300,000	
	Investment in Company S.		500,000
(D1)	Inventory (to increase from $100,000 to $120,000)	20,000	
(D2)	Equipment (to increase from $300,000 to $400,000)	100,000	
(D3)	Goodwill ($700,000 price minus $620,000 fair value assets).	80,000	
(D)	Investment in Company S ($700,000 price minus $500,000 book value eliminated above)		200,000

The balance sheet column of Worksheet 2-2 includes the subsidiary accounts at full fair value and reflects the $80,000 of goodwill included in the purchase price. The formal balance sheet for Company P, based on the worksheet, would be exactly the same as shown above for the asset acquisition.

Purchase of a subsidiary at a price in excess of the fair values of the subsidiary equity is as simple as the case just presented, especially where there are a limited number of assets to adjust to fair value. For more involved purchases, where there are many accounts to adjust and/or the price paid is not high enough to adjust all accounts to full fair value, a more complete analysis is needed. We will now proceed to develop these tools.

Analysis of Complicated Purchases—100% Interest

The previous examples assumed the purchase of the subsidiary for cash. However, most purchases are accomplished by the parent issuing common stock (or, less often, preferred stock) in exchange for the subsidiary common shares being acquired. This avoids the depletion of cash and, if other criteria are met, allows the subsidiary shareholders to have a tax-free exchange. In most cases, the shares are issued by a publicly traded parent company that provides a readily determinable market price for the shares issued. The investment in the subsidiary is then recorded at the fair value of the shares issued. Less frequently, a nonpublicly traded parent may issue

6

OBJECTIVE

Apply zone and price analyses to guide the adjustment process to reflect the price paid for the controlling interest.

shares to subsidiary shareholders. In these cases, the fair values are determined for the net assets of the subsidiary company, and the total estimated fair value of the subsidiary company is recorded as the cost of the investment.

In order to illustrate the complete procedures used to record the investment in and the consolidation of a subsidiary, we will revisit the Johnson Company example used in Chapter 1 (page 10). This will also allow us to continue to compare the procedures used for a stock purchase with those used for an asset acquisition in Chapter 1. The balance sheet of the Johnson Company on December 31, 20X1, when Acquisitions Inc. purchased 100% of its shares, was as follows:

Johnson Company Balance Sheet December 31, 20X1				
Assets			**Liabilities and Equity**	
Current assets:			Current liabilities	$ 5,000	
Accounts receivable.	$28,000		Bonds payable	20,000	
Inventory	40,000		Total liabilities		$ 25,000
Total		$ 68,000		
Long-term assets:			Stockholders' equity:		
Land.	$10,000		Common stock, $1 par . . .	$ 1,000	
Buildings (net)	40,000		Paid-in capital in excess		
Equipment (net)	20,000		of par.	59,000	
Patent (net)	15,000		Retained earnings	68,000	
Total		85,000	Total		128,000
Total assets		$153,000	Total liabilities and equity . . .		$153,000

Assume that Acquisitions Inc. exchanges 7,000 shares of its common stock for the 1,000 shares of Johnson common stock (7 to 1 exchange ratio). The fair value per share is $50, and the par value is $1 per share. Acquisitions Inc. also makes the following additional payments:

1. $10,000 to attorneys and accountants for direct acquisition costs.
2. $5,000 to a brokerage company for stock issuance costs.

Acquisitions Inc. would record the investment as follows:

Investment in Johnson Company (7,000 shares × $50		
fair value per share + $10,000 direct acquisition cost)	360,000	
Common Stock, $1 Par (7,000 shares × $1)		7,000
Paid-In Capital in Excess of Par ($350,000 − $7,000 par)		343,000
Cash (for direct acquisition costs).		10,000

The payment of the issue costs would reduce the amount assigned to the shares issued as follows:

Paid-In Capital in Excess of Par	5,000	
Cash (to investment company)		5,000

Acquisitions Inc. is aware that it will have to consolidate this investment into its financial statements. It realizes that the $360,000 price paid does not agree with the book value of the underlying equity ($128,000). When consolidating, it will be eliminating a $360,000 investment against a stockholders' equity of $128,000. The difference is the amount of adjustment that will be needed for the subsidiary's accounts. Knowing this, Johnson would prepare a comparison of recorded book versus estimated fair values for assets and liabilities. Assets will be arranged by their priorities as follows:

Johnson Company Book and Estimated Fair Values
December 31, 20X1

Assets	Book Value	Fair Value	Liabilities and Equity	Book Value	Fair Value
Priority assets:					
Accounts receivable.	$ 28,000	$ 28,000	Current liabilities	$ 5,000	$ 5,000
Inventory	40,000	45,000	Bonds payable	20,000	21,000
Total priority assets . . .	**$ 68,000**	**$ 73,000**	**Total liabilities**	**$ 25,000**	**$ 26,000**
Nonpriority assets:					
Land	$ 10,000	$ 50,000			
Buildings (net)	40,000	80,000			
Equipment (net)	20,000	50,000			
Patent (net)	15,000	30,000			
Brand-name copyright*	0	40,000			
Total nonpriority assets	**$ 85,000**	**$250,000**	**Value of net assets**		
Total assets	**$153,000**	**$323,000**	**(assets – liabilities)**	**$128,000**	**$297,000**

*Previously unrecorded assets.

The comparison includes the priorities or the accounts as discussed in Chapter 1.

Zone Analysis. A zone analysis, based on fair values used in Chapter 1 (page 27), is prepared as follows:

Zone Analysis	Group Total	Cumulative Total
Priority accounts (fair value priority assets – liabilities)	$ 47,000	$ 47,000
Nonpriority accounts (at fair value)	250,000	297,000

From the zone analysis, we can do a *price analysis*.

Price Analysis.

- **Extraordinary gain:** A price **below $47,000** will have no value assigned to nonpriority accounts or to goodwill. Only the priority accounts will be recorded at fair value. The amount below $47,000 would result in an extraordinary gain.
- **Bargain:** A price **between $47,000 and $297,000** will lead to nonpriority accounts being assigned less than full fair value, and result in no goodwill being recorded. Priority accounts are always recorded at fair value.
- **Premium price:** A price **above $297,000** will allow all identifiable accounts to be adjusted to full fair value and lead to recording goodwill for any excess of the price paid over $297,000.

A *price analysis schedule* compares the price paid to the above cumulative zone limits and determines the amount available to each group of assets. For this example, the price paid exceeds the total, including nonpriority accounts, by $63,000, leading to the following price analysis:

Price (including direct acquisition costs)	**$360,000**	
Assign to priority accounts......................................	47,000	Full value
Assign to nonpriority accounts	250,000	Full value
Goodwill.	**63,000**	
Extraordinary gain	**0**	

The price analysis schedule indicates that all the accounts can be fully adjusted to fair value; therefore, no allocation will be needed.

The 2005 FASB exposure draft on business combinations would greatly simplify the "price analysis." All identifiable assets would be adjusted to full fair value regardless of the price paid. A price greater than the sum of the net identifiable assets would be goodwill; a price less than the fair value of the net identifiable assets would be a gain (ordinary).

Examine Worksheet 2-3 on page 87 for Acquisitions Inc. and its subsidiary, Johnson Company, as it would be prepared immediately after the purchase. Notice that entry (EL) eliminated total stockholders' equity of $128,000 against an investment balance of $360,000. The entry in general journal form is as follows:

Worksheet 2-3: page 87

(EL)	Common Stock, $1 Par	1,000	
	Paid-In Capital in Excess of Par	59,000	
	Retained Earnings	68,000	
	Investment in Johnson Company		128,000

7

OBJECTIVE

Create a determination and distribution of excess (D&D) schedule.

Determination and Distribution of Excess Schedule. After the (EL) entry, there is an excess of cost over book value of $232,000 ($360,000 cost − $128,000 subsidiary equity). This amount reflects the undervaluation of Johnson's accounts and is the amount of write-up to fair value that must be made in the consolidation process. The *determination and distribution of excess (D&D) schedule* compares the price paid with the subsidiary equity to predetermine the imbalance that will occur on the consolidated worksheet when the investment account amount is eliminated against the underlying subsidiary equity. The schedule then uses the price analysis schedule to guide the adjustment of subsidiary accounts. In this example, the price analysis indicated that every account can be fully adjusted to fair value.

Price paid for investment (including direct acquisition costs).		**$360,000**	
Less book value of interest purchased:			
Common stock, $1 par	$ 1,000		
Paid-in capital in excess of par	59,000		
Retained earnings	68,000		
Total equity		128,000	
Excess of cost over book value		**$232,000**	Cr.
Adjustments:			
Accounts receivable.	$ 0		
Inventory ($45,000 fair − $40,000 book)	5,000		Dr.
Current liabilities	0		
Premium on bonds payable (new account)	(1,000)		Cr.
Land ($50,000 fair − $10,000 book)	40,000		Dr.
Buildings (net) ($80,000 fair − $40,000 book)	40,000		Dr.
Equipment (net) ($50,000 fair − $20,000 book).............	30,000		Dr.
Patent (net) ($30,000 fair − $15,000 book)	15,000		Dr.

Brand-name copyright (new account)	40,000	Dr.
Goodwill (new account)	63,000	Dr.
Total adjustments.	**$232,000**	

This schedule is then used to distribute the excess in Worksheet 2-3, entry series (D), as follows in journal entry form:

(D1)	Inventory	5,000	
(D2)	Premium on Bonds Payable		1,000
(D3)	Land.	40,000	
(D4)	Buildings (net)	40,000	
(D5)	Equipment (net)	30,000	
(D6)	Patent (net).	15,000	
(D7)	Brand-Name Copyright.	40,000	
(D8)	Goodwill	63,000	
(D)	Investment in Johnson Company (balance)		232,000

The adjustments to the building (D4) and equipment (D5) are made by increasing the asset cost amount, rather than by decreasing accumulated depreciation. A more complex solution would be to restate the assets at their net fair value and eliminate all accumulated depreciation. This causes more complications in worksheets of future periods than is typically warranted.

The same D&D will be a necessary support schedule for all future worksheets because, as noted earlier, the worksheet eliminations and adjustments are not recorded on the books of either the subsidiary or the parent. The D&D prepared on the purchase date will always drive the distribution of excess entry. Separate adjustments to depreciate or amortize the adjustments will be described and recorded in Chapter 3.

The consolidated balance sheet includes the book value of parent accounts and the fair value of subsidiary accounts. The following formal consolidated balance sheet would be prepared on December 31, 20X1:

Acquisitions Inc.
Consolidated Balance Sheet
December 31, 20X1

Assets			Liabilities and Equity		
Current assets:			Current liabilities	$ 94,000	
Cash	$ 51,000		Bonds payable	120,000	
Accounts receivable.	70,000		Premium on bonds payable	1,000	
Inventory	140,000		Total liabilities		$ 215,000
Total		$ 261,000			
Long-term assets:					
Land.	$110,000				
Buildings	600,000				
Accumulated depreciation. . .	(70,000)				
Equipment	120,000		Stockholders' equity:		
Accumulated depreciation. . .	(34,000)		Common stock, $1 par	$ 20,000	
Patent (net)	30,000		Paid-in capital in excess		
Brand-name copyright.	40,000		of par	480,000	
Goodwill	63,000		Retained earnings	405,000	
Total.		859,000	Total		905,000
Total assets		$1,120,000	Total liabilities and equity		$1,120,000

Bargain Purchases—100% Interest

A *bargain purchase* is one in which the price paid does not allow nonpriority accounts to be recorded at fair value. There is no excess available for goodwill. The previous zone analysis shows that this would occur at a price less than $297,000, but greater than $47,000.

We will assume that 4,000 shares of Acquisitions Inc. common stock are issued as payment with a fair value of $50 each. We will again assume that there are direct acquisition costs of $10,000 and issue costs of $5,000. The entries to record the purchase would be as follows:

Investment in Johnson Company (4,000 shares × $50 fair value per share + $10,000 direct acquisition cost)	210,000	
Common Stock, $1 Par (4,000 shares × $1)		4,000
Paid-In Capital in Excess of Par ($200,000 − $4,000 par)		196,000
Cash (for direct acquisition costs)		10,000
Paid-In Capital in Excess of Par	5,000	
Cash (to investment company)		5,000

The price of $210,000 is compared to the same zone analysis used in the previous example:

Zone Analysis	Group Total	Cumulative Total
Priority accounts (net of liabilities)	$ 47,000	$ 47,000
Nonpriority accounts	250,000	297,000

A price analysis schedule compares the price paid to the cumulative totals in the zone analysis and determines the amount available to each group of assets. For this example, the price analysis would be as follows:

Price (including direct acquisition costs)	**$210,000**	
Assign to priority accounts	47,000	Full value
Assign to nonpriority accounts	163,000	Allocate
Goodwill	**0**	
Extraordinary gain	**0**	

The price analysis indicates that full value will be assigned to priority accounts and the $163,000 will be used to adjust the nonpriority accounts as follows:

Allocation to Nonpriority Accounts:	Fair Value	Percent	Amount to Allocate	Allocated Amount	Book Value	Adjustment
Land	$ 50,000	20%	$163,000	$ 32,600	$10,000	$22,600
Buildings (net)	80,000	32	163,000	52,160	40,000	12,160
Equipment (net)	50,000	20	163,000	32,600	20,000	12,600
Patent	30,000	12	163,000	19,560	15,000	4,560
Brand-name copyright	40,000	16	163,000	26,080	0	26,080
Total	$250,000			$163,000	$85,000	$78,000

Note that the total adjustment is for $78,000, because the subsidiary's books already included $85,000 of the total $163,000 to be allocated to this group of assets.

The determination and distribution schedule will proceed to adjust the priority accounts to full fair value and will distribute $78,000 to the nonpriority assets. The schedule is prepared as follows:

Price paid for investment (including direct
acquisition costs) **$210,000**

Less book value of interest purchased:

Common stock, $1 par	$ 1,000	
Paid-in capital in excess of par	59,000	
Retained earnings	68,000	
Total equity		128,000
Excess of cost over book value		**$ 82,000** Cr.

Adjustments:

Accounts receivable.................................	$ 0	
Inventory ($45,000 fair – $40,000 book).................	5,000	Dr.
Current liabilities	0	
Premium on bonds payable (new account)	(1,000)	Cr.
Land (from allocation schedule)........................	22,600	Dr.
Buildings (net) (from allocation schedule)	12,160	Dr.
Equipment (net) (from allocation schedule)	12,600	Dr.
Patent (net) (from allocation schedule).................	4,560	Dr.
Brand-name copyright (from allocation schedule)	26,080	Dr.
Total adjustments................................	**$ 82,000**	

Examine Worksheet 2-4 on page 88 for Acquisitions Inc. and its subsidiary, Johnson Company. Notice that entry (EL) eliminated total stockholders' equity of $128,000 against an investment balance of $210,000. The worksheet entry in journal entry form is as follows:

worksheet

Worksheet 2-4: page 88

(EL)	Common Stock, $1 Par	1,000	
	Paid-In Capital in Excess of Par	59,000	
	Retained Earnings	68,000	
	Investment in Johnson Company		128,000

The D&D schedule is then used to distribute the excess in Worksheet 2-4, entry series (D), in journal entry form as follows:

(D1)	Inventory	5,000	
(D2)	Premium on Bonds Payable		1,000
(D3)	Land...	22,600	
(D4)	Buildings (net)	12,160	
(D5)	Equipment (net)	12,600	
(D6)	Patent (net).......................................	4,560	
(D7)	Brand-name Copyright	26,080	
(D)	Investment in Johnson Company (balance)		82,000

The consolidated balance sheet values include the book value of the parent plus the adjusted values of the subsidiary accounts. Notice that there is no investment in the subsidiary on the consolidated balance sheet. The following formal consolidated balance sheet would be prepared on December 31, 20X1:

Acquisitions Inc.
Consolidated Balance Sheet
December 31, 20X1

Assets			Liabilities and Equity		
Current assets:			Current liabilities	$ 94,000	
Cash	$ 51,000		Bonds payable	120,000	
Accounts receivable.	70,000		Premium on bonds payable.	1,000	
Inventory	140,000		Total liabilities		$215,000
Total		$261,000			
Long-term assets:					
Land.	$ 92,600				
Buildings	572,160				
Accumulated depreciation. . .	(70,000)		Stockholders' equity:		
Equipment	102,600		Common stock, $1 par	$ 17,000	
Accumulated depreciation. . .	(34,000)		Paid-in capital in excess		
Patent (net)	19,560		of par	333,000	
Brand-name copyright	26,080		Retained earnings	405,000	
Total		709,000	Total		755,000
Total assets		$970,000	Total liabilities and equity		$970,000

Extraordinary Gain—100% Interest

We will assume that 500 shares of Acquisitions Inc. common stock are issued as payment with a fair value of $50 each. We will again assume that there are direct acquisition costs of $10,000 and issue costs of $5,000. The entries to record the purchase would be as follows:

Investment in Johnson Company (500 shares × $50		
fair value per share + $10,000 direct acquisition cost)	35,000	
Common Stock, $1 Par (500 shares × $1)		500
Paid-In Capital in Excess of Par ($25,000 − $500 par)		24,500
Cash (for direct acquisition costs).		10,000
Paid-In Capital in Excess of Par	5,000	
Cash (to investment company)		5,000

The price of $35,000 is compared to the same zone analysis used in the previous examples as follows:

Zone Analysis	Group Total	Cumulative Total
Priority accounts (net of liabilities)	$ 47,000	$ 47,000
Nonpriority accounts.	250,000	297,000

A price analysis schedule compares the price paid to the cumulative totals in the zone analysis and determines the amount available to each group of assets. For this example, the price analysis would be as follows:

Price (including direct acquisition costs)	**$ 35,000**	
Assign to priority accounts.......................................	$ 47,000	Full value
Assign to nonpriority accounts	0	No value
Goodwill..	**0**	
Extraordinary gain	**(12,000)**	

The determination and distribution schedule will proceed to adjust the priority accounts to full fair value. Since no value will be assigned to nonpriority accounts, the book value applicable to them is removed. An extraordinary gain becomes part of the distribution. The schedule is prepared as follows:

Price paid for investment (including direct acquisition costs)		**$ 35,000**	
Less book value of interest purchased:			
Common stock, $1 par	$ 1,000		
Paid-in capital in excess of par	59,000		
Retained earnings	68,000		
Total equity	$128,000		
Ownership interest	× 100%	128,000	
Excess of cost over book value (book value exceeds cost)		**$(93,000)**	Dr.
Adjustments:			
Accounts receivable.......................................	$ 0		
Inventory ($45,000 fair − $40,000 book)	5,000		Dr.
Current liabilities	0		
Premium on bonds payable (new account)	(1,000)		Cr.
Land (remove book value)	(10,000)		Cr.
Buildings (net) (remove book value)......................	(40,000)		Cr.
Equipment (net) (remove book value).....................	(20,000)		Cr.
Patent (net) (remove book value)	(15,000)		Cr.
Brand-name copyright (no amount available)	0		
Extraordinary gain.......................................	(12,000)		Cr.
Total adjustments................................		**$(93,000)**	

Examine Worksheet 2-5 on page 89 for Acquisitions Inc. and its subsidiary, Johnson Company, as it would be prepared immediately after the purchase. Notice that entry (EL) eliminated total stockholders' equity of $128,000 against an investment balance of $35,000. The worksheet entry in general journal form is as follows:

Worksheet 2-5: page 89

(EL)	Common Stock, $1 Par	1,000	
	Paid-In Capital in Excess of Par	59,000	
	Retained Earnings	68,000	
	Investment in Johnson Company		128,000

The investment account is overeliminated by $93,000 ($35,000 cost less $128,000 elimination). This requires that subsidiary assets be reduced and an extraordinary gain be recorded. The D&D schedule is then used to distribute this overelimination in Worksheet 2-5, entry series (D), as follows:

(D1)	Inventory	5,000	
(D2)	Premium on Bonds Payable		1,000
(D3)	Land..		10,000
(D4)	Buildings (net)		40,000
(D5)	Equipment (net)		20,000
(D6)	Patent (net)......................................		15,000
(D8)	Extraordinary Gain (Parent retained earnings)		12,000
(D)	Investment in Johnson Company (balance)	93,000	

The consolidated balance sheet values include the book value of the parent plus the adjusted values of the subsidiary accounts. The following formal consolidated balance sheet would be prepared on December 31, 20X1:

Acquisitions Inc.
Consolidated Balance Sheet
December 31, 20X1

Assets			Liabilities and Equity		
Current assets:			Current liabilities	$ 94,000	
Cash	$ 51,000		Bonds payable	120,000	
Accounts receivable........	70,000		Premium on bonds payable........	1,000	
Inventory	140,000		Total liabilities		$215,000
Total		$261,000			
Long-term assets:			Stockholders' equity:		
Land....................	$ 60,000		Common stock, $1 par	$ 13,500	
Buildings	520,000		Paid-in capital in excess		
Accumulated depreciation...	(70,000)		of par......................	161,500	
Equipment	70,000		Retained earnings	417,000	
Accumulated depreciation...	(34,000)				
Total		546,000	Total		592,000
Total assets		$807,000	Total liabilities and equity		$807,000

Notice that there is no goodwill on the consolidated balance sheet. There has been no value added to the parent's accounts for all subsidiary nonpriority accounts. Since only a balance sheet is being prepared, the extraordinary gain has been added to the parent's retained earnings.

REFLECTION

- A difference will usually exist between the price paid for a 100% interest and the underlying book value of subsidiary accounts. The difference is the total adjustment that must be made to subsidiary accounts when consolidating.

- A premium price is high enough to adjust all accounts to full fair value. Any unallocated excess is considered goodwill.

- A bargain price allows priority accounts (current assets, other marketable investments, and liabilities) to be recorded at fair value. The value remaining is not sufficient to record nonpriority assets at full fair value; instead, they are allocated the cost remaining after recording the priority accounts at fair value.

- An extraordinary gain occurs when the price paid is less than the amount assigned to the priority accounts (which are never discounted).

CONSOLIDATING A LESS THAN 100% INTEREST

8

OBJECTIVE

Explain the impact of a noncontrolling interest on worksheet procedures and financial statement preparation.

Consolidation of financial statements is required whenever the parent company controls a subsidiary. In other words, a parent company could consolidate far less than a 100% ownership interest. Several important ramifications may arise when less than 100% interest is consolidated.

◆ The parent's investment account is eliminated against only its ownership percentage of the underlying subsidiary equity accounts. The noneliminated portion of the subsidiary equity is termed the *noncontrolling interest (NCI)*. The NCI is typically shown on the consolidated balance sheet in total and is not broken into par, paid-in capital in excess of par, and retained earnings. The most common placement of the NCI on the balance sheet is to show it as a liability or to display it in the "mezzanine" which is between liabilities and stockholders' equity. A 2005 FASB exposure draft on consolidated financial statements[2] would require the noncontrolling interest to be displayed as a part of stockholders' equity. This text will follow the proposal.

◆ The entire amount of every subsidiary nominal (income statement) account is merged with the nominal accounts of the parent to calculate consolidated income. *The noncontrolling interest is allocated its percentage ownership times the reported income of the subsidiary only.* The precise methods and display of this interest are discussed in Chapter 3. In the past, this share of income has often been treated as another expense in the consolidated income statement. The 2005 FASB exposure draft would require that it not be shown as an expense, but rather as a distribution of consolidated income. This text will follow the proposed procedure.

◆ Current practice is to *adjust subsidiary accounts to fair value only for the parent's percentage interest.* Thus, if the book value of a subsidiary asset is $50,000 and the fair value is $80,000, an 80% parent owner would adjust the asset by only $24,000 (80% × $30,000 book/fair value difference). This text will use this approach, which is called the "Proprietary Theory of Consolidation." The 2005 FASB exposure draft suggests adjusting subsidiary assets to 100% of their fair value. This is a radical departure from current practice and will not be used in the text. The new method is explained in the special appendix to the chapters on business combinations.

Analysis of Complicated Purchase—Less than 100% Interest

When less than a 100% interest is purchased, zone analysis, price analysis, and the determination and distribution of excess procedures are applied only to the percentage interest purchased. We will now revisit the example involving the purchase of an interest in Johnson Company, as found on pages 66 to 67. We will assume that Acquisitions Inc. exchanges 5,600 shares of its common stock for 800 shares (an 80% interest) of Johnson Company stock (7 to 1 exchange ratio). The fair value of the shares issued is $50, and the par value is $1. The following additional payments are again made:

1. $10,000 to attorneys and accountants for direct acquisition costs.
2. $5,000 to a brokerage company for stock issuance costs.

---

2 FASB Exposure Draft, "Consolidated Financial Statements, Including Accounting and Reporting of Noncontrolling Interests in Subsidiaries—a replacement of ARB. 51" (Proposed Statements of the Financial Accounting Standards Board) June 30, 2005.

Acquisitions Inc. would record the investment as follows:

Investment in Johnson Company (5,600 shares × $50 fair value per share + $10,000 direct acquisition cost)	290,000	
Common Stock, $1 Par (5,600 shares × $1)		5,600
Paid-In Capital in Excess of Par ($280,000 − $5,600 par)		274,400
Cash (for direct acquisition costs).		10,000

The payment of the issue costs would again reduce the amount assigned to the shares issued as follows:

Paid-in Capital in Excess of Par	5,000	
Cash (to investment company)		5,000

Zone analysis is now performed on the 80% interest using the fair values shown on page 67. Adding an *ownership portion* modifies the zone analysis schedule. The parent may adjust only 80% of each account to fair value. The cumulative totals are also based on an 80% interest.

Zone Analysis	Group Total	Ownership Portion	Cumulative Total
Ownership percentage		80%	
Priority accounts (net of liabilities)	$ 47,000	$ 37,600	$ 37,600
Nonpriority accounts.	250,000	200,000	237,600

Premium Price. A price analysis schedule compares the price paid to the zone limits (used for the prior example) and determines the amount available to each group of assets. For this example, the price analysis would be as follows:

Price (including direct acquisition costs)	**$290,000**	
Assign to priority accounts, controlling share	$ 37,600	Full value
Assign to nonpriority accounts, controlling share	200,000	Full value
Goodwill.	**52,400**	
Extraordinary gain	**0**	

The price analysis schedule indicates that the parent's 80% share of all accounts can be fully adjusted to fair value. Goodwill is recorded for the excess of the $290,000 price over the $237,600 fair value of the parent's 80% share of the subsidiary's net assets.

Examine Worksheet 2-6 on page 90 for Acquisitions Inc. and its subsidiary, Johnson Company. Notice that entry (EL) eliminated only 80% of the subsidiary's equity ($102,400) against an investment balance of $290,000. The worksheet entry in journal form is as follows:

Worksheet 2-6: page 90

(EL)	Common Stock, $1 Par, 80%	800	
	Paid-In Capital in Excess of Par, 80%	47,200	
	Retained Earnings, 80%	54,400	
	Investment in Johnson Company		102,400

There is an excess of cost over book value of $187,600 ($290,000 price − $102,400 equity). As before, this amount reflects the undervaluation of the parent's share of Johnson's accounts and is the amount of write-up to fair value that must be made in the consolidation process. The D&D schedule compares the price paid with 80% of the subsidiary equity. Notice that a new line was added to the schedule to reduce the total subsidiary equity to the portion owned by the parent. The D&D then uses the price analysis schedule to guide the adjustment of subsidiary accounts. In this example, the parent's share of every account can be adjusted to fair value as follows:

Price paid for investment (including direct

acquisition costs)			**$290,000**	
Less book value of interest purchased:				
Common stock, $1 par	$	1,000		
Paid-in capital in excess of par		59,000		
Retained earnings		68,000		
Total equity.	$	128,000		
Ownership interest	×	80%	102,400	
Excess of cost over book value			**$187,600**	Cr.

Adjustments:

Accounts receivable.	$	0	
Inventory, 80% of ($45,000 fair − $40,000 book)		4,000	Dr.
Current liabilities		0	
Premium on bonds payable, 80% of $1,000		(800)	Cr.
Land, 80% of ($50,000 fair − $10,000 book).		32,000	Dr.
Buildings (net), 80% of ($80,000 fair − $40,000 book)		32,000	Dr.
Equipment (net), 80% of ($50,000 fair − $20,000 book)		24,000	Dr.
Patent (net), 80% of ($30,000 fair − $15,000 book).		12,000	Dr.
Brand-name copyright, 80% of $40,000		32,000	Dr.
Goodwill		52,400	Dr.
Total adjustments.		**$187,600**	

The D&D schedule is then used to distribute this excess in Worksheet 2-6, entry series (D), in journal entry form as follows:

(D1)	Inventory	4,000	
(D2)	Premium on Bonds Payable		800
(D3)	Land.	32,000	
(D4)	Buildings (net)	32,000	
(D5)	Equipment (net)	24,000	
(D6)	Patent (net).	12,000	
(D7)	Brand-Name Copyright.	32,000	
(D8)	Goodwill	52,400	
(D)	Investment in Johnson Company (balance)		187,600

The consolidated balance sheet values are the book value of the parent plus the adjusted values of the subsidiary's accounts. In this case, the parent's 80% interest in subsidiary accounts is at fair value, and the 20% NCI remains at book value. The following formal consolidated balance sheet would be prepared on December 31, 20X1:

Acquisitions Inc.
Consolidated Balance Sheet
December 31, 20X1

Assets			Liabilities and Equity		
Current assets:			Current liabilities		$ 94,000
Cash	$ 51,000		Bonds payable		120,000
Accounts receivable.	70,000		Premium on bonds payable.		800
Inventory	139,000		Total liabilities		$ 214,800
Total		$ 260,000			

(continued)

Assets		Liabilities and Equity	
Long-term assets:			
Land	$102,000		
Buildings	592,000		
Accumulated depreciation. . .	(70,000)		
Equipment	114,000	Stockholders' equity:	
Accumulated depreciation. . .	(34,000)	**Noncontrolling interest**	**$ 25,600**
Patent (net)	27,000	Common stock, $1 par	18,600
Brand-name copyright	32,000	Paid-in capital in excess of par . . .	411,400
Goodwill	52,400	Retained earnings	405,000
Total	815,400	Total	860,600
Total assets	$1,075,400	Total liabilities and equity	$1,075,400

Notice that the NCI is shown only in the aggregate as a subdivision of stockholders' equity.

Bargain Purchase. The procedures for a bargain purchase with less than a 100% interest are basically the same as that for a 100% interest, except that all adjustments are limited to the ownership percentage interest. As an example, assume that Acquisitions Inc. issued only 4,000 shares of its common stock for an 80% interest in Johnson Company and incurred the same direct acquisition and issue costs. The entries to record the purchase would be as follows:

Investment in Johnson Company (4,000 shares × $50		
fair value per share + $10,000 direct acquisition cost)	210,000	
Common Stock, $1 Par (4,000 shares × $1)		4,000
Paid-In Capital in Excess of Par ($200,000 − $4,000 par)		196,000
Cash (for direct acquisition costs)		10,000

The payment of the issue costs would again reduce the amount assigned to the shares issued as follows:

Paid-In Capital in Excess of Par	5,000	
Cash (to investment company)		5,000

A price analysis schedule compares the price paid to the cumulative totals in the previous zone analysis and determines the amount available to each group of assets. For this example, the price analysis would be as follows:

Price (including direct acquisition costs)	**$210,000**	
Assign to priority accounts, controlling share	$ 37,600	Full value
Assign to nonpriority accounts, controlling share	172,400	Allocate
Goodwill	**0**	
Extraordinary gain	**0**	

The price analysis schedule indicates that the parent's share of nonpriority accounts will be discounted and that there will be no goodwill. The *allocation schedule* for nonpriority accounts is as follows:

	Fair Value	Percent	Amount to Allocate	Allocated Amount	80% Book Value	Adjustment
Allocation to nonpriority accounts:						
Land.....................................	$ 50,000	20%	$172,400	$ 34,480	$ 8,000	$ 26,480
Buildings (net)	80,000	32	172,400	55,168	32,000	23,168
Equipment (net)	50,000	20	172,400	34,480	16,000	18,480
Patent....................................	30,000	12	172,400	20,688	12,000	8,688
Brand-name copyright....................	40,000	16	172,400	27,584	0	27,584
Total.....................................	$250,000			$172,400	$68,000	$104,400

Note that the *amount to allocate* applies to only the controlling share of all accounts. Therefore, this amount must be compared to only 80% of the subsidiary recorded book value. The NCI remains at book value as in the prior example.

Examine Worksheet 2-7 on page 91 for Acquisitions Inc. and its subsidiary, Johnson Company. Notice that entry (EL) eliminated 80% of the subsidiary's equity of $102,400 against an investment balance of $210,000. The worksheet entry in journal form is as follows:

Worksheet 2-7: page 91

(EL)	Common Stock, $1 Par, 80%	800	
	Paid-In Capital in Excess of Par, 80%	47,200	
	Retained Earnings, 80%	54,400	
	Investment in Johnson Company		102,400

There is an excess of cost over book value of $107,600. This amount reflects the undervaluation of the parent's share of Johnson's accounts and is the amount of write-up to fair value that must be made in the consolidation process. The determination and distribution of excess schedule compares the price paid with 80% of the subsidiary.

Price paid for investment (including direct acquisition costs)			**$210,000**	
Less book value of interest purchased:				
Common stock, $1 par		$ 1,000		
Paid-in capital in excess of par		59,000		
Retained earnings		68,000		
Total equity		$128,000		
Ownership interest	×	80%	102,400	
Excess of cost over book value			**$107,600**	Cr.
Adjustments:				
Accounts receivable.................................	$	0		
Inventory, 80% × ($45,000 fair − $40,000 book)		4,000		Dr.
Current liabilities		0		
Premium on bonds payable, 80% × $1,000		(800)		Cr.
Land (from allocation schedule).......................		26,480		Dr.
Buildings (net) (from allocation schedule)		23,168		Dr.
Equipment (net) (from allocation schedule)		18,480		Dr.
Patent (net) (from allocation schedule)...................		8,688		Dr.
Brand-name copyright (from allocation schedule)		27,584		Dr.
Total adjustments...............................			**$107,600**	

This schedule is then used to distribute the excess in Worksheet 2-7, entry series (D), as follows:

(D1)	Inventory	4,000	
(D2)	Premium on Bonds Payable		800
(D3)	Land	26,480	
(D4)	Buildings (net)	23,168	
(D5)	Equipment (net)	18,480	
(D6)	Patent (net)	8,688	
(D7)	Brand-Name Copyright	27,584	
(D)	Investment in Johnson Company (balance)		107,600

Extraordinary Gain. We will assume that 400 shares of Acquisitions Inc. common stock are issued as payment with a fair value of $50 each. We will again assume that there are direct acquisition costs of $10,000 and issue costs of $5,000. The entries to record the purchase would be as follows:

Investment in Johnson Company (400 shares × $50		
fair value per share + $10,000 direct acquisition cost)	30,000	
Common Stock, $1 Par (400 shares × $1)		400
Paid-In Capital in Excess of Par ($20,000 – $400 par)		19,600
Cash (for direct acquisition costs)		10,000
Paid-In Capital in Excess of Par	5,000	
Cash (to investment company)		5,000

A price analysis schedule compares the price paid to the cumulative totals in the zone analysis and determines the amount available to each group of assets. For this example, the price analysis would be as follows:

Price (including direct acquisition costs)	**$30,000**	
Assign to priority accounts, controlling share	$ 37,600	Full value
Assign to nonpriority accounts, controlling share	0	
Goodwill	**0**	
Extraordinary gain	**7,600**	

The determination and distribution schedule will proceed to adjust the controlling share of priority accounts to fair value. Since no value will be assigned to nonpriority accounts, the 80% (controlling share) book value applicable to them is removed. An extraordinary gain becomes part of the distribution. The schedule is prepared as follows:

Price paid for investment (including direct			
acquisition costs)			$ 30,000
Less book value of interest purchased:			
Common stock, $1 par	$	1,000	
Paid-in capital in excess of par		59,000	
Retained earnings		68,000	
Total equity	$	128,000	
Ownership interest	×	80%	102,400
Excess of cost over book value (book value			
exceeds cost)			**$(72,400)** Dr.

(continued)

Adjustments:

Accounts receivable.	$ 0	
Inventory, 80% × ($45,000 fair − $40,000 book).	4,000	Dr.
Current liabilities	0	
Premium on bonds payable (80% × $1,000)	(800)	Cr.
Land (remove 80% of book value)	(8,000)	Cr.
Buildings (net) (remove 80% of book value)	(32,000)	Cr.
Equipment (net) (remove 80% of book value)	(16,000)	Cr.
Patent (net) (remove 80% of book value)	(12,000)	Cr.
Brand-name copyright (no amount available)	0	
Extraordinary gain.	(7,600)	Cr.
Total adjustments	**$(72,400)**	

Eighty percent of the nonpriority accounts would be eliminated on the consolidated worksheet. Only the 20% NCI share of the subsidiary nonpriority accounts would be extended to the consolidated balance sheet.

The 2005 FASB exposure draft on business combinations would adjust all subsidiary assets and liabilities to 100% of fair value. This means that the noncontrolling interest's share of all accounts would also be adjusted to full fair value. Goodwill would even be recorded applicable to the noncontrolling interest. As is the case with a 100% purchase, there would be goodwill recorded when the price paid exceeds the fair value of the controlling interest in net assets at fair value and a gain (ordinary) would be recorded when the price paid is less than the controlling interest in net assets at fair value.

REFLECTION

- A less than 100% interest requires that zone and price analyses use only the parent ownership portion of all subsidiary accounts.

- Account adjustments are limited to the parent interest times the fair/book value difference.

- The noncontrolling interest percentage of all subsidiary assets remains at book value.

- The noncontrolling share of subsidiary equity appears as a single line item amount within the equity section of the balance sheet.

9

OBJECTIVE

Show the impact of preexisting goodwill on the consolidation process.

PREEXISTING GOODWILL

If a subsidiary is purchased and it has goodwill on its books, it is ignored in the zone and price analyses, since it has no priority. The only complication caused by existing goodwill is that the D&D schedule will adjust existing goodwill, rather than only recording new goodwill. Let us return to the example involving Johnson Company on page 66 and change only two facts: assume Johnson had goodwill of $40,000 and that its retained earnings was $40,000 greater. The modified comparison of values would be as follows:

Johnson Company Book and Estimated Fair Values December 31, 20X1					
Assets	Book Value	Fair Value	Liabilities and Equity	Book Value	Fair Value
Priority assets:					
Accounts receivable.	$ 28,000	$ 28,000	Current liabilities	$ 5,000	$ 5,000
Inventory	40,000	45,000	Bonds payable	20,000	21,000
Total priority assets	**$ 68,000**	**$ 73,000**	**Total liabilities**	**$ 25,000**	**$ 26,000**

(continued)

Assets	Book Value	Fair Value	Liabilities and Equity	Book Value	Fair Value
Nonpriority assets:					
Land.......................	$ 10,000	$ 50,000			
Buildings (net)	40,000	80,000			
Equipment (net)	20,000	50,000			
Patent (net).................	15,000	30,000			
Brand-name copyright*.......	0	40,000			
Goodwill.................	**40,000**	**?**			
Total nonpriority assets ...	**$125,000**	**$250,000**	**Value of net assets**		
Total assets	**$193,000**	**$323,000**	**(assets – liabilities)**.....	**$168,000**	**$297,000**

*Previously unrecorded asset.

No amount is entered for the fair value of goodwill since that is determined by the price paid. Zone analysis is based only on priority accounts and nonpriority accounts remaining other than goodwill, so it remains unchanged.

Let us revisit the example on page 75, where an 80% interest is purchased for $290,000. There would be absolutely no change in the zone and price analyses on page 76. There would, however, be some modifications to the determination and distribution of excess schedule as shown below.

Price paid for investment (including direct acquisition costs)		**$290,000**	
Less book value of interest purchased:			
Common stock, $1 par	$ 1,000		
Paid-in capital in excess of par	59,000		
Retained earnings **(greater by $40,000)**	108,000		
Total equity......................................	$168,000		
Ownership interest	× 80%	134,400	
Excess of cost over book value		**$155,600**	Cr.
Adjustments:			
Accounts receivable......................................	$ 0		
Inventory, 80% of $5,000.................................	4,000		Dr.
Current liabilities	0		
Premium on bonds payable, 80% of $1,000	(800)		Cr.
Land, 80% of $40,000	32,000		Dr.
Buildings (net), 80% of $40,000.........................	32,000		Dr.
Equipment (net), 80% of $30,000........................	24,000		Dr.
Patent (net), 80% of $15,000	12,000		Dr.
Brand-name copyright, 80% of $40,000	32,000		Dr.
Goodwill ($52,400 − existing 80% × $40,000).............	20,400		Dr.
Total adjustments..................................		**$155,600**	

Note that instead of goodwill being recorded for the full $52,400 indicated in the price analysis, the controlling interest in goodwill is adjusted to $52,400. Total subsidiary existing goodwill is $40,000. The NCI portion of goodwill (20% × $40,000) cannot be adjusted. The parent's share of existing goodwill is $32,000. It must be adjusted by $20,400 to bring it to the required $52,400 balance.

Existing Goodwill in a Bargain

Let us assume that the price paid for the 80% interest in Johnson was $210,000 (same as example on page 78). Again, the price analysis and the nonpriority account allocation schedules on pages 78 and 79 remain unchanged. The modified determination and distribution of excess schedule would appear as follows:

Price paid for investment (including direct acquisition costs)		**$210,000**	
Less book value of interest purchased:			
Common stock, $1 par	$ 1,000		
Paid-in capital in excess of par	59,000		
Retained earnings ($40,000 greater)	108,000		
Total equity.	$ 168,000		
Ownership interest	× 80%	134,400	
Excess of cost over book value		**$ 75,600**	Cr.
Adjustments:			
Accounts receivable.	$ 0		
Inventory, 80% × $5,000	4,000		Dr.
Current liabilities	0		
Premium on bonds payable, 80% × $1,000	(800)		Cr.
Land (from allocation schedule)	26,480		Dr.
Buildings (net) (from allocation schedule)	23,168		Dr.
Equipment (net) (from allocation schedule)	18,480		Dr.
Patent (net) (from allocation schedule)	8,688		Dr.
Brand-name copyright (from allocation schedule)	27,584		Dr.
Goodwill (remove 80% × $40,000 existing)	**(32,000)**		**Cr.**
Total adjustments.		**$ 75,600**	

Notice that goodwill, applicable to the controlling interest, is entirely eliminated. No goodwill can be applicable to the parent's interest unless all other accounts have been adjusted to full fair value for the parent's ownership portion.

REFLECTION

- Goodwill on the subsidiary's books at the time of the purchase is ignored in zone and price analyses.

- The D&D schedule shows an adjustment for the difference between total goodwill (from price analysis) and the parent's share of existing goodwill.

10

OBJECTIVE

Define push-down account-
ing, and explain when it
may be used and its impact.

PUSH-DOWN ACCOUNTING

Thus far, it has been assumed that the subsidiary's statements are unaffected by the parent's purchase of a controlling interest in the subsidiary. None of the subsidiary's accounts is adjusted on
the subsidiary's books. In all preceding examples, adjustments to reflect fair value are made only
on the consolidated worksheet. This is the most common but not the only accepted method.

Some accountants object to the inconsistency of using book values in the subsidiary's separate statements while using fair value adjusted values when the same accounts are included in
the consolidated statements. They would advocate *push-down accounting*, whereby the subsidiary's accounts are adjusted to reflect the fair value adjustments. In accordance with the new
basis of accounting, retained earnings are eliminated, and the balance (as adjusted for fair value
adjustments) is added to paid-in capital. It is argued that the purchase of a controlling interest
gives rise to a new basis of accountability for the interest traded, and the subsidiary accounts
should reflect those values.

If the push-down method were applied to the example of a 100% purchase for $360,000 on
page 66, the following entry would be made by the subsidiary on its books:

Inventory	5,000	
Premium on Bonds Payable		1,000
Land.	40,000	
Buildings	40,000	
Equipment	30,000	
Patent.	15,000	
Brand-Name Copyright.	40,000	
Goodwill	63,000	
Paid-In Capital in Excess of Par		232,000

This entry would raise the subsidiary equity to $360,000. The $360,000 investment
account would be eliminated against the $360,000 subsidiary equity with no excess remaining.
If there is a noncontrolling interest, adjustments on the subsidiary books would be limited to
the controlling ownership percentage.

The SEC staff has adopted a policy of requiring push-down accounting, in some cases, for
the separately published statements of a subsidiary. The existence of any significant noncontrolling interests (usually above 5%) and/or significant publicly held debt or preferred stock generally eliminates the requirement to use push-down accounting. **Note that the consolidated
statements are unaffected by this issue**. The only difference is in the placement of the adjustments from the determination and distribution of excess schedule. The conventional approach,
which is used in this text, makes the adjustments on the consolidated worksheet. The push-
down method makes the same adjustments directly on the books of the subsidiary. Under the
push-down method, the adjustments are already made when consolidation procedures are
applied. Since all accounts are adjusted to reflect fair values, the investment account is eliminated against subsidiary equity with no excess. The difference in methods affects only the presentation on the subsidiary's separate statements.

REFLECTION

- Push-down accounting revalues subsidiary accounts directly on the books of the subsidiary
based on adjustments indicated in the D&D schedule.

- Since assets are revalued before the consolidation process starts, no distribution of excess
(to adjust accounts) is required on the consolidated worksheet.

Worksheet 2-1

100% Interest; Price Equals Book Value
Company P and Subsidiary Company S
Worksheet for Consolidated Balance Sheet
December 31, 20X1

Worksheet 2-1 (see page 63)

		Trial Balance		Eliminations & Adjustments		Consolidated Balance Sheet	
		Company P	Company S	Dr.	Cr.		
1	Cash	300,000				300,000	1
2	Accounts Receivable	300,000	200,000			500,000	2
3	Inventory	100,000	100,000			200,000	3
4	Investment in Company S	500,000			(EL) 500,000		4
5							5
6	Equipment (net)	150,000	300,000			450,000	6
7	Goodwill						7
8	Current Liabilities	(150,000)	(100,000)			(250,000)	8
9	Bonds Payable	(500,000)				(500,000)	9
10	Common Stock—Company S		(200,000)	(EL) 200,000			10
11	Retained Earnings—Company S		(300,000)	(EL) 300,000			11
12	Common Stock—Company P	(100,000)				(100,000)	12
13	Retained Earnings—Company P	(600,000)				(600,000)	13
14	Totals	0	0	500,000	500,000	0	14

Eliminations and Adjustments:

(EL) Eliminate the investment in the subsidiary against the subsidiary equity accounts.

Worksheet 2-2

100% Interest; Price Exceeds Book Value
Company P and Subsidiary Company S
Worksheet for Consolidated Balance Sheet
December 31, 20X1

Worksheet 2-2 (see page 65)

| | Trial Balance | | Eliminations & Adjustments | | Consolidated | |
	Company P	Company S	Dr.	Cr.	Balance Sheet	
1 Cash	100,000				100,000	1
2 Accounts Receivable	300,000	200,000			500,000	2
3 Inventory	100,000	100,000	(D1) 20,000		220,000	3
4 Investment in Company S	700,000			(EL) 500,000		4
5				(D) 200,000		5
6 Equipment (net)	150,000	300,000	(D2) 100,000		550,000	6
7 Goodwill			(D3) 80,000		80,000	7
8 Current Liabilities	(150,000)	(100,000)			(250,000)	8
9 Bonds Payable	(500,000)				(500,000)	9
10 Common Stock—Company S		(200,000)	(EL) 200,000			10
11 Retained Earnings—Company S		(300,000)	(EL) 300,000			11
12 Common Stock—Company P	(100,000)				(100,000)	12
13 Retained Earnings—Company P	(600,000)				(600,000)	13
14 Totals	0	0	700,000	700,000	0	14

Eliminations and Adjustments:

(EL) Eliminate the investment in the subsidiary against the subsidiary equity accounts.
(D)   Distribute $200,000 excess of cost over book value as follows:
(D1) Inventory, $20,000.
(D2) Equipment, $100,000.
(D3) Goodwill, $80,000.

Worksheet 2-3

100% Interest; Price Exceeds Market Value of Identifiable Net Assets

Acquisitions Inc. and Subsidiary Johnson Company
Worksheet for Consolidated Balance Sheet
December 31, 20X1

Worksheet 2-3 (see page 68)

		Trial Balance		Eliminations & Adjustments		Consolidated Balance Sheet	
		Acquisitions	Johnson	Dr.	Cr.		
1	Cash	51,000	0			51,000	1
2	Accounts Receivable	42,000	28,000			70,000	2
3	Inventory	95,000	40,000	(D1) 5,000		140,000	3
4	Investment in Johnson Company	360,000			(EL) 128,000		4
5					(D) 232,000		5
6	Land	60,000	10,000	(D3) 40,000		110,000	6
7	Buildings	500,000	60,000	(D4) 40,000		600,000	7
8	Accumulated Depreciation	(50,000)	(20,000)			(70,000)	8
9	Equipment	60,000	30,000	(D5) 30,000		120,000	9
10	Accumulated Depreciation	(24,000)	(10,000)			(34,000)	10
11	Patent (net)		15,000	(D6) 15,000		30,000	11
12	Brand-Name Copyright			(D7) 40,000		40,000	12
13	Goodwill			(D8) 63,000		63,000	13
14	Current Liabilities	(89,000)	(5,000)			(94,000)	14
15	Bonds Payable	(100,000)	(20,000)			(120,000)	15
16	Discount (premium)				(D2) 1,000	(1,000)	16
17	Common Stock—Johnson		(1,000)	(EL) 1,000			17
18	Paid-In Capital in Excess of Par—Johnson		(59,000)	(EL) 59,000			18
19	Retained Earnings—Johnson		(68,000)	(EL) 68,000			19
20	Common Stock—Acquisitions	(20,000)				(20,000)	20
21	Paid-In Capital in Excess of Par—Acquisitions	(480,000)				(480,000)	21
22	Retained Earnings—Acquisitions	(405,000)				(405,000)	22
23	Totals	0	0	361,000	361,000	0	23

Eliminations and Adjustments:

(EL) Eliminate investment in subsidiary against subsidiary equity accounts.
(D) Distribute $232,000 excess of cost over book value as follows:
(D1) Inventory, $5,000.
(D2) Premium on bonds payable, ($1,000).

(D3) Land, $40,000.
(D4) Buildings, $40,000.
(D5) Equipment, $30,000.
(D6) Patent, $15,000.
(D7) Brand-name copyright, $40,000.
(D8) Goodwill, $63,000.

Worksheet 2-4

100% Interest; Price Exceeds Fair Value of Priority Accounts
Acquisitions Inc. and Subsidiary Johnson Company
Worksheet for Consolidated Balance Sheet
December 31, 20X1

Worksheet 2-4 (see page 71)

		Trial Balance		Eliminations & Adjustments		Consolidated Balance Sheet	
		Acquisitions	Johnson	Dr.	Cr.		
1	Cash	51,000	0			51,000	1
2	Accounts Receivable	42,000	28,000			70,000	2
3	Inventory	95,000	40,000	(D1) 5,000		140,000	3
4	Investment in Johnson	210,000			(EL) 128,000		4
5					(D) 82,000		5
6	Land	60,000	10,000	(D3) 22,600		92,600	6
7	Buildings	500,000	60,000	(D4) 12,160		572,160	7
8	Accumulated Depreciation	(50,000)	(20,000)			(70,000)	8
9	Equipment	60,000	30,000	(D5) 12,600		102,600	9
10	Accumulated Depreciation	(24,000)	(10,000)			(34,000)	10
11	Patent (net)		15,000	(D6) 4,560		19,560	11
12	Brand-Name Copyright			(D7) 26,080		26,080	12
13	Goodwill			(D8) 0		0	13
14	Current Liabilities	(89,000)	(5,000)			(94,000)	14
15	Bonds Payable	(100,000)	(20,000)			(120,000)	15
16	Discount (premium)				(D2) 1,000	(1,000)	16
17	Common Stock—Johnson		(1,000)	(EL) 1,000			17
18	Paid-In Capital in Excess of Par—Johnson		(59,000)	(EL) 59,000			18
19	Retained Earnings—Johnson		(68,000)	(EL) 68,000			19
20	Common Stock—Acquisitions	(17,000)				(17,000)	20
21	Paid-In Capital in Excess of Par—Acquisitions	(333,000)				(333,000)	21
22	Retained Earnings—Acquisitions	(405,000)				(405,000)	22
23	Totals	0	0	211,000	211,000	0	23

Eliminations and Adjustments:

(EL) Eliminate investment in subsidiary against subsidiary equity accounts.
(D) Distribute $82,000 excess of cost over book value as follows:
(D1) Inventory, $5,000.
(D2) Premium on bonds payable, ($1,000).
(D3) Land, $22,600.

(D4) Buildings, $12,160.
(D5) Equipment, $12,600.
(D6) Patent, $4,560.
(D7) Brand-name copyright, $26,080.
(D8) No amount available for goodwill.

Worksheet 2-5

100% Interest; Price Is Less than Fair Value of Priority Accounts

Acquisitions Inc. and Subsidiary Johnson Company
Worksheet for Consolidated Balance Sheet
December 31, 20X1

Worksheet 2-5 (see page 73)

		Trial Balance		Eliminations & Adjustments		Consolidated Balance Sheet	
		Acquisitions	Johnson	Dr.	Cr.		
1	Cash	51,000	0			51,000	1
2	Accounts Receivable	42,000	28,000			70,000	2
3	Inventory	95,000	40,000	(D1) 5,000		140,000	3
4	Investment in Johnson	35,000			(EL) 128,000		4
5				(D) 93,000			5
6	Land	60,000	10,000		(D3) 10,000	60,000	6
7	Buildings	500,000	60,000		(D4) 40,000	520,000	7
8	Accumulated Depreciation	(50,000)	(20,000)			(70,000)	8
9	Equipment	60,000	30,000		(D5) 20,000	70,000	9
10	Accumulated Depreciation	(24,000)	(10,000)			(34,000)	10
11	Patent (net)		15,000		(D6) 15,000		11
12	Brand-Name Copyright			(D7) 0			12
13	Goodwill						13
14	Current Liabilities	(89,000)	(5,000)			(94,000)	14
15	Bonds Payable	(100,000)	(20,000)			(120,000)	15
16	Discount (premium)				(D2) 1,000	(1,000)	16
17	Common Stock—Johnson		(1,000)	(EL) 1,000			17
18	Paid-In Capital in Excess of Par—Johnson		(59,000)	(EL) 59,000			18
19	Retained Earnings—Johnson		(68,000)	(EL) 68,000			19
20	Common Stock—Acquisitions	(13,500)				(13,500)	20
21	Paid-In Capital in Excess of Par—Acquisitions	(161,500)				(161,500)	21
22	Retained Earnings—Acquisitions	(405,000)			(D8) 12,000	(417,000)	22
23	Totals	0	0	226,000	226,000	0	23

Eliminations and Adjustments:

(EL) Eliminate investment in subsidiary against subsidiary equity accounts.
(D) Distribute $93,000 excess of book value over cost as follows:
(D1) Inventory, $5,000.
(D2) Premium on bonds payable, ($1,000).
(D3) Land, ($10,000).
(D4) Building is eliminated; no value available.
(D5) Equipment is eliminated; no value available.
(D6) Patent is eliminated; no value available.
(D7) No amount available for brand-name copyright.
(D8) No goodwill; record extraordinary gain. Since this is a balance sheet only, extraordinary gain is credited to retained earnings.

Worksheet 2-6

80% Interest; Price Exceeds Fair Value of Priority Accounts

Acquisitions Inc. and Subsidiary Johnson Company
Worksheet for Consolidated Balance Sheet
December 31, 20X1

Worksheet 2-6 (see page 76)

	Trial Balance		Eliminations & Adjustments		NCI	Consolidated Balance Sheet	
	Acquisitions	Johnson	Dr.	Cr.			
Cash	51,000	0				51,000	1
Accounts Receivable	42,000	28,000				70,000	2
Inventory	95,000	40,000	(D1) 4,000			139,000	3
Investment in Johnson	290,000			(EL) 102,400			4
				(D) 187,600			5
Land	60,000	10,000	(D3) 32,000			102,000	6
Buildings	500,000	60,000	(D4) 32,000			592,000	7
Accumulated Depreciation	(50,000)	(20,000)				(70,000)	8
Equipment	60,000	30,000	(D5) 24,000			114,000	9
Accumulated Depreciation	(24,000)	(10,000)				(34,000)	10
Patent (net)		15,000	(D6) 12,000			27,000	11
Brand-Name Copyright			(D7) 32,000			32,000	12
Goodwill			(D8) 52,400			52,400	13
Current Liabilities	(89,000)	(5,000)				(94,000)	14
Bonds Payable	(100,000)	(20,000)				(120,000)	15
Discount (premium)				(D2) 800		(800)	16
Common Stock—Johnson		(1,000)	(EL) 800		(200)		17
Paid-In Capital in Excess of Par—Johnson		(59,000)	(EL) 47,200		(11,800)		18
Retained Earnings—Johnson		(68,000)	(EL) 54,400		(13,600)		19
Common Stock—Acquisitions	(18,600)					(18,600)	20
Paid-In Capital in Excess of Par—Acquisitions	(411,400)					(411,400)	21
Retained Earnings—Acquisitions	(405,000)					(405,000)	22
Noncontrolling Interest					(25,600)	(25,600)	23
Totals	0	0	290,800	290,800	(25,600)	0	24

Eliminations and Adjustments:

(EL)   Eliminate investment in subsidiary against 80% of the subsidiary's equity accounts.
(D)   Distribute $187,600 excess of cost over book value as follows:
(D1)   Inventory, $4,000.
(D2)   Premium on bonds payable, ($800).
(D3)   Land, $32,000.
(D4)   Buildings, $32,000.

(D5)   Equipment, $24,000.
(D6)   Patent, $12,000.
(D7)   Brand-name copyright, $32,000.
(D8)   Goodwill, $52,400.

Worksheet 2-7

80% Purchase, Bargain
Acquisitions Inc. and Subsidiary Johnson Company
Worksheet for Consolidated Balance Sheet
December 31, 20X1

Worksheet 2-7 (see page 79)

		Trial Balance		Eliminations & Adjustments		NCI	Consolidated Balance Sheet	
		Acquisitions	Johnson	Dr.	Cr.			
1	Cash	51,000	0				51,000	1
2	Accounts Receivable	42,000	28,000				70,000	2
3	Inventory	95,000	40,000	(D1) 4,000			139,000	3
4	Investment in Johnson	210,000			(EL) 102,400			4
5					(D) 107,600			5
6	Land	60,000	10,000	(D3) 26,480			96,480	6
7	Buildings	500,000	60,000	(D4) 23,168			583,168	7
8	Accumulated Depreciation	(50,000)	(20,000)				(70,000)	8
9	Equipment	60,000	30,000	(D5) 18,480			108,480	9
10	Accumulated Depreciation	(24,000)	(10,000)				(34,000)	10
11	Patent (net)		15,000	(D6) 8,688			23,688	11
12	Brand-Name Copyright			(D7) 27,584			27,584	12
13	Goodwill			(D8) 0				13
14	Current Liabilities	(89,000)	(5,000)				(94,000)	14
15	Bonds Payable	(100,000)	(20,000)				(120,000)	15
16	Discount (premium)				(D2) 800		(800)	16
17	Common Stock—Johnson		(1,000)	(EL) 800		(200)		17
18	Paid-In Capital in Excess of Par—Johnson		(59,000)	(EL) 47,200		(11,800)		18
19	Retained Earnings—Johnson		(68,000)	(EL) 54,400		(13,600)		19
20	Common Stock—Acquisitions	(17,000)					(17,000)	20
21	Paid-In Capital in Excess of Par—Acquisitions	(333,000)					(333,000)	21
22	Retained Earnings—Acquisitions	(405,000)					(405,000)	22
23	Noncontrolling Interest					(25,600)	(25,600)	23
24	Totals	0	0	210,800	210,800	(25,600)	0	24

Eliminations and Adjustments:

(EL) Eliminate investment in subsidiary against 80% of the subsidiary's equity accounts.
(D) Distribute $107,600 excess of cost over book value as follows:
(D1) Inventory, $4,000.
(D2) Land, $26,480.

(D3) Premium on bonds payable, ($800).
(D4) Buildings, $23,168.
(D5) Equipment, $18,480.
(D6) Patent, $8,688.
(D7) Brand-name copyright, $27,584.

UNDERSTANDING THE ISSUES

1. Johnson Company is considering an investment in the common stock of Bickler Company. What are the accounting issues surrounding the recording of income in future periods if Johnson purchases:

   a. 10% of Bickler's outstanding shares.
   b. 30% of Bickler's outstanding shares.
   c. 100% of Bickler's outstanding shares.
   d. 80% of Bickler's outstanding shares.

2. A parent must normally consolidate a company if it owns over 50% of the outstanding voting common stock of that company. In your own words, explain how a parent could gain control without an over 50% interest in a company.

3. What does the elimination process accomplish?

4. Padro Company purchases a controlling interest in Salto Company. Salto had identifiable net assets with a cost of $400,000 and a fair value of $600,000. It was agreed that the total fair value of Salto's common stock was $900,000. What adjustments will be made to Salto's accounts, and what new accounts and amounts will be recorded if:

   a. Padro purchases 100% of Salto's common stock for $900,000.
   b. Padro purchases 80% of Salto's common stock for $720,000.

5. Pillow Company is purchasing a 100% interest in the common stock of Sleep Company. Sleep's balance sheet amounts at book and fair value are as follows:

Account	Book Value	Fair Value
Current assets	$ 200,000	$ 250,000
Fixed assets	350,000	800,000
Liabilities	(200,000)	(200,000)

   What adjustments to recorded values of Sleep Company's accounts will be made in the consolidation process (including the creation of new accounts), if the price paid for the 100% is:

   a. $1,000,000.
   b. $500,000.
   c. $30,000.

6. Pillow Company is purchasing an 80% interest in the common stock of Sleep Company. Sleep's balance sheet amounts at book and fair value are as follows:

Account	Book Value	Fair Value
Current assets	$ 200,000	$ 250,000
Fixed assets	350,000	800,000
Liabilities	(200,000)	(200,000)

   What adjustments to recorded values of Sleep Company's accounts will be made in the consolidation process (including the creation of new accounts), if the price paid for the 100% is:

   a. $800,000.
   b. $600,000.
   c. $30,000.

7. Pillow Company is purchasing an 80% interest in the common stock of Sleep Company. Sleep's balance sheet amounts at book and fair value are as follows:

Account	Book Value	Fair Value
Current assets	$ 200,000	$ 250,000
Fixed assets	350,000	800,000
Liabilities	(200,000)	(200,000)

What will be the amount of the noncontrolling interest in the consolidated balance sheet, and how will it be displayed in the consolidated balance sheet?

EXERCISES

Exercise 2-1 *(LO 1)* **Investment recording methods.** Solara Corporation is considering investing in Focus Corporation, but is unsure about what level of ownership should be undertaken. Solara and Focus have the following reported incomes:

	Solara	Focus
Sales	$640,000	$370,000
Cost of goods sold	300,000	230,000
Gross profit	$340,000	$140,000
Selling and administrative expenses	120,000	75,000
Net income	$220,000	$ 65,000

Focus paid $15,000 in cash dividends to its investors. Prepare a pro forma income statement for Solara Corporation that compares income under 10%, 20%, and 70% ownership levels.

Exercise 2-2 *(LO 4)* **Asset compared to stock purchase.** Glass Company is thinking about acquiring Plastic Company. Glass Company is considering two methods of accomplishing control and is wondering how the accounting treatment will differ under each method. Glass Company has estimated that the fair values of Plastic's net assets are equal to their book values, except for the equipment, which is understated by $20,000.

The following balance sheets have been prepared on the date of acquisition:

Assets	Glass	Plastic
Cash	$540,000	$ 20,000
Accounts receivable	50,000	70,000
Inventory	50,000	100,000
Property, plant, and equipment (net)	230,000	270,000
Total assets	$870,000	$460,000

Liabilities and Equity	Glass	Plastic
Current liabilities	$140,000	$ 80,000
Bonds payable	250,000	100,000
Stockholders' equity:		
Common stock ($ 100 par)	200,000	150,000
Retained earnings	280,000	130,000
Total liabilities and equity	$870,000	$460,000

1. Assume Glass Company purchased the net assets directly from Plastic Company for $530,000.

   a. Prepare the entry that Glass Company would make to record the purchase.
   b. Prepare the balance sheet for Glass Company immediately following the purchase.

2. Assume that 100% of the outstanding stock of Plastic Company is purchased from the former stockholders for a total of $530,000.

     a. Prepare the entry that Glass Company would make to record the purchase.
     b. State how the investment would appear on Glass's unconsolidated balance sheet prepared immediately after the purchase.
     c. Indicate how the consolidated balance sheet would appear.

Exercise 2-3 *(LO 6)* **Simple price zone analysis.** Flower Company is considering the cash purchase of 100% of the outstanding stock of Vase Company. The terms are not set, and alternative prices are being considered for negotiation. The balance sheet of Vase Company shows the following values:

Assets		Liabilities and Equity	
Cash equivalents	$ 60,000	Current liabilities	$ 60,000
Inventory	120,000	Common stock ($5 par).	100,000
Land.	50,000	Paid-in capital in excess of par	150,000
Building (net)	200,000	Retained earnings	120,000
Total assets.	$430,000	Total liabilities and equity	$430,000

Appraisals reveal that the inventory has a fair value of $160,000 and that the land and building have fair values of $100,000 and $300,000, respectively. The questions to be answered concern the price to be paid for Vase's common stock.

1. Above what price would goodwill be recorded?
2. Below what price would fixed assets be recorded at less-than-full fair value?
3. Below what price would an extraordinary gain be recorded?

Exercise 2-4 *(LO 6, 7)* **Recording purchase with goodwill.** Wood'n Wares Inc. purchased all the outstanding stock of Pine Inc. for $950,000. Wood'n Wares also paid $10,000 in direct acquisition costs and $3,000 for indirect acquisition costs. Just before the investment, the two companies had the following balance sheets:

Assets	Wood'n Wares Inc.	Pine Inc.
Accounts receivable	$ 900,000	$ 500,000
Inventory	600,000	200,000
Depreciable fixed assets (net)	1,500,000	600,000
Total assets.	$3,000,000	$1,300,000

Liabilities and Equity		
Current liabilities	$ 950,000	$ 400,000
Bonds payable	500,000	200,000
Common stock ($10 par).	400,000	300,000
Paid-in capital in excess of par	500,000	380,000
Retained earnings	650,000	20,000
Total liabilities and equity	$3,000,000	$1,300,000

Appraisals for the assets of Pine Inc. indicate that fair values differ from recorded book values for the inventory and for the property, plant, and equipment, which have fair values of $250,000 and $700,000, respectively.

1. Prepare the entry to record the purchase of the Pine Inc. common stock including all acquisition costs.
2. Prepare a zone analysis and a determination and distribution of excess schedule for the investment in Pine Inc.
3. Prepare the elimination entries that would be made on a consolidated worksheet.

Exercise 2-5 *(LO 6, 7)* **Purchase at alternative prices.** Libra Company is purchasing 100% of the outstanding stock of Gemini Company, which has the following balance sheet on the date of acquisition:

Assets		Liabilities and Equity	
Accounts receivable	$ 300,000	Current liabilities	$ 250,000
Inventory	200,000	Bonds payable	200,000
Property, plant, and		Common stock ($5 par)	200,000
equipment (net)	500,000	Paid-in capital in excess of par	300,000
Computer software	125,000	Retained earnings	175,000
Total assets	$1,125,000	Total liabilities and equity	$1,125,000

Appraisals indicate that the following fair values should be acknowledged:

Inventory	$215,000
Property, plant, and equipment	700,000
Bonds payable	210,000
Computer software	130,000

1. Above what price would goodwill be recorded?
2. Below what price would an extraordinary gain be recorded?

   Prepare the zone analysis, the determination and distribution of excess schedule, and the worksheet elimination entries that would be made if:

3. The price paid for the 100% interest was $1,000,000.
4. The price paid for the 100% interest was $810,000.

Exercise 2-6 *(LO 6, 7, 9)* **Bargain purchase, allocation.** Lancaster Company is purchasing 100% of the outstanding common stock of Villard Company for $600,000 plus $20,000 of direct acquisition costs. The following balance sheet was prepared for Villard on the date of the purchase:

Assets		Liabilities and Equity	
Inventory	$ 50,000	Current liabilities	$150,000
Mineral rights	250,000	Common stock ($5 par)	100,000
Equipment (net)	150,000	Paid-in capital in excess of par	300,000
Goodwill	50,000	Retained earnings	(50,000)
Total assets	$500,000	Total liabilities and equity	$500,000

Appraisals are as follows for the assets of Villard Company:

Inventory	$ 10,000
Mineral rights	700,000
Equipment	100,000

Based on the preceding facts,

1. Prepare a zone analysis and a determination and distribution of excess schedule.
2. Prepare the elimination entries that would be made on a consolidated worksheet prepared on the date of purchase.

Exercise 2-7 *(LO 6, 7, 8)* **80% purchase, goodwill.** Quincy Company purchased 80% of the common stock of Cooker Company for $700,000 plus direct acquisition costs of $30,000. At the time of the purchase, Cooker Company had the following balance sheet:

Assets		Liabilities and Equity	
Cash equivalents...............	$ 120,000	Current liabilities...............	$ 200,000
Inventory.....................	200,000	Bonds payable	400,000
Land.........................	100,000	Common stock ($5 par).........	100,000
Building (net).................	450,000	Paid-in capital in excess of par	150,000
Equipment (net)	230,000	Retained earnings..............	250,000
Total assets..................	$1,100,000	Total liabilities and equity	$1,100,000

Fair values differ from book values for all assets other than cash equivalents. The fair values are as follows:

Inventory	$300,000
Land.............................	200,000
Building	600,000
Equipment	200,000

Based on the preceding facts,

1. Prepare a zone analysis and a determination and distribution of excess schedule.
2. Prepare the elimination entries that would be made on a consolidated worksheet prepared on the date of purchase.

Exercise 2-8 *(LO 6, 7, 8)* **80% purchase, alternative prices.** Venus Company purchased 8,000 shares of Saturn Company for $82 per share. Just prior to the purchase, Saturn Company had the following balance sheet:

Assets		Liabilities and Equity	
Cash	$ 20,000	Current liabilities.................	$250,000
Inventory	280,000	Common stock ($5 par)............	50,000
Property, plant, and		Paid-in capital in excess of par	130,000
equipment (net)...............	400,000	Retained earnings	370,000
Goodwill	100,000		
Total assets..................	$800,000	Total liabilities and equity	$800,000

Venus Company believes that the inventory has a fair value of $400,000 and that the property, plant, and equipment is worth $500,000. Business consultants have suggested that the goodwill is worth no more than $50,000. Based on these facts,

1. Prepare a zone analysis and a determination and distribution of excess schedule.
2. Prepare the elimination entries that would be made on a consolidated worksheet prepared on the date of acquisition.
3. Prepare the elimination entries that would be made on a consolidated worksheet prepared on the date of acquisition assuming Venus pays $64 per share.

Exercise 2-9 *(LO 10)* **Push-down accounting.** On January 1, 20X7, Knight Corporation purchased all the outstanding shares of Craig Company for $950,000. It has been decided that Craig Company will use push-down accounting principles to account for this transaction. The current balance sheet is stated at historical cost.

The following balance sheet was prepared for Craig Company on January 1, 20X7:

Assets			Liabilities and Equity		
Current assets:			Current liabilities		$ 90,000
Cash	$ 80,000		Long-term liabilities:		
Accounts receivable.	260,000		Bonds payable.	$300,000	
			Deferred taxes	50,000	350,000
Prepaid expenses.	20,000	$ 360,000	Stockholders' equity:		
Property, plant, and equipment:			Common stock ($10 par).	$300,000	
Land.	$200,000		Retained earnings	420,000	720,000
Building (net)	600,000	800,000			
Total assets.		$1,160,000	Total liabilities and equity		$1,160,000

Knight Corporation received the following appraisals for Craig Company's assets and liabilities:

Accounts receivable	$280,000
Land.	230,000
Building (net)	700,000
Bonds payable	280,000
Deferred tax liability	40,000

1. Record the investment.
2. Record the adjustments on the books of Craig Company.
3. Prepare the entries that would be made on the consolidated worksheet to eliminate the investment.

PROBLEMS

Problem 2-1 *(LO 4, 5, 6, 7)* **100% purchase, goodwill, consolidated balance sheet.** On July 1, 20X6, Rose Company exchanged 18,000 of its $35 fair value ($10 par value) shares for all the outstanding shares of Daisy Company. Rose paid direct acquisition costs of $20,000 and $5,000 in stock issuance costs. The two companies had the following balance sheets on July 1, 20X6:

↳ indirect expense treated as PIC

Assets	Rose	Daisy
Other current assets.	$ 50,000	$ 70,000
Inventory	120,000	60,000
Land.	100,000	40,000
Buildings (net)	300,000	120,000
Equipment (net)	430,000	110,000
Total assets.	$1,000,000	$400,000

Liabilities and Equity	Rose	Daisy
Current liabilities	$ 180,000	$ 60,000
Common stock ($10 par).	400,000	200,000
Retained earnings	420,000	140,000
Total liabilities and equity	$1,000,000	$400,000

effect from JE's

(20,000) (5000) = 95.000
+ 5.000 = 185.000
+60.000 = 200.000
+ 30.000 = 450.000
(35.000) = 505.000

$ 1,685.000

(continued)

The following fair values differ from book values for Daisy's assets:

Inventory	$ 65,000
Land	100,000
Building	150,000
Equipment	75,000

Required ▶ ▶ ▶ ▶ ▶

1. Record the investment in Daisy Company and any other entry necessitated by the purchase.
2. Prepare a zone analysis and a determination and distribution of excess schedule.
3. Prepare a consolidated balance sheet for July 1, 20X6, immediately subsequent to the purchase.

Problem 2-2 *(LO 4, 5, 6, 7, 8)* **80% purchase, goodwill, consolidated balance sheet.** Using the data given in Problem 2-1, assume that Rose Company exchanged 18,000 of its $35 fair value ($10 par value) shares for 16,000 of the outstanding shares of Daisy Company.

Required ▶ ▶ ▶ ▶ ▶

1. Record the investment in Daisy Company and any other entry necessitated by the purchase.
2. Prepare a determination and distribution of excess schedule.
3. Prepare a consolidated balance sheet for July 1, 20X6, immediately subsequent to the purchase.

Problem 2-3 *(LO 4, 5, 6, 7)* **100% purchase, bargain, elimination entries only.** On March 1, 20X5, Carlson Enterprises purchased a 100% interest in Express Corporation for $400,000.

Express Corporation had the following balance sheet on February 28, 20X5:

Express Corporation
Balance Sheet
For the Month Ended February 28, 20X5

Assets		Liabilities and Equity	
Accounts receivable	$ 60,000	Current liabilities	$ 50,000
Inventory	80,000	Bonds payable	100,000
Land	40,000	Common stock	50,000
Buildings	300,000	Paid-in capital in excess of par	250,000
Accum. depr.—building	(120,000)	Retained earnings	70,000
Equipment	220,000		
Accum. depr.—equipment	(60,000)		
Total assets	$ 520,000	Total liabilities and equity	$520,000

Carlson Enterprises received an independent appraisal on the fair values of Express Corporation's assets. The controller has reviewed the following figures and accepts them as reasonable.

Inventory	$100,000
Land	40,500
Buildings	202,500
Equipment	162,000
Bonds payable	95,000

Required ▶ ▶ ▶ ▶ ▶

1. Record the investment in Express Corporation.
2. Prepare a zone analysis and a determination and distribution of excess schedule.
3. Prepare the elimination entries that would be made on a consolidated worksheet prepared on the date of acquisition.

Problem 2-4 *(LO 6, 7, 10)* **100% purchase, goodwill, push-down accounting.** On March 1, 20X5, Collier Enterprises purchased a 100% interest in Robby Corporation for $480,000. It was decided that Robby Corporation will apply push-down accounting principles to account for this acquisition.

Robby Corporation had the following balance sheet on February 28, 20X5:

Robby Corporation
Balance Sheet
For the Month Ended February 28, 20X5

Assets		Liabilities and Equity	
Accounts receivable	$ 60,000	Current liabilities	$ 50,000
Inventory	80,000	Bonds payable	100,000
Land........................	40,000	Common stock................	50,000
Buildings	300,000	Paid-in capital in excess of par ...	250,000
Accum. depr.—building	(120,000)	Retained earnings	70,000
Equipment	220,000		
Accum. depr.—equipment	(60,000)		
Total assets.................	$ 520,000	Total liabilities and equity	$520,000

Collier Enterprises received an independent appraisal on the fair values of Robby Corporation's assets. The controller has reviewed the following figures and accepts them as reasonable.

Inventory	$100,000
Land....................................	55,000
Buildings	200,000
Equipment	150,000
Bonds payable	98,000

1. Record the investment in Robby Corporation.
2. Prepare a zone analysis and a determination and distribution of excess schedule.
3. Give Robby Corporation's adjusting entry.

◄ ◄ ◄ ◄ ◄ **Required**

Problem 2-5 *(LO 4, 5, 6, 7)* **100% purchase, goodwill, worksheet.** On December 31, 20X1, Adam Company purchased 100% of the common stock of Scott Company for $475,000. On this date, any excess of cost over book value was attributed to accounts with fair values that differed from book values. These accounts of the Scott Company had the following fair values:

Inventory	$140,000
Land....................................	45,000
Buildings and equipment....................	225,000
Bonds payable	105,000
Copyrights..............................	25,000

The following comparative balance sheets were prepared for the two companies immediately after the purchase:

	Adam	Scott
Cash	$ 160,000	$ 40,000
Accounts receivable	70,000	30,000
Inventory	130,000	120,000

(continued)

	Adam	Scott
Investment in Scott Company.	$ 475,000	
Land.	50,000	$ 35,000 US, 000
Buildings and equipment.	350,000	230,000
Accumulated depreciation	(100,000)	(50,000)
Copyrights.	40,000	10,000
Total assets.	$1,175,000	$415,000
Current liabilities	$ 192,000	$ 65,000
Bonds payable		100,000
Common stock ($10 par), Adam.	100,000	
Common stock ($5 par), Scott.		50,000
Paid-in capital in excess of par	250,000	70,000
Retained earnings	633,000	130,000
Total liabilities and equity	$1,175,000	$415,000

Required ▶ ▶ ▶ ▶ ▶

1. Prepare zone and price analyses and a determination and distribution of excess schedule for the investment in Scott Company.
2. Complete a consolidated worksheet for Adam Company and its subsidiary Scott Company as of December 31, 20X1.

Problem 2-6 *(LO 4, 5, 6, 7, 8)* **80% purchase, goodwill, worksheet.** Using the data given in Problem 2-5, assume that Adam Company purchased 80% of the common stock of Scott Company for $475,000.

Required ▶ ▶ ▶ ▶ ▶

1. Prepare zone and price analyses and a determination and distribution of excess schedule for the investment in Scott Company.
2. Complete a consolidated worksheet for Adam Company and its subsidiary Scott Company as of December 31, 20X1.

Use the following information for Problems 2-7 through 2-10:

    In an attempt to expand its operations, Pantera Company acquired Sader Company on January 1, 20X1. Pantera paid cash in exchange for the common stock of Sader. On the date of acquisition, Sader had the following balance sheet:

Sader Company
Balance Sheet
January 1, 20X1

Assets		Liabilities and Equity	
Accounts receivable	$ 20,000	Current liabilities	$ 40,000
Inventory	50,000	Bonds payable	100,000
Land.	40,000	Common stock, $1 par	10,000
Buildings	200,000	Paid-in capital in excess	
Accumulated depreciation	(50,000)	of par	90,000
Equipment	60,000	Retained earnings	60,000
Accumulated depreciation	(20,000)		
Total assets.	$300,000	Total liabilities and equity	$300,000

    An appraisal indicates that the following assets exist and have fair values that differed from their book values:

Inventory	$ 55,000
Land...............................	70,000
Buildings	250,000
Equipment	60,000
Copyright	50,000

Problem 2-7 *(LO 4, 5, 6, 7)* **100% purchase, goodwill, limited adjustments, worksheet.**

Use the preceding information for Pantera's purchase of Sader common stock. Assume Pantera purchased 100% of the common stock for $410,000. Pantera had the following balance sheet immediately after the purchase:

Pantera Company
Balance Sheet
January 1, 20X1

Assets		Liabilities and Equity	
Cash	$ 51,000	Current liabilities	$ 80,000
Accounts receivable	65,000	Bonds payable	200,000
Inventory	80,000	Common stock.................	20,000
Land........................	100,000	Paid-in capital in excess of par	180,000
Investment in Sader	410,000	Retained earnings	446,000
Buildings	250,000		
Accumulated depreciation	(80,000)		
Equipment	90,000		
Accumulated depreciation	(40,000)		
Total assets................	$926,000	Total liabilities and equity	$926,000

◄ ◄ ◄ ◄ ◄ **Required**

1. Prepare a zone analysis and a determination and distribution of excess schedule for the investment in Sader.
2. Complete a consolidated worksheet for Pantera Company and its subsidiary Sader Company as of January 1, 20X1.

Problem 2-8 *(LO 4, 5, 6, 7)* **100% purchase, bargain, limited adjustments, worksheet.**

Use the preceding information for Pantera's purchase of Sader common stock. Assume Pantera purchased 100% of the common stock for $250,000. Pantera had the following balance sheet immediately after the purchase:

Pantera Company
Balance Sheet
January 1, 20X1

Assets		Liabilities and Equity	
Cash	$211,000	Current liabilities	$ 80,000
Accounts receivable	65,000	Bonds payable	200,000
Inventory	80,000	Common stock..............	20,000
Land......................	100,000	Paid-in capital in excess of par .	180,000
Investment in Sader	250,000	Retained earnings	446,000
Buildings	250,000		
Accumulated depreciation	(80,000)		
Equipment	90,000		
Accumulated depreciation	(40,000)		
Total assets..............	$926,000	Total liabilities and equity ...	$926,000

Required ▶ ▶ ▶ ▶ ▶

1. Prepare a zone analysis and a determination and distribution of excess schedule for the investment in Sader.
2. Complete a consolidated worksheet for Pantera Company and its subsidiary Sader Company as of January 1, 20X1.

Problem 2-9 *(LO 4, 5, 6, 7, 8)* **80% purchase, goodwill, limited adjustments, worksheet.** Use the preceding information for Pantera's purchase of Sader common stock. Assume Pantera purchased 80% of the common stock for $360,000. Pantera had the following balance sheet immediately after the purchase:

Pantera Company
Balance Sheet
January 1, 20X1

Assets		Liabilities and Equity	
Cash	$101,000	Current liabilities	$ 80,000
Accounts receivable	65,000	Bonds payable	200,000
Inventory	80,000	Common stock	20,000
Land	100,000	Paid-in capital in excess of par	180,000
Investment in Sader	360,000	Retained earnings	446,000
Buildings	250,000		
Accumulated depreciation	(80,000)		
Equipment	90,000		
Accumulated depreciation	(40,000)		
Total assets	$926,000	Total liabilities and equity	$926,000

Required ▶ ▶ ▶ ▶ ▶

1. Prepare a zone analysis and a determination and distribution of excess schedule for the investment in Sader.
2. Complete a consolidated worksheet for Pantera Company and its subsidiary Sader Company as of January 1, 20X1.

For Wed 9/29

No Goodwill

Problem 2-10 *(LO 4, 5, 6, 7, 8)* **80% purchase, bargain, limited adjustments, worksheet.** Use the preceding information for Pantera's purchase of Sader common stock. Assume Pantera purchased 80% of the common stock for $200,000. Pantera had the following balance sheet immediately after the purchase:

Pantera Company
Balance Sheet
January 1, 20X1

Assets		Liabilities and Equity	
Cash	$261,000	Current liabilities	$ 80,000
Accounts receivable	65,000	Bonds payable	200,000
Inventory	80,000	Common stock	20,000
Land	100,000	Paid-in capital in excess of par	180,000
Investment in Sader	200,000	Retained earnings	446,000
Buildings	250,000		
Accumulated depreciation	(80,000)		
Equipment	90,000		
Accumulated depreciation	(40,000)		
Total assets	$926,000	Total liabilities and equity	$926,000

1. Prepare a zone analysis and a determination and distribution of excess schedule for the investment in Sader. ◄ ◄ ◄ ◄ ◄ **Required**
2. Complete a consolidated worksheet for Pantera Company and its subsidiary Sader Company as of January 1, 20X1.

Use the following information for Problem 2-11 through 2-14:

Purnell Corporation acquired Soma Corporation on December 31, 20X1. Soma had the following balance sheet on the date of acquisition:

Soma Corporation
Balance Sheet
December 31, 20X1

Assets		Liabilities and Equity	
Accounts receivable	$ 50,000	Current liabilities	$ 90,000
Inventory	120,000	Bonds payable	200,000
Land	100,000	Common stock, $1 par	10,000
Buildings	300,000	Paid-in capital in excess	
Accumulated depreciation	(100,000)	of par	190,000
Equipment	140,000	Retained earnings	140,000
Accumulated depreciation	(50,000)		
Patent	10,000		
Goodwill	60,000		
Total assets	$ 630,000	Total liabilities and equity	$630,000

An appraisal has been performed to determine whether the book values of Soma's net assets reflect their fair values. The appraiser also determined that several intangible assets existed, although they were not recorded. The following assets and liabilities had fair values that differed from their book values:

Inventory	$150,000
Land	200,000
Buildings	400,000
Equipment	200,000
Patent	150,000
Computer software	50,000
Bonds payable	210,000

Problem 2-11 *(LO 4, 5, 6, 7, 9)* **100% purchase, goodwill, several adjustments, worksheet.** Use the preceding information for Purnell's purchase of Soma common stock. Assume Purnell exchanged 24,000 shares of its own stock for 100% of the common stock of Soma. The stock had a market value of $50 per share and a par value of $1. Purnell had the following trial balance immediately after the purchase:

(continued)

Purnell Company
Trial Balance
December 31, 20X1

Cash	170,000
Accounts Receivable	300,000
Inventory	410,000
Land	800,000
Investment in Soma	1,200,000
Buildings	2,800,000
Accumulated Depreciation	(500,000)
Equipment	600,000
Accumulated Depreciation	(230,000)
Current Liabilities	(150,000)
Bonds Payable	(300,000)
Common Stock ($1 par)	(100,000)
Paid-In Capital in Excess of Par	(3,900,000)
Retained Earnings	(1,100,000)
Total	0

Required ▶ ▶ ▶ ▶ ▶

1. Prepare a zone analysis and a determination and distribution of excess schedule for the investment in Soma.
2. Complete a consolidated worksheet for Purnell Company and its subsidiary Soma Company as of December 31, 20X1.

Problem 2-12 *(LO 4, 5, 6, 7, 9)* **100% purchase, bargain, several adjustments, worksheet.** Use the preceding information for Purnell's purchase of Soma common stock. Assume Purnell exchanged 16,000 shares of its own stock for 100% of the common stock of Soma. The stock had a market value of $50 per share and a par value of $1. Purnell had the following trial balance immediately after the purchase:

Purnell Company
Trial Balance
December 31, 20X1

Cash	170,000
Accounts Receivable	300,000
Inventory	410,000
Land	800,000
Investment in Soma	800,000
Buildings	2,800,000
Accumulated Depreciation	(500,000)
Equipment	600,000
Accumulated Depreciation	(230,000)
Current Liabilities	(150,000)
Bonds Payable	(300,000)
Common Stock ($1 par)	(92,000)
Paid-In Capital in Excess of Par	(3,508,000)
Retained Earnings	(1,100,000)
Total	0

Required ▶ ▶ ▶ ▶ ▶

1. Prepare a zone analysis and a determination and distribution of excess schedule for the investment in Soma.
2. Complete a consolidated worksheet for Purnell Company and its subsidiary Soma Company as of December 31, 20X1.

Problem 2-13 *(LO 4, 5, 6, 7, 8, 9)* **80% purchase, goodwill, several adjustments, worksheet.** Use the preceding information for Purnell's purchase of Soma common stock. Assume Purnell exchanged 19,000 shares of its own stock for 80% of the common stock of Soma. The stock had a market value of $50 per share and a par value of $1. Purnell had the following trial balance immediately after the purchase:

Purnell Company
Trial Balance
December 31, 20X1

Cash	170,000
Accounts Receivable	300,000
Inventory	410,000
Land	800,000
Investment in Soma	950,000
Buildings	2,800,000
Accumulated Depreciation	(500,000)
Equipment	600,000
Accumulated Depreciation	(230,000)
Current Liabilities	(150,000)
Bonds Payable	(300,000)
Common Stock ($1 par)	(95,000)
Paid-in Capital in Excess of Par	(3,655,000)
Retained Earnings	(1,100,000)
Total	0

1. Prepare a zone analysis and a determination and distribution of excess schedule for the investment in Soma. ◄ ◄ ◄ ◄ ◄ **Required**
2. Complete a consolidated worksheet for Purnell Company and its subsidiary Soma Company as of December 31, 20X1.

Problem 2-14 *(LO 4, 5, 6, 7, 8, 9)* **80% purchase, bargain, several adjustments, worksheet.** Use the preceding information for Purnell's purchase of Soma common stock. Assume Purnell exchanged 10,000 shares of its own stock for 80% of the common stock of Soma. The stock had a market value of $50 per share and a par value of $1. Purnell had the following trial balance immediately after the purchase:

Purnell Company
Trial Balance
December 31, 20X1

Cash	170,000
Accounts Receivable	300,000
Inventory	410,000
Land	800,000
Investment in Soma	500,000
Buildings	2,800,000
Accumulated Depreciation	(500,000)
Equipment	600,000
Accumulated Depreciation	(230,000)
Current Liabilities	(150,000)
Bonds Payable	(300,000)

(continued)

Common Stock ($1 par)	(86,000)
Paid-In Capital in Excess of Par	(3,214,000)
Retained Earnings	(1,100,000)
Total	0

Required ▶ ▶ ▶ ▶ ▶

1. Prepare a zone analysis and a determination and distribution of excess schedule for the investment in Soma.
2. Complete a consolidated worksheet for Purnell Company and its subsidiary Soma Company as of December 31, 20X1.

Case 2-1

Consolidating a Bargain Purchase

Your client, Best Value Hardware Stores, has come to you for assistance in evaluating an opportunity to purchase a controlling interest in a hardware store in a neighboring city. The store under consideration is a closely held family corporation. Owners of 60% of the shares are willing to sell you the 60% interest, 30,000 common stock shares in exchange for 7,500 of Best Value shares, which have a fair value of $40 each and a par value of $10 each.

Your client sees this as a good opportunity to enter a new market. The controller of Best Value knows, however, that all is not well with the store being considered. The store, Al's Hardware, has not kept pace with the market and has been losing money. It also has a major lawsuit against it stemming from alleged faulty electrical components it supplied which caused a fire. The store is not insured for the loss. Legal counsel advises that the store will likely pay $300,000 in damages.

The following balance sheet was provided by Al's Hardware as of December 31, 20X1:

Assets		Liabilities and Equity	
Cash	$ 180,000	Current liabilities	$ 425,000
Accounts receivable	460,000	8% Mortgage payable	600,000
Inventory	730,000	Common stock ($5 par)	250,000
Land	120,000	Paid-in capital in	
Building	630,000	excess of par	750,000
Accum. depr.—building	(400,000)	Retained earnings	(80,000)
Equipment	135,000		
Accum. depr.—equipment . . .	(85,000)		
Goodwill	175,000		
Total assets	$1,945,000	Total liabilities and equity . .	$1,945,000

Your analysis raises substantial concerns about the values shown. You have gathered the following information:

1. Aging of the accounts receivable reveals the need for a $110,000 allowance for bad debts.
2. The inventory has many obsolete items; the fair value is $600,000.
3. Appraisals for long-lived assets are as follows:

Land	$100,000
Building	300,000
Equipment	100,000

4. The goodwill resulted from the purchase of another hardware store that has since been consolidated into the existing location. The goodwill was attributed to customer loyalty.

5. Liabilities are fairly stated except that there should be a provision for the estimated loss on the lawsuit.

On the basis of your research, you are convinced that the statements of Al's Hardware are not representative and need major restatement. Your client is not interested in being associated with statements that are not accurate.

Your client asks you to make recommendations on two concerns:

1. Does the price asked seem to be a real bargain? It is suggested that you consider the fair value of the entire equity of Al's Hardware and then decide if the price is reasonable for a 60% interest.
2. If the deal were completed, what accounting methods would you recommend either on the books of Al's Hardware or in the consolidation process? Al's Hardware would remain a separate legal entity with a substantial noncontrolling interest.

Consolidated Statements: Subsequent to Acquisition

Learning Objectives

When you have completed this chapter, you should be able to

1. Show how an investment in a subsidiary account is maintained under the simple equity, sophisticated equity, and cost methods.

2. Complete a consolidated worksheet using the simple equity method for the parent's investment account.

3. Complete a consolidated worksheet using the cost method for the parent's investment account.

4. Describe the special worksheet procedures that are used for an investment maintained under the sophisticated equity method.

5. Distribute and amortize multiple adjustments resulting from the difference between the price paid for an investment in a subsidiary and the subsidiary equity eliminated.

6. Demonstrate the worksheet procedures used for investments purchased during the financial reporting period.

7. Demonstrate an understanding of when goodwill impairment loss exists and how it is calculated.

8. (Appendix) Explain the impact of tax-related complications arising on the purchase date.

This chapter's mission is to teach the procedures needed to prepare consolidated income statements, retained earnings statements, and balance sheets in periods subsequent to the acquisition of a subsidiary. There are several worksheet models to master. This variety is caused by the alternative methods available to a parent for maintaining its investment in a subsidiary account. Accounting principles do not address the method used by a parent to record its investment in a subsidiary that is to be consolidated. The method used is of no concern to standard setters since the investment account is always eliminated when consolidating. Thus, the method chosen to record the investment usually is based on convenience.

In the preceding chapter, worksheet procedures included asset and liability adjustments to reflect fair values on the date of the purchase. This chapter discusses the subsequent depreciation and amortization of these asset and liability revaluations in conjunction with its analysis of worksheet procedures for preparing consolidated financial statements.

This chapter does not deal with the income tax issues of the consolidated company except to the extent that they are reflected in the original acquisition price. The chapter appendix on pages 134 to 135 considers tax issues that arise as part of the original purchase.

ACCOUNTING FOR THE INVESTMENT IN A SUBSIDIARY

A parent may choose one of two basic methods when accounting for its investment in a subsidiary: the *equity method* or the *cost method*. The equity method records as income an ownership percentage of the reported income of the subsidiary, whether or not it was received by the

1

OBJECTIVE

Show how an investment in a subsidiary account is maintained under the simple equity, sophisticated equity, and cost methods.

parent. The cost method treats the investment in the subsidiary like a passive investment by recording income only when dividends are declared by the subsidiary.

Equity Method

The equity method views the earning of income by a controlled subsidiary as sufficient reason to record the parent's share of that income.

The equity method records as income the parent's ownership interest percentage multiplied by the subsidiary reported net income. The income is added to the parent's investment account. In a like manner, the parent records its share of a subsidiary loss and lowers its investment account for its share of the loss. Dividends received from the subsidiary are viewed as a conversion of a portion of the investment account into cash; thus, dividends reduce the investment account balance. The investment account at any point in time can be summarized as follows:

Investment in Subsidiary (equity method)

Original cost	less: Ownership interest × Reported losses of subsidiary since acquisition
plus: Ownership interest × Reported income of subsidiary since acquisition	less: Ownership interest × Dividends declared by subsidiary since acquisition
equals: Equity-adjusted balance	

The real advantage of using the simple equity method when consolidating is that every dollar of change in the stockholders' equity of the subsidiary is recorded on a pro rata basis in the investment account. This method expedites the elimination of the investment account in the consolidated worksheets in future periods. It is favored in this text because of its simplicity.

For some unconsolidated investments, the sophisticated equity method is required by APB Opinion No. 18, *The Equity Method of Accounting for Investments in Common Stock*. According to this Opinion, a company's investment should be adjusted for amortizations when the investor has an "influential" investment of 20% or more of another company's voting stock. For example, assume that the price paid for an investment in a subsidiary exceeded underlying book value and that the determination and distribution of excess schedule attributed the entire excess to a building. Just as a building will decrease in value and should be depreciated, so should that portion of the price paid for the investment attributed to the building also be amortized. If the estimated life of the building is 10 years, then the portion of the investment price attributed to the building should be amortized over 10 years. This would be accomplished by reducing the investment income each year by the amortization, which means that the income posted to the investment account each year is also less by the amount of the amortization.

The sophisticated equity method is required for influential investments (normally 20% to 50% interests) and for those rare subsidiaries that are not consolidated. Its use for these types of investments is fully discussed in Chapter 5. The sophisticated equity method also is used by some parent companies to maintain the investment in a subsidiary that is to be consolidated. This better reflects the investment account in the parent-only statements, but such statements may not be used as the primary statements for external reporting purposes. Parent-only statements may be used as supplemental statements only when the criteria for consolidated statements are met. The use of this method for investments to be consolidated makes recording the investment income and the elimination of the investment account more difficult than under the simple equity method.

Cost Method

When the cost method is used, the investment in subsidiary account is retained at its original cost-of-acquisition balance. No adjustments are made to the account for income as it is earned by the subsidiary. Income on the investment is limited to dividends received from the subsidiary. The cost method is acceptable for subsidiaries that are to be consolidated because, in the consolidation process, the investment account is eliminated entirely.

The cost method is the most common method used in practice by parent companies. It is simple to use during the accounting period and avoids the risk of incorrect adjustments. Typically, the correct income of the subsidiary is not known until after the end of the accounting period. Awaiting its determination would delay the parent company's closing procedures. Companies that use the cost method may convert to the simple equity method as part of the consolidation process.

Example of the Equity and Cost Methods

The simple equity, sophisticated equity, and cost methods will be illustrated by an example covering two years. This example, which will become the foundation for several consolidated worksheets in this chapter, is based on the following facts:

1. The D&D schedule that follows was prepared on the date of purchase. This schedule is similar to that of the preceding chapter but is modified to indicate the period over which adjustments to the subsidiary book values will be allocated. This expanded format will be used in preparing all future worksheets.
2. Income during 20X1 was $30,000 for Company S; dividends declared by Company S at the end of 20X1 totaled $10,000.
3. During 20X2, Company S had a loss of $10,000 and declared dividends of $5,000.
4. The balance in Company S's retained earnings account on December 31, 20X2, is $55,000.

The journal entries and resulting investment account balances shown below and on pages 112 and 113 record this information on the books of Company P using the simple equity, cost, and sophisticated equity methods. Note that the only difference between the sophisticated and simple equity methods is that the former reduces investment income each year for an amount equal to the amortization of the patent ($1,000).

REFLECTION

- The simple equity method records investment income equal to the parent ownership interest multiplied by the reported subsidiary income.

- The sophisticated equity method records investment income equal to the parent ownership interest multiplied by the reported subsidiary income and deducts amortizations of excess related to the price paid for the investment.

- The cost method records only dividends as received.

Company P and Subsidiary Company S Determination and Distribution of Excess Schedule January 1, 20X1				
	Total	Controlling	Amort. Periods	Controlling Amort.
Price paid for investment		$145,000		
Less book value interest acquired:				
Common stock.	$100,000			
Retained earnings	50,000			
Total stockholders' equity.	$150,000			
Interest acquired	× 90%	135,000		
Excess of cost over book value (debit)		**$ 10,000**		
Patent		**$ 10,000**	**Dr. 10**	**$1,000**

Event		Simple Equity Method		
20X1				
Jan. 1	Purchase of stock	Investment in Company S	145,000	
		Cash		145,000
Dec. 31	Subsidiary income of $30,000 reported to parent	Investment in Company S	27,000	
		Subsidiary Income		27,000
31	Dividends of $10,000 declared by subsidiary	Dividends Receivable	9,000	
		Investment in Company S.............		9,000
		Investment Balance, Dec. 31, 20X1 ..		**$163,000**
20X2				
Dec. 31	Subsidiary loss of $10,000 reported to parent	Loss on Subsidiary Operations	9,000	
		Investment in Company S.............		9,000
31	Dividends of $5,000 declared by subsidiary	Dividends Receivable	4,500	
		Investment in Company S.............		4,500
		Investment Balance, Dec. 31, 20X2 ..		**$149,500**

ELIMINATION PROCEDURES

Worksheet procedures necessary to prepare consolidated income statements, retained earnings statements, and balance sheets are examined in the following section. **Recall that the consolidation process is performed independently each year since the worksheet eliminations of previous years are never recorded by the parent or subsidiary.**

The illustrations that follow are based on the facts concerning the investment in Company S, as detailed in the previous example. The procedures for consolidating an investment maintained under the simple equity method will be discussed first, followed by an explanation of how procedures would differ under the cost and sophisticated equity methods. (See the inside front cover for a complete listing of the elimination codes used in this text.)

Effect of Simple Equity Method on Consolidation

Worksheet 3-1: page 136

Examine Worksheet 3-1 on pages 136 and 137, noting that the worksheet trial balances for Company P and Company S are pre-closing trial balances and, thus, include the income statement accounts of both companies. Look at Company P's trial balance and note that Investment in Company S is now at the equity-adjusted cost at the end of the year. The balance reflects the following information:

Cost...	$145,000
Plus equity income (90% × $30,000 Company S income).........................	27,000
Less dividends received (90% × $10,000 dividends paid by Company S)	(9,000)
Balance	$163,000

If we are going to eliminate the subsidiary equity against the investment account and get the correct excess, there must be "date alignment." Date alignment means that **the investment account and subsidiary equity are at the same point in time.** On the worksheet, the investment account is adjusted through the end of the year, and the subsidiary retained earnings is still at its January 1 balance. Eliminating the entries that affected the investment balance during the current year creates date alignment. First, entry for (CY1) [for Current Year entry #1] eliminates the subsidiary income recorded against the investment account as follows:

Cost Method		Sophisticated Equity Method	
Investment in Company S 145,000		Investment in Company S 145,000	
Cash	145,000	Cash	145,000
No entry.		Investment in Company S .... 26,000[a]	
		Subsidiary Income	26,000
Dividends Receivable 9,000		Dividends Receivable 9,000	
Subsidiary (Dividend) Income	9,000	Investment in Company S.	9,000
Investment Balance, Dec. 31, 20X1	**$145,000**	**Investment Balance, Dec. 31, 20X1**	**$162,000**
No entry.		Loss on Subsidiary Operations ... 10,000[b]	
		Investment in Company S.	10,000
Dividends Receivable 4,500		Dividends Receivable 4,500	
Subsidiary (Dividend) Income	4,500	Investment in Company S.	4,500
Investment Balance, Dec. 31, 20X2	**$145,000**	**Investment Balance, Dec. 31, 20X2**	**$147,500**

[a]Parent's share of subsidiary income less amortization of excess of $1,000 per year.
[b]Parent's share of subsidiary loss (90% × $10,000) = $9,000 plus amortization of excess of $1,000 per year.

Eliminate current-year investment income and create "date alignment:"

(CY1)	Subsidiary Income (Company P account)	27,000	
	Investment in Company S.		27,000

This elimination also removes the subsidiary income account. This is appropriate because we will, instead, be including the income statement accounts of the subsidiary. The intercompany dividends paid by the subsidiary to the parent will be eliminated next as follows with entry (CY2):

Eliminate intercompany dividends:

(CY2)	Investment in Company S	9,000	
	Dividends Declared (Company S account)		9,000

After this entry, only subsidiary dividends paid to the noncontrolling shareholders will remain. These are dividends paid to the "outside world" and, as such, belong in the consolidated statements.

Once you have created "date alignment," it is appropriate to eliminate 90% of the subsidiary equity against the investment account with entry (EL) [for Elimination entry]. This entry is the same as described in Chapter 2.

Eliminate 90% subsidiary equity against investment account:

(EL)	Common Stock ($10 par), Company S (90% eliminated)	90,000	
	Retained Earnings, January 1, 20X1, Company S (90% eliminated)	45,000	
	Investment in Company S.		135,000

The excess ($145,000 balance after eliminating current year entries − $135,000) should always agree with that indicated by the D&D schedule. The next procedure is to distribute the excess with entry (D) [for Distribute entry] as indicated by the D&D schedule as follows:

	Distribute excess investment account balance to accounts to be adjusted:		
(D)	Patent..	10,000	
	Investment in Company S (remaining balance)		10,000

The D&D schedule indicated that the life of the patent was 10 years. It must now be amortized for the first year with entry (A) [for Amortization entry]:

	Amortize excess for current year:		
(A)	Patent Amortization Expense ($10,000/10 years)	1,000	
	Patent..		1,000

Patent amortization expense should be maintained in a separate account, so that it will be available for the income statement as a separate item.

The Consolidated Income Statement column follows the Eliminations & Adjustments columns. The adjusted income statement accounts of the constituent companies are used to calculate the *consolidated net income* of $69,000. This income is distributed to the controlling interest and NCI. Note that the NCI receives 10% of the $30,000 reported net income of the subsidiary, or $3,000. The controlling interest receives the balance of the consolidated net income, or $66,000.

The distribution of income is handled best by using *income distribution schedules (IDS)* which appear at the end of Worksheet 3-1. The subsidiary IDS is a "T account" which begins with the reported net income of the subsidiary. This income is termed *internally generated net income*, which connotes the income of only the company being analyzed without consideration of income derived from other members of the affiliated group. Unless the subsidiary owned shares of the parent, the subsidiary's internally generated net income is the same as its net income. In Worksheet 3-1, the subsidiary net income is multiplied by the noncontrolling ownership percentage to calculate the NCI share of income. A similar T account is used for the parent IDS. The parent's share of subsidiary net income is added to the internally generated net income of the parent, and amortizations of excess are deducted. Patent amortization is borne entirely by the controlling interest. Note that this is true for *all* excess cost over book value situations. Under the parent company theory, only the portion applicable to the purchaser's interest is acknowledged; thus, the amortization of excess affects only the controlling interest. The balance in the parent T account is the controlling share of the consolidated net income. **The IDS is a valuable self-check procedure since the sum of the income distributions should equal the consolidated net income on the worksheet.**

The NCI column of the worksheet summarizes the total ownership interest of noncontrolling stockholders on the balance sheet date. The noneliminated portion of subsidiary common stock at par, additional paid-in capital in excess of par, beginning retained earnings, the NCI share of income, and dividends declared is extended to this column. The total of this column is then extended to the consolidated balance sheet column as the noncontrolling interest. The formal balance sheet will typically show only the total NCI and will not provide information on the components of this balance.

The Controlling Retained Earnings column produces the controlling retained earnings balance on the balance sheet date. The beginning parent retained earnings balance, as adjusted by eliminations and adjustments, is extended to this column. Dividends declared by the parent are also extended to this column. The controlling share of consolidated income is extended to this column to produce the ending balance. The balance is extended to the balance sheet column as the retained earnings of the consolidated company.

The Consolidated Balance Sheet column includes the consolidated asset and liability balances. The paid-in equity balances of the parent are extended as the consolidated paid-in capital balance. As mentioned above, the aggregate balances of the NCI and the Controlling Retained Earnings are also extended to the balance sheet column.

Separate debit and credit columns may be used for the consolidated balance sheet. This arrangement may minimize errors and aid analysis. Single columns are not advocated but are used to facilitate the inclusion of lengthy worksheets in a summarized fashion.

The information for the following formal statements is taken directly from Worksheet 3-1:

Company P
Consolidated Income Statement
For Year Ended December 31, 20X1

Revenue	$ 180,000
Expenses	(110,000)
Patent amortization	(1,000)
Consolidated net income	$ 69,000
Distributed to:	
Noncontrolling interest	$ 3,000
Controlling interest.	$ 66,000

Company P
Consolidated Retained Earnings Statement
For Year Ended December 31, 20X1

	Controlling
Retained earnings, January 1, 20X1	$123,000
Consolidated net income (Company P share)	66,000
Balance, December 31, 20X1	$189,000

Company P
Consolidated Balance Sheet
December 31, 20X1

Assets		Stockholders' Equity		
Net tangible assets	$397,000	Noncontrolling interest		$ 17,000
Patent.	9,000	Controlling interest:		
		Common stock	$200,000	
		Retained earnings	189,000	389,000
Total assets	$406,000	Total stockholders' equity . . .		$406,000

There are several features of the consolidated statements that you should notice:

◆ Consolidated net income is the total income earned by the consolidated entity. The consolidated net income is then distributed to the noncontrolling interest (NCI) and the controlling interest. This is consistent with the FASB exposure draft on liabilities and equity.[1] It is common to find the NCI portion of consolidated net income treated as an expense. The controlling share of income is then incorrectly labeled "consolidated net income."

---

1 2000 FASB Exposure Draft, *Accounting for Financial Instruments with Characteristics of Liabilities, Equity, or Both* (Norwalk, CT: Financial Accounting Standards Board), October 27, 2000.

♦ The retained earnings statement shows only the controlling interest. The beginning balance is only the parent retained earnings balance, the income added is only the controlling share of consolidated net income, and, if the parent paid dividends, the parent's dividends declared would be deducted. Detail as to the subsidiary retained earnings appears only in the separate statements of the subsidiary.

♦ The consolidated balance sheet shows the NCI as a subdivision of stockholders' equity as discussed in Chapter 2. The NCI is shown only as a total and is not itemized.

Now consider consolidation procedures for 20X2 as they would apply to Companies P and S under the simple equity method. This will provide added practice in preparing worksheets and will emphasize that, at the end of each year, consolidation procedures are applied to the separate statements of the constituent firms. In essence, **each year's consolidation procedures begin as if there had never been a previous consolidation.** However, reference to past worksheets is used commonly to save time.

The separate trial balances of Companies P and S are displayed in the first two columns of Worksheet 3-2, pages 138 and 139. The investment in subsidiary account includes the simple equity-adjusted investment balance as calculated on page 112. Note that the balances in the retained earnings accounts of Companies P and S are for January 1, 20X2, because these are the pre-closing trial balances. The retained earnings amounts are calculated as follows:

Worksheet 3-2: page 138

Company P:	January 1, 20X1, balance	$123,000
	Net income, 20X1 (including Company P's share of subsidiary income under simple equity method)	67,000
	Balance, January 1, 20X2	$190,000
Company S:	January 1, 20X1, balance	$ 50,000
	Net income, 20X1	30,000
	Dividends declared	(10,000)
	Balance, January 1, 20X2	$ 70,000

As before, entry (CY1) eliminates the subsidiary income recorded by the parent, and entry (CY2) eliminates the intercompany dividends. Neither subsidiary income nor dividends declared by the subsidiary to the parent should remain in the consolidated statements. In journal form, the entries are as follows:

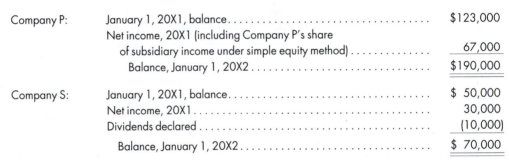

	Create "date alignment" and eliminate current-year subsidiary income:		
(CY1)	Investment in Company S	9,000	
	Subsidiary Loss		9,000
(CY2)	Investment in Company S	4,500	
	Dividends Declared (Company S account)		4,500

At this point, the investment account balance is returned to $163,000 ($149,500 on the trial balance + $9,000 loss + $4,500 dividends), which is the balance on January 1, 20X2. Date alignment now exists, and elimination of the investment account may proceed. Entry (EL) eliminates 90% of the subsidiary equity accounts against the investment account. Entry (EL) differs in amount from the prior year's (20X1) entry only because Company S's retained earnings balance has changed. Always eliminate the subsidiary's equity balances as they appear on the worksheet, not in the original D&D schedule. In journal form, entry (EL) is as follows:

	Eliminate investment account at beginning of the year balance:		
(EL)	Common Stock, Company S	90,000	
	Retained Earnings, January 1, 20X2, Company S	63,000	
	Investment in Company S		153,000

Entry (D) is exactly the same as it was on the 20X1 worksheet. It will be necessary to make this same entry every year until the mark-up caused by the purchase is fully amortized or the asset is sold. In entry form, entry (D) is as follows:

	Distribute excess of cost (patent):		
(D)	Patent...	10,000	
	Investment in Company S........................		10,000

Finally, entry (A) includes amortization of the patent for 20X1 and 20X2. The expense for 20X1 is charged to Company P retained earnings since it relates to prior-year income. The charge is made only to the parent's retained earnings because the asset adjustment applies only to the controlling interest. In journal form, the entry is as follows:

	Amortize patent for current and prior year:		
(A)	Retained Earnings, January 1, 20X2, Company P	1,000	
	Patent Amortization Expense.......................	1,000	
	Patent..		2,000

Note that the 20X3 worksheet will include three total years of amortization, and so **the entries made in prior periods' worksheets have not been recorded in either the parent's or subsidiary's books.** Even in later years, when the patent is past its 10-year life, it will be necessary to use a revised entry (D), which would adjust all prior years' amortizations to the patent as follows:

Retained Earnings, Company P (10 years × $1,000)	10,000	
Investment in Company S (the excess)		10,000

Note that the original D&D schedule prepared on the date of acquisition becomes the foundation for all subsequent worksheets. Once prepared, the schedule is used without modification.

Effect of Cost Method on Consolidation

Recall that parent companies often may choose to record their investments in a subsidiary under the cost method, whereby the investments are maintained at their original costs. Income from the investments are recorded only when dividends are declared by the subsidiary. The use of the cost method means that the investment account does not reflect changes in subsidiary equity. Rather than develop a new set of procedures for the elimination of an investment under the cost method, **the cost method investment will be converted to its simple equity balance at the beginning of the period** to create "date alignment." Then, the elimination procedures developed earlier can be applied.

Worksheet 3-3, pages 140 and 141, is a consolidated financial statements worksheet for Companies P and S for the first year of combined operations. The worksheet is based upon the entries made under the cost method, as shown on page 113. Reference to Company P's Trial Balance column in Worksheet 3-3 reveals that the investment in the subsidiary account at year-end still is stated at the original $145,000 cost and the income recorded by the parent as a result of subsidiary ownership is limited to $9,000, or 90% of the dividends declared by the subsidiary. When the cost method is used, the account title *Dividend Income may be used in place of Subsidiary Income.*

There is no need for an equity conversion at the end of the first year. Date alignment is automatic; the investment in Company S account and the subsidiary retained earnings are both as of January 1, 20X1. There is no entry (CY1) under the cost method; only entry (CY2) is needed to eliminate intercompany dividends. All remaining eliminations are the same as for 20X1 under the equity method. In journal form, the complete set of entries for 20X1 are as follows:

3

OBJECTIVE

Complete a consolidated worksheet using the cost method for the parent's investment account.

Worksheet 3-3: page 140

Eliminate current-year dividends:

(CY2)   Subsidiary Income   9,000

        Dividends Declared (Company S account)   9,000

Eliminate investment account at beginning of the year
    balance:

(EL)   Common Stock, Company S   90,000

      Retained Earnings, January 1, 20X1, Company S   45,000

        Investment in Company S.   135,000

Distribute excess of cost (patent):

(D)   Patent.   10,000

      Investment in Company S.   10,000

Amortize patent for current year:

(A)   Patent Amortization Expense.   1,000

      Patent.   1,000

The last four columns of Worksheet 3-3 are exactly the same as those for Worksheet 3-1, resulting in the same consolidated statements.

For periods after 20X1 (first year of consolidation), date alignment will not exist, and an equity conversion entry will be needed. Worksheet 3-4 on pages 142 and 143 is such an example. The worksheet is for 20X2 and parallels Worksheet 3-2 except that the cost method is in use. The balance in the investment account is still the original cost of $145,000. The retained earnings of the subsidiary is, however, at its January 1, 20X2, balance of $70,000. Note that the parent's January 1, 20X2, retained earnings balance is $18,000 less than in Worksheet 3-2 because it does not include the 20X1 undistributed subsidiary income of $18,000 ($27,000 income less $9,000 dividends received). In order to get date alignment, an equity conversion entry, (CV), is made to convert the investment account to its January 1, 20X2, simple equity balance. This conversion entry is always calculated as follows:

Worksheet 3-4: page 142

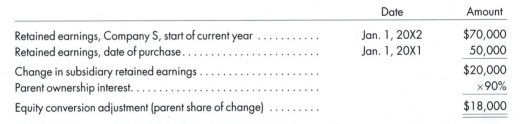

	Date	Amount
Retained earnings, Company S, start of current year	Jan. 1, 20X2	$70,000
Retained earnings, date of purchase.	Jan. 1, 20X1	50,000
Change in subsidiary retained earnings		$20,000
Parent ownership interest.		×90%
Equity conversion adjustment (parent share of change)		$18,000

Based on this calculation, the conversion entry on Worksheet 3-4 is as follows in journal entry form:

Convert investment to simple equity method as of
    Jan. 1, 20X2:

(CV)   Investment in Company S   18,000

      Retained Earnings, Jan. 1, 20X2, Company P   18,000

With date alignment created, remaining eliminations parallel Worksheet 3-2 except that there is no entry (CY1) for current-year equity income. Entry (CY2) is still used to eliminate intercompany dividends. In journal form, the remaining entries for Worksheet 3-4 are as follows:

Eliminate current-year dividends:

(CY2)	Subsidiary Income.	4,500	
	Dividends Declared (Company S account)		4,500

Eliminate investment account at beginning of the year
    balance:

(EL)	Common Stock, Company S	90,000	
	Retained Earnings, Jan. 1, 20X2, Company S	63,000	
	Investment in Company S.		153,000

Distribute excess of cost (patent):

(D)	Patent.	10,000	
	Investment in Company S.		10,000

Amortize patent for current and prior years:

(A)	Retained Earnings, Jan. 1, 20X2, Company P	1,000	
	Patent Amortization Expense.	1,000	
	Patent.		2,000

The last four columns of Worksheet 3-4 are exactly the same as those for Worksheet 3-2, as are the consolidated financial statements for 20X2.

The simplicity of this technique of converting from the cost to the simple equity method should be appreciated. At any future date, in order to convert to the simple equity method, it is necessary only to compare the balance of the subsidiary retained earnings account on the worksheet trial balance with the balance of that account on the original date of acquisition (included in the D&D schedule). Specific reference to income earned and dividends paid by the subsidiary in each intervening year is unnecessary.

Effect of Sophisticated Equity Method on Consolidation

In some cases, a parent may desire to prepare its own separate statements as a supplement to the consolidated statements. In this situation, the investment in the subsidiary must be shown on the parent's separate statements at the sophisticated equity balance. This requirement may lead the parent to maintain its subsidiary investment account under the sophisticated equity method. Two ramifications occur when such an investment is consolidated. First, the current year's equity adjustment is net of excess amortizations; second, the investment account contains only the remaining unamortized excess applicable to the investment.

The use of the sophisticated equity method complicates the elimination of the investment account in that the worksheet distribution and amortization of the excess procedures are altered. However, there is no impact on the other consolidation procedures. To illustrate, the information given in Worksheet 3-2 will be used as the basis for an example. The trial balance of Company P will show the following changes as a result of using the sophisticated equity method:

1. The Investment in Company S will be carried at $147,500 ($149,500 simple equity balance less 2 years' amortization of excess at $1,000 per year).

2. The January 1, 20X2, balance for Company P Retained Earnings will be $189,000 ($190,000 under simple equity less 1 year's amortization of excess of $1,000).

3. The subsidiary loss account of the parent will have a balance of $10,000 ($9,000 share of the subsidiary loss plus $1,000 amortization of excess).

4

OBJECTIVE

Describe the special worksheet procedures that are used for an investment maintained under the sophisticated equity method.

Based on these changes, a partial worksheet under the sophisticated equity method follows:

Company P and Subsidiary Company S
Partial Worksheet for Consolidated Financial Statements
For Year Ended December 31, 20X2

(Credit balance amounts are in parentheses.)	Trial Balance		Eliminations & Adjustments			
	Company P	Company S	Dr.		Cr.	
Investment in Company S	147,500		(CY1)	10,000	(EL)	153,000
			(CY2)	4,500	(D)	9,000
Patent			(D)	9,000	(A)	1,000
Retained Earnings, January 1, 20X2, Company P	(189,000)					
Common Stock ($10 par), Company S		(100,000)	(EL)	90,000		
Retained Earnings, January 1, 20X2, Company S		(70,000)	(EL)	63,000		
Revenue	(100,000)	(50,000)				
Expenses	80,000	60,000	(A)	1,000		
Patent Amortization						
Subsidiary Loss	10,000				(CY1)	10,000
Dividends Declared		5,000			(CY2)	4,500

Eliminations and Adjustments:

(CY1) Eliminate the current-year entries made in the investment account to record the subsidiary loss. The loss account now includes the $1,000 excess amortization.
(CY2) Eliminate intercompany dividends.
(EL)   Using the balances at the beginning of the year, eliminate 90% of the Company S equity balances against the remaining investment account.
(D)   Distribute the remaining unamortized excess on January 1, 20X2 ($10,000 on purchase date less $1,000 20X1 amortization) to the patent account.
(A)   Amortize the patent for the current year only; prior-year amortization has been recorded in the parent's investment account.

The sophisticated equity method essentially is a modification of simple equity procedures. The major difference in the consolidation procedures under the two methods is that, subsequent to the acquisition, the original excess calculated on the determination and distribution of excess schedule does not appear when the sophisticated equity method is used. Only the remaining unamortized excess appears. Since the investment account is eliminated in the consolidation process, the added complexities of the sophisticated method are not justified for most companies and seldom are applied to consolidated subsidiaries.

Determination of the Method Being Used

Before you attempt to prepare a consolidated worksheet, you need to know which of the three methods is being used by the parent to record its investment in the subsidiary. You cannot begin to eliminate the intercompany investment until that is determined. The most efficient approach is to

1. Test for the use of the cost method. If the cost method is used:

    a. *The investment account will be at the original cost shown on the determination and distribution of excess schedule.*
    b. *The parent will have recorded as its share of subsidiary income its ownership interest times the dividends declared by the subsidiary. In most cases, this income will be called "subsidiary dividend income," but some may call it "subsidiary income" or "dividend income." Therefore, do not rely on the title of the account.*

2. If the method used is not cost, check for the use of simple equity as follows:

    a. *The investment account will not be at the original cost.*

    b. *The parent will have recorded as subsidiary income its ownership percentage times the reported net income of the subsidiary.*

3. If the method used is neither cost nor simple equity, it must be the sophisticated equity method. Confirm that it is by noting that

    a. *The investment account will not be at the original cost.*

    b. *The parent will have recorded as subsidiary income its ownership percentage times the reported net income of the subsidiary minus the amortizations of excess for the current period.*

REFLECTION

- "Date alignment" is needed before an investment can be eliminated.

- For an equity method investment, date alignment means removing current-year entries to return to the beginning of the year investment balance.

- For a cost method investment, date alignment means converting the investment account to its equity-adjusted balance at the start of the year.

- Many distributions of excess must be followed by amortizations that cover the current and prior years.

- The consolidated net income derived on a worksheet is allocated to the controlling and noncontrolling interests using an income distribution schedule.

5

OBJECTIVE

Distribute and amortize multiple adjustments resulting from the difference between the price paid for an investment in a subsidiary and the subsidiary equity eliminated.

COMPLICATED PURCHASE, SEVERAL DISTRIBUTIONS OF EXCESS

In Worksheets 3-1 through 3-4, it was assumed that the entire excess of cost over book value was attributable to a patent. In reality, the excess will seldom apply to a single asset. The following example illustrates a more complicated purchase.

Paulos Company paid $690,000 to obtain 8,000 shares (80% interest) of Carlos Company on January 1, 20X1. In addition, $10,000 of direct acquisition costs were paid by Paulos. At the time of the purchase, Carlos had the following summarized balance sheet:

Carlos Company Balance Sheet
January 1, 20X1

Assets			Liabilities and Equity		
Current assets:			Current liabilities	$ 50,000	
Inventory		$ 75,000	Bonds payable, 6%, due		
			December 31, 20X4	200,000	
Long-term assets:			Total liabilities		$250,000
Land	$ 150,000				
Buildings	600,000		Stockholders' equity:		
Accumulated depreciation . . .	(300,000)		Common stock, $10 par	$100,000	
Equipment	150,000		Paid-in capital in excess of par . . .	150,000	
Accumulated depreciation . . .	(50,000)		Retained earnings	250,000	
Patent (net)	125,000		Total		500,000
Total		675,000			
Total assets		$750,000	Total liabilities and equity		$750,000

The entry to record the purchase would be as follows:

Investment in Carlos Company ($690,000 + $10,000 direct acquisition costs)...............................	700,000	
Cash (for purchase of Carlos shares)....................		690,000
Cash (for direct acquisition costs).....................		10,000

An analysis of book versus fair values is prepared as follows:

Carlos Company Book and Estimated Fair Values
December 31, 20X1

Assets	Book Value	Fair Value	Liabilities and Equity	Book Value	Fair Value
Priority assets:					
			Current liabilities	$ 50,000	$ 50,000
Inventory	$ 75,000	$ 80,000	Bonds payable*	200,000	186,750
Total priority assets	**$ 75,000**	**$ 80,000**	**Total liabilities..........**	**$250,000**	**$236,750**
Nonpriority accounts:					
Land........................	$ 150,000	$ 200,000			
Buildings (net)	300,000	500,000			
Equipment (net)	100,000	80,000			
Patent (net)	125,000	150,000			
Total nonpriority assets ...	**$675,000**	**$ 930,000**	**Market value of net assets**		
Total assets	**$750,000**	**$1,010,000**	**(assets – liabilities) .....**	**$500,000**	**$773,250**

*The bonds pay 6% nominal interest annually. There are four years to maturity. The current market interest rate is 8%. Discounting the $12,000 per year cash interest plus the $200,000 maturity value at 8% annual interest provides a present value of $186,751 (rounded to $186,750 to eliminate partial dollars when amortizing).

Zone analysis is now performed on the 80% interest using the fair values as follows:

Zone Analysis	Group Total	Ownership Portion	Cumulative Total
Ownership percentage		80%	
Priority accounts (net of liabilities)	$(156,750)	$(125,400)	$(125,400)
Nonpriority accounts..........................	930,000	744,000	618,600

Price analysis would be as follows:

Price (including direct acquisition costs)	**$700,000**	
Assign to priority accounts, controlling share	(125,400)	Full value
Assign to nonpriority accounts, controlling share	744,000	Full value
Goodwill...	**81,400**	
Extraordinary gain	**0**	

The price analysis schedule indicates that the parent's share of all accounts can be fully adjusted to fair value.

From this information, a determination and distribution excess is prepared. *Columns have been added that indicate the period of time over which the excess will be amortized and the annual amortization amount.* The schedule will now appear as follows:

Price paid for investment (including direct acquisition costs)...............................			**$700,000**			
Less book value of interest purchased:						
Common stock, $10 par	$100,000					
Paid-in capital in excess of par	150,000					
Retained earnings	250,000					
Total equity	$500,000					
Ownership interest	× 80%	400,000				

			Credit/Key	**Amort. Period**	**Amort. Amount**
Excess of cost over book value		**$300,000**			
Adjustments:					
Inventory, 80% of $5,000 fair-book value	$ 4,000		Debit D1	1	$ 4,000
Land, 80% of $50,000 fair-book value....................	40,000		Debit D2	None	
Discount on bonds payable, 80% of $13,250 fair-book value ...	10,600		Debit D3	4	2,650
Buildings (net), 80% of $200,000 fair-book value	160,000		Debit D4	20	8,000
Equipment (net), 80% of ($20,000) fair-book value	(16,000)		Debit D5	5	(3,200)
Patent (net), 80% of $25,000 fair-book value...............	20,000		Debit D6	10	2,000
Goodwill	81,400		Debit D7		
Total adjustments....................................		**$300,000**			

The following observations need to be made relative to the above determination and distribution of excess schedule:

♦ It is assumed that the inventory will be sold in the first year after the purchase. A total of $4,000 would therefore be added to the cost of goods sold for 20X1. In later periods, this adjustment will be made to controlling retained earnings.
♦ The discount on the bonds payable is being amortized on a straight-line basis over four years. If effective interest amortization were used, the amounts over the four years would be $2,352, $2,540, $2,743, and $2,965, respectively.
♦ Equipment depreciation will be reduced each year by $3,200 for five years.
♦ Theoretically, adjustments to plant and equipment should eliminate all accumulated depreciation applicable to the controlling interest. The parent's share of the assets would then start with a new basis. For the sake of simplicity, the assets are adjusted directly.
♦ Goodwill is not amortized. Impairment testing is required and could lead to impairment losses in any given period.

A summary of depreciation and amortization adjustments follows:

Account Adjustments	Life	Annual Amount	Current Year	Prior Years	Total	Key
Inventory	1	$ 4,000	$ 4,000	$0	$ 4,000	(D1)
Subject to amortization:						
Bonds payable	4	$ 2,650	$ 2,650	$0	$ 2,650	(A3)
Buildings	20	8,000	8,000	0	8,000	(A4)
Equipment	5	(3,200)	(3,200)	0	(3,200)	(A5)
Patent (net)................	10	2,000	2,000	0	2,000	(A6)
Total.................		$ 9,450	$ 9,450	$0	$ 9,450	

It is assumed that the method and life used for depreciation of fixed assets and amortization of the patent are the same as those used by the subsidiary. If that were not the case, the parent would have to recompute depreciation and patent amortization, based on their life and method and then adjust amounts recorded by the subsidiary. The "same method and life assumption" allows us to just depreciate or amortize the adjustment made in consolidation.

Take note of the following differences in Worksheet 3-6 as compared to Worksheet 3-5:

♦ The adjustment of the inventory, at the time of the purchase on January 1, 20X1, now goes to retained earnings since it is a correction of the 20X1 cost of goods sold.
♦ Amortizations of excess are made for both the current and prior years, using the following schedule:

Account Adjustments	Life	Annual Amount	Current Year	Prior Years	Total	Key
Inventory	1	$ 4,000	$ 0	$ 4,000	$ 4,000	(D1)
Subject to amortization:						
Bonds payable	4	$ 2,650	$ 2,650	$ 2,650	$ 5,300	(A3)
Buildings	20	8,000	8,000	8,000	16,000	(A4)
Equipment	5	(3,200)	(3,200)	(3,200)	(6,400)	(A5)
Patent (net)	10	2,000	2,000	2,000	4,000	(A6)
Total		$ 9,450	$ 9,450	$ 9,450	$18,900	

The amortizations of excess for prior periods and the inventory adjustment are carried to controlling retained earnings. Since only the controlling share of asset adjustments was recorded, amortizations are borne only by the controlling interest.

♦ The controlling retained earnings balance is adjusted for the above amortizations of excess before it is extended to the Retained Earnings column.

If a worksheet were prepared for December 31, 20X3, the prior years' amortizations of excess would cover two prior years as follows:

Account Adjustments	Life	Annual Amount	Current Year	Prior Years	Total	Key
Inventory	1	$ 4,000	$ 0	$ 4,000	$ 4,000	(D1)
Subject to amortization:						
Bonds payable	4	$ 2,650	$ 2,650	$ 5,300	$ 7,950	(A3)
Buildings	20	8,000	8,000	16,000	24,000	(A4)
Equipment	5	(3,200)	(3,200)	(6,400)	(9,600)	(A5)
Patent (net)	10	2,000	2,000	4,000	6,000	(A6)
Total		$ 9,450	$ 9,450	$18,900	$28,350	

Exhibit 3-1 contains the formal consolidated financial statements for Paulos Company for 20X2. Note the following features of the statements:

♦ All nominal accounts are merged, as adjusted, for amortizations to arrive at consolidated net income. The consolidated net income is then distributed to the noncontrolling and controlling interests, using the amounts from the income distribution schedules.

Exhibit 3-1
Consolidated Financial Statements for Paulos Company

Paulos Company
Consolidated Income Statement
Period Ending December 31, 20X2

Sales revenue	$700,000
Less cost of goods sold	320,000
Gross profit	$380,000

Less operating expenses:		
Depreciation expense (building and equipment).............	$ 99,800	
Other operating expenses...............................	125,000	224,800
Operating income......................................		$155,200
Interest expense......................................		14,650
Consolidated net income................................		$140,550
Distributed to noncontrolling interest......................		$ 20,000
Distributed to controlling interest........................		$120,550

Paulos Company
Retained Earnings Statement
Period Ending December 31, 20X2

Retained earnings, balance, December 31, 20X2.......................	$714,550
Net income (controlling share of consolidated net income).................	120,550
Balance, December 31, 20X2	$835,100

Paulos Company
Consolidated Balance Sheet
December 31, 20X2

Assets			Liabilities and Equity		
Current assets:			Current liabilities...........	$ 190,000	
Cash	$ 472,000		Bonds payable, 6%,		
			due Dec. 31, 20X4.......	200,000	
Inventory	330,000		Discount on bonds payable...	(5,300)	
Total current assets...........		$ 802,000	Total liabilities		$ 384,700
Long-term assets:					
Land.....................	$ 390,000				
Buildings	1,560,000				
Accumulated depreciation...	(466,000)				
Equipment	534,000		Stockholders' equity:		
Accumulated depreciation...	(173,600)		Noncontrolling interest	$ 124,000	
Patent (net)...............	116,000		Common stock...........	1,500,000	
Goodwill	81,400		Retained earnings	835,100	
Total long-term assets.....		2,041,800	Total equity.............		2,459,100
Total assets		$2,843,800	Total liabilities and equity		$2,843,800

◆ The statement of retained earnings only shows the changes in the controlling retained
earnings. The beginning balance reflects the parent company balance as adjusted for prior
years' amortization of excess amounts.
◆ The total NCI is shown as a single amount under stockholders' equity in the consolidated
balance sheet.

SUMMARY: WORKSHEET TECHNIQUE

At this point, it is wise to review the overall mechanical procedures used to prepare a consolidated worksheet. It will help you to have this set of procedures at your side for the first few worksheets you do. Later, the process will become automatic. The following procedures are designed to provide for both efficiency and correctness:

1. When recopying the trial balances, always sum them and make sure they balance before proceeding with the eliminations. At this point, you want to be sure that there are no errors in transporting figures to the worksheet. An amazing number of students' consolidated balance sheets are out of balance because their trial balances did not balance to begin with.

2. Carefully key all eliminations to aid future reference. It is suggested that a symbol, a little "p" for parent or a little "s" for subsidiary, be used to identify each worksheet adjustment entry that affects consolidated net income. This identification will make it easier to locate the adjustments that must be posted later to the income distribution schedules. Recall that any adjustment to income must be assigned to one of the company's income distribution schedules. This second step will become particularly important in the next two chapters where there will be many adjustments to income.

3. Sum the eliminations to be sure that they balance before you begin to extend the account totals.

4. Now that the eliminations are completed, crossfoot account totals and then extend them to the appropriate worksheet column. Extend each account in the order that it appears on the trial balance. Do not select just the accounts needed for a particular statement. For example, do not work only on the income statement. This can lead to errors. There may be some accounts that you will forget to extend, and you may not be aware of the errors until your balance sheet column total fails to equal zero. Extending each account in order assures that none will be overlooked and allows careful consideration of the appropriate destination of each account balance.

5. Calculate consolidated net income.

6. Prepare income distribution schedules. Verify that the sum of the distributions equals the consolidated net income on the worksheet. Distribute the NCI in income to the NCI column and distribute the controlling interest in income to the Controlling Retained Earnings column.

7. Sum the NCI column and extend that total to the Consolidated Balance Sheet column. Sum the Controlling Retained Earnings column and extend that total to the Consolidated Balance Sheet column as well.

8. Verify that the Consolidated Balance Sheet column total equals zero (or that the totals are equal if two columns are used).

GOODWILL IMPAIRMENT LOSSES

When circumstances indicate that the goodwill may have become impaired (see Chapter 1), the remaining goodwill will be estimated. If the resulting estimate is less than the book value of the goodwill, a *goodwill impairment loss* is recorded. The impairment loss is reported in the consolidated income statement for the period in which it occurs. It is presented on a before-tax basis as part of continuing operations and may appear under the caption "other gains and losses."

The parent company could handle the impairment loss in two ways:

1. The parent could record the impairment loss on its books and credit the investment in subsidiary account. This would automatically reduce the excess available for distribution, including the amount available for goodwill. This would mean that the impairment loss would already exist before consolidation procedures start. The loss would automatically be extended to the Consolidated Income column.

On the controlling IDS schedule, the loss would appear as a debit in periods subsequent to the impairment, the controlling retained earnings would already have been reduced on the parent's books, and no adjustment would be needed.

2. The impairment loss could be recorded only on the consolidated worksheet. This would adjust consolidated net income and produce a correct balance sheet. The only complication affects consolidated worksheets in periods subsequent to the impairment. The investment account, resulting goodwill, and the controlling retained earnings would be overstated. Thus, on the worksheet, an adjustment reducing the goodwill account and the controlling retained earnings would be needed.

The procedure used in this text will be to follow Option 1 and directly adjust the investment account on the parent's books. This approach would mean the price used in the D&D schedule would be reduced by the amount of the impairment.

The impairment loss is applicable only to the interest owned in the subsidiary. The impairment test must use the sophisticated equity investment balance (simple equity balance less amortizations of excess to date). For example, suppose Company P purchased an 80% interest in Company S in 20X2 and the price resulted in goodwill of $165,000. On a future balance sheet date, say December 31, 20X4, the following information applies to Company S:

Sophisticated equity method investment balance (net of amortizations of excess cost) on December 31, 20X4	$800,000
Estimated fair value of Company S	900,000
Estimated fair value of net identifiable assets	850,000

Determining if goodwill has been impaired would be calculated as shown here:

Sophisticated equity method investment balance on December 31, 20X4	$800,000
Estimated fair value of investment (80% × $900,000)	720,000

Because the investment amount exceeds the fair value, goodwill is impaired, and a loss must be calculated.

The impairment loss would be calculated as follows:

Estimated fair value of Company S	$ 900,000
Estimated fair value of net identifiable assets	850,000
Estimated goodwill	$ 50,000
80% ownership interest (80% × $50,000)	$ 40,000
Existing goodwill	165,000
Goodwill impairment loss	$(125,000)

The impairment entry on Company P's books would be as follows:

Goodwill Impairment Loss	125,000	
Investment in Company S		125,000

REFLECTION

• When the fair value of an investment is less than the sophisticated equity balance of that investment, any goodwill arising from the investment purchase is impaired, and a related loss must be recognized.

8
OBJECTIVE

(Appendix) Explain the impact of tax-related complications arising on the purchase date.

APPENDIX: TAX-RELATED ADJUSTMENTS

Recall from Chapter 1 that a deferred tax liability results when the fair value of an asset may not be used in future depreciation calculations for tax purposes. (This occurs when the purchase is a *tax-free exchange* to the seller.) In this situation, future depreciation charges for tax purposes must be based on the book value of the asset, and a liability should be acknowledged in the determination and distribution of excess schedule by creating a deferred tax liability account. Consider the following determination and distribution of excess schedule for a subsidiary that has a building with a book value for tax purposes of $120,000 and a fair value of $200,000. Assuming a tax rate of 30%, there is a deferred tax liability of $24,000 ($80,000 excess of fair value over tax basis × 30%).

As is true in all determination and distribution of excess schedules, any remaining unallocated value becomes goodwill. In the case of a tax-free exchange, the remaining unallocated value is the amount available for goodwill **less the applicable deferred tax liability**. In the example which follows, the remaining unallocated value on the determination and distribution of excess schedule is $44,000. The $44,000 excess is what is left after a 30% deferred tax liability is recorded. The goodwill to be recorded is, therefore, $44,000 divided by the net of tax rate of 70% which equals $62,857. The deferred tax liability is 30% of the goodwill recorded (30% × $62,857 = $18,857).

Price paid for investment		$ 600,000
Less interest acquired:		
Common stock	$ 100,000	
Retained earnings	400,000	
Total stockholders' equity	$ 500000	
Interest acquired	× 100%	500,000
Excess of cost over book value (debit balance)		$ 100,000
Available for long-lived assets:		
Building		80,000 Dr.
Deferred tax liability, building		**(24,000) Cr.**
Goodwill (net of deferred tax liability)		**$ 44,000 Dr.**
Distributed as follows:		
Goodwill ($44,000 ÷ 70%)		$ 62,857
Deferred tax liability (30% × $62,857)		**(18,857)**
Net goodwill		$ 44,000

The worksheet entry to distribute the excess of cost over book value would be as follows:

Building (to fair value)	80,000	
Goodwill (balance of excess)	62,857	
Deferred Tax Liability (**$24,000 + $18,857**)		42,857
Investment in Subsidiary S (excess cost after elimination of		
subsidiary equity)		100,000

Worksheet eliminations will be simpler if each deferred tax liability is recorded below the asset to which it relates. It is possible that inventory could have a fair value in excess of its book value used for tax purposes. This, too, would require the recognition of a deferred tax liability.

Recall the general rule that the fair values of the liabilities are acknowledged in full even in a bargain purchase. There is an exception to this rule with respect to the deferred tax liability that results from recording the fair value adjustments made in a purchase: **The deferred tax liability has the same priority as the asset to which it relates**. For instance, since inventory always is adjusted to full fair value, the deferred tax liability related to inventory is recognized fully as well. In the case of a depreciable asset, only a portion of the difference between book and fair value is recorded in a bargain purchase; thus, the deferred tax liability is limited to the portion of the fair-book value disparity that is recorded.

The need to recognize the deferred tax liability may complicate the distribution of the excess. Assume we have an asset that has a fair value estimated to exceed its book value by $150,000, but there is only $70,000 of excess available to distribute to the asset. Assuming a 30% tax rate, the excess would be divided by 70%, or the net-of-tax percentage, to arrive at the amount to allocate to the asset itself—in this case, $100,000 ($70,000 ÷ 70%); thus 30% of the $100,000 would be recognized as related deferred tax liability. The $70,000 excess of cost would be distributed as follows:

Excess of cost over book value available.		$70,000
Adjustment of depreciable assets:		
Asset	$100,000	
Deferred tax liability	(30 000)	70,000
		$ 0

REFLECTION

• When assets are part of a tax-free exchange, they must be accompanied by a deferred tax liability equal to the value of the forfeited tax deduction.

Worksheet 3-1

Simple Equity Method
Company P and Subsidiary Company S
Worksheet for Consolidated Financial Statements
For Year Ended December 31, 20X1

	(Credit balance amounts are in parentheses.)	Trial Balance	
		Company P	Company S
1	**Investment in Company S**	163,000	
2			
3			
4	**Patent**		
5	Other Assets (net of liabilities)	227,000	170,000
6	Common Stock ($10 par), Company P	(200,000)	
7	Retained Earnings, January 1, 20X1, Company P	(123,000)	
8	Common Stock ($10 par), Company S		(100,000)
9	Retained Earnings, January 1, 20X1, Company S		(50,000)
10	Revenue	(100,000)	(80,000)
11	**Expenses**	60,000	50,000
12	**Patent Amortization**		
13	**Subsidiary Income**	(27,000)	
14	**Dividends Declared**		10,000
15		0	0
16	**Consolidated Net Income**		
17	**To NCI (see distribution schedule)**		
18	**Balance to Controlling Interest (see distribution schedule)**		
19	Total NCI		
20	Retained Earnings, Controlling Interest, December 31, 20X1		
21			

Eliminations and Adjustments:

(CY1)   Eliminate subsidiary income against the investment account.
(CY2)   Eliminate dividends paid by subsidiary to parent. After (CY1) and (CY2), the investment account and subsidiary retained earnings
are at a common point in time. Then, elimination of the investment account can proceed.
(EL)   Eliminate the pro rata share of Company S equity balances at the beginning of the year against the investment account.
The elimination of the parent's share of subsidiary stockholders' equity leaves only the noncontrolling interest in each element
of the equity.
(D)   Distribute the $10,000 excess cost as required by the D&D schedule on page 111. In this example, Patent is recorded for $10,000.
(A)   Amortize the resulting patents over the 10-year period. The current portion is $1,000 per year ($10,000 ÷ 10 years).

Worksheet 3-1 (see page 112)

Eliminations & Adjustments				Consolidated Income Statement	NCI	Controlling Retained Earnings	Consolidated Balance Sheet	
Dr.		Cr.						
(CY2)	**9,000**	**(CY1)**	**27,000**					1
		(EL)	135,000					2
		(D)	10,000					3
(D)	10,000	**(A)**	**1,000**				9,000	4
							397,000	5
							(200,000)	6
						(123,000)		7
(EL)	90,000				(10,000)			8
(EL)	45,000				(5,000)			9
				(180,000)				10
				110,000				11
(A)	**1000**			**1,000**				12
(CY1)	**27,000**							13
		(CY2)	**9,000**		1,000			14
	182,000		182,000					15
				(69,000)				16
				3,000	**(3,000)**			17
				66,000		**(66,000)**		18
					(17,000)		(17,000)	19
						(189,000)	(189,000)	20
							0	21

Subsidiary Company S Income Distribution

Internally generated net income	$30,000
Adjusted income	$30,000
NCI share	10%
NCI	**$ 3,000**

Parent Company P Income Distribution

Patent amortization . . . . **(A)**	**$1,000**	Internally generated net income	$ 40,000
		90% × Company S adjusted income of $30,000 . .	27,000
		Controlling interest	**$66,000**

Worksheet 3-2

Simple Equity Method, Second Year
Company P and Subsidiary Company S
Worksheet for Consolidated Financial Statements
For Year Ended December 31, 20X2

	(Credit balance amounts are in parentheses.)	Trial Balance	
		Company P	Company S
1	**Investment in Company S**	149,500	
2			
3	Patent		
4	Other Assets (net of liabilities)	251,500	155,000
5	Common Stock ($10 par), Company P	(200,000)	
6	**Retained Earnings, January 1, 20X2, Company P**	(190,000)	
7	Common Stock ($10 par), Company S		(100,000)
8	Retained Earnings, January 1, 20X2, Company S		(70,000)
9	Revenue	(100,000)	(50,000)
10	Expenses	80,000	60,000
11	**Patent Amortization**		
12	**Subsidiary Loss**	9,000	
13	**Dividends Declared**		5,000
14		0	0
15	**Consolidated Net Income**		
16	**To NCI (see distribution schedule)**		
17	**Balance to Controlling Interest (see distribution schedule)**		
18	Total NCI		
19	Retained Earnings, Controlling Interest, December 31, 20X2		
20			

Eliminations and Adjustments:

(CY1) Eliminate controlling share of subsidiary loss.
(CY2) Eliminate dividends paid by subsidiary to parent. The investment account is now returned to its January 1, 20X2, balance so that elimination may proceed.
(EL)   Using balances at the beginning of the year, eliminate 90% of the Company S equity balances against the remaining investment account.
(D)   Distribute the $10,000 excess cost as indicated by the D&D schedule that was prepared on the date of acquisition.
(A)   Amortize the patent over the selected 10-year period. It is necessary to record the amortization for current and past periods, because asset adjustments resulting from the consolidation process do not appear on the separate statements of the constituent companies. Thus, entry (A) reduces Patent by $2,000 for the 20X1 and 20X2 amortizations. The amount for the current year is expensed, while the cumulative amortization for prior years is deducted from the beginning controlling retained earnings account. The NCI does not share in the adjustments because the only patent originally acknowledged is that which is applicable to the controlling interest.

Worksheet 3-2 (see page 116)

Eliminations & Adjustments				Consolidated Income Statement	NCI	Controlling Retained Earnings	Consolidated Balance Sheet	
Dr.		Cr.						
(CY1)	9,000	(EL)	153,000					1
(CY2)	4,500	(D)	10,000					2
(D)	10,000	(A)	2,000				8,000	3
							406,500	4
							(200,000)	5
(A)	1,000					(189,000)		6
(EL)	90,000				(10,000)			7
(EL)	63,000				(7,000)			8
				(150,000)				9
				140,000				10
(A)	1,000			1,000				11
		(CY1)	9,000					12
		(CY2)	4,500		500			13
	178,500		178,500					14
				(9,000)				15
				(1,000)	1,000			16
				10,000		(10,000)		17
					(15,500)		(15,500)	18
						(199,000)	(199,000)	19
							0	20

Subsidiary Company S Income Distribution

Internally generated **loss**	$ 10,000	
Adjusted income	$ 10,000	
NCI share	× 10%	
NCI	**$ 1,000**	

Parent Company P Income Distribution

Patent amortization .... (A)	**$1,000**	Internally generated net income	$ 20,000
90% × Company S adjusted income of			
$10,000....................................	9,000		
		Controlling interest	**$10,000**

Worksheet 3-3

Cost Method
Company P and Subsidiary Company S
Worksheet for Consolidated Financial Statements
For Year Ended December 31, 20X1

	(Credit balance amounts are in parentheses.)	Trial Balance	
		Company P	Company S
1	**Investment in Company S**	145,000	
2			
3	**Patent**		
4	Other Assets (net of liabilities)	227,000	170,000
5	Common Stock ($10 par), Company P	(200,000)	
6	Retained Earnings, January 1, 20X1, Company P	(123,000)	
7	Common Stock ($10 par), Company S		(100,000)
8	Retained Earnings, January 1, 20X1, Company S		(50,000)
9	Revenue	(100,000)	(80,000)
10	Expenses	60,000	50,000
11	**Patent Amortization**		
12	**Subsidiary (Dividend) Income**	(9,000)	
13	**Dividends Declared**		10,000
14		0	0
15	Consolidated Net Income		
16	To NCI (see distribution schedule)		
17	Balance to Controlling Interest (see distribution schedule)		
18	Total NCI		
19	Retained Earnings, Controlling Interest, December 31, 20X1		
20			

Eliminations and Adjustments:

(CY2) Eliminate intercompany dividends.
(EL)   Eliminate 90% of the Company S equity balances at the beginning of the year against the investment account.
(D)   Distribute the $10,000 excess cost as indicated by the D&D schedule on page 113.
(A)   Amortize the patent for the current year.

Worksheet 3-3 (see page 117)

Eliminations & Adjustments				Consolidated Income Statement	NCI	Controlling Retained Earnings	Consolidated Balance Sheet	
Dr.		Cr.						
		(EL)	135,000					1
		(D)	10,000					2
(D)	10,000	(A)	1,000				9,000	3
							397,000	4
							(200,000)	5
						(123,000)		6
(EL)	90,000				(10,000)			7
(EL)	45,000				(5,000)			8
				(180,000)				9
				110,000				10
(A)	1,000			1,000				11
(CY2)	9,000							12
		(CY2)	9,000		1,000			13
	155,000		155,000					14
				(69,000)				15
				3,000	(3,000)			16
				66,000		(66,000)		17
					(17,000)		(17,000)	18
						(189,000)	(189,000)	19
							0	20

Subsidiary Company S Income Distribution

Internally generated net income	$ 30,000
Adjusted income	$ 30,000
NCI share	× 10%
NCI	**$ 3,000**

Parent Company P Income Distribution

Patent amortization . . . . (A) $1,000	Internally generated net income	$ 40,000
	90% × Company S adjusted income of $30,000	27,000
	Controlling interest	**$66,000**

Worksheet 3-4

Cost Method, Second Year
Company P and Subsidiary Company S
Worksheet for Consolidated Financial Statements
For Year Ended December 31, 20X2

	(Credit balance amounts are in parentheses.)	Trial Balance	
		Company P	Company S
1	**Investment in Company S**	145,000	
2			
3	Patent		
4	Other Assets (net of liabilities)	251,500	155,000
5	Common Stock ($10 par), Company P	(200,000)	
6	**Retained Earnings, January 1, 20X2, Company P**	(172,000)	
7	Common Stock ($10 par), Company S		(100,000)
8	Retained Earnings, January 1, 20X2, Company S		(70,000)
9	Revenue	(100,000)	(50,000)
10	Expenses	80,000	60,000
11	Patent Amortization		
12	**Subsidiary (Dividend) Income**	(4,500)	
13	**Dividends Declared**		5,000
14		0	0
15	Consolidated Net Income		
16	To NCI (see distribution schedule)		
17	Balance to Controlling Interest (see distribution schedule)		
18	Total NCI		
19	Retained Earnings, Controlling Interest, December 31, 20X2		
20			

Eliminations and Adjustments:

(CV) Convert to simple equity method as of January 1, 20X2.
(CY2) Eliminate the current-year intercompany dividends.
(EL)   Eliminate 90% of the Company S equity balances at the beginning of the year against the investment account.
(D)   Distribute the $10,000 excess cost as indicated by the D&D schedule that was prepared on the date of acquisition.
(A)   Amortize the patent for the current year and one previous year.

Worksheet 3-4 (see page 118)

Eliminations & Adjustments				Consolidated Income Statement	NCI	Controlling Retained Earnings	Consolidated Balance Sheet	
Dr.		Cr.						
(CV)	18,000	(EL)	153,000					1
		(D)	10,000					2
(D)	10,000	(A)	2,000				8,000	3
							406,500	4
							(200,000)	5
(A)	1,000	(CV)	18,000			(189,000)		6
(EL)	90,000				(10,000)			7
(EL)	63,000				(7,000)			8
				(150,000)				9
				140,000				10
(A)	1,000			1,000				11
(CY2)	4,500							12
		(CY2)	4,500		500			13
	187,500		187,500					14
				(9,000)				15
				(1,000)	1,000			16
				10,000		(10,000)		17
					(15,500)		(15,500)	18
						(199,000)	(199,000)	19
							0	20

Subsidiary Company S Income Distribution

Internally generated **loss**	$ 10,000
Adjusted income	$ 10,000
NCI share	× 10%
NCI	**$ 1,000**

Parent Company P Income Distribution

Patent amortization	(A)	$1,000	Internally generated net income	$ 20,000
90% × Company S adjusted income of				
$10,000		9,000		
			Controlling interest	**$10,000**

Worksheet 3-5

Simple Equity Method, First Year
Paulos Company and Subsidiary Carlos Company
Worksheet for Consolidated Financial Statements
For Year Ended December 31, 20X1

	(Credit balance amounts are in parentheses.)	Trial Balance	
		Paulos	Carlos
1	Cash	100,000	50,000
2	Inventory	226,000	62,500
3	Land	200,000	150,000
4	Investment in Carlos	732,000	
5			
6			
7	Buildings	800,000	600,000
8	Accumulated Depreciation	(80,000)	(315,000)
9	Equipment	400,000	150,000
10	Accumulated Depreciation	(50,000)	(70,000)
11	Patent (net)		112,500
12	Goodwill		
13	Current Liabilities	(100,000)	
14	Bonds Payable		(200,000)
15	Discount (premium)		
16	Common Stock, Carlos		(100,000)
17	Paid-In Capital in Excess of Par, Carlos		(150,000)
18	Retained Earnings, January 1, 20X1, Carlos		(250,000)
19	Common Stock, Paulos	(1,500,000)	
20	Retained Earnings, January 1, 20X1, Paulos	(600,000)	
21	Sales	(350,000)	(200,000)
22	Cost of Goods Sold	150,000	80,000
23	Depreciation Expense—Building	40,000	15,000
24	Depreciation Expense—Equipment	20,000	20,000
25	Other Expenses	60,000	13,000
26	Interest Expense		12,000
27	Subsidiary Income	(48,000)	
28	Dividends Declared		20,000
29	Totals	0	0
30	Consolidated Net Income		
31	NCI Share		
32	Controlling Share		
33	Total NCI		
34	Retained Earnings, Controlling Interest, Dec. 31, 20X1		
35	Totals		

Worksheet 3-5 (see page 124)

Eliminations & Adjustments				Consolidated Income Statement	NCI	Controlling Retained Earnings	Consolidated Balance Sheet	
Dr.		Cr.						
							150,000	1
							288,500	2
(D2)	40,000						390,000	3
(CY2)	16,000	(CY1)	48,000					4
		(EL)	400,000					5
		(D)	300,000					6
(D4)	160,000						1,560,000	7
		(A4)	8,000				(403,000)	8
		(D5)	16,000				534,000	9
(A5)	3,200						(116,800)	10
(D6)	20,000	(A6)	2,000				130,500	11
(D7)	81,400						81,400	12
							(100,000)	13
							(200,000)	14
(D3)	10,600	(A3)	2,650				7,950	15
(EL)	80,000				(20,000)			16
(EL)	120,000				(30,000)			17
(EL)	200,000				(50,000)			18
							(1,500,000)	19
						(600,000)		20
				(550,000)				21
(D1)	4,000			234,000				22
(A4)	8,000			63,000				23
		(A5)	3,200	36,800				24
(A6)	2,000			75,000				25
(A3)	2,650			14,650				26
(CY1)	48,000							27
		(CY2)	16,000		4,000			28
	795,850		795,850					29
				(126,550)				30
				12,000	(12,000)			31
				114,550		(114,550)		32
					(108,000)		(108,000)	33
						(714,550)	(714,550)	34
							0	35

Eliminations and Adjustments:

(CY1)   Eliminate current-year entries made to record subsidiary income.
(CY2)   Eliminate dividends paid by Carlos to Paulos. The investment is now at its January 1, 20X1, balance.
(EL)   Eliminate 80% of subsidiary equity against the investment account.
(D)   Distribute $300,000 excess as follows:
(D1)   Cost of goods sold for inventory adjustment at time of purchase.
(D2)   Land adjustment.
(D3)   Record discount on bonds payable.
(D4)   Adjust building.
(D5)   Adjust equipment.
(D6)   Adjust patent.
(D7)   Record goodwill.

(A3–A6) Account Adjustments to Be Amortized	Life	Annual Amount	Current Year	Prior Years	Total	Key
Bonds payable	4	$ 2,650	$ 2,650	0	$ 2,650	(A3)
Buildings	20	8,000	8,000	0	8,000	(A4)
Equipment	5	(3,200)	(3,200)	0	(3,200)	(A5)
Patent (net).....................................	10	2,000	2,000	0	2,000	(A6)
Total...	0	$ 9,450	$ 9,450	0	$ 9,450	

Subsidiary Carlos Company Income Distribution

	Internally generated net income	$ 60,000
	Adjusted income	$ 60,000
	NCI share	× 20%
	NCI	$ 12,000

Parent Paulos Company Income Distribution

Amortizations of excess (Elim. A) .... (A3–A6)	$9,450	Internally generated net income	$ 80,000
Inventory adjustment .... (D1)	4,000	80% × Carlos adjusted income.................	48,000
		Controlling interest	$114,550

Worksheet 3-6

Simple Equity Method, Second Year
Paulos Company and Subsidiary Carlos Company
Worksheet for Consolidated Financial Statements
For Year Ended December 31, 20X2

	(Credit balance amounts are in parentheses.)	Trial Balance	
		Paulos	Carlos
1	Cash	312,000	160,000
2	Inventory	210,000	120,000
3	Land	200,000	150,000
4	Investment in Carlos	796,000	
5			
6			
7	Buildings	800,000	600,000
8	Accumulated Depreciation	(120,000)	(330,000)
9	Equipment	400,000	150,000
10	Accumulated Depreciation	(90,000)	(90,000)
11	Patent (net)		100,000
12	Goodwill		
13	Current Liabilities	(150,000)	(40,000)
14	Bonds Payable		(200,000)
15	Discount (premium)		
16	Common Stock, Carlos		(100,000)
17	Paid-In Capital in Excess of Par, Carlos		(150,000)
18	Retained Earnings, Jan. 1, 20X2, Carlos		(290,000)
19	Common Stock, Paulos	(1,500,000)	
20	Retained Earnings, Jan. 1, 20X2, Paulos	(728,000)	
21			
22	Sales	(400,000)	(300,000)
23	Cost of Goods Sold	200,000	120,000
24	Depr. Expense—Building	40,000	15,000
25	Depreciation Exp.—Equipment	20,000	20,000
26	Other Expenses	90,000	33,000
27	Interest Expense		12,000
28	Subsidiary Income	(80,000)	
29	Dividends Declared		20,000
30	Totals	0	0
31	Consolidated Net Income		
32	NCI Share		
33	Controlling Share		
34	Total NCI		
35	Retained Earnings, Controlling Interest, Dec. 31, 20X2		
36	Totals		

Worksheet 3-6 (see page 125)

Eliminations & Adjustments				Consolidated Income Statement	NCI	Controlling Retained Earnings	Consolidated Balance Sheet	
Dr.		Cr.						
							472,000	1
							330,000	2
(D2)	40,000						390,000	3
(CY2)	16,000	(CY1)	80,000					4
		(EL)	432,000					5
		(D)	300,000					6
(D4)	160,000						1,560,000	7
		(A4)	16,000				(466,000)	8
		(D5)	16,000				534,000	9
(A5)	6,400						(173,600)	10
(D6)	20,000	(A6)	4,000				116,000	11
(D7)	81,400						81,400	12
							(190,000)	13
							(200,000)	14
(D3)	10,600	(A3)	5,300				5,300	15
(EL)	80,000				(20,000)			16
(EL)	120,000				(30,000)			17
(EL)	232,000				(58,000)			18
							(1,500,000)	19
(D1)	4,000							20
(A3–A6)	9,450					(714,550)		21
				(700,000)				22
				320,000				23
(A4)	8,000			63,000				24
		(A5)	3,200	36,800				25
(A6)	2,000			125,000				26
(A3)	2,650			14,650				27
(CY1)	80,000							28
		(CY2)	16,000		4,000			29
	872,500		872,500					30
				(140,550)				31
				20,000	(20,000)			32
				120,550		(120,550)		33
					(124,000)		(124,000)	34
						(835,100)	(835,100)	35
							0	36

Eliminations and Adjustments:

(CY1)	Eliminate current-year entries made to record subsidiary income.
(CY2)	Eliminate dividends paid by Carlos to Paulos. The investment is now at its January 1, 20X2, balance.
(EL)	Eliminate 80% of subsidiary equity against the investment account.
(D)	Distribute $300,000 excess as follows:
(D1)	Cost of goods sold for inventory adjustment at time of purchase.
(D2)	Land adjustment.
(D3)	Record discount on bonds payable.
(D4)	Adjust building.
(D5)	Adjust equipment.
(D6)	Adjust patent.
(D7)	Record goodwill.

(A3–A6) Account Adjustments to Be Amortized	Life	Annual Amount	Current Year	Prior Years	Total	Key
Bonds payable	4	$ 2,650	$ 2,650	$ 2,650	$ 5,300	(A3)
Buildings	20	8,000	8,000	8,000	16,000	(A4)
Equipment	5	(3,200)	(3,200)	(3,200)	(6,400)	(A5)
Patent (net)	10	2,000	2,000	2,000	4,000	(A6)
Total		$ 9,450	$ 9,450	$ 9,450	$18,900	

Subsidiary Carlos Company Income Distribution

	Internally generated net income	$ 100,000
	Adjusted income	$ 100,000
	NCI share	× 20%
	NCI	$ 20,000

Parent Paulos Company Income Distribution

Amortizations of excess (Elim. A) . . . . (A3–A6)	$9,450	Internally generated net income.	$ 50,000
		80% × Carlos adjusted income.	80,000
		Controlling interest	$120,550

Worksheet 3-7

Intraperiod Purchase; Subsidiary Books Closed on Purchase Date
Company P and Subsidiary Company S
Worksheet for Consolidated Financial Statements
For Year Ended December 31, 20X1

	(Credit balance amounts are in parentheses.)	Trial Balance	
		Company P	Company S
1	Current Assets	187,600	87,500
2	**Investment in Company S**	**118,400**	
3			
4			
5	Goodwill		
6	Equipment	400,000	80,000
7	Accumulated Depreciation	(200,000)	(32,500)
8	Liabilities	(60,000)	(12,000)
9	Common Stock, Company P	(250,000)	
10	Retained Earnings, **Jan. 1, 20X1, Company P**	(100,000)	
11	Common Stock, Company S		(50,000)
12	Retained Earnings, **July 1, 20X1, Company S**		(58,000)
13	Sales	(500,000)	(92,000)
14	Cost of Goods Sold	350,000	60,000
15	Expenses	70,000	12,000
16	**Subsidiary Income**	**(16,000)**	
17	Dividends Declared		5,000
18			
19		0	0
20			
21	Consolidated Net Income		
22	To NCI (see distribution schedule)		
23	Balance to Controlling Interest (see distribution schedule)		
24	Total NCI		
25	Retained Earnings, Controlling Interest, December 31, 20X1		
26			

Eliminations and Adjustments:

(CY1)   Eliminate the entries made in the investment in Company S account and in the subsidiary income account to record
         the parent's 80% controlling interest in the subsidiary's second six months' income.
(CY2)   Eliminate intercompany dividends. This restores the investment account to its balance as of the July 1, 20X1 investment date.
(EL)   Eliminate 80% of the subsidiary's July 1, 20X1, equity balances against the balance of the investment account.
(D)   Distribute the excess of cost over book value of $20,000 to Goodwill in accordance with the D&D schedule.

Worksheet 3-7 (see page 129)

Eliminations & Adjustments				Consolidated Income Statement	NCI	Controlling Retained Earnings	Consolidated Balance Sheet	
Dr.		Cr.						
							275,100	1
(CY2)	4,000	(CY1)	16,000					2
		(EL)	86,400					3
		(D)	20,000					4
(D)	20,000						20,000	5
							480,000	6
							(232,500)	7
							(72,000)	8
							(250,000)	9
						(100,000)		10
(EL)	40,000				(10,000)			11
(EL)	46,400				(11,600)			12
				(592,000)				13
				410,000				14
				82,000				15
(CY1)	16,000							16
		(CY2)	4,000		1,000			17
								18
	126,400		126,400					19
								20
				(100,000)				21
				4,000	(4,000)			22
				96,000		(96,000)		23
					(24,600)		(24,600)	24
						(196,000)	(196,000)	25
							0	26

Subsidiary Company S Income Distribution

Internally generated net income **(last six months)** ...	**$20,000**
Adjusted income	$ 20,000
NCI share	× 20%
NCI	**$ 4,000**

Parent Company P Income Distribution

Internally generated net income	$ 80,000
80% × Company S adjusted income of $20,000	
(last six months)	**16,000**
Controlling interest	**$96,000**

Worksheet 3-8

Intraperiod Purchase; Subsidiary Books Not Closed on Purchase Date
Company P and Subsidiary Company S
Worksheet for Consolidated Financial Statements
For Year Ended December 31, 20X1

	(Credit balance amounts are in parentheses.)	Trial Balance	
		Company P	Company S
1	Current Assets	187,600	87,500
2	**Investment in Company S**	**118,400**	
3			
4			
5	Goodwill		
6	Equipment	400,000	80,000
7	Accumulated Depreciation	(200,000)	(32,500)
8	Liabilities	(60,000)	(12,000)
9	Common Stock, Company P	(250,000)	
10	Retained Earnings, **Jan. 1, 20X1, Company P**	(100,000)	
11	Common Stock, Company S		(50,000)
12	Retained Earnings, **Jan. 1, 20X1, Company S**		(45,000)
13	Sales	(500,000)	(182,000)
14	Cost of Goods Sold	350,000	120,000
15	Expenses	70,000	24,000
16	**Subsidiary Income**	**(16,000)**	
17	**Dividends Declared**		**10,000**
18			
19	**Purchased Income**		
20		0	0
21			
22	Consolidated Net Income		
23	To NCI (see distribution schedule)		
24	Balance to Controlling Interest (see distribution schedule)		
25	Total NCI		
26	Retained Earnings, Controlling Interest, Dec. 31, 20X1		
27			

Eliminations and Adjustments:

(CY1)   Eliminate the entries made in the investment account and in the subsidiary income account (same as Worksheet 3-7).
(CY2)   Eliminate intercompany dividends. Notice that Company P's share of the subsidiary dividends declared are from those declared after the purchase.
(EL)   Eliminate 80% of the subsidiary equity balances at the beginning of the year plus 80% of Company S's income earned as of July 1, 20X1, against the investment account. The share of preacquisition income is entered as *Purchased Income* to emphasize that this income was earned prior to the date of purchase by Company P. For elimination purposes, this account may be viewed as a supplement to retained earnings. Since the subsidiary also declared dividends *prior to July 1, 20X1*, the controlling percentage of those dividends should be eliminated in this entry by crediting Dividends Declared.
(D)   Distribute the $20,000 excess of cost over book value (same as Worksheet 3-7).

Worksheet 3-8 (see page 130)

Eliminations & Adjustments				Consolidated Income Statement		NCI		Controlling Retained Earnings	Consolidated Balance Sheet		
Dr.		Cr.									
									275,100		1
(CY2)	4,000	(CY1)	16,000								2
		(EL)	86,400								3
		(D)	20,000								4
(D)	20,000								20,000		5
									480,000		6
									(232,500)		7
									(72,000)		8
									(250,000)		9
								(100,000)			10
(EL)	40,000					(10,000)					11
(EL)	36,000					(9,000)					12
				(682,000)							13
				470,000							14
				94,000							15
(CY1)	16,000										16
		(CY2)	4,000			2,000					17
		(EL)	**4,000**								18
(EL)	**14,400**			**14,400**							19
	130,400		130,400								20
											21
				(103,600)							22
				7,600		(7,600)					23
				96,000				(96,000)			24
						(24,600)			(24,600)		25
								(196,000)	(196,000)		26
									0		27

Subsidiary Company S Income Distribution

Internally generated net income **entire year**	$ **38,000**
Adjusted income	$ 38,000
NCI share	× 20%
NCI	$ **7,600**

Parent Company P Income Distribution

Internally generated net income	$ 80,000
80% × Company S adjusted income of $20,000 **(last six months)**	16,000
Controlling interest	$ **96,000**

UNDERSTANDING THE ISSUES

1. A parent company paid $400,000 for a 100% interest in a subsidiary. At the end of the first year, the subsidiary reported net income of $30,000 and paid $5,000 in dividends. The price paid reflected understated equipment of $50,000, which will be amortized over 10 years. What would be the subsidiary income reported on the parent's unconsolidated income statement, and what would the parent's investment balance be at the end of the first year under each of these methods?

   a. The simple equity method
   b. The sophisticated equity method
   c. The cost method

2. What is meant by date alignment? Does it exist on the consolidated worksheet under the following methods, and if not, how is it created prior to elimination of the investment account under each of these methods?

   a. The simple equity method
   b. The sophisticated equity method
   c. The cost method

3. What is the noncontrolling share of consolidated net income? Does it reflect adjustments based on fair values at the purchase date? How has it been displayed in income statements in the past, and how should it be displayed?

4. A parent company purchased an 80% interest in a subsidiary on July 1, 20X1. The subsidiary reported net income of $60,000 for 20X1, earned evenly during the year. The parent's net income, exclusive of any income of the subsidiary, was $140,000. The price paid for the subsidiary exceeded book value by $100,000. The entire difference was attributed to a patent with a 10-year life.

   a. What is consolidated net income for 20X1?
   b. What is the noncontrolling share of net income for 20X1?

5. A parent company purchased an 80% interest in a subsidiary on January 1, 20X1, at a price high enough to result in goodwill. Included in the assets of the subsidiary are inventory with a book value of $50,000 and a fair value of $60,000 and equipment with a book value of $100,000 and a fair value of $150,000. The equipment has a five-year remaining life. What impact would the inventory and equipment acquired in the purchase have on consolidated net income in 20X1 and 20X2?

6. You are working on a consolidated trial balance of a parent and an 80%-owned subsidiary. What components will enter into the total noncontrolling interest, and how will it be displayed in the consolidated balance sheet?

7. It seems as if consolidated net income is always less than the sum of the parent's and subsidiary's separately calculated net incomes. Is it possible that the consolidated net income of the two affiliated companies could actually exceed the sum of their individual net incomes?

8. How would push-down accounting simplify consolidated worksheet procedures?

EXERCISES

Exercise 3-1 *(LO 1)* **Compare alternative methods for recording income.** Cooke Company purchased an 80% interest in Hill Company common stock for $360,000 cash on January 1, 20X1. At that time, Hill Company had the following balance sheet:

Assets		Liabilities and Equity	
Current assets	$ 60,000	Accounts payable	$ 60,000
Land.	100,000	Common stock ($5 par).	50,000
Equipment	350,000	Paid-in capital in excess of par	100,000
Accumulated depreciation	(150,000)	Retained earnings	150,000
Total assets.	$ 360,000	Total liabilities and equity	$360,000

Appraisals indicated that accounts are fairly stated except for the equipment which has a fair value of $225,000 and a remaining life of five years. Any remaining excess is goodwill.

Hill Company experienced the following changes in retained earnings during 20X1 and 20X2:

Retained earnings, January 1, 20X1.		$150,000
Net income, 20X1	$ 60,000	
Dividends paid in 20X1.	(10,000)	50,000
Balance, December 31, 20X1		$200,000
Net income, 20X2.	$ 40,000	
Dividends paid in 20X2.	(10,000)	30,000
Balance, December 31, 20X2		$230,000

Prepare a determination and distribution of excess schedule for the investment in Hill Company. Prepare journal entries that Cooke Company would make on its books to record income earned and/or dividends received on its investment in Hill Company during 20X1 and 20X2 under the following methods: simple equity, sophisticated equity, and cost.

Exercise 3-2 *(LO 1)* **Alternative investment models, more complex D&D.** Mast Corporation purchased a 75% interest in the common stock of Shaw Company on January 1, 20X4, for $462,500 cash. Shaw had the following balance sheet on that date:

Assets		Liabilities and Equity	
Current assets	$ 80,000	Current liabilities	$ 50,000
Inventory	40,000	Common stock ($5 par).	50,000
Land.	100,000	Paid-in capital in excess of par	150,000
Buildings and equipment (net)	200,000	Retained earnings	200,000
Patent.	30,000		
Total assets.	$450,000	Total liabilities and equity	$450,000

Appraisals indicated that the book values for inventory, buildings and equipment, and patent are below fair values. The inventory had a fair value of $50,000 and was sold during 20X4. The buildings and equipment have an appraised fair value of $300,000 and a remaining life of 20 years. The patent, which has a 10-year life, has an estimated fair value of $50,000. Any remaining excess is goodwill.

Shaw Company reported the following income earned and dividends paid during 20X4 and 20X5:

Retained earnings, January 1, 20X4.		$200,000
Net income, 20X4	$ 70,000	
Dividends paid in 20X4.	(20,000)	50,000
Balance, December 31, 20X4		$250,000
Net income, 20X5.	$ 48,000	
Dividends paid in 20X5.	(20,000)	28,000
Balance, December 31, 20X5		$278,000

Prepare a determination and distribution of excess schedule for the investment in Shaw Company and determine the balance in the Investment in Shaw Company on Mast Company's books as of December 31, 20X5, under the following methods that could be used by the parent, Mast Company: simple equity, sophisticated equity, and cost.

Exercise 3-3 *(LO 2)* **Equity method, first year, eliminations, statements.** Pepper Company purchased an 80% interest in Salt Company for $250,000 in cash on January 1, 20X1, when Salt Company had the following balance sheet:

Assets		Liabilities and Equity	
Current assets	$100,000	Current liabilities	$ 50,000
Depreciable fixed assets	200,000	Common stock ($10 par).	100,000
		Retained earnings	150,000
Total assets.	$300,000	Total liabilities and equity . . .	$300,000

Any excess of the price paid over book value is attributable only to the fixed assets, which have a 10-year remaining life. Pepper Company uses the simple equity method to record its investment in Salt Company.

The following trial balances of the two companies were prepared on December 31, 20X1:

	Pepper	Salt
Current Assets	60,000	130,000
Depreciable Fixed Assets	400,000	200,000
Accumulated Depreciation	(106,000)	(20,000)
Investment in Salt Company	266,000	
Current Liabilities.	(60,000)	(40,000)
Common Stock ($10 par)	(300,000)	(100,000)
Retained Earnings, January 1, 20X1.	(200,000)	(150,000)
Sales	(150,000)	(100,000)
Expenses	110,000	75,000
Subsidiary Income.	(20,000)	
Dividends Declared		5,000
Total	0	0

Handwritten notes in left margin: 250,000; includes ←(190,000); 5,000 Depr; Cons. NI = 60,000

Handwritten note near Subsidiary Income: 25,000 × .80 =→

Handwritten note near Salt Dividends: NI 25,00

1. Prepare a determination and distribution of excess schedule for the investment.
2. Prepare all the eliminations and adjustments that would be made on the 20X1 consolidated worksheet.
3. Prepare the 20X1 consolidated income statement and its related income distribution schedules.
4. Prepare the 20X1 consolidated balance sheet.

Exercise 3-4 *(LO 2)* **Equity method, second year, eliminations, statements.** The trial balances of Pepper and Salt companies of Exercise 3-3 for December 31, 20X2, are presented as follows:

	Pepper	Salt
Current Assets	152,000	115,000
Depreciable Fixed Assets	400,000	200,000
Accumulated Depreciation	(130,000)	(40,000)
Investment in Salt Company	270,000	
Current Liabilities.	(80,000)	
Common Stock ($10 par)	(300,000)	(100,000)
Retained Earnings, January 1, 20X2.	(260,000)	(170,000)

Sales	(200,000)	(100,000)
Expenses	160,000	85,000
Subsidiary Income	(12,000)	
Dividends Declared		10,000
Total	0	0

Pepper Company continued to use the simple equity method.

1. Prepare all the eliminations and adjustments that would be made on the 20X2 consolidated worksheet.
2. Prepare the 20X2 consolidated income statement and its related income distribution schedules.

Exercise 3-5 *(LO 4)* **Sophisticated equity method, first year, eliminations, statements.** *(Note: Read carefully. This is not the same as Exercise 3-3.)* Pepper Company purchased an 80% interest in Salt Company for $250,000 on January 1, 20X1, when Salt Company had the following balance sheet:

Assets		Liabilities and Equity	
Current assets	$100,000	Current liabilities	$ 50,000
Depreciable fixed assets	200,000	Common stock ($10 par)	100,000
		Retained earnings	150,000
Total assets	$300,000	Total liabilities and equity . . .	$300,000

Any excess of the price paid over book value is attributable only to the fixed assets, which have a 10-year remaining life. Pepper uses the sophisticated equity method to record the investment in Salt Company.

The following trial balances of the two companies were prepared on December 31, 20X1:

	Pepper	Salt
Current Assets	60,000	130,000
Depreciable Fixed Assets	400,000	200,000
Accumulated Depreciation	(106,000)	(20,000)
Investment in Salt Company	261,000	
Current Liabilities	(60,000)	(40,000)
Common Stock ($10 par)	(300,000)	(100,000)
Retained Earnings, January 1, 20X1	(200,000)	(150,000)
Sales	(150,000)	(100,000)
Expenses	110,000	75,000
Subsidiary Income (from Salt Company)	(15,000)	
Dividends Declared		5,000
Total	0	0

1. If you did not solve Exercise 3-3, prepare a determination and distribution of excess schedule for the investment.
2. Prepare all the eliminations and adjustments that would be made on the 20X1 consolidated worksheet.
3. If you did not solve Exercise 3-3, prepare the 20X1 consolidated income statement and its related income distribution schedule.
4. If you did not solve Exercise 3-3, prepare the 20X1 consolidated balance sheet.

Exercise 3-6 *(LO 4)* **Sophisticated equity method, second year, eliminations, statements.** The trial balances of Pepper and Salt companies of Exercise 3-5 for December 31, 20X2, are presented as follows:

	Pepper	Salt
Current Assets	152,000	115,000
Depreciable Fixed Assets	400,000	200,000
Accumulated Depreciation	(130,000)	(40,000)
Investment in Salt Company	260,000	
Current Liabilities.	(80,000)	
Common Stock ($10 par)	(300,000)	(100,000)
Retained Earnings, January 1, 20X2.	(255,000)	(170,000)
Sales	(200,000)	(100,000)
Expenses	160,000	85,000
Subsidiary Income (from Salt Company)	(7,000)	
Dividends Declared.		10,000
Total.	0	0

Pepper Company continued to use the sophisticated equity method.

1. Prepare all the eliminations and adjustments that would be made on the 20X2 consolidated worksheet.
2. If you did not solve Exercise 3-4, prepare the 20X2 consolidated income statement and its related income distribution schedules.

Exercise 3-7 *(LO 3)* **Cost method, first year, eliminations, statements.** *(Note: Read carefully. This is not the same as Exercise 3-3 or 3-5.)* Pepper Company purchased an 80% interest in Salt Company for $250,000 in cash on January 1, 20X1, when Salt Company had the following balance sheet:

Assets		Liabilities and Equity	
Current assets	$100,000	Current liabilities	$ 50,000
Depreciable fixed assets	200,000	Common stock ($10 par).	100,000
		Retained earnings	150,000
Total assets.	$300,000	Total liabilities and equity . . .	$300,000

Any excess of the price paid over book value is attributable only to the fixed assets, which have a 10-year remaining life. Pepper Company uses the cost method to record its investment in Salt Company.

The following trial balances of the two companies were prepared on December 31, 20X1:

	Pepper	Salt
Current Assets	60,000	130,000
Depreciable Fixed Assets	400,000	200,000
Accumulated Depreciation	(106,000)	(20,000)
Investment in Salt Company	250,000	
Current Liabilities.	(60,000)	(40,000)
Common Stock ($10 par)	(300,000)	(100,000)
Retained Earnings, January 1, 20X1.	(200,000)	(150,000)
Sales	(150,000)	(100,000)
Expenses	110,000	75,000
Dividend Income (from Salt Company)	(4,000)	
Dividends Declared.		5,000
Total.	0	0

1. If you did not solve Exercise 3-3 or 3-5, prepare a determination and distribution of excess schedule for the investment.

Using cost method — do not recognize income of subsidiary.

2. Prepare all the eliminations and adjustments that would be made on the 20X1 consolidated worksheet.
3. If you did not solve Exercise 3-3 or 3-5, prepare the 20X1 consolidated income statement and its related income distribution schedules.
4. If you did not solve Exercise 3-3 or 3-5, prepare the 20X1 consolidated balance sheet.

Exercise 3-8 *(LO 3)* **Cost method, second year, eliminations, statements.** The trial balances of Pepper and Salt companies of Exercise 3-7 for December 31, 20X2, are presented as follows:

	Pepper	Salt
Current Assets	152,000	115,000
Depreciable Fixed Assets	400,000	200,000
Accumulated Depreciation	(130,000)	(40,000)
Investment in Salt Company	250,000	
Current Liabilities	(80,000)	
Common Stock ($10 par)	(300,000)	(100,000)
Retained Earnings, January 1, 20X2	(244,000)	(170,000)
Sales	(200,000)	(100,000)
Expenses	160,000	85,000
Dividend Income (from Salt Company)	(8,000)	
Dividends Declared		10,000
Total	0	0

Pepper Company continued to use the cost method.

1. Prepare all the eliminations and adjustments that would be made on the 20X2 consolidated worksheet.
2. If you did not solve Exercise 3-4 or 3-6, prepare the 20X2 consolidated income statement and its related income distribution schedules.

Exercise 3-9 *(LO 5)* **Amortization procedures, several years.** Walt Company purchased an 80% interest in Mitchell Company common stock on January 1, 20X1. Appraisals of Mitchell's assets and liabilities were performed, and Walt ended up paying an amount that was greater than the fair value of Mitchell's net assets. The following determination and distribution of excess schedule was created on December 31, 20X1, to assist in putting together the consolidated financial statements:

Determination and Distribution of Excess Schedule

Price paid for investment		$1,100,000
Less book value interest acquired:		
Common stock	$100,000	
Paid-in capital in excess of par	150,000	
Retained earnings	350,000	
Total equity	$600,000	
Interest acquired	× 80%	480,000
Excess of cost over book value (debit)		$ 620,000

Adjustments to first priority accounts:			Life
Inventory	$	5,000	1
Investments		20,000	5
Land		40,000	—
Bonds payable		10,000	5
Buildings (net)		200,000	20

[Handwritten marginal notes:]

Ex 3-8
Must Convert to Equity Method in 2nd subsequent yr.
year 1 -
R/E 150,000
year 2
R/E - 170,000
change $20,000
× 80
own er ship 16,000
add to Inv in Salt DR
R/E - Pepper CR

always convert current year R/E to 1st year.
Record change as above.

Div Income 8,000
Div Dec 8,000

Equipment (net)	138,000	5
Patent...	18,000	10
Trademark	16,000	10
Goodwill	173,000	
Total adjustments	$ 620,000	

Prepare an amortization schedule for the years 20X1, 20X2, 20X3, and 20X4.

Exercise 3-10 *(LO 6)* **Purchase during the year, elimination entries, income statement.** Karen Company had the following balance sheet on January 1, 20X2:

Assets		Liabilities and Equity	
Current assets	$200,000	Current liabilities	$100,000
Equipment (net)	300,000	Common stock ($10 par)......	100,000
		Retained earnings	300,000
Total assets...............	$500,000	Total liabilities and equity ...	$500,000

Between January 1 and July 1, 20X2, Karen Company estimated its net income to be $30,000. On July 1, 20X2, Neiman Company purchased 80% of the outstanding common stock of Karen Company for $310,000. Any excess of book value over cost was attributed to the equipment, which had an estimated five-year life. Karen Company did not close its books on July 1.

On December 31, 20X2, Neiman Company and Karen Company prepared the following trial balances:

	Neiman	Karen
Current Assets	220,000	250,000
Equipment	500,000	300,000
Accumulated Depreciation—Equipment	(140,000)	(20,000)
Investment in Karen Company....................................	310,000	
Current Liabilities...	(200,000)	(70,000)
Common Stock ($10 par)	(200,000)	(100,000)
Retained Earnings, January 1, 20X2.............................	(430,000)	(300,000)
Sales	(300,000)	(200,000)
Cost of Goods Sold	180,000	90,000
General Expenses	60,000	50,000
Total..	0	0

1. Prepare a determination and distribution of excess schedule for the investment.
2. Prepare all the eliminations and adjustments that would be made on the December 31, 20X2, consolidated worksheet.
3. Prepare the 20X2 consolidated income statement and its related income distribution schedules.

Exercise 3-11 *(LO 7)* **Impairment loss.** Albers Company purchased an 80% interest in Baker Company on January 1, 20X1, for $850,000. The following determination and distribution of excess schedule was prepared at the time of purchase:

Price paid		$850,000
Stockholders' equity	$600,000	
Interest acquired	× 80%	480,000
Excess of cost over book value................................		$370,000
Attributed to:		
Building, 80% × $200,000 undervaluation, 20-year life...........		160,000
Goodwill		$210,000

Albers used the simple equity method for its investment in Baker. As of December 31, 20X5, Baker had earned $200,000 since it was purchased by Albers. Baker paid no dividends during 20X1–20X5.

On December 31, 20X5, the following values were available:

Fair value of Baker's identifiable net assets (100%)	$ 900,000
Estimated fair value of Baker Company (net of liabilities)	1,000,000

Determine if goodwill is impaired. If not, explain your reasoning. If so, calculate the adjustment needed to the investment account. (Albers will directly adjust its investment account for any impairment losses.)

APPENDIX EXERCISES

Exercise 3A-1*(LO 8)* **D&D for nontaxable exchange.** Rainman Corporation is considering the acquisition of Lamb Company through the purchase of Lamb's common stock. Rainman Corporation will issue 20,000 shares of its $5 par common stock, with a fair value of $25 per share, in exchange for all 10,000 outstanding shares of Lamb Company's voting common stock.

The acquisition meets the criteria for a tax-free exchange as to the seller. Because of this, Rainman Corporation will be limited for future tax returns to the book value of the depreciable assets. Rainman Corporation falls into the 30% tax bracket.

The appraisal of the assets of Lamb Company showed that the inventory has a fair value of $120,000, and the depreciable fixed assets have a fair value of $270,000. Any excess is attributed to goodwill. Lamb Company had the following balance sheet just before the acquisition:

Lamb Company
Balance Sheet
December 31, 20X5

Assets		Liabilities and Equity		
Cash	$ 40,000	Current liabilities		$ 70,000
Accounts receivable	150,000	Bonds payable		100,000
Inventory	100,000	Stockholders' equity:		
Depreciable fixed assets	210,000	Common stock ($10 par)....	$100,000	
		Retained earnings	230,000	330,000
Total assets	$500,000	Total liabilities and equity		$500,000

1. Record the acquisition of Lamb Company by Rainman Corporation.
2. Prepare a determination and distribution of excess schedule.
3. Prepare the elimination entries that would be made on the consolidated worksheet.

Exercise 3A-2*(LO 8)* **D&D and income statement for nontaxable exchange.** Lucy Company issued securities with a fair value of $465,000 for a 90% interest in Desmond Company on January 1, 20X1, at which time Desmond Company had the following balance sheet:

Assets		Liabilities and Equity	
Accounts receivable	$ 50,000	Current liabilities	$ 70,000
Inventory	80,000	Common stock ($5 par).........	100,000
Land......................	20,000	Paid-in capital in excess of par ...	130,000
Building (net)	200,000	Retained earnings	50,000
Total assets...............	$350,000	Total liabilities and equity	$350,000

It was believed that the inventory and the building were undervalued by $20,000 and $50,000, respectively. The building had a 10-year remaining life; the inventory on hand January 1, 20X1, was sold during the year. The deferred tax liability associated with the asset revaluations was to be reflected in the consolidated statements. Each company has an income tax rate of 30%. Any remaining excess is goodwill.

The separate income statements of the two companies prepared for 20X1 are as follows:

	Lucy	Desmond
Sales	$ 400,000	$150,000
Cost of goods sold......................................	(200,000)	(90,000)
Gross profit	$ 200,000	$ 60,000
General expenses	(50,000)	(25,000)
Depreciation expense	(60,000)	(15,000)
Operating income.......................................	$ 90,000	$ 20,000
Subsidiary income.......................................	18,000	
Net income before income tax	$ 108,000	$ 20,000
Provision for tax (does not include tax on subsidiary income)	(27,000)	(6,000)
Net income	$ 81,000	$ 14,000

1. Prepare a determination and distribution of excess schedule for the investment.
2. Prepare the 20X1 consolidated income statement and its related income distribution schedules.

PROBLEMS

Problem 3-1 *(LO 1)* **Alternative investment account methods, effect on eliminations.** On January 1, 20X1, Peter Company purchased an 80% interest in Saul Company by issuing 10,000 of its common stock shares with a par value of $10 per share and a fair value of $72 per share. The direct acquisition costs were $20,000. At the time of the purchase, Saul had the following balance sheet:

Assets		Liabilities and Equity	
Current assets	$100,000	Current liabilities	$ 80,000
Investments	150,000	Bonds payable	250,000
Land......................	120,000	Common stock ($10 par).........	100,000
Building (net)	350,000	Paid-in capital in excess of par	200,000
Equipment (net)	160,000	Retained earnings	250,000
Total assets..............	$880,000	Total liabilities and equity	$880,000

Appraisals indicate that book values are representative of fair values with the exception of the land and building. The land has a fair value of $190,000, and the building is appraised at $450,000. The building has an estimated remaining life of 20 years. Any remaining excess is goodwill.

The following summary of Saul's retained earnings applies to 20X1 and 20X2:

Balance, January 1, 20X1....................	$250,000
Net income for 20X1......................	60,000
Dividends paid in 20X1....................	(10,000)
Balance, December 31, 20X1	$300,000
Net income for 20X2......................	45,000
Dividends paid in 20X2....................	(10,000)
Balance, December 31, 20X2	$335,000

Required ▶ ▶ ▶ ▶ ▶   1. Prepare a determination and distribution of excess schedule for the investment in Saul Company. As a part of the schedule, indicate annual amortization of excess adjustments.

2. For 20X1 and 20X2, prepare the entries that Peter would make concerning its investment in Saul under the simple equity, sophisticated equity, and cost methods. It is suggested that you set up a worksheet with side-by-side columns for each method so that you can easily compare the entries.

3. For 20X1 and 20X2, prepare the worksheet elimination that would be made on a consolidated worksheet under the simple equity, sophisticated equity, and cost methods. It is suggested that you set up a worksheet with side-by-side columns for each method so that you can easily compare the entries.

Problem 3-2 *(LO 2)* Equity method adjustments, consolidated worksheet.

On January 1, 20X1, Peres Company purchased 80% of the common stock of Soll Company for $308,000. On this date, Soll had common stock, other paid-in capital, and retained earnings of $50,000, $100,000, and $150,000, respectively. Net income and dividends for two years for Soll Company were as follows:

	20X1	20X2
Net income	$60,000	$90,000
Dividends.	20,000	30,000

On January 1, 20X1, the only tangible assets of Soll that were undervalued were inventory and the building. Inventory, for which FIFO is used, was worth $10,000 more than cost. The inventory was sold in 20X1. The building, which is worth $25,000 more than book value, has a remaining life of 10 years, and straight-line depreciation is used. The remaining excess of cost over book value is attributable to goodwill.

1. Using this information or the information in the following trial balances, prepare a determination and distribution of excess schedule.

 **Required**

2. Peres Company carries the investment in Soll Company under the simple equity method. In general journal form, record the entries that would be made to apply the equity method in 20X1 and 20X2.

3. Compute the balance that should appear in Investment in Soll Company and in Soll Income on December 31, 20X2 (the second year). Fill in these amounts on Peres Company's trial balance for 20X2.

4. Complete a worksheet for consolidated financial statements for 20X2. Include columns for eliminations and adjustments, consolidated income, NCI, controlling retained earnings, and balance sheet.

	Peres Company	Soll Company
Inventory, December 31	100,000	50,000
Other Current Assets	148,000	180,000
Investment in Soll Company.	Note 1	
Land.	50,000	50,000
Buildings and Equipment.	350,000	320,000
Accumulated Depreciation	(100,000)	(60,000)
Goodwill		
Other Intangibles.	20,000	
Current Liabilities.	(120,000)	(40,000)
Bonds Payable.		(100,000)
Other Long-Term Liabilities	(200,000)	
Common Stock, P Company	(200,000)	
Other Paid-In Capital, P Company	(100,000)	
Retained Earnings, P Company.	(214,000)	
Common Stock, S Company		(50,000)
Other Paid-In Capital, S Company		(100,000)
		(continued)

	Peres Company	Soll Company
Retained Earnings, S Company.		(190,000)
Net Sales.	(520,000)	(450,000)
Cost of Goods Sold	300,000	260,000
Operating Expenses	120,000	100,000
Soll Income	Note 1	
Dividends Declared, P Company	50,000	
Dividends Declared, S Company		30,000

Note 1: To be calculated.

Problem 3-3 *(LO 4)* **Sophisticated equity method adjustments, consolidated worksheet.** (This is the same as Problem 3-2, except the sophisticated equity method is used.) On January 1, 20X1, Peres Company purchased 80% of the common stock of Soll Company for $308,000. On this date, Soll had common stock, other paid-in capital, and retained earnings of $50,000, $100,000, and $150,000, respectively. Net income and dividends for two years for Soll Company were as follows:

	20X1	20X2
Net income	$60,000	$90,000
Dividends.	20,000	30,000

On January 1, 20X1, the only tangible assets of Soll that were undervalued were inventory and the building. Inventory, for which FIFO is used, was worth $10,000 more than cost. The inventory was sold in 20X1. The building, which is worth $25,000 more than book value, has a remaining life of 10 years, and straight-line depreciation is used. The remaining excess of cost over book value is attributable to goodwill.

Required ▶ ▶ ▶ ▶ ▶

1. Using this information or the information in the following trial balances, prepare a determination and distribution of excess schedule.
2. Peres Company carries the investment in Soll Company under the sophisticated equity method. In general journal form, record the entries that would be made to apply the equity method in 20X1 and 20X2.
3. Compute the balance that should appear in Investment in Soll Company and in Soll Income on December 31, 20X2 (the second year). Fill in these amounts on Peres Company's trial balance for 20X2.
4. Complete a worksheet for consolidated financial statements for 20X2. Include columns for eliminations and adjustments, consolidated income, NCI, controlling retained earnings, and balance sheet.

	Peres Company	Soll Company
Inventory, December 31	100,000	50,000
Other Current Assets	148,000	180,000
Investment in Soll Company.	Note 1	
Land.	50,000	50,000
Buildings and Equipment.	350,000	320,000
Accumulated Depreciation	(100,000)	(60,000)
Goodwill		
Other Intangibles.	20,000	
Current Liabilities.	(120,000)	(40,000)
Bonds Payable.		(100,000)

Other Long-Term Liabilities	(200,000)	
Common Stock, P Company	(200,000)	
Other Paid-In Capital, P Company	(100,000)	
Retained Earnings, P Company	(204,000)	
Common Stock, S Company		(50,000)
Other Paid-In Capital, S Company		(100,000)
Retained Earnings, S Company		(190,000)
Net Sales	(520,000)	(450,000)
Cost of Goods Sold	300,000	260,000
Operating Expenses	120,000	100,000
Soll Income	Note 1	
Dividends Declared, P Company	50,000	
Dividends Declared, S Company		30,000

Note 1: To be calculated.

Problem 3-4 *(LO 3)* **Cost method, consolidated statements.** The trial balances of Chango Company and its subsidiary, Lhasa Inc., are as follows on December 31, 20X3:

	Chango	Lhasa
Current Assets	530,000	130,000
Depreciable Fixed Assets	1,805,000	440,000
Accumulated Depreciation	(405,000)	(70,000)
Investment in Lhasa Inc.	460,000	
Liabilities	(900,000)	(225,000)
Common Stock ($1 par)	(220,000)	
Common Stock ($5 par)		(50,000)
Paid-In Capital in Excess of Par	(1,040,000)	(15,000)
Retained Earnings, January 1, 20X3	(230,000)	(170,000)
Revenues	(460,000)	(210,000)
Expenses	450,000	170,000
Dividends Declared	10,000	
Total	0	0

On January 1, 20X1, Chango Company exchanged 20,000 shares of its common stock, with a fair value of $23 per share, for all the outstanding stock of Lhasa Inc. Any excess of cost over book value was attributed to goodwill. The stockholders' equity of Lhasa Inc. on the purchase date was as follows:

Common stock ($5 par)	$ 50,000
Paid-in capital in excess of par	15,000
Retained earnings	135,000
Total equity	$200,000

1. Prepare a determination and distribution of excess schedule for the investment.
2. Prepare the 20X3 consolidated statements, including the income statement, retained earnings statement, and balance sheet. (A worksheet is not required.)

◀ ◀ ◀ ◀ ◀ **Required**

Problem 3-5 *(LO 3)* **Cost method, worksheet, statements.** Bell Corporation purchased all of the outstanding stock of Stockdon Corporation for $220,000 in cash on January 1, 20X7. On the purchase date, Stockdon Corporation had the following condensed balance sheet:

Assets		Liabilities and Equity	
Cash	$ 60,000	Liabilities	$150,000
Inventory	40,000	Common stock ($10 par).........	100,000
Land........................	120,000	Paid-in capital in excess of par	50,000
Buildings (net)	180,000	Retained earnings	100,000
Total assets.................	$400,000	Total liabilities and equity	$400,000

Any excess of book value over cost was attributable to the building, which is currently over-stated on Stockdon's books. All other assets and liabilities have book values equal to fair values. The building has an estimated 10-year life with no salvage value.

The trial balances of the two companies on December 31, 20X7, appear as follows:

	Bell	Stockdon
Cash	180,000	143,000
Inventory	60,000	30,000
Land..	120,000	120,000
Buildings (net)	600,000	162,000
Investment in Stockdon Corporation	220,000	
Accounts Payable	(405,000)	(210,000)
Common Stock ($3 par)	(300,000)	
Common Stock ($10 par)		(100,000)
Paid-In Capital in Excess of Par	(180,000)	(50,000)
Retained Earnings, January 1, 20X7....................	(255,000)	(100,000)
Sales	(210,000)	(40,000)
Cost of Goods Sold	120,000	35,000
Other Expenses	45,000	10,000
Dividends Declared.................................	5,000	
Total..	0	0

Required ▶ ▶ ▶ ▶ ▶

1. Prepare a determination and distribution of excess schedule for the investment.
2. Prepare the 20X7 consolidated worksheet. Include columns for the eliminations and adjustments, the consolidated income statement, the controlling retained earnings, and the consolidated balance sheet.
3. Prepare the 20X7 consolidated statements, including the income statement, retained earnings statement, and balance sheet.

Problem 3-6 *(LO 2)* **Equity method, 80% interest, worksheet, statements.** Scully Company prepared the following balance sheet on January 1, 20X1:

Assets		Liabilities and Equity	
Current assets	$ 50,000	Liabilities	$140,000
Land........................	75,000	Common stock ($10 par).........	100,000
Buildings	350,000	Paid-in capital in excess of par	120,000
Accumulated depreciation		Retained earnings (deficit)........	(25,000)
—Buildings	(140,000)		
Total assets.................	$ 335,000	Total liabilities and equity	$335,000

On this date, Prescott Company purchased 8,000 shares of Scully Company's outstanding stock for a total price of $270,000. Also on this date, the buildings were understated by $40,000 and had a 10-year remaining life. Any remaining discrepancy between the price paid and book value was attributed to goodwill. Since the purchase, Prescott Company has used the simple equity method to record the investment and its related income.

Prescott Company and Scully Company have prepared the following separate trial balances on December 31, 20X2:

	Prescott	Scully
Current Assets	180,000	115,000
Land	150,000	75,000
Buildings	590,000	350,000
Accumulated Depreciation—Buildings	(265,000)	(182,000)
Investment in Scully Company	294,000	
Liabilities	(175,000)	(133,000)
Common Stock ($10 par)	(200,000)	(100,000)
Paid-In Capital in Excess of Par		(120,000)
Retained Earnings, Jan. 1, 20X2	(503,000)	15,000
Sales	(360,000)	(120,000)
Cost of Goods Sold	179,000	50,000
Expenses	120,000	45,000
Subsidiary Income	(20,000)	
Dividends Declared	10,000	5,000
Total	0	0

1. Prepare a determination and distribution of excess schedule for the investment.
2. Prepare the 20X2 consolidated worksheet. Include columns for the eliminations and adjustments, the consolidated income statement, the NCI, the controlling retained earnings, and the consolidated balance sheet. Prepare supporting income distribution schedules.
3. Prepare the 20X2 consolidated statements including the income statement, retained earnings statement, and the balance sheet.

◄ ◄ ◄ ◄ ◄ **Required**

Problem 3-7 *(LO 6)* **Interperiod purchase.** Jeter Corporation purchased 80% of the outstanding stock of Summer Company for $275,000 on May 1, 20X1. Summer Company had the following stockholders' equity:

Common stock ($5 par)	$150,000
Retained earnings	50,000
Total equity	$200,000

The fair values of Summer's assets and liabilities agreed with the book values, except for the equipment and the building. The equipment was undervalued by $10,000 and was thought to have a five-year life; the building was undervalued by $50,000 and was thought to have a 20-year life. The remaining excess of cost over book value is attributable to goodwill. Jeter Corporation uses the simple equity method to record its investments.

Since the purchase date, both firms have operated separately, and no intercompany transactions have occurred. Summer Company did not close its books on the date of acquisition. Therefore, the income amounts in the trial balance reflect amounts earned during the whole year. Income is earned evenly throughout the year.

The separate trial balances of the firms on December 31, 20X1, are as follows:

	Jeter Corporation	Summer Company
Cash	296,600	97,000
Land	160,000	90,000
Buildings	225,000	135,000
Accumulated Depreciation—Buildings	(100,000)	(50,000)
Equipment	450,000	150,000
Accumulated Depreciation—Equipment	(115,000)	(60,000)
Investment in Summer Company	284,600	

(continued)

	Jeter Corporation	Summer Company
Liabilities	(480,000)	(150,000)
Common Stock ($100 par)	(400,000)	
Common Stock ($5 par)		(150,000)
Paid-In Capital in Excess of Par	(40,000)	
Retained Earnings, January 1, 20X1	(251,600)	(50,000)
Sales	(460,000)	(120,000)
Cost of Goods Sold	220,000	60,000
Other Expenses	210,000	48,000
Subsidiary Income	(9,600)	
Dividends Declared	10,000	
Total	0	0

Required ▶ ▶ ▶ ▶ ▶

1. Prepare a determination and distribution of excess schedule for the investment.
2. Prepare the 20X1 consolidated worksheet. Include columns for the eliminations and adjustments, the consolidated income statement, the NCI, the controlling retained earnings, and the consolidated balance sheet. Prepare supporting income distribution schedules as well.
3. Prepare the 20X1 consolidated statements, including the income statement, retained earnings statement, and balance sheet.

Problem 3-8 *(LO 3, 5)* **Cost method, 80% interest, worksheet, several adjustments.** Detner International purchased 80% of the outstanding stock of Hughes Company for $1,600,000 plus $8,000 of direct acquisition costs on January 1, 20X5. At the purchase date, the inventory, the equipment, and the patents of Hughes Company had fair values of $10,000, $50,000, and $100,000, respectively, in excess of their book values. The other assets and liabilities of Hughes Company had book values equal to their fair values. The inventory was sold during the month following the purchase. The two companies agreed that the equipment had a remaining life of eight years and the patents, 10 years. On the purchase date, the owners' equity of Hughes Company was as follows:

Common stock ($10 stated value)	$1,000,000
Additional paid-in capital	300,000
Retained earnings	400,000
Total equity	$1,700,000

During the next two years, Hughes Company had income and paid dividends as follows:

	Income	Dividends
20X5	$ 90,000	$30,000
20X6	150,000	30,000

The trial balances of the two corporations as of December 31, 20X7, are as follows:

	Detner International	Hughes Company
Current Assets	624,000	505,000
Equipment (net)	1,320,000	940,000
Patents	100,000	35,000
Other Assets	1,620,000	730,000
Investment in Hughes Company	1,608,000	
Accounts Payable	(658,000)	(205,000)
Common Stock ($5 par)	(2,000,000)	
Common Stock ($10 par)		(1,000,000)

Paid-In Capital in Excess of Par	(1,200,000)	(300,000)
Retained Earnings, January 1, 20X7.	(1,255,000)	(580,000)
Sales	(905,000)	(425,000)
Cost of Goods Sold	470,000	170,000
Other Expenses	250,000	100,000
Dividend Income	(24,000)	
Dividends Declared.	50,000	30,000
Total.	0	0

The remaining excess of cost over book value is attributable to goodwill.   ◀ ◀ ◀ ◀ ◀ **Required**

1. Prepare the original determination and distribution of excess schedule for the investment.
2. Prepare the 20X7 consolidated worksheet for December 31, 20X7. Include columns for the eliminations and adjustments, the consolidated income statement, the controlling retained earnings, and the consolidated balance sheet.

Use the following information for Problems 3-9 through 3-12:

Pcraft Corporation builds powerboats. On January 1, 20X1, Pcraft acquired Sailair Corporation, a company that manufactures sailboats. Pcraft paid cash in exchange for Sailair common stock. Sailair had the following balance sheet on January 1, 20X1:

Sailair Corporation
Balance Sheet
January 1, 20X1

Assets		Liabilities and Equity	
Accounts receivable	$ 32,000	Current liabilities	$ 90,000
Inventory	40,000	Bonds payable	100,000
Land.	60,000	Common stock, $1 par	10,000
Buildings	250,000	Paid-in capital in excess of par . . .	90,000
Accumulated depreciation . . .	(50,000)	Retained earnings	112,000
Equipment	100,000		
Accumulated depreciation . . .	(30,000)		
Total assets.	$402,000	Total liabilities and equity	$402,000

An appraisal indicated that the following assets and liabilities had fair values that differed from their book values:

Inventory (sold during 20X1)	$ 38,000
Land.	150,000
Buildings (20-year life)	300,000
Equipment (5-year life).	100,000
Bonds payable (5-year life)	96,000

Any remaining excess is attributed to goodwill.

Problem 3-9 *(LO 2, 5)* **100%, equity method worksheet, several adjustments, third year.** Refer to the preceding information for Pcraft's acquisition of Sailair's common stock. Assume that Pcraft paid $500,000 for 100% of Sailair common stock. Pcraft uses the simple equity method to account for its investment in Sailair. Pcraft and Sailair had the following trial balances on December 31, 20X3:

	Pcraft	Sailair
Cash	80,000	60,000
Accounts Receivable	90,000	55,000
Inventory	120,000	86,000
Land.	100,000	60,000
Investment in Sailair.	595,000	
Buildings	800,000	300,000
Accumulated Depreciation	(220,000)	(80,000)
Equipment	150,000	100,000
Accumulated Depreciation	(90,000)	(72,000)
Current Liabilities.	(60,000)	(102,000)
Bonds Payable.		(100,000)
Common Stock	(100,000)	(10,000)
Paid-In Capital in Excess of Par	(900,000)	(90,000)
Retained Earnings, January 1, 20X3.	(385,000)	(182,000)
Sales	(800,000)	(350,000)
Cost of Goods Sold	450,000	210,000
Depreciation Expense—Buildings.	30,000	15,000
Depreciation Expense—Equipment.	15,000	14,000
Other Expenses	140,000	68,000
Interest Expense.		8,000
Subsidiary Income.	(35,000)	
Dividends Declared.	20,000	10,000
Totals	0	0

Required ▶ ▶ ▶ ▶ ▶

1. Prepare a zone analysis and a determination and distribution of excess schedule for the investment in Sailair.
2. Complete a consolidated worksheet for Pcraft Corporation and its subsidiary Sailair Corporation as of December 31, 20X3. Prepare supporting amortization and income distribution schedules.

Problem 3-10 *(LO 3, 5)* **100%, cost method worksheet, several adjustments, third year.** Refer to the preceding information for Pcraft's acquisition of Sailair's common stock. Assume that Pcraft paid $500,000 for 100% of Sailair common stock. Pcraft uses the cost method to account for its investment in Sailair. Pcraft and Sailair had the following trial balances on December 31, 20X3:

	Pcraft	Sailair
Cash	80,000	60,000
Accounts Receivable	90,000	55,000
Inventory	120,000	86,000
Land.	100,000	60,000
Investment in Sailair.	500,000	
Buildings	800,000	300,000
Accumulated Depreciation	(220,000)	(80,000)
Equipment	150,000	100,000
Accumulated Depreciation	(90,000)	(72,000)
Current Liabilities.	(60,000)	(102,000)
Bonds Payable.		(100,000)
Common Stock	(100,000)	(10,000)
Paid-In Capital in Excess of Par	(900,000)	(90,000)
Retained Earnings, January 1, 20X3.	(315,000)	(182,000)
Sales	(800,000)	(350,000)

Cost of Goods Sold	450,000	210,000
Depreciation Expense—Buildings	30,000	15,000
Depreciation Expense—Equipment	15,000	14,000
Other Expenses	140,000	68,000
Interest Expense		8,000
Dividend Income	(10,000)	
Dividends Declared	20,000	10,000
Totals	0	0

1. Prepare a zone analysis and a determination and distribution of excess schedule for the ◄ ◄ ◄ ◄ ◄ **Required**
   investment in Sailair.
2. Complete a consolidated worksheet for Pcraft Corporation and its subsidiary Sailair Corporation as of December 31, 20X3. Prepare supporting amortization and income distribution schedules.

Problem 3-11 *(LO 3, 5)* **70%, cost method worksheet, several adjustments, first year.** Refer to the preceding information for Pcraft's acquisition of Sailair's common stock. Assume that Pcraft paid $400,000 for 70% of Sailair common stock. Pcraft uses the cost method to account for its investment in Sailair. Pcraft and Sailair had the following trial balances on December 31, 20X1:

	Pcraft	Sailair
Cash	177,000	31,000
Accounts Receivable	80,000	35,000
Inventory	90,000	52,000
Land	100,000	60,000
Investment in Sailair	400,000	
Buildings	800,000	250,000
Accumulated Depreciation	(200,000)	(60,000)
Equipment	150,000	100,000
Accumulated Depreciation	(75,000)	(44,000)
Current Liabilities	(50,000)	(88,000)
Bonds Payable		(100,000)
Common Stock	(100,000)	(10,000)
Paid-In Capital in Excess of Par	(900,000)	(90,000)
Retained Earnings, January 1, 20X1	(300,000)	(112,000)
Sales	(750,000)	(300,000)
Cost of Goods Sold	400,000	180,000
Depreciation Expense—Buildings	30,000	10,000
Depreciation Expense—Equipment	15,000	14,000
Other Expenses	120,000	54,000
Interest Expense		8,000
Dividend Income	(7,000)	
Dividends Declared	20,000	10,000
Total	0	0

1. Prepare a zone analysis and a determination and distribution of excess schedule for the ◄ ◄ ◄ ◄ ◄ **Required**
   investment in Sailair.
2. Complete a consolidated worksheet for Pcraft Corporation and its subsidiary Sailair Corporation as of December 31, 20X1. Prepare supporting amortization and income distribution schedules.

Problem 3-12 *(LO 3, 5)* **70%, cost method worksheet, several adjustments, third year.** Refer to the preceding information for Pcraft's acquisition of Sailair's common stock.

Assume that Pcraft paid $400,000 for 70% of Sailair common stock. Pcraft uses the cost method to account for its investment in Sailair. Pcraft and Sailair had the following trial balances on December 31, 20X3:

	Pcraft	Sailair
Cash	177,000	60,000
Accounts Receivable	90,000	55,000
Inventory	120,000	86,000
Land	100,000	60,000
Investment in Sailair	400,000	
Buildings	800,000	300,000
Accumulated Depreciation	(220,000)	(80,000)
Equipment	150,000	100,000
Accumulated Depreciation	(90,000)	(72,000)
Current Liabilities	(60,000)	(102,000)
Bonds Payable		(100,000)
Common Stock	(100,000)	(10,000)
Paid-In Capital in Excess of Par	(900,000)	(90,000)
Retained Earnings, January 1, 20X3	(315,000)	(182,000)
Sales	(800,000)	(350,000)
Cost of Goods Sold	450,000	210,000
Depreciation Expense—Buildings	30,000	15,000
Depreciation Expense—Equipment	15,000	14,000
Other Expenses	140,000	68,000
Interest Expense		8,000
Dividend Income	(7,000)	
Dividends Declared	20,000	10,000
Total	0	0

Required ▶ ▶ ▶ ▶ ▶

1. Prepare a zone analysis and a determination and distribution of excess schedule for the investment in Sailair.
2. Complete a consolidated worksheet for Pcraft Corporation and its subsidiary Sailair Corporation as of December 31, 20X3. Prepare supporting amortization and income distribution schedules.

Problem 3-13 *(LO 4, 5)* **100%, sophisticated equity method, several excesses, third year.** Refer to the preceding information for Pcraft's acquisition of Sailair's common stock. Assume that Pcraft paid $500,000 for 100% of Sailair common stock. Pcraft uses the sophisticated equity method to account for its investment in Sailair. Pcraft and Sailair had the following trial balances on December 31, 20X3:

	Pcraft	Sailair
Cash	80,000	60,000
Accounts Receivable	90,000	55,000
Inventory	120,000	86,000
Land	100,000	60,000
Investment in Sailair	561,600	
Buildings	800,000	300,000
Accumulated Depreciation	(220,000)	(80,000)
Equipment	150,000	100,000
Accumulated Depreciation	(90,000)	(72,000)
Current Liabilities	(60,000)	(102,000)
Bonds Payable		(100,000)
Common Stock	(100,000)	(10,000)

Paid-In Capital in Excess of Par	(900,000)	(90,000)
Retained Earnings, January 1, 20X3...............................	(363,400)	(182,000)
Sales	(800,000)	(350,000)
Cost of Goods Sold	450,000	210,000
Depreciation Expense—Buildings................................	30,000	15,000
Depreciation Expense—Equipment..............................	15,000	14,000
Other Expenses...	140,000	68,000
Interest Expense..		8,000
Subsidiary Income..	(23,200)	
Dividends Declared...	20,000	10,000
Total..	0	0

1. Prepare a zone analysis and a determination and distribution of excess schedule for the investment in Sailair. ◄ ◄ ◄ ◄ ◄ **Required**
2. Complete a consolidated worksheet for Pcraft Corporation and its subsidiary Sailair Corporation as of December 31, 20X3. Prepare supporting amortization and income distribution schedules.

Use the following information for Problems 3-14 through 3-18:

Fast Cool Company and HD Air Company are both manufacturers of air conditioning equipment. On January 1, 20X1, Fast Cool acquired the common stock of HD Air by exchanging its own $1 par, $20 fair value common stock. On the date of acquisition, HD Air had the following balance sheet:

HD Air Company
Balance Sheet
January 1, 20X1

Assets		Liabilities and Equity	
Accounts receivable	$ 40,000	Current liabilities	$ 30,000
Inventory	60,000	Mortgage payable	200,000
Land.....................	50,000	Common stock, $1 par	100,000
Buildings	400,000	Paid-in capital in excess of par ...	200,000
Accumulated depreciation ...	(50,000)	Retained earnings	180,000
Equipment	150,000		
Accumulated depreciation ...	(30,000)		
Patent (net)................	40,000		
Goodwill	50,000		
Total assets..............	$710,000	Total liabilities and equity	$710,000

Fast Cool requested that an appraisal be done to determine whether the book value of HD Air's net assets reflected their fair values. The appraiser determined that several intangible assets existed, although they were unrecorded. If the intangible assets did not have an observable market, the appraiser estimated their value. The following are the fair values and estimates determined by the appraiser:

Inventory (sold during 20X1)..................................	$ 65,000
Land...	100,000
Buildings (20-year life)	500,000
Equipment (5-year life)..	100,000
Patent (5-year life)	50,000
Mortgage payable (5-year life)	205,000
Production backlog (2-year life)................................	10,000

Any remaining excess is attributed to goodwill.

Problem 3-14 *(LO 2, 5)* **100%, complicated excess, first year.** Refer to the preceding information for Fast Cool's acquisition of HD Air's common stock. Assume Fast Cool issued 40,000 shares of its $20 fair value common stock for 100% of HD Air's common stock. Fast Cool uses the simple equity method to account for its investment in HD Air. Fast Cool and HD Air had the following trial balances on December 31, 20X1:

	Fast Cool	HD Air
Cash	147,000	37,000
Accounts Receivable	70,000	100,000
Inventory	150,000	60,000
Land	60,000	50,000
Investment in HD Air	837,500	
Buildings	1,200,000	400,000
Accumulated Depreciation	(176,000)	(67,500)
Equipment	140,000	150,000
Accumulated Depreciation	(68,000)	(54,000)
Patent (net)		32,000
Goodwill		50,000
Current Liabilities	(80,000)	(40,000)
Mortgage Payable		(200,000)
Common Stock	(100,000)	(100,000)
Paid-In Capital in Excess of Par	(1,500,000)	(200,000)
Retained Earnings, January 1, 20X1	(400,000)	(180,000)
Sales	(700,000)	(400,000)
Cost of Goods Sold	380,000	210,000
Depreciation Expense—Buildings	10,000	17,500
Depreciation Expense—Equipment	7,000	24,000
Other Expenses	50,000	85,000
Interest Expense		16,000
Subsidiary Income	(47,500)	
Dividends Declared	20,000	10,000
Total	0	0

Required ▶ ▶ ▶ ▶ ▶

1. Prepare a zone analysis and a determination and distribution of excess schedule for the investment in HD Air.

2. Complete a consolidated worksheet for Fast Cool Company and its subsidiary HD Air Company as of December 31, 20X1. Prepare supporting amortization and income distribution schedules.

Problem 3-15 *(LO 2, 5)* **100%, complicated excess, equity, second year.** Refer to the preceding information for Fast Cool's acquisition of HD Air's common stock. Assume Fast Cool issued 40,000 shares of its $20 fair value common stock for 100% of HD Air's common stock. Fast Cool uses the simple equity method to account for its investment in HD Air. Fast Cool and HD Air had the following trial balances on December 31, 20X2:

	Fast Cool	HD Air
Cash	396,000	99,000
Accounts Receivable	200,000	120,000
Inventory	120,000	95,000
Land	60,000	50,000
Investment in HD Air	895,000	
Buildings	1,200,000	400,000
Accumulated Depreciation	(200,000)	(85,000)

Equipment	140,000	150,000
Accumulated Depreciation	(80,000)	(78,000)
Patent (net)		24,000
Goodwill		50,000
Current Liabilities	(150,000)	(50,000)
Mortgage Payable		(200,000)
Common Stock	(100,000)	(100,000)
Paid-In Capital in Excess of Par	(1,500,000)	(200,000)
Retained Earnings, January 1, 20X2	(680,500)	(217,500)
Sales	(700,000)	(500,000)
Cost of Goods Sold	380,000	260,000
Depreciation Expense—Buildings	10,000	17,500
Depreciation Expense—Equipment	7,000	24,000
Other Expenses	50,000	115,000
Interest Expense		16,000
Subsidiary Income	(67,500)	
Dividends Declared	20,000	10,000
Total	0	0

1. Prepare a zone analysis and a determination and distribution of excess schedule for the **◄ ◄ ◄ ◄ ◄ Required** investment in HD Air.
2. Complete a consolidated worksheet for Fast Cool Company and its subsidiary HD Air Company as of December 31, 20X2. Prepare supporting amortization and income distribution schedules.

Problem 3-16 *(LO 2, 5)* **100% bargain, complicated equity, second year.** Refer to the preceding information for Fast Cool's acquisition of HD Air's common stock. Assume Fast Cool issued 25,000 shares of its $20 fair value common stock for 100% of HD Air's common stock. Fast Cool uses the simple equity method to account for its investment in HD Air. Fast Cool and HD Air had the following trial balances on December 31, 20X2:

	Fast Cool	HD Air
Cash	396,000	99,000
Accounts Receivable	200,000	120,000
Inventory	120,000	95,000
Land	60,000	50,000
Investment in HD Air	595,000	
Buildings	1,200,000	400,000
Accumulated Depreciation	(200,000)	(85,000)
Equipment	140,000	150,000
Accumulated Depreciation	(80,000)	(78,000)
Patent (net)		24,000
Goodwill		50,000
Current Liabilities	(150,000)	(50,000)
Mortgage Payable		(200,000)
Common Stock	(85,000)	(100,000)
Paid-In Capital in Excess of Par	(1,215,000)	(200,000)
Retained Earnings, January 1, 20X2	(680,500)	(217,500)
Sales	(700,000)	(500,000)
Cost of Goods Sold	380,000	260,000
Depreciation Expense—Buildings	10,000	17,500
Depreciation Expense—Equipment	7,000	24,000
Other Expenses	50,000	115,000
		(continued)

	Fast Cool	HD Air
Interest Expense..		16,000
Subsidiary Income..	(67,500)	
Dividends Declared...	20,000	10,000
Total...	0	0

Required ▶ ▶ ▶ ▶ ▶

1. Prepare a zone analysis and a determination and distribution of excess schedule for the investment in HD Air.
2. Complete a consolidated worksheet for Fast Cool Company and its subsidiary HD Air Company as of December 31, 20X2. Prepare supporting amortization and income distribution schedules.

Problem 3-17 *(LO 2, 5)* **80%, first year, complicated excess.** Refer to the preceding information for Fast Cool's acquisition of HD Air's common stock. Assume Fast Cool issued 35,000 shares of its $20 fair value common stock for 80% of HD Air's common stock. Fast Cool uses the simple equity method to account for its investment in HD Air. Fast Cool and HD Air had the following trial balances on December 31, 20X1:

	Fast Cool	HD Air
Cash	145,000	37,000
Accounts Receivable	70,000	100,000
Inventory	150,000	60,000
Land...	60,000	50,000
Investment in HD Air	730,000	
Buildings	1,200,000	400,000
Accumulated Depreciation	(176,000)	(67,500)
Equipment	140,000	150,000
Accumulated Depreciation	(68,000)	(54,000)
Patent (net)...		32,000
Goodwill		50,000
Current Liabilities..	(80,000)	(40,000)
Mortgage Payable...		(200,000)
Common Stock	(95,000)	(100,000)
Paid-In Capital in Excess of Par	(1,405,000)	(200,000)
Retained Earnings, January 1, 20X1........................	(400,000)	(180,000)
Sales	(700,000)	(400,000)
Cost of Goods Sold	380,000	210,000
Depreciation Expense—Buildings...........................	10,000	17,500
Depreciation Expense—Equipment..........................	7,000	24,000
Other Expenses	50,000	85,000
Interest Expense...		16,000
Subsidiary Income..	(38,000)	
Dividends Declared.......................................	20,000	10,000
Total...	0	0

Required ▶ ▶ ▶ ▶ ▶

1. Prepare a zone analysis and a determination and distribution of excess schedule for the investment in HD Air.
2. Complete a consolidated worksheet for Fast Cool Company and its subsidiary HD Air Company as of December 31, 20X1. Prepare supporting amortization and income distribution schedules.

Problem 3-18 *(LO 2, 5)* **80%, second year, complicated excess.** Refer to the preceding information for Fast Cool's acquisition of HD Air's common stock. Assume Fast Cool issued 35,000 shares of its $20 fair value common stock for 80% of HD Air's common stock. Fast

Cool uses the simple equity method to account for its investment in HD Air. Fast Cool and HD Air had the following trial balances on December 31, 20X2:

	Fast Cool	HD Air
Cash	392,000	99,000
Accounts Receivable	200,000	120,000
Inventory	120,000	95,000
Land	60,000	50,000
Investment in HD Air	776,000	
Buildings	1,200,000	400,000
Accumulated Depreciation	(200,000)	(85,000)
Equipment	140,000	150,000
Accumulated Depreciation	(80,000)	(78,000)
Patent (net)		24,000
Goodwill		50,000
Current Liabilities	(150,000)	(50,000)
Mortgage Payable		(200,000)
Common Stock	(95,000)	(100,000)
Paid-In Capital in Excess of Par	(1,405,000)	(200,000)
Retained Earnings, January 1, 20X2	(671,000)	(217,500)
Sales	(700,000)	(500,000)
Cost of Goods Sold	380,000	260,000
Depreciation Expense—Buildings	10,000	17,500
Depreciation Expense—Equipment	7,000	24,000
Other Expenses	50,000	115,000
Interest Expense		16,000
Subsidiary Income	(54,000)	
Dividends Declared	20,000	10,000
Total	0	0

◄ ◄ ◄ ◄ ◄ **Required**

1. Prepare a zone analysis and a determination and distribution of excess schedule for the investment in HD Air.
2. Complete a consolidated worksheet for Fast Cool Company and its subsidiary HD Air Company as of December 31, 20X2. Prepare supporting amortization and income distribution schedules.

APPENDIX PROBLEMS

Problem 3A-1(*LO 8*) **D&D only, nontaxable exchange, tax.** On December 31, 20X5, Bryant Company exchanged 10,000 of its $10 par value shares for a 90% interest in Joshua Company. The purchase was recorded at the $80 per share fair value of Bryant shares. Joshua Company had the following balance sheet on the date of the purchase:

Assets		Liabilities and Equity	
Cash	$ 100,000	Current liabilities	$ 130,000
Accounts receivable	200,000	Deferred rental income	120,000
Inventory	150,000	Bonds payable	250,000
Investment in marketable securities	150,000	Common stock ($10 par)	100,000
Depreciable fixed assets	400,000	Paid-in capital in excess of par	150,000
		Retained earnings	250,000
Total assets	$1,000,000	Total liabilities and equity	$1,000,000

It was determined that the following fair values differed from book values for the assets of Joshua Company:

Inventory	$200,000
Depreciable fixed assets (net)	500,000
Investment in marketable securities	170,000

The purchase is a tax-free exchange to the seller, which means Bryant Company will use the book value of Joshua's assets for tax purposes. The tax rate for both firms is 30%.

Required ▶ ▶ ▶ ▶ ▶   Record the investment and prepare a determination and distribution of excess schedule.

Suggestion: Asset adjustments should be accompanied by the appropriate deferred tax liability.

Problem 3A-2*(LO 2, 8)* **Worksheet for nontaxable exchange.** The balance sheets of Tip Company and Kim Company as of December 31, 20X6, are as follows:

	Tip	Kim
Cash	$ 1,200,000	$ 50,000
Accounts receivable	2,400,000	300,000
Inventory	11,200,000	1,500,000
Prepayments	422,000	47,000
Depreciable fixed assets	18,978,000	2,100,000
Investment in Kim Company	2,400,000	
Total assets	$36,600,000	$3,997,000
Payables	$ 7,200,000	$1,750,000
Accruals	1,615,000	400,000
Common stock ($100 par)	10,000,000	1,000,000
Retained earnings	17,785,000	847,000
Total liabilities and equity	$36,600,000	$3,997,000

An appraisal on December 31, 20X6, which was considered carefully and approved by the boards of directors of both companies, placed a total replacement value, less depreciation, of $3,000,000 on Kim's depreciable fixed assets.

Tip Company offered to purchase all the assets of Kim Company, subject to its liabilities, as of December 31, 20X6, for $3,000,000. However, 20% of the stockholders of Kim Company objected to the price because it did not include any consideration for goodwill, which they believed to be worth at least $500,000. A counterproposal was made, and a final agreement was reached. In exchange for its own shares, Tip acquired 80% of the common stock of Kim at the agreed-upon fair value of $300 per share. The purchase is structured as a tax-free exchange to the seller; thus, Tip will use the book value of the assets for future tax purposes. The tax rate for both companies is 30%.

Required ▶ ▶ ▶ ▶ ▶   Prepare a consolidated worksheet and a consolidated balance sheet as of December 31, 20X6. Include a determination and distribution schedule.

(AICPA adapted)

Intercompany Transactions: Merchandise, Plant Assets, and Notes

Learning Objectives

When you have completed this chapter, you should be able to

1. Explain why transactions between members of a consolidated firm should not be reflected in the consolidated financial statements.

2. Defer intercompany profits on merchandise sales when appropriate and eliminate the double counting of sales between affiliates.

3. Defer profits on intercompany sales of long-term assets and realize the profits over the period of use and/or at the time of sale to a firm outside the consolidated group.

4. Eliminate intercompany loans and notes.

The elimination of the parent's investment in a subsidiary and the adjustments that may result from the elimination process are only the start of the procedures that are necessary to consolidate a parent and a subsidiary. It is common for affiliated companies to transact business with one another. The more integrated the affiliates are with respect to operations, the more common intercompany transactions become. This chapter considers the most often encountered types of intercompany transactions. These include intercompany sales of merchandise and fixed assets as well as loans between members of the consolidated group.

Transactions between the separate legal and accounting entities must be recorded on each affiliate's books. The consolidation process starts with the assumption that these transactions are recorded properly on the separate books of the parent and the subsidiary. However, consolidated statements are those that portray the parent and its subsidiary as a single economic entity. There should not be any intercompany transactions found in these consolidated statements. Only the effect of those transactions between the consolidated company and the companies outside the consolidated company should appear in the consolidated statements. Intercompany transactions must be eliminated as part of the consolidation process. For each type of intercompany transaction, sound reasoning will be developed to support the worksheet procedures. The guiding principle shall come from answering this question: **From the standpoint of a single consolidated company, what accounts and amounts should remain in the financial statements?**

The worksheet eliminations for intercompany transactions are the same no matter what method is used by the parent to maintain its investment in the subsidiary account. The examples in this chapter assume the use of the simple equity method. This is done because any investment that is maintained under the cost method is converted to the simple equity method on the consolidation worksheet.

INTERCOMPANY MERCHANDISE SALES

It is common to find that the goods sold by one member of an affiliated group have been purchased from another member of the group. One company may produce component parts that are assembled by its affiliate that sells the final product. In other cases, the product may be produced entirely by one member company and sold on a wholesale basis to another member

1

OBJECTIVE

Explain why transactions between members of a consolidated firm should not be reflected in the consolidated financial statements.

company that is responsible for selling and servicing the product to the final users. Taken as a whole, these different examples of merchandise sales represent the most common type of intercompany transaction and must be understood as a basic feature of consolidated reporting.

Sales between affiliated companies will be recorded in the normal manner on the books of the separate companies. Remember that each company is a separate legal entity maintaining its own accounting records. Thus, sales to and purchases from an affiliated company are recorded as if they were transactions made with a company outside the consolidated group, and the separate financial statements of the affiliated companies will include these purchase and sale transactions. However, when the statements of the affiliates are consolidated, such sales become transfers of goods within the consolidated entity. Since these sales do not involve parties outside the consolidated group, they cannot be acknowledged in consolidated statements.

Following are the procedures for consolidating affiliated companies engaged in intercompany merchandise sales:

1. The intercompany sale must be eliminated to avoid double counting. To understand this requirement, assume that Company P sells merchandise costing $1,000 to a subsidiary, Company S, for $1,200. Company S, in turn, sells the merchandise to an outside party for $1,500. If no elimination is made, the consolidated income statement would show the following with respect to the two transactions:

Sales	$2,700	($1,500 outside sale plus $1,200 sale to Company S)
Less cost of goods sold	2,200	($1,000 cost to Company P plus $1,200 purchase by Company S)
Gross profit	$ 500	(18.5% gross profit rate)

While the gross profit is correct, sales and the cost of goods sold are inflated because they are included twice. As a result, the gross profit percentage is understated, since the $500 gross profit appears to relate to $2,700 of sales rather than to the outside sale of $1,500. The intercompany sale must be eliminated from the consolidated statements. All that should remain on the consolidated income statement with respect to the two transactions is as follows:

Sales	$1,500	(only the final sale to the outside party)
Less cost of goods sold	1,000	(only the purchase from the outside party)
Gross profit	$ 500	(33⅓% gross profit rate)

When the goods sold between the affiliated companies are manufactured by the selling affiliate, the consolidated cost of goods sold includes only those costs that can be inventoried, such as labor, materials, and overhead, and may not include any profit.

The intercompany sale, though eliminated, does have an effect on the distribution of consolidated net income to the controlling interest and NCI. This is true because the reported net income of the subsidiary reflects the intercompany sales price, and the subsidiary's separate income statement becomes the base from which the noncontrolling share of income is calculated. In effect, the intercompany transfer price becomes an agreement as to how a portion of combined net income will be divided. For example, if Company S is an 80%-owned subsidiary, the NCI will receive 20% of the $300 profit made on the final sale by Company S, or $60. If the intercompany transfer price is increased from $1,200 to $1,300 and the final sales price remains at $1,500, Company S would earn only $200, and the NCI would receive 20% of $200, or $40.

2. Often, intercompany sales will be made on credit. Thus, intercompany trade balances will appear in the separate accounts of the affiliated companies. From a consolidated viewpoint, intercompany receivables and payables represent internal agreements to transfer funds. As such, **this internal debt should not appear on consolidated statements and must be eliminated.** Only debt transactions with entities outside the consolidated group should appear on the consolidated balance sheet.

3. **No profit on intercompany sales may be recognized until the profit is realized by a sale to an *outside* party.** This means that any profit contained in the ending inventory of intercompany goods must be eliminated and its recognition deferred until the period in which the goods are sold to outsiders. In the example described in item 1, assume that the sale by Company P to Company S was made on December 30, 20X1, and that Company S did not sell the goods until March 20X2. From a consolidated viewpoint, there can be no profit recognized until the outside sale occurs in March of 20X2. At that time, consolidation theory will acknowledge a $500 profit, of which $200 will be distributed to Company P and $300 will be distributed to Company S as part of the 20X2 consolidated net income. However, until that time, the $200 profit on the intercompany sale recorded by Company P must be deferred. In addition, not only must the $1,200 intercompany sale be eliminated, but the inventory on December 31, 20X1, must be reduced by $200 (the amount of the intercompany profit) to its $1,000 cost to the consolidated companies.

Care must be taken in calculating the profit applicable to intercompany inventory. It is most convenient when the gross profit rate is provided so that it can be multiplied by the inventory value to arrive at the intercompany profit. In some instances, however, the profit on sales may be stated as a percentage of cost. For example, one might be told that the cost of units is "marked up" 25% to arrive at the intercompany sales price. If the inventory sales price is $1,000, it cannot be multiplied by 25% to calculate the intercompany profit because the 25% applies to the *cost*, and not the sales price, at which the inventory is stated. Instead, the gross profit rate, which is a percentage of sales price, should be calculated. The easiest method of accomplishing this is to pick the theoretical cost of $1 and mark it up by 25% (the given percentage of cost) to $1.25 and ask: "What is the gross profit percentage?" In this example, it is $0.25 ÷ $1.25, or 20%. From this point, the $1,000 inventory value can be multiplied by 20% to arrive at the intercompany profit of $200.

The worksheet procedures to eliminate the effects of intercompany inventory sales are discussed in the next four sections as follows:

1. There are no intercompany goods in the beginning or ending inventories.
2. Intercompany goods remain in the ending inventory.
3. There are intercompany goods in the ending inventory, and there were intercompany goods in the beginning inventory. This is the most common situation.
4. Instead of the perpetual inventory method assumed in sections 1–3 above, the companies use the periodic inventory method. There are intercompany goods in the ending inventory, and there were intercompany goods in the beginning inventory.

No Intercompany Goods in Purchasing Company's Inventories

In the simplest case, which is illustrated in Worksheet 4-1, pages 196 and 197, all goods sold between the affiliates have been sold, in turn, to outside parties by the end of the accounting period. Worksheet 4-1 is based on the following assumptions:

Worksheet 4-1: page 196

1. Company S is an 80%-owned subsidiary of Company P. On January 1, 20X1, Company P purchased its interest in Company S at a price equal to its pro rata share of Company S's book value. Company P uses the equity method to record the investment.
2. Companies P and S had the following separate income statements for 20X1:

	Company P	Company S
Sales	$700,000	$500,000
Less cost of goods sold	510,000	350,000
Gross profit	$190,000	$150,000
Other expenses	(90,000)	(75,000)
Subsidiary income	60,000	
Net income	$160,000	$ 75,000

Note that under the equity method, Company P's income includes 80% of the reported income of Company S.

3. During the year, Company S sold goods that cost $80,000 to Company P for $100,000 (a 20% gross profit). Company P then sold all of the goods purchased from Company S to outside parties for $150,000. Company P had not paid $25,000 of the invoices received from Company S for the goods. (Note that it is assumed in this and Worksheets 4-2 and 4-3 that a **perpetual** inventory system is used.) Consider the journal entries made by each affiliate:

Company S

Accounts Receivable (from Company P)	100,000	
Sales (to Company P)		100,000
Cost of Goods Sold (to Company P)	80,000	
Inventory		80,000
Cash	75,000	
Accounts Receivable (from Company P)		75,000

Company P

Inventory	100,000	
Accounts Payable (to Company S)		100,000
Accounts Receivable (from outside parties)	150,000	
Sales (to outside parties)		150,000
Cost of Goods Sold (to outside parties)	100,000	
Inventory		100,000
Accounts Payable (to Company S)	75,000	
Cash		75,000

The elimination entries for Worksheet 4-1 in journal entry form are as follows:

(CY1)	Eliminate current-year equity income:			
	Subsidiary Income		60,000	
	Investment in Company S			60,000
(EL)	Eliminate 80% of subsidiary equity against investment in subsidiary account:			
	Common Stock ($10 par), Company S		80,000	
	Retained Earnings, January 1, 20X1, Company S		56,000	
	Investment in Company S			136,000
(IS)	Eliminate intercompany merchandise sales:			
	Sales		100,000	
	Cost of Goods Sold			100,000
(IA)	Eliminate intercompany unpaid trade balances at year-end:			
	Accounts Payable		25,000	
	Accounts Receivable			25,000

Entry (IS) is a simplified summary entry that can be further analyzed with the following entry:

Sales (to Company P)	100,000	
Cost of Goods Sold (by Company S to Company P— the intercompany sale)		80,000
Cost of Goods Sold (by Company P to outside parties— the profit recorded by Company S)		20,000

The preceding expanded entry removes the cost of goods sold with respect to the intercompany sale and removes the intercompany profit from the sales made by the parent to outside parties. Note that the parent recorded the cost of the goods sold to outside parties at $100,000, which contains $20,000 of Company S's profit. As shown in the expanded (IS) entry above, the true cost of the goods to the consolidated company is $80,000 ($100,000 less the 20% internal gross profit).

Entry (IA) eliminates the intercompany receivables/payables still remaining unpaid at the end of the year. Income distribution schedules are used in Worksheet 4-1 to distribute the $175,000 of consolidated net income to the noncontrolling and controlling interests. It should be noted that all of the above procedures remain unchanged if the parent is the seller of the intercompany goods.

Intercompany Goods in Purchasing Company's Ending Inventory

Let us now change the example in Worksheet 4-1 to assume that Company P did not resell $40,000 of the total of $100,000 of goods it purchased from Company S. This means that $40,000 of goods purchased from Company S remain in Company P's ending inventory. As shown below, Company S (the intercompany seller) will have the same entries as presented on page 184, and Company P will have the following revised entries:

2

OBJECTIVE

Defer intercompany profits on merchandise sales when appropriate and eliminate the double counting of sales between affiliates.

Company S

Accounts Receivable (from Company P)	100,000	
Sales (to Company P)		100,000
Cost of Goods Sold (to Company P)	80,000	
Inventory		80,000
Cash	75,000	
Accounts Receivable (from Company P)		75,000

Company P

Inventory	100,000	
Accounts Payable (to Company S)		100,000
Accounts Receivable (from outside parties)	90,000	
Sales (to outside parties)		90,000
Cost of Goods Sold (to outside parties)	60,000	
Inventory		60,000
Accounts Payable (to Company S)	75,000	
Cash		75,000

Let us now consider what has happened to the $100,000 of goods sold to Company P by Company S:

$80,000 is the original cost of the goods sold by Company S that should be removed from the consolidated cost of goods sold since it is derived from the intercompany sale and not the outside sale.

$12,000 is the intercompany profit included in the goods sold by Company P to outside parties. The cost of these sales should be reduced by $12,000 (20% × $60,000) to arrive at the true cost of the goods to the consolidated company.

$8,000 is the intercompany profit remaining in the Company P ending inventory. This inventory, now at $40,000, should be reduced by $8,000 (20% × $40,000) to $32,000. Another way to view this is that 60% of the original intercompany goods (60% × $100,000 = $60,000) have been sold to outside parties. Thus, only the profit on these sales (20% × $60,000 = $12,000) has been realized.

If we follow the above analysis to the letter, we would make the following elimination in entry form:

Sales (by Company S to Company P) 100,000	
Cost of Goods Sold (by Company S)	80,000
Cost of Goods Sold (by Company P)	12,000
Inventory, December 31, 20X1 (held by Company P)	8,000

Worksheet 4-2: page 198

In practice, this entry is cumbersome in that it requires an analysis of the destiny of all inter-company sales. The approach used in Worksheet 4-2, pages 198 and 199, is simplified first to eliminate the intercompany sales under the assumption that all goods have been resold, and then to adjust for those goods still remaining in the inventory. This method simplifies work-sheet procedures, including the distribution of combined net income. In journal form, the sim-plified entries are:

(CY1)	Eliminate current-year equity income:		
	Subsidiary Income	60,000	
	Investment in Company S		60,000
(EL)	Eliminate 80% of subsidiary equity against investment in subsidiary account:		
	Common Stock ($10 par), Company S	80,000	
	Retained Earnings, January 1, 20X1, Company S	56,000	
	Investment in Company S		136,000
(IS)	Eliminate intercompany merchandise sales:		
	Sales	100,000	
	Cost of Goods Sold		100,000
(EI)	Eliminate intercompany profit in ending inventory:		
	Cost of Goods Sold	8,000	
	Inventory, December 31, 20X1		8,000
(IA)	Eliminate intercompany unpaid trade balance at year-end:		
	Accounts Payable	25,000	
	Accounts Receivable		25,000

The $8,000 is viewed as the unrealized intercompany inventory profit that may not be real-ized until a later period when the goods are sold to outside parties.

The unrealized intercompany profit is subtracted from the seller's income distribution schedule. In the income distribution schedules for Worksheet 4-2, the unrealized profit of $8,000 is deducted from the subsidiary's internally generated net income of $75,000. The adjusted net income of $67,000 is apportioned, with $13,400 (20%) distributed to the noncon-trolling interest and $53,600 (80%) distributed to the controlling interest.

There is no change in worksheet elimination procedures if the parent is the seller and the subsidiary has intercompany goods in its ending inventory; only the distribution of combined net income changes. To illustrate, assume the parent, Company P, is the seller of the intercom-pany goods. The income distribution schedules would be prepared as follows:

Subsidiary Company S Income Distribution

	Internally generated net income	$ 75,000
	Adjusted income	$ 75,000
	NCI share	× 20%
	NCI	$ 15,000

Parent Company P Income Distribution

Unrealized profit in ending inventory . . . . **(EI)**	**$8,000**	Internally generated net income	$100,000
		80% × Company S adjusted income of $75,000	60,000
		Controlling interest	$152,000

Intercompany Goods in Purchasing Company's Beginning and Ending Inventories

When intercompany goods are included in the purchaser's beginning inventory, the inventory value includes the profit made by the seller. The intercompany seller of the goods has included in the prior period such sales in its separate income statement as though the transactions were consummated. Thus, the beginning retained earnings balance of the seller also includes the profit on these goods. While this profit should be reflected on the separate books of the affiliates, it should not be recognized when a consolidated view is taken. Remember: **Profit must not be recognized in a consolidated statement until it is realized in the subsequent period through the sale of goods to an outside party.** Therefore, in the consolidating process, the beginning inventory of intercompany goods must be reduced to its cost to the consolidated company. Likewise, the retained earnings of the consolidated entity must be reduced by deleting the profit that was recorded in prior periods on intercompany goods contained in the buyer's beginning inventory.

To illustrate, using the example of Company P and Company S from Worksheet 4-3 on pages 200 and 201, assume the two companies have the following individual income data for **20X2**:

Worksheet 4-3: page 200

	Company P	Company S
Sales	$ 800,000	$ 600,000
Less cost of goods sold	610,000	**440,000**
Gross profit	$ 190,000	$ 160,000
Other expenses	(120,000)	(100,000)
Subsidiary income	48,000	
Net income	$ 118,000	$ 60,000

Assume the following additional facts:

1. Company P's 20X2 beginning inventory includes $40,000 of the goods purchased from Company S in **20X1**. The gross profit rate on the sale was 20%.
2. Company S sold $120,000 of goods to Company P during **20X2**.
3. Company S recorded a 20% gross profit on these sales.
4. At the end of **20X2**, Company P still owed $60,000 to Company S for the purchases.
5. Company P also had $30,000 of the intercompany purchases in its **20X2** ending inventory.

Worksheet 4-3 contains the **20X2** year-end trial balances of Company P and Company S. The elimination entries in journal entry form are as follows:

(CY1)	Eliminate current-year equity income:		
	Subsidiary Income	48,000	
	Investment in Company S		48,000
(EL)	Eliminate subsidiary equity against investment in subsidiary account:		
	Common Stock ($10 par), Company S	80,000	
	Retained Earnings, January 1, 20X2, Company S	116,000	
	Investment in Company S		196,000
(BI)	Eliminate intercompany profit in beginning inventory and reduce current-year cost of goods sold:		
	Retained Earnings, January 1, 20X2, Company P	6,400	
	Retained Earnings, January 1, 20X2, Company S	1,600	
	Cost of Goods Sold		8,000
(IS)	Eliminate intercompany merchandise sales:		
	Sales	120,000	
	Cost of Goods Sold		120,000

(continued)

(EI)	Eliminate intercompany profit in ending inventory:		
	Cost of Goods Sold	6,000	
	Inventory, December 31, 20X2		6,000
(IA)	Eliminate intercompany unpaid trade balance at year-end:		
	Accounts Payable	60,000	
	Accounts Receivable		60,000

Entry (BI) adjusts for the intercompany profit contained in the beginning inventory. At the start of 20X2, Company P included $40,000 of goods purchased from Company S in its beginning inventory. During 20X2, the inventory was debited to Cost of Goods Sold at $40,000. The cost of goods sold must now be reduced to cost by removing the $8,000 intercompany profit. The intercompany profit also was included in last year's income by the subsidiary. That income was closed to Retained Earnings. Thus, the beginning retained earnings of Company S are overstated by $8,000. That $8,000 is divided between the noncontrolling and controlling interest in retained earnings. Subsidiary retained earnings have been 80% eliminated, and only the 20% noncontrolling interest remains. The other 80% of beginning retained earnings is included in Company P's retained earnings through the use of the equity method.

Note that once the controlling share of subsidiary retained earnings is eliminated, there is a transformation of what was **subsidiary** retained earnings into what now is **NCI** in retained earnings. Entries (IS), (EI), and (IA) eliminate the intercompany sales, ending inventory, and trade accounts in the same manner as was done in Worksheet 4-2. After all eliminations and adjustments are made, the consolidated net income of $132,000 is distributed as shown in the income distribution schedules. **The adjustments for intercompany inventory profits are reflected in the *selling company's schedule*.**

It might appear that the intercompany goods in the beginning inventory are always assumed to be sold in the current period, since the deferred profit of the previous period is realized during the current period as reflected by the seller's income distribution schedule. That assumption need not be made, however. Even if part of the beginning inventory is unsold at year-end, it still would be a part of the $30,000 ending inventory, on which $6,000 of profit is deferred. Note that the use of the LIFO method for inventories could cause a given period's inventory profit to be deferred indefinitely. Unless otherwise stated, the examples and problems of this text will assume a FIFO flow.

Worksheet 4-3 assumed the intercompany merchandise sales were made by the subsidiary. Procedures would differ as follows if the sales were made by the parent:

1. The beginning inventory profit would be subtracted entirely from the beginning controlling retained earnings since only the parent recorded the profit.
2. The adjustments for the beginning and ending inventory profits would be included in the parent income distribution schedule and not in the subsidiary schedule.

Eliminations for Periodic Inventories

In Worksheets 4-1 through 4-3, the cost of goods sold was included in the trial balances, since both the parent and the subsidiary used a perpetual inventory system. However, in Worksheet 4-4 on pages 202 and 203, a periodic inventory system is used. In this illustration, which is based on the same facts as Worksheet 4-3, the following differences in worksheet procedures result from the use of a periodic inventory system:

1. The 20X2 beginning inventories of $70,000 and $40,000, rather than the ending inventories, appear as assets in the trial balances. The beginning inventories less the intercompany profit in Company P's beginning inventory are extended to the Consolidated Income Statement column as a debit.
2. The purchases accounts, rather than the cost of goods sold, appear in the trial balances and, after adjustment, are extended to the Consolidated Income Statement column.
3. Entry (BI) credits the January 1 inventory to eliminate the intercompany profit.
4. Entry (IS) credits the purchases account, which is still open under the periodic method, and makes the usual debit to the sales account.

Worksheet 4-4: page 202

5. The ending inventories of both Company P and Company S are entered in each company's trial balances as both a debit (the balance sheet amount) and a credit (the adjustment to the cost of goods sold). These inventories are recorded at the price paid for them, which, for intercompany goods, includes the intercompany sales profit. Entry (EI) removes the $6,000 intercompany profit applicable to the ending inventory. The balance sheet inventory is reduced to $104,000. The $104,000 credit balance is extended to the Consolidated Income Statement column.

The elimination entries in journal entry form are as follows:

(CY1)	Eliminate current-year equity income:		
	Subsidiary Income.	48,000	
	Investment in Company S.		48,000
(EL)	Eliminate subsidiary equity against investment in		
	subsidiary account:		
	Common Stock ($10 par), Company S.	80,000	
	Retained Earnings, January 1, 20X2, Company S	116,000	
	Investment in Company S.		196,000
(BI)	Eliminate intercompany profit in beginning inventory and		
	reduce current-year cost of goods sold:		
	Retained Earnings, January 1, 20X2, Company P	6,400	
	Retained Earnings, January 1, 20X2, Company S	1,600	
	Cost of Goods Sold		8,000
(IS)	Eliminate intercompany merchandise sales:		
	Sales	120,000	
	Purchases.		120,000
(EI)	Eliminate intercompany profit in ending inventory:		
	Cost of Goods Sold	6,000	
	Inventory, December 31, 20X2, Asset.		6,000
(IA)	Eliminate intercompany unpaid trade balance at year-end:		
	Accounts Payable	60,000	
	Accounts Receivable		60,000

Effect of Lower-of-Cost-or-Market Method on Inventory Profit

Intercompany inventory in the hands of the purchaser may have been written down by the purchaser to a market value below its intercompany transfer cost. Assume that, for $50,000, Company S purchased goods that cost its parent company $40,000. Assume further that Company S has all the goods in its ending inventory but has written them down to $42,000, the lower market value at the end of the period. As a result of this markdown, the inventory needs to be reduced by only another $2,000 to reflect its cost to the consolidated company ($40,000). The only remaining issue is how to defer the $2,000 inventory profit in the income distribution schedules. As before, such profit is deferred by entering it as a debit on the intercompany seller's schedule. In the subsequent period, the profit will be realized by the seller.

It may seem strange that the $8,000 of profit written off is treated as realized, since it is not deducted in the seller's distribution schedule. This procedure is proper, however, since the $8,000 loss recognized by the buyer is offset by allowing the seller to realize the $8,000 profit. Only the remaining $2,000 of profit needs to be deferred. Had the inventory been written down to $40,000 or less, there would be no need to defer the offsetting profit in the consolidated worksheet or in the income distribution schedules.

Losses on Intercompany Sales

Assume a parent sells goods to a subsidiary for $5,000 and the goods cost the parent $6,000. If the market value of the goods is $5,000 or less, the loss may be recognized in the consolidated income statement, even if the goods remain in the subsidiary's ending inventory. Such a loss can be recognized under the lower-of-cost-or-market principle that applies to inventory. However, if the intercompany sales price is below market value, the part of the loss that results from the price being below market value cannot be recognized until the subsidiary sells the goods to an outside party. Elimination procedures would be similar, but opposite in direction, to those used for unrealized gains.

REFLECTION

- Merchandise sales between affiliated companies are eliminated; only the purchase and sale to the "outside world" should remain in the statements.

- The profit must be removed from the beginning inventory by reducing the cost of goods sold and the retained earnings.

- The profit must be removed from the ending inventory both by reducing the inventory and by increasing the cost of goods sold. The deduction of the inventory from the goods available for sale is too great prior to this adjustment.

- Unpaid intercompany trade payables/receivables resulting from intercompany merchandise sales are eliminated.

3

OBJECTIVE

Defer profits on intercompany sales of long-term assets and realize the profits over the period of use and/or at the time of sale to a firm outside the consolidated group.

INTERCOMPANY PLANT ASSET SALES

Any plant asset may be sold between members of an affiliated group, and such a sale may result in a gain for the seller. The buyer will record the asset at a price that includes the gain, and when the sale involves a depreciable asset, the buyer will base future depreciation charges on the price paid. While these recordings are proper for the companies as separate entities, they must not be reflected in the consolidated statements. Consolidation theory views the sale as an *internal transfer of assets*. There is no basis for recognizing a gain at the time of the internal transfer. A gain on the sale of a nondepreciable asset cannot be recorded on the consolidated statements until the asset is resold to the outside world. However, the recognition of a gain on the sale of a depreciable asset does not have to wait until resale occurs. Instead, the intercompany gain is amortized over the depreciable life of the asset. The buyer's normal intent is to use the asset, not to resell it. Since the asset is overstated by the amount of the intercompany gain, subsequent depreciation is overstated as well. The consolidation process reduces depreciation in future years so that depreciation charges in the consolidated statements reflect the original cost of the asset to the consolidated company. While the gain is deferred in the year of sale, it is realized later through the increased combined net income resulting from the reduction in depreciation expense in subsequent periods. The decrease in depreciation expense for each and every period is equal to the difference between the depreciation based on the intercompany sales price and the depreciation based on the book value of the asset on the sale date.

Intercompany Sale of a Nondepreciable Asset

One member of an affiliated group may sell land to another affiliate and record a gain. For consolidating purposes, there has been no sale; thus, there is no cause to recognize a gain. Since the asset is not depreciable, the entire gain must be deferred until the land is sold to an outside party. This deferment may be permanent if there is no intent to sell at a later date. For example, assume that in 20X1 Company S (80% owned) sells land to its parent company, Company P. The sale price is $30,000, and the original cost of the land to Company S was $20,000. Consolidation theory would rule that, until Company P sells the land to an outside party, recognition of the $10,000 profit must be deferred. Elimination (LA) eliminates the intercompany gain in the year of sale.

	Partial Trial Balance		Eliminations & Adjustments	
	Company P	Company S	Dr.	Cr.
Land	30,000			(LA) 10,000
Gain on Sale of Land		(10,000)	(LA) 10,000	

As usual, the selling company's income distribution schedule would reflect the deferment of the gain.

In subsequent years, assuming the land is not sold by Company P, the gain must be removed from the consolidated retained earnings. Since the sale was made by Company S, which is an 80%-owned subsidiary of Company P, the controlling interest must absorb 80% of the deferment, while the noncontrolling interest must absorb 20%. For example, the adjustments in 20X2 would be as follows:

	Partial Trial Balance		Eliminations & Adjustments	
	Company P	Company S	Dr.	Cr.
Land	30,000			(LA) 10,000
Retained Earnings, January 1, 20X2, Company P	(100,000)*		(LA) 8,000	
Retained Earnings, January 1, 20X2, Company S		(20,000)*	(LA) 2,000	

*arbitrary balance

Now, assume Company P sells the land in 20X3 to an outside party for $45,000, recording a gain of $15,000. When this sale occurs, the $10,000 intercompany gain also is realized. The following elimination would remove the previously unrealized gain from the consolidated retained earnings and would add it to the gain already recorded by Company P. The retained earnings adjustment is allocated 80% to the controlling interest and 20% to the noncontrolling interest, since the original sale was made by the subsidiary.

	Partial Trial Balance		Eliminations & Adjustments	
	Company P	Company S	Dr.	Cr.
Gain on Sale of Land	(15,000)			(LA) 10,000
Retained Earnings, January 1, 20X3, Company P	(120,000)*		(LA) 8,000	
Retained Earnings, January 1, 20X3, Company S		(15,000)*	(LA) 2,000	

*arbitrary balance

The income distribution schedule would add the $10,000 gain to the 20X3 internally generated net income of Company S. At this point, it should be clear that the gain on the intercompany sale was deferred, not eliminated. The original gain of $10,000 eventually is credited to the subsidiary. Thus, the gain does affect the noncontrolling share of consolidated net income at a future date. Any sale of a nondepreciable asset should be viewed as an agreement between the controlling and noncontrolling interests regarding the future distribution of consolidated net income.

When a parent sells a nondepreciable asset to a subsidiary, the worksheet procedures are the same, except for these areas:

1. The deferment of the gain in the year of the intercompany sale and the recognition of the gain in the year of the sale of the asset to an outside party flow through only the parent company income distribution schedule.

2. In the years subsequent to the intercompany sale through the year the land is sold to an external company, the related adjustment is made exclusively through the controlling retained earnings.

Intercompany Sale of a Depreciable Asset

Turning to the case where a depreciable plant asset is sold between affiliates, the following example illustrates the worksheet procedures necessary for the **deferment of a gain on the sale *over the asset's useful life.*** Assume that the parent, Company P, sells a machine to a subsidiary, Company S, for $30,000 on January 1, 20X1. Originally, the machine cost $32,000. Accumulated depreciation as of January 1, 20X1, is $12,000. Therefore, the book value of the machine is $20,000, and the reported gain on the sale is $10,000. Further assume that Company S (the buyer) believes the asset has a five-year remaining life; thus, it records straight-line depreciation of $6,000 ($30,000 cost ÷ 5 years) annually.

The eliminations recognize the gain over the five-year life of the asset by reducing annual depreciation charges. For consolidated reporting purposes, depreciation is based on the asset's $20,000 book value to the consolidated company. Worksheet 4-5, on pages 204 and 205, is based on the following additional facts:

Worksheet 4-5: page 204

1. Company P owns an 80% investment in Company S. The amount paid for the investment was equal to the book value of Company S's underlying equity. The simple equity method is used by Company P to record its investment.

2. There were no beginning or ending inventories, and the companies had the following separate income statements for 20X1:

	Company P	Company S
Sales	$ 200,000	$100,000
Cost of goods sold	(150,000)	(59,000)
Gross profit	$ 50,000	$ 41,000
Depreciation expense	(30,000)	(16,000)
Gain on sale of machine	10,000	
Subsidiary income (80%)	20,000	
Net income	$ 50,000	$ 25,000

The elimination entries in journal entry form are:

(CY1)	Eliminate current-year equity income:		
	Subsidiary Income	20,000	
	Investment in Company S		20,000
(EL)	Eliminate subsidiary equity against investment in subsidiary account:		
	Common Stock ($10 par), Company S	40,000	
	Retained Earnings, January 1, 20X1, Company S	60,000	
	Investment in Company S		100,000
(F1)	Eliminate intercompany gain on machine sale and reduce machine to cost:		
	Gain on Sale of Machinery	10,000	
	Machinery		10,000

(F2) Reduce machinery depreciation to amount based on book value:

Accumulated Depreciation—Machinery.....................	2,000	
Depreciation Expense		2,000

Entry (F1) eliminates the $10,000 intercompany gain and restates the asset at its book value of $20,000 on the date of the intercompany sale.

Entry (F2) reduces the depreciation expense for the year by the difference between depreciation based on:

1. The book value [($32,000 − $12,000 = $20,000 depreciable base) ÷ 5 years = $4,000] and
2. The intercompany sales price ($30,000 depreciable base ÷ 5 years = $6,000).

The allocation of consolidated net income of $47,000 is shown in the income distribution schedules. Note that Company S (the buyer in this example) must absorb depreciation based on the agreed-upon sales price, and it is the controlling interest that realizes the benefit of the reduced depreciation as the asset is used. Also, note that the realizable profit for Company P (the seller) in any year is the depreciation absorbed by the buyer minus the depreciation for consolidated purposes ($6,000 − $4,000). If the sale had been made by Company S, the profit deferment and recognition entries would flow through its income distribution schedule.

Worksheets for periods subsequent to the sale of the machine must correct the current-year nominal accounts and remove the unrealized profit in the beginning consolidated retained earnings. Worksheet 4-6, on pages 206 and 207, portrays a consolidated worksheet for 20X2, based on the following separate income statements of Company P and Company S:

worksheet

	Company P	Company S	Worksheet 4-6: page 206
Sales	$ 250,000	$120,000	
Cost of goods sold.......................................	(180,000)	(80,000)	
Gross profit	$ 70,000	$ 40,000	
Depreciation expense	(20,000)	(16,000)	
Subsidiary income (80%)	19,200		
Net income	$ 69,200	$ 24,000	

The elimination entries in journal entry form are as follows:

(CY1) Eliminate current-year equity income:

Subsidiary Income......................................	19,200	
Investment in Company S.............................		19,200

(EL) Eliminate subsidiary equity against investment in subsidiary account:

Common Stock ($10 par), Company S....................	40,000	
Retained Earnings, January 1, 20X2, Company S	80,000	
Investment in Company S.............................		120,000

(F1) Eliminate remaining intercompany gain on machine sale, reduce machine to cost, and adjust accumulated depreciation for prior year:

Retained Earnings, Company P, January 1, 20X2	8,000	
Accumulated Depreciation—Machinery....................	2,000	
Machinery		10,000

(F2) Reduce current-year machinery depreciation to amount based on book value:

Accumulated Depreciation—Machinery....................	2,000	
Depreciation Expense		2,000

Entry (F1) in this worksheet corrects the asset's net book value, accumulated depreciation, and retained earnings as of the beginning of the year. Since the sale was by the parent, only the controlling interest in beginning retained earnings is adjusted. Had the sale been by the subsidiary, the adjustment would have been split 20/80 to the noncontrolling and controlling interests, respectively, in beginning retained earnings.

Entry (F2) corrects the depreciation expense, and the accumulated depreciation accounts for the current year. The resulting consolidated net income of $76,000 is distributed as shown in the income distribution schedules that follow Worksheet 4-6. During each year, Company S must absorb the larger depreciation expense that resulted from its purchase of the asset. Company P has the right to realize $2,000 more of the original deferred profit.

REFLECTION

- The gain on an intercompany sale of land cannot be recognized until (if ever) the land is sold to the "outside world." The gain is deducted from the land account. In the year of intercompany sale, the gain is eliminated; in later periods, retained earnings is reduced for the amount of the gain.

- A gain on the intercompany sale of a fixed asset is eliminated in the period of sale. The gain is recognized over the depreciable life of the asset as a reduction in each period's depreciation expense.

4
OBJECTIVE

Eliminate intercompany loans and notes.

INTERCOMPANY DEBT

Typically, a parent company is larger than any one of its subsidiaries and can secure funds under more favorable terms. Because of this, a parent company often will advance cash to a subsidiary. The parent may accept a note from the subsidiary as security for the loan, or the parent may discount a note that the subsidiary received from a customer. In most cases, the parent will charge a competitive interest rate for the funds advanced to the subsidiary.

In the examples that follow, the more common situation in which the parent is the lender is assumed. If the subsidiary were the lender, the theory and practice would be identical, with the only differences being the books on which the applicable accounts appear and the procedure for the distribution of combined net income.

Assume that on July 1, 20X1, an 80%-owned subsidiary, Company S, borrows $10,000 from its parent, Company P, signing a one-year, 8% note, with interest payable on the due date. This intercompany loan will cause the following accounts and their balances to appear on the December 31, 20X1, trial balances of the separate affiliated companies:

Parent Company P		Subsidiary Company S	
Notes Receivable..................	10,000	Notes Payable..................	(10,000)
Interest Income...................	(400)	Interest Expense.................	400
Interest Receivable...............	400	Interest Payable................	(400)

While this information is required on the books of the separate companies, it should not appear on the consolidated statements. The procedures needed to eliminate this intercompany note and its related interest amounts are demonstrated in Worksheet 4-7, pages 208 and 209.

The elimination entries in journal entry form are as follows:

(CY1)	Eliminate current-year equity income:		
	Subsidiary Income....................................	8,000	
	Investment in Company S............................		8,000

worksheet

Worksheet 4-7: page 208

(EL)	Eliminate subsidiary equity against investment in subsidiary account:		
	Common Stock ($10 par), Company S.	40,000	
	Retained Earnings, January 1, 20X1, Company S	80,000	
	Investment in Company S.		120,000
(LN1)	Eliminate intercompany note and accrued interest:		
	Note Payable to Company P	10,000	
	Accrued Interest Payable.	400	
	Note Receivable from Company S.		10,000
	Accrued Interest Receivable.		400
(LN2)	Eliminate intercompany interest income and expense:		
	Interest Income.	400	
	Interest Expense		400

Entry (LN1) eliminates the intercompany receivable and payable for the note and the accrued interest on the note. Entry (LN2) eliminates the intercompany interest income and expense amounts. In this worksheet, it is assumed that the intercompany note is the only note recorded. However, sometimes an intercompany note and its related interest expense, revenue, and accruals are commingled with notes to outside parties. Before the trial balances are entered on the worksheet and before consolidation is attempted, intercompany interest expense and revenue must be accrued properly on the books of the parent and subsidiary.

After all the necessary worksheet eliminations are made, the effect of the note on the distribution of consolidated net income must be considered. There might be a temptation to increase the noncontrolling share of consolidated net income by $400 as a result of eliminating the interest expense on the intercompany note, but it is not correct to do so. Even though the interest does not appear on the consolidated income statement, it is a legitimate expense for Company S as a separate entity and a legitimate revenue for Company P as a separate entity. In essence, Company S has agreed to transfer $400 to Company P for interest during 20X1, and the NCI must respect this agreement when calculating its share of consolidated net income. Thus, the basis for calculating the noncontrolling share is the net income of Company S as a separate entity. The NCI receives 20% of this $10,000 net income which is net of the $400 of intercompany interest expense.

A parent receiving a note from a subsidiary subsequently may discount the note at a nonaffiliated financial institution in order to receive immediate cash. This results in a note receivable discounted being recorded by the parent. From a consolidated viewpoint, there is a note payable to outside parties. Consolidation procedures should eliminate the internal note receivable against the note receivable discounted. This elimination will result in the note, now payable to an outside party, being extended to the consolidated balance sheet. Intercompany interest accrued prior to the discounting is eliminated. Interest paid by the subsidiary subsequent to the discounting is paid to the outside party and is not eliminated. The net interest expense or revenue on the discounting of the note is a transaction between the parent and the outside party and, thus, is not eliminated. When consolidated statements are prepared, however, it is desirable to net the interest expense on the note recorded by the maker subsequent to the discounting of the note against the net interest expense or revenue on the discounting transaction.

REFLECTION

- Intercompany debt balances, including accrued interest receivable/payable, are eliminated.

- Intercompany interest expense/revenue is also eliminated. These amounts are equal; thus, there is no effect on consolidated net income.

Worksheet 4-1

Intercompany Sales; No Intercompany Goods in Inventories
Company P and Subsidiary Company S
Worksheet for Consolidated Financial Statements
For Year Ended December 31, **20X1**

	(Credit balance amounts are in parentheses.)	Trial Balance	
		Company P	Company S
1	**Accounts Receivable**	110,000	150,000
2	Inventory, December 31, 20X1	70,000	40,000
3	Investment in Company S	196,000	
4			
5	Other Assets	314,000	155,000
6	**Accounts Payable**	(80,000)	(100,000)
7	Common Stock ($10 par), Company P	(200,000)	
8	Retained Earnings, January 1, 20X1, Company P	(250,000)	
9	Common Stock ($10 par), Company S		(100,000)
10	Retained Earnings, January 1, 20X1, Company S		(70,000)
11	**Sales**	(700,000)	(500,000)
12	**Cost of Goods Sold**	510,000	350,000
13	Expenses	90,000	75,000
14	Subsidiary Income	(60,000)	
15		0	0
16	Consolidated Net Income		
17	To NCI (see distribution schedule)		
18	Balance to Controlling Interest (see distribution schedule)		
19	Total NCI		
20	Retained Earnings, Controlling Interest, December 31, 20X1		
21			

Eliminations and Adjustments:

(CY1)   Eliminate the entry recording the parent's share of subsidiary net income.

(EL)   Eliminate against the investment in Company S account the pro rata portion of the subsidiary equity balances (80%) owned by the parent. To simplify the elimination, there is no discrepancy between the cost and book values of the investment in this example. Also, note that the worksheet process is expedited by always eliminating the intercompany investment first.

(IS)   Eliminate the intercompany sales to avoid double counting. Now only Company S's original purchase from third parties and Company P's final sale to third parties remain in the consolidated income statement.

(IA)   Eliminate the $25,000 intercompany trade balances resulting from the intercompany sale.

Worksheet 4-1 (see page 183)

Eliminations & Adjustments		Consolidated Income Statement	NCI	Controlling Retained Earnings	Consolidated Balance Sheet	
Dr.	Cr.					
	(IA) 25,000				235,000	1
					110,000	2
	(CY1) 60,000					3
	(EL) 136,000					4
					469,000	5
(IA) 25,000					(155,000)	6
					(200,000)	7
				(250,000)		8
(EL) 80,000			(20,000)			9
(EL) 56,000			(14,000)			10
(IS) 100,000		(1,100,000)				11
	(IS) 100,000	760,000				12
		165,000				13
(CY1) 60,000						14
321,000	321,000					15
		(175,000)				16
		15,000	(15,000)			17
		160,000		(160,000)		18
			(49,000)		(49,000)	19
				(410,000)	(410,000)	20
					0	21

Subsidiary Company S Income Distribution

Internally generated net income	$ 75,000
Adjusted income	$ 75,000
NCI share	× 20%
NCI	$ 15,000

Parent Company P Income Distribution

Internally generated net income	$100,000
80% × Company S adjusted income of $75,000.	60,000
Controlling interest	$160,000

Worksheet 4-2

Intercompany Goods in Ending Inventory
Company P and Subsidiary Company S
Worksheet for Consolidated Financial Statements
For Year Ended December 31, **20X1**

	(Credit balance amounts are in parentheses.)	Trial Balance	
		Company P	Company S
1	Accounts Receivable	110,000	150,000
2	**Inventory, December 31, 20X1**	**70,000**	**40,000**
3	Investment in Company S	196,000	
4			
5	Other Assets	314,000	155,000
6	Accounts Payable	(80,000)	(100,000)
7	Common Stock ($10 par), Company P	(200,000)	
8	Retained Earnings, January 1, 20X1, Company P	(250,000)	
9	Common Stock ($10 par), Company S		(100,000)
10	Retained Earnings, January 1, 20X1, Company S		(70,000)
11	Sales	(700,000)	(500,000)
12	**Cost of Goods Sold**	**510,000**	**350,000**
13	Expenses	90,000	75,000
14	Subsidiary Income	(60,000)	
15		0	0
16	Consolidated Net Income		
17	To NCI (see distribution schedule)		
18	Balance to Controlling Interest (see distribution schedule)		
19	Total NCI		
20	Retained Earnings, Controlling Interest, December 31, 20X1		
21			

Eliminations and Adjustments:

(CY1) Eliminate the entry recording the parent's share of subsidiary net income.
(EL)   Eliminate 80% of the subsidiary equity balances against the investment in Company S account. There is no excess of cost or book value in this example.
(IS)   Eliminate the intercompany sale.
(EI)   Eliminate intercompany profit in ending inventory.
(IA)   Eliminate the intercompany trade balances.

Worksheet 4-2 (see page 186)

Eliminations & Adjustments				Consolidated Income Statement	NCI	Controlling Retained Earnings	Consolidated Balance Sheet	
Dr.		Cr.						
		(IA)	25,000				235,000	1
		(EI)	**8,000**				102,000	2
		(CY1)	60,000					3
		(EL)	136,000					4
							469,000	5
(IA)	25,000						(155,000)	6
							(200,000)	7
						(250,000)		8
(EL)	80,000				(20,000)			9
(EL)	56,000				(14,000)			10
(IS)	100,000			(1,100,000)				11
(EI)	**8,000**	(IS)	100,000	768,000				12
				165,000				13
(CY1)	60,000							14
	329,000		329,000					15
				(167,000)				16
				13,400	(13,400)			17
				153,600		(153,600)		18
					(47,400)		(47,400)	19
						(403,600)	(403,600)	20
							0	21

Subsidiary Company S Income Distribution

Unrealized profit in ending inventory .... **(EI) $8,000**	Internally generated net income	$ 75,000
	Adjusted income	$ 67,000
	NCI share	× 20%
	NCI	$ 13,400

Parent Company P Income Distribution

	Internally generated net income	$100,000
	80% × Company S adjusted income of $67,000	53,600
	Controlling interest	$153,600

Worksheet 4-3

Intercompany Goods in Beginning and Ending Inventories
Company P and Subsidiary Company S
Worksheet for Consolidated Financial Statements
For Year Ended December 31, **20X2**

	(Credit balance amounts are in parentheses.)	Trial Balance	
		Company P	Company S
1	Accounts Receivable	160,000	170,000
2	**Inventory, December 31, 20X2**	**60,000**	**50,000**
3	Investment in Company S	244,000	
4			
5	Other Assets	354,000	165,000
6	Accounts Payable	(90,000)	(80,000)
7	Common Stock ($10 par), Company P	(200,000)	
8	**Retained Earnings, January 1, 20X2, Company P**	**(410,000)**	
9	Common Stock ($10 par), Company S		(100,000)
10	**Retained Earnings, January 1, 20X2, Company S**		**(145,000)**
11			
12	Sales	(800,000)	(600,000)
13	**Cost of Goods Sold**	**610,000**	**440,000**
14			
15	Expenses	120,000	100,000
16	Subsidiary Income	(48,000)	
17		0	0
18	Consolidated Net Income		
19	To NCI (see distribution schedule)		
20	Balance to Controlling Interest (see distribution schedule)		
21	Total NCI		
22	Retained Earnings, Controlling Interest, December 31, 20X2		
23			

Eliminations and Adjustments:

(CY1)   Eliminate the entry recording the parent's share of subsidiary net income.
(EL)   Eliminate 80% of the subsidiary equity balances against the investment in Company S account. There is no excess of cost or book value in this example.
(BI)   Eliminate the intercompany profit of $8,000 (20% × $40,000) in the beginning inventory by reducing both the cost of goods sold and the beginning retained earnings accounts. 20% of the decrease in retained earnings is shared by the noncontrolling interest, since, in this case, the *selling company was the subsidiary*. If the parent had been the seller, only the controlling interest in retained earnings would be decreased. It should be noted that the $8,000 profit is shifted from 20X1 to 20X2, since, as a result of the entry, the 20X2 consolidated cost of goods sold balance is reduced by $8,000. This procedure emphasizes the concept that intercompany inventory profit is not eliminated but only deferred until inventory is sold to an outsider.
(IS)   Eliminate the intercompany sales to avoid double counting.
(EI)   Eliminate the intercompany profit of $6,000 (20% × $30,000) recorded by Company S for the intercompany goods contained in Company P's ending inventory, and increase the cost of goods sold balance by this same amount.
(IA)   Eliminate the intercompany trade balances.

Worksheet 4-3 (see page 187)

Eliminations & Adjustments				Consolidated Income Statement	NCI	Controlling Retained Earnings	Consolidated Balance Sheet	
Dr.		Cr.						
		(IA)	60,000				270,000	1
		(EI)	**6,000**				104,000	2
		(CY1)	48,000					3
		(EL)	196,000					4
							519,000	5
(IA)	60,000						(110,000)	6
							(200,000)	7
(BI)	**6,400**					(403,600)		8
(EL)	80,000				(20,000)			9
(EL)	116,000							10
(BI)	**1,600**				(27,400)			11
(IS)	120,000			(1,280,000)				12
(EI)	**6,000**	**(BI)**	**8,000**					13
		(IS)	120,000	928,000				14
				220,000				15
(CY1)	48,000							16
	438,000		438,000					17
				(132,000)				18
				12,400	(12,400)			19
				119,600		(119,600)		20
					(59,800)		(59,800)	21
						(523,200)	(523,200)	22
							0	23

Subsidiary Company S Income Distribution

Unrealized profit in ending inventory, 20% × $30,000 . . . .**(EI)**	**$6,000**	Internally generated net income	$ 60,000
		Realized profit in beginning inventory, 20% × $40,000 . . . .**(BI)**	**8,000**
		Adjusted income	$ 62,000
		NCI share	× 20%
		NCI	$ 12,400

Parent Company P Income Distribution

Internally generated net income.	$ 70,000
80% × Company S adjusted income of $62,000	49,600
Controlling interest.	$119,600

Worksheet 4-4

Intercompany Goods in Beginning and Ending Inventories; Periodic Inventory
Company P and Subsidiary Company S
Worksheet for Consolidated Financial Statements
For Year Ended December 31, **20X2**

	(Credit balance amounts are in parentheses.)	Trial Balance	
		Company P	Company S
1	Accounts Receivable	160,000	170,000
2	**Inventory, January 1, 20X2**	**70,000**	**40,000**
3	Investment in Company S	244,000	
4			
5	Other Assets	354,000	165,000
6	Accounts Payable	(90,000)	(80,000)
7	Common Stock ($10 par), Company P	(200,000)	
8	**Retained Earnings, January 1, 20X2, Company P**	**(410,000)**	
9	Common Stock ($10 par), Company S		(100,000)
10	**Retained Earnings, January 1, 20X2, Company S**		**(145,000)**
11			
12	Sales	(800,000)	(600,000)
13	**Purchases**	**600,000**	**450,000**
14	**Inventory, December 31, 20X2: Asset**	**60,000**	**50,000**
15	**Cost of Goods Sold**	**(60,000)**	**(50,000)**
16	Expenses	120,000	100,000
17	Subsidiary Income	(48,000)	
18		0	0
19	Consolidated Net Income		
20	To NCI (see distribution schedule)		
21	Balance to Controlling Interest (see distribution schedule)		
22	Total NCI		
23	Retained Earnings, Controlling Interest, December 31, 20X2		
24			

Eliminations and Adjustments:

(CY1)   Eliminate the entry recording the parent's share of subsidiary net income.

(EL)   Eliminate 80% of the subsidiary equity balances against the investment in Company S account. There is no excess of cost or book value in this example.

(BI)   Eliminate the intercompany profit of $8,000 (20% × $40,000) in the beginning inventory by reducing both the cost of goods sold and the beginning retained earnings accounts. 20% of the decrease in retained earnings is shared by the noncontrolling interest, since, in this case, the *selling company was the subsidiary*. If the parent had been the seller, only the controlling interest in retained earnings would be decreased. It should be noted that the $8,000 profit is shifted from 20X1 to 20X2, since, as a result of the entry, the 20X2 consolidated cost of goods sold balance is reduced by $8,000. This procedure emphasizes the concept that intercompany inventory profit is not eliminated but only deferred until inventory is sold to an outsider.

(IS)   Eliminate the intercompany sales to avoid double counting.

(EI)   Enter the combined ending inventories of Company P and Company S, $60,000 and $50,000, respectively, less the intercompany profit of $6,000 (20% × $30,000) recorded by Company S for the intercompany goods contained in Company P's ending inventory.

(IA)   Eliminate the intercompany trade balances.

Worksheet 4-4 (see page 188)

Eliminations & Adjustments				Consolidated Income Statement	NCI	Controlling Retained Earnings	Consolidated Balance Sheet	
Dr.		Cr.						
		(IA)	60,000				270,000	1
		(BI)	**8,000**	102,000				2
		(CY1)	48,000					3
		(EL)	196,000					4
							519,000	5
(IA)	60,000						(110,000)	6
							(200,000)	7
(BI)	**6,400**					(403,600)		8
(EL)	80,000				(20,000)			9
(EL)	116,000							10
(BI)	**1,600**				(27,400)			11
(IS)	120,000			(1,280,000)				12
		(IS)	120,000	930,000				13
		(EI)	6,000				104,000	14
(EI)	6,000			(104,000)				15
				220,000				16
(CY1)	48,000							17
	438,000		438,000					18
				(132,000)				19
				12,400	(12,400)			20
				119,600		(119,600)		21
					(59,800)		(59,800)	22
						(523,200)	(523,200)	23
							0	24

Subsidiary Company S Income Distribution

Unrealized profit in ending inventory, 20% × $30,000 .... **(EI) $6,000**	Internally generated net income	$ 60,000[a]	
	Realized profit in beginning inventory, 20% × $40,000 .... **(BI)**	**8,000**	
	Adjusted income	$ 62,000	
	NCI share	× 20%	
	NCI	$ 12,400	

[a][$600,000 − ($40,000 + $450,000 − $50,000) − $100,000 = $60,000]

Parent Company P Income Distribution

Internally generated net income	$ 70,000[b]
80% × Company S adjusted income of $62,000	49,600
Controlling interest	$119,600

[b][$800,000 − ($70,000 + $600,000 − $60,000) − $120,000 = $70,000]

Worksheet 4-5

Intercompany Sale of Depreciable Asset
Company P and Subsidiary Company S
Worksheet for Consolidated Financial Statements
For Year Ended December 31, **20X1**

	(Credit balance amounts are in parentheses.)	Trial Balance			
		Company P		Company S	
1	Current Assets	15,000			20,000
2	**Machinery**	50,000	(a)		230,000
3	**Accumulated Depreciation—Machinery**	(25,000)	(b)		(100,000)
4	Investment in Company S	120,000			
5					
6	Common Stock ($10 par), Company P	(100,000)			
7	Retained Earnings, January 1, 20X1, Company P	(10,000)			
8	Common Stock ($10 par), Company S				(50,000)
9	Retained Earnings, January 1, 20X1, Company S				(75,000)
10	Sales	(200,000)			(100,000)
11	Cost of Goods Sold	150,000			59,000
12	**Depreciation Expense**	30,000	(b)		16,000
13	**Gain on Sale of Machine**	(10,000)			
14	Subsidiary Income	(20,000)			
15		0			0
16	Consolidated Net Income				
17	To NCI (see distribution schedule)				
18	Balance to Controlling Interest (see distribution schedule)				
19	Total NCI				
20	Retained Earnings, Controlling Interest, December 31, 20X1				
21					

Notes to Trial Balance:

(a)   Includes machine purchased for $30,000 from Company P on January 1, 20X1.
(b)   Includes $6,000 depreciation on machine purchased from Company P on January 1, 20X1.

Eliminations and Adjustments:

(CY1)   Eliminate the entry recording the parent's share of subsidiary net income for the current year.
(EL)   Eliminate 80% of the subsidiary equity balances against the investment account. There is no excess to be distributed.
(F1)   Eliminate the $10,000 gain on the intercompany sale of the machine, and reduce machine to book value.
(F2)   Reduce the depreciation expense and accumulated depreciation accounts to reflect the depreciation ($4,000 per year) based on the consolidated book value of the machine, rather than the depreciation ($6,000 per year) based on the sales price.

Worksheet 4-5 (see page 192)

Eliminations & Adjustments		Consolidated Income Statement	NCI	Controlling Retained Earnings	Consolidated Balance Sheet	
Dr.	Cr.					
					35,000	1
	(F1) 10,000				270,000	2
(F2) 2,000					(123,000)	3
	(CY1) 20,000					4
	(EL) 100,000					5
					(100,000)	6
				(10,000)		7
(EL) 40,000			(10,000)			8
(EL) 60,000			(15,000)			9
		(300,000)				10
		209,000				11
	(F2) 2,000	44,000				12
(F1) 10,000						13
(CY1) 20,000						14
132,000	132,000					15
		(47,000)				16
		5,000	(5,000)			17
		42,000		(42,000)		18
			(30,000)		(30,000)	19
				(52,000)	(52,000)	20
					0	21

Subsidiary Company S Income Distribution

Internally generated net income	$25,000
Adjusted income	$25,000
NCI share	× 20%
NCI	$ 5,000

Parent Company P Income Distribution

Unrealized gain on sale of machine ....(F1) **$10,000**	Internally generated net income (including sale of machine) $30,000
	80% × Company S adjusted income of $25,000 20,000
	Gain realized through use of machine sold to subsidiary .... (F2) **2,000**
	Controlling interest $42,000

Worksheet 4-6

Intercompany Sale of Depreciable Asset
Company P and Subsidiary Company S
Worksheet for Consolidated Financial Statements
For Year Ended December 31, **20X2**

	(Credit balance amounts are in parentheses.)	Trial Balance			
		Company P		Company S	
1	Current Assets	85,000			60,000
2	**Machinery**	50,000	(a)		230,000
3	**Accumulated Depreciation—Machinery**	(45,000)	(b)		(116,000)
4					
5	Investment in Company S	139,200			
6					
7	Common Stock ($10 par), Company P	(100,000)			
8	**Retained Earnings, January 1, 20X2, Company P**	**(60,000)**			
9	Common Stock ($10 par), Company S				(50,000)
10	Retained Earnings, January 1, 20X2, Company S				(100,000)
11	Sales	(250,000)			(120,000)
12	**Cost of Goods Sold**	180,000			80,000
13	**Depreciation Expense**	20,000	(c)		16,000
14	Subsidiary Income	(19,200)			
15		0			0
16	Consolidated Net Income				
17	To NCI (see distribution schedule)				
18	Balance to Controlling Interest (see distribution schedule)				
19	Total NCI				
20	Retained Earnings, Controlling Interest, December 31, 20X2				
21					

Notes to Trial Balance:

(a)   Includes machine purchased for $30,000 from Company P on January 1, 20X1.
(b)   Includes $12,000 accumulated depreciation ($6,000 per year) on machine purchased from Company P on January 1, 20X1.
(c)   Includes $6,000 depreciation on machine purchased from Company P on January 1, 20X1.

Eliminations and Adjustments:

(CY1)   Eliminate the entry recording the parent's share of subsidiary net income for the current year.
(EL)   Eliminate 80% of the subsidiary equity balances against the investment account. There is no excess to be distributed.
(F1)   Eliminate the gain on the intercompany sale as it is reflected in beginning retained earnings on the parent's trial balance. Since the sale was made by the parent, Company P, the entire unrealized gain at the beginning of the year (now $8,000) is removed from the controlling retained earnings beginning balance. If the sale had been made by the subsidiary, the adjustment of beginning retained earnings would be split 80% to the controlling interest and 20% to the noncontrolling interest.
(F2)   Reduce the depreciation expense and accumulated depreciation accounts to reflect the depreciation based on the consolidated book value of the asset on the date of sale. This entry will bring the accumulated depreciation account to its correct consolidated year-end balance.

Worksheet 4-6 (see page 193)

Eliminations & Adjustments		Consolidated Income Statement	NCI	Controlling Retained Earnings	Consolidated Balance Sheet	
Dr.	Cr.					
					145,000	1
	(F1) 10,000				270,000	2
(F1) 2,000					(157,000)	3
(F2) 2,000						4
	(CY1) 19,200					5
	(EL) 120,000					6
					(100,000)	7
(F1) 8,000				(52,000)		8
(EL) 40,000			(10,000)			9
(EL) 80,000			(20,000)			10
		(370,000)				11
		260,000				12
	(F2) 2,000	34,000				13
(CY1) 19,200						14
151,200	151,200					15
		(76,000)				16
		4,800	(4,800)			17
		71,200		(71,200)		18
			(34,800)		(34,800)	19
				(123,200)	(123,200)	20
					0	21

Subsidiary Company S Income Distribution

Internally generated net income	$ 24,000
Adjusted income	$ 24,000
NCI share	× 20%
NCI	$ 4,800

Parent Company P Income Distribution

Internally generated net income	$50,000
80% of Company S adjusted income of $24,000	19,200
Gain realized through use of machine sold to subsidiary . . . . **(F2)**	**2,000**
Controlling interest	$71,200

Worksheet 4-7

Intercompany Notes
Company P and Subsidiary Company S
Worksheet for Consolidated Financial Statements
For Year Ended December 31, **20X1**

	(Credit balance amounts are in parentheses.)	Trial Balance	
		Company P	Company S
1	Cash	35,000	20,400
2	**Note Receivable from Company S**	**10,000**	
3	**Interest Receivable**	**400**	
4	Property, Plant, and Equipment (net)	140,000	150,000
5	Investment in Company S	128,000	
6			
7	**Note Payable to Company P**		**(10,000)**
8	**Interest Payable**		**(400)**
9	Common Stock, Company P	(100,000)	
10	Retained Earnings, January 1, 20X1, Company P	(200,000)	
11	Common Stock, Company S		(50,000)
12	Retained Earnings, January 1, 20X1, Company S		(100,000)
13	Sales	(120,000)	(50,000)
14	**Interest Income**	**(400)**	
15	Subsidiary Income	(8,000)	
16	Cost of Goods Sold	75,000	20,000
17	Other Expenses	40,000	19,600
18	**Interest Expense**		**400**
19		0	0
20	Consolidated Net Income		
21	To NCI (see distribution schedule)		
22	Balance to Controlling Interest (see distribution schedule)		
23	Total NCI		
24	Retained Earnings, Controlling Interest, December 31, 20X5		
25			

Eliminations and Adjustments:

(CY1)   Eliminate the parent's share (80%) of subsidiary net income.
(EL)   Eliminate the controlling portion (80%) of the Company S January 1, 20X1, stockholders' equity against the investment in Company S account. No excess results.
(LN1)   Eliminate the intercompany note and accrued interest applicable to the note. This entry removes the internal note from the consolidated balance sheet.
(LN2)   Eliminate the intercompany interest expense and revenue. Since an equal amount of expense and revenue is eliminated, there is no change in the combined net income as a result of this entry.

Worksheet 4-7 (see page 194)

Eliminations & Adjustments		Consolidated Income Statement	NCI	Controlling Retained Earnings	Consolidated Balance Sheet	
Dr.	Cr.					
					55,400	1
	(LN1) 10,000					2
	(LN1) 400					3
					290,000	4
	(CY1) 8,000					5
	(EL) 120,000					6
(LN1) 10,000						7
(LN1) 400						8
					(100,000)	9
				(200,000)		10
(EL) 40,000			(10,000)			11
(EL) 80,000			(20,000)			12
		(170,000)				13
(LN2) 400						14
(CY1) 8,000						15
		95,000				16
		59,600				17
	(LN2) 400					18
138,800	138,800					19
		(15,400)				20
		2,000	(2,000)			21
		13,400		(13,400)		22
			(32,000)		(32,000)	23
				(213,400)	(213,400)	24
					0	25

Subsidiary Company S Income Distribution

Internally generated net income	$ 10,000
Adjusted income	$ 10,000
NCI share	× 20%
NCI	$ 2,000

Parent Company P Income Distribution

Internally generated net income	$ 5,400
80% × Company S adjusted income of $10,000	8,000
Controlling interest	$13,400

UNDERSTANDING THE ISSUES

1. During 20X1, Company P sold $40,000 of goods to subsidiary Company S at a profit of $10,000. One-fourth of the goods remain unsold at year-end. If there were no adjustments made on the consolidated worksheet, what would be incorrect on the consolidated income statement and balance sheet?

2. During 20X1, Company P sold $40,000 of goods to subsidiary Company S at a profit of $10,000. One-fourth of the goods remain unsold at year-end. What specific procedures are needed on the consolidated worksheet to deal with these issues?

3. Company S is 80% owned by Company P. Near the end of 20X1, Company S sold merchandise with a cost of $4,000 to Company P for $6,000. Company P sold the merchandise to a nonaffiliated firm in 20X2 for $10,000. How much total profit should be recorded on the consolidated income statements in 20X1 and 20X2? How much profit should be awarded to the controlling and noncontrolling interests in 20X1 and 20X2?

4. Subsidiary Company S is 80% owned by Company P. Company S sold a machine with a book value of $100,000 to Company P for $150,000. The asset has a five-year life and is depreciated under the straight-line method. The president of Company S thinks it has scored a $50,000 immediate profit for the noncontrolling interest. Explain how much profit the noncontrolling interest will realize and when it will be awarded.

5. Company S is an 80%-owned subsidiary of Company P. Company S needed to borrow $500,000 on January 1, 20X1. The best interest rate it could secure was 10% annual. Company P has a better credit rating and decided to borrow the funds needed from a bank at 8% annual and then loaned the money to Company S at 9.5% annual.

   a. Is Company S better off as a result of borrowing the funds from Company P?
   b. What are the interest revenue and expense amounts recorded by Company P and Company S during 20X2?
   c. How much interest expense and/or interest revenue should appear in the 20X1 consolidated income statement?

EXERCISES

Exercise 4-1 *(LO 1, 2)* **Gross profit: separate firms versus consolidated.** Solvent is an 80%-owned subsidiary of Painter Company. The two affiliates had the following separate income statements for 20X1 and 20X2:

	Solvent Company		Painter Company	
	20X1	20X2	20X1	20X2
Sales revenue	$250,000	$300,000	$500,000	$540,000
Cost of goods sold	150,000	180,000	310,000	360,000
Gross profit	$100,000	$120,000	$190,000	$180,000
Expenses	45,000	56,000	120,000	125,000
Net income	$ 55,000	$ 64,000	$ 70,000	$ 55,000

Solvent sells at the same gross profit percentage to all customers. During 20X1, Solvent sold goods to Painter for the first time in the amount of $100,000. $20,000 of these sales remained in Painter's ending inventory. During 20X2, sales to Painter by Solvent were $110,000, of which $30,000 of sales were still in Painter's December 31, 20X2, inventory.

Prepare consolidated income statements including the distribution of income to the controlling and noncontrolling interests for 20X1 and 20X2.

Exercise 4-2 *(LO 2)* Inventory profits with lower-of-cost-or-market adjustment.

Hide Corporation is a wholly owned subsidiary of Seek Company. During 20X1, Hide sold all of its production to Seek Company for $400,000, a price that includes a 20% gross profit. 20X1 is the first year that such intercompany sales were made. By year-end, Seek sold 80% of the goods it had purchased for $416,000. The balance of the intercompany goods, $80,000, remained in the ending inventory and was adjusted to a lower fair value of $70,000. The adjustment was a charge to the cost of goods sold.

1. Determine the gross profit on sales recorded by both companies.
2. Determine the gross profit to be shown on the consolidated income statement.

Exercise 4-3 *(LO 2)* Distribution of income with inventory profits.
Nick Company is an 80%-owned subsidiary of Van Corporation. The separate income statements of the two companies for 20X2 are as follows:

	Van Corporation	Nick Company
Sales	$ 220,000	$120,000
Cost of goods sold	(150,000)	(90,000)
Gross profit	$ 70,000	$ 30,000
Other expenses	(40,000)	(12,000)
Other income	5,000	
Operating income	$ 35,000	$ 18,000
Subsidiary income	14,400	
Net income	$ 49,400	$ 18,000

The following facts apply to 20X2:

a. Nick Company sold $70,000 of goods to Van Corporation. The gross profits on sales to Van and to unrelated companies are equal and have not changed from the previous years.
b. Van Corporation held $15,000 of the goods purchased from Nick Company in its beginning inventory and $20,000 of such goods in ending inventory.
c. Van Corporation billed Nick Company $5,000 for computer services. The charge was expensed by Nick Company and treated as other income by Van Corporation.

Prepare the consolidated income statement for 20X2, including the distribution of the consolidated net income to the controlling and noncontrolling interests. The supporting income distribution schedules should be prepared as well.

Exercise 4-4 *(LO 3)* Machinery sale.
On January 1, 20X2, Jungle Company sold a machine to Safari Company for $30,000. The machine had an original cost of $24,000, and accumulated depreciation on the asset was $9,000 at the time of the sale. The machine has a five-year remaining life and will be depreciated on a straight-line basis with no salvage value. Safari Company is an 80%-owned subsidiary of Jungle Company.

1. Explain the adjustments that would have to be made to arrive at consolidated net income for the years 20X2 through 20X6 as a result of this sale.
2. Prepare the elimination that would be required on the December 31, 20X2, consolidated worksheet as a result of this sale.
3. Prepare the entry for the December 31, 20X3, worksheet as a result of this sale.

Exercise 4-5 *(LO 3)* Land and building profit.
Wavemasters Inc. owns an 80% interest in Sayner Development Company. In a prior period, Sayner Development purchased a parcel of land for $50,000. During 20X1, it constructed a building on the land at a cost of $500,000. The land

and building were sold to Wavemasters at the very end of 20X1 for $750,000, of which $100,000 was for the land. It is estimated that the building has a 20-year life with no salvage value.

1. Prepare all worksheet eliminations that would be made on the 20X1 consolidated worksheet as a result of the real estate sale.
2. Prepare all worksheet eliminations that would be made on the 20X3 consolidated worksheet as a result of the 20X1 real estate sale.

Exercise 4-6 *(LO 3)* **Fixed asset sales by parent and subsidiary.** The separate income statements of Dark Company and its 90%-owned subsidiary, Light Company, for the year ended December 31, 20X2, are as follows:

	Dark Company	Light Company
Sales	$ 700,000	$ 280,000
Cost of goods sold	(450,000)	(190,000)
Gross profit	$ 250,000	$ 90,000
Other expenses	(180,000)	(70,000)
Other income	20,000	
Operating income	$ 90,000	$ 20,000
Subsidiary income	18,000	
Net income	$ 108,000	$ 20,000

The following additional facts apply:

a. On January 1, 20X1, Light Company purchased a building, with a book value of $100,000 and an estimated 20-year life, from Dark Company for $180,000. The building was being depreciated on a straight-line basis with no salvage value.
b. On January 1, 20X2, Light Company sold a machine with a book value of $50,000 to Dark Company for $60,000. The machine had an expected life of five years and is being depreciated on a straight-line basis with no salvage value. Light Company is a dealer for the machine.

Prepare the December 31, 20X2, consolidated income statement and supporting income distribution schedules.

Exercise 4-7 *(LO 2, 3)* **Merchandise and fixed asset sale.** Peninsula Company owns an 80% controlling interest in Sandbar Company. Sandbar regularly sells merchandise to Peninsula, which then sells to outside parties. The gross profit on all such sales is 40%. On January 1, 20X1, Peninsula sold land and a building to Sandbar. Tax assessments divide the value of the parcel 20% to land and 80% to structures. Pertinent information for the companies is summarized as follows:

	Peninsula	Sandbar
Internally generated net income, 20X1	$520,000	$250,000
Internally generated net income, 20X2	340,000	235,000
Intercompany merchandise sales, 20X1		100,000
Intercompany merchandise sales, 20X2		120,000
Intercompany inventory, December 31, 20X1		15,000
Intercompany inventory, December 31, 20X2		20,000
Cost of real estate sold on January 1, 20X1	600,000	
Sale price for real estate on January 1, 20X1	800,000	
Depreciable life of building		20 years

Prepare income distribution schedules for 20X1 and 20X2 for Peninsula and Sandbar as they would be prepared to distribute income to the noncontrolling and controlling interests in support of consolidated worksheets.

Exercise 4-8 *(LO 4)* **Intercompany note.** Saratoga Company owns 80% of the outstanding common stock of Windsor Company. On May 1, 20X3, Windsor Company arranged a one-year, $50,000 loan from Saratoga Company. The loan agreement specified that interest would accrue at the rate of 6% per annum and that all interest would be paid on the maturity date of the loan. The financial reporting period ends on December 31, 20X3, and the note originating from the loan remains outstanding.

1. Prepare the entries that both companies would have made on their separate books, including the accrual of interest.
2. Prepare the eliminations, in entry form, that would be made on a consolidated worksheet prepared as of December 31, 20X3.

Exercise 4-9 *(LO 4)* **Intercompany note discounted.** Assume the same facts as in Exercise 4-8, but in addition, assume that Saratoga was itself in need of cash. It discounted the note received from Windsor at the First Bank on July 1, 20X3, at a discount rate of 8% per annum.

1. Prepare the entries that both companies would make on their separate books, including interest accruals.
2. Prepare the eliminations, in entry form, that would be made on a consolidated worksheet prepared as of December 31, 20X3.

PROBLEMS

Problem 4-1 *(LO 2)* **100%, equity, ending inventory.** On January 1, 20X1, 100% of the outstanding stock of Solid Company was purchased by Plaid Corporation for $3,200,000. At that time, the book value of Solid's net assets was $2,800,000. The excess is attributable to equipment with a 10-year life.

The following trial balances of Plaid Corporation and Solid Company were prepared on December 31, 20X1:

	Plaid Corporation	Solid Company
Cash	810,000	170,000
Accounts Receivable	425,000	365,000
Inventory	600,000	275,000
Property, Plant, and Equipment (net)	4,000,000	2,300,000
Investment in Solid Company	3,410,000	
Accounts Payable	(35,000)	(100,000)
Common Stock ($10 par)	(1,000,000)	(400,000)
Paid-In Capital in Excess of Par	(1,500,000)	(200,000)
Retained Earnings, January 1, 20X1	(5,500,000)	(2,200,000)
Sales	(12,000,000)	(1,000,000)
Cost of Goods Sold	7,000,000	750,000
Other Expenses	4,000,000	40,000
Subsidiary Income	(210,000)	
Total	0	0

Throughout 20X1, sales to Plaid Corporation made up 40% of Solid's revenue and produced a 30% gross profit rate. At year-end, Plaid Corporation had sold $300,000 of the goods purchased from Solid Company and still owed Solid $25,000. None of the Solid products were in Plaid's January 1, 20X1, beginning inventory.

Prepare the worksheet necessary to produce the consolidated income statement and balance ◄ ◄ ◄ ◄ ◄ **Required** sheet of Plaid Corporation and its subsidiary for the year ended December 31, 20X1. Include the determination and distribution of excess schedule.

Problem 4-2 *(LO 2)* **80%, cost, beginning and ending inventory.** On April 1, 20X1, Baxter Corporation purchased 80% of the outstanding stock of Crystal Company for $425,000. A condensed balance sheet of Crystal Company at the purchase date follows:

Assets		Liabilities and Equity	
Current assets	$180,000	Liabilities	$100,000
Long-lived assets (net)	320,000	Equity.	400,000
Total assets.	$500,000	Total liabilities and equity	$500,000

All book values approximated fair values on the purchase date. Any excess cost is attributed to goodwill.

The following information has been gathered pertaining to the first two years of operation since Baxter's purchase of Crystal Company stock:

a. Intercompany merchandise sales are summarized as follows:

Date	Transaction	Sales	Gross Profit	Merchandise Remaining in Purchaser's Ending Inventory
April 1, 20X1 to	Baxter to Crystal	$35,000	15%	$9,000
March 31, 20X2	Crystal to Baxter	20,000	20	3,500
April 1, 20X2 to	Baxter to Crystal	32,000	22	6,000
March 31, 20X3	Crystal to Baxter	30,000	25	3,000

b. On March 31, 20X3, Baxter owed Crystal $10,000, and Crystal owed Baxter $5,000 as a result of the intercompany sales.

c. Baxter paid $25,000 in cash dividends on March 20, 20X2 and 20X3. Crystal paid its first cash dividend on March 10, 20X3, giving each share of outstanding common stock a $0.15 cash dividend.

d. The trial balances of the two companies as of March 31, 20X3, follow:

	Baxter Corporation	Crystal Company
Cash	216,200	44,300
Accounts Receivable (net)	290,000	97,000
Inventory	310,000	80,000
Investment in Crystal Company	425,000	
Land.	1,081,000	150,000
Building and Equipment	1,850,000	400,000
Accumulated Depreciation	(940,000)	(210,000)
Goodwill	60,000	
Accounts Payable	(242,200)	(106,300)
Bonds Payable.	(400,000)	
Common Stock ($0.50 par)	(250,000)	
Common Stock ($1 par)		(200,000)
Paid-In Capital in Excess of Par	(1,250,000)	(100,000)
Retained Earnings, April 1, 20X2	(1,105,000)	(140,000)
Sales	(880,000)	(630,000)
Dividend Income (from Crystal Company)	(24,000)	
Cost of Goods Sold	704,000	504,000
Other Expenses	130,000	81,000
Dividends Declared.	25,000	30,000
Total	0	0

1. Prepare the worksheet necessary to produce the consolidated financial statements of Baxter ◀ ◀ ◀ ◀ ◀ **Required**
   Corporation and its subsidiary for the year ended March 31, 20X3. Include the determination and distribution of excess schedule and the income distribution schedules.

2. Prepare the formal consolidated income statement for the fiscal year 20X2–20X3.

Use the following information for Problems 4-3 and 4-4:

On January 1, 20X1, Panther Corporation acquired 70% of the common stock of Spider Corporation for $350,000. On this date, Spider had the following balance sheet:

Spider Corporation
Balance Sheet
January 1, 20X1

Assets		Liabilities and Equity	
Accounts receivable	$ 60,000	Accounts payable	$ 40,000
Inventory	40,000	Bonds payable	100,000
Land	60,000	Common stock, $1 par	10,000
Buildings	200,000	Paid-in capital in excess of par .	90,000
Accumulated depreciation	(50,000)	Retained earnings	112,000
Equipment	72,000		
Accumulated depreciation	(30,000)		
Total assets	$352,000	Total liabilities and equity . . .	$352,000

Buildings, which have a 20-year life, are understated by $150,000. Equipment, which has a 5-year life, is understated by $58,000. Any remaining excess is considered to be goodwill. Panther uses the simple equity method to account for its investment in Spider.

Panther and Spider had the following trial balances on December 31, 20X2:

	Panther Corporation	Spider Corporation
Cash	116,000	132,000
Accounts Receivable	90,000	45,000
Inventory	120,000	56,000
Land	100,000	60,000
Investment in Spider	378,000	
Buildings	800,000	200,000
Accumulated Depreciation	(220,000)	(65,000)
Equipment	150,000	72,000
Accumulated Depreciation	(90,000)	(46,000)
Accounts Payable	(60,000)	(102,000)
Bonds Payable		(100,000)
Common Stock	(100,000)	(10,000)
Paid-In Capital in Excess of Par	(800,000)	(90,000)
Retained Earnings, January 1, 20X2	(325,000)	(142,000)
Sales	(800,000)	(350,000)
Cost of Goods Sold	450,000	208,500
Depreciation Expense—Buildings	30,000	7,500
Depreciation Expense—Equipment	15,000	8,000
Other Expenses	140,000	98,000
Interest Expense		8,000
Subsidiary Income	(14,000)	
Dividends Declared	20,000	10,000
Totals	0	0

Problem 4-3 *(LO 2)* **70%, equity, beginning and ending inventory, subsidiary seller.** Refer to the preceding facts for Panther's acquisition of Spider common stock. On January 1, 20X2, Panther held merchandise acquired from Spider for $8,000. This beginning inventory had an applicable gross profit of 25%. During 20X2, Spider sold $30,000 worth of merchandise to Panther. Panther held $6,000 of this merchandise at December 31, 20X2. This ending inventory had an applicable gross profit of 30%. Panther owed Spider $6,000 on December 31 as a result of these intercompany sales.

Required ▶ ▶ ▶ ▶ ▶

1. Prepare a zone analysis and a determination and distribution of excess schedule for the investment in Spider.
2. Complete a consolidated worksheet for Panther Corporation and its subsidiary Spider Corporation as of December 31, 20X2. Prepare supporting amortization and income distribution schedules.

Problem 4-4 *(LO 2)* **70%, equity, beginning and ending inventory, parent and subsidiary seller.** Refer to the preceding facts for Panther's acquisition of Spider common stock. On January 1, 20X2, Panther held merchandise acquired from Spider for $10,000. This beginning inventory had an applicable gross profit of 25%. During 20X2, Spider sold $40,000 worth of merchandise to Panther. Panther held $6,000 of this merchandise at December 31, 20X2. This ending inventory had an applicable gross profit of 30%. Panther owed Spider $11,000 on December 31 as a result of this intercompany sale.

On January 1, 20X2, Spider held merchandise acquired from Panther for $15,000. This beginning inventory had an applicable gross profit of 40%. During 20X2, Panther sold $60,000 worth of merchandise to Spider. Spider held $22,000 of this merchandise at December 31, 20X2. This ending inventory had an applicable gross profit of 35%. Spider owed Panther $12,000 on December 31 as a result of this intercompany sale.

Required ▶ ▶ ▶ ▶ ▶

1. Prepare a zone analysis and a determination and distribution of excess schedule for the investment in Spider.
2. Complete a consolidated worksheet for Panther Corporation and its subsidiary Spider Corporation as of December 31, 20X2. Prepare supporting amortization and income distribution schedules.

Problem 4-5 *(LO 2)* **80%, equity, beginning and ending inventory, write-down, note.** On January 1, 20X1, Silvio Corporation exchanged on a 1-for-3 basis common stock it held in its treasury for 80% of the outstanding stock of Jenkins Company. Silvio Corporation common stock had a market price of $40 per share on the exchange date.

On the date of the acquisition, the stockholders' equity section of Jenkins Company was as follows:

Common stock ($5 par)	$ 450,000
Paid-in capital in excess of par	180,000
Retained earnings	370,000
Total	$1,000,000

Also on that date, Jenkins Company's book values approximated fair values, except for the land, which was undervalued by $75,000. The remaining excess is attributable to goodwill.

Information regarding intercompany transactions for 20X3 follows:

a. Silvio Corporation sells merchandise to Jenkins Company, realizing a 30% gross profit. Sales during 20X3 were $140,000. Jenkins had $25,000 of the 20X2 purchases in its beginning inventory for 20X3 and $35,000 of the 20X3 purchases in its ending inventory for 20X3.

b. Jenkins signed a 12%, four-month, $10,000 note to Silvio in order to cover the remaining balance of its payables on November 1, 20X3. No new merchandise was purchased after this date.

c. Jenkins wrote down to $28,000 the merchandise purchased from Silvio Corporation and remaining in its 20X3 ending inventory.

The trial balances of Silvio Corporation and Jenkins Company as of December 31, 20X3, are as follows:

	Silvio Corporation	Jenkins Company
Cash	140,000	205,200
Accounts Receivable	285,000	110,000
Interest Receivable	1,500	
Notes Receivable	50,000	
Inventory	470,000	160,000
Land	350,000	300,000
Depreciable Fixed Assets	1,110,000	810,000
Accumulated Depreciation	(500,000)	(200,000)
Intangibles	60,000	
Investment in Jenkins Company	1,128,000	
Accounts Payable	(611,500)	(175,000)
Interest Payable		(200)
Common Stock ($1 par)	(400,000)	
Common Stock ($5 par)		(450,000)
Paid-In Capital in Excess of Par	(1,235,000)	(180,000)
Retained Earnings, January 1, 20X3	(958,500)	(470,000)
Treasury Stock (at cost)	315,000	
Sales	(1,020,000)	(500,000)
Interest Income	(1,500)	
Subsidiary Income	(88,000)	
Cost of Goods Sold	705,000	300,000
Other Expenses	200,000	90,000
Totals	0	0

Prepare the worksheet necessary to produce the consolidated financial statements of Silvio   ◀ ◀ ◀ ◀ ◀ **Required**
Corporation and its subsidiary for the year ended December 31, 20X3. Include the determination and distribution of excess schedule and the income distribution schedules.

Problem 4-6 *(LO 3)* **80%, equity, fixed asset sales by subsidiary and parent.** On September 1, 20X1, Parcel Corporation purchased 80% of the outstanding common stock of Sack Corporation for $152,000. On that date, Sack's net book values equaled fair values, and there was no excess of cost or book value resulting from the purchase. Parcel has been maintaining its investment under the simple equity method.

Over the next three years, the intercompany transactions between the companies were as follows:

a. On September 1, 20X1, Sack sold its four-year-old delivery truck to Parcel for $14,000 in cash. At that time, Sack had depreciated the truck, which had cost $15,000, to its $5,000 salvage value. Parcel estimated on the date of the sale that the asset had a remaining useful life of three years and no salvage value.

b. On September 1, 20X2, Parcel sold equipment to Sack for $103,000. Parcel originally paid $80,000 for the equipment and planned to depreciate it over 20 years, assuming no salvage value. However, Parcel had the property for only 10 years and carried it at a net book value of $40,000 on the sale date. Sack will use the equipment for 10 years, at which time Sack expects no salvage value.

Both companies use straight-line depreciation for all assets.

Trial balances of Parcel Corporation and Sack Corporation as of the August 31, 20X3, year-end are as follows:

	Parcel Corporation	Sack Corporation
Cash	120,000	50,000
Accounts Receivable (net)	115,000	18,000
Notes Receivable..........................		10,000
Inventory	175,000	34,000
Investment in Sack Corporation......................	217,440	
Plant and Equipment	990,700	295,000
Accumulated Depreciation	(170,000)	(85,000)
Other Assets	28,000	
Accounts Payable	(80,000)	(50,200)
Notes Payable.....................................	(25,000)	
Bonds Payable, 12%.............................	(300,000)	
Common Stock ($10 par)	(290,000)	(70,000)
Paid-In Capital in Excess of Par	(110,000)	(62,000)
Retained Earnings, September 1, 20X2	(498,850)	(118,000)
Sales	(920,000)	(240,000)
Cost of Goods Sold	598,000	132,000
Selling and General Expenses......................	108,000	80,000
Subsidiary Income................................	(23,040)	
Interest Income...................................		(800)
Interest Expense..................................	37,750	
Gain on Sale of Equipment	(63,000)	
Dividends Declared...............................	90,000	7,000
Totals	0	0

Required ▶ ▶ ▶ ▶ ▶   Prepare the worksheet necessary to produce the consolidated financial statements of Parcel Corporation and its subsidiary for the year ended August 31, 20X3. Include the income distribution schedules.

Use the following information for Problems 4-7 and 4-8:
On January 1, 20X1, Polka Company acquired Salsa Company. Polka paid $440,000 for 80% of Salsa's common stock. On the date of acquisition, Salsa had the following balance sheet:

Salsa Company
Balance Sheet
January 1, 20X1

Assets		Liabilities and Equity	
Accounts receivable	$ 60,000	Accounts payable	$ 40,000
Inventory	40,000	Bonds payable	100,000
Land......................	60,000	Common stock, $1 par	10,000
Buildings	200,000	Paid-in capital in excess of par ...	90,000
Accumulated depreciation	(50,000)	Retained earnings	112,000
Equipment	72,000		
Accumulated depreciation	(30,000)		
Total assets...............	$352,000	Total liabilities and equity	$352,000

Buildings, which have a 20-year life, are understated by $100,000. Equipment, which has a five-year life, is understated by $38,000. Any remaining excess is considered goodwill. Polka uses the simple equity method to account for its investment in Salsa.

Polka and Salsa had the following trial balances on December 31, 20X2:

	Polka Company	Salsa Company
Cash	24,000	132,000
Accounts Receivable	90,000	45,000
Inventory	120,000	56,000
Land	100,000	60,000
Investment in Salsa	472,000	
Buildings	800,000	200,000
Accumulated Depreciation	(220,000)	(65,000)
Equipment	150,000	72,000
Accumulated Depreciation	(90,000)	(46,000)
Accounts Payable	(60,000)	(102,000)
Bonds Payable		(100,000)
Common Stock	(100,000)	(10,000)
Paid-In Capital in Excess of Par	(800,000)	(90,000)
Retained Earnings, January 1, 20X2	(325,000)	(142,000)
Sales	(800,000)	(350,000)
Cost of Goods Sold	450,000	208,500
Depreciation Expense—Buildings	30,000	7,500
Depreciation Expense—Equipment	15,000	8,000
Other Expenses	160,000	98,000
Gain on Fixed Asset Sale	(20,000)	
Interest Expense		8,000
Subsidiary Income	(16,000)	
Dividends Declared	20,000	10,000
Totals	0	0

Problem 4-7 *(LO 2, 3)* **80%, equity, several excess distributions, fixed asset sale.**
Refer to the preceding facts for Polka's acquisition of Salsa common stock. On January 1, 20X2, Polka held merchandise sold to it from Salsa for $12,000. This beginning inventory had an applicable gross profit of 25%. During 20X2, Salsa sold merchandise to Polka for $75,000. On December 31, 20X2, Polka held $18,000 of this merchandise in its inventory. This ending inventory had an applicable gross profit of 30%. Polka owed Salsa $20,000 on December 31 as a result of this intercompany sale.

On January 1, 20X2, Polka sold equipment with a book value of $30,000 to Salsa for $50,000. During 20X2, the equipment was used by Salsa. Depreciation is computed over a five-year life, using the straight-line method.

1. Prepare a zone analysis and a determination and distribution of excess schedule for the investment in Salsa.  **◄ ◄ ◄ ◄ ◄ Required**
2. Complete a consolidated worksheet for Polka Company and its subsidiary Salsa Company as of December 31, 20X2. Prepare supporting amortization and income distribution schedules.

Problem 4-8 *(LO 2, 3)* **80%, equity, several excess distributions, fixed asset sale by parent and subsidiary.** Refer to the preceding facts for Polka's acquisition of Salsa common stock. On January 1, 20X2, Salsa held merchandise sold to it from Polka for $20,000. During 20X2, Polka sold merchandise to Salsa for $100,000. On December 31, 20X2, Salsa held $25,000 of this merchandise in its inventory. Polka has a gross profit of 30%. Salsa owed Polka $15,000 on December 31 as a result of this intercompany sale.

On January 1, 20X1, Salsa sold equipment to Polka at a profit of $30,000. Depreciation is computed over a six-year life, using the straight-line method. The gain shown for 20X2 is on sales to outside parties.

Required ▶ ▶ ▶ ▶ ▶

1. Prepare a zone analysis and a determination and distribution of excess schedule for the investment in Salsa.
2. Complete a consolidated worksheet for Polka Company and its subsidiary Salsa Company as of December 31, 20X2. Prepare supporting amortization and income distribution schedules.

Problem 4-9 *(LO 2, 4)* **90%, cost, merchandise, note payable.** The December 31, 20X2 trial balances of the Pettie Corporation and its 90%-owned subsidiary Sunny Corporation are as follows:

	Pettie Corporation	Sunny Corporation
Cash	75,000	45,500
Accounts and Other Current Receivables	410,900	170,000
Inventory	920,000	739,400
Property, Plant, and Equipment (net)	1,000,000	400,000
Investment in Sunny Corporation........................	1,200,000	
Accounts Payable and Other Current Liabilities	(140,000)	(305,900)
Common Stock ($10 par)	(500,000)	
Common Stock ($10 par)		(200,000)
Retained Earnings, January 1, 20X2........................	(2,800,000)	(650,000)
Dividends Declared..		1,000
Sales	(2,000,000)	(650,000)
Dividend Income	(900)	
Interest Expense..		5,000
Interest Income..	(5,000)	
Cost of Goods Sold	1,500,000	400,000
Other Expenses	340,000	45,000
Totals	0	0

Pettie's investment in Sunny was purchased for $1,200,000 in cash on January 1, 20X1, and is accounted for by the cost method. On January 1, 20X1, Sunny had the following equity balances:

Common stock................	$200,000
Retained earnings	600,000
Total equity	$800,000

Pettie's excess of cost over book value on Sunny's investment has been identified appropriately as goodwill.

Sunny borrowed $100,000 from Pettie on June 30, 20X2, with the note maturing on June 30, 20X3, at 10% interest. Correct accruals have been recorded by both companies.

During 20X2, Pettie sold merchandise to Sunny at an aggregate invoice price of $300,000, which included a profit of $75,000. As of December 31, 20X2, Sunny had not paid Pettie for $90,000 of these purchases, and 10% of the total merchandise purchased from Pettie still remained in Sunny's inventory.

Sunny declared a $1,000 cash dividend in December 20X2 payable in January 20X3.

Required ▶ ▶ ▶ ▶ ▶

Prepare the worksheet required to produce the consolidated statements of Pettie Corporation and its subsidiary, Sunny Corporation, for the year ending December 31, 20X2. Include the determination and distribution of excess schedule and the income distribution schedules.

(AICPA adapted)

Problem 4-10 *(LO 2, 3)* **80%, equity, several excess distributions, merchandise, equipment sales.** On January 1, 20X1, Peanut Company acquired 80% of the common

stock of Sam Company for $200,000. On this date, Sam had total owners' equity of $200,000. During 20X1 and 20X2, Peanut appropriately accounted for its investment in Sam using the simple equity method.

Any excess of cost over book value is attributable to inventory (worth $12,500 more than cost), to equipment (worth $25,000 more than book value), and to goodwill. FIFO is used for inventories. The equipment has a remaining life of four years, and straight-line depreciation is used. On January 1, 20X2, Peanut held merchandise acquired from Sam for $20,000. During 20X2, Sam sold merchandise to Peanut for $40,000, $10,000 of which is still held by Peanut on December 31, 20X2. Sam's usual gross profit is 50%.

On December 31, 20X1, Peanut sold equipment to Sam at a gain of $15,000. During 20X2, the equipment was used by Sam. Depreciation is being computed using the straight-line method, a five-year life, and no salvage value.

The following trial balances were prepared for the Peanut and Sam companies for December 31, 20X2:

	Peanut Company	Sam Company
Inventory, December 31	130,000	50,000
Other Current Assets	241,000	235,000
Investment in Sam Company	308,000	
Other Long-Term Investments	20,000	
Land	140,000	80,000
Buildings and Equipment	375,000	200,000
Accumulated Depreciation	(120,000)	(30,000)
Other Intangibles		20,000
Current Liabilities	(150,000)	(70,000)
Bonds Payable		(100,000)
Other Long-Term Liabilities	(200,000)	(50,000)
Common Stock, Peanut Company	(200,000)	
Other Paid-In Capital, Peanut Company	(100,000)	
Retained Earnings, Peanut Company	(320,000)	
Common Stock, Sam Company		(50,000)
Other Paid-In Capital, Sam Company		(50,000)
Retained Earnings, Sam Company		(150,000)
Net Sales	(600,000)	(315,000)
Cost of Goods Sold	350,000	150,000
Operating Expenses	150,000	60,000
Subsidiary Income	(84,000)	
Dividends Declared, Peanut Company	60,000	
Dividends Declared, Sam Company		20,000
Totals	0	0

◄ ◄ ◄ ◄ ◄ **Required**

Complete the worksheet for consolidated financial statements for the year ended December 31, 20X2. Include the necessary determination and distribution of excess schedule and income distribution schedules.

Problem 4-11 *(LO 2, 3)* **80%, cost, several excess distributions, merchandise, equipment sales.** (This is the same as Problem 4-10 except for use of the cost method.) On January 1, 20X1, Peanut Company acquired 80% of the common stock of Sam Company for $200,000. On this date, Sam had total owners' equity of $200,000, which included retained earnings of $100,000. During 20X1 and 20X2, Peanut accounted for its investment in Sam using the cost method.

Any excess of cost over book value is attributable to inventory (worth $12,500 more than cost), to equipment (worth $25,000 more than book value), and to goodwill. FIFO is used for inventories. The equipment has a remaining life of four years, and straight-line depreciation is used.

On January 1, 20X2, Peanut held merchandise acquired from Sam for $20,000. During 20X2, Sam sold merchandise to Peanut for $40,000, $10,000 of which is still held by Peanut on December 31, 20X2. Sam's usual gross profit is 50%.

On December 31, 20X1, Peanut sold equipment to Sam at a gain of $15,000. During 20X2, the equipment was used by Sam. Depreciation is being computed using the straight-line method, a five-year life, and no salvage value.

The following trial balances were prepared for the Peanut and Sam companies for December 31, 20X2:

	Peanut Company	Sam Company
Inventory, December 31	130,000	50,000
Other Current Assets	241,000	235,000
Investment in Sam Company	200,000	
Other Long-Term Investments	20,000	
Land	140,000	80,000
Buildings and Equipment	375,000	200,000
Accumulated Depreciation	(120,000)	(30,000)
Other Intangibles		20,000
Current Liabilities	(150,000)	(70,000)
Bonds Payable		(100,000)
Other Long-Term Liabilities	(200,000)	(50,000)
Common Stock, Peanut Company	(200,000)	
Other Paid-In Capital, Peanut Company	(100,000)	
Retained Earnings, Peanut Company	(280,000)	
Common Stock, Sam Company		(50,000)
Other Paid-In Capital, Sam Company		(50,000)
Retained Earnings, Sam Company		(150,000)
Net Sales	(600,000)	(315,000)
Cost of Goods Sold	350,000	150,000
Operating Expenses	150,000	60,000
Dividend Income	(16,000)	
Dividends Declared, Peanut Company	60,000	
Dividends Declared, Sam Company		20,000
Totals	0	0

Required ▶ ▶ ▶ ▶ ▶   Complete the worksheet for consolidated financial statements for the year ended December 31, 20X2. Include any necessary determination and distribution of excess schedule and income distribution schedules.

Use the following information for Problems 4-12 and 4-13:

On January 1, 20X1, Purple Company acquired Simple Company. Purple paid $300,000 for 80% of Simple's common stock. On the date of acquisition, Simple had the following balance sheet:

Simple Company
Balance Sheet
January 1, 20X1

Assets		Liabilities and Equity	
Accounts receivable	$ 50,000	Accounts payable	$ 60,000
Inventory	60,000	Bonds payable	200,000
Land	100,000	Common stock, $1 par	10,000
Buildings	150,000	Paid-in capital in excess of par	90,000

Accumulated depreciation	(50,000)	Retained earnings	60,000
Equipment	100,000		
Accumulated depreciation	(30,000)		
Goodwill	40,000		
Total assets..............	$420,000	Total liabilities and equity	$420,000

Buildings, which have a 20-year life, are understated by $100,000. Equipment, which has a five-year life, is understated by $50,000. Any remaining excess is goodwill. Purple uses the simple equity method to account for its investment in Simple.

Problem 4-12 *(LO 2, 3)* **80%, equity, several excess distributions, inventory, fixed assets, parent and subsidiary sales.** Refer to the preceding facts for Purple's acquisition of Simple common stock. On January 1, 20X2, Simple held merchandise sold to it from Purple for $14,000. This beginning inventory had an applicable gross profit of 40%. During 20X2, Purple sold merchandise to Simple for $60,000. On December 31, 20X2, Simple held $12,000 of this merchandise in its inventory. This ending inventory had an applicable gross profit of 35%. Simple owed Purple $8,000 on December 31 as a result of this intercompany sale.

Purple held $12,000 worth of merchandise in its beginning inventory from sales from Simple. This beginning inventory had an applicable gross profit of 25%. During 20X2, Simple sold merchandise to Purple for $30,000. Purple held $16,000 of this inventory at the end of the year. This ending inventory had an applicable gross profit of 30%. Purple owed Simple $6,000 on December 31 as a result of this intercompany sale.

On January 1, 20X1, Purple sold equipment to Simple at a profit of $40,000. Depreciation on this equipment is computed over an eight-year life, using the straight-line method.

On January 1, 20X2, Simple sold equipment with a book value of $30,000 to Purple for $54,000. This equipment has a six-year life and is depreciated using the straight-line method. Purple and Simple had the following trial balances on December 31, 20X2:

	Purple Company	Simple Company
Cash	92,400	65,500
Accounts Receivable	130,000	36,000
Inventory	105,000	76,000
Land..	100,000	100,000
Investment in Simple	387,600	
Buildings	800,000	150,000
Accumulated Depreciation	(250,000)	(60,000)
Equipment	210,000	220,000
Accumulated Depreciation	(115,000)	(80,000)
Goodwill...		40,000
Accounts Payable	(70,000)	(78,000)
Bonds Payable..		(200,000)
Common Stock	(100,000)	(10,000)
Paid-In Capital in Excess of Par	(800,000)	(90,000)
Retained Earnings, January 1, 20X2...................	(325,000)	(142,000)
Sales	(800,000)	(350,000)
Cost of Goods Sold	450,000	208,500
Depreciation Expense—Buildings......................	30,000	5,000
Depreciation Expense—Equipment.....................	25,000	23,000
Other Expenses	140,000	92,000
Gain on Fixed Asset Sale...............................		(24,000)

(continued)

Intercompany Bonds, Cash Flow, EPS, and Unconsolidated Investments

Learning Objectives

When you have completed this chapter, you should be able to

1. Explain the alternatives a parent company has if it wishes to acquire outstanding subsidiary bonds from outside owners.

2. Follow the procedures used to retire intercompany bonds on a consolidated worksheet.

3. Demonstrate an understanding of the effect of a business combination on cash flow in and after the period of the purchase.

4. Compute earnings per share for a consolidated firm.

5. Apply consolidation-type procedures to influential investments.

6. (Appendix) Be able to apply consolidation procedures to a worksheet that is arranged in a vertical format.

This chapter first focuses on intercompany bond holdings, which create a long-term debtor-creditor relationship between the members of a consolidated group. The usual impetus for these transactions is the parent's ability to borrow larger amounts of capital at more favorable terms than would be available to the subsidiary. In addition, the parent company may desire to manage all capital needs of the consolidated company for better control of all capital sources.

Typically, the subsidiary has issued bonds which appear on its balance sheet as long-term liabilities. The parent company may purchase the bonds and list them on its balance sheet as an investment. However, when consolidated statements are prepared, the intercompany bond purchase, in effect, should be viewed as a retirement of the bonds.

There are special reporting issues applicable to consolidated firms. Some unique procedures are needed to prepare a consolidated statement of cash flows. Fortunately, they require only minor changes in the procedures used in your prior accounting courses. Also, only minor adjustments of typical earnings per share procedures are needed for consolidated companies.

This chapter concludes with a discussion of the use of the sophisticated equity method for investments that are not consolidated. These investments require the use of procedures that parallel those used in consolidations. The end result is that the income reported from the investee is the same as if the investee were consolidated and the controlling interest in subsidiary income were calculated.

The appendix demonstrates the application of consolidation procedures to the vertical style worksheet which stacks the statements in the following order: income statement, statement of retained earnings, and balance sheet.

INTERCOMPANY INVESTMENT IN BONDS

To secure long-term funds, one member of a consolidated group (typically a subsidiary) may sell its bonds directly to another member of the group. Clearly, such a transaction results in intercompany debt which must be eliminated from the consolidated statements. On the worksheet,

1
OBJECTIVE

Explain the alternatives a parent company has if it wishes to acquire outstanding subsidiary bonds from outside owners.

the investment in bonds recorded by one company must be eliminated against the bonds payable of the other. In addition, the applicable interest expense recorded by one affiliate must be eliminated against the applicable interest revenue recorded by the other affiliate. Interest accruals recorded on the books of the separate companies must be eliminated as well.

A subsidiary may have outstanding bonds, and the parent may loan the subsidiary the funds needed to retire the bonds. The bonds would be retired on the subsidiary's books. There would however be intercompany debt between the parent and the subsidiary that would have to be eliminated on future consolidated statements.

There are also situations where one affiliate (usually the subsidiary) has outstanding bonds that have been purchased by parties that are not members of the affiliated group, and a decision is made by another affiliate (usually the parent) to purchase these bonds. The parent purchases the subsidiary bonds from the outside parties and holds them as an investment. This creates an intercompany investment in bonds, where each affiliate continues to accrue and record interest on the bonds. The intercompany bonds are treated as a liability on the subsidiary's books and as an investment on the parent company's books. However, from a consolidated viewpoint, the bonds have been retired and the debt to outside parties has been liquidated. The purchase of intercompany bonds has the following ramifications when consolidating:

1. Consolidated statements prepared for the period in which the bonds are purchased must portray the intercompany bond purchase as a retirement of the bonds. It is possible, but unlikely, that the bonds will be purchased at book value. The price paid for the bonds may exceed their book value, creating a loss on retirement. If the price paid for the bonds is less than their book value, there will be a gain on retirement. The resulting gain or loss on retirement will be recognized on the consolidated income statement.

2. For all periods during which the intercompany investment exists, the intercompany bonds, interest accruals, and interest expense/revenue must be eliminated since the bonds no longer exist from a consolidated viewpoint.

The complexity of the elimination procedures depends on whether the bonds originally were issued at face value or at a premium or discount. Additionally, one must exercise extra care in the application of elimination procedures when only a portion of the outstanding bonds is purchased intercompany.

<table>
<tr><td>

2

OBJECTIVE

Follow the procedures used to retire intercompany bonds on a consolidated worksheet.

</td>
<td>

Bonds Originally Issued at Face Value

When bonds are sold at face value by a subsidiary to outside parties, there will not be an "issuance" discount or premium. The parent may later purchase the bonds at a price greater or less than the face value, which will create a "purchase" premium or discount on the bonds purchased by the parent.

To illustrate the procedures required for intercompany bonds originally issued at face value, assume a subsidiary, Company S, issued five-year, 8% bonds at face value of $100,000 to outside parties on January 1, 20X1. Interest is paid each January 1 for the preceding year. On January 2, 20X3, the parent, Company P, purchased the bonds from the outside parties for $103,600.

</td></tr>
</table>

Company S will continue to list the $100,000 bond debt and to record interest expense of $8,000 during 20X3, 20X4, and 20X5. However, Company P will record a bond investment of $103,600 and will amortize $1,200 per year, for the remaining life of the bond, by reducing the investment account and reducing interest revenue. Though the interest method of amortization is preferable, the straight-line method is permitted if results are not materially different. This initial example and most others in this chapter use the straight-line method in order to simplify analysis. A summary example is used to demonstrate the interest method of amortization.

Although the investment and liability accounts continue to exist on the separate books of the affiliated companies, retirement has occurred from a consolidated viewpoint. Debt with a book value of $100,000 was retired by a payment of $103,600, and there is a $3,600 loss on retirement. If a consolidated worksheet is prepared on the day the bonds are purchased, Bonds Payable would be eliminated against Investment in Company S Bonds, and a *loss on retirement* would be reported on the consolidated income statement.

The following abbreviated worksheet displays the procedures used to retire the bonds as part of the elimination process:

	Partial Trial Balance		Eliminations & Adjustments	
	Co. P	Co. S	Dr.	Cr.
Investment in Company S Bonds	103,600			(B) 103,600
Bonds Payable		(100,000)	(B) 100,000	
Loss on Bond				
Retirement			(B) 3,600	

This partial worksheet, prepared on January 2, 20X3, is only hypothetical since, in reality, there will be no consolidated worksheet prepared until December 31, 20X3, the end of the period. During 20X3, Companies P and S will record the transactions for interest as follows:

Company P		Company S	
Interest Receivable..............	8,000	Interest Expense.............	8,000
Investment in Company S		Interest Payable	8,000
Bonds..................	1,200	To record interest expense.	
Interest Income..............	6,800		
To record interest revenue net			
of $1,200 per year premium			
amortization.			

These entries will be reflected in the trial balances of the December 31, 20X3, consolidated worksheet, shown in Worksheet 5-1 on pages 254 and 255. Note that Investment in Company S Bonds reflects the premium amortization since the balance is $102,400 ($103,600 original cost − $1,200 amortization). On this worksheet, it is assumed that Investment in Company S Stock reflects a 90% interest purchased at a price equal to the book value of the underlying equity, and the simple equity method is used by Company P to record the investment in stock.

Worksheet 5-1: page 254

Entries (CY1) and (EL) eliminate the intercompany stock investment. Entry (B1) eliminates the intercompany bonds at their year-end balances and the intercompany interest expense and revenue recorded during the year. Entry (B2) eliminates the year-end interest accruals made by the parent and the subsidiary. In journal entry form, elimination entries are as follows:

(CY1)	*Eliminate current-year equity income:*		
	Subsidiary Income.....................................	10,800	
	Investment in Company S Stock..........................		10,800
(EL)	*Eliminate 90% of subsidiary equity:*		
	Common Stock ($10 par), Company S......................	72,000	
	Retained Earnings, January 1, 20X3, Company S	18,000	
	Investment in Company S Stock..........................		90,000
(B1)	*Eliminate intercompany bonds and interest expense:*		
	Bonds Payable.......................................	100,000	
	Investment in Company S Bonds		102,400
	Interest Income......................................	6,800	
	Interest Expense.....................................		8,000
	Loss on Bond Retirement	3,600	
(B2)	*Eliminate intercompany accrued interest:*		
	Interest Payable.....................................	8,000	
	Interest Receivable...................................		8,000

The amount of the gain or loss is the sum of the difference between the remaining book value of the investment on bonds compared to the debt and the difference between interest expense and debt. For this example

Investment in Bonds Balance, December 31, 20X3	$102,400	
Bonds Payable, December 31, 20X3	100,000	$2,400
Interest Expense, 20X3	$ 8,000	
Interest Revenue, 20X3	6,800	1,200
Loss, January 2, 20X3		$3,600

As a result of the elimination entries, the consolidated income statement will include the retirement loss and will exclude intercompany interest payments and accruals. The consolidated balance sheet will not list the intercompany bonds payable or investment in bonds accounts.

The only remaining problem is the distribution of consolidated net income to the controlling and noncontrolling interests. The income distribution schedule shows Company S absorbing all of the retirement loss. It is most common to view the purchasing affiliate as a mere agent of the issuing affiliate. Therefore, it is the issuer, not the purchaser, that must bear the gain or loss on retirement. Even though the debt is retired from a consolidated viewpoint, it still exists internally. Company P has a right to collect the interest as part of its share of Company S's operations. Based on the value of the debt on January 2, 20X3, the interest expense/revenue is $6,800. The interest cost of $8,000 recorded by Company S must be corrected to reflect the internal interest expense of $6,800. The income distribution schedule increases the income of Company S to reflect the adjustment ($1,200) to interest expense. It should be noted that the retirement loss borne by Company S will entirely offset the adjustments to interest expense by the time the bonds mature. If the parent, Company P, had issued the bonds to outside parties and if the subsidiary, Company S, later had purchased them, the only change would be that the income distribution schedule of Company P would absorb the loss on retirement and the interest adjustment.

The worksheet procedures that would be needed at the end of 20X4 are shown in Worksheet 5-2 on pages 256 and 257. The interest revenue and expense have been recorded on the books of the separate companies. The investment in Company S bonds account on the parent's books reflects its book value at the end of 20X4.

The eliminations in journal entry form are as follows:

Worksheet 5-2: page 256

(CY1)	*Eliminate current-year equity income:*			
	Subsidiary Income		19,800	
	Investment in Company S Stock			19,800
(EL)	*Eliminate 90% of subsidiary equity:*			
	Common Stock ($10 par), Company S		72,000	
	Retained Earnings, January 1, 20X4, Company S		28,800	
	Investment in Company S Stock			100,800
(B1)	*Eliminate intercompany bonds and interest expense:*			
	Bonds Payable		100,000	
	Investment in Company S Bonds			101,200
	Interest Income		6,800	
	Interest Expense			8,000
	Retained Earnings, January 1, 20X4, Company P		2,160	
	Retained Earnings, January 1, 20X4, Company S		240	
(B2)	*Eliminate intercompany accrued interest:*			
	Interest Payable		8,000	
	Interest Receivable			8,000

Entry (B1) eliminates the intercompany bonds at their year-end balances and the intercompany interest expense and revenue. Recall that the original retirement loss was $3,600 when the bonds had three years to maturity. By the start of the second period, 20X4, $1,200 of that loss was already amortized on the separate books of the affiliates. The loss remaining is $2,400 [it is verified in the explanation to entry (B1) in Worksheet 5-2]. This remaining loss is debited to Retained Earnings since the retirement occurred in a prior period. The adjustment is allocated to noncontrolling and controlling beginning retained earnings since the bonds were issued by the subsidiary.

The 20X4 consolidated income statement will not include intercompany interest. The income distribution schedules for Worksheet 5-2 reflect the fact that the debt still existed internally during the period. However, the interest expense recorded by Company S is reduced to reflect the interest cost based on the January 2, 20X3, purchase price.

If Company S was the purchaser and Company P the issuer of the bonds, Worksheet 5-2 would differ as follows:

1. The January 1, 20X4, retained earnings adjustment would be absorbed completely by the controlling retained earnings, since the parent company would be the issuer absorbing the loss.
2. The income distribution schedule of the parent would contain the interest adjustment.

Bonds Not Originally Issued at Face Value

The principles of eliminating intercompany investments in bonds are not altered by the existence of an "issuance" premium or discount. The numerical calculations just become more complex. To illustrate, assume Company S issued $100,000 of five-year, 8% bonds on January 1, 20X1. The market interest rate approximated 9% and, as a result, the bonds sold at a discount of $3,890. Interest is paid each December 31. On each interest payment date, the discount is amortized $778 ($3,890 ÷ 5 years) by decreasing the discount and by increasing interest expense. On December 31, 20X3, the balance of the discount is $1,556 [$3,890 − (3 × $778 annual amortization)].

The parent, Company P, purchased the bonds for $103,600 on December 31, 20X3, after interest had been paid. The parent will amortize $1,800 of the investment each subsequent December 31, reducing the parent's interest income to $6,200 ($8,000 cash − $1,800 amortization) for 20X4 and 20X5.

The following abbreviated December 31, 20X3 (date of purchase) worksheet lists the investment in Company S bonds account, the bonds payable account, and the remaining issuance discount. Eliminating the $103,600 price paid for the bonds by Company P against the book value of $98,444 ($100,000 − $1,556) creates a loss on retirement of $5,156, which is carried to consolidated net income. Worksheet procedures may be aided by linking the bonds payable and the related discount or premium on the worksheet. This is done on our worksheets by circling the amounts in the trial balance and in the eliminations.

	Partial Trial Balance		Eliminations & Adjustments	
	Company P	Company S	Dr.	Cr.
Investment in Company S Bonds	103,600			(B) 103,600
Bonds Payable, 8%		(100,000)	(B) 100,000	
Discount on Bonds Payable		1,556		(B) 1,556
Loss on Bond				
Retirement			(B) 5,156	
Interest Expense		8,778*		

*$8,000 cash + $778 straight-line amortization.

Interest expense on the books of Company S is extended to the consolidated income statement, since this interest was incurred as a result of transactions with outside parties. There would be no interest adjustment for 20X3, since the bonds were not purchased by the parent until December 31, 20X3. The income distribution schedules accompanying the worksheet would assess the retirement loss against the issuer, Company S.

The implications of these intercompany bonds on the 20X4 consolidated worksheet are reflected in Worksheet 5-3 on pages 258 and 259. Assume Company P acquired a 90% interest in the common stock of Company S at a price equal to the book value of the underlying equity. The simple equity method is used by the parent to record the investment in the stock of Company S. The trial balances include the following items:

Worksheet 5-3: page 258

1. The investment in Company S bonds at its amortized balance on December 31, 20X4, $101,800 ($103,600 − $1,800 amortization),
2. The interest revenue (adjusted for $1,800 amortization) of $6,200 on the books of Company P,
3. The discount on bonds account at its amortized December 31, 20X4, balance of $778, and
4. The interest expense (adjusted for discount amortization) of $8,778 ($8,000 cash + $778 amortization) on the books of Company S.
5. There is no accrued interest receivable/payable since interest was paid on December 31, 20X4.

The eliminations in journal entry form are as follows:

(CY1)	*Eliminate current-year equity income:*		
	Subsidiary Income.	8,874	
	Investment in Company S Stock		8,874
(EL)	*Eliminate 90% of subsidiary equity:*		
	Common Stock ($10 par), Company S.	36,000	
	Retained Earnings, January 1, 20X4, Company S	99,000	
	Investment in Company S Stock		135,000
(B)	*Eliminate intercompany bonds and interest expense:*		
	Bonds Payable.	100,000	
	Discount on Bonds		778
	Investment in Company S Bonds		101,800
	Interest Income.	6,200	
	Interest Expense		8,778
	Retained Earnings, January 1, 20X4, Company P	4,640	
	Retained Earnings, January 1, 20X4, Company S	516	

Entry (B) eliminates the investment in bonds against the bonds payable and the applicable remaining discount. Entry (B) also eliminates interest expense and revenue. Be sure to understand the calculation of the adjustment to beginning retained earnings, which is explained in the entry (B) information. The loss at the start of the year is the sum of the loss remaining at year-end and the loss amortized on the books of the separate affiliates during the year.

Again, the consolidated income statement does not include intercompany interest. However, the Company S income distribution schedule does reflect the adjustment of Company S's interest expense. The original $8,778 interest expense has been replaced by a $6,200 expense, based on the purchase price paid by Company P. The smaller interest expense compensates the subsidiary for the retirement loss absorbed in a previous period.

Purchase of Only a Portion of the Bonds

The preceding examples assume that the parent company purchases all of the outstanding bonds of the subsidiary. In such cases, all of the subsidiary bonds are retired on the worksheet. There may be cases, however, where the parent purchases only a portion of the subsidiary's outstanding bonds. Suppose, for example, that the parent purchased 80% of the subsidiary's outstanding bonds. Only the 80% interest in the bonds would be eliminated on the consolidated worksheet, and only the interest expense and revenue applicable to 80% of the bonds would be eliminated on the worksheet. **The 20% interest in the subsidiary bonds owned by persons outside the control group remains as a valid debt of the consolidated company and is not eliminated.** It is a common error for students to eliminate the 80% interest in intercompany bonds owned by a parent against 100% of the bonds issued by the subsidiary. Such a mistake improperly eliminates valid debt and greatly miscalculates the gain or loss on retirement. It also should be noted that the interest paid to persons outside the control group should remain a part of the consolidated statements. Only the interest paid to the affiliated company is to be eliminated.

Interest Method of Amortization

The procedures used to eliminate intercompany bonds are not altered by the interest method of amortization; only the dollar values change. To illustrate the calculations, assume that Company S issued $100,000 of five-year, 8% bonds on January 1, 20X1. The market interest rate on that date was 9%, so that the bonds sold at a discount of $3,890. Interest on the bonds is paid each December 31. The discount amortization for the term of the bonds follows:

Year	Debt Balance, January 1	Effective Interest	Nominal Interest	Discount Amortization
20X1	$96,110	$8,650 (0.09 × $96,110)	$8,000	$ 650
20X2	96,760 ($96,110 + $650)	8,708 (0.09 × $96,760)	8,000	708
20X3	97,468 ($96,760 + $708)	8,772 (0.09 × $97,468)	8,000	772
20X4	98,240 ($97,468 + $772)	8,842 (0.09 × $98,240)	8,000	842
20X5	99,082 ($98,240 + $842)	8,918* (0.09 × $99,082)	8,000	918
*Includes $1 rounding error.				$3,890

On December 31, 20X3, after interest had been paid, the bonds were purchased by parent Company P at a price to yield 6%. Based on present value computations, $103,667 was paid for the bonds. The premium on the bonds would be amortized by Company P as follows:

Year	Investment Balance, January 1	Effective Interest	Nominal Interest	Premium Amortization
20X4	$103,667	$6,220 (0.06 × $103,667)	$8,000	$1,780
20X5	101,887 ($103,667 − $1,780)	6,113 (0.06 × $101,887)	8,000	1,887
				$3,667

The following abbreviated December 31, 20X3 (date of purchase), worksheet lists the investment in Company S bonds account, the bonds payable account, and the remaining issuance discount. Eliminating the $103,667 price paid by Company P against the book value of $98,240 ($100,000 − $1,760) creates a loss on retirement of $5,427 that is carried to consolidated net income.

	Partial Trial Balance		Eliminations & Adjustments	
	Company P	Company S	Dr.	Cr.
Investment in Company S Bonds	103,667			(B) 103,667
Bonds Payable, 8%		(100,000)	(B) 100,000	
Discount on Bonds Payable		1,760		(B) 1,760
Loss on Bond Retirement			(B) 5,427	
Interest Expense		8,772*		

*See preceding discount amortization schedule for issuer.

Worksheet 5-4: page 260

The differences in the 20X4 consolidated worksheet caused by the interest method of amortization are shown in Worksheet 5-4 on pages 260 and 261. Note particularly the change in the Company S income distribution schedule. The original 9% interest, totaling $8,842, has been replaced by the $6,220 of interest calculated using the 6% rate.

The eliminations in journal entry form are as follows:

(CY1)   *Eliminate current-year equity income:*
     Subsidiary Income   8,820
        Investment in Company S Stock   8,820

(EL)   *Eliminate 90% of subsidiary equity:*
     Common Stock ($10 par), Company S   36,000
     Retained Earnings, January 1, 20X4, Company S   99,180
        Investment in Company S Stock   135,180

(B)   *Eliminate intercompany bonds and interest expense:*
     Bonds Payable   100,000
        Discount on Bonds   918
        Investment in Company S Bonds   101,887
     Interest Income   6,220
        Interest Expense   8,842
     Retained Earnings, January 1, 20X4, Company P   4,884
     Retained Earnings, January 1, 20X4, Company S   543

REFLECTION

- When the parent buys subsidiary bonds, the bonds cease to exist, from a consolidated viewpoint. They are retired on the consolidated worksheet by elimination.

- When the intercompany bonds are eliminated, there will be a difference between the amortized cost and the price paid; this creates a gain or loss on retirement.

- In periods subsequent to the intercompany purchase, the bonds must continue to be eliminated, and retained earnings is adjusted for the remaining retirement gain or loss that has not already been amortized.

- Intercompany interest expense/revenue and accrued interest receivable/payable are also eliminated.

CONSOLIDATED STATEMENT OF CASH FLOWS

3
OBJECTIVE

Demonstrate an understanding of the effect of a business combination on cash flow in and after the period of the purchase.

FASB Statement of Financial Accounting Standards No. 95 requires that a statement of cash flows accompany a company's published income statement and balance sheet. The process of preparing a consolidated statement of cash flows is similar to that which is used for a single company, a topic covered in depth in intermediate accounting texts. Since the analysis of changes in cash of a consolidated entity begins with consolidated statements, intercompany transactions will have been eliminated and, thus, will not cause any complications. However, because of the parent–subsidiary relationship, there are some situations that require special consideration. These situations are discussed in the following paragraphs.

Cash Acquisition of Controlling Interest

The cash purchase of a controlling interest in a company is considered an *investing activity* and would appear as a cash outflow in the cash flows from investing activities section of the statement of cash flows. It also is necessary to explain the total increase in consolidated assets and the addition of the NCI to the consolidated balance sheet. This is a result of the requirement that the statement of cash flows disclose investing and *financing activities* that affect the company's financial position even though they do not impact cash.

To illustrate the disclosure required, consider an example of a cash purchase of an 80% interest in a company. Assume Company S had the following balance sheet on January 1, 20X1, when Company P acquired an 80% interest for $540,000 in cash:

Assets		Liabilities and Equity	
Cash and cash equivalents	$ 50,000	Long-term liabilities	$150,000
Inventory	60,000	Common stock ($10 par).	200,000
Equipment (net)	190,000	Retained earnings	350,000
Building (net)	400,000		
Total assets.	$700,000	Total liabilities and equity	$700,000

Assume the fair values of the equipment and building are $250,000 and $425,000, respectively, and any remaining excess of cost is attributed to goodwill. The estimated remaining life of the equipment is five years and of the building is 10 years.

The following zone analysis would be prepared:

	Group Total	Ownership Portion	Cumulative Total
Ownership percentage		80%	
Priority accounts (net of liabilities)	$ (40,000)	$ (32,000)	$ (32,000)
Nonpriority accounts	675,000	540,000	508,000

Price Analysis

Price (including direct acquisition costs)	$540,000	
Assign to priority accounts, controlling share	(32,000)	Full value
Assign to nonpriority accounts, controlling share	540,000	Full value
Goodwill	32,000	

The price analysis schedule indicates that the parent's share of all accounts can be fully adjusted to fair value.

From this information, a determination and distribution of excess would be prepared:

	Company	Controlling Interest		Amortization Periods	Controlling Amortization
Price paid for investment including direct acquisition costs....		$540,000			
Less book value of interest purchased:					
Common stock ($10 par)............................	$200,000				
Retained earnings	350,000				
Total equity......................................	$550,000				
Ownership interest................................	× 80%	440,000			
Excess of cost over book value adjustments..............		$100,000	Cr.		
Equipment (net), 80% of $60,000		(48,000)	Dr.	5	$9,600
Buildings (net), 80% of $25,000		(20,000)	Dr.	10	2,000
Goodwill..		$ 32,000	Dr.		

The effect of the purchase on the balance sheet accounts of the consolidated company for 20X1 would be as follows:

	Debit	Credit
Cash ($540,000 paid − $50,000 subsidiary cash)		490,000
Inventory	60,000	
Equipment ($190,000 book value + $48,000 excess)	238,000	
Building ($400,000 book value + $20,000 excess)	420,000	
Goodwill	32,000	
Long-term liabilities		150,000
Noncontrolling interest (20% × $550,000 subsidiary equity)		110,000
Total..	750,000	750,000

The disclosure of the purchase on the statement of cash flows would be summarized as follows:

Under the heading "Cash flows from investing activities:"

> Payment for purchase of Company S, net
> of cash acquired .... $(490,000)

In the supplemental schedule of noncash financing and investing activity:

> Company P purchased 80% of the common stock of Company S for $540,000. In conjunction with the acquisition, liabilities were assumed and an NCI was created as follows:

Adjusted value of assets acquired ($700,000 book value + $100,000 excess)................	$800,000
Cash paid for common stock	540,000
Balance (noncash)............................	$260,000
Liabilities assumed.............................	$150,000
NCI	$110,000

Noncash Acquisition of Controlling Interest

Suppose that instead of paying cash for its controlling interest, Company P issued 10,000 shares of its $10 par stock for the controlling interest. Further assume the shares had a market value of

$54 each. Since the acquisition price is the same ($540,000), the determination and distribution of excess schedule would not change. The analysis of balance sheet account changes would be as follows:

	Debit	Credit
Cash ($50,000 subsidiary cash).	50,000	
Inventory	60,000	
Equipment ($190,000 book value + $48,000 excess)	238,000	
Building ($400,000 book value + $20,000 excess)	420,000	
Goodwill	32,000	
Long-term liabilities		150,000
Noncontrolling interest (20% × $550,000 subsidiary equity)		110,000
Common stock, $10 par, Company P.		100,000
Paid-in capital in excess of par, Company P		440,000
Total.	800,000	800,000

The disclosure of the purchase on the statement of cash flows would be summarized as follows:

Under the heading "Cash flows from investing activities:"

Cash acquired in purchase of Company S	$50,000

In the supplemental schedule of noncash financing and investing activity:

Company P acquired 80% of the common stock of Company S in exchange for 10,000 shares of Company P common stock valued at $540,000. In conjunction with the acquisition, liabilities were assumed and a noncontrolling interest was created as follows:

Adjusted value of assets acquired ($700,000 book value + $100,000 excess).	$800,000
Common stock issued	$540,000
Liabilities assumed.	$150,000
Noncontrolling interest	$110,000

In the past, when an acquisition qualified as a pooling of interests, all prior financial statements were consolidated retroactively which required that cash flow analyses proceed from a comparison of the consolidated balance sheets of the current and previous periods. Due to the retroactive application of the pooling of interests, there was no difference between the comparative statements as a result of the pooling. The impact of the pooling on the consolidated stockholders' equity was disclosed in the period the pooling was consummated.

Adjustments Resulting from Business Combinations

A business combination will have ramifications on the statements of cash flows prepared in subsequent periods. A purchase may create amortizations of excess deductions (noncash items) which need to be adjusted. In addition, there may be impact resulting from additional purchases of subsidiary shares and/or dividend payments by the subsidiary. Intercompany bonds and nonconsolidated investments also need to be considered for their impact.

Amortization of Excesses. Income statements prepared for periods including or following a purchase of another company will include the amortization of the excesses that are shown on the determination and distribution of excess schedule as well as book value depreciation and amortization recorded by both the parent and subsidiary. These amortizations of the excesses, while reflected in consolidated net income, do not require the use of cash; thus, under the indirect method, they must be included as an adjustment to consolidated net income to arrive at cash flows from operating activities. Using the facts of the preceding examples, the following adjustments would appear on the cash flows statement for 20X1:

Cash from operating activities:	
Consolidated net income.	$XXX,XXX
Add amortizations resulting from business combination:	
Depreciation on equipment ($48,000 ÷ 5)	9,600
Depreciation on building ($20,000 ÷ 10).	2,000

In addition, cash from operating activities would be adjusted for depreciation and amortizations of book value recorded by the constituent companies on their separate books.

Purchase of Additional Subsidiary Shares. The purchase of additional shares directly from the subsidiary results in no added cash flowing into the consolidated company. The transfer of cash within the consolidated company would not appear in the consolidated statement of cash flows. However, the purchase of additional shares from the noncontrolling interest does result in an outflow of cash. From a consolidated viewpoint, it is the equivalent of purchasing treasury shares. Thus, it would be listed under *financing activities.*

Subsidiary Dividends. Dividends paid by the subsidiary to the parent are a transfer of cash within the consolidated entity and thus would not appear in the consolidated statement of cash flows. However, dividends paid by the subsidiary to noncontrolling shareholders represent a flow of cash to parties outside the consolidated group and would appear as an outflow under the cash flows from financing activities heading of the consolidated statement of cash flows.

Purchase of Intercompany Bonds. The purchase of intercompany bonds from parties outside the consolidated company affects a cash flow from one member of the consolidated group to parties outside the consolidated entity. Recall that the purchase of intercompany bonds is viewed as a retirement of the bonds on the consolidated worksheet. The consolidated statement of cash flows also treats the purchase of the bonds as a retirement of the consolidated company's debt and includes the cash outflow under cash flows from financing activities. Since the process of constructing a cash flows statement starts with the consolidated income statement and balance sheet, intercompany interest payments and amortizations of premiums and/or discounts already are eliminated and will not enter into the analysis of consolidated cash flows. Only cash interest payments to bondholders outside the consolidated entity are important to the analysis and should be included in cash flows from *operating* activities.

Nonconsolidated Investments. Investments in the stock of companies not included in the consolidated group result in income to the consolidated entity. Where the investment is accounted for under the cost method, cash dividends received are included in cash flows from operating activities. However, where the equity method is applied, only that portion of the income received in cash may be included in cash from operating activities. For example, the investee may report income of $50,000 and pay dividends of $10,000. Assume further that the consolidated company paid $20,000 more than book value for its 30% interest and regards the excess as attributable to equipment with a 10-year life. Investment income under the equity method would be calculated as follows:

30% of reported income of $50,000	$15,000
Less amortization of excess cost ($20,000 ÷ 10)	2,000
Equity income	$13,000

Only $3,000 (30% × $10,000) was received in the form of cash dividends; thus, the $13,000 of income would be reduced to only $3,000 of cash from operating activities. The $10,000 of undistributed income would be adjusted out of net income to arrive at cash from operating activities.

Preparation of Consolidated Statement of Cash Flows

A complete example of the process of preparing a consolidated statement of cash flows is presented in this section. Assume Company P originally purchased an 80% interest in Company S on January 1, 20X1. In addition, Company P purchased a 20% interest in Company E on January 2, 20X2, and accounted for the investment under the sophisticated equity method. The following determination and distribution of excess schedules were prepared for each investment:

Price paid for investment in Company S		$365,000
Less book value interest acquired:		
Common stock ($10 par)...............	$ 50,000	
Paid-in capital in excess of par	150,000	
Retained earnings	100,000	
Total stockholders' equity.............	$300,000	
Interest acquired	× 80%	240,000

			Amortization Periods	Controlling Amortization
Excess of cost over book value (debit)	$ 125,000			
Equipment, 80% × $31,250	**25,000**	**Dr.**	**5**	**$5,000**
Goodwill...	**$100,000**			

For the January 2, 20X2, 20% investment in nonconsolidated Company E:

Price paid for investment in Company E		$255,000
Less interest acquired:		
Common stock.......................................	$ 500,000	
Retained earnings	750,000	
Total equity..	$1,250,000	
Interest acquired	× 20%	250,000
Equipment (10-year life)		$ 5,000

Since this investment is not consolidated, there will be no recording of the increased value of the equipment. This information is used only to amortize the excess cost in future income statements. Because of this, there are no debits or credits accompanying the distribution of the excess. The following consolidated statements were prepared for Company P and its subsidiary, Company S, for 20X3:

Company P and Subsidiary Company S Consolidated Income Statement For Year Ended December 31, 20X3		
Sales		$ 900,000
Less cost of goods sold..............................		525,000
Gross profit		$ 375,000
Less expenses:		
General and administrative...........................	$150,500	
Depreciation	**70,000***	**220,500**
Operating income..................................		$ 154,500
Investment income (equity method).................		**15,500****
Consolidated net income.............................		$ 170,000
Distributed to:		
NCI		11,200
Controlling interest................................		$ 158,800

*Includes $5,000 of depreciation resulting from the excess of the subsidiary equipment's fair value over book value on January 1, 20X1, the date on which the 80% interest was acquired.

**20% of Company E net income of $80,000 less $500 amortization of equipment. (Dividends received were $2,000.)

Company P and Subsidiary Company S
Consolidated Retained Earnings Statement
For Year Ended December 31, 20X3

Retained earnings, January 1, 20X3	$440,000
Add distribution of consolidated net income	158,800
Less dividends declared	(50,000)
Balance, December 31, 20X3	$548,800

Company P and Subsidiary Company S
Consolidated Balance Sheet
December 31, 20X2 and 20X3

Assets	20X3	20X2
Cash and cash equivalents	$ 179,000	$ 160,000
Inventory	210,000	180,000
Accounts receivable	154,000	120,000
Property, plant, and equipment	1,330,000	1,250,000
Accumulated depreciation	(370,000)	(300,000)
Goodwill	100,000	100,000
Investment in Company E (20%)	333,500	320,000
Total assets	$1,936,500	$1,830,000

Liabilities and Stockholders' Equity	20X3	20X2
Accounts payable	$ 156,500	$ 166,000
Bonds payable	300,000	300,000
Noncontrolling interest	79,200	72,000
Controlling interest:		
Common stock, par	200,000	200,000
Paid-in capital in excess of par	652,000	652,000
Retained earnings	548,800	440,000
Total liabilities and stockholders' equity	$1,936,500	$1,830,000

The following additional facts are available to aid in the preparation of a consolidated statement of cash flows:

1. Company P purchased a new piece of equipment during 20X3 for $80,000.
2. In 20X3, Company P declared and paid $50,000 in dividends and Company S declared and paid $20,000 in dividends.

Illustration 5-1 is a worksheet approach to calculating a statement of cash flows under the *indirect method.* Explanations 1 through 6 use changes in balance sheet accounts to analyze cash from operations. This information is taken from the income statement and is implied from changes in current assets and current liabilities. Explanation 7 reflects the only investing activity in this example. Explanations 8 and 9 show the financing activities. The worksheet provides the information needed to develop the statement of cash flows located on page 242.

If the *direct method* of disclosing cash from operating activities is used, the cash flows from operating activities section of the statement of cash flows would be prepared as follows:

Cash flows from operating activities:

Cash from customers ($900,000 sales − $34,000 increase in accounts receivable) . .	$ 866,000
Cash from investments (dividends received)	2,000
Cash to suppliers ($525,000 cost of goods sold + $30,000 inventory increase + $9,500 decrease in accounts payable).	(564,500)
Cash for general and administrative expenses	(150,500)
Net cash provided by operating activities.	$ 153,000

Illustration 5-1
Company P and Subsidiary Company S
Worksheet for Analysis of Cash: Indirect Approach
For Year Ended December 31, 20X3

	Account Change		Explanations				Balance
	Debit	Credit		Debit		Credit	
Inventory	30,000		(4)	30,000			0
Accounts receivable	34,000		(3)	34,000			0
Property, plant, and equipment.	80,000		(7)	80,000			0
Accumulated depreciation		70,000			(2)	70,000	0
Goodwill	0						0
Investment in Company E (20%)	13,500		(6)	13,500			0
Accounts payable	9,500		(5)	9,500			0
Bonds payable							0
Noncontrolling interest		7,200	(9)	4,000	(1)	11,200	0
Controlling interest:							
Common stock, par							0
Paid-in excess of par							0
Retained earnings		108,800	(8)	50,000	(1)	158,800	0
	167,000	186,000		221,000		240,000	
Net change in cash	19,000	0		19,000		0	
Cash from Operations:							
Consolidated net income.			(1)	170,000			
Depreciation expense			(2)	70,000			
Increase in accounts receivable.					(3)	34,000	
Increase in inventory					(4)	30,000	
Decrease in accounts payable					(5)	9,500	
Equity income in excess of dividends.					(6)	13,500	
Net cash provided by operating activities.				153,000			
Cash from Investing:							
Purchase of equipment					(7)	80,000	
Net cash used in investing activities						80,000	
Cash from Financing:							
Dividend payment to controlling interest					(8)	50,000	
Dividend payment to noncontrolling interest					(9)	4,000	
Net cash used in investing activities						54,000	
Net cash provided.				19,000			

Company P and Subsidiary Company S
Consolidated Statement of Cash Flows
For Year Ended December 31, 20X3

Cash flows from operating activities:		
Consolidated net income................................		$170,000
Adjustments to reconcile net income to net cash:		
Depreciation expense	$ 70,000	
Increase in accounts receivable......................	(34,000)	
Increase in inventory	(30,000)	
Decrease in accounts payable.......................	(9,500)	
Equity income from Company E in excess of		
dividends received...............................	(13,500)	
Total adjustments		(17,000)
Net cash provided by operating activities...................		$153,000
Cash flows from investing activities:		
Purchase of equipment.............................		(80,000)
Cash flows from financing activities:		
Dividend payments to controlling interests..................	$(50,000)	
Dividend payments to noncontrolling interest................	(4,000)	
Net cash used in financing activities.....................		(54,000)
Net increase in cash and cash equivalents		$ 19,000
Cash and cash equivalents at beginning of year...............		160,000
Cash and cash equivalents at year-end........................		$179,000

REFLECTION

- Subsequent to the period of purchase, the only impact of consolidations on cash flow is the added amortization and depreciation caused by the purchase.

- A purchase of a subsidiary for cash is in the "investing" section of the cash flow statement. The cash outflow is net of the cash received.

- A purchase of a subsidiary by issuing securities is a noncash investing/financing activity that must be disclosed in the notes to the cash flow statement. Any subsidiary cash received in the purchase is a positive cash flow under "investing."

- The parent purchase of subsidiary bonds is treated as a retirement and is a financing activity.

- The parent purchase of additional shares of subsidiary stock is viewed as a treasury stock transaction and is considered a financing activity.

CONSOLIDATED EARNINGS PER SHARE

4

OBJECTIVE

Compute earnings per share for a consolidated firm.

The computation of *consolidated earnings per share (EPS)* remains virtually the same as that for single entities. For the purpose of this discussion, all calculations will be made only on an annual basis. ***Basic earnings per share (BEPS)* is calculated by dividing only the controlling interest in consolidated net income by parent company outstanding stock.** The calculation of *diluted earnings per share (DEPS)* is not complicated when applied to the consolidated company, provided that the subsidiary company has no dilutive securities. As long as no such securities exist, the controlling interest's share of consolidated net income is divided by the number of outstanding parent company shares. The numerator and denominator adjustments caused by parent company dilutive securities can be considered in the normal manner.

When the subsidiary has dilutive securities, the calculation of consolidated DEPS becomes a two-stage process. First, the DEPS of the subsidiary must be calculated. Then, the consolidated DEPS is calculated using as a component of the calculation the adjusted DEPS of the subsidiary. This two-stage process handles subsidiary dilutive securities, which require the possible issuance of subsidiary company shares. A further complication occurs when the subsidiary has outstanding dilutive options, warrants, and/or convertible securities, which may require the issuance of parent company shares.

First, consider the calculation of consolidated DEPS when the subsidiary has outstanding dilutive securities, which may require the issuance of subsidiary company shares only. The EPS model for a single entity is modified in two ways:

1. Only the parent's adjusted internally generated net income, the parent's income adjusters, and the parent's share adjusters enter the formula directly.
2. The parent's share of subsidiary's income is entered indirectly by multiplying the number of equivalent subsidiary shares owned by the parent times the subsidiary DEPS.

The basic model by which to compute consolidated EPS in this situation is as follows:

$$\text{Consolidated DEPS} = \frac{\begin{pmatrix}\text{Parent's} \\ \text{adjusted} \\ \text{internally} \\ \text{generated} \\ \text{net income}\end{pmatrix} + \begin{pmatrix}\text{Parent's DEPS} \\ \text{income} \\ \text{adjustments}\end{pmatrix} + \begin{pmatrix}\text{Parent-} \\ \text{owned} \\ \text{equivalent} \\ \text{shares}\end{pmatrix} \times \begin{pmatrix}\text{Subsidiary} \\ \text{DEPS}\end{pmatrix}}{\begin{pmatrix}\text{Parent's common} \\ \text{stock outstanding}\end{pmatrix} + \begin{pmatrix}\text{Parent's share} \\ \text{adjustments}\end{pmatrix}}$$

The parent's adjusted internally generated net income includes adjustments for unrealized profits (on sales to the subsidiary) recorded during the current period and for realization of profits deferred from previous periods. It is also adjusted for the amortizations of excess resulting from the original purchase of the subsidiary. **This would be all of the adjustments that appear on the parent's income distribution schedule, except for the inclusion of the parent's share of subsidiary income.** Likewise, the income used to compute the subsidiary DEPS must be adjusted for intercompany transactions (as shown in the subsidiary income distribution schedule). To illustrate the computation of consolidated DEPS, assume the following data concerning the subsidiary:

Net income (adjusted for intercompany profits)	$22,000
Preferred stock cash dividend	$2,000
Interest paid on convertible bonds	$3,000
Common stock shares outstanding	5,000
Warrants to purchase one share of common stock	1,000
Warrants held by parent	500
Convertible bonds outstanding (convertible into 10 shares of common stock)	200
Convertible bonds held by parent	180

$$\frac{\text{Subsidiary}}{\text{DEPS}} = \frac{\$22,000 - \overset{(1)}{\$2,000} + \overset{(2)}{\$3,000}}{5,000 + \underset{(3)}{2,000} + \underset{(4)}{500}} = \$3.07$$

(1) Dividend on nonconvertible preferred stock, none of which is owned by the parent.
(2) Income adjustment for convertible bonds which are dilutive.
(3) Share adjustment associated with convertible debentures, 200 bonds × 10 shares per bond.
(4) Share adjustment (treasury stock method—see Chapter 8) associated with the warrants. It is assumed that, using the average fair value of the stock, 500 shares could be purchased with the proceeds of the sale and that 500 additional new shares would be issued.

Assume the parent owns 80% of the subsidiary and has an adjusted internally generated net income of $40,000 and 10,000 shares of common stock outstanding. Also assume the parent has dilutive bonds outstanding, which are convertible into 3,000 shares of common stock and the interest paid on these bonds was $5,000. The consolidated DEPS would be computed as follows:

$$\text{Consolidated DEPS} = \frac{\overset{(1)}{\$40,000 + \$5,000} + \overset{(2)}{\$18,574}}{\underset{(3)}{10,000 + 3,000}} = \$4.89$$

(1) Income adjustment from interest on parent company convertible bonds, which are dilutive.

(2) Subsidiary common shares owned by parent

     (80% × 5,000)   4,000

     Parent-owned equivalent shares applicable to convertible

     bonds (90% × 2,000)*   1,800

     Parent-owned equivalent shares applicable to warrants

     (50% × 500)**   250

     Total parent-owned equivalent shares   6,050

     Parent's interest in subsidiary income

     (6,050 shares × $3.07 subsidiary DEPS) $18,574

(3) Shares assumed to be issued in exchange for parent company convertible bonds (a CSE).

   *Parent owns 180 (or 90%) of 200 subsidiary bonds.

**Parent owns 500 (or 50%) of 1,000 subsidiary warrants.

If the dilutive subsidiary securities enable the holder to acquire common stock of the parent, these securities are not included in the computation of subsidiary DEPS. However, these securities must be included in the parent's share adjustment in computing consolidated DEPS. The basic model by which to compute consolidated DEPS in this situation is as follows:

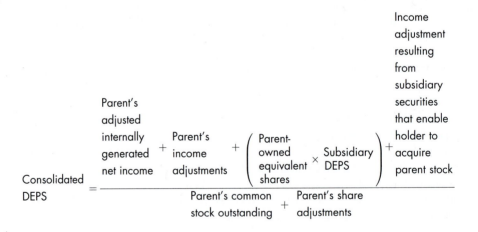

To illustrate, assume the following facts for a parent owning 90% of the outstanding subsidiary shares:

Parent internally adjusted net income $20,000

Parent company common stock shares outstanding   10,000

Parent company dilutive convertible bonds:

     Interest expense $1,000

     Shares to be issued in conversion   2,000

Subsidiary adjusted net income $7,000

Subsidiary common stock shares outstanding   4,000

Subsidiary preferred stock convertible into parent common stock:

Dividend requirement	$1,200
Number of preferred shares.	1,000
Number of parent company common shares required	2,000
Subsidiary common stock warrants to acquire 100 parent shares	100

The first step is to calculate the subsidiary's BEPS as follows:

$$\frac{\text{Subsidiary}}{\text{DEPS}} = \frac{\$7,000 - \$1,200 \text{ preferred dividends}}{4,000 \text{ outstanding shares}} = \$1.45$$

Note that the subsidiary convertible preferred stock and stock warrants are not satisfied with subsidiary shares and, thus, are not considered converted for the purpose of calculating subsidiary EPS. The consolidated DEPS would be computed as follows:

$$\frac{\text{Consolidated}}{\text{DEPS}} = \frac{\overset{(1)}{\$20,000} + \overset{}{\$1,000} + \overset{(2)}{[3,600 \times \$1.45]} + \overset{(3)}{\$1,200}}{\underset{(4)}{10,000 + (2,000 + 2,000 + 50)}} = \$1.95$$

(1) $1,000 income adjustment associated with the parent company convertible security.

(2) The parent's share of subsidiary EPS. Again, since the subsidiary's preferred stock and warrants are not convertible into subsidiary shares, the total parent-owned equivalent shares is 90% × 4,000.

(3) Income adjustment representing the dividend on subsidiary preferred shares that would not be paid if the shares were converted into common stock of the parent. Note that 100% of the adjustment is added back, even though the parent's interest in the subsidiary is less than 100%.

(4) The parent's share adjustment consisting of 2,000 shares traceable to the parent company convertible security; 2,000 shares traceable to the subsidiary preferred stock that is convertible into parent common stock; and 50 incremental shares traceable to the subsidiary warrants to acquire parent common stock. It is assumed that 50 of the 100 shares required to satisfy the warrants can be purchased with the proceeds of the exercise and 50 new shares must be issued.

Special analysis is required in computing consolidated BEPS and DEPS when an acquisition occurs during a reporting period. When the acquisition is a pooling of interests, the computations of both BEPS and DEPS include subsidiary income and securities for the entire period. However, when the acquisition is a purchase, only subsidiary income since the acquisition date is included, and the number of subsidiary shares is weighted for the partial period.

REFLECTION

- Prior to calculating consolidated EPS, the subsidiary's EPS (including dilution adjustments that add more subsidiary shares) is calculated.

- The parent's numerator for EPS includes its own internally generated net income plus its share of subsidiary EPS.

- The parent also adjusts its numerator and denominator for dilative parent company securities and subsidiary securities that are satisfied by issuing parent company shares.

5

OBJECTIVE

Apply consolidation-type
procedures to influential
investments.

EQUITY METHOD FOR UNCONSOLIDATED INVESTMENTS

The equity method for unconsolidated investments requires that income of the investee is recorded as earned, unrelated to when it is paid to the investor as dividends. The equity method is required for the following types of investments:

1. *Influential investments.* Influence is described as "representation on the board of directors, participation in policy-making processes, material intercompany transactions, interchange of managerial personnel, or technological dependency."[1] When the investor holds 20% or more of the voting shares of an investee, influence is assumed and the sophisticated equity method is required unless the investor takes on the burden of proof to show that influence does not exist, in which case the cost method would be used.[2] When the investment falls below 20%, the presumption is that influence does not exist, and the cost method is to be used unless the investor can show that influence does exist despite the low percentage of ownership. Since the most common use of the sophisticated equity method is for influential (20% to 50%) investments, such investments are used in subsequent illustrations.

2. *Corporate joint ventures.* A corporate joint venture is a separate, specific project organized for the benefit of several corporations. An example would be a research project undertaken jointly by several members of a given industry. The member corporations typically participate in the management of the venture and share the gains and losses. Since such an arrangement does not involve passive investors, the sophisticated equity method is required.

3. *Unconsolidated subsidiaries.* A parent may own over 50% of the shares of a subsidiary but may meet one of the exceptions (control is temporary or does not rest with the majority owner) to the requirement that subsidiaries be consolidated. However, if influence does exist, the sophisticated equity method would be used for the investment.

The use of the equity method requires that the investment in common stock appear as a single, equity-adjusted amount on the balance sheet of the investor. The investor's income statement will include the investor's share of the investee ordinary income as a single amount in the ordinary income section. The investor's share of investee discontinued operations and extraordinary items will appear as single amounts in the sections of the investor's income statement that correspond to the placement of these items in the investee's statement.

Calculation of Equity Income

In its basic form, the equity method requires the investor to recognize its pro rata share of investee reported income. Dividends, when received, do not constitute income, but are viewed instead as a partial liquidation of the investment. In reality, however, the price paid for the investment usually will not agree with the underlying book value of the investee, which requires that any amortization of an excess of cost or book value be treated as an adjustment of the investor's pro rata share of investee income. It is very likely that the reported income of the investee will include gains and losses on transactions with the investor. As was true in consolidations, these gains and losses cannot be recognized until they are confirmed by a transaction between the affiliated group and unrelated parties. The proper application of the sophisticated equity method will mean that the income recognized by the investor will be the same as it would be under consolidation procedures. In fact, the sophisticated equity method sometimes is referred to as "one-line consolidation."

Amortization of Excesses. A determination and distribution of excess schedule is prepared for a sophisticated equity method investment just as it would be if the investment were to be

---

1 Opinions of the Accounting Principles Board No. 18, *The Equity Method of Accounting for Investments in Common Stock* (New York: American Institute of Certified Public Accountants, 1971), par. 17.

2 For examples of situations that may overcome the presumption of influence, see FASB Interpretation No. 35, *Criteria for Applying the Equity Method of Accounting for Investments in Common Stock* (Stamford: Financial Accounting Standards Board, 1981).

consolidated. For example, assume the following schedule was prepared by Excel Corporation for a 25% interest in Flag Company acquired on January 1, 20X1:

Price paid		$250,000
Less interest acquired:		
Common stock ($10 par)	$200,000	
Retained earnings, January 1, 20X1	600,000	
Total stockholders' equity	$800,000	
Interest acquired	× 25%	200,000
Excess of cost over book value		$ 50,000
Less excess attributable to equipment with a five-year remaining		
life and undervalued by $80,000, 25% × $80,000		20,000
Goodwill (not amortized)		$ 30,000

As a practical matter, it may not be possible to relate the excess to specific assets, in which case the entire excess may be considered goodwill. However, an attempt should be made to allocate the excess in the same manner as would be done for the purchase of a controlling interest in a subsidiary.

The determination and distribution of excess schedule indicates the pattern of amortization to be followed. The required amortizations must be made directly through the investment account since the distributions shown on the schedule are not recorded in the absence of consolidation procedures. The debit and credit indicators have been dropped from the determination and distribution of excess schedule since there will not be any worksheet adjustments in the absence of consolidation. Assuming Flag Company reported net income of $60,000 for 20X1, Excel Corporation would make the following entry for 20X1:

Investment in Flag Company	11,000	
Investment Income		11,000

Income is calculated as follows:

25% × Flag reported net income of $60,000	$15,000
Less amortizations of excess cost:	
Equipment, $20,000 ÷ 5	4,000
Investment income, net of amortizations	$11,000

If an investment is acquired for less than book value, the excess of book value over cost would be amortized based on the life of assets to which it pertains. This procedure would increase investment income in the years of amortization.

Intercompany Transactions by Investee. The investee may sell inventory to the investor. As would be true if the investment were consolidated, the share of the investee's profit on goods still held by the investor at the end of a period cannot be included in income of that period. Instead, the profit must be deferred until the goods are sold by the investor. Since the two firms are separate reporting entities, the intercompany sales and related debt cannot be eliminated. Only the investor's share of the investee's profit on unsold goods in the hands of the investor is deferred. In a like manner, the investor may have plant assets that were purchased from the investee. The investor's share of the investee's gains and losses on these sales also must be deferred and allocated over the depreciable life of the asset. Profit deferments should be handled in an income distribution schedule similar to that used for consolidated worksheets. To illustrate, assume the following facts for the example of the 25% investment in Flag by Excel. Again, note that income tax is not being considered in this illustration:

1. Excel had the following merchandise acquired from Flag Company in its ending inventories:

Year	Amount	Gross Profit of Flag Company
20X1	$30,000	40%
20X2	40,000	45

2. Excel purchased a truck from Flag Company on January 1, 20X1, for $20,000. The truck is being depreciated over a four-year life on a straight-line basis with no salvage value. The truck had a net book value of $16,000 when it was sold by Flag.
3. Flag Company had an income of $60,000 in 20X1 and $70,000 in 20X2.
4. Flag declared and paid $10,000 in dividends in 20X2.

Based on these facts, Excel Corporation would prepare the following income distribution schedules:

20X1 Income Distribution for Investment in Flag Company

Gain on sale of truck, to be amortized over four years	$ 4,000	Reported income of Flag Company.	$60,000
Profit in Excel ending inventory, 40% × $30,000	12,000	Realization of ¼ of profit on sale of truck	1,000
		Adjusted income of Flag Company	$45,000
		Ownership interest, 25%.	$11,250
		Less amortization of excess cost:	
		Equipment	4,000
		Investment income, net of amortizations.	$ 7,250

20X2 Income Distribution for Investment in Flag Company

Profit in Excel ending inventory, 40% × $40,000	$18,000	Reported income of Flag Company.	$70,000
		Profit in Excel beginning inventory, 40% × $30,000	12,000
		Realization of ¼ of profit on sale of truck	1,000
		Adjusted income of Flag Company	$65,000
		Ownership interest, 25%.	$16,250
		Less amortization of excess cost:	
		Equipment	4,000
		Income from investment.	$12,250

The schedules would lead to the following entries to record investment income:

20X1	Investment in Flag Company	7,250	
	Investment Income		7,250
20X2	Investment in Flag Company	12,250	
	Investment Income		12,250

In addition, the following entry would be made in 20X2 to record dividends received:

Cash	2,500	
Investment in Flag Company		2,500

It should be noted that only the investor's share of intercompany gains and losses is deferred. The investee's remaining stockholders are not affected by the Excel Corporation investment.

Unusual Equity Adjustments

There are several unusual situations involving the investee that require special procedures for the proper recording of investment income. These situations are described in the following paragraphs.

Investee with Preferred Stock. In the absence of consolidation, an investment in preferred stock does not require elimination. However, the existence of preferred stock in the capital structure of the investee requires that the investor's equity adjustment be based on only that portion of investee income available for common stockholders. Dividends declared on preferred stock must be subtracted from income of the investee. When the preferred stock has cumulative or participation rights, the claim of preferred stockholders must be subtracted from the investee income each period to arrive at the income available for common stockholders.

Investee Stock Transactions. The investee corporation may engage in transactions with its common stockholders, such as issuing additional shares, retiring shares, or engaging in treasury stock transactions. Each of these transactions affects the investor's equity interest. A comparison is made of the investor's ownership interest before and after the investee stock transaction. An increase in the investor's interest is treated as a gain, while a decrease is recorded as a loss.

Write-Down to Market Value. The investment in another company is subject to reduction to a lower market value if it appears that a relatively permanent fall in value has occurred. The fact that the current market value of the shares is temporarily less than the equity-adjusted cost of the shares is not sufficient cause for a write-down. When the sophisticated equity method is used and a permanent decline in value occurs, a reduction would be made to the equity-adjusted cost. The equity method would continue to be applied subsequent to the write-down. There can be no subsequent write-ups, however, other than through normal equity adjustments.

Zero Investment Balance. It is possible that an investee will suffer losses to the extent that the continued application of the equity method could produce a negative balance in the investment account. Equity adjustments are to be discontinued when the investment balance becomes zero.[3] Further losses are acknowledged only by memo entries, which are needed to maintain the total unrecorded share of losses. If the investee again becomes profitable, the investor must not record income on the investment until its subsequent share of income equals the previously unrecorded share of losses.

 To illustrate these procedures, assume Grate Corporation has a 35% investment in Dittmar Company, with a sophisticated equity-adjusted cost of $30,000 on January 1, 20X1, and Dittmar reports the following results:

Period	Income (loss)
20X1	$(80,000)
20X2	(50,000)
20X3	(20,000)
20X4	90,000

---

3 According to APB Opinion No. 18 (par. 19i), any net advance to the investee that the investor may have on its books also is available to offset the inventory's share of investee losses until the receivable is reduced to a zero balance.

The following T-account summarizes entries for 20X1 through 20X4 (taxes are ignored):

Investment in Dittmar Company			
Equity-adjusted balance, January 1, 20X1	$30,000	Equity loss for 20X1, 35% × $80,000 Dittmar loss	$28,000
		Recorded equity loss for 20X2, 35% × $50,000 Dittmar loss = $17,500; loss limited to investment balance	2,000
Balance, January 1, 20X2.....................	$ 0		
		Memo entries: Unrecorded 20X2 loss, $17,500 − $2,000	$15,500
Memo entry: Unrecorded share of 20X4 Dittmar income........	22,500	Unrecorded loss for 20X3, 35% × $20,000 Dittmar loss	7,000
Actual entries resumed: Recorded equity income, 20X4, 35% × $90,000 Dittmar income, less amount to cover unrecorded losses ($15,500 + $7,000)	$ 9,000		
Balance, December 31, 20X4	$ 9,000		

Intercompany Transactions by Investor. An investor may sell merchandise and/or plant assets to an investee at a gain or loss. When influence is deemed to exist, it might seem appropriate to defer the entire gain or loss until the asset is resold or depreciated by the investee. However, an interpretation of APB Opinion No. 18 requires the entire gain or loss to be deferred only when the transaction is with a controlled (over 50%-owned) investee and is not at arm's length. In all other cases, it is appropriate to defer only a gain or loss that is in proportion to the investor's ownership interest.[4]

To illustrate, assume Grant Corporation, which owns a 35% interest in Hartwig Company, sold $50,000 of merchandise to Hartwig at a gross profit of 40%. Of this merchandise, $20,000 is still in Hartwig's 20X1 ending inventory. Grant needs to defer only profit equal to the $8,000 (40% × $20,000) unrealized gross profit multiplied by its 35% interest, or $2,800. Grant would make the following entry on December 31, 20X1:

Sales	2,800	
Deferred Gross Profit on Sales to Investee		2,800

Assuming the investor recorded the provision for income tax prior to this adjustment, the tax applicable to the unrealized gain would be deferred by the following entry, which is based on a 30% tax rate:

Deferred Tax Expense (30% × $2,800)	840	
Provision for Income Tax		840

The deferred gross profit and the related tax deferment would be realized in the period in which the goods are sold to outside parties. The deferred profit and related tax effects on plant asset sales would be realized in proportion to the depreciation recorded by the investee company.

It may occur that the investor will purchase outstanding bonds of the investee. Unlike consolidation procedures, the bonds are not assumed to be retired since the investor and investee are separate reporting entities. Similarly, a purchase of investor bonds by the investee is not a retirement of the bonds. Thus, no adjustments to income are necessary as a result of intercompany bond holdings.

---

4 Accounting Interpretations, *The Equity Method of Accounting for Investments in Common Stock: Accounting Interpretations of APB Opinion No. 18* (New York: American Institute of Certified Public Accountants, 1971), par. 1.

Gain or Loss of Influence. An investor may own less than a 20% interest in an investee, in which case the cost method ordinarily would be used to record investment income. If the investor subsequently buys sufficient additional shares to have its total interest equal to or exceed 20%, the investor must retroactively apply the sophisticated equity method to the total holding period of the investment. APB Opinion No. 18 requires an adjustment of retained earnings for the period prior to the time the 20% interest is achieved.

It is possible that an investor will own 20% or more of the voting shares of the investee but will sell a portion of the shares so that the ownership interest falls below 20%. In such a case, the sophisticated equity method is discontinued as of the sale date. However, there is no adjustment back to the cost method. The balance of the investment account remains at its equity-adjusted balance on the sale date. Should influence be attained again, a retroactive ("catch-up") equity adjustment would be made.

When all or part of an investment recorded under the sophisticated equity method is sold, the gain or loss is based on the equity-adjusted balance as of the sale date. An adjustment also would be necessary for deferred tax balances applicable to the investment.

Disclosure Requirements

Since a significant portion of the investor's income may be derived from investments, added disclosures are required in order to properly inform the readers of the financial statements. For investments of 20% or more, the investor must disclose the name of each investee, the percentage of ownership in each investee, and the disparity between the cost and underlying book value for each investment. If the sophisticated equity method is not being applied, the reasons must be given. When investments are material with respect to the investor's financial position or income, the financial statements of the investees should be included as supplemental information.

When a market value for the investment is available, it should be disclosed. However, if the investor owns a relatively large block of a subsidiary's shares, quoted market values would have little relevance because the sale of an entire controlling interest would involve different motivations and would result in a unique value.

REFLECTION

- The sophisticated equity method is used for "influential" investments.

- The sophisticated equity income is based on the investee's adjusted (for intercompany profits) income less amortizations of excess from the D&D. Note that this process includes adjustment for only investee-generated intercompany transactions.

- The investor must make a separate adjustment for its share of unrealized profits on sales to the investee.

- The investor cannot adjust its investment below a zero balance by recording its share of investee losses. If the investee becomes profitable, income equal to the unrecorded losses must be excluded from income.

- An initial ownership interest may not be "influential." If a second block is purchased, so as to make the total interest "influential," the prior block is retroactively converted to the sophisticated equity method.

- If an interest is sold down to a level that is no longer influential, the remaining interest stays at its equity-adjusted cost. The use of the equity method is discontinued in future periods.

APPENDIX: THE VERTICAL WORKSHEET

The text has used the *horizontal worksheet format* for all worksheet examples. Columns for eliminations and adjustments, consolidated income, NCI, controlling retained earnings, and the balance sheet are arranged horizontally in adjacent columns. This format makes it convenient

6

OBJECTIVE

Be able to apply consolidation procedures to a worksheet that is arranged in a vertical format.

to extend account balances from one column to the next. This is the format that you used for trial balance working papers in introductory and intermediate accounting. It is also the most common worksheet format used in practice. The horizontal format is used in all worksheet problems except those that relate to this appendix.

The alternative format is the *vertical format*. Rather than beginning the worksheet with the trial balances of the parent and the subsidiary, this format begins with the completed income statements, statements of retained earnings, and the balance sheets of the parent and subsidiary. This method, which is seldom used in practice and harder to master, has been used on the CPA Exam.

The vertical format is used in Worksheet 5-5 on pages 262 and 263. This worksheet is based on the same facts used for Worksheet 3-6 (an equity method example for the second year of a purchase with a complicated distribution of excess cost). Worksheet 5-5 is based on the determination and distribution of excess schedule.

Worksheet 5-5: page 262

Price paid for investment (including direct

acquisition costs)....................................		**$700,000**			

Less book value of interest purchased:

Common stock, $10 par	$ 100,000					
Paid-in capital in excess of par	150,000					
Retained earnings	250,000					
Total equity	$ 500,000					
Ownership interest	× 80%	400,000				
Excess of cost over book value		**$300,000**	Credit/Key	**Amort. Period**	**Amort. Amount**	

Adjustments:

Inventory, 80% of $5,000 fair-book value	$ 4,000		Debit D1	1	$ 4,000
Land, 80% of $50,000 fair-book value.....................	40,000		Debit D2	None	
Discount on bonds payable, 80% of $13,250 fair-book value . . .	10,600		Debit D3	4	2,650
Buildings (net), 80% of $200,000 fair-book value	160,000		Debit D4	20	8,000
Equipment (net), 80% of ($20,000) fair-book value	(16,000)		Debit D5	5	(3,200)
Patent (net), 80% of $25,000 fair-book value................	20,000		Debit D6	10	2,000
Goodwill	81,400		Debit D7		
Total adjustments.................................		**$300,000**			

The schedule of worksheet amortizations is as follows:

Account Adjustments	Life	Annual Amount	Current Year	Prior Years	Total	Key
Inventory	1	$ 4,000	$ 0	$ 4,000	$ 4,000	(D1)
Subject to amortization:						
Bonds payable	4	$ 2,650	$ 2,650	$ 2,650	$ 5,300	(A3)
Buildings	20	8,000	8,000	8,000	16,000	(A4)
Equipment	5	(3,200)	(3,200)	(3,200)	(6,400)	(A5)
Patent (net)................	10	2,000	2,000	2,000	4,000	(A6)
Total....................		$ 9,450	$ 9,450	$ 9,450	$18,900	

Note that the original separate statements are stacked vertically upon each other. Be sure to follow the carrydown procedure as it is applied to the separate statements. Inspect Worksheet 5-5. The net income from the income statement is allocated to the NCI and controlling interest using the IDS schedules. The IDS share of income is carried to the NCI retained earnings and the parent share is carried down to controlling retained earnings. The NCI retained earnings is carried down to the NCI line and then transferred vertically to the balance sheet. Then, the ending controlling retained earnings balance is carried down to the balance sheet.

Understand that there are no differences in the elimination and adjustment procedures as a result of this alternative format. Compare the elimination entries to those in Worksheet 3-6.

Even though there is no change in the eliminations, there are two areas of caution. First, the order in which the accounts appear is reversed; that is, nominal accounts precede balance sheet accounts. This difference in order will require care in making eliminations. Second, the eliminations to retained earnings must be made against the January 1 beginning balances, not the December 31 ending balances. The ending retained earnings balances are never adjusted but are derived after all eliminations have been made.

The complicated aspect of the vertical worksheet is the the mechanical carrydown procedure used to create the retained earnings statement and the balance sheet. Arrows are used in Worksheet 5-5 to emphasize the carrydown procedure. Note that the net income line in the retained earnings statement and the retained earnings lines on the balance sheet are never available to receive eliminations. These balances are always carried down. The net income balances are derived from the same income distribution schedules used in Worksheet 3-6.

Worksheet 5-6 on pages 264 and 265 is another example of a vertical format worksheet. It includes intercompany inventory and fixed asset transactions. The facts for the example are as follows:

Worksheet 5-6: page 264

1. Company P purchased an 80% interest in Company S on January 1, 20X1. At that time, the following determination and distribution of excess schedule was prepared:

Price paid		$500,000
Less interest acquired:		
Common stock ($5 par)	$200,000	
Retained earnings, January 1, 20X1	350,000	
Total stockholders' equity	$550,000	
Interest acquired	× 80%	440,000
Excess of cost over book value attributed to goodwill		$ 60,000

2. Company P accounts for the investment under the simple equity method.

3. Company S sells merchandise to Company P to yield a gross profit of 20%. Sales totaled $150,000 during 20X2. There were $40,000 of such goods in Company P's beginning inventory and $50,000 of such goods in Company P's ending inventory. As of December 31, 20X2, Company P had not paid the $20,000 owed for the purchases.

4. On July 1, 20X1, Company P sold a new machine that cost $20,000 to Company S for $25,000. At that time, both companies believed that the machine had a five-year remaining life; both companies use straight-line depreciation.

5. Company S declared and paid $20,000 in dividends during 20X2.

Notice that the worksheet eliminations in Worksheet 5-6 are identical to those required for the horizontal format.

REFLECTION

- On vertical worksheets for consolidations subsequent to acquisition, the income statement accounts appear at the top, followed by the retained earnings statement accounts, and then the balance sheet accounts.

- Net income is carried down to the retained earnings section.

- Ending retained earnings is then carried down to the balance sheet section.

- On a vertical worksheet, the eliminating and adjusting entries are the same as those on a trial balance worksheet.

Worksheet 5-1

Intercompany Investment in Bonds, Year of Acquisition; Straight-Line Method of Amortization
Company P and Subsidiary Company S
Worksheet for Consolidated Balance Sheet
For Year Ended December 31, 20X3

| | (Credit balance amounts are in parentheses.) | Trial Balance | |
		Company P	Company S
1	Other Assets	56,400	220,000
2	**Interest Receivable**	**8,000**	
3	Investment in Company S Stock (90%)	100,800	
4			
5	**Investment in Company S Bonds (100%)**	**102,400**	
6	**Interest Payable**		**(8,000)**
7	**Bonds Payable, 8%**		**(100,000)**
8	Common Stock ($10 par), Company P	(100,000)	
9	Retained Earnings, January 1, 20X3, Company P	(120,000)	
10	Common Stock ($10 par), Company S		(80,000)
11	Retained Earnings, January 1, 20X3, Company S		(20,000)
12	Operating Revenue	(100,000)	(80,000)
13	Operating Expense	70,000	60,000
14	**Interest Income**	**(6,800)**	
15	**Interest Expense**		**8,000**
16	Subsidiary Income	(10,800)	
17	**Loss on Bond Retirement**		
18		0	0
19	Consolidated Net Income		
20	To NCI (see distribution schedule)		
21	Balance to Controlling Interest (see distribution schedule)		
22	Total NCI		
23	Retained Earnings, Controlling Interest, December 31, 20X3		
24			

Eliminations and Adjustments:

(CY) Eliminate the entry recording the parent's share of subsidiary net income for the current year. This entry returns the investment in Company S stock account to its January 1, 20X3 balance to aid the elimination process.

(EL) Eliminate 90% of the subsidiary equity balances of January 1, 20X3, against the investment in stock account. No excess results.

(B1) Eliminate intercompany interest revenue and expense. Eliminate the balance of the investment in bonds against the bonds payable. Note that the investment in bonds is at its end-of-the-year amortized balance. The loss on retirement at the date the bonds were purchased is calculated as follows:

Loss remaining at year-end:		
Investment in bonds at December 31, 20X3	$102,400	
Less: Carrying value of bonds at December 31, 20X3	100,000	$2,400
Loss amortized during year:		
Interest expense eliminated	$ 8,000	
Less: Interest revenue eliminated	6,800	1,200
Loss at January 2, 20X3.		$3,600

(B2) Eliminate intercompany interest payable and receivable.

Worksheet 5-1 (see page 229)

Eliminations & Adjustments			Consolidated Income Statement	NCI	Controlling Retained Earnings	Consolidated Balance Sheet	
Dr.		Cr.					
						276,400	1
	(B2)	8,000					2
	(CY1)	10,800					3
	(EL)	90,000					4
	(B1)	102,400					5
(B2)	8,000						6
(B1)	100,000						7
						(100,000)	8
					(120,000)		9
(EL)	72,000			(8,000)			10
(EL)	18,000			(2,000)			11
			(180,000)				12
			130,000				13
(B1)	6,800						14
		(B1) 8,000					15
(CY1)	10,800						16
(B1)	3,600		3,600				17
	219,200	219,200					18
			(46,400)				19
			960	(960)			20
			45,440		(45,440)		21
				(10,960)		(10,960)	22
					(165,440)	(165,440)	23
						0	24

Subsidiary Company S Income Distribution

Loss on bond retirement . . . . **(B1)**	**$3,600**	Internally generated net income,		
		including interest expense		**$12,000**
		Interest adjustment		
		($3,600 ÷ 3) . . . .**(B1)**		**1,200**
		Adjusted income	$	9,600
		NCI share	×	10%
		NCI	$	960

Parent Company P Income Distribution

Internally generated net income,		
including interest revenue		**$36,800**
90% × Company S adjusted income of		
$9,600		8,640
Controlling interest		$ 45,440

Worksheet 5-2

Intercompany Investment in Bonds, Year Subsequent to Acquisition; Straight-Line Method of Amortization
Company P and Subsidiary Company S
Worksheet for Consolidated Financial Statements
For Year Ended December 31, 20X4

	(Credit balance amounts are in parentheses.)	Trial Balance	
		Company P	Company S
1	Other Assets	94,400	242,000
2	Interest Receivable	8,000	
3	Investment in Company S Stock (90%)	120,600	
4			
5	**Investment in Company S Bonds (100%)**	**101,200**	
6	Interest Payable		(8,000)
7	Bonds Payable, 8%		(100,000)
8	Common Stock ($10 par), Company P	(100,000)	
9	**Retained Earnings, January 1, 20X4, Company P**	**(167,600)**	
10	Common Stock ($10 par), Company S		(80,000)
11	**Retained Earnings, January 1, 20X3, Company S**		**(32,000)**
12			
13	Operating Revenue	(130,000)	(100,000)
14	Operating Expense	100,000	70,000
15	Subsidiary Income	(19,800)	
16	Interest Expense		8,000
17	Interest Income	(6,800)	
18		0	0
19	Consolidated Net Income		
20	To NCI (see distribution schedule)		
21	Balance to Controlling Interest (see distribution schedule)		
22	Total NCI		
23	Retained Earnings, Controlling Interest, December 31, 20X4		
24			

Eliminations and Adjustments:

(CY) Eliminate the entry recording the parent's share of subsidiary net income for the current year.
(EL) Eliminate 90% of the subsidiary equity balances of January 1, 20X4, against the investment in stock account. There is no excess to be distributed.
(B1) Eliminate intercompany interest revenue and expense. Eliminate the balance of the investment in bonds against the bonds payable. Note that the investment in bonds is at its end-of-the-year amortized balance. The remaining unamortized loss on retirement at the start of the year is calculated as follows:

Loss remaining at year-end:
Investment in bonds at December 31, 20X4 . . . . $101,200
Less: Carrying value of bonds at December 31, 20X4 . . . . 100,000 $1,200

Loss amortized during year:
Interest expense eliminated . . . . $ 8,000
Less: Interest revenue eliminated 6,800   1,200

Remaining loss at January 1, 20X4 . . . . $2,400

The remaining unamortized loss of $2,400 on January 1, 20X4, is allocated 90% to the controlling retained earnings and 10% to the noncontrolling retained earnings since the bonds were issued by the subsidiary.
(B2) Eliminate intercompany interest payable and receivable.

Worksheet 5-2 (see page 230)

| Eliminations & Adjustments | | Consolidated Income Statement | NCI | Controlling Retained Earnings | Consolidated Balance Sheet | |
Dr.	Cr.					
					336,400	1
	(B2) 8,000					2
	(CY1) 19,800					3
	(EL) 100,800					4
	(B1) 101,200					5
(B2) 8,000						6
(B1) 100,000						7
					(100,000)	8
(B1) 2,160				(165,440)		9
(EL) 72,000			(8,000)			10
(EL) 28,800			(2,960)			11
(B1) 240						12
		(230,000)				13
		170,000				14
(CY1) 19,800						15
	(B1) 8,000					16
(B1) 6,800						17
237,800	237,800					18
		(60,000)				19
		2,320	(2,320)			20
		57,680		(57,680)		21
			(13,280)		(13,280)	22
				(223,120)	(223,120)	23
					0	24

Subsidiary Company S Income Distribution

Internally generated net income, including interest expense		$22,000
Interest adjustment ($3,600 ÷ 3) . . . .**(B1)**		1,200
Adjusted income		$23,200
NCI share		× 10%
NCI		$ 2,320

Parent Company P Income Distribution

Internally generated net income, including interest revenue		$36,800
90% × Company S adjusted income of $23,200		20,880
Controlling interest		$57,680

Worksheet 5-3

Intercompany Bonds, Subsequent Period; Straight-Line Method of Amortization
Company P and Subsidiary Company S
Worksheet for Consolidated Financial Statements
For Year Ended December 31, 20X4

	(Credit balance amounts are in parentheses.)	Trial Balance	
		Company P	Company S
1	Other Assets	59,400	259,082
2	Investment in Company S Stock	143,874	
3			
4	Investment in Company S Bonds	101,800	
5	Bonds Payable		(100,000)
6	**Discount on Bonds**		778
7	Common Stock, Company P	(100,000)	
8	**Retained Earnings, January 1, 20X4, Company P**	(160,000)	
9	Common Stock, Company S		(40,000)
10	**Retained Earnings, January 1, 20X4, Company S**		(110,000)
11			
12	Sales	(80,000)	(50,000)
13	**Interest Income**	(6,200)	
14	Cost of Goods Sold	50,000	31,362
15	**Interest Expense**		8,778
16	Subsidiary Income	(8,874)	
17		0	0
18	Consolidated Net Income		
19	To NCI (see distribution schedule)		
20	Balance to Controlling Interest (see distribution schedule)		
21	Total NCI		
22	Retained Earnings, Controlling Interest, December 31, 20X4		
23			

Eliminations and Adjustments:

(CY1) Eliminate the entry recording the parent's share of subsidiary net income for the current year.
(EL)   Eliminate 90% of the January 1, 20X4, subsidiary equity balances against the January 1, 20X4, investment in Company S stock balance. No excess results.
(B)   Eliminate intercompany interest revenue and expense. Eliminate the balance of the investment in bonds against the bonds payable. Note that the investment in bonds and the discount on bonds are at their end-of-the-year amortized balances. The remaining unamortized loss on retirement at the start of the year is calculated as follows:

Loss remaining at year-end:			
Investment in bonds at December 31, 20X4		$101,800	
Less: Bonds payable at December 31, 20X4	$100,000		
Discount on bonds at December 31, 20X4	(778)	99,222	$2,578
Loss amortized during year:			
Interest expense eliminated		$ 8,778	
Less: Interest revenue eliminated		6,200	2,578
Remaining loss at January 1, 20X4			$5,156

Since from the consolidated viewpoint the bonds were retired in the prior year and since the bonds were issued by the subsidiary, the remaining unamortized loss of $5,156 on January 1, 20X4, is allocated 90% to the controlling retained earnings and 10% to the noncontrolling retained earnings.

Worksheet 5-3 (see page 232)

Eliminations & Adjustments		Consolidated Income Statement	NCI	Controlling Retained Earnings	Consolidated Balance Sheet	
Dr.	Cr.					
					318,482	1
	(CY1) 8,874					2
	(EL) 135,000					3
	(B) 101,800					4
(B) 100,000						5
	(B) 778					6
					(100,000)	7
(B) 4,640				(155,360)		8
(EL) 36,000			(4,000)			9
(EL) 99,000			(10,484)			10
(B) 516						11
		(130,000)				12
(B) 6,200						13
		81,362				14
	(B) 8,778					15
(CY1) 8,874						16
255,230	255,230					17
		(48,638)				18
		1,244	(1,244)			19
		47,394		(47,394)		20
			(15,728)		(15,728)	21
				(202,754)	(202,754)	22
					0	23

Subsidiary Company S Income Distribution

	Internally generated net income, including interest expense	$ 9,860
	Interest adjustment ($8,778 − $6,200) . . . .(B)	**2,578**
	Adjusted income	$ 12,438
	NCI share	× 10%
	NCI	$ 1,244

Parent Company P Income Distribution

	Internally generated net income, including interest revenue	$36,200
	90% × Company S adjusted income of $12,438	11,194
	Controlling interest	$47,394

Worksheet 5-4

Intercompany Bonds; Interest Method of Amortization
Company P and Subsidiary Company S
Worksheet for Consolidated Financial Statements
For Year Ended December 31, 20X4

	(Credit balance amounts are in parentheses.)	Trial Balance	
		Company P	Company S
1	Other Assets	59,333	259,082
2	Investment in Company S Stock	144,000	
3			
4	**Investment in Company S Bonds**	**101,887**	
5	**Bonds Payable**		**(100,000)**
6	**Discount on Bonds**		**918**
7	Common Stock, Company P	(100,000)	
8	Retained Earnings, January 1, 20X4, Company P	(160,180)	
9	Common Stock, Company S		(40,000)
10	Retained Earnings, January 1, 20X4, Company S		(110,200)
11			
12	Sales	(80,000)	(50,000)
13	**Interest Income**	**(6,220)**	
14	Cost of Goods Sold	50,000	31,358
15	**Interest Expense**		**8,842**
16			
17	Subsidiary Income	(8,820)	
18		0	0
19	Consolidated Net Income		
20	To NCI (see distribution schedule)		
21	Balance to Controlling Interest (see distribution schedule)		
22	Total NCI		
23	Retained Earnings, Controlling Interest, December 31, 20X4		
24			

Eliminations and Adjustments:

(CY1)   Eliminate the entry recording the parent's share of subsidiary net income for the current year.
(EL)   Eliminate 90% of the January 1, 20X4, subsidiary equity balances against the January 1, 20X4, investment in Company S stock balance. No excess results.
(B)   Eliminate intercompany interest revenue and expense. Eliminate the balance of the investment in bonds against the bonds payable. Note that the investment in bonds and the discount on bonds are at their end-of-the-year amortized balances. The remaining unamortized loss on retirement at the start of the year is calculated as follows:

Loss remaining at year-end:			
Investment in bonds at December 31, 20X4		$101,887	
Less: Bonds payable at December 31, 20X4.	$100,000		
Discount on bonds at December 31, 20X4	(918)	99,082	$2,802
Loss amortized during year:			
Interest expense eliminated		$ 8,842	
Less: Interest revenue eliminated		6,220	2,622
Remaining loss at January 1, 20X4			$5,427

Since from the consolidated viewpoint the bonds were retired in the prior year and since the bonds were issued by the subsidiary, the remaining unamortized loss of $5,427 on January 1, 20X4, is allocated 90% to the controlling retained earnings and 10% to the noncontrolling retained earnings.

Worksheet 5-4 (see page 234)

Eliminations & Adjustments		Consolidated Income Statement	NCI	Controlling Retained Earnings	Consolidated Balance Sheet	
Dr.	Cr.					
					318,415	1
	(CY1) 8,820					2
	(EL) 135,180					3
	(B) 101,887					4
(B) 100,000						5
	(B) 918					6
					(100,000)	7
(B) 4,884				(155,296)		8
(EL) 36,000			(4,000)			9
(EL) 99,180			(10,477)			10
(B) 543						11
		(130,000)				12
(B) 6,220						13
		81,358				14
	(B) 8,842					15
						16
(CY1) 8,820						17
255,647	255,647					18
		(48,642)				19
		1,242	(1,242)			20
		47,400		(47,400)		21
			(15,719)		(15,719)	22
				(202,696)	(202,696)	23
					0	24

Subsidiary Company S Income Distribution

Internally generated net income, including interest expense	$ 9,800
Interest adjustment ($8,842 – $6,220)......................(B)	**2,622**
Adjusted income	$ 12,422
NCI share	× 10%
NCI	$ 1,242

Parent Company P Income Distribution

Internally generated net income, including interest revenue	$36,220
90% × Company S adjusted income of $12,422	11,180
Controlling interest	$47,400

Worksheet 5-6

Vertical Worksheet Alternative
Company P and Subsidiary Company S
Worksheet for Consolidated Financial Statements
For Year Ended December 31, **20X2**

Worksheet 5-6 (see page 253)

(Credit balance amounts are in parentheses.)	Trial Balance		Eliminations & Adjustments		NCI	Consolidated	
	Company P	Company S	Dr.	Cr.			
Income Statement							1
Sales	(600,000)	(530,000)	(IS) 150,000			(980,000)	2
Cost of goods sold	400,000	280,000	(EI) 10,000	(IS) 150,000 (BI) 8,000		532,000	3
Depreciation expense	40,000	50,000		(F2) 1,000		89,000	4
Other expenses	60,000	70,000				130,000	5
Subsidiary income	(104,000)		(CY1) 104,000				6
							7
Net income	(204,000)	(130,000)				(229,000)	8
NCI (see distribution schedule)					(25,600)		9
Controlling interest (see distribution schedule)						(203,400)	10
							11
Retained Earnings Statement							12
Retained earnings, January 1, 20X2, Company P	(600,000)		(BI) 6,400			(589,100)	13
			(F1) 4,500				14
Retained earnings, January 1, 20X2, Company S		(400,000)	(EL) 320,000		(78,400)		15
							16
			(BI) 1,600				17
Net income (carrydown)	(204,000)	(130,000)			(25,600)	(203,400)	18
Dividends declared		20,000		(CY2) 16,000	4,000		19
Retained earnings, December 31, 20X2	(804,000)	(510,000)					20
NCI, retained earnings, December 31, 20X2					(100,000)		21
Controlling interest, retained earnings, December 31, 20X2						(792,500)	22
							23
Balance Sheet							24
Inventory	300,000	250,000		(EI) 10,000		540,000	25
Accounts receivable	120,000	180,000		(IA) 20,000		280,000	26
Plant assets	236,000	400,000		(F1) 5,000		631,000	27
Accumulated depreciation	(100,000)	(60,000)	(F1) 500 (F2) 1,000			(158,500)	28
Investment in Company S	628,000		(CY2) 16,000				29
				(CY1) 104,000			30
				(EL) 480,000			31
				(D) 60,000			32
Goodwill			(D) 60,000			60,000	33
Current liabilities	(80,000)	(60,000)	(IA) 20,000			(120,000)	34
Common stock ($5 par), Company S		(200,000)	(EL) 160,000		(40,000)		35
Common stock ($10 par), Company P	(300,000)					(300,000)	36
Retained earnings (carrydown)	(804,000)	(510,000)					37
Retained earnings, controlling interest, December 31, 20X2						(792,500)	38
Retained earnings, NCI, December 31, 20X2					(100,000)		39
Total NCI					(140,000)	(140,000)	40
Totals	0	0	854,000	854,000		0	41

Eliminations and Adjustments:

(CY1) Eliminate the current-year entries recording the parent's share (80%) of subsidiary net income.

(CY2) Eliminate intercompany dividends.

(EL) Eliminate the pro rata portion of the subsidiary equity balances owned by the parent (80%) against the balance of the investment account.

(D) Distribute the excess to the goodwill account according to the determination and distribution of excess schedule.

(IS) Eliminate the intercompany sales made during 20X2.

(BI) Eliminate the intercompany profit in the beginning inventory, 20% (0.25 ÷ 1.25) multiplied by $40,000. Since it was a subsidiary sale, the profit is shared 20% by the NCI.

(EI) Eliminate the intercompany profit (20%) applicable to the $50,000 of intercompany goods in the ending inventory.

(IA) Eliminate the intercompany trade balances.

(F1) Eliminate the intercompany gain remaining on January 1, 20X2, applicable to the sale of the machine by Company P ($5,000 original gain less one-half-year's gain of $500).

(F2) Reduce the depreciation expense and accumulated depreciation accounts ($1,000 for the current year) in order to reflect depreciation based on the original cost.

Subsidiary Company S Income Distribution		
Unrealized profit in ending inventory	Internally generated net income	$130,000
(20% × $50,000) .... (EI) $10,000	Realized profit in beginning inventory	
	(20% × $40,000) .... (BI)	8,000
	Adjusted income	$128,000
	NCI share	×20%
	NCI	**$25,600**

Parent Company P Income Distribution		
	Internally generated net income	$ 100,000
	Gain realized on sale of machine .... (F2)	1,000
	80% × Company S adjusted income of	
	$128,000	102,400
	Controlling interest	**$203,400**

UNDERSTANDING THE ISSUES

1. Subsidiary Company S has $1,000,000 of bonds outstanding. The bonds have 10 years to maturity and pay interest at 12% annually. The parent has an average annual borrowing cost of 9% and wishes to reduce the interest cost of the consolidated company. What methods could be used to maintain the subsidiary as the debtor?

2. Subsidiary Company S has $1,000,000 of bonds outstanding at 12% annual interest. The bonds have 10 years to maturity. If the parent, Company P, is able to purchase the bonds at a price that reflects 10% annual interest, what effect will the purchase have on income in the current and future years? What would the effects be if the purchase price reflected a 13% annual interest rate? Your response need not be quantified.

3. Subsidiary Company S has $1,000,000 of bonds outstanding at 12% annual interest. The bonds have 10 years to maturity. If the parent, Company P, is able to purchase the bonds at a price that reflects 10% annual interest, how will the noncontrolling interest be affected in the current and future years? Your response need not be quantified.

4. Company P purchased $100,000 of subsidiary Company S's bonds for $95,000 on January 1, 20X1. The bonds were issued at face value, pay interest at 10% annually, and have five years to maturity. What will the impact of this transaction be on consolidated net income for the current and future four years? Assuming a 20% noncontrolling interest, how will the NCI be affected in the current and next four years? Quantify your response.

5. P Company acquired 100% of the common stock of the S Company for an agreed-upon price of $800,000. The book value of the net assets is $600,000, which includes $50,000 of subsidiary cash equivalents. How will this transaction affect the cash flow statement of the consolidated firm in the period of the purchase, if:

   a. P Company pays $800,000 cash to purchase the stock?
   b. P Company pays $500,000 cash and signs 5-year notes for $300,000? All Company S shareholders receive notes.
   c. P Company exchanges only common stock with the shareholders of Company S?

6. What will be the effect of the above purchase on cash flow statements prepared in periods after the year of the purchase?

7. (Issue 1 with a noncontrolling interest.) P Company acquired 80% of the common stock of the S Company for an agreed-upon price of $640,000. The book value of the net assets is $600,000, which includes $50,000 of subsidiary cash equivalents. How will this transaction affect the cash flow statement of the consolidated firm in the period of the purchase, if:

   a. P Company pays $640,000 cash to purchase the stock?
   b. P Company pays $400,000 cash and signs 5-year notes for $240,000? 80% of the Company S shareholders receive notes.
   c. P Company exchanges only common stock with the 80% of the shareholders of Company S?

8. Company P had internally generated net income of $200,000 (excludes share of subsidiary income). Company P has 100,000 shares of outstanding common stock. Subsidiary Company S has a net income of $60,000 and 40,000 shares of outstanding common stock. What is consolidated basic EPS, if:

   a. Company P owns 100% of the Company S shares?
   b. Company P owns 80% of the Company S shares?

9. Company P had internally generated net income of $200,000 (excludes share of subsidiary income). Company P has 100,000 shares of outstanding common stock.

Subsidiary Company S has a net income of $60,000 and 40,000 shares of outstanding common stock. Company P owns 100% of the Company S shares. What is consolidated diluted EPS, if:

   a. Company S has outstanding stock options for Company S shares, which cause a dilutive effect of 2,000 additional shares of Company S shares?
   b. Company S has outstanding stock options for Company P shares, which cause a dilutive effect of 2,000 additional shares of Company P shares?
   c. Company P has outstanding stock options for Company P shares, which cause a dilutive effect of 2,000 additional shares of Company P shares?

10. Company R paid $200,000 for a 30% interest in Company E on January 1, 20X1. Company E's total stockholders' equity on that date was $500,000. The excess price was attributed to equipment with a 10-year life. During 20X1, Company E reported net income of $40,000 and paid total dividends of $10,000. Calculate:

   a. Company R's investment income for 20X1.
   b. Company R's investment balance on December 31, 20X1.
   c. Explain in words the investment balance on December 31, 20X1.

11. Company R owns a 30% interest in Company E, which it acquired at book value. Company E reported net income of $50,000 for 20X1 (ignore taxes). There was an intercompany sale of equipment at a gain of $20,000 on January 1, 20X1. The equipment has a 5-year life. What is Company R's investment income for 20X1 and what adjusting entry (if any) does Company R need to make as a result of the equipment sale, if:

   a. Company E made the sale?
   b. Company R made the sale?

12. Company E reported net income of $100,000 for 20X1. Assume the income was earned evenly throughout the year. Dividends of $10,000 were paid on December 31. What will Company R report as investment income under the following ownership situations, if:

   a. Company R owned a 10% interest from 7/1 to 12/31?
   b. Company R owned a 10% interest from 1/1 to 6/30 and a 25% interest from 7/1 to 12/31?
   c. Company R owned a 30% interest from 1/1 to 6/30 and a 10% interest from 7/1 to 12/31?

13. Company R purchased a 25% interest in Company E on January 1, 1995, at its book value of $20,000. From 1995 until 1999, Company E earned a total of $200,000. From 2000 until 2004, it lost $300,000. In 20X5, Company E reported net income of $30,000. What is Company R's investment income for 20X5, and what is its balance in the investment in Company E account on December 31, 20X5?

EXERCISES

Exercise 5-1 *(LO 1)* **Options to lower interest cost.** Marcus Engineering is a large corporation with the ability to obtain financing by selling its bonds at favorable rates. Currently, it pays 7% interest on its 10-year bond issues. In the past year, Marcus purchased an 80% interest in a subsidiary, Patel Industries. Patel Industries has $1,000,000 of bonds outstanding that mature in six years. Interest is paid annually at a stated rate of 10%. The bonds were issued at face value. Interest rates have come down, but Patel Industries could still expect to pay 9% to 9.5% interest on a long-term issue. Patel Industries is a smaller company with a lower credit rating than Marcus.

Marcus would like to reduce interest costs on the Patel Industries debt. The company has asked your advice on whether it should purchase the bonds or loan Patel Industries the money to retire its own debt. Compare the options with a focus on the impact on consolidated statements.

Exercise 5-2 *(LO 1)* **Effect of intercompany bonds on income.** Dennis Company is an 80%-owned subsidiary of Kay Industries. Dennis Company issued 10-year, 8% bonds in the amount of $1,000,000 on January 1, 20X1. The bonds were issued at face value, and interest is payable each January 1. On January, 1, 20X3, Kay Industries purchased all of the Dennis bonds for $968,000. Kay will amortize the discount on a straight-line basis. For the years ending (a) December 31, 20X3, and (b) December 31, 20X4, determine the effects of this transaction.

1. On consolidated net income.
2. On the distribution of income to the controlling and noncontrolling interests.

Exercise 5-3 *(LO 2)* **Bond eliminations, straight-line.** Casper Company is an 80%-owned subsidiary of Dien Corporation. Casper Company issued $100,000 of 9%, 10-year bonds for $95,000 on January 1, 20X1. Annual interest is paid on January 1. Dien Corporation purchased the bonds on January 1, 20X5, for $101,800. Both companies are using the straight-line method to amortize the premium/discount on the bonds.

1. Prepare the eliminations and adjustments that would be made on the December 31, 20X5, consolidated worksheet as a result of this purchase.
2. Prepare the eliminations and adjustments that would be made on the December 31, 20X6, consolidated worksheet.

Exercise 5-4 *(LO 2)* **Bond eliminations, effective interest.** On January 1, 20X4, Dunbar Corporation, an 85%-owned subsidiary of Garfield Industries, received $48,055 for $50,000 of 8%, five-year bonds it issued when the market rate was 9%. When Garfield Industries purchased these bonds for $47,513 on January 2, 20X6, the market rate was 10%. Given the following effective interest amortization schedules for both companies, calculate the gain or loss on retirement and the interest adjustments to the issuer's income distribution schedules over the remaining term of the bonds.

Dunbar (issuer)

Date	Effective Interest (9%)	Nominal Interest	Discount Amortization	Balance
1/1/X4				$48,055
1/1/X5	$4,325	$4,000	$325	48,380
1/1/X6	4,354	4,000	354	48,734
1/1/X7	4,386	4,000	386	49,120
1/1/X8	4,421	4,000	421	49,541
1/1/X9	4,459	4,000	459	50,000

Garfield (purchaser)

Date	Effective Interest (10%)	Nominal Interest	Discount Amortization	Balance
1/1/X6				$47,513
1/1/X7	$4,751	$4,000	$751	48,264
1/1/X8	4,826	4,000	826	49,091
1/1/X9	4,909	4,000	909	50,000

Exercise 5-5 *(LO 2)* **Bond eliminations, partial purchase, straight line.** Carlton Company is an 80%-owned subsidiary of Mirage Company. On January 1, 20X1, Carlton sold $100,000 of 10-year, 7% bonds for $101,000. Interest is paid annually on January 1. The market rate for this type of bond was 9% on January 2, 20X3, when Mirage purchased 60% of the Carlton bonds for $53,600. Discounts may be amortized on a straight-line basis.

1. Prepare the eliminations and adjustments required for this bond purchase on the December 31, 20X3, consolidated worksheet.
2. Prepare the eliminations and adjustments required on the December 31, 20X4, consolidated worksheet.

Exercise 5-6 *(LO 2)* **Bond calculations, effective interest.** Lift Industries, a 90%-owned subsidiary of Shark Incorporated, issued $100,000 of 12-year, 8% bonds on January 1, 20X5, to yield 7% interest. Interest is paid annually on January 1. The effective interest method is used to amortize the premium. Shark purchased the bonds for $94,005 on January 2, 20X8, when the market rate of interest was 9%. On the purchase date, the remaining premium on the bonds was $6,516. Lift's 20X8 net income was $500,000.

1. Prepare the eliminations and adjustments required for this purchase on the December 31, 20X8, consolidated worksheet.
2. Prepare the 20X8 income distribution schedule for the NCI.

Exercise 5-7 *(LO 3)* **Cash flow, cash payment, year of purchase.** Batton Company purchased an 80% interest in Ricky Company for $500,000 cash on January 1, 20X3. Any excess of cost over book value was attributed to goodwill. To help pay for the acquisition, Batton Company issued 5,000 shares of its common stock with a fair value of $60 per share. Ricky's balance sheet on the date of the purchase was as follows:

Assets		Liabilities and Equity	
Cash	$ 20,000	Current liabilities	$110,000
Inventory	140,000	Bonds payable	100,000
Property, plant,		Common stock ($10 par)........	200,000
and equipment (net)...........	550,000	Retained earnings	300,000
Total assets	$710,000	Total liabilities and equity	$710,000

Controlling share of net income for 20X3 was $145,000, net of the noncontrolling interest of $10,000. Batton declared and paid dividends of $10,000, and Ricky declared and paid dividends of $5,000. There were no purchases or sales of property, plant, or equipment during the year. Based on the following information, prepare a statement of cash flows using the indirect method for Batton Company and its subsidiary for the year ended December 31, 20X3. Any supporting schedules should be in good form.

	Batton Company December 31, 20X2	Consolidated December 31, 20X3
Cash	$ 300,000	$ 304,000
Inventory	220,000	454,000
Property, plant, and equipment (net)	800,000	1,230,000
Goodwill		100,000
Current liabilities	(160,000)	(284,000)
Bonds payable	(200,000)	(300,000)
Noncontrolling interest		(109,000)
Controlling common stock, $10 par	(200,000)	(250,000)
Controlling paid-in capital in excess of par	(300,000)	(550,000)
Retained earnings	(460,000)	(595,000)
Totals	$ 0	$ 0

Exercise 5-8 *(LO 3)* **Cash flow, issue stock, year of purchase.** Duckworth Corporation purchased an 80% interest in Poladna Corporation on January 1, 20X3, in exchange for 5,000 Duckworth shares (market value of $18) plus $155,000 cash. The appraisal showed that some of Poladna's equipment, with a four-year estimated remaining life, was undervalued by

$20,000. The excess is attributed to goodwill. The following is Poladna Corporation's balance sheet on December 31, 20X2:

Assets		Liabilities and Equity	
Cash	$ 30,000	Current liabilities	$ 30,000
Inventory	30,000	Long-term liabilities	40,000
Property, plant, and equipment...	300,000	Common stock ($10 par)........	150,000
Accumulated depreciation	(90,000)	Retained earnings	50,000
Total assets................	$270,000	Total liabilities and equity	$270,000

Comparative balance sheet data are as follows:

	December 31, 20X2 (Parent only)	December 31, 20X3 (Consolidated)
Cash	$ 100,000	$ 95,000
Inventory	60,000	84,200
Property, plant, and equipment...................	950,000	1,342,000
Accumulated depreciation	(360,000)	(574,000)
Goodwill		69,000
Current liabilities	(80,000)	(115,000)
Long-term liabilities	(100,000)	(130,000)
Noncontrolling interest		(43,000)
Controlling interest:		
Common stock ($10 par).......................	(350,000)	(400,000)
Additional paid-in capital	(50,000)	(90,000)
Retained earnings	(170,000)	(238,200)
Totals	$ 0	$ 0

The following information relates to the activities of the two companies for 20X3:

a. Poladna paid off $10,000 of its long-term debt.
b. Duckworth purchased production equipment for $76,000.
c. Consolidated net income was $104,200; the NCI's share was $6,000. Depreciation expense taken by Duckworth and Poladna on their separate books was $92,000 and $28,000, respectively.
d. Duckworth paid $30,000 in dividends; Poladna paid $15,000.

Prepare the consolidated statement of cash flows for the year ended December 31, 20X3, for Duckworth Corporation and its subsidiary, Poladna Corporation.

Exercise 5-9 *(LO 3)* **Cash flow, subsequent to year of purchase.** Paridon Motors purchased an 80% interest in Super Battery Company on January 1, 20X2, for $700,000 cash. At that date, Super Battery Company had the following stockholders' equity:

Common stock ($10 par)......................	$100,000
Paid-in capital in excess of par	300,000
Retained earnings	250,000
Total stockholders' equity....................	$650,000

Any excess of cost over book value was attributed to goodwill. A statement of cash flows is being prepared for 20X5. For each of the following situations, indicate the impact on the cash flow statement for 20X5:

a. Adjustment resulting from the original purchase of the controlling interest.
b. Super Battery Company issued 2,000 shares of common stock for $90 per share on January 1, 20X5. At the time, the stockholders' equity of Super Battery was $800,000. Paridon Motors purchased 1,000 shares.

c. Paridon Motors purchased at 102, $100,000 of face value, 10% annual interest bonds issued by Super Battery Company at face value on January 1, 20X3. Paridon purchased the bonds on January 1, 20X5.

d. Super Battery purchased a production machine from Paridon Motors on July 1, 20X5, for $80,000. Paridon's cost was $60,000, and accumulated depreciation was $20,000.

Exercise 5-10 *(LO 5)* **Equity income recording.** Trailer Corporation purchased a 25% interest in Like Company for $110,000 on January 1, 20X7. The following determination and distribution of excess schedule was prepared:

Price paid		$110,000
Less interest acquired:		
Common stock ($10 par)	$200,000	
Retained earnings	100,000	
Total stockholders' equity	$300,000	
Interest acquired	× 25%	75,000
Excess of cost over book value		$ 35,000
Less excess attributable to equipment, 25% × $40,000 (10-year life)		10,000
Goodwill		$ 25,000

Like Company earned income of $20,000 in 20X7 and $24,000 in 20X8. Like Company declared a 25-cent per share cash dividend on December 22, 20X8, payable January 12, 20X9, to stockholders of record on December 30, 20X8.

During 20X8, Like sold merchandise costing $10,000 to Trailer for $15,000. Twenty percent of the merchandise was still in Trailer's ending inventory on December 31, 20X8.

Prepare the equity adjustment required by APB Opinion No. 18 on Trailer's books on December 31, 20X7, and December 31, 20X8, to account for its investment in Like Company. Assume Trailer Corporation makes no adjustment except at the end of each calendar year.

Exercise 5-11 *(LO 5)* **Equity method investment with intercompany profits.** Turf Company purchased a 30% interest in Minnie Company for $90,000 on January 1, 20X1, when Minnie had the following stockholders' equity:

Common stock ($10 par)	$100,000
Paid-in capital in excess of par	20,000
Retained earnings	130,000
Total	$250,000

The excess cost was due to a building that is being amortized over 20 years.

Since the investment, Minnie had consistently sold goods to Turf to realize a 40% gross profit. Such sales totaled $50,000 during 20X3. Minnie had $10,000 of such goods in its beginning inventory and $40,000 in its ending inventory.

On January 1, 20X3, Turf sold a machine with a book value of $15,000 to Minnie for $20,000. The machine has a five-year life and is being depreciated on a straight-line basis.

Minnie reported a net income of $60,000 before taxes for 20X3. Minnie paid $5,000 in dividends in 20X3.

Prepare all entries caused by Turf's investment in Minnie for 20X3 (ignore tax ramifications). Assume that Turf has recorded the tax on its internally generated income. Turf has properly recorded the investment in previous periods.

Exercise 5-12 *(LO 5)* **Equity income with intercompany profits.** Spancrete Corporation acquired a 30% interest in the outstanding stock of Werl Corporation on January 1, 20X5. At that time, the following determination and distribution of excess schedule was prepared:

Price paid	$125,000

Less interest acquired:

Common stock...	$150,000	
Retained earnings	160,000	
Total stockholders' equity...............................	$310,000	
Interest acquired	× 30%	93,000
Excess of cost over book value attributable to equipment (10-year life).....		$ 32,000

During 20X5, Spancrete purchased $200,000 of goods from Werl. Of these purchases, $20,000 were in the December 31, 20X5, ending inventory. During 20X6, Spancrete purchased $250,000 of goods from Werl. Of these purchases, $30,000 were in the December 31, 20X6, ending inventory. Werl's gross profit rate is 30%. Also, Spancrete purchased a machine from Werl for $15,000 on January 1, 20X6. The machine had a book value of $10,000 and a five-year remaining life. Werl reported net income of $90,000 and paid $20,000 on dividends during 20X6.

Prepare an income distribution schedule for Werl, and record the entries to adjust the investment in Werl for 20X6.

Exercise 5-13 *(LO 5)* Equity method, change in interest.

Hanson Corporation purchased a 10% interest in Novic Company on January 1, 20X6, and an additional 15% interest on January 1, 20X8. These investments cost Hanson Corporation $80,000 and $110,000, respectively.

The following stockholders' equities of Novic Company are available:

	December 31, 20X5	December 31, 20X7
Common stock ($10 par)........................	$500,000	$500,000
Retained earnings	250,000	300,000
Total equity	$750,000	$800,000

Any excess of cost over book value on the original investment was attributed to goodwill. Any excess on the second purchase is attributable to equipment with a four-year life.

Novic Company had income of $30,000, $30,000, and $40,000 for 20X6, 20X7, and 20X8, respectively. Novic paid dividends of $0.20 per share in 20X7 and 20X8.

Ignore income tax considerations, and assume adjusting entries are made at the end of the calendar year only.

1. Prepare the cost-to-equity conversion entry, as required by APB Opinion No. 18, on January 1, 20X8, when Hanson's investment in Novic Company first exceeded 20%. Any supporting schedules should be in good form.
2. Prepare the December 31, 20X8, equity adjustment on Hanson's books. Provide supporting calculations in good form.

Exercise 5-14 *(LO 5)* Sale of equity method investment.

On January 1, 20X7, Lund Corporation purchased a 30% interest in Aluma-Boat Company for $200,000. At the time of the purchase, Aluma-Boat had total stockholders' equity of $400,000. Any excess of cost over the equity purchased was attributed in part to machinery worth $50,000 more than book value with a remaining useful life of five years. Any remaining excess would be allocated to goodwill.

Aluma-Boat reported the following income and dividend distributions in 20X7 and 20X8:

	20X7	20X8
Income.........................	$50,000	$45,000
Dividends declared and paid	10,000	10,000

Lund sold its investment in Aluma-Boat Company on January 2, 20X9, for $230,000. Record the sale of the investments. Carefully schedule the investment account balance at the time of the sale.

PROBLEMS

Problem 5-1 *(LO 2)* **Eliminations, equity, 100%, bonds with straight-line.** Since its 100% acquisition of Drew Corporation stock on December 31, 20X2, Justin Corporation has maintained its investment under the equity method. However, due to Drew's earning potential, the price included a $40,000 payment for goodwill. At the time of the purchase, the fair value of Drew's assets equaled their book value.

On January 2, 20X4, Drew Corporation issued 10-year, 9% bonds at a face value of $50,000. The bonds pay interest each December 31. On January 2, 20X6, Justin Corporation purchased all of Drew Corporation's outstanding bonds for $48,400. The premium is amortized on a straight-line basis. They have been included in Justin's long-term investment in bonds account. Below are the trial balances of both companies on December 31, 20X6:

	Justin Corp.	Drew Corp.
Cash	71,100	67,500
Accounts Receivable	450,000	75,000
Inventory	200,000	65,000
Investment in Bonds	48,600	
Plant and Equipment (net)	2,420,000	196,000
Investment in Drew Corporation	350,000	
Accounts Payable	(275,000)	(18,000)
Bonds Payable (9%)		(50,000)
Common Stock, Justin ($10 par)	(1,000,000)	
Paid-In Capital in Excess of Par, Justin	(750,000)	
Retained Earnings, Justin, January 1, 20X6	(730,000)	
Common Stock, Drew ($10 par)		(100,000)
Paid-In Capital in Excess of Par, Drew		(130,000)
Retained Earnings, Drew, January 1, 20X6		(80,000)
Sales	(2,500,000)	(540,000)
Cost of Goods Sold	1,000,000	405,000
Other Expenses	720,000	105,000
Interest Income	(4,700)	
Interest Expense	0	4,500
Total	0	0

◄ ◄ ◄ ◄ ◄ Required

1. Prepare the worksheet entries needed to eliminate the intercompany debt on December 31, 20X6.
2. Prepare a consolidated income statement for the year ended December 31, 20X6.

Note: No worksheet is required.

Problem 5-2 *(LO 2)* **Cost method, 90%, straight-line bonds.** On January 1, 20X1, Patrick Company purchased 90% of the common stock of Stuart Company for $350,000. On this date, Stuart had common stock, other paid-in capital, and retained earnings of $100,000, $40,000, and $210,000, respectively. The excess of cost over book value is due to goodwill. In both 20X1 and 20X2, Patrick has accounted for the investment in Stuart using the cost method.

On January 1, 20X1, Stuart sold $100,000 par value of 10-year, 8% bonds for $94,000. The bonds pay interest semiannually on January 1 and July 1 of each year. On December 31, 20X1, Patrick purchased all of Stuart's bonds for $96,400. The bonds are still held on December 31, 20X2. Both companies have correctly recorded all entries relative to bonds and interest, using straight-line amortization for premium or discount.

The trial balances of Patrick Company and its subsidiary were as follows on December 31, 20X2:

	Patrick Company	Stuart Company
Interest Receivable.	4,000	
Other Current Assets	249,200	315,200
Investment in Stuart Company	350,000	
Investment in Stuart Bonds	96,800	
Land.	80,000	60,000
Buildings and Equipment.	400,000	280,000
Accumulated Depreciation	(120,000)	(60,000)
Interest Payable		(4,000)
Other Current Liabilities.	(98,000)	(56,000)
Bonds Payable, 8%		(100,000)
Discount on Bonds Payable		4,800
Other Long-Term Liabilities	(200,000)	
Common Stock, Patrick Company.	(100,000)	
Other Paid-In Capital, Patrick Company	(200,000)	
Retained Earnings, Patrick Company	(365,000)	
Common Stock, Stuart Company		(100,000)
Other Paid-In Capital, Stuart Company.		(40,000)
Retained Earnings, Stuart Company		(260,000)
Net Sales.	(640,000)	(350,000)
Cost of Goods Sold	360,000	200,000
Operating Expenses	168,400	71,400
Interest Expense.		8,600
Interest Income.	(8,400)	
Divdend Income.	(27,000)	
Dividends Declared	50,000	30,000
Total	0	0

Required ▶ ▶ ▶ ▶ ▶   Prepare the worksheet necessary to produce the consolidated financial statements of Patrick and its subsidiary Stuart for the year ended December 31, 20X2. Round all computations to the nearest dollar.

Problem 5-3 *(LO 2)* **80%, cost method, straight-line bonds, fixed asset sale.** On January 1, 20X3, Warehouse Outlets had the following balances in its stockholders' equity accounts: Common Stock ($10 par), $800,000; Paid-In Capital in Excess of Par, $625,000; and Retained Earnings, $450,000. General Appliances purchased 64,000 shares of Warehouse Outlets' common stock for $1,700,000 on that date. Any excess of cost over book value was attributed to goodwill.

Warehouse Outlets issued $500,000 of eight-year, 11% bonds on December 31, 20X2. The bonds sold for $476,000. General Appliances purchased one-half of these bonds in the market on January 1, 20X5, for $259,000. Both companies use the straight-line method of amortization of premiums and discounts.

On July 1, 20X6, General Appliances sold to Warehouse Outlets an old building with a book value of $167,500, remaining life of 10 years, and $30,000 salvage value, for $195,000. The building is being depreciated on a straight-line basis. Warehouse Outlets paid $20,000 in cash and signed a mortgage note with its parent for the balance. Interest, at 11% of the unpaid balance, and principal payments are due annually beginning July 1, 20X7. (For convenience, the mortgage balances are not divided into current and long-term portions.)

The trial balances of the two companies at December 31, 20X6, are as follows:

	General Appliances	Warehouse Outlets
Cash	401,986	72,625
Accounts Receivable (net)	752,500	105,000
Interest Receivable.	9,625	
Inventory	1,950,000	900,000
Investment in Warehouse Outlets	1,700,000	
Investment in 11% Bonds.	256,000	
Investment in Mortgage	175,000	
Property, Plant, and Equipment	9,000,000	2,950,000
Accumulated Depreciation	(1,695,000)	(940,000)
Accounts Payable	(670,000)	(80,000)
Interest Payable	(18,333)	(9,625)
Bonds Payable, 11%	(2,000,000)	(500,000)
Discount on Bonds Payable	10,470	12,000
Mortgage Payable.		(175,000)
Common Stock ($5 par)	(3,200,000)	
Common Stock ($10 par)		(800,000)
Paid-In Capital in Excess of Par	(4,550,000)	(625,000)
Retained Earnings, January 1, 20X6.	(1,011,123)	(770,000)
Sales	(9,800,000)	(3,000,000)
Gain on Sale of Building	(27,500)	
Interest Income.	(35,625)	
Dividend Income	(48,000)	
Cost of Goods Sold	4,940,000	1,700,000
Depreciation Expense	717,000	95,950
Interest Expense.	223,000	67,544
Other Expenses	2,600,000	936,506
Dividends Declared.	320,000	60,000
Total.	0	0

Prepare the worksheet necessary to produce the consolidated financial statements of General ◄ ◄ ◄ ◄ ◄ **Required**
Appliances and its subsidiary for the year ended December 31, 20X6. Include the determination and distribution of excess and income distribution schedules.

Use the following information for Problems 5-4 and 5-5:

On January 1, 20X4, Packard Company acquired an 80% interest in the common stock of Stackner Company for $350,000. Stackner had the following balance sheet on the date of acquisition:

Stackner Company
Balance Sheet
January 1, 20X4

Assets		Liabilities and Equity	
Accounts receivable	$ 40,000	Accounts payable	$ 42,297
Inventory	20,000	Bonds payable	100,000
Land.	35,000	Discount on bonds payable	(2,297)
Buildings	250,000	Common stock, $10 par	10,000
Accumulated depreciation . . .	(50,000)	Paid-in capital in excess of par . . .	90,000
Equipment	120,000		
Accumulated depreciation . . .	(60,000)	Retained earnings	115,000
Total assets.	$355,000	Total liabilities and equity	$355,000

(continued)

> Buildings (20-year life) are undervalued by $75,000. Equipment (five-year life) is undervalued by $60,000. Any remaining excess is considered to be goodwill.

Problem 5-4 *(LO 2)* **80%, equity, straight-line bonds purchased this year, inventory profits.** Refer to the preceding facts for Packard's acquisition of 80% of Stackner's common stock. Packard uses the simple equity method to account for its investment in Stackner. On January 1, 20X5, Stackner held merchandise acquired from Packard for $15,000. During 20X5, Packard sold $50,000 worth of merchandise to Stackner. Stackner held $20,000 of this merchandise at December 31, 20X5. Stackner owed Packard $10,000 on December 31 as a result of these intercompany sales. Packard has a gross profit rate of 30%.

Stackner issued $100,000 of 8%, 10-year bonds for $96,719 on January 1, 20X1. Annual interest is paid on December 31. Packard purchased the bonds on January 1, 20X5 for $100,930. Both companies use the straight-line method to amortize the premium/discount on the bonds. Packard and Stackner used the following bond amortization schedules:

	Stackner				Packard		
Period	Cash	Interest	Balance	Period	Cash	Interest	Balance
Jan. X1			$ 96,719	Jan. X1			
Jan. X2	$8,000	$8,328	97,047	Jan. X2			
Jan. X3	8,000	8,328	97,375	Jan. X3			
Jan. X4	8,000	8,328	97,703	Jan. X4			
Jan. X5	8,000	8,328	98,031	Jan. X5			$100,930
Jan. X6	8,000	8,328	98,360	Jan. X6	$8,000	$7,845	100,775
Jan. X7	8,000	8,328	98,688	Jan. X7	8,000	7,845	100,620
Jan. X8	8,000	8,328	99,016	Jan. X8	8,000	7,845	100,465
Jan. X9	8,000	8,328	99,344	Jan. X9	8,000	7,845	100,310
Jan. Y0	8,000	8,328	99,672	Jan. Y0	8,000	7,845	100,155
Jan. Y1	8,000	8,328	100,000	Jan. Y1	8,000	7,845	100,000

Packard and Stackner had the following trial balances on December 31, 20X5:

	Packard Company	Stackner Company
Cash	71,070	32,032
Accounts Receivable	90,000	60,000
Inventory	100,000	30,000
Land	150,000	45,000
Investment in Stackner	385,738	
Investment in Stackner Bonds	100,775	
Buildings	500,000	250,000
Accumulated Depreciation	(300,000)	(70,000)
Equipment	200,000	120,000
Accumulated Depreciation	(100,000)	(84,000)
Accounts Payable	(55,000)	(25,000)
Bonds Payable		(100,000)
Discount on Bonds Payable		1,640
Common Stock	(100,000)	(10,000)
Paid-In Capital in Excess of Par	(600,000)	(90,000)
Retained Earnings, Jan. 1, 20X5	(400,000)	(145,000)
Sales	(600,000)	(220,000)
Cost of Goods Sold	410,000	120,000
Depreciation Expense—Buildings	30,000	10,000
Depreciation Expense—Equipment	15,000	12,000

Other Expenses	110,000	45,000
Interest Revenue	(7,845)	
Interest Expense		8,328
Subsidiary Income	(19,738)	
Dividends Declared	20,000	10,000
Total	0	0

Prepare the worksheet necessary to produce the consolidated financial statements for Packard Company and its subsidiary Stackner Company for the year ended December 31, 20X5. Include the determination and distribution of excess and income distribution schedules. ◀ ◀ ◀ ◀ ◀ **Required**

Problem 5-5 *(LO 2)* **80%, equity, straight-line bonds purchased last year, inventory profits.** Refer to the preceding facts for Packard's acquisition of 80% of Stackner's common stock. Packard uses the simple equity method to account for its investment in Stackner. On January 1, 20X6, Stackner held merchandise acquired from Packard for $20,000. During 20X6, Packard sold $60,000 worth of merchandise to Stackner. Stackner held $25,000 of this merchandise at December 31, 20X6. Stackner owed Packard $12,000 on December 31 as a result of these intercompany sales. Packard has a gross profit rate of 30%.

Stackner issued $100,000 of 8%, 10-year bonds for $96,719 on January 1, 20X1. Annual interest is paid on December 31. Packard purchased the bonds on January 1, 20X5, for $100,930. Both companies use the straight-line method to amortize the premium/discount on the bonds. Packard and Stackner used the following bond amortization schedules:

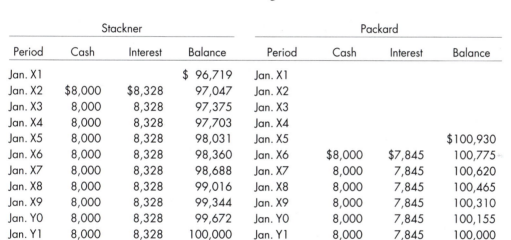

	Stackner				Packard		
Period	Cash	Interest	Balance	Period	Cash	Interest	Balance
Jan. X1			$ 96,719	Jan. X1			
Jan. X2	$8,000	$8,328	97,047	Jan. X2			
Jan. X3	8,000	8,328	97,375	Jan. X3			
Jan. X4	8,000	8,328	97,703	Jan. X4			
Jan. X5	8,000	8,328	98,031	Jan. X5			$100,930
Jan. X6	8,000	8,328	98,360	Jan. X6	$8,000	$7,845	100,775
Jan. X7	8,000	8,328	98,688	Jan. X7	8,000	7,845	100,620
Jan. X8	8,000	8,328	99,016	Jan. X8	8,000	7,845	100,465
Jan. X9	8,000	8,328	99,344	Jan. X9	8,000	7,845	100,310
Jan. YO	8,000	8,328	99,672	Jan. YO	8,000	7,845	100,155
Jan. Y1	8,000	8,328	100,000	Jan. Y1	8,000	7,845	100,000

Packard and Stackner had the following trial balances on December 31, 20X6:

	Packard Company	Stackner Company
Cash	101,710	61,032
Accounts Receivable	110,000	60,000
Inventory	120,000	45,000
Land	150,000	45,000
Investment in Stackner	403,075	
Investment in Stackner Bonds	100,620	
Buildings	500,000	250,000
Accumulated Depreciation	(330,000)	(80,000)
Equipment	200,000	120,000
Accumulated Depreciation	(115,000)	(96,000)
Accounts Payable	(35,000)	(25,000)
		(continued)

	Packard Company	Stackner Company
Bonds Payable.		(100,000)
Discount on Bonds Payable		1,312
Common Stock	(100,000)	(10,000)
Paid-In Capital in Excess of Par	(600,000)	(90,000)
Retained Earnings, January 1, 20X6.	(442,223)	(159,672)
Sales	(700,000)	(230,000)
Cost of Goods Sold	480,000	125,000
Depreciation Expense—Buildings.	30,000	10,000
Depreciation Expense—Equipment.	15,000	12,000
Other Expenses	125,000	43,000
Interest Revenue.	(7,845)	
Interest Expense.		8,328
Subsidiary Income.	(25,337)	
Dividends Declared	20,000	10,000
Total.	0	0

Required ▶ ▶ ▶ ▶ ▶   Prepare the worksheet necessary to produce the consolidated financial statements for Packard Company and its subsidiary Stackner Company for the year ended December 31, 20X6. Include the determination and distribution of excess and income distribution schedules.

Use the following information for Problems 5-6 and 5-7:

On January 1, 20X4, Postman Company acquired Sparkle Company. Postman paid $400,000 for 80% of Sparkle's common stock. On the date of acquisition, Sparkle had the following balance sheet:

Sparkle Company
Balance Sheet
January 1, 20X4

Assets		Liabilities and Equity	
Accounts receivable	$ 90,000	Accounts payable	$ 17,352
Inventory	50,000	Bonds payable	100,000
Land.	60,000	Premium on bonds payable. . .	2,648
Buildings	100,000	Common stock, $1 par	10,000
Accumulated depreciation . . .	(30,000)	Paid-in capital in excess	
Equipment	80,000	of par	90,000
Accumulated depreciation . . .	(30,000)	Retained earnings	100,000
Total assets.	$320,000	Total liabilities and equity . .	$320,000

Buildings, which have a 20-year life, are undervalued by $130,000. Equipment, which has a five-year life, is undervalued by $50,000. Any remaining excess is considered to be goodwill.

Problem 5-6 *(LO 2)* **80%, equity, effective interest bonds purchased this year, inventory profits.** Refer to the preceding facts for Postman's acquisition of 80% of Sparkle's common stock. Postman uses the simple equity method to account for its investment in Sparkle. On January 1, 20X5, Postman held merchandise acquired from Sparkle for $9,000. During 20X5, Sparkle sold $20,000 worth of merchandise to Postman. Postman held $12,000 of this merchandise at December 31, 20X5. Postman owed Sparkle $7,000 on December 31 as a result of these intercompany sales. Sparkle has a gross profit rate of 25%.

Sparkle issued $100,000 of 8%, 10-year bonds for $103,432 on January 1, 20X1, when the market rate was 7.5%. Annual interest is paid on December 31. Postman purchased the bonds for $95,514 on January 1, 20X5, when the market rate was 9%. Both companies use the effective interest method to amortize the premium/discount on the bonds. Postman and Sparkle prepared the following bond amortization schedules:

Sparkle				Postman			
Period	Cash	Interest	Balance	Period	Cash	Interest	Balance
Jan. X1			$103,432.04	Jan. X1			
Jan. X2	$8,000	$7,757.40	103,189.44	Jan. X2			
Jan. X3	8,000	7,739.21	102,928.65	Jan. X3			
Jan. X4	8,000	7,719.65	102,648.30	Jan. X4			
Jan. X5	8,000	7,698.62	102,346.92	Jan. X5			$ 95,514.08
Jan. X6	8,000	7,676.02	102,022.94	Jan. X6	$8,000	$8,596.27	96,110.35
Jan. X7	8,000	7,651.72	101,674.66	Jan. X7	8,000	8,649.93	96,760.28
Jan. X8	8,000	7,625.60	101,300.26	Jan. X8	8,000	8,708.43	97,468.71
Jan. X9	8,000	7,597.52	100,897.78	Jan. X9	8,000	8,772.18	98,240.89
Jan. Y0	8,000	7,567.33	100,465.12	Jan. Y0	8,000	8,841.68	99,082.57
Jan. Y1	8,000	7,534.88	100,000.00	Jan. Y1	8,000	8,917.43	100,000.00

Postman and Sparkle had the following trial balances on December 31, 20X5:

	Postman	Sparkle
Cash	144,486	99,347
Accounts Receivable	90,000	60,000
Inventory	120,000	55,000
Land	200,000	60,000
Investment in Sparkle	429,859	
Investment in Sparkle Bonds	96,110	
Buildings	600,000	100,000
Accumulated Depreciation	(310,000)	(40,000)
Equipment	150,000	80,000
Accumulated Depreciation	(90,000)	(50,000)
Accounts Payable	(55,000)	(25,000)
Bonds Payable		(100,000)
Discount on Bonds Payable		(2,023)
Common Stock	(100,000)	(10,000)
Paid-in Capital in Excess of Par	(800,000)	(90,000)
Retained Earnings, January 1, 20X5	(300,000)	(120,000)
Sales	(850,000)	(320,000)
Cost of Goods Sold	500,000	200,000
Depreciation Expense—Buildings	30,000	5,000
Depreciation Expense—Equipment	15,000	10,000
Other Expenses	140,000	70,000
Interest Revenue	(8,596)	
Interest Expense		7,676
Subsidiary Income	(21,859)	
Dividends Declared	20,000	10,000
Total	0	0

Prepare the worksheet necessary to produce the consolidated financial statements for Postman Company and its subsidiary Sparkle Company for the year ended December 31, 20X5. Include the determination and distribution of excess and income distribution schedules. ◄ ◄ ◄ ◄ ◄ **Required**

Problem 5-7 *(LO 2)* **80%, equity, effective interest bonds purchased last year, in-ventory profits.**   Refer to the preceding facts for Postman's acquisition of 80% of Sparkle's common stock. Postman uses the simple equity method to account for its investment in Sparkle. On January 1, 20X6, Postman held merchandise acquired from Sparkle for $12,000. During 20X6, Sparkle sold $25,000 worth of merchandise to Postman. Postman held $10,000 of this merchandise at December 31, 20X6. Postman owed Sparkle $6,000 on December 31 as a result of these intercompany sales. Sparkle has a gross profit rate of 25%.

Sparkle issued $100,000 of 8%, 10-year bonds for $103,432 on January 1, 20X1, when the market rate was 7.5%. Annual interest is paid on December 31. Postman purchased the bonds for $95,514 on January 1, 20X5, when the market rate was 9%. Both companies use the effective interest method to amortize the premium/discount on the bonds. Postman and Sparkle prepared the following bond amortization schedules:

		Sparkle				Postman	
Period	Cash	Interest	Balance	Period	Cash	Interest	Balance
Jan. X1			$103,432.04	Jan. X1			
Jan. X2	$8,000	$7,757.40	103,189.44	Jan. X2			
Jan. X3	8,000	7,739.21	102,928.65	Jan. X3			
Jan. X4	8,000	7,719.65	102,648.30	Jan. X4			
Jan. X5	8,000	7,698.62	102,346.92	Jan. X5			$ 95,514.08
Jan. X6	8,000	7,676.02	102,022.94	Jan. X6	$8,000	$8,596.27	96,110.35
Jan. X7	8,000	7,651.72	101,674.66	Jan. X7	8,000	8,649.93	96,760.28
Jan. X8	8,000	7,625.60	101,300.26	Jan. X8	8,000	8,708.43	97,468.71
Jan. X9	8,000	7,597.52	100,897.78	Jan. X9	8,000	8,772.18	98,240.89
Jan. Y0	8,000	7,567.33	100,465.12	Jan. Y0	8,000	8,841.68	99,082.57
Jan. Y1	8,000	7,534.88	100,000.00	Jan. Y1	8,000	8,917.43	100,000.00

Postman and Sparkle had the following trial balances on December 31, 20X6:

	Postman Company	Sparkle Company
Cash	290,486	99,347
Accounts Receivable	120,000	91,000
Inventory	140,000	55,000
Land	200,000	60,000
Investment in Sparkle	435,737	
Investment in Sparkle Bonds	96,760	
Buildings	600,000	100,000
Accumulated Depreciation	(340,000)	(45,000)
Equipment	150,000	80,000
Accumulated Depreciation	(105,000)	(60,000)
Accounts Payable	(40,000)	(34,000)
Bonds Payable		(100,000)
Premium on Bonds Payable		(1,675)
Common Stock	(100,000)	(10,000)
Paid-In Capital in Excess of Par	(800,000)	(90,000)
Retained Earnings, January 1, 20X6	(475,455)	(137,324)
Sales	(900,000)	(350,000)
Cost of Goods Sold	530,000	230,000
Depreciation Expense—Buildings	30,000	5,000
Depreciation Expense—Equipment	15,000	10,000
Other Expenses	155,000	80,000
Interest Revenue	(8,650)	
Interest Expense		7,652

Subsidiary Income.	(13,878)	
Dividends Declared.	20,000	10,000
Total.	0	0

◄ ◄ ◄ ◄ ◄ Required Prepare the worksheet necessary to produce the consolidated financial statements for Postman Company and its subsidiary Sparkle Company for the year ended December 31, 20X6. Include the determination and distribution of excess and income distribution schedules.

Problem 5-8 *(LO 2)* **CPA Objective, equipment, merchandise, bonds.** The problem below is an example of a question of the CPA "Other Objective Format" type as it was applied to the consolidations area. A mark-sensing answer sheet was used on the exam. You may just supply the answer which should be accompanied by calculations where appropriate.

Presented below are selected amounts from the separate unconsolidated financial statements of Poe Corporation and its 90%-owned subsidiary, Shaw Company, at December 31, 20X2. Additional information follows:

	Poe Corporation	Shaw Company
Selected income statement amounts:		
Sales	$ 710,000	$ 530,000
Cost of goods sold	490,000	370,000
Gain on the sale of equipment.		21,000
Earnings from investment in subsidiary		
(sophisticated equity)	61,000	
Interest expense		16,000
Depreciation	25,000	20,000
Selected balance sheet amounts:		
Cash	50,000	15,000
Inventories	229,000	150,000
Equipment	440,000	360,000
Accumulated depreciation.	(200,000)	(120,000)
Investment in Shaw (sophisticated equity balance)	189,000	
Investment in bonds	(100,000)	
Discount on bonds	(9,000)	
Bonds payable.		(200,000)
Common stock	(100,000)	(10,000)
Additional paid-in capital	(250,000)	(40,000)
Retained earnings	(402,000)	(140,000)
Selected statement of retained earnings amounts:		
Beginning balance, December 31, 20X1	272,000	100,000
Net income	210,000	70,000
Dividends paid.	80,000	30,000

Additional information is as follows:

1. On January 2, 20X2, Poe purchased 90% of Shaw's 100,000 outstanding common stock for cash of $155,000. On that date, Shaw's stockholders' equity equaled $150,000, and the fair values of Shaw's assets and liabilities equaled their carrying amounts. Poe has accounted for the acquisition as a purchase. Any remaining excess is considered to be goodwill.
2. On September 4, 20X2, Shaw paid cash dividends of $30,000.
3. On December 31, 20X2, Poe recorded its equity in Shaw's earnings.

Required ▶ ▶ ▶ ▶ ▶   1. Items (a) through (c) below represent transactions between Poe and Shaw during 20X2. Determine the dollar amount effect of the consolidating adjustment on 20X2 consolidated net income. Ignore income tax considerations.

Items to be answered:

a. On January 3, 20X2, Shaw sold equipment with an original cost of $30,000 and a carrying value of $15,000 to Poe for $36,000. The equipment had a remaining life of three years and was depreciated using the straight-line method by both companies.

b. During 20X2, Shaw sold merchandise to Poe for $60,000, which included a profit of $20,000. At December 31, 20X2, half of this merchandise remained in Poe's inventory.

c. On December 31, 20X2, Poe paid $91,000 to purchase 50% of the outstanding bonds issued by Shaw. The bonds mature on December 31, 20X8, and were originally issued at par. The bonds pay interest annually on December 31, and the interest was paid to the prior investor immediately before Poe's purchase of the bonds.

2. Items (a) through (1) below refer to accounts that may or may not be included in Poe's and Shaw's consolidated financial statements. The list on the right refers to the various possibilities of those amounts to be reported in Poe's consolidated financial statements for the year ended December 31, 20X2. Consider all transactions stated above in determining your answer. Ignore income tax considerations.

Items to be answered:	*Responses to be selected:*
a. Cash	1. Sum of amounts on Poe's and Shaw's separate unconsolidated financial statements.
b. Equipment	
c. Investment in subsidiary	2. Less than the sum of amounts on Poe's and Shaw's separate unconsolidated financial statements, but not the same as the amount on either.
d. Bonds payable	
e. NCI	
f. Common stock	3. Same as amount for Poe only.
g. Beginning retained earnings	4. Same as amount for Shaw only.
h. Dividends paid	5. Eliminated entirely in consolidation.
i. Gain on retirement of bonds	6. Shown in consolidated financial statements but not in separate unconsolidated financial statements.
j. Cost of goods sold	
k. Interest expense	7. Neither in consolidated nor in separate unconsolidated financial statements.
l. Depreciation expense	

(AICPA adapted)

Problem 5-9 *(LO 3)* **Cash flow, year subsequent to purchase.** Marc Company is an 80%-owned subsidiary of Luis Company. The interest in Marc was purchased on January 1, 20X1, for $640,000 cash. At that date, Marc had stockholders' equity of $650,000. The excess price was attributed to equipment with a five-year life undervalued by $25,000 and to goodwill.

The following comparative consolidated trial balances apply to Luis Company and its subsidiary, Marc:

	December 31, 20X1	December 31, 20X2
Cash	$ 16,000	$ 39,500
Inventory	120,000	160,000
Accounts receivable	200,000	300,000
Property, plant, and equipment	3,000,000	3,350,000
Accumulated depreciation	(1,080,000)	(1,280,000)
Investment in Charles Corporation (30%)		244,500
Goodwill	100,000	100,000
Accounts payable	(117,000)	(200,000)
Bonds payable	(100,000)	(400,000)
Noncontrolling interest	(138,000)	(151,000)

Controlling interest:

Common stock, par	(1,000,000)	(1,000,000)
Additional paid-in capital	(650,000)	(650,000)
Retained earnings	(351,000)	(513,000)
Totals	$ 0	$ 0

The following 20X2 information is available for the Luis and Marc companies:

a. Marc purchased equipment for $50,000.
b. Marc issued $300,000 of long-term bonds and later used the proceeds to purchase a new building.
c. On January 1, 20X2, Luis purchased 30% of the outstanding common stock of Charles Corporation for $230,000. This is an influential investment. Charles's stockholders' equity was $700,000 on the date of the purchase. Any excess cost is attributed to equipment with a 10-year life. Charles reported net income of $80,000 in 20X2 and paid dividends of $25,000.
d. Controlling share of consolidated income for 20X2 was $262,000; the noncontrolling interest in consolidated net income was $16,000. Luis paid $100,000 in dividends in 20X2; Marc paid $15,000 in dividends in 20X2.

Prepare the consolidated statement of cash flows for 20X2 using the indirect method. Any ◄ ◄ ◄ ◄ ◄ **Required** supporting calculations should be in good form.

Problem 5-10 *(LO 3)* **Cash flow, year of partial noncash purchase.** Billing Enterprises purchased a 90% interest in the common stock of Raush Corporation on January 1, 20X1, for an agreed-upon price of $500,000. Billing issued $400,000 of bonds to Raush shareholders plus $100,000 cash as payment. Raush's balance sheet on the acquisition date was as follows:

Assets		Liabilities and Equity	
Cash	$ 60,000	Accounts payable	$ 45,000
Accounts receivable	95,000	Long-term liabilities	120,000
Plant assets (net).	460,000	Common stock ($10 par).	150,000
		Retained earnings	300,000
Total assets.	$615,000	Total liabilities and equity	$615,000

Raush's equipment was understated by $20,000 and had a remaining depreciable life of five years. Any remaining excess was attributed to goodwill.

In addition to the bonds issued as part of the purchase, Billing sold additional bonds in the amount of $100,000.

Consolidated net income for 20X1 was $92,700. The controlling interest was $87,700, and the noncontrolling interest was $5,000. Raush paid $10,000 in dividends to all shareholders, including Billing Enterprises.

No plant assets were purchased or sold during 20X1.

Comparative balance sheet data are as follows:

	December 31, 20X0 Parent Only	December 31, 20X1 Consolidated
Cash	$ 82,000	$ 182,700
Accounts receivable	120,000	161,000
Plant assets (net).	870,000	1,276,000
Goodwill		77,000
Accounts payable	(52,000)	(80,000)
Bonds payable		(500,000)
Long-term liabilities	(80,000)	(40,000)
		(continued)

	December 31, 20X0 Parent Only	December 31, 20X1 Consolidated
Noncontrolling interest		(49,000)
Controlling interest:		
Common stock ($10 par).	(200,000)	(200,000)
Additional paid-in capital	(300,000)	(300,000)
Retained earnings	(440,000)	(527,700)
Totals	$ 0	$ 0

Required ▶ ▶ ▶ ▶ ▶   Prepare a consolidated statement of cash flows using the indirect method for the year ended December 31, 20X1. Supporting schedules should be in good form.

Problem 5-11 *(LO 4)* **Consolidated EPS.** On January 1, 20X2, Peanut Corporation acquired an 80% interest in Sunny Corporation. Information regarding the income and equity structure of the two companies as of the year ended December 31, 20X4, is as follows:

	Peanut Corporation	Sunny Corporation
Internally generated net income	$55,000	$56,000
Common shares outstanding during the year	20,000	12,000
Warrants to acquire Peanut stock, outstanding during the year	2,000	1,000
5% convertible (into Sunny's shares), $100 par preferred share,		
outstanding during the year.		800
Nonconvertible preferred shares outstanding	1,000	

Additional information is as follows:

a. The warrants to acquire Peanut stock were issued in 20X3. Each warrant can be exchanged for one share of Peanut common stock at an exercise price of $12 per share.
b. Each share of convertible preferred stock can be converted into two shares of Sunny common stock. The preferred stock pays an annual dividend totaling $4,000. Peanut owns 60% of the convertible preferred stock.
c. The nonconvertible preferred stock was issued on July 1, 20X4, and paid a six-month dividend totaling $500.
d. Relevant market prices per share of Peanut common stock during 20X4 are as follows:

	Average
1st Quarter	$10
2nd Quarter	12
3rd Quarter.	13
4th Quarter.	16

Required ▶ ▶ ▶ ▶ ▶   Compute the basic and diluted consolidated EPS for the year ended December 31, 20X4. Use quarterly share averaging.

Problem 5-12 *(LO 5)* **Equity income, inventory, fixed asset sale.** Heinrich Company purchased an influential 25% interest in Fink Company on January 1, 20X6, for $320,000. At that time, Fink's stockholders' equity was $1,000,000.

Fink Company assets had fair value similar to book value except for a building that was undervalued by $40,000. The building had an estimated remaining life of 20 years. Any remaining excess was attributed to goodwill.

The following additional information is available:

a. On July 1, 20X6, Heinrich sold a machine to Fink for $24,000. The cost of the machine to Heinrich was $16,000. The machine is being depreciated on a straight-line basis over 10 years.

b. Heinrich provides management services to Fink at a billing rate of $15,000 per year. This arrangement started in 20X6.

c. Fink has sold merchandise to Heinrich since 20X7. Sales were $10,000 in 20X7 and $25,000 in 20X8. The merchandise is sold to provide a gross profit rate of 25%. Heinrich had $2,000 of these goods in its December 31, 20X7, inventory and $3,000 of such goods in its December 31, 20X8, inventory.

d. The income earned and dividends paid by Fink are as follows:

Year	Income	Dividends
20X6	$48,000	$10,000
20X7	50,000	10,000
20X8	65,000	10,000

Prepare all entries necessitated by Heinrich's investment in Fink Company for 20X6 through 20X8 using the equity method for an influential investment. Supporting schedules should be in good form. Ignore taxes. ◀ ◀ ◀ ◀ ◀ **Required**

Problem 5-13 *(LO 5)* **Equity income, taxation, inventory, fixed asset sale.** On January 1, 20X6, Ashland Company purchased a 25% interest in Cramer Company for $195,000. Ashland Company prepared the following determination and distribution of excess schedule:

Price paid for investment		$195,000
Less book value of interest acquired:		
Common stock ($5 par)	$ 100,000	
Paid-in capital in excess of par	200,000	
Retained earnings	150,000	
Total stockholders' equity.	$ 450,000	
Interest acquired	× 25%	112,500
Excess of cost over book value (debit)		$ 82,500
Equipment, 25% × $30,000 (10-year life)		7,500 Dr.
Goodwill		$ 75,000 Dr.

The following additional information is available:

a. Cramer Company sold a machine to Ashland Company for $30,000 on July 1, 20X7. At this date, the machine had a book value of $25,000 and an estimated future life of five years. Straight-line depreciation (to the nearest month) is being used.

b. The following applies to Ashland Company sales to Cramer Company for 20X7 and 20X8:

	20X7	20X8
Intercompany merchandise in beginning inventory		$4,000
Sales for the year.	$10,000	$15,000
Intercompany merchandise in ending inventory.	$4,000	$5,000
Gross profit on sales	40%	40%

c. Internally generated net income for the two companies is as follows:

	20X6	20X7	20X8
Ashland Company	$140,000	$150,000	$155,000
Cramer Company.	60,000	80,000	100,000

d. Cramer paid dividends of $5,000, $10,000, and $10,000 in 20X6, 20X7, and 20X8, respectively.

Required ▶ ▶ ▶ ▶ ▶   Prepare all adjustments to Ashland Company's investment in the Cramer Company account on December 31, 20X6, 20X7, and 20X8. Supporting calculations and schedules should be in good form.

APPENDIX PROBLEMS

Problem 5A-1 *(LO 6)* **Equity method adjustments, vertical consolidated worksheet.** (Same as Problem 3-2 in Chapter 3 except vertical format worksheet is used.) On January 1, 20X1, Peres Company purchased 80% of the common stock of Soll Company for $308,000. On this date, Soll had common stock, other paid-in capital, and retained earnings of $50,000, $100,000, and $150,000, respectively. Net income and dividends for two years for Soll Company were as follows:

	20X1	20X2
Net income	$60,000	$90,000
Dividends.	20,000	30,000

On January 1, 20X1, the only tangible assets of Soll that were undervalued were inventory and the building. Inventory, for which FIFO is used, was worth $10,000 more than cost. The inventory was sold in 20X1. The building, which is worth $25,000 more than book value, has a remaining life of 10 years, and straight-line depreciation is used. The remaining excess of cost over book value is attributable to goodwill.

Required ▶ ▶ ▶ ▶ ▶   1. Using this information or the information in the following statements, prepare a determination and distribution of excess schedule.
2. Peres Company carries the Investment in Soll Company under the simple equity method. In general journal form, record the entries that would be made to apply the equity method in 20X1 and 20X2.
3. Complete the vertical worksheet for consolidated financial statements for 20X2.

Statement—Accounts	Peres Company	Soll Company
Income Statement:		
Net Sales	(520,000)	(450,000)
Cost of Goods Sold	300,000	260,000
Operating Expenses	120,000	100,000
Subsidiary Income	(72,000)	
Noncontrolling Interest in Income		
Net Income.	(172,000)	(90,000)
Retained Earnings Statement:		
Balance, Jan. 1, 20X2, P Company	(214,000)	
Balance, Jan. 1, 20X2, S Company		(190,000)
Net Income (from above)	(172,000)	(90,000)
Dividends Declared, P Company.	50,000	
Dividends Declared, S Company		30,000
Balance, December 31, 20X2.	(336,000)	(250,000)
Consolidated Balance Sheet:		
Inventory December 31	100,000	50,000
Other Current Assets	148,000	180,000
Investment in Soll Company.	Note 1	
Land.	50,000	50,000
Building and Equipment.	350,000	320,000

Accumulated Depreciation	(100,000)	(60,000)
Goodwill		
Other Intangibles	20,000	
Current Liabilities	(120,000)	(40,000)
Bonds Payable		(100,000)
Other Long-Term Liabilities	(200,000)	
Common Stock, P Company	(200,000)	
Other Paid-In Capital, P Company	(100,000)	
Common Stock, S Company		(50,000)
Other Paid-In Capital, S Company		(100,000)
Retained Earnings, December 31, 20X2 (from above)	(336,000)	(250,000)
Total	0	0

Note 1: To be calculated.

Problem 5A-2 *(LO 6)* Equity method, later period, vertical worksheet, several excess adjustments.

Booker Enterprises purchased an 80% interest in Kobe International for $850,000 on January 1, 20X5. Booker Enterprises also paid $4,000 in direct acquisition costs. On the purchase date, Kobe International had the following stockholders' equity:

Common stock ($10 par)	$150,000
Paid-in capital in excess of par	200,000
Retained earnings	400,000
	$750,000

Also on the purchase date, it was determined that Kobe International's assets were understated as follows:

Equipment, 10-year remaining life	$80,000
Land	20,000
Building, 20-year remaining life	60,000

The remaining excess of cost over book value was attributed to goodwill.

The following summarized statements of Booker Enterprises and Kobe International are for the year ended December 31, 20X7:

	Booker Enterprises	Kobe International
Income Statements:		
Sales	(650,000)	(320,000)
Cost of Goods Sold	260,000	240,000
Operating Expenses	170,000	70,000
Depreciation Expense	65,000	30,000
Subsidiary (Income)/Loss	16,000	
Net (Income)/Loss	(139,000)	20,000
Retained Earnings:		
Retained Earnings, Jan. 1, 20X7, Booker	(625,000)	
Retained Earnings, Jan. 1, 20X7, Kobe		(460,000)
Net (Income)/Loss	(139,000)	20,000
Dividends Declared		10,000
Retained Earnings, December 31, 20X7	(764,000)	(430,000)

(continued)

	Booker Enterprises	Kobe International
Balance Sheets:		
Cash	334,000	170,000
Inventory	135,000	400,000
Land...	145,000	150,000
Buildings	900,000	500,000
Accumulated Depreciation—Building	(345,000)	(360,000)
Equipment	350,000	250,000
Accumulated Depreciation—Equipment	(135,000)	(90,000)
Investment in Kobe International	828,000	
Liabilities	(248,000)	(40,000)
Bonds Payable..		(200,000)
Common Stock, Booker................................	(1,200,000)	
Common Stock, Kobe		(150,000)
Paid-In Capital in Excess of Par		(200,000)
Retained Earnings, Dec. 31, 20X7	(764,000)	(430,000)
Balance	0	0

Required ▶ ▶ ▶ ▶ ▶

Using the vertical format, prepare a consolidated worksheet for December 31, 20X7. Precede the worksheet with a determination and distribution of excess schedule. Include income distribution schedules to allocate the consolidated net income to the noncontrolling and controlling interests.

Suggestion: Remember that all adjustments to retained earnings are to beginning retained earnings, and it is the beginning balance of the subsidiary retained earnings account which is subject to elimination. Carefully follow the "carrydown" procedure to calculate the ending retained earnings balances.

Problem 5A-3 *(LO 6)* **Cost method, later period, vertical worksheets.** Harvard Company purchased a 90% interest in Benz Company for $740,000 on January 1, 20X1. The investment has been accounted for under the cost method. At the time of the purchase, a building owned by Benz was understated by $180,000; it had a 20-year remaining life on the purchase date. The remaining excess was attributed to goodwill. The stockholders' equity of Benz Company on the purchase date was as follows:

Common stock ($10 par).....................	$350,000
Retained earnings	200,000
Total equity	$550,000

The following summarized statements are for the year ending December 31, 20X2. (Credit balance amounts are in parentheses.)

	Harvard	Benz
Income Statements:		
Sales	(580,000)	(280,000)
Cost of Goods Sold	285,000	155,000
Operating Expenses	140,000	55,000
Depreciation Expense	72,000	30,000
Dividend Income	(9,000)	
Net Income..	(92,000)	(40,000)
Retained Earnings Statements:		
Retained Earnings, Jan. 1, 20X2, Harvard	(484,000)	
Retained Earnings, Jan. 1, 20X2, Benz..............		(320,000)
Net Income	(92,000)	(40,000)
Dividends Declared	20,000	10,000
Retained Earnings, December 31, 20X2	(556,000)	(350,000)

Balance Sheets:

Cash	310,000	170,000
Inventory	260,000	340,000
Land...	99,000	150,000
Building	800,000	500,000
Accumulated Depreciation—Building	(380,000)	(360,000)
Equipment	340,000	250,000
Accumulated Depreciation—Equipment	(190,000)	(90,000)
Investment in Benz Company..............................	740,000	
Current Liabilities.....................................	(123,000)	(60,000)
Bonds Payable..		(200,000)
Common Stock, Harvard................................	(800,000)	
Paid-In Capital in Excess of Par, Harvard..................	(500,000)	
Common Stock, Benz		(350,000)
Retained Earnings, Dec. 31, 20X2	(556,000)	(350,000)
Balance	0	0

Using the vertical format, prepare a consolidated worksheet for December 31, 20X2. Precede the worksheet with a determination and distribution of excess schedule. Include income distribution schedules to allocate the consolidated net income to the noncontrolling and controlling interests.   ◄ ◄ ◄ ◄ ◄ **Required**

Suggestion: Remember that all adjustments to retained earnings are to beginning retained earnings, and it is the beginning balance of the subsidiary retained earnings account which is subject to elimination. One of the adjustments to the parent retained earnings account is the cost-to-equity conversion entry. Be sure to follow the carrydown procedure to calculate the ending retained earnings balances.

Problem 5A-4 *(LO 6)* **Vertical worksheet, 100%, cost, fixed asset and merchandise sales.** Arther Corporation acquired all of the outstanding $10 par voting common stock of Trent Inc. on January 1, 20X2, in exchange for 50,000 shares of its $10 par voting common stock. On December 31, 20X1, the common stock of Arther had a closing market price of $15 per share on a national stock exchange. The retained earnings balance of Trent Inc. was $156,000 on the date of the acquisition. The acquisition was accounted for appropriately as a purchase. Both companies continued to operate as separate business entities maintaining separate accounting records with years ending December 31.

On December 31, 20X4, after year-end adjustments but before the nominal accounts were closed, the companies had the following condensed statements:

	Arther Corporation	Trent Inc.
Income Statement:		
Sales	(1,900,000)	(1,500,000)
Dividend Income (from Trent Inc.)	(40,000)	
Cost of Goods Sold	1,180,000	870,000
Operating Expenses	550,000	440,000
(includes depreciation)		
Net Income....................................	(210,000)	(190,000)
Retained Earnings Statements:		
Retained Earnings, January 1, 20X4..............	(250,000)	(206,000)
Net Income	(210,000)	(190,000)
Dividends Paid.................................	40,000	
Balance, December 31, 20X4...................	(460,000)	(356,000)
Balance Sheet:		
Cash	285,000	150,000
Accounts Receivable (net)	430,000	350,000

(continued)

	Arther Corporation	Trent Inc.
Inventories	530,000	410,000
Land, Building, and Equipment	660,000	680,000
Accumulated Depreciation	(185,000)	(210,000)
Investment in Trent Inc. (at cost)	750,000	
Accounts Payable and Accrued Expenses	(670,000)	(544,000)
Common Stock (10 par).	(1,200,000)	(400,000)
Additional Paid-In Capital	(140,000)	(80,000)
Retained Earnings, December 31, 20X2.	(460,000)	(356,000)
Totals	0	0

Additional information is as follows:

a. There have been no changes in the common stock and additional paid-in capital accounts since the one necessitated in 20X2 by Arther's acquisition of Trent Inc.
b. At the acquisition date, the market value of Trent's machinery exceeded book value by $54,000. This excess is being amortized over the asset's estimated average remaining life of six years. The fair values of Trent's other assets and liabilities were equal to book values. Any remaining excess is goodwill.
c. On July 1, 20X2, Arther sold a warehouse facility to Trent for $129,000 in cash. At the date of sale, Arther's book values were $33,000 for the land and $66,000 for the undepreciated cost of the building. Trent allocated the $129,000 purchase price to the land for $43,000 and to the building for $86,000. Trent is depreciating the building over its estimated five-year remaining useful life by the straight-line method with no salvage value.
d. During 20X4, Arther purchased merchandise from Trent at an aggregate invoice price of $180,000, which included a 100% markup on Trent's cost. At December 31, 20X4, Arther owed Trent $75,000 on these purchases, and $36,000 of the merchandise purchased remained in Arther's inventory.

Required ▶ ▶ ▶ ▶ ▶   Complete the vertical worksheet necessary to prepare the consolidated income statement and retained earnings statement for the year ended December 31, 20X4, and a consolidated balance sheet as of December 31, 20X4, for Arther Corporation and its subsidiary. Formal consolidated statements and journal entries are not required. Include the determination and distribution of excess schedule and the income distribution schedules.

(AICPA adapted)

Problem 5A-5 *(LO 6)* **Vertical worksheet, 80%, cost, several excess distributions, merchandise, equipment sales.** (This is similar to Problem 4-12, except that it uses the vertical worksheet format.) On January 1, 20X1, Peanut Company acquired 80% of the common stock of Sam Company for $200,000. On this date, Sam had total owners' equity of $200,000, which included retained earnings of $100,000. During 20X1 and 20X2, Peanut has accounted for its investment in Sam using the simple equity method.

Any excess of cost over book value is attributable to inventory (worth $12,500 more than cost), to equipment (worth $25,000 more than book value), and to goodwill. FIFO is used for inventories. The equipment has a remaining life of four years, and straight-line depreciation is used. Any remaining excess is attributed to goodwill.

On January 1, 20X2, Peanut held merchandise acquired from Sam for $20,000. During 20X2, Sam sold merchandise to Peanut for $40,000, $10,000 of which is still held by Peanut on December 31, 20X2. Sam's usual gross profit is 50%.

On December 31, 20X1, Peanut sold equipment to Sam at a gain of $15,000. During 20X2, the equipment was used by Sam. Depreciation is being computed using the straight-line method, a five-year life, and no salvage value.

The following condensed statements were prepared for the Peanut and Sam companies for December 31, 20X2:

	Peanut Company	Sam Company
Income Statements:		
Net Sales	(600,000)	(315,000)
Cost of Goods Sold	350,000	150,000
Operating Expenses	150,000	60,000
Subsidiary Income	(84,000)	
Net Income	(184,000)	(105,000)
Retained Earnings Statements:		
Balance, January 1, 20X2, Peanut Company	(320,000)	
Balance, January 1, 20X2, Sam Company		(150,000)
Net Income (from above)	(184,000)	(105,000)
Dividends Declared, Peanut Company	60,000	
Dividends Declared, Sam Company		20,000
Balance, December 31, 20X2	(444,000)	(235,000)
Consolidated Balance Sheets:		
Inventory, December 31	130,000	50,000
Other Current Assets	241,000	235,000
Investment in Sam Company	308,000	
Other Long-Term Investments	20,000	
Land	140,000	80,000
Building and Equipment	375,000	200,000
Accumulated Depreciation	(120,000)	(30,000)
Other Intangibles		20,000
Current Liabilities	(150,000)	(70,000)
Bonds Payable		(100,000)
Other Long-Term Liabilities	(200,000)	(50,000)
Common Stock, Peanut Company	(200,000)	
Other Paid-In Capital, Peanut Company	(100,000)	
Common Stock, Sam Company		(50,000)
Other Paid-In Capital, Sam Company		(50,000)
Retained Earnings, Dec. 31, 20X2	(444,000)	(235,000)
Totals	0	0

Complete the worksheet for consolidated financial statements for the year ended December 31, 20X2. Include any necessary determination and distribution of excess schedule and income distribution schedules.

Analysis of FASB Exposure Drafts for Business Combinations by Impact on Chapters 1–5

Learning Objective

When you have completed this appendix, you will understand the changes that are likely to occur for accounting for business combinations.

On June 30, 2005, the FASB issued two exposure drafts that have a major impact on the accounting methods used for business combinations. The exposure drafts are:

◆ Consolidated Financial Statements, Including Accounting and Reporting of Noncontrolling Interests in Subsidiaries—a replacement of ARB No. 51.
◆ Business Combinations—a replacement of FASB Statement No. 141.

Under the new procedures, all identifiable assets and liabilities will be recorded at full fair value regardless of the price paid for the interest or the size of the controlling interest. A price above the net fair value of the identifiable assets results in goodwill. A lesser price results in a gain.

The accounts of the subsidiary will be adjusted to full fair value only once, the date control is achieved. Any change in the controlling interest that does not cause a loss of control is viewed as an equity transaction with no impact on income.

Consolidated income will be defined as the income of the entire entity, which will then be allocated to the controlling interest and the NCI. The NCI will be displayed on the balance sheet as a portion of stockholders' equity.

SUMMARY OF MAJOR CHANGES

◆ Identifiable assets and liabilities of the acquired company will always be recorded at fair value using the guidance of the Exposure Draft on Fair Value Measurements. A price above the sum of the fair values of the net identifiable assets results in goodwill. A price below the sum of the fair values of the net identifiable assets results in a gain (not extraordinary).
◆ All value measurements are made on the "acquisition date." This is the date that control is transferred to the buyer. This may be a date other than the closing date if there is an agreement to that effect.
◆ All acquisition costs are expensed; none are included in the price paid.
◆ Any liability for contingent consideration must be estimated and included in the price paid. Later adjustments affect income of later periods. Goodwill is not adjusted upon the payment of later consideration.
◆ When there is a less than 100% purchase, all subsidiary accounts are adjusted to 100% of fair value in the consolidation process. The NCI (noncontrolling interest) shares in the fair value adjustments. Goodwill is also attributed to the NCI. It is presumed that the goodwill would be proportional to that recorded on the controlling interest, unless it can be demonstrated that the price reflects a control premium. In that case, the goodwill applicable to the NCI would be separately determined.
◆ The current text presentation of NCI is affirmed. The NCI portion of equity is included as a single amount in the equity section of the consolidated balance sheet. The income statement must show consolidated net income and then the distribution to the controlling interest and the NCI. The distribution of other comprehensive income to the controlling interest and NCI must also be disclosed. It should be noted that for most companies, the current practice is to treat the NCI as a liability or to locate it in the "mezzanine" between debt and equity.

1

OBJECTIVE

Business combinations: Purchase Method Procedures (including Combinations Between Mutual Enterprises) and Certain Issues Related to the Accounting for and Reporting of Noncontrolling (Minority) Interests (as of March 8, 2005)

Currently, the NCI portion of consolidated net income is often shown as an expense and consolidated net income refers to only the controlling share of income.

◆ Procedures for block purchases are specified. When control is achieved and there is a prior noncontrolling interest, that prior interest is adjusted to fair value and is added to the price paid for the later block to form a combined single block. When control exists at the time of the purchase of a new block, the transaction is viewed as an equity transaction, with no impact on income.

◆ Procedures for the sale of a controlling interest not resulting in a loss of control are specified. The difference between the sales price and the carrying value is an adjustment to equity and is an adjustment to paid-in capital in excess of par or retained earnings (if negative effect).

◆ When a portion of the controlling interest is sold and results in a loss of control, both the shares sold and the shares retained are adjusted to fair value.

CHANGES AS THEY IMPACT EACH CHAPTER
CHAPTER 1

It is presumed that the fair value of the consideration given determines the fair value of the company purchased. If, however, the value of the consideration given is not clear, the fair value of the business acquired must be estimated using fair value measurements. The FASB Exposure Draft on Fair Value Measurement provides guidance in estimating the fair value of the business.

All identifiable assets and liabilities will be recorded at fair value using the new guidance on fair values that will result from the FASB Exposure Draft on Fair Value Measurement.

In-process R&D is to be estimated and included as an asset. The in-process R&D value cannot be increased for expenditures after the acquisition date. The amount assigned to in-process R&D is to be impairment tested in future periods.

Contingent gains and losses of the acquired business, which would otherwise not be recorded, are to be estimated at fair value.

There will be no discounting of assets in a bargain purchase. If the price paid is less than the sum of the fair values of the net identifiable assets, a gain (not extraordinary) is recorded on the purchase. There is to be a close evaluation of fair values before a gain is recorded.

All acquisition costs, including direct acquisition costs (added to cost in the past), are to be expensed. No mention is made of issue costs. Presumably, they would follow the normal practice of reducing the value assigned to the securities issued (current practice).

Where there is contingent consideration, an estimated liability should be recorded for the estimated fair value of the amount to be paid. Any change in that estimate impacts income of later periods. There can be no recording of added goodwill subsequent to the acquisition date. It would appear that the procedure for contingencies based on the share price of the issuer would remain the same since they do not affect the amount paid for the acquired firm.

Application Example. Let us assume that the company to be acquired by Acquisitions Inc. has the following balance sheet.

		Johnson Company Balance Sheet December 31, 20X1	
Cash	$ 40,000	Current liabilities	$ 25,000
Marketable investments	60,000	8%, 5-year bond payable	100,000
Inventory	100,000	Total liabilities	$125,000
Equipment (net)	80,000		
Land	30,000	Common stock, $1 par	$ 10,000
Buildings (net)	150,000	Paid-in capital in excess of par	140,000
		Retained earnings	185,000
		Total equity	$335,000
Total assets	$460,000	Liabilities plus equity	$460,000

Note 1: A customer list with significant value exists.

Note 2: There is an unrecorded warranty liability on prior product sales.

Fair values for all accounts have been established in conformity with the FASB Exposure Draft on Fair Value Measurement as follows:

Account	Method of Estimation	Fair Value
Cash	Book value	$ 40,000
Marketable investment	Level 1—market value	66,000
Inventory	Level 1—market value	110,000
Equipment	Level 1—market value	145,000
Land	Level 2—adjusted market value	72,000
Buildings	Level 2—adjusted market value	288,000
Customer list	Level 3—other estimate, discounted cash flow	123,300
Current liabilities	Book value	(25,000)
Bonds payable		(100,000)
Premium on bonds payable	Level 3—other estimate, discounted cash flow	(4,100)
Warranty liability	Level 3—other estimate, discounted cash flow	(11,912)
Fair value of net identifiable assets		$ 703,288

Recording the Purchase. The price paid for the company being purchased is normally measured as the sum of the consideration (total assets) exchanged for the business. This would be the sum of the cash, other assets, debt securities issued, and any stock issued by the acquiring company. In a rare case, the fair value of the company being purchased may be more determinable than the consideration given. This could be the case where stock is issued which is not publicly traded and the fair value of the business acquired is more measurable.

The basic procedures to record the purchase are:
◆ All accounts identified are measured at estimated fair value as demonstrated above. This is true even if the consideration given for a company is less than the sum of the fair values of the net assets (assets minus liabilities assumed, $703,288 in above example).
◆ If the total consideration given for a company exceeds the fair value of its net identifiable assets ($703,288), the excess price paid is recorded as Goodwill.
◆ In a rare case, where total consideration given for a company is less than the fair value of its net identifiable assets ($703,288), the excess of the net assets over the price paid is recorded as a gain in the period of the purchase.
◆ All acquisition costs are expensed in the period of the purchase. These costs could include the fees of accountants and lawyers that were necessary to negotiate and consummate the purchase. In the past, these costs were included as part of the price paid for the company purchased.

Examples of Recording a Purchase. Prior to attempting to record a purchase, an analysis should be made comparing the price paid for the company with the fair value of the net assets acquired.

◆ If the price exceeds the sum of the fair value of the net identifiable assets acquired, the excess price is goodwill.
◆ If the price is less than the sum of the fair value of the net identifiable assets acquired, the price deficiency is a gain.

1. Price paid exceeds fair value of net identifiable assets acquired.

Acquisitions Inc. issues 40,000 shares of its $1 par value common stock shares with a market value of $20 each for Johnson Company, illustrated above. Acquisitions Inc. pays related acquisition costs of $35,000.

Value analysis:

Total price paid (consideration given), 40,000 shares × $20 market value	$ 800,000
Total fair value of net assets acquired from Johnson Company	(703,288)
Goodwill	$ 96,712
Expense acquisition costs	35,000

Entries to record purchase and related costs are as follows:

	Dr.	Cr.
To record purchase of net assets:		
Cash	40,000	
Marketable Investments	66,000	
Inventory	110,000	
Equipment	145,000	
Land	72,000	
Buildings	288,000	
Customer List	123,300	
Goodwill	**96,712**	
Current Liabilities		25,000
Bonds Payable		100,000
Premium on Bonds Payable		4,100
Warranty Liability		11,912
Common Stock, $1 par, 40,000 shares issued		40,000
Paid-In Capital in Excess of Par ($20 per share × 40,000 shares less $40,000 assigned to par)		760,000
Dr. = Cr. Check Totals	941,012	941,012
To record acquisition costs:		
Acquisition Expense	35,000	
Cash		35,000

2. Price paid is less than fair value of net identifiable assets acquired.

Acquisitions Inc. issues 25,000 shares of its $1 par value common stock shares with a market value of $20 each for Johnson Company, illustrated above. Acquisitions Inc. pays related acquisition costs of $35,000.

Value analysis:

Total price paid (consideration given), 25,000 shares × $20 market value	$ 500,000
Total fair value of net assets acquired from Johnson Company	(703,288)
Gain on purchase of business	$ 203,288
Expense acquisition costs	35,000

Entries to record purchase and related costs are as follows:

	Dr.	Cr.
To record purchase of net assets:		
Cash	40,000	
Marketable Investments	66,000	
Inventory	110,000	
Equipment	145,000	
Land	72,000	
Buildings	288,000	
Customer List	123,300	
Current Liabilities		25,000
Bonds Payable		100,000
Premium on Bonds Payable		4,100
Warranty Liability		11,912
Common Stock, $1 par, 25,000 shares issued		25,000
Paid-In Capital in Excess of Par ($20 per share × 25,000 shares less $25,000 assigned to par)		475,000
Gain on Purchase of Business		**203,288**
Dr. = Cr. Check Totals	844,300	844,300

To record acquisition costs:

Acquisition Expense	35,000	
Cash		35,000

CHAPTER 1 EXERCISES AND PROBLEMS

Exercise SA1-1 Bargain purchase. Carp Corporation is purchasing the net assets of Bass Company on December 31, 20X6, when Bass Company has the following balance sheet:

Assets		Liabilities and Equity	
Current assets	$100,000	Liabilities	$ 90,000
Land.	50,000	Common stock ($10 par).	200,000
Buildings (net)	200,000	Retained earnings	140,000
Equipment (net)	60,000		
Patents	20,000		
Total assets.	$430,000	Total liabilities and equity	$430,000

Carp has obtained the following fair values for Bass Company accounts:

Current assets	$120,000
Land.	80,000
Buildings	250,000
Equipment	150,000
Patents	20,000
Liabilities	92,000

Direct acquisition costs are $18,000, and indirect acquisition costs are $5,000.

Prepare the entries to record the purchase of Bass Company assuming the cash payment by Carp Corporation to Bass Company is $400,000. Carp Corporation will assume the liabilities of Bass Company. Value analysis is recommended.

Problem SA1-1 Alternate consideration, bargain. Kent Corporation is considering the purchase of Williams Incorporated. Kent has asked you, its accountant, to evaluate the various offers it might make to Williams Incorporated. The December 31, 20X1, balance sheet of Williams is as follows:

Williams Incorporated
Balance Sheet
December 31, 20X1

Assets			Liabilities and Equity		
Current assets:			Accounts payable		$ 40,000
Accounts receivable. . .	$ 50,000				
Inventory	300,000				
		$350,000	Stockholders' equity:		
Noncurrent assets:			Common stock	$ 40,000	
Land.	$ 20,000		Paid-in capital in excess of par . .	110,000	
Building (net)	70,000	90,000	Retained earnings	250,000	400,000
Total assets.		$440,000	Total liabilities and equity		$440,000

The following fair values differ from existing book values:

Inventory	$250,000
Land	40,000
Building	120,000

Required ▶ ▶ ▶ ▶ ▶   Record the purchase entry for Kent Corporation that would result under each of the alternative offers. Value analysis is suggested.

1. Kent Corporation issues 20,000 of its $10 par common stock with a fair value of $25 per share for the net assets of Williams Incorporated.
2. Kent Corporation pays $385,000 in cash.

CHAPTER 2

The price paid by the parent company for the controlling interest will no longer include direct acquisition costs, as they are expensed at purchase date.

We will illustrate consolidation procedures using the 80% acquisition of Sample Company by Parental Inc. Presented below are the balance sheet amounts and the fair values of the assets and liabilities of Sample Company as of December 31, 20X1.

Assets	Book Value	Market Value		Book Value	Market Value
Accounts receivable	20,000	20,000	Current liabilities	40,000	40,000
Inventory	50,000	55,000	Bonds payable	100,000	100,000
Land	40,000	70,000	**Total liabilities**	**140,000**	**140,000**
Buildings	200,000	250,000			
Accumulated depreciation	(50,000)		**Stockholders' equity:**		
Equipment	60,000	60,000	Common stock, $1 par	10,000	
Accumulated depreciation	(20,000)		Paid-in excess of par	90,000	
Copyright		50,000	Retained earnings	100,000	
Goodwill	40,000	TBD	Total equity	200,000	
Total assets	**340,000**	**505,000**	**Net assets**	**200,000**	**365,000**

Assume that Parental Inc. issued 16,800 shares of its $1 par value common stock for 80% (8,000 shares) of the outstanding shares of Sample Company. The fair value of a share of Parental Inc. stock is $25. Parental also pays $20,000 in accounting and legal fees to accomplish the purchase. Parental would make the following entry to record the purchase:

	Dr.	Cr.
To record the purchase:		
Investment in Sample Company (16,800 shares issued × $25 fair value)	420,000	
Common Stock, $1 par value (16,800 shares × $1 par)		16,800
Paid-In Capital in Excess of Par ($420,000 − $16,800 par value)		403,200
To record the costs of the acquisition:		
Acquisition Expense (closed to retained earnings since we are		
examining only balance sheets)	20,000	
Cash		20,000

The separate "zone" and "price" analyses of the current text will be replaced by a single "valuation analysis" for the entire entity. The following "value analysis" would be prepared for the 80% interest:

Value Analysis Schedule			
	Parent Price (80%)	NCI Value (20%)	Company Fair Value
1. Company fair value..............................	$420,000	$105,000	$525,000
2. Fair value of net assets excluding goodwill..............	292,000	73,000	365,000
3. Goodwill—Fair value of company exceeds fair value of net assets excluding goodwill...........................	128,000	32,000	160,000
4. Gain—Parent price is less than the parent share of fair value of net assets excluding goodwill........................	N/A	N/A	N/A

Several assumptions went into the above calculation:

◆ Line 1, Company fair value—It is assumed that if the parent would pay $420,000 for an 80% interest, then the entire subsidiary company is worth $525,000 ($420,000/80%). We will refer to this as the "implied value" of the subsidiary company. Assuming this to be true, the NCI is worth 20% of the total subsidiary company value (20% × $525,000 = $105,000). This approach assumes that the price the parent would pay is directly proportional to the size of the interest purchased. We will later study the situation where this presumption is defeated.

◆ Line 2, Fair value of net assets excluding goodwill—The fair values of the subsidiary accounts are from the comparison of book and fair values. All identifiable liabilities and all liabilities will be adjusted to 100% of fair value regardless of the size of the controlling interest purchased.

◆ Line 3, Goodwill—The total goodwill is the excess of the "Company Fair Value" over the fair value of the subsidiary net assets. It is proportionately allocated to the controlling interest and NCI.

Determination and Distribution of Excess Schedule

The D&D schedules in the existing text only analyze, and adjust to fair value, the controlling interest. The D&D must be modified to also revalue the NCI based on the price paid for the controlling interest. The D&D that follows revalues the entire entity, including the NCI.

Determination and Distribution of Excess Schedule				
	Implied Company Value	Parent Price	NCI Value	Worksheet Distribution
Fair value of subsidiary	525,000	420,000	105,000	
Less book value interest acquired:				
Common stock, $1 par	10,000			
Paid-in excess of par	90,000			
Retained earnings	100,000			
Total equity......................................	200,000			
Interest acquired		80.00%	20.00%	
Book value..		160,000	40,000	
Excess of fair value over book value	325,000	260,000	65,000	

(continued)

	Implied Company Value	Parent Price	NCI Value	Worksheet Distribution
Adjustment of identifiable accounts:				
Inventory ($55,000 fair – $50,000 book value)	5,000		—	**debit D1**
Land ($70,000 fair – $40,000 book value)	30,000		—	**debit D2**
Buildings ($250,000 – $150,000 net book value)	100,000		—	**debit D3**
Equipment ($60,000 fair – $40,000 net book value)	20,000		—	**debit D4**
Copyright ($50,000 fair – $0 book value)	50,000			**debit D5**
Goodwill ($160,000 fair – $40,000 book value)	120,000			**debit D6**
Gain (not applicable).	—	—	—	
Total	325,000			

Note the following features of the revised D&D schedule:

◆ The "fair value of subsidiary" line contains the implied value of the entire company, the parent price paid, and the implied value of the NCI from the above "Value Analysis" schedule.

◆ The total stockholders' equity of the subsidiary (equal to the net assets of the subsidiary at book value) is allocated 80/20 to the controlling interest and the NCI.

◆ The excess of fair value over book value is shown for the company, the controlling interest, and the NCI. This line means that the entire adjustment of subsidiary net assets will be $325,000. The controlling interest paid $260,000 more than the underlying book value of subsidiary net assets. This is the excess that will appear on the worksheet when the parent's 80% share of subsidiary stockholders' equity is eliminated against the investment account. Finally, the NCI share of the increase to fair value is $65,000.

◆ All subsidiary assets and liabilities will be increased to 100% of fair value, just as would be the case for a 100% purchase.

◆ Goodwill will be adjusted by the $120,000 difference between the new estimated goodwill ($160,000) and that which is already recorded ($40,000).

Worksheet A2-1: page 307

The D&D provides complete guidance for the worksheet eliminations. Study Worksheet A2-1 on page 307 and note the following:

◆ Elimination "EL" eliminated the subsidiary equity purchased (80% in this example) against the investment account as follows:

(EL)	Common Stock, $1 par, Sample	8,000	
	Paid-In Excess of Par, Sample	72,000	
	Retained Earnings, Sample	80,000	
	Investment in Sample Company.		160,000

◆ The "D" series eliminations distribute the excess applicable to the controlling interest plus the increase in the NCI (labeled "NCI") to the appropriate accounts, as indicated by the D&D schedule. The adjustment of the NCI is carried to subsidiary retained earnings. Recall, however, that only the total NCI will appear on the consolidated balance sheet. Worksheet eliminations are as follows:

(D1)	Inventory	5,000
(D2)	Land.	30,000
(D3)	Buildings	100,000
(D4)	Equipment	20,000
(D5)	Copyright	50,000

(D6)	Goodwill ($160,000 total − $40,000 existing goodwill)	120,000	
(D)	Investment in Sample Company (remaining excess after "EL")....................		260,000
(NCI)	Retained Earnings—Sample (NCI share of fair market adjustment).........................		65,000
	Check Totals	325,000	325,000

The amounts that will appear on the consolidated balance sheet are shown in the final column of Worksheet A2-1. The components of the NCI are summed and presented as a single amount in the balance sheet column. Notice that we have consolidated 100% of the fair values of subsidiary accounts with the existing book values of parent company accounts. The balance sheet columns of the worksheet will show the components of controlling equity (par, paid-in excess, and retained earnings) and the total NCI.

Formal Balance Sheet

The formal consolidated balance sheet resulting from the 80% purchase of Sample Company, in exchange for 16,800 Parental shares, has been taken from the balance sheet column of Worksheet A2-1.

Parental Inc.
Consolidated Balance Sheet
December 31, 20X1

Assets			Liabilities and Equity		
Current assets:			Current liabilities	$120,000	
Cash	$ 84,000		Bonds payable	300,000	
Accounts receivable........	92,000		Total liabilities		$ 420,000
Inventory	135,000				
Total		$ 311,000			
Long-term assets:			Stockholders' equity:		
Land....................	$ 170,000		Common stock, $1 par	$ 36,800	
Buildings	800,000		Paid-in capital in excess		
			of par	603,200	
Accumulated depreciation...	(130,000)		Retained earnings	456,000	
Equipment	320,000		Total controlling equity....		1,096,000
Accumulated depreciation...	(60,000)		Noncontrolling interest	105,000	
Copyright (net)............	50,000		Total equity.............		1,201,000
Goodwill (net)	160,000				
Total		1,310,000			
Total assets		$1,621,000	Total liabilities and equity		$1,621,000

Adjustment of Goodwill Applicable to NCI

The NCI goodwill value can be reduced below its implied value if there is evidence that the implied value exceeds the real fair value of the NCI's share of goodwill. This could occur when a parent pays a premium to achieve control, which is not dependent on the size of the ownership interest.

The NCI share of goodwill could be reduced to zero, but the NCI share of the fair value of net tangible assets is never reduced. The total NCI can never be less than the NCI percentage of the fair value of the net assets (in this case, it cannot be less than 20% × $365,000 = $73,000).

If the fair value of the NCI was estimated to be $90,000 ($15,000 less than the value implied by parent purchase price), the value analysis would be modified as follows (changes are boldfaced):

Value Analysis Schedule			
	Parent Price (80%)	NCI Value (20%)	Company Fair Value
1. Company fair value.	$420,000	**$90,000**	**$510,000**
2. Fair value of net assets **excluding goodwill**.	292,000	73,000	365,000
3. Goodwill—Fair value of company exceeds fair value of net assets excluding goodwill	128,000	17,000	**145,000**
4. Gain—Parent price is less than the parent share of fair value of net assets excluding goodwill	N/A		

Several assumptions went into the above calculation:

◆ Line 1, Company fair value—This is now the sum of the price paid by the parent plus the newly estimated fair value of the NCI.
◆ Line 2, Fair value of net assets **excluding goodwill**—The fair values of the subsidiary accounts are from the comparison of book and fair values. These values are never less than fair value.
◆ Line 3, Goodwill—The total goodwill is the excess of the "Company Fair Value" over the fair value of the subsidiary net assets.

The revised D&D schedule with changes (from the previous example) in boldfaced type would be:

Determination and Distribution of Excess Schedule				
	Company Value	Parent Price	NCI Value	Worksheet Distribution
Fair value of subsidiary	**510,000**	420,000	**90,000**	
Less book value interest acquired:				
Common stock, $1 par	10,000			
Paid-in excess of par	90,000			
Retained earnings	100,000			
Total equity.	200,000			
Interest acquired		80.00%	20.00%	
Book value.		160,000	40,000	
Excess of fair value over book value	**310,000**	260,000	**50,000**	
Adjustment of identifiable accounts:				
Inventory ($55,000 fair − $50,000 book value)	5,000		—	debit D1
Land ($70,000 fair − $40,000 book value).	30,000		—	debit D2
Buildings ($250,000 − $150,000 net book value)	100,000		—	debit D3
Equipment ($60,000 fair − $40,000 net book value)	20,000		—	debit D4
Copyright ($50,000 fair − $0 book value).	50,000			debit D5
Goodwill ($145,000 fair − $40,000 book value)	**105,000**			debit D6
Gain (not applicable)	—	—	—	
Total	**310,000**			

If goodwill becomes impaired in a future period, the impairment charge would be allocated to the controlling interest and the NCI based on the percentage of total goodwill each equity interest received on the D&D. In the original example, where goodwill on the NCI was assumed to be proportional to that recorded on the controlling interest, the impairment charge would be allocated 80/20 to the controlling interest and NCI. In the above example, where goodwill was not proportional, a new percentage would be developed as follows:

	Value	Percentage of Total
Goodwill applicable to parent from value analysis schedule	$128,000	88.28%
Goodwill applicable to NCI from value analysis schedule	17,000	11.72%
Total goodwill	$145,000	

Gain on Purchase of Subsidiary

Let us now study the same example, except that the price paid will be low enough to result in a gain. Assume that Parental Inc. issued 10,000 shares of its $1 par value common stock for 80% of the outstanding shares of Sample Company. The fair value of a share of Parental Inc. stock is $25. Parental also pays $20,000 in accounting and legal fees to complete the purchase. Parental would make the following journal entry to record the purchase:

	Dr.	Cr.
To record the purchase:		
Investment in Sample Company (10,000 shares issued × $25 fair value)......................................	250,000	
Common Stock, $1 par value (10,000 shares × $1 par)		10,000
Paid-In Capital in Excess of Par ($250,000 – $10,000 par value)......................................		240,000
To record the costs of the acquisition:		
Acquisition Expense (closed to retained earnings since we are examining only balance sheets)	20,000	
Cash.......................................		20,000

Refer back to the prior comparison of book and fair values for the subsidiary. The following value analysis would be prepared for the 80% interest:

Value Analysis Schedule	Parent Price (80%)	NCI Value (20%)	Company Fair Value
1. Company fair value............................	$250,000	$62,500 73,000	$323,000
2. Fair value of net assets **excluding goodwill**.........	292,000	73,000	365,000
3. Goodwill—Fair value of company exceeds fair value of net assets excluding goodwill	N/A	N/A	
4. Gain—Parent price is less than the parent share of fair value of net assets excluding goodwill	42,000		

Several assumptions went into the above calculation:

◆ Line 1, Company fair value—It is assumed that if the parent would pay $250,000 for an 80% interest, then the entire subsidiary company is worth $312,500 ($250,000/80%). We will refer to this as the "implied value" of the subsidiary company. Assuming this to be true, the NCI is worth 20% of the total subsidiary company value (20% × $312,500 = $62,500). The NCI value, however, can never be less than its share of net identifiable assets ($73,000). Thus, the NCI share of company value is raised to $73,000 (replacing the $62,500).

◆ Line 2—Fair value of net assets **excluding goodwill**—The fair values of the subsidiary accounts are from the comparison of book and fair values.

◆ Line 3—There can be no goodwill when the price paid is less than the fair value of the parent's share of the fair value of net identifiable assets. Thus, the line is marked N/A (Not Applicable).

◆ Line 4—The only gain recognized is that applicable to the controlling interest.

The following D&D would be prepared:

Determination and Distribution of Excess Schedule

	Company Value	Parent Price	NCI Value	Worksheet Distribution
Fair value of subsidiary	323,000	250,000	73,000	
Less book value interest acquired:				
Common stock, $1 par	10,000			
Paid-in excess of par	90,000			
Retained earnings	100,000			
Total equity.	200,000			
Interest acquired		80.00%	20.00%	
Book value.		160,000	40,000	
Excess of cost over book value (debit)	123,000	90,000	33,000	
Adjustment of identifiable accounts:				
Inventory ($55,000 fair − $50,000 book value)	5,000		—	debit D1
Land ($70,000 fair − $40,000 book value).	30,000		—	debit D2
Buildings ($250,000 − $150,000 net book value)	100,000		—	debit D3
Equipment ($60,000 fair − $40,000 net book value)	20,000		—	debit D4
Copyright ($50,000 fair − $0 book value).	50,000			debit D5
Goodwill ($0 fair value − $40,000 book value)	(40,000)			credit D6
Gain (only applies to the controlling interest)	(42,000)	—	—	credit D7
Total.	123,000			

Worksheet A2-2: page 308

Worksheet A2-2 on page 308 is the consolidated worksheet for the $250,000 price. The D&D provides complete guidance for the worksheet eliminations:

◆ Elimination "EL" eliminated the subsidiary equity purchased (80% in this example) against the investment account as follows:

(EL)	Common Stock, $1 par	8,000	
	Paid-In Excess of Par	72,000	
	Retained Earnings	80,000	
	Investment in Sample Company.		160,000

◆ The "D" series eliminations distribute the excess applicable to the controlling interest plus the increase in the NCI (labeled "NCI") to the appropriate accounts as indicated by the D&D schedule. Worksheet eliminations are as follows:

(D1)	Inventory	5,000
(D2)	Land.	30,000
(D3)	Buildings	100,000

(D4)	Equipment	20,000	
(D5)	Copyright	50,000	
(D6)	Goodwill (existing goodwill eliminated)		40,000
(D7)	Gain on Purchase of Subsidiary (since we are dealing		
	only with a balance sheet, this would be credited		
	to Controlling Retained Earnings)		42,000
(D)	Investment in Sample Company (remaining excess		
	after "EL")		90,000
(NCI)	Retained Earnings—Sample (NCI		
	share of fair market adjustment)		33,000
	Check Totals	205,000	205,000

Valuation Schedule Strategy

Here are steps to valuation that will always work if scheduled as shown below:

1. Enter value for cell C2 (sum of fair values of company's net identifiable assets), and then enter appropriate percentage of that value into cells A2 and B2. These amounts are fixed regardless of the price paid by the parent. They will never change.

Step 1:

	A 80% Parent	B 20% NCI	C Company
1. Company fair value.			
2. Fair value of net identifiable assets	**292,000**	**3,000**	**65,000**
3. Goodwill			
4. Gain			—

2. Enter price paid $420,000 for controlling interest by the parent in cell A1.

Step 2:

	A 80% Parent	B 20% NCI	C Company
1. Company fair value.	**420,000**		
2. Fair value of net identifiable assets	292,000	73,000	365,000
3. Goodwill			
4. Gain			—

3. Compare A1, the price paid by the parent, and A2, the parent's share of the fair value of the company's net identifiable assets:

a. If A1>A2, enter A3, which is the goodwill applicable to the parent. Then complete cell B1. Normally, this amount will be proportional to A1. It can be a lesser amount but never less than cell B2. The proportionate value would be 20%/80% for this example. Calculate values for C1, B2, and B3.

Step 3(a):

	A 80% Parent	B 20% NCI	C Company
1. Company fair value.	420,000	**90,000***	
2. Fair value of net identifiable assets	292,000	73,000	365,000
3. Goodwill	**128,000**		
4. Gain			—

*Greater than 73,000 and less than 20%/80% × 420,000 = 105,000

Complete remaining cells:

	A 80% Parent	B 20% NCI	C Company
1. Company fair value.	420,000	90,000*	**510,000**
2. Fair value of net identifiable assets	292,000	73,000	365,000
3. Goodwill	128,000	**17,000**	**145,000**
4. Gain			—

b. If A2>A1, enter A4, which is the gain applicable to the parent. Then enter cell B1 equal to B2 (the NCI cannot have a gain). Calculate value for C1. Cell C4 = A4.

Try it for Parent price of $250,000:

Step 1:

	A 80% Parent	B 20% NCI	C Company
1. Company fair value.			
2. Fair value of net identifiable assets	**292,000**	**73,000**	**365,000**
3. Goodwill			
4. Gain			—

Step 2:

	A 80% Parent	B 20% NCI	C Company
1. Company fair value.	**250,000**		
2. Fair value of net identifiable assets	292,000	73,000	365,000
3. Goodwill			
4. Gain	**42,000**		—

Step 3(b):

	A 80% Parent	B 20% NCI	C Company
1. Company fair value.	250,000	**73,000**	
2. Fair value of net identifiable assets	292,000	73,000	365,000
3. Goodwill			
4. Gain	42,000		—

Complete remaining cells:

	A 80% Parent	B 20% NCI	C Company
1. Company fair value.	250,000	73,000	**323,000**
2. Fair value of net identifiable assets	292,000	73,000	365,000
3. Goodwill			
4. Gain	42,000		**42,000**

Gain on Parent Asset Transferred to Subsidiary to Acquire Interest

The parent must bring to fair value any assets, other than cash, that it exchanges for the controlling interest. If those assets are retained and used by the subsidiary company, the gain must be eliminated in the consolidation process.

Assets transferred would be retained by the subsidiary when either:

1. the assets are transferred to the former shareholders of the subsidiary company and the shareholders sell the assets to the subsidiary company, or
2. the assets are transferred directly to the subsidiary company in exchange for newly issued shares or treasury shares.

The gain would be deferred using the procedures demonstrated in Chapter 4 for the parent sale of a fixed asset to the subsidiary.

Worksheet A2-1

80% Interest: Price Exceeds Fair Value of Net Identifiable Assets
Parental Inc. and Subsidiary Sample Company
Worksheet for Consolidated Balance Sheet
December 31, 20X1

(Facts on page 300)

(Credit balance amounts are in parentheses.)	Balance Sheet		Eliminations & Adjustments		NCI	Consolidated Balance Sheet	
	Parental	Sample	Dr.	Cr.			
Cash	84,000	0				84,000	1
Accounts Receivable	72,000	20,000				92,000	2
Inventory	80,000	50,000	(D1) 5,000			135,000	3
Land	100,000	40,000	(D2) 30,000			170,000	4
Investment in Sample Company	420,000			(EL) 160,000			5
				(D) 260,000			6
Buildings	500,000	200,000	(D3) 100,000			800,000	7
Accumulated Depreciation	(80,000)	(50,000)				(130,000)	8
Equipment	240,000	60,000	(D4) 20,000			320,000	9
Accumulated Depreciation	(40,000)	(20,000)				(60,000)	10
Copyright			(D5) 50,000			50,000	11
Goodwill		40,000	(D6) 120,000			160,000	12
Current Liabilities	(80,000)	(40,000)				(120,000)	13
Bonds Payable	(200,000)	(100,000)				(300,000)	14
Common Stock—Sample		(10,000)	(EL) 8,000		(2,000)		15
Paid-In Excess—Sample		(90,000)	(EL) 72,000		(18,000)		16
Retained Earnings—Sample		(100,000)	(EL) 80,000	(NCI) 65,000	(85,000)		17
Common Stock—Parental	(36,800)					(36,800)	18
Paid-In Excess—Parental	(603,200)					(603,200)	19
Retained Earnings—Parental	(456,000)					(456,000)	20
Totals	0	0	485,000	485,000			21
NCI					(105,000)	(105,000)	22
							23
Totals						0	24

Eliminations and Adjustments:

(EL)   Eliminate 80% subsidiary equity against investment account.
(NCI)   Adjust NCI to fair value.
(D)   Distribute remaining excess in investment account plus NCI adjustment to:
(D1)   Inventory.
(D2)   Land.

(D3)   Building (recorded cost is increased without removing accumulated depreciation). The alternative is to debit Accumulated Depreciation for $50,000 and the building for $50,000. This would restate the asset at fair value.
(D4)   Equipment (recorded cost is increased without removing accumulated depreciation). The alternative is to debit Accumulated Depreciation for $20,000. This would restate the asset at fair value.
(D5)   Copyright.
(D6)   Goodwill.

Worksheet A2-2

80% Interest: Price Is Less than Fair Value of Net Identifiable Assets
Parental Inc. and Subsidiary Sample Company
Worksheet for Consolidated Balance Sheet
December 31, 20X1

(Facts on page 304)

(Credit balance amounts are in parentheses.)	Balance Sheet Parental	Sample	Eliminations & Adjustments Dr.	Cr.	NCI	Consolidated Balance Sheet	
Cash	254,000	0				254,000	1
Accounts Receivable	72,000	20,000				92,000	2
Inventory	80,000	50,000	(D1) 5,000			135,000	3
Land	100,000	40,000	(D2) 30,000			170,000	4
Investment in Sample Company	250,000			(EL) 160,000			5
				(D) 90,000			6
Buildings	500,000	200,000	(D3) 100,000			800,000	7
Accumulated Depreciation	(80,000)	(50,000)				(130,000)	8
Equipment	240,000	60,000	(D4) 20,000			320,000	9
Accumulated Depreciation	(40,000)	(20,000)				(60,000)	10
Copyright			(D5) 50,000			50,000	11
Goodwill		40,000		(D6) 40,000			12
Current Liabilities	(80,000)	(40,000)				(120,000)	13
Bonds Payable	(200,000)	(100,000)				(300,000)	14
Common Stock—Sample		(10,000)	(EL) 8,000		(2,000)		15
Paid-In Excess—Sample		(90,000)	(EL) 72,000		(18,000)		16
Retained Earnings—Sample		(100,000)	(EL) 80,000	(NCI) 33,000	(53,000)		17
Common Stock—Parental	(36,800)					(36,800)	18
Paid-In Excess—Parental	(603,200)					(603,200)	19
Retained Earnings—Parental	(456,000)			(D7) 42,000		(498,000)	20
Totals	0	0	365,000	365,000			21
NCI					(73,000)	(73,000)	22
							23
Totals						0	24

Eliminations and Adjustments:

(EL) Eliminate 80% subsidiary equity against investment account.
(NCI) Adjust NCI to fair value.
(D) Distribute remaining excess in investment account plus NCI adjustment to:
(D1) Inventory.
(D2) Land.

(D3) Building (recorded cost is increased without removing accumulated depreciation). The alternative is to debit Accumulated Depreciation for $50,000 and the building for $50,000. This would restate the asset at fair value.
(D4) Equipment (recorded cost is increased without removing accumulated depreciation). The alternative is to debit Accumulated Depreciation for $20,000. This would restate the asset at fair value.
(D5) Copyright.
(D6) Goodwill.

CHAPTER 2 EXERCISES AND PROBLEMS

Exercise SA2-1 80% purchase, goodwill.   Quincy Company purchased 80% of the common stock of Cooker Company for $720,000 and paid direct acquisition costs of $10,000. At the time of the purchase, Cooker Company had the following balance sheet:

Assets		Liabilities and Equity	
Cash equivalents	$ 120,000	Current liabilities	$ 200,000
Inventory . . . . :	200,000	Bonds payable	400,000
Land.	100,000	Common stock ($5 par).	100,000
Building (net)	450,000	Paid-in capital in excess of par .	150,000
Equipment (net)	230,000	Retained earnings	250,000
Total assets.	$1,100,000	Total liabilities and equity . . .	$1,100,000

Fair values differ from book values for all assets other than cash equivalents. The fair values are as follows:

Inventory	$300,000
Land.	200,000
Building	600,000
Equipment	200,000

Based on the preceding facts, do the following.

1. Prepare a value analysis schedule and a determination and distribution of excess schedule.
2. Prepare the elimination entries that would be made on a consolidated worksheet prepared on the date of purchase.

Exercise SA2-2 80% purchase, alternative prices.   Venus Company purchased 8,000 shares of Saturn Company for $82 per share. Just prior to the purchase, Saturn Company had the following balance sheet:

Assets		Liabilities and Equity	
Cash	$ 20,000	Current liabilities	$250,000
Inventory	280,000	Common stock ($5 par).	50,000
Property, plant, and		Paid-in capital in excess of	
equipment (net)	400,000	par	130,000
		Retained earnings	370,000
Goodwill	100,000		
Total assets.	$800,000	Total liabilities and equity	$800,000

Venus Company believes that the inventory has a fair value of $400,000 and that the property, plant, and equipment is worth $500,000.

1. Prepare a value analysis schedule and a determination and distribution of excess schedule.   ◄ ◄ ◄ ◄ ◄ **Required**
2. Prepare the elimination entries that would be made on a consolidated worksheet prepared on the date of acquisition.
3. Prepare the value analysis schedule and the determination and distribution of excess schedule and the elimination entries that would be made on a consolidated worksheet prepared on the date of acquisition assuming Venus pays $64 per share.

Problem SA2-1 80% purchase at less than fair value of net identifiable assets, elimination entries only.

On March 1, 20X5, Penson Enterprises purchased an 80% interest in Express Corporation for $320,000. Express Corporation had the following balance sheet on February 28, 20X5:

Express Corporation
Balance Sheet
February 28, 20X5

Assets		Liabilities and Equity	
Accounts receivable	$ 60,000	Current liabilities	$ 50,000
Inventory	80,000	Bonds payable	100,000
Land	40,000	Common stock ($10 par)	50,000
Buildings	300,000	Paid-in capital in excess of par	250,000
Accum. depreciation—buildings	(120,000)	Retained earnings	70,000
Equipment	220,000		
Accum. depreciation—equipment	(60,000)		
Total assets	$ 520,000	Total liabilities and equity	$520,000

Penson Enterprises received an independent appraisal on the fair values of Express Corporation's assets. The controller has reviewed the following figures and accepts them as reasonable.

Accounts receivable	$ 60,000
Inventory	100,000
Land	50,000
Buildings	200,000
Equipment	162,000
Current liabilities	50,000
Bonds payable	95,000

Required ▶ ▶ ▶ ▶ ▶

1. Record the investment in Express Corporation.
2. Prepare a value analysis schedule and a determination and distribution of excess schedule.
3. Prepare the elimination entries that would be made on a consolidated worksheet prepared on the date of acquisition.

Problem SA2-2 80% purchase, goodwill, several adjustments, worksheet.

Parton Corporation acquired Soma Corporation on December 31, 20X1. Parton exchanged shares of its $1 par, $50 fair value stock for 80% of the common stock of Soma. Soma had the following balance sheet on the date of acquisition:

Soma Corporation
Balance Sheet
December 31, 20X1

Assets		Liabilities and Equity	
Accounts receivable	$ 50,000	Current liabilities	$ 90,000
Inventory	120,000	Bonds payable	200,000
Land	100,000	Common stock ($1 par)	10,000
Buildings	300,000	Paid-in capital in excess	
Accumulated depreciation	(100,000)	of par	190,000
Equipment	140,000	Retained earnings	140,000
Accumulated depreciation	(50,000)		
Patent	10,000		
Goodwill	60,000		
Total assets	$ 630,000	Total liabilities and equity	$630,000

An appraisal has been performed to determine whether the book values of Soma's net assets reflect their fair values. The appraiser also determined that several intangible assets existed, although they were not recorded. The following assets and liabilities had fair values that differed from their book values:

Accounts receivable	$ 50,000
Inventory	100,000
Land	200,000
Buildings	400,000
Equipment	200,000
Patent	150,000
Computer software	50,000
Current liabilities	90,000
Bonds payable	210,000

Use the preceding information for Parton's purchase of Soma common stock. Assume Parton exchanged 19,000 shares of its own stock for 80% of the common stock of Soma. The stock had a market value of $50 per share and a par value of $1. Parton had the following trial balance immediately after the purchase:

Parton Corporation Trial Balance December 31, 20X1 (Parent only)	
Cash	170,000
Accounts Receivable	300,000
Inventory	410,000
Land	800,000
Investment in Soma	950,000
Buildings	2,800,000
Accumulated Depreciation	(500,000)
Equipment	600,000
Accumulated Depreciation	(230,000)
Current Liabilities	(150,000)
Bonds Payable	(300,000)
Common Stock ($1 par)	(95,000)
Paid-In Capital in Excess of Par	(3,655,000)
Retained Earnings	(1,100,000)
Total	0

1. Prepare a value analysis schedule and a determination and distribution of excess schedule for the investment in Soma.
2. Complete a consolidated worksheet for Parton Corporation and its subsidiary Soma Corporation as of December 31, 20X1.

CHAPTER 3

The changes to Chapter 3 can be summarized as follows:

♦ Identifiable assets and liabilities have been adjusted to 100% of fair value regardless of the parent ownership percentage. This means that the entire adjustment to fair value must be amortized in subsequent periods. Since the NCI will share in the amortizations of excess, **all amortizations of excess will now flow through the Subsidiary IDS schedule. Amortizations for prior periods will be allocated to the retained earnings of the controlling interest and NCI.**

Worksheet A3-1: page 316

♦ In the period of a bargain purchase (parent price is less than controlling share of fair value of net identifiable assets), the parent will record a gain on the purchase of the subsidiary. The NCI does not share in the gain on the purchase. In later periods, the gain will be credited to only controlling retained earnings.

Worksheet A3-1 on pages 316 to 317 is an example of an 80% purchase with goodwill. The following table shows book and fair values of Carlos Company on the date of purchase:

	Book Value	Market Value	Life		Book Value	Market Value	Life
Assets:							
				Current liabilities	50,000	50,000	1
Inventory	75,000	80,000	1	Bonds payable	200,000	186,760	4
Land.	150,000	200,000	—	**Total liabilities**	**250,000**	**236,760**	
Buildings	600,000	500,000	20	Stockholders' equity:			
Accumulated							
depreciation	(300,000)			Common stock.	100,000		
Equipment	150,000	80,000	5	Paid-in excess of par	150,000		
Accumulated				Retained earnings	250,000		
depreciation	(50,000)						
Patent.	125,000	150,000	10				
Existing							
goodwill.	—			Total equity	500,000		
Total assets	**750,000**	**1,010,000**		**Net assets**	**500,000**	**773,260**	

The parent company, Paulos, paid $720,000 for an 80% interest in Carlos Company on January 1, 20X1. It is assumed that the goodwill applicable to the NCI is proportional to that reflected in the parent's purchase price. The following value analysis schedule was prepared:

Value Analysis Schedule			
	Parent Price (80%)	NCI Value (20%)	Company Fair Value
1. Company fair value.	$720,000	$180,000	$900,000
2. Fair value of net assets **excluding goodwill**.	618,592	154,648	773,240
3. Goodwill—Fair value of company exceeds fair value of net assets excluding goodwill	101,408	25,352	126,760
4. Gain—Parent price is less than the parent share of fair value of net assets excluding goodwill	N/A		

Based on the above information, the following D&D schedule is prepared:

Determination and Distribution of Excess Schedule				
	Company Value	Parent Price	NCI Value	Worksheet Distribution
Fair value of subsidiary	900,000	720,000	180,000	
Less book value interest acquired:				
Common stock	100,000			
Paid-in excess of par	150,000			
Retained earnings	250,000			

Total equity...........	500,000		
Interest acquired		80.00%	20.00%
Book value of interest.........		400,000	100,000
Excess of cost over book value			
(debit)	400,000	320,000	80,000

Allocated to:

		Life		Amortization per Year
Accounts receivable	—	—		
Inventory	5,000	1	debit D1	
Land......................	50,000	—	debit D2	
Buildings	200,000	20	debit D3	10,000
Equipment	(20,000)	5	credit D4	(4,000)
Patent.....................	25,000	10	debit D5	2,500
Goodwill	126,760		debit D6	
Accounts payable	—			
Discount on bonds payable....	13,240	4	debit D7	3,310
Gain (not applicable)	—			
Total adjustments	400,000			

Worksheet A3-1 is prepared as of December 31, 20X2, the end of the second year. Eliminations in journal entry form are as follows:

	Eliminate subsidiary income recorded by the parent company:		
(CY1)	Subsidiary Income.....................................	80,000	
	Investment in Carlos..................................		80,000
	Eliminate dividends paid by Carlos to Paulos:		
(CY2)	Investment in Carlos..................................	16,000	
	Dividends Declared by Carlos.........................		16,000
	Eliminate 80% of Carlos equity against investment in Carlos:		
(EL)	Common Stock, Carlos	80,000	
	Paid-In Capital in Excess of Par, Carlos.....................	120,000	
	Retained Earnings, Carlos..............................	232,000	
	Investment in Carlos..................................		432,000
	Distribute excess of cost over book value:		
(D1)	Retained Earnings, Paulos (80% of $5,000 prior-year amount) ..	4,000	
(D1)	Retained Earnings, Carlos (20% of $5,000 prior-year amount) ..	1,000	
(D2)	Land...	50,000	
(D3)	Buildings	200,000	
(D4)	Equipment		20,000
(D5)	Patent..	25,000	
(D6)	Goodwill	126,760	
(D7)	Discount on Bonds Payable	13,240	
(D)	Investment in Carlos (noneliminated excess)		320,000
(NCI)	Retained Earnings—Carlos (to adjust NCI to fair value)		80,000
	Amortize excess for current year as shown on schedule following entry:		
(A3)	Depreciation Expense—Building........................	10,000	

Worksheet A3-1

Simple Equity Method, Second Year
Paulos Company and Subsidiary Carlos Company

Worksheet for Consolidated Financial Statements
For the Year Ended December 31, 20X2

	(Credit balance amounts are in parentheses.)	Trial Balance Paulos	Trial Balance Carlos
1	Cash	312,000	160,000
2	Inventory	210,000	120,000
3	Land	200,000	150,000
4	Investment in Carlos	816,000	
5			
6			
7			
8	Buildings	800,000	600,000
9	Accumulated Depreciation	(120,000)	(330,000)
10	Equipment	400,000	150,000
11	Accumulated Depreciation	(90,000)	(90,000)
12	Patent (net)		100,000
13			
14	Goodwill		0
15	Current Liabilities	(150,000)	(40,000)
16	Bond Payable	0	(200,000)
17	Discount (Premium)		
18			
19	Common Stock—Carlos		(100,000)
20	Paid-In Excess—Carlos		(150,000)
21	Retained Earnings, January 1, 20X2—Carlos		(290,000)
22			
23			
24			
25	Common Stock—Paulos	(1,500,000)	
26	Retained Earnings, January 1, 20X2—Paulos	(748,000)	
27			
28			
29			
30			
31	Sales	(400,000)	(300,000)
32	Cost of Goods Sold	200,000	120,000
33	Depreciation Expense—Building	40,000	15,000
34	Depreciation Expense—Equipment	20,000	20,000
35	Patent Amortization Expense		
36	Other Expenses	90,000	33,000
37	Interest Expense		12,000
38			
39	Subsidiary Income	(80,000)	
40	Dividends Declared—Carlos		20,000
41	Totals	0	0
42	Consolidated Net Income		
43	NCI Share		
44	Controlling Share		
45	Total NCI		
46	Retained Earnings—Controlling Interest, December 31, 20X2		
47	Totals		

Pe...

Balance, January 1, 20X2......
Net income ....
Dividends paid ....
Balance, December 31, 20X2 ..

Asse...

Current assets:
  Cash ....
  Inventory ....
Total current assets...........
Long-term assets:
  Land......................
  Buildings ....
  Accumulated depreciation...
  Equipment ....
  Accumulated depreciation...
  Patent (net)...............
  Goodwill ....
  Total long-term assets .....
Total assets ....

(Facts on page 312)

Eliminations and Adjustments		Consolidated Income Statement	NCI	Controlling Retained Earnings	Consolidated Balance Sheet	
Dr.	Cr.					
					472,000	1
					330,000	2
(D2) 50,000					400,000	3
	(CY1) 80,000					4
(CY2) 16,000						5
	(EL) 432,000					6
	(D) 320,000					7
(D3) 200,000					1,600,000	8
	(A3) 20,000				(470,000)	9
	(D4) 20,000				530,000	10
(A4) 8,000					(172,000)	11
(D5) 25,000					120,000	12
	(A5) 5,000					13
(D6) 126,760					126,760	14
					(190,000)	15
					(200,000)	16
(D7) 13,240						17
0	(A7) 6,620				6,620	18
(EL) 80,000			(20,000)			19
(EL) 120,000			(30,000)			20
(EL) 232,000			(134,638)			21
	(NCI) 80,000					22
(D1) 1,000						23
(A3–A7) 2,362						24
					(1,500,000)	25
						26
(D1) 4,000						27
(A3–A7) 9,448						28
	(CV)					29
				(734,552)		30
		(700,000)				31
		320,000				32
(A3) 10,000		65,000				33
0	(A4) 4,000	36,000				34
(A5) 2,500		2,500				35
		123,000				36
(A7) 3,313		15,310				37
						38
(CY1) 80,000						39
	(CY2) 16,000		4,000			40
983,620	983,620					41
		(138,190)				42
		17,638	(17,638)			43
		120,552		(120,552)		44
			(198,276)		(198,276)	45
				(855,104)	(855,104)	46
					0	47

CHAPTER 3 PROBLEMS

Problem SA3-1 Equity meth...
ary 1, 20X1, Peres Company p...
$308,000. Soll has common st...
$100,000, and $150,000, respec...
follows:

Net income ....
Dividends......

On January 1, 20X1, the onl...
and the building. Inventory, for...
inventory was sold in 20X1. The...
remaining life of 10 years, and s...
over book value is attributed to g...

Elimir

(CY1
(CY2

(EL)

(D)
(D1)
(D2)
(D3)
(D4)
(D5)
(D6)
(D7)
(A)

A

In

S

T

C

N

The only addition to Chapter 4 is the possible deferral of a gain that may have existed on parent assets that were transferred to the subsidiary as part of the original purchase (see Chapter 2's portion of this update). The gain would be deferred in the same manner as a gain on the parent sale of a fixed asset to the subsidiary.

CHAPTER 5

Nothing in this chapter is directly impacted by the exposure draft.

Multinational Accounting and Other Reporting Concerns

Chapter 6: *Foreign Currency Transactions*

Chapter 7: *Translation of Foreign Financial Statements*

In today's evolving global economy, companies buy goods and services from foreign sources, manufacture goods in a number of different countries, and sell their products to customers throughout the world. The complexities of the many international transactions have required accounting to become more international in nature. Efforts are underway to develop accounting principles that are comparable or harmonious between trading nations.

As international trading expands, accounting principles must address how to account for transactions involving different currencies. Since changes in currency exchange rates expose trading parties to potential gains or losses, the economic consequences of such rate changes must be measured. Also, companies often use different strategies to reduce risk. Hedging strategies, including the use of such derivatives as forward contracts, options, and currency swaps, add complexity to accounting for these transactions.

Companies also invest in foreign entities. These investments create a need to translate foreign entity financial statements from one currency into another. Specialized accounting procedures are used for the required translation or remeasurement from the foreign currency into the domestic currency of the investor.

Interim reporting and segmental reporting are designed to provide timely and relevant information for decision making. Both types of reporting involve the application of special accounting principles. Timely reporting of interim information serves as an indicator of annual results. Segmental reports, arising from growing diversification in companies domestically and globally, communicate useful financial information about segmental assets and performance.

Foreign Currency Transactions

Learning Objectives

When you have completed this chapter, you should be able to

1. Explain the floating international monetary system, and identify factors that influence rates of exchange between currencies.

2. Define the various terms associated with exchange rates, including spot rates, forward rates, premiums, and discounts.

3. Account for a foreign currency transaction, including the measurement of exchange gain or loss.

4. Identify the contexts in which a company may be exposed to foreign currency exchange risk.

5. Understand the characteristics of derivatives and the common types used to hedge foreign currency exchange rate risk.

6. Explain the accounting treatment given various types of foreign currency hedges.

The global economy has increased the trade between nations to levels previously thought unimaginable. For example, total export trade in goods for the United States had reached $906 billion in the year 2005. U.S. import of goods had reached $1,673 billion in the same time frame. During this period of time, trading levels with the top five trading nations were as follows:

	Exports			Imports	
Nation	(in billions)	% of Total	Nation	(in billions)	% of Total
Canada	$211.9	23.4	Canada	$ 290.4	17.4
Mexico	120.4	13.3	China	243.5	14.6
Japan	55.5	6.1	Mexico	170.1	10.2
China	41.9	4.6	Japan	138.0	8.2
United Kingdom	38.6	4.3	Germany	84.8	5.1
Total all nations	906.0	100.0	Total all nations	1,673.5	100.0

Companies in the United States and throughout the world are expanding their markets into a number of countries as evidenced by the following disclosures (to be discussed more fully in Chapter 12) regarding international sales:

Company	Nike, Inc.	Ford Motor	McDonald's	Sony
Year-End Allocation of Net Revenue	May 31, 2005 (in millions)	December 31, 2005 (in billions)	December 31, 2005 (in millions)	March 31, 2005 (in millions)
United States	$ 5,129.3	$ 80.6	$ 2,421.6	$18,479
Europe	4,281.6	30.0	7,071.8	15,070
Asia Pacific	1,897.3	7.7	2,815.8	
Japan				19,634
Others	2,431.5	35.2	8,151.0	13,729
Total	$13,739.7	$153.5	$20,460.2	$66,912

When parties from two different nations transact business, each would normally like to use its own national currency. Since it is impossible to use more than one currency as the medium of exchange, a currency must be selected, and rates of exchange must be established between the two competing currencies.

For example, if a U.S. footwear manufacturer purchases leather from a German supplier, the transaction must be settled in either U.S. dollars or euros. If euros are chosen, a rate of exchange between the U.S. dollar and the euro must be determined in order to record the transaction on the American company's books in dollars. Given that rates of exchange vary, the number of U.S. dollars needed to acquire the necessary euros also could change between the time the order is placed and the goods are paid for. If, during this time, more dollars are needed to acquire the necessary euros to pay for the leather, the U.S. purchaser is exposed to an additional business risk. The more volatility there is in exchange rates, the more risk to which the party is exposed. Similarly, if the dollar is used as the medium of exchange, this risk would still exist, but it would be transferred to the German vendor.

It is readily apparent that the currency decision becomes an important factor in negotiating such transactions. Due to the volatility of currency exchange rates, companies transacting business in foreign markets should aggressively control and measure exchange risk. Management should develop a model that enables them to forecast the direction, magnitude, and timing of exchange rate changes. This model, in turn, can be used to develop a strategy to minimize foreign exchange losses and maximize foreign exchange gains.

Business transactions that are settled in a currency other than that of the domestic (home country) currency are referred to, in this text, as *foreign currency transactions* and require the use of special terminology. One of the transacting parties will settle the transaction in its own domestic currency and also measure the transaction in its domestic currency. For example, a German company may sell inventory to a U.S. company and require payment in euros. The currency used to settle the transaction is referred to as the *denominated currency* and would be the euro in this case. The other transacting party will settle the transaction in a foreign currency but will need to measure the transaction in its domestic currency. For example, a U.S. company that purchases inventory from a German company must settle the resulting accounts payable in euros and yet must measure the purchase of inventory and the accounts payable in terms of U.S. dollars. The currency used to measure or record the transaction is referred to as the *measurement currency* and would be the U.S. dollar in this case. Whenever a transaction is denominated in a currency different from the measurement currency, exchange rate risk exists, and exchange rates must be used for measurement purposes. The process of expressing a transaction in the measurement currency when it is denominated in a different currency is referred to as a *foreign currency translation*.

THE INTERNATIONAL MONETARY SYSTEM

1

OBJECTIVE

Explain the floating international monetary system, and identify factors that influence rates of exchange between currencies.

Denominating a transaction in a currency other than the entity's domestic currency requires the establishment of a rate of exchange between the currencies. The international monetary system establishes rates of exchanges between currencies through the use of a variety of systems. The selection of a particular monetary system and the resulting exchange rates have a significant effect on international business and the risk associated with such business.

Alternative International Monetary Systems

Several major international monetary systems have been employed over time, and previous systems have occasionally been reestablished. Prior to 1944, the *gold system* provided a strict apolitical system based on gold. The currencies of nations were backed by or equivalent to some physical measure of gold. To illustrate, suppose Nation A has 1 million currency units backed by 1,000 ounces of gold and Nation B has 2 million currency units also backed by 1,000 ounces of gold. With gold as the common denominator, exchange rates between currencies could be established. In the above example, one unit of Nation A's currency could be exchanged for two units of Nation B's currency. A nation's supply of gold, therefore, influenced its money supply, rates of exchange, prices, and international trading levels (imports and exports).

In 1944, the *Bretton Woods Agreement*, which created the International Monetary Fund (IMF) and a *fixed rate exchange system*, was signed. The fixed rate system required each nation to set a par value for its currency in terms of gold or the U.S. dollar. In turn, the U.S. dollar's value was defined in terms of gold. Modest variations from a currency's par value were allowed, and each nation could adjust its money supply in order to maintain its par value. The IMF could provide support to a nation in order to maintain its par value. Changes in a currency's par value were referred to as *devaluations* and *revaluations*.

As pressures to maintain the par values established by the fixed rate system increased, pressure was placed on the U.S. dollar. The ability of the dollar to support the system became questionable, and fears arose that countries with dollar surpluses might seek to convert these dollars into gold. In 1971, the U.S. government, for all practical purposes, terminated the Bretton Woods Agreement by suspending the convertibility of the dollar into gold.

Currencies temporarily became part of a *floating system* where rates of exchange were in response to the supply and demand factors affecting a currency. Shortly thereafter, the IMF accepted the *Smithsonian Agreement* which devalued the U.S. dollar and did not allow for the convertibility of the dollar into gold. Par values of currencies were established along with a wider margin of acceptable values around the par value. The Smithsonian Agreement was short-lived, and in response to increasing pressures on the U.S. dollar, the fixed rate system was abandoned in 1973.

Today, the international monetary system is a floating system whereby the factors of supply and demand primarily define currency exchange rates. Each nation's central bank may intervene in order to move its currency toward a target rate of exchange. This intervention results in a managed, or "dirty" float, versus an unmanaged, or "clean" float. Supply and demand factors along with possible central bank intervention result in much more uncertainty and risk than that experienced in a fixed rate system. A number of factors beyond supply and demand affect exchange rates including but not limited to a nation's trade balances, money supply, economic stability, interest rates, and governmental intervention.

Although the present international monetary system is best described as a floating system, there are a number of special variations within the system. Some nations still maintain a fixed system whereby the rate of exchange is established by their central bank. However, because these fixed rates are changed frequently, sometimes daily, they may be viewed as a controlled or "dirty" float. A currency that is frequently adjusted downward, such as those in less developed nations, is referred to as a "crawling peg" currency. Tiered systems also exist whereby special rates are established for certain types of transactions, such as import and export sales and dividend payments, to accomplish desired political and economic objectives. For example, to encourage exports and to discourage capital withdrawal, a foreign government may establish favorable official rates for export sales and less favorable exchange rates for the payment of dividends to investors in other countries. The forces of supply and demand, however, occasionally make it difficult for a government to maintain an official exchange rate. In response, the government either devalues or revalues its currency.

The Mechanics of Exchange Rates

An exchange rate is a measure of how much of one currency may be exchanged for another currency. These rates may be in the form of either *direct* or *indirect quotes* made by a foreign currency trader who is usually employed by a large commercial bank. A direct quote measures how much of the domestic currency must be exchanged to receive one unit of the foreign currency (1 FC). Direct quotes allow the party using the quote to understand the price of the foreign currency in terms of its own "base" or domestic currency. This method is frequently used in the United States, and direct quotes are published daily in financial papers such as *The Wall Street Journal* or on Web sites such as http://www.x-rates.com/. Indirect quotes, also known as European terms, measure how many units of foreign currency will be received for one unit of the domestic currency. Thus, if the direct quote for a foreign currency (FC) is $0.25, then 1 FC would cost $0.25. The indirect quote would be the reciprocal of the direct quote, or 4 FC per dollar ($1.00 divided by $0.25).

2

OBJECTIVE

Define the various terms associated with exchange rates, including spot rates, forward rates, premiums, and discounts.

Exchange Rate Quotes	
Direct Quote	Indirect Quote
1 FC = $0.25	$1 = 4 FC

The business news often reports that a currency has strengthened (gained) or weakened (lost) relative to another currency. Assuming a direct quote system, such changes measure the difference between the new rate and the old rate, as a percentage of the old rate. For example, if the dollar strengthened or gained 20% against a foreign currency from its previous rate of $0.25, the dollar would now command more FC (i.e., the FC would be cheaper to buy). To be exact, the new exchange rate would be $0.20 [$0.25 − (20% × 0.25)]. Therefore, *the strengthening currency would be evidenced by a reduction in the directly quoted amount and an increase in the indirectly quoted amount.* The opposite would be true for a weakening of the domestic currency. The reaction to a strengthening or weakening of a currency depends on what type of transaction is contemplated. For example, an American exporter would want a weaker dollar because the foreign importer would need fewer of its currency units to acquire a dollar's worth of U.S. goods. Thus, U.S. goods would cost less in terms of the foreign currency. If the dollar strengthened so that one could acquire more foreign currency units for a dollar, importers would benefit. Therefore, U.S. companies and citizens would have to spend fewer U.S. dollars to buy the imported goods.

Changes Relative to Another Currency

A Strengthening U.S Currency		A Weakening U.S. Currency	
Before:	1 FC = $0.25	Before:	1 FC = $0.25
After:	1 FC = $0.20	After:	1 FC = $0.30
Result:	The dollar gained 20%.	Result:	The dollar lost 20%.
	($0.25 − $0.20 = $0.05;		($0.25 − $0.30 = −$0.05;
	$0.05 ÷ $0.25 = 20%)		−$0.05 ÷ 0.25 = −20%)

Exchange rates often are quoted in terms of a buying rate (the bid price) and a selling rate (the offered price). The buying and selling rates represent what the currency broker (normally a large commercial bank) is willing to pay to acquire or sell a currency. The difference or spread between these two rates represents the broker's commission and is often referred to as the points. The spread is influenced by several factors, including the supply of and demand for the currency, the number of transactions taking place, currency risk, and the overall volatility of the market. For example, assume a currency broker agrees to pay $0.20 to a holder of a foreign currency and agrees to sell that currency to a buyer of foreign currency for $0.22. In this case, the broker will receive a commission of $0.02 ($0.22 − $0.20). In the United States, rates generally are quoted between the U.S. dollar and a foreign currency. However, rates between two foreign currencies are also quoted and are referred to as cross rates.

Exchange rates fall into two primary groups. A *spot rate* is the rate of exchange for a currency with delivery, selling, or buying of the currency normally occurring within two business days. In addition to exchange rates governing the immediate delivery of currency, *forward rates* apply to the exchange of different currencies at a future point in time. An agreement to exchange currencies at a specified price with delivery at a specified future point in time is a *forward contract.* Although not all currencies are quoted in forward rates, virtually all major trading nations have forward rates.

Although future exchange dates typically are quoted in 30-day intervals, contracts can be written to cover any number of days. To illustrate a forward contract, assume the forward rate to buy a FC to be delivered in 90 days is $1.650. This means that, after the specified time from the inception of the contract date (90 days), one FC will be exchanged for $1.650, regardless of what the spot rate is at that time.

Inception of Contract ◄————— 90 Days —————►	Settlement of Contract
Forward Rate	Exchange Rate
1 FC = $1.650	1 FC = $1.650 (Regardless of what the spot rate is on that day.)
Spot Rate	Spot Rate
1 FC = $1.640	1 FC = $1.655

Several aspects of spot rates and forward rates are noteworthy. First, typically both rates are constantly changing. Spot rates are revised daily; as they change, forward rates for the *remaining time* covered by a given forward contract also change even though the forward rate at inception is fixed. When there is no more remaining time, the current forward rate becomes the spot rate. Therefore, the value of a forward contract changes over the forward period. For instance, in the above example, if the forward rate is 1 FC = $1.652 with 30 days remaining, the right to *buy* FC at the original fixed forward rate of 1 FC = $1.650 suggests that the value of the forward contract has increased. Rather than paying a forward rate of $1.652 to acquire FC in 30 days, the holder of the original forward contract must only pay the fixed rate of $1.650. Second, the ultimate value of the forward contract must be assessed by comparing the fixed forward rate against the spot rate at the settlement date. In the above example, at the settlement date, the holder of the contract will pay the fixed rate of 1 FC = $1.650 to buy an FC rather than the spot rate of 1 FC = $1.655. The total change in value is represented by the difference between the original fixed forward rate and the spot rate at settlement date. Finally, the difference between a forward rate and a spot rate represents a premium or discount which is traceable to a number of factors. This difference between the spot and forward rates represents the time value of the forward contract.

If the forward rate is greater than the spot rate at inception of the contract, the contract is said to be at a *premium* (as in the above example). The opposite situation results in a discount. Quoting premiums or discounts (known as forward differentials) relative to the spot rate, rather than forward rates, is common industry practice.

Forward Rates
Employ a Forward Exchange Contract

At a Premium	At a Discount
Forward Rate > Spot Rate	Forward Rate < Spot Rate
(At inception of contract)	(At inception of contract)

At inception, the difference between the forward and spot rates represents a contract expense or income to the purchaser of the forward contract. A number of factors influence forward rates and, thus, account for the difference between a forward rate and a spot rate. A primary factor is the interest rate differential between holding an investment in foreign currency and holding an investment in domestic currency over a period of time. It is for this reason that the difference between a forward rate is referred to as the *time value* of the forward contract. For example, if a broker sold a contract to deliver foreign currency in 30 days, the interest differential would be the difference between

1. The interest earned on investing foreign currency for the 30 days prior to delivery date and
2. The 30 days of interest lost on the domestic currency that was not invested but was used to acquire the foreign currency needed for delivery.

Assume that the spot rate is 1 FC = $0.60 and that you want to determine a six-month forward rate. Further, assume that the dollar could be invested at 4.5% and the FC could be invested at 7.25%. The forward rate would be calculated as follows:

	U.S. Dollars	Foreign Currency (FC)
Value today	$600.00	1,000 FC
Interest rate	4.5%	7.25 %
Six months of interest	$ 13.50	36.25 FC
Value in six months	$613.50	1,036.25 FC

6-month forward rate = $613.50 ÷ 1,036.25 FC = 1 FC = $0.592

The forward rate for a currency can also be derived by the following formula:

$$\text{Forward rate} = \text{Direct spot rate at the beginning of period } t \times \frac{1 + \text{Interest rate for domestic investment during period } t}{1 + \text{Interest rate for foreign country investment during period } t}$$

Using the formula to solve the previous example results in the following, based on six-month interest rates:

$$\text{Forward rate of } \$0.592 = \$0.60 \times \frac{1 + 0.0225}{1 + 0.03625}$$

If the interest yield on the FC is greater than the yield on the U.S. dollar, the forward rate will be less than the spot rate (contract sells at a discount). The forward contract will sell at a premium if the opposite is true. The forward rate based on interest differentials will be slightly different from the quoted forward rate because the quoted rate includes a commission to the foreign currency broker. Furthermore, other factors in addition to interest differentials could be incorporated into the forward rate. These other factors include the volatility of the spot rates, the time period covered by the contract, expectations of future exchange rate changes, and the political and economic environments of a given country.

The student of international accounting should have an understanding of the international monetary system and exchange rates. As previously mentioned, changes in exchange rates represent an additional business risk when transactions are denominated in a foreign currency. The accounting for foreign currency transactions measures this risk and demonstrates the use of both spot and forward rates.

REFLECTION

- The current international monetary system is a floating system in which rates of exchange between currencies change in response to a variety of factors including trade balances, interest rates, money supply, and other economic factors.

- Spot rates represent the current rate of exchange between two currencies. A forward rate represents a future rate of exchange at a future point in time. If the forward rate exceeds the spot rate, the contract is at a premium rather than a discount.

ACCOUNTING FOR FOREIGN CURRENCY TRANSACTIONS

3

OBJECTIVE

Account for a foreign currency transaction, including the measurement of exchange gain or loss.

Assume a U.S. company sells mining equipment to a foreign company and the equipment must be paid for in 30 days with U.S. dollars. This transaction is denominated in dollars and will be measured by the U.S. company in dollars. Changes in the exchange rate between the U.S. dollar and the foreign currency from the transaction date to the settlement date will not expose the U.S. company to any risk of gain or loss from exchange rate changes. Now assume that the same transaction occurs except that the transaction is to be settled in the foreign currency. Because this transaction is denominated in the foreign currency and will be measured by the U.S. company in dollars, changes in the exchange rate subsequent to the transaction date expose the U.S. company to the risk of an exchange rate loss or gain. If the U.S. dollar strengthens, relative to the foreign currency, the U.S. company will experience a loss because it is holding an asset (a receivable of foreign currency) whose price and value have declined. If the dollar weakens, the opposite effect would be experienced. Whether a transaction is settled in dollars versus a foreign currency is a matter that is negotiated between the transacting parties and is influenced by a number of factors. For one of the parties, the currency will be a foreign currency; for the other party, the currency will be its domestic currency. A bank wire transfer is generally used to transfer currency between parties in different countries. When a bank wire transfer is used, the owing party instructs its bank to reduce its bank account by the appropriate amount. Its bank in turn notifies the receiving party's bank to add a corresponding translated amount to the receiving party's bank account. Therefore, the bank wire transfer, through the use of electronic means, eliminates the need to physically transfer currencies between transacting parties.

To summarize, *changes in exchange rates do not affect transactions that are both denominated and measured in the reporting entity's currency.* Therefore, these transactions require no special accounting treatment. However, *if a transaction is denominated in a foreign currency and measured in the reporting entity's currency, changes in the exchange rate between the transaction date and settlement date result in a gain or loss to the reporting entity.* These gains or losses are referred to as exchange gains or losses, and their recognition requires special accounting treatment.

Effect of Rate Changes	
No Exchange Gain or Loss	Exchange Gain or Loss
Transactions are denominated and measured in the reporting entity's currency.	Transactions are denominated in the foreign currency and measured in the reporting entity's currency.

Originally, two methods were proposed for the treatment of exchange gains or losses arising from foreign currency transactions. After considering the merits of these two methods, the FASB adopted the *two-transactions method* which views the initial foreign currency transaction as one transaction. The effect of any subsequent changes in the exchange rates and the resulting exchange gain or loss are viewed as a second transaction. Therefore, the initial transaction is recorded independently of the settlement transaction. This method is consistent with accepted accounting techniques, which normally account for the financing of a transaction as a separate and distinct event. (The required two-transactions method is used in all instances with one exception. The exception relates to a hedge on a foreign currency commitment that is discussed later in this chapter. Therefore, unless otherwise stated, the two-transactions method will be used throughout the chapter.)

In order to illustrate the two-transactions method, assume that a U.S. company sells mining equipment on June 1, 20X4, to a foreign company, with the corresponding receivable to be paid or settled on July 1, 20X4. The equipment has a selling price of $306,000 and a cost of $250,000. On June 1, 20X4, the foreign currency is worth $1.70, and on July 1, 20X4, the foreign currency is worth $1.60. Illustrations 6-1 and 6-2 present the entries to record the sale of the mining equipment, assuming that the transaction is denominated in dollars ($306,000) and then in foreign currency (180,000). Note that, when the transaction is denominated in dollars (in Illustration 6-1), the U.S. company does not experience an exchange gain or loss. However, because the foreign company measures the transaction in foreign currency but denominates the transaction in dollars, it experiences an exchange loss. In substance, the value of the foreign company's accounts payable changed because it was denominated in a foreign currency (dollars, in this case), that is, in a currency other than its own. In order to emphasize that the value of certain asset or liability balances is not fixed and will change over time, these changing accounts are identified in boldface type throughout the text.

When the transaction is denominated in foreign currency, as in Illustration 6-2, the U.S. company experiences an exchange loss (or gain). The exchange loss (or gain) is accounted for separately from the sales transaction and does not affect the U.S. company's gross profit on the sale. This separately recognized exchange gain or loss is not viewed as an extraordinary item, but should be included in determining income from continuing operations for the period and, if material, should be disclosed in the financial statements or in a note to the statements. Finally, it is important to note in Illustration 6-2 that the foreign company does not experience an exchange gain or loss. This is because the foreign company both measured and denominated the transaction in foreign currency.

Unsettled Foreign Currency Transactions

If a foreign currency transaction is unsettled at year-end, an unrealized gain or loss should be recognized to reflect the change in the exchange rate occurring between the transaction date and the end of the reporting period (e.g., year-end). This treatment focuses on accrual accounting and the fact that exchange gains and losses occur over time rather than only at the date of settlement or payment. Therefore, at any given time the asset or liability arising from a foreign currency transaction that is denominated in a foreign currency *should be measured at its fair value* as suggested by current spot rates. The changes in fair value, both positive and negative, are recognized in current earnings. In essence, the asset or liability is *marked-to-market.*

Illustration 6-1
Transaction Denominated in **Dollars:** Two-Transactions Method

U.S. Company (dollars)			Foreign Company (foreign currency—FC)		
June 1, 20X4					
Accounts Receivable	306,000		Equipment	180,000*	
Sales Revenue		306,000	**Accounts Payable—FC** . . .		**180,000**
Cost of Goods Sold	250,000				
Inventory		250,000			
July 1, 20X4					
Cash	306,000		**Accounts Payable—FC**	**180,000**	
Accounts Receivable		306,000	Exchange Loss	11,250	
			Cash		191,250**

Note: The U.S. company experienced no exchange gain or loss because its transaction was both denominated and measured in dollars. However, under the two-transactions method, the foreign company did experience an exchange loss since its transaction was measured in foreign currency and denominated in dollars. The decrease in the value of the foreign currency relative to the U.S. dollar means more foreign currency must be paid to cover the liability.

*($306,000 ÷ $1.70 = 180,000 FC)
**($306,000 ÷ $1.60 = 191,250 FC)

Illustration 6-2
Transaction Denominated in **Foreign Currency (FC):** Two-Transactions Method

U.S. Company (dollars)			Foreign Company (foreign currency)		
June 1, 20X4					
Accounts Receivable—FC	**306,000**		Equipment	180,000	
Sales Revenue		306,000	Accounts Payable		180,000
Cost of Goods Sold	250,000				
Inventory		250,000			
July 1, 20X4					
Cash	288,000*		Accounts Payable	180,000	
Exchange Loss	18,000**		Cash		180,000
Accounts Receivable—FC . .		**306,000**			

Note: The loss is considered to be part of a separate financing decision and unrelated to the original sales transaction.

*The company received 180,000 FC when the exchange rate was 1 FC = $1.60 (180,000 FC × $1.60 = $288,000). Normally, the company would not physically receive FC but would have the dollar equivalent wired to its bank account. Through the use of a bank wire transfer, the foreign company's account would be debited for the number of FC, and the U.S. company's bank account would be credited for the applicable number of dollars, given the exchange rate.
**The decrease in the value of the FC from $1.70 to $1.60 results in an exchange loss to the U.S. company since the FC it received is less valuable than it was at the transaction date [180,000 × ($1.60 − $1.70) = −$18,000].

To illustrate the accounting for unsettled transactions, assume a U.S. company purchases goods from a foreign company on November 1, 20X1. The purchase in the amount of 1,000 foreign currencies (FC) is to be paid for on February 1, 20X2, in foreign currency. To record or measure the transaction, the domestic company would make the following entry, assuming an exchange rate of 1 FC = $0.50:

Inventory	500	
Accounts Payable—FC		500

Purchase of inventory for 1,000 FC when the exchange rate is 1 FC = $0.50.

Assuming the exchange rate on the December 31, 20X1, year-end is 1 FC = $0.52, the following entry would be necessary:

Exchange Loss [1,000 × ($0.52 − $0.50)]*	20	
Accounts Payable—FC		20

To accrue the exchange loss on the unperformed portion of the foreign currency transaction when 1 FC = $0.52.

*The increase in the value of each FC from $0.50 to $0.52 results in a loss to the domestic company since, as of year-end, the company would have to pay out more dollars than originally recorded in order to eliminate the liability.

If the transaction had been settled at year-end, the domestic company would have had to expend $520 to acquire 1,000 FC. Therefore, a loss of $20 is traceable to the unperformed portion of the transaction. Some theorists have suggested that an exchange gain or loss should not be recognized prior to settlement because the gain or loss has not been "realized" through settlement. This position fails to recognize the merits of accrual accounting and is in conflict with the position of the FASB, which requires that the assets or liabilities that are denominated in a foreign currency be measured at fair value with the recognition of resulting unrealized gains or losses being recognized in current earnings.

Finally, assuming an exchange rate of 1 FC = $0.55 on the settlement date (February 1, 20X2), the domestic entity would make the following entry to record the settlement:

Accounts Payable—FC ($500 + $20)	520	
Exchange Loss [1,000 × ($0.55 − $0.52)]	30	
Cash		550

To record payment of liability for 1,000 FC, when 1 FC = $0.55.

Note that the company experiences a $50 loss due to changes in the exchange rate. This is allocated between 20X1 and 20X2 in accordance with accrual accounting.

REFLECTION

- If a transaction is denominated in a foreign currency, there is exposure to risk associated with exchange rate changes.

- Assets or liabilities that are denominated in foreign currency are to be measured at fair value using spot exchange rates at the date of measurement. In essence, such accounts are marked-to-market. Exchange gains and losses are recorded in current earnings even if not yet realized.

THE EXPOSURE TO FOREIGN CURRENCY EXCHANGE RISK AND THE USE OF DERIVATIVES

4

OBJECTIVE

Identify the contexts in which a company may be exposed to foreign currency exchange risk.

When business is conducted between parties with different currencies, one of the transacting parties will be exposed to the exchange rate risk associated with having a transaction denominated in a foreign currency. Companies may be exposed to foreign currency exchange risk in several situations including the following:

1. *An actual existing foreign currency transaction that results in the recognition of assets or liabilities.* As previously illustrated, the risk to be hedged against is the risk that exchange rates may change between the transaction date and the settlement date.

2. *A firm commitment to enter into a foreign currency transaction.* Such a commitment is an agreement between two parties that specifies all significant terms related to the prospective transaction including prices or amounts of consideration stated in foreign currency units. Beginning at the date of the commitment, the risk to be hedged against is the risk that the value of the commitment, which is fixed in a foreign currency amount, could be adversely affected by subsequent changes in exchange rates. For example, a commitment to purchase inventory for a fixed amount of foreign currency could have a value of $10,000 at the commitment date but, due to exchange rate changes, have a value of $11,000 at the transaction date thus resulting in a higher inventory cost than anticipated.

3. *A forecasted foreign currency transaction that has a high probability of occurrence.* Such a forecasted transaction, unlike a commitment or an existing transaction, does not provide an entity with any present rights or obligations and does not have any fixed prices or rates. Because fixed prices or rates are not present, an entity is exposed to the risk that future cash flows may vary due to changes in prices and exchange rates. The risk being hedged against is the risk associated with exchange rate changes. For example, if a manufacturer forecasted needing raw materials to meet future production, even if material prices to be paid in foreign currency did not change in the future, the dollar equivalent cash flows associated with the forecasted purchase could change over time due to changes in exchange rates.

4. *An investment in a foreign subsidiary.* Translating the financial statements of a foreign subsidiary expressed in foreign currency into the domestic currency of the investor entity can affect the equity of the investor entity. The risk being hedged against is the risk that the translation will reduce the investor's equity due to adverse changes in exchange rates. Such a hedge is known as a *hedge of a net investment.*

The risk associated with (4) above will be discussed in the next chapter. However, the risk associated with the first three situations above is traceable to the risk of changes in exchange rates over the time periods prior to when payment is made on a transaction as illustrated in the following table:

Situation 3	Situation 2	Situation 1	
Company forecasts a transaction	Company commits to a transaction	Transaction occurs	Payment is made on the transaction

Derivatives: Characteristics and Types

As stated above, a company can be exposed to the risk associated with changes in currency exchange rates in a number of contexts. Common strategies to hedge against such risks involve the use of derivative financial instruments.

A financial instrument represents a right, through a contractual agreement between two opposite parties called *counterparties,* to receive or deliver cash or another financial instrument on potentially favorable or unfavorable terms. Financial instruments include cash, equity and debt investments, and derivatives. A derivative is a type of financial instrument that has several distinguishing characteristics that have been set forth by the FASB. These are the characteristics of a derivative:

1. Derives its value from changes in the rate or price of a related asset or liability. The rate or price is known as an underlying.

2. The quantity or number of units specified by a derivative is known as the notional amount.

3. Requires little or no initial investment upon inception.

4. Allows for net settlement in that the derivative contract can be settled in exchange for cash, without having to actually buy or sell the related asset or liability.

CHARACTERISTICS OF DERIVATIVES

5

OBJECTIVE

Understand the characteristics of derivatives and the common types used to hedge foreign currency exchange rate risk.

A critical characteristic of a derivative and the basis for its name is that the instrument derives its value from changes in the value of a related asset or liability. The rates or prices that relate to the asset or liability underlying the derivative are referred to as *underlyings*. The underlying may take a variety of forms, including a commodity price, stock price, foreign currency exchange rate, or interest rate. **It is important to note that the underlying is not the asset or liability itself, but rather its price or rate.** For example, the underlying in a forward contract is not the foreign currency itself but rather the currency exchange rate. Changes in the underlying price or rate cause the value of the derivative to change. For example, if the forward exchange rate underlies the value of the forward contract, an increase in the forward rate will cause a forward contract to buy foreign currency to increase in value.

In order to fully value a derivative, one must know the number of units (quantity) that is specified in the derivative instrument. This is called the *notional amount*, and it determines the total dollar value of a derivative, traceable to movement or changes in the underlying. For example, if the forward contract to buy foreign currency increases in value, the total magnitude of this increase in value depends on how many foreign currency units, for example 100,000 units, can be sold under the terms of the contract. **Both the underlying price or rate and the notional amount are necessary in order to determine the total value of a derivative at any point in time.**

Typically, a derivative requires little or no initial investment because it is an investment in a change in value traceable to an underlying, rather than an investment in the actual asset or liability to which the underlying relates. The holder of a forward contract to buy foreign currency to be used at a future date involves no initial investment, whereas the holder of actual foreign currency to be used at a future date has already made an investment in the currency.

Many derivatives do not require the parties to the contract, the counterparties, to actually deliver an asset that is associated with the underlying in order to realize the value of a derivative. For example, the holder of a forward contract to buy foreign currency could sell the contract. The ability to settle the contract in exchange for cash, without actually buying or selling the related asset or liability, is referred to as *net settlement*.

COMMON TYPES OF DERIVATIVES

The number of financial instruments that have the characteristics of a derivative has continued to expand, and, in turn, these instruments have become increasingly complex. However, within the context of hedging the risk associated with foreign currency exchange rate risk, two common types of derivatives are forward contracts and options (the use of foreign currency swaps are beyond the scope of this chapter).

A *foreign currency forward contract* is an executory contract to buy or sell a specified amount of foreign currency, at a specified fixed rate with delivery at a specified future point in time. The party that agrees to sell the asset is said to be in a *short position,* and the party that agrees to buy the asset is said to be in a *long position.* The specified fixed rate in the contract is known as a *forward rate.* The specified future date is referred to as the *forward date.* Forward contracts are not formally regulated on an organized exchange, and the parties are exposed to a risk that default of the contract could occur. However, the lack of formal regulation means that such contracts can be customized in response to specialized needs regarding notional amounts and forward dates.

The value of a forward contract is zero at inception and typically does not require an initial cash outlay. However, over time, movement in the rate of the underlying results in a change in value of the forward contract. **The total change in the value of a forward contract is measured as the difference between the forward rate and the spot rate at the forward date.** For example, on April 1, a party (called the *writer*) writes a contract in which she/he agrees to sell (short position) to another party (called the *holder*) who agrees to buy (long position) 1,000,000 FC (for example, euros) at a specific price of $0.16 per FC with delivery in 90 days (June 29). The relationship between the parties is as follows:

If the spot rate at the end of the forward period is $0.18, the total change in value is determined as follows:

1,000,000 FC at a forward rate (on April 1) of $0.16 (1,000,000 × $0.16)	$160,000
1,000,000 FC at a spot rate (on June 29) of $0.18 (1,000,000 × $0.18)	180,000
Gain in value to holder	$ 20,000

This is a gain because on June 29 the holder received something with a fair value greater than the fair value given up that day. (Conversely, this would be a loss to the writer.) The holder of the forward contract could buy foreign currencies for $160,000 on the forward date compared to the spot value of $180,000 at that time and experience an immediate $20,000 gain. It is important to note that the value of the currency at the final spot rate could have been less than $160,000. In that case, the holder would have experienced a loss and the writer a gain. When the value of a derivative can change in both directions (gain or loss), it is said to have a *symmetric return profile.* It is also important to note that in the case of a forward contract, if the holder of the contact experiences a gain (loss) in value, then the writer of the contract simultaneously experiences a loss (gain) in value.

The forward rate is a function of a number of variables and as these variables change over the life of the contract, the value of the forward contract also changes. Also, because *the forward rates represent values in the future, the current value is represented by the present value of the future rates.* Continuing with the example involving foreign currencies, assume the following forward rate information throughout the 90-day term of the contract:

Remaining Term of Contract	Forward Rate	Notional Amount	Total Forward Value	Cumulative Change in Forward Value
90 days	$0.160	1,000,000	$160,000	
60 days	0.170	1,000,000	170,000	$10,000
30 days	0.170	1,000,000	170,000	10,000
0 days	0.180	1,000,000	180,000	20,000

Assuming a 6% discount rate, the change in value of the forward contract over time is as follows:

	60 Days Remaining	30 Days Remaining	Total Life of Contract
Cumulative change in forward value.	$10,000	$10,000	$20,000
Present value of cumulative change:			
60 days at 6%	$ 9,901		
30 days at 6%		$ 9,950	
0 days at 6%			$20,000
Previously recognized gain or loss	0	(9,901)	(9,950)
Current period gain or loss	$ 9,901	$ 49	$10,050

Note that the total change in the value of the forward contract is $20,000 ($9,901 + $49 + $10,050), which is recognized over the term of the contract as the net present value of changes in the forward rates. Even if the forward rates did not change between two valuation dates (as they barely did between 60 and 30 days here), the value of the contract would change because the remaining term of the forward contract continues to decrease and the present value of the forward value increases. Also, note that *the stated forward rate at the expiration date of the contract is equal to the spot rate at that date.* This is due to the fact that at expiration of the contract the forward date is the same as the current date.

A *foreign currency option* represents a right, rather than an obligation, to either buy or sell some quantity of a particular foreign currency. The option is valid for a specified period of time and calls for a specified buy or sell rate or price, referred to as the *strike price* or *exercise price.*

If an option allows the holder to *buy* an underlying, it is referred to as a *call option*. An option that allows the holder to *sell* an underlying is referred to as a *put option*. Options are actively traded on organized exchanges or may be negotiated on a case-by-case basis between counterparties (over-the-counter contracts). Option contracts require the holder to make an initial non-refundable cash outlay, known as the *premium,* as represented by the option's current value. The premium is paid, in part, because the writer of the option takes more risk than the holder of the option. The holder can allow the option to expire, while the writer must comply if the holder chooses to exercise it.

During the option period, the strike price of the option on the underlying is generally different from the current value of an underlying. The following terms are used to describe the relationship between the strike price and the current price (note that the premium is not considered in these relationships):

Option Type	Strike Price Is Equal to Current Price	Strike Price Is Greater than Current Price	Strike Price Is Less than Current Price
Call (buy) option	At-the-money	Out-of-the-money	In-the-money
Put (sell) option	At-the-money	In-the-money	Out-of-the-money

As the above table suggests, in-the-money is a favorable condition as compared to being out-of-the-money, which is an unfavorable condition. The original premium is not considered when describing whether an option is or is not in-the-money. However, it is important to note that the original premium certainly is considered when determining whether an investment in an option has experienced an overall profit. The holder of an option has a right, rather than an obligation, and will not exercise the option unless it is in-the-money. In that case, the holder will experience a gain, and the writer will experience a loss. However, if the option is not in-the-money, the option will not be exercised, the holder will limit her/his loss to the amount of the option premium, and the writer will limit her/his gain to the amount of the premium. Therefore, in theory, the opportunities for gain and loss are characterized as follows:

	Potential for	
	Gain	Loss
Holder of option	Unlimited	Limited to amount of premium
Writer of option	Limited to amount of premium	Unlimited

Because the counterparties do not have equal opportunity for both upside and downside changes in value, options are said to have an asymmetric or one-sided return profile.

Options are traded on an organized exchange and over the counter; therefore, their current value is quoted in terms of present dollars on a frequent basis. The current value of an option depends on forward periods and spot prices. The difference between the strike and spot prices, at any point in time, measures the intrinsic value of the option, so changes in spot prices will change the intrinsic value of the option. Changes in the length of the remaining forward period will affect the time value of the option. The time value is measured as the difference between an option's current value and its intrinsic value as in the following illustration:

◆ If the option is in-the-money, the option has intrinsic value. For example, if an investor has a 90-day call (buy) option to buy 100,000 FC at a strike price of $1.10 per FC and the current spot rate is $1.12 FC, the option is in-the-money and has an intrinsic value of $2,000 (100,000 × $0.02). An option that is out-of-the-money or at-the-money has no intrinsic value.

◆ The difference between the current value of an option and its intrinsic value represents time value. For example, if the 90-day call (buy) option has a current value of $2,200, the time value component is $200 (the current value of $2,200, less the intrinsic value of $2,000). The time value of an option represents a discounting factor and a volatility factor.

◆ The discounting factor relates to the fact that the strike price does not have to be paid currently, but rather at the time of exercise. Therefore, the holder of an option to buy FC could benefit from an appreciation in the value of FC without actually having to currently pay out the cash to purchase the FC.

- The volatility factor relates to the volatility of the underlying relative to the fixed strike price and reflects the potential for gain on the option. Underlyings with more price volatility present greater opportunities for gains if the option is in-the-money. Therefore, higher volatility increases the value of an option. Note that volatility could also lead to an out-of-the-money situation. However, this possibility can be disregarded because, unlike forward contracts, the risk for an option is asymmetric since the holder can avoid unfavorable outcomes by allowing the option to expire.

To illustrate the value components of an option, assume that a put (sell) option allows for the sale of 100,000 FC in 60 days at a strike or exercise price of $0.50 per FC. The value of the option would consist of the following:

	Initial Date of Purchase	End of 30 Days	End of 60 Days
Value of 100,000 FC at the current spot rate	$51,000	$49,000	$48,000
Assumed total value of option	1,300	1,650	2,000
Intrinsic value (never less than zero)	0 (option is out-of-the-money)	1000 (in-the-money ($50,000 vs. $49,000)	2000 (in-the-money ($50,000 vs. $48,000)
Time value (total value less intrinsic value)	1,300	650	0

ACCOUNTING FOR DERIVATIVES THAT ARE DESIGNATED AS A HEDGE

As previously discussed, transactions that are denominated in a foreign currency and measured in an entity's domestic currency are exposed to risk associated with exchange rate changes. In turn the rate changes result in exchange gains or losses associated with the related asset or liability denominated in foreign currency. Derivative instruments can be used to hedge against the exchange risk associated with these transactions. If the asset or liability (the hedged item) experiences an unfavorable change in value, a properly structured hedge (the hedging instrument) could be effective in providing a change in value in the opposite direction such that there is no adverse effect. If a derivative is properly structured for this purpose, it seems that the change in the value of the derivative (the hedging instrument) should be recognized in the same accounting period as is the change in the value of the related asset or liability (the hedged item). Hedges are generally designated as either *fair value* or *cash flow*. A **fair value hedge** is used to offset changes in the fair value of items with fixed exchange prices or rates. Fair value hedges include hedges against a change in the fair value of

- A recognized foreign currency denominated asset or liability.
- An unrecognized foreign currency firm commitment.

A **cash flow hedge** is used to establish fixed prices or rates when future cash flows could vary due to changes in prices or rates. Cash flow hedges include hedges against the change in cash flows associated with

- A forecasted foreign currency transaction.
- The forecasted functional-currency-equivalent cash flows associated with a recognized asset or liability.
- An unrecognized foreign currency firm commitment.

Special Accounting for Fair Value Hedges

The hedged item in a fair value hedge is either a recognized asset or liability or a firm commitment. Recognized assets or liabilities in a fair value hedge result from actual past transactions such as a purchase of inventory denominated in foreign currency. Commitments relate to transactions that have not yet occurred, such as a contract to purchase inventory denominated in foreign currency. A commitment is a binding agreement between two parties that specifies all significant terms related to the prospective transaction. Such terms include the quantity to be exchanged, the timing of the transaction, and a fixed price (e.g., the number of foreign currency units). The agreement also includes a large enough disincentive to make performance of the contract probable.

Because the number of foreign currency units in an existing transaction or a firm commitment is fixed, subsequent changes in currency exchange rates affect the value of a recognized asset, liability, or commitment. For example, if an entity has purchased inventory and has a recognized accounts payable to be settled in FC, changes in exchange rates will change the value of the payable. Similarly, if an entity has a firm commitment to purchase inventory, changes in the exchange rates will change the value of the commitment.

Many accounting principles do not allow for the *recognition in current earnings of both increases and decreases* in the value of recognized assets, liabilities, or firm commitments. However, if the risk of such changes in value is covered by a fair value hedge, special accounting treatment is allowed that provides for the recognition of such changes in earnings. In a qualifying fair value hedge, the gain or loss on the derivative hedging instrument and the offsetting loss or gain on the hedged item are both recognized currently in earnings. For instance, assume a recognized account payable is to be settled in FC. An increase in the rate of exchange between the FC and the domestic currency will result in a higher value of the payable. If the payable is hedged, both the exchange loss on the payable and the change in the value of the derivative instrument used as a hedge are recognized in earnings.

In order to qualify for special fair value hedge accounting, the derivative hedging instrument and the hedged item must satisfy a number of criteria. A critical criterion is that an entity must have formal documentation of the hedging relationship and the entity's risk-management objective and strategy. The entity must indicate the reason for undertaking the designated hedge, identify the hedged item and the derivative hedging instrument, and explain the nature of the risk being hedged. This criterion must be satisfied at inception and cannot be retroactively applied after an entity has determined whether hedging would be appropriate. Another important criterion is that the hedging relationship must be assessed both at inception and on an ongoing basis to determine if it is highly effective in offsetting the identified risks. Although specific quantitative guidelines are not available to define *highly effective,* the FASB expects a high correlation to exist between changes in the value of the derivative instrument and in the fair value of the hedged item such that the respective changes in value would be substantially offset. Generally speaking, a hedge would be totally effective if the terms (such as notional amount, maturity dates, quality/condition, delivery locations, etc.) of the hedging instrument and the hedged item are the same. This approach is known as *critical terms analysis.* It is important to note that in practice the terms of a derivative do not always align with the terms of the related asset or liability and therefore other approaches to assessing effectiveness must be employed. Management must also describe how it will assess hedge effectiveness. Generally, hedge ineffectiveness is the difference between the gains or losses on the derivative and the hedged item. However, the portion of the gain or loss representing time value may be excluded from the assessment of effectiveness and included in current earnings. Additional criteria which must be met by fair value hedges are set forth in greater detail in several FASB statements of financial accounting standards.[1] Assuming the necessary criteria are satisfied for treatment as a fair value hedge, the hedge will qualify for special accounting treatment. The gain or loss on the derivative hedging instrument will be recognized currently in earnings, along with the change in value on the hedged item, and an appropriate adjustment to the basis of the hedged item will be recorded. If the cumulative change in the value of the derivative instrument does not exactly offset the cumulative change in the value of the hedged item, the difference is recognized currently in earnings. Because both hedge effectiveness and hedge ineffectiveness are recognized currently in earnings, it is not necessary to separately account for that portion of the hedge which is considered to be ineffective.

---

1 See Statement of Financial Accounting Standards No. 133, Statement of Financial Accounting Standards No. 138, and Statement of Financial Accounting Standards No. 149.

Special Accounting for Cash Flow Hedges

The hedged item in a cash flow hedge is one in which future cash flows could be affected due to a particular risk such as the change in foreign currency exchange rates. A forecasted transaction is well suited to the use of a cash flow hedge. Because fixed prices or rates are not present in a forecasted transaction, an entity is exposed to the risk that future cash flows may vary due to changes in prices/rates. For example, if an entity forecasted purchasing raw materials from a foreign vendor with the invoice payable in FC, the cash flows needed to acquire the materials could change because the price of the materials could change between the forecast date and the purchase date. However, even if that did not occur, the necessary cash flows could also be affected because of changes in the exchange rate between the foreign and domestic currencies. Another application of a cash flow hedge could involve an existing liability, denominated in FC, which bears interest at a variable rate of interest. The cash flows associated with interest could be affected due to not only the variability of interest rates but also changes in the exchange rate.

A nonderivative financial instrument may not be used as the hedging instrument in a foreign currency cash flow hedge. Furthermore, as is the case with a fair value hedge, special hedge accounting is not available for a cash flow hedge unless a number of criteria are satisfied. Cash flow hedges must also meet the criteria regarding documentation and assessment of effectiveness. Additional necessary criteria are set forth in greater detail in several FASB statements of financial accounting standards.[2] If the derivative instrument and the hedged item satisfy the criteria, then the cash flow hedge will qualify for special accounting. The effective portion of the gain or loss on the derivative instrument will be reported in *other comprehensive income (OCI)*,[3] and the ineffective portion, if any, will be recognized currently in earnings. As with fair value hedges, a portion of the derivative instrument's gain or loss may be excluded from the assessment of effectiveness. That portion of the gain or loss will be recognized currently in earnings rather than as a component of other comprehensive income. The amounts reported in OCI will be reclassified into recognized earnings in the same period in which the hedged item affects earnings. For example, assume that a forecasted sale of inventory is hedged. Once the inventory is sold and recognized in earnings, the applicable amount, the OCI gain or loss, will also be recognized in earnings. If the forecasted transaction were a purchase of a depreciable asset, the applicable portion of the OCI would be recognized in earnings when the asset's depreciation expense is recognized.

EXAMPLES OF THE ACCOUNTING FOR FAIR VALUE HEDGES

As previously stated, fair value hedges may be used to hedge against changes in the fair value of either a recognized foreign currency denominated asset or liability or an unrecognized foreign currency firm commitment. Assuming the necessary criteria are satisfied, the fair value hedge will be given special accounting treatment. This special treatment allows for the recognition in current earnings of both the gain or loss on the derivative hedging instrument and the offsetting loss or gain on the hedged item.

Hedging an Existing Foreign Currency Denominated Asset or Liability

The gain or loss associated with the foreign currency exposure of a recognized, foreign currency denominated asset or liability as measured by changes in the spot rate is generally recognized in earnings. However, this recognition does not prevent such exposed positions from being hedged with a fair value hedge or a cash flow hedge.[4] Therefore, recognized foreign currency denominated assets or liabilities may be the subject of a fair value or cash flow hedge and receive special hedge accounting treatment if all necessary qualifying criteria for such accounting are satisfied.

6

OBJECTIVE

Explain the accounting treatment given various types of foreign currency hedges.

---

2 Ibid.

3 Other comprehensive income is not included in the income statement; it bypasses the traditional income statement but is shown as a component of equity.

4 Statement of Financial Accounting Standards No. 138, *Accounting for Certain Derivative Instruments and Certain Hedging Activities* (Norwalk, CT: Financial Accounting Standards Board, 2000), par. 4j.

However, it is important to note that only derivative instruments can be designated as a hedge of a foreign currency denominated asset or liability.

Illustration of Hedging with a Forward Contract. Assume that a U.S. company purchases inventory from a foreign vendor with subsequent payment due in FC, a foreign currency denominated liability, and that the company acquires a forward contract to buy FC. If prior to settlement, the dollar weakens relative to the FC, the accounts payable will increase in value resulting in an exchange loss. However, the forward contract to buy FC (an asset) will increase in value if the dollar weakens.

Additional information supporting this illustration is as follows:

1. On November 1, 20X1, the company bought inventory from a foreign vendor with payment due on February 1, 20X2, in the amount of 100,000 FC.

2. On November 1, 20X1, the company purchased a forward contract to buy 100,000 FC on February 1, 20X2, at a forward rate of 1 FC = $0.506.

3. Selected spot and forward rates are as follows:

Date	Spot Rate	Forward Rate for Remaining Term of Contract
November 1, 20X1	1 FC = $0.50	1 FC = $0.506
December 31, 20X1	1 FC = 0.52	1 FC = 0.530
February 1, 20X2	1 FC = 0.55	1 FC = 0.550

4. Changes in the value of the forward contract are to be discounted at a 6% rate.

5. Changes in the value of the forward contract over time are as follows:

	November 1— 90 Days Remaining	December 31— 30 Days Remaining	Transaction Date
Number of FC	100,000	100,000	100,000
Spot rate 1 FC	$0.500	$0.520	$0.550
Forward rate for remaining time – 1 FC	$0.506	$0.530	$0.550
Initial forward rate – 1 FC		$0.506	$0.506
Fair value of forward contract:			
Original forward value		$ 50,600	$ 50,600
Current forward value		53,000	55,000
Change—gain (loss)—in forward value		$ 2,400	$ 4,400
Present value of change:			
$n = 1, i = 6\%/12$		$ 2,388	
$n = 0, i = 6\%/12$			$ 4,400
Change in value from prior period:			
Current present value		$ 2,388	$ 4,400
Prior present value		0	2,388
Change in present value		$ 2,388	$ 2,012

Illustration 6-3 presents the entries to record the foreign currency transaction and the related forward contract. Once again, in order to emphasize that the value of certain account balances is not fixed and will change over time, these accounts are identified in boldface type.

Illustration 6-3
Hedging a Foreign Currency Denominated Liability

Relating to the Purchase of Inventory			Relating to the Forward Contract		
November 1, 20X1					
Inventory	50,000		**Forward Contract Receivable—FC**	50,600	
Accounts Payable—FC		50,000	Forward Contract Payable—$		50,600
Purchase of inventory			Purchase of contract to buy		
for 100,000 FC when			100,000 FC at a forward rate		
1 FC = $0.50.			of 1 FC = $0.506.[a]		
December 31, 20X1					
Exchange Loss	2,000		**Forward Contract Receivable—FC**	2,388	
Accounts Payable—FC		2,000	Gain on Contract		2,388
To accrue the exchange loss on			To record the change in the value of		
the FC denominated payable			the forward contract.		
when the spot rate is $0.52.					
			Note that the above entry includes the entire		
			change in the value of the contract including both		
			the effective and ineffective portion of the		
			contract.		
February 1, 20X2					
Accounts Payable—FC	52,000		**Forward Contract Receivable—FC**	2,012	
Exchange Loss	3,000		Gain on Contract		2,012
Foreign Currency		55,000	To record change in the value of the		
To record settlement			forward contract.		
of the liability when					
1 FC = $0.55.			Foreign Currency[b]	55,000	
			Forward Contract Payable—$	50,600	
			Forward Contract Receivable—FC		55,000
			Cash		50,600
			To record settlement of contract.[c]		

[a]Noting the offsetting nature of the two accounts, an alternative for this entry would be a memo entry to describe the commitment resulting from the contract. Such treatment emphasizes the executory nature of the contract and is most common in practice. However, recognizing the forward contract with entries helps in understanding the relationships in using forward contracts. If no entry were made at inception, subsequent changes in the value of the hedging instrument would still be recognized by either debiting or crediting a "forward contract" in the case of an unrealized gain or loss, respectively. It should be noted that no separate accounting is given to the contract.

[b]Generally, the company would not physically receive the foreign currency. Instead, a bank wire transfer would be used to settle the transaction. The currency broker would debit the domestic company's bank account for the necessary number of dollars and credit the foreign company's bank account for the necessary number of foreign currencies. If a bank wire transfer were used, the entry would be as follows:

Cash	4,400	
Forward Contract Payable — $	50,600	
Forward Contract Receivable — FC		55,000

[c]If a memo entry was initially used to account for the forward contract, the settlement of the contract would be recorded as follows:

Foreign Currency	55,000	
Forward Contract—FC		4,400
Cash		50,600

To summarize, the accounting for the hedge of a foreign currency denominated asset or liability is characterized as follows:

1. The accounting for the hedging instrument is separate from the accounting for the foreign currency denominated asset or liability.
2. The hedging instrument will be carried at fair value, and changes in value over time will be recognized as an unrealized gain or loss and be reported in earnings.
3. The change in value of the hedging instrument consists of a change in the instrument's intrinsic value and its time value. The total change in value of the instrument, including both hedge effectiveness and hedge ineffectiveness, is reported currently in earnings.
4. Changes in the value of the hedging instrument should be accrued at the end of a reporting period.
5. The gains (losses) on the hedging instrument will offset or net against the losses (gains) on the foreign currency transaction (the hedged item).
6. A hedge would be fully effective or "perfect" if the critical terms (nature of the underlying, notional amount, delivery dates, settlement date, type of currency, etc.) of the hedging instrument matched the terms of the hedged item. In a perfect hedge, the net offset amount will merely equal the change in the time value of the hedging instrument.
7. In the case of a forward contract, technically there is no need to record the contract at inception because it is an executory contract. In reality, most companies follow this no recording practice but do keep supporting schedules detailing contracts. Even if this practice is followed, the forward contract is marked-to-market in order to reflect changes in the value of the underlying foreign currency. These changes in fair value are recorded by the company. For instructional purposes, forward contracts will be recorded at inception. Note, however, that the forward contract receivable and forward contract payable accounts will be netted against each other for presentation purposes. This netting results in balance sheet amounts equal to those that would have existed if no entry had been made at inception to record the hedging instrument.

The hedge accounted for in Illustration 6-3 was effective in that the losses associated with the changing value of the FC denominated account payable were offset by the positive changes in the value of the forward contract. Instead of a $5,000 exchange loss, the company incurred only a $600 loss, which represents the premium on the forward rate of 0.506 versus the spot rate of 0.50 on the inception date of the forward contract. If financial statements were presented on December 31, 20X1, the purchase and hedge would be reported as follows:

Income Statement		Balance Sheet	
		Assets:	
Exchange loss	$(2,000)	Inventory	$ 50,000
Unrealized gain on contract	2,388	Forward contract receivable—FC . . .	$ 52,988
Net gain	$ 388	Forward contract payable—$	(50,600)
		Net contract.	$ 2,388
		Liabilities:	
		Accounts payable—FC	$ 52,000

The overall effect of the hedge presented in Illustration 6-3 is summarized as follows:

	Without the Hedge	With the Hedge
Exchange gain (loss) on foreign currency denominated asset or liability [100,000 FC × ($0.55 − $0.50)]	$(5,000)	$(5,000)
Gain on forward contract [100,000 FC × ($0.55 − $0.506)]		4,400
Net income effect	$(5,000)	$ (600)

The net effect on income represents the original premium on the forward contract of $600 [100,000 × (forward rate of $0.506 versus original spot rate of $0.500)].

It is important to note that a hedge may also eliminate exchange gains associated with a foreign currency denominated asset or liability. For instance, when a forward contract establishes a forward rate, it is possible that changes in the spot rate may not move in the same direction or may not move as much as had been expected. Considering the previous transactions, assume the same facts except that the spot rates are as follows:

Date	Spot Rate
November 1, 20X1	1 FC = $0.50
December 31, 20X1	1 FC = $0.49
February 1, 20X2	1 FC = $0.48

In effect, the hedge eliminated potential exchange gains, and the company paid the same $600 premium for the forward contract:

	Without the Hedge	With the Hedge
Exchange gain (loss) on foreign currency transaction [100,000 FC × ($0.48 − $0.50)]	$2,000	$ 2,000
Loss on forward contract [100,000 FC × ($0.48 − $0.506)]		(2,600)
Net income effect	$2,000	$ (600)

Although this hedge had a negative impact on earnings, it did eliminate the uncertainty associated with exchange rate risk. By entering into a forward contract on the date of the transaction, the company established a known payment amount of $50,600. Illustration 6-3 involved the use of a forward contract to buy FC in order to settle the FC denominated accounts payable. A forward contract may also be used to sell FC when an FC denominated receivable is settled. For example, if a U.S. company sold inventory to a foreign customer and the resulting account receivable was denominated in FC, the company would receive FC. The company could acquire a forward contract to sell FC upon receipt from the foreign customer. If the dollar strengthened relative to the FC, the U.S. company's receivable would decrease in value. However, a forward contract to sell FC in this scenario would increase in value and serve as a hedge against the losses on the receivable.

Illustration of Hedging with a Foreign Currency Option. Assume that a U.S. company sold inventory to a foreign customer with subsequent collection due in FC, a foreign currency denominated asset, and that the company acquired a put option to sell FC.

Additional information supporting this illustration is as follows:

1. On November 1, 20X1, the company sold inventory, with a cost of $32,000, to a foreign customer with payment due on February 1, 20X2, in the amount of 100,000 FC.

2. On November 1, 20X1, the company purchased a put option to sell 100,000 FC on February 1, 20X2, at a strike price of 1 FC = $0.51. An option premium of $400 was paid.

3. Spot rates, option values, and changes in value over time are as follows:

	November 1 20X1	December 31 20X1	February 1 20X2
Strike price 1 FC	$0.51	$0.51	$0.51
Spot rate 1 FC	$0.515	$0.498	$0.495
Fair value of options	$ 400	$1,300	$1,500
Intrinsic value of option	0	1,200	1,500
Time value of option	$ 400	$ 100	$ 0

Illustration 6-4 presents the entries to record the foreign currency transaction and the related option. Once again, in order to emphasize that the value of certain account balances is not fixed and will change over time, these accounts are identified in boldface type.

Illustration 6-4
Hedging a Foreign Currency Denominated Asset

Relating to the Sale of Inventory			Relating to the Put Option		
November 1, 20X1					
Accounts Receivable—FC	51,500		**Investment in Put Option**	400	
Sales Revenue		51,500	Cash		400
			To record purchase of option.		
Cost of Sales	32,000				
Inventory		32,000			
To record sale of inventory.					
December 31, 20X1					
Exchange Loss	1,700		**Investment in Put Option**	900	
Accounts Receivable—FC		1,700	Gain on Option		900
To accrue the exchange loss on the FC denominated receivable when the spot rate is $0.498.			To record the change in the value of the put option.		
			Note that the above entry includes the entire change in the value of the option including both the effective (intrinsic value) and ineffective (time value) portion.		
February 1, 20X2					
Foreign Currency	49,500		**Investment in Put Option**	200	
Exchange Loss	300		Gain on Option		200
Accounts Receivable—FC		49,800	To record change in the value of the put option.		
To record settlement of the receivable when 1 FC = $0.495.					
			Cash	51,000	
			Foreign Currency		49,500
			Investment in Put Option		1,500
			To record net settlement of the option.		

The overall effect of the hedge presented in Illustration 6-4 is summarized as follows:

	Without the Hedge	With the Hedge
Exchange gain (loss) on foreign currency denominated asset or liability [100,000 FC × ($0.515 − $0.495)]	$(2,000)	$(2,000)
Gain on option ($1,500 − $400)		1,100
Net income effect	$(2,000)	$ (900)

As a result of the hedge, the net effect on income represents two components: (a) the fact that the option's intrinsic value of $1,500 only offsets $2,000 of the exchange loss on the receivable and (b) the $400 cost of the original premium on the option.

Special Hedging Complications

The previous examples assumed that the term of the hedging instrument covered the same period of time as the settlement period, which is defined as the period of time between the transaction date and the settlement date of the foreign currency denominated asset or liability. However, it is possible that a hedging instrument could cover a period of time different from the settlement period. The previous examples also assumed that the hedging instrument was for the same number of foreign currency units as required by the foreign currency transaction. It also is possible that a hedging instrument could be for a number of foreign currency units different from the number of units required by the transaction.

Hedging Instrument Expires Before Settlement Date. Prior to the expiration date of a hedging instrument, it is possible for the holder of the contract to settle the contract in exchange for cash. Net settlement is a characteristic of all derivatives such as a forward contract. However, if the contract expires before the settlement date of the underlying hedged transaction, the holder of the hedging instrument has several alternatives for dealing with the contract. For example, assuming that a forward contract to sell foreign currency expires before the customer remits the foreign currency, the seller may: (a) roll over the forward contract, (b) purchase the necessary foreign currency to satisfy the contract and acquire a new forward contract to sell the foreign currency when the customer pays, or (c) simply purchase the necessary foreign currency to satisfy the contract and deal with the foreign currency when it is received.

Transactions and hedging instruments may be settled on different dates. For example, some currency brokers will extend a forward contract for a short time at the original forward rate as a courtesy to their clients. However, if settlement is not expected soon, the original contract may be rolled over into a new contract to settle on the anticipated date of payment. Rather than rolling over a forward contract, the needed FC can be purchased to settle the forward contract. When the hedged transaction is ultimately settled, the FC received could then be sold at the spot rate. Obviously, this route creates exposure to the risk that spot rates will change between the time of purchasing FC and receiving FC from the customer. In order to avoid this exposure, a new forward contract to sell FC could be employed.

Hedging Instrument Expires After Settlement Date. Hedging instruments can also expire after the settlement date. For example, suppose a customer paying in foreign currency accelerates the payment date in order to improve his/her current ratio. Assuming the seller has hedged the transaction with a forward contract, they once again have several options: (a) hold the foreign currency until the date of the original forward contract, (b) roll the contract back and sell the foreign currency immediately, (c) sell the foreign currency immediately and sell the forward contract to another party, and (d) sell the foreign currency immediately and acquire FC at the spot rate when the forward contract is settled. Alternative (d) results in a speculative position. (There is no hedged transaction, and it is discouraged by many company policy statements.) If a forward contract expires after the settlement date, any gain or loss that accrues on the forward contract after the transaction settlement date is recognized as a component of current operating income.

Hedging Instrument's Notional Amount Different from Transaction Amount. If a hedging instrument is for a smaller number of foreign currency units than the foreign currency transaction, the contract gain or loss is recognized as a partial hedge on the exposed position. However, if the forward contract is for a greater number of foreign currency units than the exposed asset or liability position, special treatment is required. That portion of the hedging instrument which exceeds the exposed position is considered to be a speculative hedge and is accounted for as an investment. The gain or loss on that portion of the contract which exceeds the exposed position is accordingly accounted for as an investment gain or loss.

Hedging an Identifiable Foreign Currency Firm Commitment

An identifiable firm commitment is a binding agreement between two parties that specifies all significant terms related to a yet-to-be-executed transaction. If the commitment requires ultimate settlement in a fixed amount of FC, then exposure to exchange rate risk exists. Because the terms and prices of the commitment in FC are fixed, changes in FC exchange rates affect the value of the commitment or the cash flows associated with the commitment. For example, assume a commitment to buy inventory in 60 days for 500,000 FC. If at the date of the commitment the spot rate is 1 FC = $0.25 and the 60-day forward rate is 1 FC = $0.258, changes in these rates could be used to suggest the change in the relative dollar value of the commitment. If 30 days after the commitment date the spot rate is 1 FC = $0.254 and the remaining 30-day forward rate is 1 FC = $0.264, it would appear that the commitment has lost value. Clearly, it appears that the commitment will require more dollars to settle than was previously estimated.

Furthermore, because the commitment terms (e.g., pay 500,000 FC) are fixed, the commitment cannot be renegotiated to take into consideration the fact that the dollar has weakened relative to the FC. Changes in the value of a commitment can be suggested by either changes in spot rates or forward rates over time. In either case, the suggested change reflects value at the transaction date, versus commitment date, and therefore must be discounted to reflect the change in value at the present time. Using the above example and a discount rate of 6%, the change in value of the above commitment after the first 30 days would be measured as follows:

	Based on Spot Rates	Based on Forward Rates
Rate at:		
Commitment date.	$ 0.250	$ 0.258
30 days later	0.254	0.264
Change in rate.	0.004	0.006
Number of FC	500,000	500,000
Change in value	$ 2,000	$ 3,000
Present value of change where n = 1		
month and i = 6%/12.	$ 1,990	$ 2,985

In order to avoid the unfavorable effect of exchange rate changes on the firm commitment, an entity could designate a derivative instrument as a hedge against unfavorable outcomes. The hedge of a firm commitment can be designated as either a fair value hedge or a cash flow hedge assuming the necessary respective criteria are satisfied. More often than not, a fair value hedge will be employed, and such a hedge will be illustrated below.

The special accounting for a fair value hedge of a firm foreign currency commitment is characterized as follows:

1. The accounting for the hedge (the hedging instrument) is separate from the accounting for the foreign currency commitment (the hedged item). If the commitment were not hedged, no special accounting treatment would be given the commitment.
2. The hedging instrument will be carried at fair value, and changes in value over time will be recognized as an unrealized gain or loss and be reported currently in earnings.
3. The change in the value of the hedging instrument consists of a change in the instrument's intrinsic value and its time value. Changes in both the intrinsic and time values are reported currently in earnings and therefore will not be separately accounted for.
4. Changes in the value of the hedging instrument should be accrued at the end of a reporting period.
5. A hedge would be fully effective or "perfect" if the critical terms (nature of the underlying, notional amount, delivery dates, settlement date, type of currency, etc.) of the hedging instrument matched the terms of the hedged item. It is permitted, but not required, to exclude the time value of the derivative instrument from the assessment of hedge effectiveness.
6. Management must set forth how the gain or loss on the firm commitment will be measured. The resulting gain or loss in value will be reported currently in earnings. The change in the value of the firm commitment from the time of the commitment to the transaction date is recognized as a firm commitment asset or liability. This recognized change in value will result in an adjustment to the basis of the committed item. The gains (losses) on the hedging instrument will offset or net against the losses (gains) on the commitment (the hedged item).
7. If the hedge is perfectly effective, the change in the value of the firm commitment will result in an adjustment, at the date of the transaction, to the basis of the committed item so that the effect of exchange rate changes on fixed prices can be offset. The result is that the dollar basis of the transaction is established at the commitment date rather than the later transaction date, and the targeted values at the date of the commitment can be realized.
8. That portion of the hedging instrument which exceeds the notional amount of the commitment is considered to be a speculative hedge and is accounted for accordingly. Therefore, the special accounting treatment given a fair value hedge is not extended to the portion of the hedge which is deemed to be ineffective.

To illustrate, assume that on March 31, a U.S. company commits to selling specialty equipment to a foreign customer with delivery and payment in 90 days. The firm commitment calls for a selling price of 100,000 FC, and it is estimated that the cost to manufacture the equipment will be $55,000. Assume that the spot rate at the date of the commitment is 1 FC = $0.85. If the spot rate were to remain constant over time, management would be able to realize a target gross profit on the sale of $30,000 [(100,000 FC × $0.85) – $55,000]. However, management fears that the FC could weaken relative to the dollar and the target gross profit margin could be reduced. For example, if the rate of exchange at the transaction date were 1 FC = $0.80, the gross profit would be reduced to $25,000 [(100,000 FC × $0.80) – $55,000]. Recognizing that it may be desirable to establish the dollar basis of a transaction at the commitment date rather than the later transaction date, management could enter into a hedge.

To continue the above example, assume that at the date of the commitment, management decides to hedge the commitment by acquiring a forward contract to sell FC in 90 days. Management has elected to include both the change in intrinsic value and time value in the measurement of hedge effectiveness. The change in the value of the firm commitment will be measured by changes in the forward rates. Assume that a 6% discount rate is to be used.

Selected rates and changes in value are presented in the table below. It is important to note the following:

1. The forward contract calls for the sale of FC. Therefore, as remaining forward rates fall below the original forward rate (FC can be sold forward for fewer dollars), the contract increases in value and gains are experienced.

2. The difference between the initial spot and forward rates, referred to as the spot-forward difference, represents the time value of the contract and is either a premium or discount. In the present case, the spot-forward difference is a loss. The initial forward rate to sell is less than the initial spot value of the FC. This loss is included in the assessment of hedge effectiveness as so elected at inception of the hedge although management could have elected to exclude it from hedge effectiveness. The hedge is expected to be fully effective or "perfect" because the critical terms (nature of the underlying, notional amount, delivery dates, settlement date, type of currency, etc.) of the hedging instrument match the terms of the hedged item.

3. Changes in the value of the firm commitment are measured as changes in the forward rate over time. As the forward rates decrease over time, the commitment to sell becomes less valuable.

	March 31—90 Days Remaining	60 Days Remaining	30 Days Remaining	Transaction Date
Number of FC	100,000	100,000	100,000	100,000
Spot rate 1 FC	$0.850	$0.840	$0.820	$0.800
Forward rate for remaining time – 1 FC	$0.845	$0.838	$0.814	$0.800
Initial forward rate – 1 FC		$0.845	$0.845	$0.845
Fair value of forward contract:				
Original forward value		$ 84,500	$ 84,500	$ 84,500
Current forward value		83,800	81,400	80,000
Change—gain (loss)—in forward value		$ 700	$ 3,100	$ 4,500
Present value of change:				
n = 2, i = 6%/12		$ 693		
n = 1, i = 6%/12			$ 3,085	
n = 0, i = 6%/12				$ 4,500
Change in value from prior period:				
Current present value		$ 693	$ 3,085	$ 4,500
Prior present value		0	693	3,085
Change in present value		$ 693	$ 2,392	$ 1,415

Entries by the U.S. company to record the fair value hedge are set forth in Illustration 6-5. An analysis of the entries in Illustration 6-5 reveals that the fair value hedge was effective in accomplishing the concerns of the U.S. company. At the commitment date, the commitment to receive FC had a value of $85,000 (ignoring the time value of money), represented by 100,000 FC at a then spot rate of 1 FC = $0.85. Nevertheless, the company was concerned that the FC would weaken, resulting in a reduction of the targeted gross profit. In fact, the value of the commitment to receive FC did lose value over time as evidenced by a declining spot rate. However, by hedging the commitment, the company was able to ultimately adjust the basis of the sales transaction and, with the exception of the forward contract discount, attain the targeted gross profit. Note that the account "Firm Commitment" serves the purpose of fixing the basis of the sales by the amount of the loss on firm commitment recognized during the commitment period. The effect of the above fair value hedge on reported income can be summarized as follows:

Illustration 6-5
Hedge of an Identifiable Foreign Currency Commitment

Relating to the Commitment and Sale of Equipment

March 31
Memo: Company commits to sell equipment.

60 days remaining
| Loss on Firm Commitment | 693 | |
| Firm Commitment | | 693 |

To record the loss on commitment measured by change in the forward rates.

30 days remaining
| Loss on Firm Commitment | 2,392 | |
| Firm Commitment | | 2,392 |

To record the loss on commitment.

0 days remaining
| Loss on Firm Commitment | 1,415 | |
| Firm Commitment | | 1,415 |

To record the loss on commitment.

Foreign Currency	80,000	
Firm Commitment	4,500	
Sales Revenue		84,500

To record sale and adjustment to basis of sale.

| Cost of Sales | 55,000 | |
| Equipment Inventory | | 55,000 |

To record cost of sales.

Relating to the Forward Contract

March 31
| Forward Contract Receivable—$ | 84,500 | |
| Forward Contract Payable—FC | | 84,500 |

Purchase of contract to sell 100,000 at a forward rate of 1 FC — $0.845.

60 days remaining
| Forward Contract Payable—FC | 693 | |
| Gain on Contract | | 693 |

To record change in value due to forward rate changes.

30 days remaining
| Forward Contract Payable—FC | 2,392 | |
| Gain on Contract | | 2,392 |

To record change in value due to forward rate changes.

0 days remaining
| Forward Contract Payable—FC | 1,415 | |
| Gain on Contract | | 1,415 |

To record change in value due to forward rate changes.

| Forward Contract Payable—FC | 80,000 | |
| Foreign Currency | | 80,000 |

To record settlement of forward contract.

| Cash | 84,500 | |
| Forward Contract Receivable—$ | | 84,500 |

To record receipt of cash from broker.

	Targeted Position	Without the Hedge	With the Hedge
Sales price.....................................	$85,000	$80,000	$84,500
Cost of sales....................................	55,000	55,000	55,000
Gross profit	$30,000	$25,000	$29,500

If the commitment had not been hedged, the actual gross profit on the sale would have been reduced from the targeted gross profit of $30,000 to $25,000. However, the fair value hedge was effective in maintaining the targeted gross profit. This was accomplished at a cost of $500, which represents the time value (the original discount – a forward rate less than the spot rate) on the forward contract [($0.845 – $0.850) (100,000 FC)]. This hedge was highly effective in that the loss on the commitment ($4,500) was perfectly offset by the gain on the forward contract ($4,500). Although this hedge was highly effective in offsetting losses on the commitment, it is important to remember that forward rates could have increased over time, and the hedge would have effectively eliminated gains on the commitment.

If financial statements were presented on April 30, with 60 days remaining on the hedge, the sale and hedge would be reported as follows:

Income Statement		Balance Sheet	
		Assets:	
Loss on firm commitment	$(693)	Forward contract receivable—$ ...	$84,500
Gain on contract	693	Forward contract payable—FC....	83,807
		Net contract...................	$ 693
Net loss	$ (0)	Liabilities:	
		Firm commitment	$ 693

The special accounting treatment given a fair value hedge of a firm commitment continues during the commitment period unless

- The necessary criteria to qualify as a fair value hedge are no longer satisfied,
- The derivative instrument expires or is sold, terminated, or exercised,
- The entity no longer designates the derivative as a fair value hedge, or
- The hedging relationship is no longer considered highly effective based on management's policies.

Furthermore, note that the treatment given a fair value hedge does not continue beyond the point in time where the commitment actually becomes a transaction. If the term of the derivative instrument extends beyond the transaction date, any exchange gains or losses after the transaction date are treated as shown in Illustration 6-3.

Foreign currency commitments are frequently hedged through the use of forward contracts. However, other forms of derivative and nonderivative instruments may be effective. For example, in the above illustration, management could have acquired a put option to sell foreign currency at the transaction date. Alternatively, management could have borrowed dollars for a short term with a promise to repay the loan with a fixed number of FC. The FC received from the sales transaction could have been used to settle the loan denominated in FC. Regardless of the instrument used, the goal of a fair value hedge of a commitment is to reduce the exposure that exchange rate changes may have on the value or amount of the U.S. (domestic) currency to be received or paid. Although the above illustration focused on a commitment involving the receipt of FC in connection with a sale, it is also possible that a commitment might involve the payment of FC. For example, if a company was committed to acquire inventory to be paid for in FC, changes in exchange rates could result in the inventory costing more than anticipated. Such increases in the cost of inventory could reduce gross profits associated with the subsequent sale of the inventory.

EXAMPLES OF THE ACCOUNTING FOR CASH FLOW HEDGES

As previously stated, cash flow hedges may be used to hedge against changes in the cash flows of either a forecasted foreign currency transaction, the forecasted functional currency equivalent cash flows associated with a recognized asset or liability, and an unrecognized foreign currency firm commitment. Assuming the necessary criteria are satisfied, the cash flow hedge will be given special accounting treatment. This special treatment is characterized as follows:

1. The effective portion of the gain or loss on the derivative instrument will be reported in other comprehensive income (OCI).

2. Although not required, a portion of the derivative instrument's gain or loss represented by the time value may be excluded from the assessment of hedge effectiveness. If the time value is excluded, changes in time value will be recognized currently in earnings rather than as a component of other comprehensive income.

3. The amounts reported in OCI will be reclassified into recognized earnings in the same period in which the hedged item affects earnings.

4. Given a hedge of a forecasted transaction, special rules relate to how much of the change in the value of the derivative instrument can be recognized in OCI relative to the change in the forecasted transaction. These rules will be discussed in a subsequent section.

Hedging a Foreign Currency Forecasted Transaction

A forecasted transaction is one that is expected to occur in the future at market prices that will be in existence at the time of the transaction. This is in contrast to a foreign currency commitment, which involves market prices that have been previously determined or committed to at the time of the commitment. Because the transaction is forecasted and has not yet occurred, a forecasted transaction does not provide an entity with any present rights or obligations and therefore does not have any fixed prices or rates. Because, unlike a firm commitment, no terms are fixed, an entity is exposed to the risk that future cash flows associated with the forecasted transaction could change. For example, if a company forecasted a purchase of inventory, the cost of the inventory could change. Furthermore, if the forecasted transaction were denominated in FC, not only could the FC price change, but the number of dollars needed to acquire the necessary FC could also change. To illustrate, assume that a company forecasts purchasing inventory for 100,000 FC and that the current spot rate is 1 FC = $1.10. The entity is exposed to the risk that the actual cost of the inventory could exceed 100,000 FC and that the FC could strengthen relative to the dollar. For example, if it turned out that the inventory actually cost 105,000 FC and that 1 FC × $1.14, then the transaction that was forecasted to cost $110,000 (100,000 FC × $1.10) would actually cost $119,700 (105,000 FC × $1.14).

The objective of a hedge of a forecasted transaction is to reduce the variability of cash flows associated with the transaction by fixing exchange rates. As previously stated, qualifying cash flow hedges are given special accounting treatment and in the case of a forecasted transaction it is important to note the following:

1. The accounting for the hedge (the hedging instrument) is separate from the accounting for the forecasted foreign currency transaction (the hedged item). Furthermore, since the hedged item is a forecasted transaction, which obviously has not yet occurred or been firmly committed to, no accounting is necessary until the forecasted transaction actually takes place. Therefore, there are no recognized gains or losses in the value of the forecasted transaction being concurrently recognized along with changes in the value of the hedging instrument.

2. The cumulative amount of OCI, resulting from changes in the value of the hedging instrument, cannot exceed the cumulative change in the value of expected/forecasted cash flows. If the cumulative amount of OCI exceeds the cumulative change in the value of expected/forecasted cash flows, the difference is removed from OCI and recognized currently as earnings. For example, if a derivative instrument increases $1,000 in value and the forecasted cash flows decrease in value by $900, a $900 gain will be shown as OCI, and a $100 gain will

be recognized in current earnings. In essence, if the hedge is over effective, that amount will be taken to earnings rather than OCI.

3. If the change in value of a derivative instrument is less than the change in value of the fore-casted transaction, all of the change in value of the derivative instrument is recognized as a component of other comprehensive income. However, the excess change in value of the fore-casted transaction is not recognized. To do so would allow partial recognition of a transaction that has not yet occurred. For example, assume a derivative instrument changes $1,000 in value and the forecasted cash flows change in value by $1,200. Only $1,000 of the change in value is recognized as a component of other comprehensive income and the $200 difference is not accounted for.

4. If the hedge is under effective, then all of the change value will be recorded as a component of OCI.

5. Changes in the value of the hedging instrument should be accrued at the end of a reporting period.

6. When the forecasted transaction actually affects earnings (versus occurs), the change in the hedging instrument's value recognized as a component of OCI is reclassified into current earnings.

7. If the hedge is perfectly effective, the variability of forecasted cash flows due to changes in exchange rates will be reduced. The component of OCI that is reclassified into current earnings when the forecasted transaction actually affects earnings will reduce the effect that changes in exchange rates have had on the underlying cash flows. The result of the hedge is that resulting cash flows are fixed at an exchange rate rather that being allowed to vary as would be the case without a hedge.

8. The deferral of a loss on a cash flow hedge as a component of OCI is not appropriate if it is likely to result in a combined basis/cost that exceeds the fair value of the resulting asset or liability. For example, assume a derivative loss associated with a forecasted purchase of equipment will, when combined with the expected cost of the equipment, result in a total cost in excess of the item's fair value. If this is expected, the derivative's loss should be recognized immediately in earnings, to the extent that it exceeds the equipment's fair value.

9. If all or part of a transaction is still forecasted, there may be some gain or loss on a corresponding derivative that is still being classified as a component of OCI. On an ongoing basis, it is important to make sure that the gain (loss) on a derivative that remains as a component of OCI does not more than offset the cumulative loss (gain) in the value of the remaining forecasted transaction. If excessive amounts are classified as OCI, such excess amounts must be reclassified as a component of current earnings. For example, if the balance in OCI related to a forecasted transaction represents a gain on the hedging instrument of $10,000 and the loss in value of the remaining forecasted transaction is $8,000, the excess OCI balance of $2,000 must be reclassified as a component of current earnings.

Illustration of Hedging a Forecasted Transaction with an Option. To illustrate the special accounting for a cash flow hedge of a forecasted transaction, assume the following:

1. On June 1, a company forecasted the purchase of 5,000 units of inventory from a foreign vendor. The purchase would probably occur on September 1 and require the payment of 100,000 FC.

2. It is anticipated that the inventory could be further processed and delivered to customers by early October.

3. On June 1, the company purchased an out-of-the-money call option to buy 100,000 FC at a strike price of 1 FC = $0.55 during September. An option premium of $900 was paid.

4. Effectiveness of the hedge is measured by comparing changes in the option's intrinsic value with changes in the forecasted cash flows based on changes in the spot rates for FC. Changes in the time value of the option will be excluded from the assessment of hedge effectiveness. The hedge is expected to be fully effective because the critical terms (nature of underlying, notional amounts, delivery dates, settlement date, type of currency, etc.) of the hedging instrument match the terms of the hedged item.

5. Spot rates, option values, and changes in value over time are as follows:

	June 1	June 30	July 31	September 1
Strike price 1 FC	$0.55	$0.55	$0.55	$0.55
Spot rate 1 FC	$0.53	$0.552	$0.57	$0.575
Fair value of options	$ 900	$ 1,350	$ 2,400	$ 2,600
Intrinsic value of option	0	200	2,000	2,500
Time value of option	$ 900	$ 1,150	$ 400	$ 100
Cumulative change – gain/(loss) in:				
Intrinsic value		$ 200	$ 2,000	$ 2,500
Value of expected cash flows				
(change in spot rates over time)		$(2,200)	$(4,000)	$(4,500)
Lesser (in absolute amount) of derivative's				
cumulative gain (loss) or loss (gain) in value				
of expected/forecasted cash flows		$ 200	$ 2,000	$ 2,500

6. On September 1, the company purchased 5,000 units of inventory at a cost of 103,000 FC. The option was settled/sold on September 1 at its fair value of $2,600.

7. After incurring further processing costs of $20,000, the inventory was sold for $95,000 on October 5.

Illustration 6-6 presents the necessary entries to account for the cash flow hedge of the above forecasted transaction and the subsequent actual transactions.

Illustration 6-6
Using an Option as a Cash Flow Hedge of a Forecasted Transaction

The following entries relate to the hedge. There is no corresponding transaction.

June 1

Investment in Call Option	900	
Cash		900
To record purchase of option.		

June 30

Investment in Call Option ($1,350 – $900)	450	
Gain on Option		250
OCI [(0.552 – 0.55) × 100,000 FC]		200
To record change in the value of the option.		

The change in the time value is excluded from the assessment of hedge effectiveness. The portion of the gain recorded in OCI equals the change in the option's intrinsic value, which was zero on June 1 because the strike price of $0.55 was greater than the spot rate of $0.53.

July 31

Investment in Call Option ($2,400 – $1,350)	1,050	
Loss on Option	750	
OCI [(0.57 – 0.552) × 100,000 FC]		1,800
To record change in the value of the option.		

September 1

Investment in Call Option	200	
Loss on Option	300	
OCI		500
To record change in the value of the option.		

Cash	2,600	
Investment in Call Option...		2,600
To record net settlement of option.		

The remaining entries relate to the inventory purchase and subsequent sale. There is no hedge outstanding.

Inventory	59,225	
Cash		59,225
To record payment of 103,000 FC × $0.575.		

Inventory	20,000	
Cash		20,000
To record additional processing costs.		

October 5

Cash	95,000	
Sales Revenue		95,000
To record sale of inventory.		

Cost of Sales ($59,225 + $20,000)	79,225	
Inventory		79,225
To recognize cost of sales.		

OCI (balance)	2,500	
Cost of Sales		2,500
To adjust cost of sales by the gain accumulated in OCI.		

An analysis of the entries in Illustration 6-6 reveals that the cash flow hedge was effective in accomplishing the concerns of the U.S. company. At the time of the forecasted transaction, the company anticipated purchasing inventory for 100,000 FC. At a current spot rate of 1 FC = $0.53, the cash outflow would have been $53,000. However, as the spot rate began to increase, the cost of the inventory would increase, and the potential gross profit on its eventual sale would decrease. At the date of the transaction, the spot rate was 1 FC = $0.575. If the price of the inventory had remained at 100,000 FC, the cost of the inventory would have been $57,500. Acquiring an option to buy FC allowed the company to reduce the variability of cash flows and acquire FC at a fixed strike price of 1 FC = $0.550. The effect of the cash flow hedge of the forecasted transaction can be summarized as follows:

	Without the Call Option	With the Call Option
Sales price of inventory	$ 95,000	$ 95,000
Cost of sales – Raw materials.................................	(59,225)	(59,225)
Cost of sales – Processing costs	(20,000)	(20,000)
Gross profit	$ 15,775	$ 15,775
Adjustment to cost of sales due to change in the intrinsic value of the option		2,500
Adjusted gross profit	$ 15,775	$ 18,275
Unrealized loss on hedge excluded from assessment of hedge effectiveness		(800)
Net income effect	$ 15,775	$ 17,475

The adjusted gross profit resulting from the use of a hedge results from the following:

Sales revenue	$ 95,000
Locked in cost of sales on 100,000 FC at the strike price of $0.550	(55,000)
No hedge on the additional cost of 3,000 FC at the transaction date spot rate of $0.575	(1,725)
Processing costs	(20,000)
Adjusted gross profit	$ 18,275

An analysis of the entries also shows that the balance in OCI at any point in time never exceeded the lesser (in absolute amounts) of the derivative's cumulative gain (loss) in intrinsic value or the loss (gain) in the value of the expected/forecasted cash flows (as measured by changes in spot rates).

The cash flow hedge was effective in reducing the variability of cash flows and was accomplished at a cost of $800, which represents the change in the time value of the option over the holding period ($900 − $100). Once again, remember that the variability of cash flows may also produce a positive effect. For example, if the spot rate had decreased, the purchase of inventory would have required even less cash flow than originally forecasted, and additional gross profit may have resulted. However, an option is a useful derivative to employ in such situations. Remember that the option represents a right, rather than an obligation, to buy FC. If spot rates had declined below the strike price, the holder of the out-of-the-money option could have elected not to exercise and merely recognized the option premium of $900 as a loss. If a forward contract to buy FC had been employed, the holder would have been obligated to exercise or settle the contract. In that case, the hedging instrument would have had an unfavorable effect, offsetting the positive effects associated with variable cash flows.

If financial statements were presented at June 30, the hedge would be reported as follows:

Income Statement		Balance Sheet	
		Assets:	
Gain on option	$250	Investment in options	$1,350
		Stockholders' Equity:	
		Other comprehensive income—Gain on option	$ 200

The special accounting treatment given a cash flow hedge of a forecasted transaction continues unless

◆ The necessary criteria to qualify as a cash flow hedge are no longer satisfied,
◆ The derivative instrument expires or is sold, terminated, or exercised,
◆ The derivative instrument is no longer designated as a hedge on a forecasted transaction, or
◆ The hedging relationship is no longer highly effective based on management's policies.

Once a forecasted transaction actually occurs, it is possible at that time to designate the original derivative, if not expired, or a new derivative as a hedge on any exposed asset or liability resulting from the actual transaction. However, if the forecasted transaction is no longer probable, the gain or loss accumulated in OCI should be recognized immediately in earnings.

Illustration of Hedging a Forecasted Transaction with a Forward Contract. To illustrate the special accounting for a cash flow hedge of a forecasted transaction with a forward contract, assume the same facts as presented above in the case of hedging with an option except the following:

1. On June 1, the company purchased a forward contract to buy 100,000 FC at a forward rate of 1 FC = $0.542 on September 1.
2. Effectiveness of the hedge is measured by comparing changes in the spot rates (intrinsic value) with changes in the forecasted cash flows based on changes in the spot rates for FC. Changes in the time value of the forward will be excluded from the assessment of hedge effectiveness. The hedge is expected to be fully effective because the critical terms (nature of

underlying, notional amounts, delivery dates, settlement date, type of currency, etc.) of the hedging instrument match the terms of the hedged item.

3. Spot rates, forward rates, and changes in value over time are as follows:

	June 1	June 30	July 31	September 1
Number of FC	100,000	100,000	100,000	100,000
Spot rate 1 FC	$0.530	$0.552	$0.570	$0.575
Forward rate for remaining time – 1 FC	$0.542	$0.560	$0.572	$0.575
Initial forward rate – 1 FC		$0.542	$0.542	$0.542
Fair value of forward contract:				
Original forward value		$ 54,200	$ 54,200	$ 54,200
Current forward value		56,000	57,200	57,500
Change—gain (loss)—in forward value		$ 1,800	$ 3,000	$ 3,300
Present value of change:				
n = 2, i = 6%/12.....................		$ 1,782		
n = 1, i = 6%/12.....................			$ 2,985	
n = 0, i = 6%/12.....................				$ 3,300
Change in value from prior period:				
Current present value..................		$ 1,782	$ 2,985	$ 3,300
Prior present value		0	1,782	2,985
Change in present value		$ 1,782	$ 1,203	$ 315
Amortization of time value		400[a]	400	400
Increase (decrease) in OCI				
		$ 2,182	$ 1,603	$ 715

[a]The time value of the forward contract is represented by original contract premium or discount. In the present case, the premium is $1,200 [100,000 × ($0.542 forward rate − $0.530 spot rate)]. Amortization of the contract premium or discount over the life of the contract can be accomplished using several methods. However, straight-line amortization is allowed by the FASB and is used throughout the text examples and end-of-chapter materials. Furthermore, other available methods are more complex than straight-line.

Using a forward contract as the hedging instrument, Illustration 6-7 presents the necessary entries to account for the cash flow hedge of the above forecasted transaction and the subsequent actual transactions.

Illustration 6-7
Using a Forward Contract as a Cash Flow Hedge of a Forecasted Transaction

The following entries relate to the hedge. There is no corresponding transaction.

June 1
Forward Contract Receivable—FC... 54,200
  Forward Contract Payable—$..   54,200
    To record purchase of contract to buy 100,000 FC at a forward rate of 1 FC = $0.542.

June 30
Forward Contract Receivable—FC... 1,782
Premium Expense 400
  OCI...   2,182
    To record change in the value of the forward contract and record the amortization of the contract premium.

July 31

Forward Contract Receivable—FC..	1,203	
Premium Expense	400	
OCI		1,603
To record change in the value of the forward contract and record the amortization of the contract premium.		

September 1

Forward Contract Receivable—FC..	315	
Premium Expense	400	
OCI		715
To record change in the value of the forward contract and record the amortization of the contract premium.		

Foreign Currency..	57,500	
Forward Contract Payable—$	54,200	
Forward Contract Receivable—FC..	57,500	
Cash		54,200

The remaining entries relate to the inventory purchase and subsequent sale. There is no hedge outstanding.

Inventory	59,225	
Cash		59,225
To record payment of 103,000 FC × $0.575.		

Inventory	20,000	
Cash		20,000
To record additional processing costs.		

October 5

Cash	95,000	
Sales Revenue		95,000
To record sale of inventory.		

Cost of Sales ($59,225 + $20,000)	79,225	
Inventory		79,225
To recognize cost of sales.		

OCI (balance)	4,500	
Cost of Sales		4,500
To adjust cost of sales by the gain accumulated in OCI.		

An analysis of the entries in Illustration 6-7 reveals that the cash flow hedge was effective in accomplishing the concerns of the U.S. company. Given the use of a forward contract, the effect of the cash flow hedge of the forecasted transaction can be summarized as follows:

	Without the Forward Contract	With the Forward Contract
Sales price of inventory	$ 95,000	$ 95,000
Cost of sales – Raw materials..................................	(59,225)	(59,225)
Cost of sales – Processing costs	(20,000)	(20,000)
Gross profit	$ 15,775	$ 15,775
		(continued)

	Without the Forward Contract	With the Forward Contract
Adjustment to cost of sales.		4,500
Adjusted gross profit	$ 15,775	$ 20,275
Unrealized loss on hedge excluded from assessment of hedge effectiveness		(1,200)
Net income effect	$ 15,775	$ 19,075

The adjusted gross profit resulting from the use of a hedge results from the following:

Sales revenue	$ 95,000
Locked in cost of sales on 100,000 FC at the spot rate of $0.530	(53,000)
No hedge on the additional cost of 3,000 FC at the transaction date spot rate of $0.575	(1,725)
Processing costs.	(20,000)
Adjusted gross profit	$ 20,275

The above gross profit of $20,275 based on the use of a forward contract is $2,000 greater than the gross profit of $18,275 traceable to the earlier hedge of a forecasted transaction using an option (Illustration 6-5). The difference is traceable to the fact that the forward contract was able to lock in the purchase of inventory at a cost of $53,000 (100,000 × $0.53 spot rate) compared to the option that locked in a cost of inventory of $55,000 (100,000 × $0.55 strike price).

Summary of Hedging Transactions

When transactions are denominated in one currency and measured in another, changes in currency exchange rates can expose the transacting party to potential exchange gains or losses. In order to reduce the uncertainty associated with exchange rate changes, forward contracts and other derivatives are often used to hedge against the exposure associated with:

- A forecasted foreign currency transaction,
- An unrecognized foreign currency commitment, or
- A recognized foreign currency denominated asset or liability.

The following table summarizes some of the details relating to these risk-management techniques.

	Transaction Is Forecasted	Commit to Transaction	Transaction Occurs
	Hedge of a Forecasted Transaction	Hedge of an Identifiable Firm Commitment	Hedge of a Denominated FC Asset or Liability
1. Type of hedge.	Cash flow hedge.	Fair value hedge or cash flow hedge. Most often fair value.	Fair value hedge or cash flow hedge. Most often fair value.
2. Basic purpose of hedge.	Hedge against changes in the cash flows due to exchange rate risk occurring between the time of the probable forecasted transaction and the resulting actual transaction.	Hedge against exchange rate risk occurring between the commitment date and the transaction date.	Hedge the exchange rate risk between the transaction date and the payment/settlement date.

(continued)

	Transaction Is Forecasted	Commit to Transaction	Transaction Occurs
	Hedge of a Forecasted Transaction	Hedge of an Identifiable Firm Commitment	Hedge of a Denominated FC Asset or Liability
3. Measurement of the value of a forward contract at a point in time.	Measured as the net present value of the difference between the notional amount at the forward rate at inception and the notional amount at the now current forward rate.	Measured as the net present value of the difference between the notional amount at the forward rate at inception and the notional amount at the now current forward rate.	Measured as the net present value of the difference between the notional amount at the forward rate at inception and the notional amount at the now current forward rate.
4. Measurement of the value of an option at a point in time.	Measured as the quoted option value.	Measured as the quoted option value.	Measured as the quoted option value.
5. Recognition over time of changes in the value of the derivative.	Changes in value are recognized as a component of other comprehensive income (OCI). When the resulting transaction affects earnings, an offsetting amount of OCI is also recognized currently in earnings.	Changes in value are recognized currently as a component of income.	Changes in value are recognized currently as a component of income.
6. Portion of the change in value of a derivative that is excluded from assessment of hedge effectiveness.	May exclude that portion traceable to the time value of the derivative.	May exclude that portion traceable to the time value of the derivative.	May exclude that portion traceable to the time value of the derivative.
7. Measurement of the time value of a derivative at inception.	For a forward contract, the difference between the initial forward rate and the initial spot rate times the notional amount. For an option, the total value of the option at inception less the intrinsic value at inception.	For a forward contract, the difference between the initial forward rate and the initial spot rate times the notional amount. For an option, the total value of the option at inception less the intrinsic value at inception.	For a forward contract, the difference between the initial forward rate and the initial spot rate times the notional amount. For an option, the total value of the option at inception less the intrinsic value at inception.
8. If excluded from the assessment of hedge effectiveness, recognition of the change in time value.	Recognized currently in earnings with an offsetting amount being recorded in OCI.	Recognized currently in earnings. There is no need to separately account for the ineffective portion.	Recognized currently in earnings. There is no need to separately account for the ineffective portion.
9. Recognition of the gain or loss on the hedged item.	No gain or loss—forecasted transaction is not recorded.	Recognized currently in earnings and results in an adjustment to the basis of the hedged transaction.	Recognized currently in earnings.
10. Measurement of the gain or loss on the hedged item.	No gain or loss—forecasted transaction is not recorded.	Measured as the change in spot or forward rates between the date of the commitment and the transaction date.	Measured as the change in spot or forward rates between the date of the commitment and the settlement date.
11. Effect on the basis of the resulting transaction.	Fixes the dollar basis of the actual transaction.	Fixes the dollar basis of the actual transaction.	None.

Disclosures Regarding Hedges of Foreign Currency Exposure

Disclosures regarding foreign currency hedges are required by the FASB as part of its broader disclosure requirements for derivative instruments and hedging activity. More specific disclosure requirements also exist for fair value and cash flow hedges.

REFLECTION

- A company may be exposed to foreign currency exchange risk in several contexts including foreign currency transactions, commitments, and/or forecasted transactions.

- In a hedge of an existing foreign currency transaction, both the hedging instrument and the hedged transaction are measured at fair value with resulting gains or losses being recognized currently in earnings.

- A hedge of a foreign currency commitment is a fair value hedge that is given special accounting treatment. Changes in the fair value of both the hedging instrument and the commitment are recognized currently in earnings. When the transaction occurs, the hedged item is adjusted for the accumulated gain or loss on the commitment.

- A hedge of a forecasted foreign currency transaction is a cash flow hedge that is given special accounting treatment. Changes in the fair value of the hedging instrument are recognized as a component of other comprehensive income (OCI). Components of OCI are subsequently recognized in earnings in the same period(s) as the actual transaction affects earnings.

UNDERSTANDING THE ISSUES

1. If the U.S. dollar was expected to strengthen relative to a foreign currency (FC), what effect might this have on a U.S. exporter?

2. A U.S. company purchases inventory from a foreign vendor, and purchases are denominated in the foreign currency (FC). The U.S. dollar is expected to weaken against the FC. Explain how a forward contract might be employed as a hedge against exchange rate risk.

3. Explain how a U.S. company's commitment to purchase inventory with settlement in foreign currency (FC) might become less attractive over time and how adverse effects on earnings could be reduced.

4. If a forecasted purchase of equipment were to be denominated in foreign currency (FC), how would the change in value of a cash flow hedge of the forecasted transaction be accounted for?

EXERCISES

Exercise 6-1 *(LO 3)* **Purchase and sale denominated in euros.** Frankfurt Engineering, Inc., a U.S. company, reconditions and sells injection molding equipment. Reconditioning facilities exist in the United States, Germany, and South Korea. The German facility had the following transactions:

a. Purchased used equipment from a French equipment broker for 200,000 euros to be paid for in 30 days on June 1, 20X5.
b. Incurred reconditioning costs of 80,000 euros uniformly throughout June 20X5.
c. Paid the French equipment broker on June 28, 20X5.

d. Sold the reconditioned equipment for 350,000 euros with terms of net 30 on July 15, 20X5.
e. Collected 350,000 euros in connection with the above sale on August 10, 20X5.

Relevant spot rates are as follows:

	1 euro =
June 1, 20X5	$1.1705
June 20X5 average	1.1707
June 28, 20X5	1.1709
July 15, 20X5	1.1710
August 10, 20X5	1.1712

Prepare the entries to record the above transactions on the books of the U.S. company.

Exercise 6-2 *(LO 2)* **Spot rates and forward rates.** On January 1, 20X5, one U.S. dollar can be exchanged for eight foreign currencies (FC). The dollar can be invested short term at a rate of 4%, and the FC can be invested at a rate of 5%.

1. Calculate the direct and indirect spot exchange rates as of January 1, 20X5.
2. Calculate the 180-day forward rate to buy FC (assume 365 days per year).
3. If the spot rate is 1 CA$ = $0.740 and the 90-day forward rate is $0.752, what does this suggest about interest rates in the two countries?
4. Explain why a weak dollar relative to the FC would likely increase U.S. exports.
5. Discuss what would happen to the forward rate if the dollar strengthened relative to the FC.

Exercise 6-3 *(LO 3, 5)* **Measuring changes in value of FC transaction and a forward contract.** Dettner Corporation purchased inventory from a foreign vendor in the amount of 75,000 FC on December 1 of the current year. On this same date, Dettner entered into a 90-day forward contract to buy FC. Dettner has a calendar year-end, and payment is due to the vendor on March 1 of the next year. When measuring changes in the current value of the forward contract, Dettner uses the present values of changes in the forward value of contracts. The discount rate is 6%.

Various spot and forward rates are as follows:

	December 1	December 31	March 1
Spot rate	$1.40	$1.43	$1.48
Forward rate	1.45	1.47	1.48

Prepare a schedule that calculates the value of accounts payable, the cumulative gain/loss on the transaction, and the forward contract for all relevant dates.

Exercise 6-4 *(LO 3, 6)* **Hedge with forward contract.** Stark Inc. placed an order for inventory costing 500,000 FC with a foreign vendor on April 15 when the spot rate was 1 FC = $0.683. Stark received the goods on May 1 when the spot rate was 1 FC = $0.687. Also on May 1, Stark entered into a 90-day forward contract to purchase 500,000 FC at a forward rate of 1 FC = $0.693. Payment was made to the foreign vendor on August 1 when the spot rate was 1 FC = $0.696. Stark has a June 30 year-end. On that date, the spot rate was 1 FC = $0.691, and the forward rate on the contract was 1 FC = $0.695. Changes in the current value of the forward contract are measured as the present value of the changes in the forward rates over time. The relevant discount rate is 6%.

1. Prepare all relevant journal entries suggested by the above facts.
2. Prepare a partial income statement and balance sheet as of the company's June 30 year-end that reflect the above facts.

Exercise 6-5 *(LO 4, 5)* **Hedge with forward contract or loan with FC payoff.** Cortez Electronics buys subassemblies from a foreign vendor. On June 1, 20X9, the company committed to acquire subassemblies costing 400,000 foreign currency units (FC). The parts will be

	Spot Rate	Forward Rate for 30 Days from November 1	Forward Rate for 60 Days from November 30
November 1	1 FC = $1.12	1 FC = $1.132	
November 15	1 FC = $1.13		
November 30	1 FC = $1.15		1 FC = $1.146
December 31...............	1 FC = $1.14		1 FC = $1.138

Required ▶ ▶ ▶ ▶ ▶   Assuming that the company's year-end is December 31, for each of the above transactions determine the current-year effect on earnings. All necessary discounting should be determined by using a 6% discount rate. For transactions C and D, the time value of the hedging instrument is excluded from hedge effectiveness and is to be separately accounted for.

Problem 6-2 *(LO 5)* **Hedge forecasted transactions, forward contracts.** Riker International is building a water purification system in Mexico that will sell for $1,200,000. Although most of the costs incurred will be paid for in U.S. dollars, the company is forecasting that several necessary purchases of project components will be denominated in foreign currency (FC). The forecasted costs are as follows:

> May 31:   Purchase of fluid movement equipment—cost of 200,000 FC with payment due June 30.
> June 30:   Purchase of standby generators—cost of 100,000 FC with payment due June 30.

On May 15, Riker acquired a forward contract to buy 300,000 FC for delivery on June 30 in order to hedge the above forecasted transactions. The time value of the forward contract will be excluded from the assessment of hedge effectiveness and amortized over the term of the contract.

Other construction costs related to the project include $300,000 in May, $200,000 in June, and $250,000 in July. The project was completed in late July, and the company was paid the selling price. The completed contract method is used to account for the project.

Selected spot and forward rates are as follows:

	Spot Rate	Forward Rate for June 30
May 15	1 FC = $1.100	1 FC = $1.108
May 31	1 FC = $1.110	1 FC = $1.112
June 30	1 FC = $1.120	1 FC = $1.120

Required ▶ ▶ ▶ ▶ ▶   1. Prepare all necessary entries for the months April through June. Use a 6% discount rate for all necessary discounting.
2. Compute the gross profit to be recognized on the above project.

Problem 6-3 *(LO 3, 5)* **Income statement effects of transactions, commitments, and hedging.** Clayton Industries sells medical equipment worldwide. On March 1 of the current year, the company sold equipment, with a cost of $160,000, to a foreign customer for 200,000 euros payable in 60 days. At the same time, the company purchased a forward contract to sell 200,000 euros in 60 days. In another transaction, the company committed, on March 15, to deliver equipment in May to a foreign customer in exchange for 300,000 euros payable in June. This equipment is anticipated to have a completed cost of $210,000. On March 15, the company hedged the commitment by acquiring a forward contract to sell 300,000 in 90 days. Changes in the value of the commitment are based on changes in forward rates and all discounting is based on a 6% discount rate.

Various spot and forward rates for the euro are as follows:

	Spot Rate	Forward Rate for 60 Days from March 1	Forward Rate for 90 Days from March 15
March 1...........................	$1.180	$1.181	
March 15	1.181	1.180	$1.179
March 31	1.179	1.178	1.177
April 30...........................	1.175		1.174

For individual months of March and April, calculate the income statement effect of: ◄ ◄ ◄ ◄ ◄ **Required**

1. The foreign currency transaction.
2. The hedge on the foreign currency transaction.
3. The foreign currency commitment.
4. The hedge on the foreign currency commitment.

Problem 6-4 *(LO 3, 6)* **Hedging foreign currency transactions and commitments.** Medical Distributors, Inc., is a U.S. company that buys and sells used medical equipment throughout the United States and Canada. During the month of June, the company had the following transactions with Canadian parties:

1. Purchased used equipment on June 1 from a hospital located in Toronto for 220,000 Canadian dollars (CA$) payable in 45 days. On the same day, the company paid $1,000 for a call option to buy 220,000 Canadian dollars during July at a strike price of 1 CA$ = $0.726. The option had a fair value of $3,200 on June 30.
2. Sold equipment on June 1 for 300,000 Canadian dollars to be paid in 30 days. At the same time, the company purchased a forward contract to sell the Canadian dollars in 30 days.
3. Committed to buy equipment on June 15 from a Montreal health care provider for 400,000 Canadian dollars in 45 days. At the same time, the company purchased a forward contract to buy 400,000 Canadian dollars in 45 days.
4. Paid 30,000 Canadian dollars on June 20 to refurbish the equipment purchased on June 1.
5. Sold the equipment purchased on June 1 on June 20 for 310,000 Canadian dollars to be received in 30 days.
6. Collected the 300,000 Canadian dollars on June 30 from the sale on June 1.

Selected spot and forward rates are as follows:

	Spot Rate 1 CA$ =	Forward Rate 1 CA$ =
June 1	$0.720	30-day sell rate = $0.729
June 15	0.729	45-day buy rate = $0.731
June 20	0.732	
June 30	0.735	30-day buy rate = $0.737

Prepare all of the necessary journal entries to record the above activities during the month of   ◄ ◄ ◄ ◄ ◄ **Required**
June. Changes in the value of the commitment are based on changes in forward rates. All necessary discounting should be determined using a 6% discount rate.

Problem 6-5 *(LO 3, 5, 6)* **FC bank loan, hedge of forecasted inventory purchase, impact on earnings.** Wagner Corporation transacts business in a number of foreign currencies and had the following activities during the current year. On July 1, the company signed a 60-day, 400,000 foreign currency A (FCA) note with a foreign bank. The note is to be repaid in FCA and bears simple interest at the rate of 7.2%. The company used the proceeds of the note to purchase manufacturing equipment. The equipment will be depreciated by the straight-line method over a useful life of 15 years (salvage value is to be ignored).

On July 15, the company committed to purchase inventory from a foreign vendor with a delivery date of August 31. Payment of 250,000 foreign currency B (FCB) is due on September 30. In order to limit its exposure on this transaction, on July 15, the company hedged the commitment by acquiring a contract to buy 250,000 FCB for delivery on September 30. Forward rates for a contract to buy FCB on September 30 are as follows:

On July 15	$1.060
On July 31	1.061
On August 31	1.068

On September 1, the company shipped (f.o.b. shipping point) inventory to a foreign customer with payment due on October 15. These items were the inventory that the company ordered on July 15, as discussed previously. The sales price was $336,000.

Selected spot rates are as follows:

	1 FCA =	1 FCB =
July 1	$0.62	
July 15		$1.04
July 31	0.66	1.05
August 1	0.65	
August 31	0.64	1.05
September 1		1.06
September 30	0.67	1.07

Required ▶ ▶ ▶ ▶ ▶

1. Prepare a schedule by month that details the effect on net income of the above transactions for the months of July, August, and September. Changes in the value of the commitment are based on changes in forward rates. Use a 6% discount rate for all necessary discounting.
2. Prepare all necessary entries through the end of July.

Problem 6-6 *(LO 5)* **Comparison of strategies: no hedge, hedge commitment, hedge transaction.** Boyd Enterprises has begun to purchase certain component parts from a foreign vendor. These purchases will be denominated in foreign currency units (FC), and the company is trying to evaluate various alternative methods of paying for the purchases. The company does not expect to order from the foreign vendor more than twice a year and with the following terms:

Commitment (order date)	30 days before delivery
Delivery	f.o.b. destination
Payment date	60 days after receipt

Various alternative methods of payment are as follows:

Option A   Do not hedge the exposed liability position.
Option B   Hedge the commitment with a forward contract due on payment date.
Option C   Hedge the transaction at delivery date versus commitment date.

The company wants to evaluate the options under two alternative assumptions regarding spot and forward rates. The assumptions are as follows:

	Assumption 1	Assumption 2
Spot rate at commitment date	$1.200	$1.20
Spot rate at delivery date	1.224	1.17
Spot rate on payment date	1.289	1.12
Spot rate 30 days after payment date	1.320	1.10
90-day forward rate at commitment date	1.210	1.18
120-day forward rate at commitment date	1.220	1.17
60-day forward rate at delivery date	1.230	1.19

Required ▶ ▶ ▶ ▶ ▶

Prepare a schedule that shows the effect on net income for each of the payment options, given the assumptions regarding exchange rates. Assume that the average purchase is for 100,000 FC. Changes in the value of the commitment are based on changes in forward rates. All necessary discounting should be determined using a 6% discount rate.

Problem 6-7 *(LO 6)* **Hedge a commitment to sell.** On February 1, Pettit Corporation committed to sell inventory with a cost of $75,000 to a foreign company for 100,000 FC. Delivery of the inventory will occur on April 1 with payment due on May 1. In anticipation of this sale, Pettit entered into a 90-day forward contract to sell 100,000 FC on May 1. Changes

in the value of the commitment are based on changes in forward rates. All necessary discounting should be determined using a 6% discount rate.

Relevant spot and forward rates are as follows:

	February 1	March 1	April 1	May 1
Spot rate	$0.90	$0.87	$0.85	$0.81
Forward rate	0.91	0.87	0.83	0.81

1. Given all of the above information, calculate what the total impact on earnings will be.
2. Prepare all relevant monthly journal entries to record the above information and reconcile the impact on earnings to your response to Requirement 1.

◄ ◄ ◄ ◄ ◄ **Required**

Translation of Foreign Financial Statements

Learning Objectives

When you have completed this chapter, you should be able to

1. Define the functional currency, and identify factors suggesting the functional currency.

2. Explain the objectives of the translation process.

3. Apply the functional currency translation process to a trial balance, and calculate the translation adjustment.

4. Explain how the translation adjustment is accounted for and how a hedge may be employed.

5. Describe the consolidation process and the sophisticated equity method, giving particular attention to modifications due to translation.

6. Apply the remeasurement process to a trial balance, and explain how to account for the remeasurement gain or loss.

7. Differentiate between the two methods for converting functional currency to the parent/investor's currency, and explain the circumstances under which each should be used.

The magnitude of U.S. investment abroad has increased significantly in response to a more global economy, a reduction in trade barriers, and the growth of international capital markets. Similarly, these same factors have encouraged an increase in foreign investment in the United States. The size and growth of these investment patterns are suggested by the following statistics.

U.S. Direct Investment Abroad: Position and Balance of Payment Flows
(in millions of dollars)

	2000	2001	2002	2003	2004
Direct investment position* at historical cost.	$1,316,247	$1,460,352	$1,616,548	$1,791,891	$2,063,998
Direct investment position at market value.	2,694,014	2,314,934	2,022,588	2,718,203	3,287,373
Capital outflows (inflows):					
Equity capital.	$ 78,041	$ 60,942	$ 42,707	$ 19,206	$ 80,686
Reinvested earnings.	77,018	52,307	65,756	1,098,344	153,822
Intercompany debt.	(12,341)	11,624	26,483	(9,634)	(5,214)
Total.	$ 142,718	$ 124,873	$ 134,946	$ 119,406	$ 229,294
Income**	$ 133,692	$ 110,029	$ 124,940	$ 171,229	$ 209,338

*Direct investment position is the value of U.S. direct investors' equity in, and net outstanding loans to, their foreign affiliates. The equity includes reinvested earnings.
**Income is the return on the direct investment position abroad. It consists of the parent's share of the foreign affiliate's net income and the net interest received by the parent on outstanding debt with the affiliate.

Source: U.S. Department of Commerce—Bureau of Economic Analysis.

The previous chapter identified a variety of transactions that may occur between a domestic (U.S.) company and a foreign entity. These transactions were not dependent on the domestic company's having any type of ownership interest in the foreign entity. However, as the preceding statistics suggest, many domestic companies do have an ownership interest in or control of foreign companies, and accounting for these interests presents special problems. The accounting treatments of domestic and foreign entity relationships that involve some degree of control are summarized as follows:

Domestic Entity	Foreign Entity	Accounting Treatment
Home office	Branch	Branch accounting
Parent	Subsidiary	Consolidated financial statements or separate financial statements
Investor	Investee	Investment in foreign entity at market or equity

The above relationships suggest the need to combine or consolidate the foreign entity financial statements with those of the domestic entity. The financial statements of a foreign entity typically are measured in the currency of that foreign country. This currency usually is different from the reporting currency of the domestic entity. Therefore, a methodology must be developed to express the foreign entity's financial statements in the reporting currency of the domestic entity. The process of expressing amounts denominated or measured in foreign currencies into amounts measured in the reporting currency (dollars) of the domestic entity (U.S.) is referred to as *foreign currency translation*.

In addition to establishing a methodology for translation, the process is complicated by the reality that the foreign financial statements may have been prepared using accounting principles that are different from those of the domestic reporting entity. There are a number of differences between generally accepted accounting principles (GAAP) employed in the United States and principles employed in financial statements of certain foreign entities. Therefore, prior to translation, the statements of a foreign entity must be adjusted to reflect the principles (GAAP) employed by the domestic reporting entity. For example, a foreign subsidiary may not be required to capitalize leases although the lease would be capitalized if GAAP followed by the parent company were employed. Before proceeding with translation, the accounting for these leases must be adjusted to conform with the principles employed by the reporting entity. The international efforts to harmonize accounting principles are eliminating the need for such adjustments.

STATEMENT OF FINANCIAL ACCOUNTING STANDARDS NO. 52

1

OBJECTIVE

Define the functional currency, and identify factors suggesting the functional currency.

In late 1981, after considering two exposure drafts, the FASB issued Statement of Financial Accounting Standards No. 52, *Foreign Currency Translation*. FASB Statement No. 52 adopted a *functional currency* approach which focuses on whether the domestic reporting entity's cash flows will be indirectly or directly affected by changes in the exchange rates of the foreign entity's currency. Assume a foreign entity operates exclusively in its own country using only its currency (see Illustration 7-1a). It is questionable whether changes in the exchange rate between its currency and that of the parent entity would directly affect the parent's cash flows. After all, how could changes in the rate of exchange between the foreign currency and the dollar affect you if your transactions were primarily denominated in the foreign currency? However, if a foreign entity operates or functions in a currency other than its own currency, exchange rate changes between these currencies presumably will directly affect cash flows of the foreign entity and ultimately the cash flows of the parent (see Illustration 7-1b). For example, if the foreign subsidiary has to convert one foreign currency into another type of foreign currency (FC-A) in order to pay a foreign supplier, this additional use of cash will ultimately affect cash flows of the parent. If the foreign subsidiary has less cash, then the parent would, in turn, expect to receive less cash from its investment in the subsidiary. In this instance, the resulting effect should be the same as if transactions were denominated in a foreign currency.

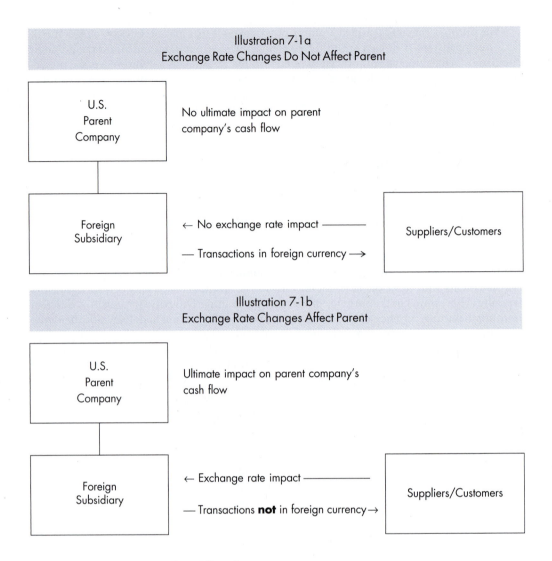

Functional Currency Identification

In order to achieve the objectives of the translation process, it is critical to identify the foreign entity's functional currency. The functional currency is the currency of the primary economic environment in which the entity generates and expends cash. For example, assume a French company that is a subsidiary of a U.S. company purchases labor and materials and pays for these items with euros (see Illustration 7-2a). The finished product of the company is sold, and payment is received in euros. In this situation, changes in the exchange rate between the euro and the dollar of the U.S. parent do not generally have an economic impact on the French company or its U.S. parent. Because of this, the French company's day-to-day operations are not dependent on the economic environment of the U.S. parent's currency (dollars). Therefore, the euro would be considered the functional currency of the French company.

The functional currency of an entity is not always that of its own country. Assume the French company discussed above received most of its debt capital in the form of dollars from an American bank and that its products were sold primarily in the United States with payment being received in dollars (see Illustration 7-2b). In this case, changes in the exchange rate between the euro and the dollar would have an impact on the French company's cash flows and ultimately those of the parent. The French company's day-to-day operations are dependent on the economic environment of the U.S. parent's currency (dollars). Changes in the foreign entity's assets and liabilities will, or will have the potential to, immediately impact the cash flows of the U.S. parent. In this case, the functional currency is that of the parent (U.S. dollars). It is important to note that a foreign entity may have a functional currency which is not its domestic currency or that of the parent entity. Thus, the French company could have the Japanese yen as its functional currency, rather than the euro or the dollar, if the yen is the currency that primarily influences the company's cash flows (see Illustration 7-2c). This might be the case if the French company's financing, sales, and purchases of goods and services are denominated in yen.

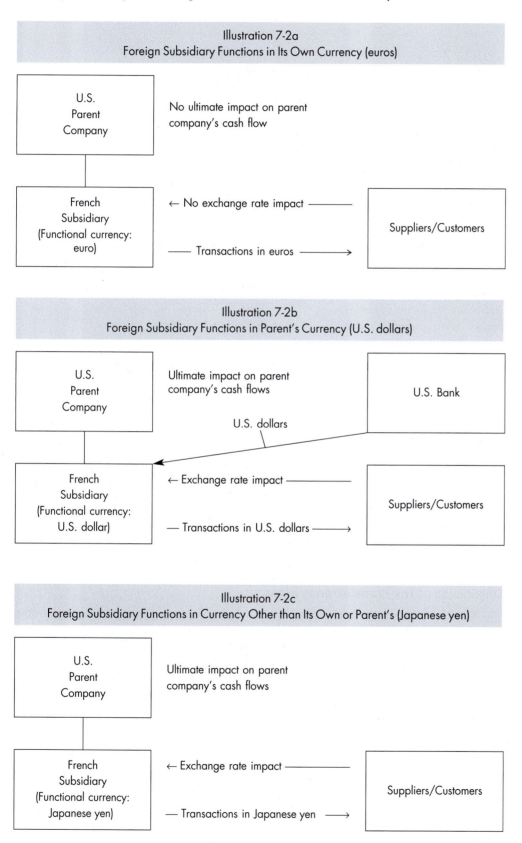

Illustration 7-2a
Foreign Subsidiary Functions in Its Own Currency (euros)

U.S. Parent Company

No ultimate impact on parent company's cash flow

French Subsidiary (Functional currency: euro)

← No exchange rate impact ———

—— Transactions in euros ———→

Suppliers/Customers

Illustration 7-2b
Foreign Subsidiary Functions in Parent's Currency (U.S. dollars)

U.S. Parent Company

Ultimate impact on parent company's cash flows

U.S. Bank

U.S. dollars

French Subsidiary (Functional currency: U.S. dollar)

← Exchange rate impact ———

—— Transactions in U.S. dollars ———→

Suppliers/Customers

Illustration 7-2c
Foreign Subsidiary Functions in Currency Other than Its Own or Parent's (Japanese yen)

U.S. Parent Company

Ultimate impact on parent company's cash flows

French Subsidiary (Functional currency: Japanese yen)

← Exchange rate impact ———

—— Transactions in Japanese yen ———→

Suppliers/Customers

Identification of the functional currency is not subject to definitive criteria. However, certain basic economic factors should be considered in making this identification.[1] Some of these factors are summarized in Exhibit 7-1.

Exhibit 7-1
Factors Suggesting the Functional Currency

Indicator	Foreign Entity's Currency Is the Functional Currency	Parent's Currency Is the Functional Currency
Cash flows	Cash flows are primarily in the currency of the foreign entity. Such flows do not impact the parent's cash flows.	Cash flows directly impact the parent's cash flows and are readily available to the parent.
Sales price	Sales prices are influenced by local factors rather than exchange rates.	Sales prices are influenced by international factors and exchange rate changes.
Sales market	There is an active and primarily local market.	The sales market is primarily in the parent's country.
Expenses	Goods and services are acquired locally and denominated in local currencies.	Goods and services are acquired from the parent's country.
Financing	Financing is secured locally and denominated in local currencies. Debt is serviced through local operations.	Financing is secured primarily from the parent or is denominated in the parent's currency.
Intercompany transaction and arrangements	Intercompany transaction volume is low. Major interrelationships between foreign and parent operations do not exist.	Intercompany transaction volume is high. There are major interrelationships between entities. A foreign entity holds major assets and obligations of the parent.

These factors should be considered both individually and collectively in order to identify the functional currency. The selection of a functional currency should be applied consistently over time, unless significant changes suggest that the functional currency has changed. Changes should not be accounted for on a retroactive basis.

Although these factors focus on the parent's currency as a possible functional currency, remember that the functional currency may be one other than that of the foreign entity or the parent.

2

OBJECTIVE

Explain the objectives of the translation process.

Objectives of the Translation Process

The focus of FASB Statement No. 52 is critical to achieving the objectives of translation. The compatibility resulting from translating various financial statements into a common reporting currency is a practical necessity. However, this process should not alter the significance of the results and relationships experienced by the individual consolidated entity. Consistent with this underlying concern, the translation process should accomplish the following objectives. The first objective is explained in this section. The second objective is explained later in the chapter.

1. Provide information that is generally compatible with the expected economic effects of a rate change on an enterprise's cash flows and equity.

---

1 Statement of Financial Accounting Standards No. 52, Foreign Currency Translation (Stamford: Financial Accounting Standards Board, 1981), par. 42.

2. Reflect in consolidated statements the financial results and relationships of the individual consolidated entities as measured in their functional currencies in conformity with U.S. generally accepted accounting principles.[2]

The first objective recognizes that exchange rate changes may or may not have any substantial or direct effect on the cash flows and economic well-being of the related entities. If the foreign entity conducts business in its own currency, exchange rate changes relative to the parent would not affect the cash flow or economic well-being of the foreign entity. Thus, translation should not impact reported income. For example, assume that a foreign subsidiary borrows 1,000 foreign currencies (FC) from a bank in order to purchase a tract of land for 1,000 FC when the rate of exchange is 1 FC = $1 (see Illustration 7-3a). If the land were to be sold for 1,000 FC when the rate of exchange is 1 FC = $0.80, 1,000 FC would be available to repay the loan. Neither the foreign entity's nor the parent's cash flows, or their economic well-being, would have been adversely affected by the change in exchange rates.

However, if the foreign entity conducts business primarily in another currency (e.g., the parent's currency), changes in the exchange rate would affect the cash flow or economic well-being of the foreign entity. Therefore, the effect of translation should be included in reported income. To illustrate, assume the same facts as in the above example except that the funds necessary to purchase the land were borrowed from a U.S. bank in dollars and then converted to FC with ultimate repayment of the loan due in dollars (see Illustration 7-3b). If the land were to be sold for 1,000 FC and the proceeds converted to U.S. dollars when 1 FC = $0.80, only $800 would be available to repay the loan. The French subsidiary would then need to use more cash in order to pay off the remaining $200 of debt. This would have a negative impact on the cash flows of the subsidiary and ultimately on those of the U.S. parent. Therefore, the change in exchange rates would have an effect on both the potential cash flows available to the parent and the parent's economic well-being. This adverse effect of the exchange rate changes should be reflected in the current-period net income.

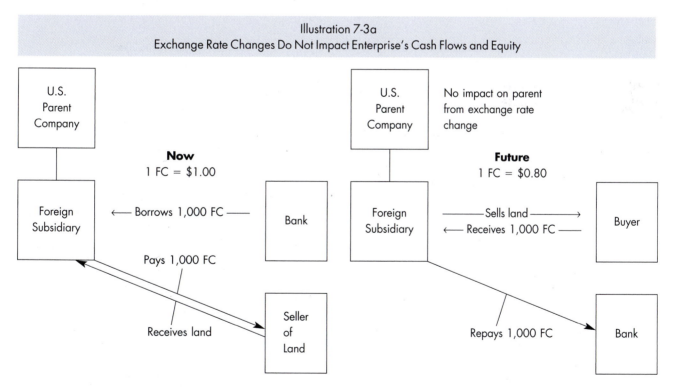

Illustration 7-3a
Exchange Rate Changes Do Not Impact Enterprise's Cash Flows and Equity

Note: Parent's net cash flow is adversely affected, so parent's economic well-being is affected.

---

2 *Ibid.*, par. 4.

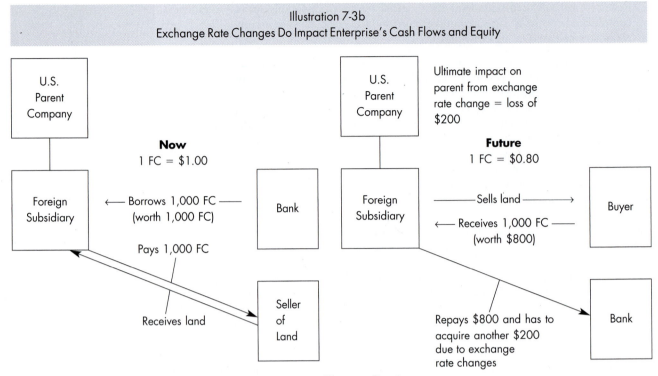

Illustration 7-3b
Exchange Rate Changes Do Impact Enterprise's Cash Flows and Equity

Note: Parent's net cash flow is adversely affected, so parent's economic well-being is affected.

The expected economic effects of rate changes must be properly reflected in financial statements and may be analyzed as follows:

Expected Economic Effect of Rate Changes	Accounting Response to Effect of Rate Changes
Cash inflows increase, and/or cash outflows decrease. Economic well-being is affected.	Translation losses should be included in net income.
Cash inflows decrease, and/or cash outflows increase. Economic well-being is affected.	Translation gains should be included in net income.
Cash inflows and/or outflows are not affected. Economic well-being is not affected.	No translation gain or loss should be included in net income. The effect of rate changes will not be realized until the parent's investment in the foreign entity is disposed of or liquidated. Therefore, the effect of translation does not affect current net income and is shown as a separate component of other comprehensive income.

Expected Economic Effects of Rate Changes when the Functional Currency Is Not the Foreign Currency. The first objective of translation seeks to provide accounting information that is consistent or compatible with the expected economic effects of rate changes. This objective is satisfied by focusing on the functional currency and may be demonstrated by consideration of the following example. Assume that a foreign subsidiary is formed on January 1, Year 1, when the rate of exchange is 1 foreign currency (FC) = $1.50. At the date of formation, the subsidiary

1. Received a $30,000 equity investment in dollars from the parent company's sale of stock;
2. Received a $120,000 loan in dollars from a U.S. bank; and
3. Purchased a parcel of land for 100,000 FC payable in dollars.

At the end of Year 1 when the rate of exchange is 1 FC = $2.00, the parcel of land is sold for 100,000 FC collectible in dollars. Shortly thereafter, dollars will be remitted to the U.S. bank and the parent.

When evaluating the factors used to identify the functional currency, it would appear that the dollar, not the foreign currency, is the functional currency, because financing is denominated in dollars, acquisitions of goods and services are paid for in dollars, and sales are receivable in dollars. Furthermore, the substance of these transactions suggests that the foreign subsidiary is merely a conduit through which the U.S. parent conducts business and experiences dollar cash flows. Therefore, if the translation process is sound, it should provide information that is compatible with the expected economic effects of rate changes. In this particular example, the translated dollar amounts for the subsidiary should be identical to the dollar balances that would have resulted had the U.S. parent engaged in these transactions without the foreign subsidiary serving as a conduit. In that case, entries in column A would have been appropriate.

Entries if the parent records the transactions—measured in U.S. dollars are as follows:

			Column A	
Jan. 1	Cash		150,000	
	Owners' Equity			30,000
	Loans Payable			120,000
	To record receipt of $30,000 from stock sale and $120,000 from loan proceeds.			
	Land		150,000	
	Cash			150,000
	To record purchase of land (100,000 × $1.50 direct rate).			
Dec. 31	Cash		200,000	
	Land			150,000
	Gain on Sale			50,000
	To record sale of land (100,000 × $2.00 direct rate).			

Resulting financial statements at year-end—measured in U.S. dollars are as follows:

Balance Sheet

Cash	$200,000
Loan payable	$120,000
Owners' equity:	
Original amount	30,000
Net income	50,000
	$200,000

Income Statement

Gain on sale	$50,000

Ratios

Debt-to-equity	1.50 to 1	(120/80)
Current ratio*	1.67 to 1	(200/120)
Return on equity	167%	(50/30)

*Assumes loan is a current liability.

If the U.S. parent engaged in the transactions through a foreign subsidiary, the entries in column B would be appropriate.

Entries if the foreign subsidiary records the transactions—measured in FC are as follows:

			Column B
Jan. 1	Cash	100,000	
	Owners' Equity		20,000
	Loans Payable		80,000
	To record receipt of $30,000 equity investment		
	($30,000 ÷ 1.5) and $120,000 loan ($120,000 ÷ 1.5)		
	when the exchange rate was 1FC = $1.50.		
	Land..	100,000	
	Cash		100,000
	To record purchase of land for 100,000 FC.		
Dec. 31	Loan Payable..	20,000	
	Exchange Gain on Loan		20,000
	To adjust $120,000 loan payable, which is denominated		
	in dollars, to an equivalent amount of FC due to change in		
	rate from 1 FC = $1.50 to 1 FC = $2.00		
	[($120,000 ÷ 2.0) − ($120,000 ÷ 1.5)].		
	Cash	100,000	
	Land.......................................		100,000
	To record sale of land for 100,000 FC.		

Resulting financial statements at year-end—measured in FC and translated into U.S. dollars are as follows:

Balance Sheet

	Foreign Currency		Relevant Exchange Rate	U.S. Dollars
Cash	100,000	FC	2.00	$200,000
Loan payable.................................	60,000	FC	2.00	$120,000
Owners' equity:				
Original amount	20,000		1.50	30,000
Net income	20,000		(see below)	50,000
	100,000	FC		$200,000

Income Statement

	Foreign Currency	Relevant Exchange Rate	U.S. Dollars
Exchange gain on loan	20,000 FC	2.00	$ 40,000
Translation adjustment		**(to balance)**	**10,000**
	20,000 FC		$ 50,000

Ratios

	Foreign Currency		Relevant Exchange Rate	U.S. Dollars
Debt-to-equity.................................	1.50 to 1	(60/40)	1.50 to 1	(120/80)
Current ratio	1.67 to 1	(100/60)	1.67 to 1	(200/120)
Return on equity...........................	100%	(20/20)	167%	(50/30)

The goal of translating the FC statements was to produce identical values to those that would have resulted if the U.S. parent had engaged in the same transactions. A comparison of the above financial statements compared to those that would have resulted had the U.S. parent recorded the transactions reveals that the values are identical. The relevant exchange rates necessary to accomplish this goal are dependent upon a proper identification of the functional currency. The first objective of the translation process has been satisfied, and the results confirm the following:

1. The foreign subsidiary merely acted as a conduit through which the U.S. parent operated.
2. The foreign subsidiary's translated financial statements are identical to those statements that would have resulted had the transactions been originally recorded in the dollar functional currency.
3. The transactions of the foreign entity had an immediate or potentially immediate impact on the dollar cash flows and equity; therefore, the impact was included in net income.

If the proceeds from the sale of the land were subsequently remitted to the U.S. bank and the parent, the proceeds of 100,000 FC collectible in dollars would result in $200,000 being available. The U.S. bank would receive $120,000 (ignoring interest for purposes of discussion). The remaining $80,000 would be distributed to the parent, which is $50,000 more than its original investment of $30,000. Therefore, the exchange rate change did have a potentially immediate effect on the cash flows and economic well-being of the parent and should be included in net income of the period in which exchange rates change. (This example parallels the one in the previous Illustration 7-2b.) Furthermore, if the rate had not changed, the proceeds of 100,000 FC collectible in dollars would have resulted in $150,000 (the rate remains at 1 FC = $1.50), of which $120,000 would have been remitted to the U.S. bank. The remaining $30,000 is the same as the parent's original investment, and clearly the absence of an exchange rate change had no effect on the parent's potentially immediate cash flows and/or economic well-being.

Expected Economic Effects of Rate Changes when the Functional Currency Is the Foreign Currency. If the foreign currency (FC) is the functional currency, rate changes are not expected to have an immediate impact on the parent's cash flows (as shown in the previous Illustration 7-3a). Therefore, in response to rate changes, the accounting information should not include any translation adjustment in the determination of current net income. Instead, translation adjustments should be classified as a separate component of other comprehensive income. This component would be recognized as a component of net income when realized through the liquidation or disposition of the foreign entity. In order to demonstrate these concepts, consider the following example:

Assume a foreign subsidiary is formed on January 1, Year 1, when the rate of exchange is 1 FC = $1.50. At the date of formation, the subsidiary

1. Received 20,000 FC from the U.S. parent;
2. Received an 80,000 FC loan from a local bank; and
3. Purchased a parcel of land from a local party for 100,000 FC.

At the end of Year 1 when the rate of exchange is 1 FC = $2.00, the parcel of land is sold to a local party for 100,000 FC.

When evaluating the factors used to identify a functional currency, it would appear that the FC is the functional currency because financing is denominated in FC, acquisitions of goods and services are paid for in FC, and sales prices are based on local economics and are collected in FC. Furthermore, the substance of these transactions suggests that the foreign subsidiary operates independently of the U.S. parent, and its day-to-day operations are not dependent on the economic environment of the U.S. parent's currency but on that of the foreign country. Consider the following analysis of the foreign entity's activities:

Entries if the foreign subsidiary records the transactions—measured in FC are as follows:

Jan. 1	Cash	100,000	
	Owners' Equity		20,000
	Loans Payable		80,000
	To record receipt of 20,000 FC from equity investment		
	and 80,000 FC from loan proceeds.		
	Land...	100,000	
	Cash		100,000
	To record purchase of land for 100,000 FC.		
Dec. 31	Cash	100,000	
	Land..		100,000
	To record sale of land for 100,000 FC.		

Resulting financial statements at year-end—measured in FC and translated into U.S. dollars (using the functional method) are as follows:

Balance Sheet

	Foreign Currency	Relevant Exchange Rate	U.S. Dollars
Cash	100,000 FC	2.00	$200,000
Loan payable................................	80,000 FC	2.00	$160,000
Owners' equity:			
Original amount	20,000	1.50	30,000
Net income	0		0
Translation adjustment—other			
comprehensive income...............		**(to balance)**	10,000
	100,000 FC		$200,000

Ratios

Debt-to-equity...............................	4.00 to 1 (80/20)	4.00 to 1 (160/40)
Current ratio	1.25 to 1 (100/80)	1.25 to 1 (200/160)
Return on equity............................	0% (0/20)	0% (0/30)

In comparing the results of the above example to that of the prior example, where the foreign entity was merely a conduit and the functional currency was the dollar, several important differences surface.

♦ The exchange rate change required an adjustment to the loan payable when the dollar was the functional currency but not when the foreign currency was the functional currency.
♦ When the FC is the functional currency, changes in the exchange rate did not produce a gain with respect to the loan because the loan is denominated in FC and rate changes have no impact on the settlement value of the loan.

◆ There is no indication that the exchange rate changes will immediately impact the parent's cash flows or equity. Therefore, to include the translation adjustment as a component of net income would not be compatible with the economic effects of the rate change. It is quite likely that the foreign entity will redeploy available cash by buying more goods and services and/or by repaying the loan. In either case, cash flows are not being remitted to the parent. Because the impact on the parent's cash flows is unclear, the translation adjustment is included as a separate component of other comprehensive income rather than as net income.

It is important to note that the translation adjustment amount may be temporary and, in fact, either increase or decrease over time. For example, if the trial balance of the subsidiary at the end of Year 2 is the same as it was at the end of Year 1 and the rate of exchange returns to 1 FC = $1.50, then the balance of the cumulative translation adjustment will be zero. However, if the exchange rate increases to 1 FC = $2.20, the balance of the cumulative translation adjustment will increase.

If there is a balance in the cumulative translation adjustment included as a component of other comprehensive income, its impact on the parent's cash flows and/or economic well-being is normally not considered to be immediate or potentially immediate unless the parent liquidates or disposes of its investment in the foreign subsidiary. At that time, the separate component of other comprehensive income should be transferred to the income statement and recognized as a component of net income. To illustrate, assume that in the above example the foreign subsidiary is liquidated after having sold the land. Keeping in mind that the FC is the functional currency, 80,000 FC of cash would be used to repay the loan (ignoring interest for purposes of discussion), and this would leave 20,000 FC of cash. In the final liquidation transaction, the 20,000 FC of cash is remitted to the parent in exchange for its equity investment. The 20,000 FC received by the parent has a value of $40,000 (assuming the exchange rate remains at 1 FC = $2.00). When compared to the historical basis of the parent's original $30,000 investment in the equity of the subsidiary, the current equity of $40,000 represents a $10,000 realized gain which may now be recognized in net income.

As a second objective of the translation process, the FASB stated that the translation process should produce (consolidated) financial statements that reflect the financial results and relationships of the individual entities as measured in their functional currency. In both of the above examples, this objective was evident by the following ratio analysis:

	First Example: U.S. Dollar = Functional Currency			Second Example: FC = Functional Currency	
	If Parent Records Statements in U.S. Dollars	If Subsidiary Records Statements in FC	Translated Statements	Statements in FC	Translated Statements
Debt-to-equity	1.50 to 1	1.50 to 1	1.50 to 1	4.00 to 1	4.00 to 1
Current ratio*	1.67 to 1	1.67 to 1	1.67 to 1	1.25 to 1	1.25 to 1
Return on equity	167%	100%	167%	0%	0%

*Assumes loan is a current liability.

The above illustrations emphasize the importance of properly identifying the functional currency. The expected economic effects of rate changes vary, and the foreign subsidiary's financial statements differ significantly, depending upon the identification of the functional currency. The translation process set forth by the FASB achieves its objectives when the functional currency is properly identified.

Relative to a parent/subsidiary relationship, a summary of the critical observations associated with the identification of the functional currency is as follows:

	When the Functional Currency	
	Is Not the Foreign Currency	Is the Foreign Currency
Nature of the subsidiary entity.	Operates as a conduit through which transactions occur in the parent's functional currency.	Operates as an independent entity through which transactions occur in the subsidiary's functional currency.
Exchange rate changes.	Affect the economic well-being of the parent.	Do not affect the economic well-being of the parent.
Effect of exchange rate changes on net income.	The effect is a gain or loss which is recognized as a component of net income.	The effect is not currently recognized as a component of net income but rather as a component of other comprehensive income.
Effect of exchange rate changes on the parent's cash flows.	Changes have an immediate or potentially immediate impact on cash flows.	Changes do not have an immediate or potentially immediate impact on cash flows. The impact on cash flows is currently unclear.
Financial relationships between accounts.	Relationships subsequent to translation are different than they were prior to translation, therefore reflecting the economic effect of exchange rate changes.	Relationships subsequent to translation retain the same values as they had prior to translation. Exchange rate changes do not have an economic effect on the parent.

Adoption of a translation method that fails to properly reflect the economic effects of rate changes may produce misleading results. Prior to FASB Statement No. 52, financial statements were subject to the major criticism that they resulted in the recognition of major translation gains and losses that distorted earnings and had no effect on cash flows. The functional currency approach adopted in FASB Statement No. 52 does not remeasure foreign operations as though they originally had been conducted in the domestic reporting currency. Rather, this approach retains the financial results and relationships that were influenced by the economic environment in which the foreign entity operates.

REFLECTION

- The functional currency is the primary currency in which an entity experiences cash inflows and outflows. Evaluating cash flows, marketing practices, financing arrangements, and procurement of necessary factors of production may identify this currency.

- Given a functional currency, the objectives of translation are to provide information that is reflective of the economic effects of exchange rate changes. Translation should also reflect the financial results and relationships of entities consistent with their functional currency and U.S. GAAP.

3

OBJECTIVE

Apply the functional currency translation process to a trial balance, and calculate the translation adjustment.

BASIC TRANSLATION PROCESS: FUNCTIONAL CURRENCY TO REPORTING CURRENCY

Before beginning the translation process, **the financial statements of the foreign entity must be adjusted to conform with generally accepted accounting principles.** Although this is a very important step in the accounting process, the specifics are not covered in this text. It is assumed that all of the adjustments to GAAP have already been made. The next step in the translation process is to identify the functional currency of the foreign entity.

- If the functional currency is determined to be the foreign entity's local currency, the *current rate method* is used to translate. This is also called the *functional* or *translation method*.

♦ If the foreign entity's local currency is not the functional currency, the *historical rate method* is used to translate. This is also called the *temporal* or *remeasurement method*.

In the following pages, both the current rate/functional method and the historical rate/temporal method will be fully illustrated.

The basic translation process is applied to a foreign subsidiary's trial balance prior to its inclusion in consolidated financial statements, home and branch combined statements, or the computation of equity income for influential foreign investments.

With respect to consolidated financial statements, recall that one of the primary criteria to determine if consolidation is appropriate deals with the extent of control the parent entity exercises over the subsidiary. For foreign subsidiaries, effective control is determined, in part, by currency restrictions and the possibility of nationalization of the operations by foreign governments. Assuming consolidation is appropriate, the financial statements of the foreign entity must be translated into dollars according to the principles expressed in FASB Statement No. 52. Then intercompany eliminations are made, and the statements are consolidated according to the principles of consolidation discussed earlier in this text.

Demonstrating the Current Rate/Functional Method

If the foreign entity's currency is the functional currency, then the current rate method would be used for translation. **The current rate/functional method requires that**

1. All assets and liabilities are translated at the current exchange rate at the date of translation.
2. Elements of income are translated at the current exchange rates that existed at the time the revenues and expense were recognized. As a practical consideration, income elements normally are translated at a weighted-average exchange rate for the period.
3. Equity accounts other than retained earnings are translated at the historical exchange rate on the date of investment in the subsidiary.
4. Retained earnings are translated in layers.
   a. Retained earnings that exist on the date of investment are translated at the historical rate on the date of investment.
   b. Income additions to retained earnings since the initial acquisition are included as translated in item (2).
   c. Reductions for dividends are translated at the historical exchange rates at the date of declaration.
5. Components of the statement of cash flows are translated at the exchange rates in effect at the time of the cash flows. Operations are translated at the rate used for income elements [see item (2) above]. The reconciliation of the change in cash and cash equivalents during the period should include the effect of exchange rate changes on cash balances.
6. The translation process will result in a cumulative translation adjustment which is classified as a component of other comprehensive income (OCI) expressed in the parent/investor's currency (U.S. dollars) rather than as a component of net income.

Illustration 7-4 demonstrates the translation of a subsidiary's financial statements, measured in its local currency (the functional currency), into U.S. dollars for the purpose of preparing consolidated financial statements and is based on the following facts:

1. Sori Corporation, a foreign corporation, began operations on January 1, 20X0. On January 1, 20X1, when net assets totaled 100,000 FC, 90% of Sori stock was acquired by Pome Corporation, a U.S. corporation. Sori's functional currency is the foreign currency, and it maintains its records in the functional currency.
2. Sales to Pome are billed in the foreign currency, and all receivables from Pome have been collected except for the amount shown in the account Due from Pome. All other sales are billed in the foreign currency as well. The level of sales and purchases was constant over the year. None of the inventory purchased from Sori remains in Pome's ending inventory.
3. Selected exchange rates between the functional currency and the dollar are as follows:

Date	Rate
January 1, 20X0	1 FC = $0.98
January 1, 20X1	1 FC = 1.00
December 31, 20X1	1 FC = 1.05
20X1 average	1 FC = 1.03

Illustration 7-4
Sori Corporation
Trial Balance Translation
December 31, 20X1

Account	Balance in Functional Currency	Relevant Exchange Rate (Dollars/FC)	Balance in Dollars
Cash	10,000 FC	1.05	$ 10,500
Accounts Receivable	21,000	1.05	22,050
Allowance for Doubtful Accounts	(1,000)	1.05	(1,050)
Due from Pome	14,000	1.05	14,700
Inventory (at Market, Cost = 32,000) . .	30,000	1.05	31,500
Prepaid Insurance	3,000	1.05	3,150
Land.	18,000	1.05	18,900
Depreciable Assets	120,000	1.05	126,000
Accumulated Depreciation	(15,000)	1.05	(15,750)
Cost of Goods Sold	180,000	1.03	185,400
Depreciation Expense	10,000	1.03	10,300
Income Tax Expense	30,000	1.03	30,900
Other Expenses	23,000	1.03	23,690
Total (Note B).	443,000 FC		$460,290
Accounts Payable	20,000 FC	1.05	$ 21,000
Taxes Payable	30,000	1.05	31,500
Accrued Interest Payable	1,000	1.05	1,050
Mortgage Payable—Land	10,000	1.05	10,500
Common Stock	80,000	1.00	80,000
Retained Earnings (January 1, 20X1) . .	20,000	Note A	20,000
Sales—Pome	80,000	1.03	82,400
Sales—Other	200,000	1.03	206,000
Gain on Sale of Depreciable Assets. . . .	2,000	1.03	2,060
Cumulative Translation Adjustment (to balance)			**5,780**
Total (Note B).	443,000 FC		$460,290

Note A: The beginning balance of retained earnings normally is equal to the translated value of the previous period's ending retained earnings. However, since 20X1 is the first year Pome has owned Sori, the beginning balance is set equal to the January 1, 20X1 (acquisition date), balance of retained earnings in foreign currency translated at the January 1, 20X1, spot rate (in this case, 1.00). The balance sheet for 20X1 would show a translated value for retained earnings equal to the translated beginning balance of retained earnings plus the translated value of net income less dividends translated at the rate existing on the declaration date.

Note B: If the accounts in this trial balance were arranged in balance sheet and income statement order, the following totals would be calculated:

Total revenues and gains.	282,000 FC	$290,460
Total expenses.	243,000	250,290
Net income	39,000 FC	$ 40,170
Total assets	200,000 FC	$210,000

Total liabilities	61,000 FC	$ 64,050
Total equity (including NI)	139,000	140,170
Total liabilities and equity (including NI)	200,000 FC	$204,220
Cumulative translation adjustment to balance . . .		5,780
Total liabilities and equity (December 31, 20X1)	200,000 FC	$210,000

Accounting for the Cumulative Translation Adjustment.

Translation adjustments result from the process of translating foreign financial statements from their functional currency into the domestic entity's reporting currency. Because various exchange rates (current, historical, and weighted-average) are used in the translation process, the basic equality of the balance sheet equation is not preserved. Therefore, from a mechanical viewpoint, the translation adjustment is an amount necessary to balance a translated entity's trial balance. Translation adjustments do not exist in terms of the functional currency and have no immediate effect on the cash flows of the foreign or domestic entity. At the time of the translation, exchange rate fluctuations do not have an economic impact on the foreign entity or its domestic parent. Furthermore, any potential impact on the reporting (parent) entity is uncertain and remote. Therefore, as discussed above, it would be improper to include the translation adjustment in current reported net income. However, the translation adjustment must be reported somewhere. Rather than being included as a component of reported earnings, the translation should be included as a component of other comprehensive income. It is important to remember that the translation adjustment on the trial balance is a cumulative amount which changes from period to period.

Direct Calculation of the Current Period Translation Adjustment.

Although the translation adjustment is a balancing amount necessary to satisfy the balance sheet equation, the current period's (not cumulative) adjustment may be calculated directly as follows:

1. The change in exchange rates during the period multiplied by the amount of net assets (i.e., owners' equity) held by the domestic investor at the beginning of the period; plus
2. The difference between the weighted-average exchange rate used in translating income elements and the end-of-period exchange rate multiplied by the increase or decrease in net assets for the period traceable to net income, excluding capital transactions; plus (minus)
3. The increase (decrease) in net assets as a result of capital transactions, including investments by the domestic investor during the period (e.g., stock issuances, retirements, and dividends), multiplied by the difference between the end-of-period exchange rate and the exchange rate at the time of the transaction.

Based on the information given in Illustration 7-4, the direct calculation of the translation adjustment is as follows:

Reconciliation of Annual Translation Adjustment

Net assets at beginning of period multiplied by the change in exchange rates during the period [0[a] × ($1.05 − $1.00)]	$ 0
Increase in net assets (excluding capital transactions) multiplied by the difference between the current rate and the average rate used to translate income [39,000 FC[b] × ($1.05 − $1.03)]	780
Increase in net assets due to capital transactions (including investments by the domestic investor) multiplied by the difference between the current rate and the rate at the time of the capital transaction [100,000 FC[c] × ($1.05 − $1.00)]	5,000
Translation adjustment	$5,780

[a]Although Sori Corporation began operations in 20X0, the parent company, Pome Corporation, had not acquired an interest until 20X1. Therefore, Pome had no investment in Sori as of the beginning of 20X1.
[b]This is the net income for the period (see Illustration 7-4).
[c]This is the original capital balance as of the date of the parent's acquisition.

4

OBJECTIVE

Explain how the translation adjustment is accounted for and how a hedge may be employed.

The above reconciliation is not a required disclosure but may help in understanding the factors which contribute to the translation adjustment. Note that the reconciliation explains only the $5,780 translation adjustment traceable to 20X1. After the first year of operation, the annual translation adjustments will be accumulated and presented as a component of other comprehensive income. For example, if Sori Corporation has a translation adjustment of $4,400 traceable to 20X2, the accumulated other comprehensive income portion of equity on the balance sheet at the end of 20X2 will show a cumulative translation adjustment of $10,180 ($5,780 + $4,400).

Accomplishing the Objectives of Translation. The translation demonstrated in Illustration 7-4 has accomplished the objectives of translation as presented in FASB Statement No. 52. The economic effect of the exchange rate change (i.e., translation adjustment) has been presented as an increase in stockholders' equity. The spot rate had increased from a beginning-of-year rate of 1 FC = $1.00 to an end-of-period rate of 1 FC = $1.05. This change indicates that the foreign currency strengthened relative to the dollar. Therefore, the domestic company's investment in the net assets of the foreign subsidiary has increased as evidenced by the increase in stockholders' equity. However, because the foreign entity's currency is the functional currency, exchange rate changes do not have an immediate effect on the cash flows of the foreign or domestic entity. Thus, the translation adjustment is not reported as a component of current net income but rather as a component of other comprehensive income. Therefore, the presentation is compatible with the expected economic effects of exchange rate changes. In addition, the translated financial statements reflect the same financial results and relationships of the foreign company as originally measured in its functional currency. For instance, the following ratios indicate that the original relationships have been preserved after translation:

Ratio	Before Translation	After Translation
Current	1.51 (77,000 ÷ 51,000)	1.51 (80,850 ÷ 53,550)
Debt-to-equity	0.44 (61,000 ÷ 139,000)*	0.44 (64,050 ÷ 145,950)**
Gross profit percent	36% (100,000 ÷ 280,000)	36% (103,000 ÷ 288,400)

 *See Illustration 7-4, Note B.
**After translation equity includes the cumulative translation adjustment ($140,170 + $5,780).

Subsequent Recognition of the Translation Adjustment. Although translation adjustments have no immediate effect on reported earnings, they may ultimately affect income when there is a *partial or complete sale or complete or substantially complete liquidation of the investment in the foreign entity.*[3] Unfortunately, the FASB has not defined what constitutes a substantially complete liquidation. Given such a sale or liquidation, some or all of the accumulated translation adjustment included in equity would be removed and included as part of the gain or loss on disposition of the investment. For example, assume a company owns 100% of a foreign entity, its investment account has a balance of $4,200,000, and its owners' equity includes accumulated other comprehensive income containing a debit of $320,000 representing the accumulated translation adjustment. If the entire investment in the subsidiary is sold for $4,750,000, the translation adjustment does affect the gain on sale as follows:

Proceeds from sale of investment.................	$ 4,750,000
Basis of investment account.....................	(4,200,000)
	$ 550,000
Balance in cumulative translation adjustment	(320,000)
Gain on sale of investment......................	$ 230,000

It is important to note that if only a portion of the investment in the subsidiary were sold, then only a pro rata portion of the translation adjustment would have been allocated to the sale.

---

3 See FASB Interpretation No. 37, *Accounting for Translation Adjustments upon Sale of Part of an Investment in a Foreign Entity* (Norwalk, CT: Financial Accounting Standards Board, 1983) and Statement of Financial Accounting Standards No. 52, *op. cit.,* pars. 110 and 119.

Consolidating the Foreign Subsidiary

5

OBJECTIVE

Describe the consolidation process and the sophisticated equity method, giving particular attention to modifications due to translation.

Once a foreign subsidiary's financial statements have been translated into the reporting currency, certain eliminations and adjustments due to intercompany transactions generally will be required. With regard to the exchange rate that should be used to translate such transactions, the FASB concluded that **all intercompany balances, except for intercompany profits and losses, should be translated at the rates used for all other accounts. Intercompany profits and losses should be translated using the exchange rate that existed at the date of the sale or transfer.** As a practical matter, however, *average rates or approximations may be used* to translate such profits and losses.

The facts of Illustration 7-4 are used here to demonstrate the consolidation process. Assume Pome Corporation paid 105,000 FC for its 90% interest in Sori Corporation. Recall that at the time of acquisition (January 1, 20X1), Sori equity consisted of 80,000 FC of common stock and 20,000 FC of retained earnings. Upon acquisition of Sori, Pome recorded its investment as follows:

Investment in Sori..	105,000	
Cash (105,000 × $1.00)		105,000

Assuming that any excess is traceable to patents with a 10-year useful life, the excess of cost over book value is determined as follows:

Price paid		105,000 FC
Equity purchased:		
Common stock..	80,000 FC	
Retained earnings	20,000	
Total...	100,000 FC	
90% Interest acquired		90,000
Excess cost traceable to patents....................................		15,000 FC

Notice that the determination of excess is calculated in the foreign currency. The excess will be translated into the parent's currency separately. Assume that Pome used the simple equity method to account for its investment in Sori. The following translation would be required to determine the subsidiary income recorded by Pome. Note that under the current rate method the weighted-average exchange rate for the year is used to translate income items.

Account	Balance in Functional Currency	Relevant Exchange Rate (Dollars/FC)	Balance in Dollars
Sales—Pome.............................	80,000 FC	1.03	$ 82,400
Sales—Other.............................	200,000	1.03	206,000
Gain on Sale of Depreciable Assets	2,000	1.03	2,060
Cost of Goods Sold	(180,000)	1.03	(185,400)
Depreciation Expense	(10,000)	1.03	(10,300)
Income Tax Expense	(30,000)	1.03	(30,900)
Other Expenses (including interest)	(23,000)	1.03	(23,690)
Net Income	39,000 FC		$ 40,170
Pome's share		×	90%
Pome's interest in Sori net income (in dollars)			$ 36,153

The parent's entry to record its interest in the foreign subsidiary's undistributed income would be as follows:

Investment in Sori..	36,153	
Subsidiary Income		36,153

Worksheet 7-1: page 406

Worksheet 7-1, pages 406 and 407, shows the consolidated financial statements of the Pome and Sori corporations. The trial balance amounts for Pome are assumed, and Sori's balances are based on Illustration 7-4. Entries (CY1) and (EL) in the worksheet follow the usual procedures of eliminating the current-period entry recording the parent's share of the subsidiary net income and its share of the subsidiary equity accounts as of the beginning of the period. Entry **(CT)** allocates 90% of Sori's cumulative adjustment to the controlling interest. These entries do not require any translating because the balances being eliminated have already been translated into U.S. dollars.

Entries (D) and (A) for the distribution of asset markups and their amortizations, however, do require translation. The calculations for entry (D) are as follows:

Distribution of Asset Markup	FC	Exchange Rate	U.S. Dollars
Accounts:			
Depreciable Assets and Patents......................	15,000	1.05*	$15,750 DR
Investment in Sori Corporation	15,000	1.00**	15,000 CR
Cumulative Translation Adjustment—Pome (to balance).....			750 CR

*Use the current exchange rate for asset markup as used in the current rate method for all asset accounts.
**Use the date of investment exchange rate for crediting the investment account because the objective of the entry is to eliminate this balance, and it was initially recorded at a 1.00 exchange rate.

Calculations for entry (A) are as follows:

Amortization of Asset Markups	FC	Exchange Rate	U.S. Dollars
Accounts:			
Accumulated Depreciation and Amortization (15,000/10)...	1,500	1.05*	$1,575 CR
Depreciation and Amortization Expense..................	1,500	1.03**	1,545 DR
Cumulative Translation Adjustment—Pome (to balance)......			30 DR

*Use the current exchange rate for accumulated depreciation and amortization as used in the current rate method for all asset accounts.
**Use the weighted-average exchange rate for expenses as used in the current rate method for all income items.

Entries (IA) and (IS) follow the usual worksheet eliminations and adjustments for intercompany transactions and require no additional translation.

The consolidation procedures just discussed also are applicable to periods subsequent to the first year of acquisition. Although the methodology is the same, the following should be noted:

1. The parent must continue to recognize its interest in the amortization of any original excess of cost over book value.
2. Any additional cumulative adjustment traceable to the excess of cost over book value should continue to be recognized.

When consolidating a foreign subsidiary, special attention must be paid to the elimination of intercompany profits. This is true only when the foreign entity's currency is the functional currency. The problem arises because the exchange rates used to translate receivables and payables resulting from intercompany transactions are different from the rates which existed at the date of the intercompany transaction. In order to illustrate this point, assume that a U.S. parent sold inventory to a foreign subsidiary and that none of the inventory had been sold by the subsidiary as of the end of the period. In the consolidation process, it would be appropriate to eliminate the parent's receivable and the subsidiary's corresponding payable. Furthermore, the unrealized intercompany profit on the unsold inventory must also be eliminated. For purposes of discussion, assume that the intercompany transaction is denominated in foreign currencies in the amount of 1,000 FC and that relevant exchange rates are as follows:

Date of sale   1 FC = $1.00   End of period   1 FC = $1.20

Relevant balances at the end of the period would be as follows:

	Value in FC	Exchange Rate	Value in U.S. Dollars
Parent's Accounts			
Accounts Receivable	1,000	1.20	$1,200
Sales Revenue	1,000	1.00	1,000
Cost of Sales (assume 80%)			800
Subsidiary's Accounts (translated using current rate method):			
Accounts Payable	1,000	1.20	$1,200
Inventory	1,000	1.20	1,200

It is clear from the preceding schedule of account balances that the dollar values of the parent's accounts receivable and the subsidiary's accounts payable are equal and could be eliminated against each other. However, the problem arises with the elimination of the unrealized intercompany profit included in the ending inventory of the subsidiary. If the profit of 20% were eliminated using the translated value of the inventory, then $240 (20% × $1,200) of profit would be eliminated, which does not agree with the $200 of intercompany profit which actually existed at the date of the transaction. However, if the intercompany profit is eliminated using the rate of exchange which existed at the date of the transaction, no inconsistency exists. At the date of the transaction, the inventory had a dollar equivalent of $1,000 (1,000 FC × $1), and the 20% unrealized profit of $200 (20% × $1,000) would be the appropriate amount of profit to eliminate against the parent's gross profit of $200 (sales revenue of $1,000 versus the cost of sales of $800). Therefore, the exchange rate at the date of the original transaction must *always* be used to determine the amount of unrealized profit to be eliminated. Once again, this complication will be encountered only when translating from the functional currency into the parent's reporting currency.

Gains and Losses Excluded from Income

The other comprehensive income section of equity in which cumulative translation adjustments are reported also should include gains and losses attributable to:

1. Foreign currency transactions that are designated and effective as economic hedges of a net investment in a foreign entity, beginning with the designation date.
2. Intercompany foreign currency transactions that are long-term investments in nature (i.e., settlement is not planned or anticipated in the foreseeable future) when the entities involved in the transaction are consolidated, combined, or accounted for by the equity method in the reporting enterprise's financial statements.[4]

Foreign Currency Transactions as Hedges of a Net Investment in a Foreign Entity. When translating foreign financial statements from their functional currency into dollars, a translation adjustment is produced and classified as a component of other comprehensive income (OCI). Noting that OCI is a component of owners' equity, the translation adjustment has the effect of either increasing or decreasing the parent company's equity as a result of its net investment in the foreign subsidiary. A parent company would certainly want to minimize any adverse impact on equity and may decide to hedge against such impacts. This is referred to as a hedge of a net investment in a foreign entity. Not knowing whether the impact of translation on equity will be positive or negative, some companies hedge net investments as a matter of policy. Such hedges may be accomplished through the use of a nonderivative or derivative instrument. The purpose of the hedging strategy is to offset the negative (positive) effect of the translation adjustment on the net investment with the gain (loss) on the hedging instrument. Statement of Financial Accounting Standards (SFAS) No. 133, as amended by SFAS No. 138, states that the gain or loss on a designated and effecitve hedge of a net investment should be classified in the same

---

manner as is the translation adjustment. Therefore, if the translation adjustment is classified as a component of other comprehensive income, the gain or loss on the accompanying hedge would also be classified as a component of other comprehensive income. As discussed in a subsequent section of this chapter, in some instances, the translation adjustment may be classified as a component of net income. In these instances, the gain or loss on a hedge of a net investment would also be similarly classified.

In order to demonstrate a hedge of a net investment in a foreign entity, recall the facts surrounding Illustration 7-4 and Worksheet 7-1. The facts supporting Illustration 7-4 were based on a parent company (Pome Corporation) acquiring a 90% interest in a subsidiary company (Sori Corporation) when the subsidiary's net equity was 100,000 FC. Initially not knowing whether the translation adjustment would have a positive or negative impact on equity, assume that the parent company, as a matter of policy, hedged its net investment in the foreign subsidiary. Assume that in order to hedge its investment on January 1, 20X1, the parent company secured a foreign bank loan denominated in the foreign currency when the spot rate was 1 FC = $1.00. The bank loan has a principal amount of 90,000 FC (90% of the subsidiary's equity). Interest calculations are ignored for purposes of this example. The bank loan is designated as a hedge of the net investment and is considered to have satisfied all necessary criteria. Because exchange rates have changed, the value of the hedging instrument has also changed as follows:

Value of loan payable at December 31, 20X1 (90,000 FC × $1.050) . . .	$94,500
Value of loan payable at inception (90,000 FC × $1.000)	90,000
Change in value of loan payable	$ 4,500

The entry to record the change in value of the payable is as follows:

Translation Adjustment (OCI)	4,500	
Loan Payable		4,500

Illustration 7-4 presented the translation of a foreign subsidiary's (Sori Corporation) financial statements into dollars. The translation resulted in a current-year translation adjustment of $5,780. The net amount of the translation adjustment that impacts the parent company's (Pome Corporation) OCI is determined as follows based on Worksheet 7-1:

Current-year translation adjustment (from Illustration 7-4)	$5,780
Portion allocated to noncontrolling interest (Worksheet 7-1)	(578)
Subtotal	$5,202
Increase due to distribution of excess and amortization	
[Worksheet 7-1 entry (D)]	750
Decrease due to amortization of excess	
[Worksheet 7-1 entry (A)]	(30)
Current-year translation adjustment allocated to parent company	$5,922

The above $5,922 translation adjustment would be shown as a component of the parent's OCI. Offset against this amount would be the $4,500 traceable to the hedge of the net investment. Therefore, the hedge was considered to be effective.

Note that the effectiveness of the hedging instrument (the FC denominated bank loan) against the net investment in the subsidiary is as follows:

Effect on parent's OCI of translation	$5,922	credit
Effect on OCI of hedge on net investment	4,500	debit
Net effect on OCI.	$1,422	credit

If the change in the value of the hedging instrument exceeds the related translation adjustment recognized during the period of the hedge, the excess is ineffective and recognized in earnings. In the above example, none of the hedge was ineffective. However, if the hedge had involved a loan for 130,000 FC, the change in the value of the loan payable would have been $6,500 [130,000 FC × ($1.05 − $1.00)] which would have exceeded the related translation adjustment. Therefore, the excess change in value that does not offset the translation adjustment would be recognized in current earnings.

The foreign currency strengthened against the dollar resulting in an increase in equity due to the translation adjustment. In retrospect, the parent should not have hedged its investment even though the hedge was effective in offsetting the effect on OCI of the translation. Once again, we are reminded that exchange rates may not actually change as one had hoped or anticipated.

The above example involved the hedge of a net investment with a nonderivative instrument. However, it is also possible to employ a derivative instrument such as a forward contract or foreign currency option and be accorded the same accounting treatment.

Intercompany Foreign Currency Transactions of a Long-Term Nature. The second example of an exchange gain or loss that may be excluded from income and be included as a component of equity relates to certain long-term investment transactions between a domestic company and its foreign subsidiary. For example, assume a U.S. parent borrows funds from a French subsidiary with the loan being denominated in euros. If the settlement of the loan is not planned or anticipated in the foreseeable future, the effect of rate changes on the loan also would not have a foreseeable effect on the income of the U.S. parent. Therefore, the effect of rate changes on long-term investment transactions should be reflected in owners' equity as other comprehensive income, not current net income.

Unconsolidated Investments: Translation for the Cost or Equity Method

Unconsolidated foreign investments are accounted for by either the cost method or the sophisticated equity method. Under the cost method, a complete translation of the foreign financial statements is not necessary. The parent company must record the cost basis of its investment in dollars. If the cost is incurred in foreign currency, the exchange rate at the date of acquisition should be used. Investment income is translated at the exchange rate at the date dividends are declared.

If the parent's interest in the foreign subsidiary is considered influential, the subsidiary will not be consolidated and the sophisticated equity method should be employed. This method requires the adjustment of subsidiary income or loss for the amortization of differences between book and market values of the investment and any intercompany profits or losses. Application of this method to an investment in a foreign entity will be demonstrated using the facts of Illustration 7-4.

Assume Pome Corporation paid 35,000 FC ($35,000) for a 30% interest in Sori Corporation on January 1, 20X1. Furthermore, assuming that any excess is traceable to patents with a 10-year useful life, the excess of cost over book value is determined as follows:

Price paid		35,000 FC
Equity purchased:		
Common stock	80,000 FC	
Retained earnings	20,000	
Total	100,000 FC	
30% Interest acquired		30,000
Excess cost traceable to patents		5,000 FC

Pome's interest in the adjusted net income of Sori is calculated as follows:

Sori net income translated into dollars	$40,170
Pome's share	× 30%
Pome's interest in Sori net income	$12,051
Amortization of excess related to the patents	
(5,000 FC ÷ 10 years × $1.03 average rate)	(515)
Pome's equity share of Sori net income adjusted for amortization of excess	$11,536

The investor also must recognize its interest in the cumulative translation adjustment for 20X1, calculated as follows:

Cumulative translation adjustment (from Illustration 7-4)	$5,780
Pome's share	× 30%
Pome's interest in the cumulative translation adjustment	$1,734

The following entries are to record Pome's interest in the foreign entity under the sophisticated equity method:

20X1				
Jan. 1	Investment in Sori Corporation		35,000	
	Cash			35,000
	To record the initial investment of 35,000 FC			
	when the spot rate was 1 FC = $1.00.			
Dec. 31	Investment in Sori Corporation		13,270	
	Subsidiary Income			11,536
	Cumulative Translation Adjustment			1,734
	To record share of net income adjusted for the			
	amortization of excess and share of cumulative			
	translation adjustment.			

Notice that under the sophisticated equity method the investor recorded both the amortization of the excess of cost over book value and its share of the current year's translation adjustment.

REFLECTION

- If the foreign entity's currency is the functional currency, the current rate method is used and the translation process is as follows: all assets and liabilities are translated at current rates, net income at weighted-average rates, and equity accounts (excluding retained earnings) at historical rates.

- The translation is based on the premise that changes in exchange rates will have no immediate effect on the cash flows or economic well-being of the foreign entity or parent/ investor. Therefore, the resulting translation adjustment is classified as a component of other comprehensive income and generally is not recognized in current earnings until there is a sale or liquidation of the foreign subsidiary.

- The net investment in a foreign entity may be hedged and the change in value of the hedging instrument will be recognized as a component of other comprehensive income.

- The consolidation of a parent and a foreign subsidiary involves special adjustments involving the excess over cost and the elimination of intercompany profits. Under the sophisticated equity method, the parent must recognize its proportional interest in the translation adjustment.

REMEASURED FINANCIAL STATEMENTS: FOREIGN CURRENCY TO FUNCTIONAL CURRENCY

6

OBJECTIVE

Apply the remeasurement process to a trial balance, and explain how to account for the remeasurement gain or loss.

The previous illustrations of the translation process assumed that the currency of the foreign entity was the functional currency. However, there are certain instances when the functional currency is not the currency of the foreign entity. In these instances, the financial statements of the foreign entity must be remeasured into the functional currency before the financial statements can be translated into the parent's domestic currency. The remeasurement process is intended to produce financial statements that are the same as if the foreign entity's transactions had been originally recorded in the functional currency. In essence, *the historical exchange rates between the functional currency and the foreign currency are used to remeasure certain accounts.* The adjustment resulting from the remeasurement process is referred to as a *remeasurement gain or loss* and is included as a component of net income.

If the foreign entity's currency is not the functional currency, then the historical rate method is used for remeasurement/translation. The historical rate/temporal method requires that:

1. Monetary assets and all liabilities are translated at the current exchange rate at the date of translation. All other assets are translated at the historical exchange rate on the date the assets were acquired. (Use the historical rate on the date of the investment if assets were acquired before the investment was made in the foreign entity.)
2. Elements of income are translated at the weighted-average exchange rate for the period except for items that can be specifically identified with a date of acquisition. For example, use the historical rate on the date inventory and fixed assets were acquired for translating cost of goods sold and depreciation expense, respectively.
3. Equity accounts are translated as they were for the current method.
    a. Equity and retained earnings balances on the date of investment are translated at the historical exchange rate on that date.
    b. Income additions to retained earnings are included as translated in item (2).
    c. Dividend deductions to retained earnings are translated at the historical exchange rates at the date of declaration.
4. The remeasurement process will result in a remeasurement gain or loss that is classified as a component of net income expressed in the functional currency rather than as a component of other comprehensive income.

The remeasurement process is encountered in two situations. One situation arises when the entity's books of record (accounting records) and resulting financial statements are prepared in a currency that is not the functional currency. Another situation arises when the foreign entity is in a highly inflationary economy. In that case, the functional currency is the domestic entity's reporting currency (dollars for U.S. parent companies).

Books of Record Not Maintained in Functional Currency

Perhaps one of the most common situations in which the books of record are not maintained in the functional currency is when the functional currency is the parent/investor's currency. For example, assume that a U.S. company has a Mexican subsidiary. That parent invested dollars in that subsidiary, and dollar-denominated loans were arranged on behalf of the subsidiary. As shown in Illustration 7-5, the Mexican company acquires raw materials from Japanese suppliers that are paid in U.S. dollars and sells the manufactured products throughout Central and North America. The subsidiary's sales are denominated in dollars, and distributions of earnings are remitted to the parent in dollars. Based on the above information, it is clear that the Mexican company's functional currency is the U.S. dollar even though it maintains its books of record (BR) in Mexican pesos.

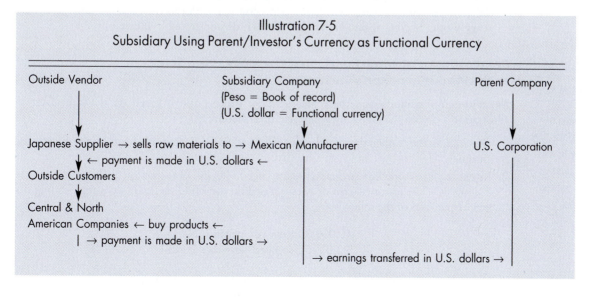

Illustration 7-5
Subsidiary Using Parent/Investor's Currency as Functional Currency

| Outside Vendor | Subsidiary Company (Peso = Book of record) (U.S. dollar = Functional currency) | Parent Company |

Japanese Supplier → sells raw materials to → Mexican Manufacturer   U.S. Corporation
    ↓ ← payment is made in U.S. dollars ←
Outside Customers
    ↓
Central & North
American Companies ← buy products ←
    | → payment is made in U.S. dollars →
                                          | → earnings transferred in U.S. dollars →

It is also possible that a foreign entity that maintains its books of record in its domestic currency may have a functional currency that is not the parent/investor's currency. For instance, as shown in Illustration 7-6, assume a Mexican subsidiary of an American company purchases materials from Belgian vendors with amounts due payable in euros. The materials are assembled in Mexico and then returned to Belgium for resale. Sales revenues are collected in euros. Considering the factors used to identify the functional currency, the euro would be the Mexican company's functional currency. However, the Mexican company maintains its books of record (accounting records) in pesos although its functional currency is the euro. In this example, a two-step process is involved. First, the financial statements prepared in pesos would have to be remeasured into euros, the functional currency. Second, the remeasured financial statements would have to be translated into dollars.

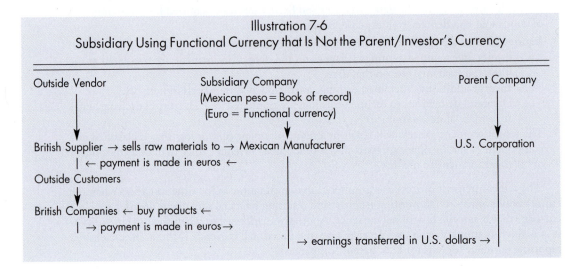

Illustration 7-6
Subsidiary Using Functional Currency that Is Not the Parent/Investor's Currency

If the books of record are not maintained in the functional currency, a remeasurement process, which differs significantly from the functional currency approach of FASB Statement No. 52, is employed in order to express trial balance amounts in the functional currency.

Furthermore, *the adjustment resulting from the remeasurement is included as a component of net income rather than as a component of other comprehensive income.* It is important to remember that once the trial balance is remeasured into the functional currency, further translation may or may not be necessary. Possible scenarios are as follows:

1. Books of record currency (not U.S. dollars) remeasured to U.S. dollar functional currency. Therefore, no further translation is necessary. This is demonstrated in Illustration 7-7.

2. Books of record currency (not U.S. currency) remeasured into functional currency (not U.S. dollars). Therefore, further translation is necessary in order to translate the functional currency (not U.S. dollars) into U.S. dollars. This is demonstrated in Illustration 7-8.

Remeasurement when Functional Currency Is the Same as the Parent/Investor's Currency

Illustration 7-7 demonstrates the remeasurement process and is based on the same facts as Illustration 7-4 with the following additional information:

1. The U.S. dollar, rather than the books of record (BR), is determined to be the functional currency.

2. Inventory is recorded at its market value of 30,000 FC even though its historical cost is 32,000 FC. The historical cost of sales is based on the FIFO method of costing. Ending inventory consists of the following:

10,000 FC acquired October 1, 20X1
22,000 FC acquired November 1, 20X1

3. The prepaid insurance represents amounts that were incurred on October 1, 20X1.
4. The depreciable assets, with 10-year lives, were acquired as follows:

> 80,000 FC acquired on January 1, 20X0*
> 60,000 FC acquired on July 1, 20X1
>
> *20,000 FC of these assets were sold on July 1, 20X1, for $19,760 U.S.

5. The cost of sales consists of the following purchases:

> 20,000 FC acquired December 1, 20X0
> 60,000 FC acquired March 1, 20X1
> 80,000 FC acquired July 1, 20X1
> 20,000 FC acquired October 1, 20X1

6. The other expenses include 3,000 FC of insurance expense that was originally prepaid on October 1, 20X1. The balance of other expenses was incurred uniformly throughout the year.
7. The land and the related mortgage were acquired on March 1, 20X1.
8. Selected exchange rates between the FC and the U.S. dollar functional currency are as follows:

Jan. 1, 20X0	1 FC = $0.98	July 1, 20X1	1 FC = $1.04
July 1, 20X0	1 FC = 1.01	Oct. 1, 20X1	1 FC = 1.045
Dec. 1, 20X0	1 FC = 0.99	Nov. 1, 20X1	1 FC = 1.043
Jan. 1, 20X1	1 FC = 1.00	Dec. 31, 20X1	1 FC = 1.05
Mar. 1, 20X1	1 FC = 1.015	20X1 average	1 FC = 1.03

A special remeasurement rule is necessary for inventory when the rule of cost or market value, whichever is lower, is applied. Before the rule is applied, the inventory cost and market values must be expressed in the functional currency. A possible result is for an inventory write-down to occur in the functional currency, even if no write-down is suggested in the books of record currency. It also is possible for a write-down in the books of record currency to no longer be appropriate in the functional currency. This special rule is demonstrated in Illustration 7-7.

In reviewing Illustration 7-7, it is important to note the following:

1. If amounts are to be remeasured at historical exchange rates that are traceable to transactions occurring prior to the parent's date of acquisition, they should be remeasured at the *historical exchange rate existing at the parent's date of acquisition.*
2. The remeasurement gain or loss is recognized as a component of income rather than as a component of other comprehensive income. Remeasurement gains or losses from prior years would be included in the remeasured amount of retained earnings at the beginning of the current year.
3. Because the functional currency is the U.S. dollar in this example, only the remeasurement process was necessary. If the functional currency had been in a different currency than that of the parent, it would have been necessary to first remeasure into the functional currency and then translate into the currency of the parent/investor. For example, if the book of record currency (BR) is the Japanese yen, the functional currency is the euro, and the currency of the parent/investor is the U.S. dollar, it would be necessary to remeasure the Japanese yen into euros and then translate the euros to U.S. dollars.
4. The remeasurement process resulted in a gain that favorably affects net income. This is because the FC strengthened against the dollar and made the parent's net investment in the subsidiary more valuable. If the FC had weakened, a remeasurement loss would have likely occurred. If the parent's management felt a remeasurement loss might occur, it might employ some type of financial instrument to hedge against the loss.

5. If the investor is using the equity method of accounting for its investment in the investee, income from the investment should include the investor's share of the remeasurement gain or loss. Therefore, the investment account must be adjusted to reflect the investor's interest in the remeasurement gain or loss. For example, if an investor has a 30% interest in an investee and there is a current remeasurement gain of $50,000, the following entry would be made under the equity method:

Investment in Investee 15,000
   Investment Income   15,000

Illustration 7-7
Sori Corporation
Trial Balance Remeasurement
December 31, 20X1

Account	Balance in Books of Record (BR) Currency	Relevant Exchange Rate (Dollars/FC)	Balance in Functional Currency (Dollars)
Cash	10,000 BR	1.050	$ 10,500
Accounts Receivable	21,000	1.050	22,050
Allowance for Doubtful Accounts	(1,000)	1.050	(1,050)
Due from Pome	14,000	1.050	14,700
Inventory (at Market, Cost = 32,000)	30,000	Note A	31,500
Prepaid Insurance	3,000	1.045	3,135
Land	18,000	1.015	18,270
Depreciable Assets	120,000	Note B	122,400
Accumulated Depreciation	(15,000)	Note C	(15,120)
Cost of Goods Sold	180,000	Note D	185,000
Depreciation Expense	10,000	Note E	10,120
Income Tax Expense	30,000	1.030	30,900
Other Expenses	23,000	Note F	23,735
Total	443,000 BR		$456,140
Accounts Payable	20,000 BR	1.050	$ 21,000
Taxes Payable	30,000	1.050	31,500
Accrued Interest Payable	1,000	1.050	1,050
Mortgage Payable—Land	10,000	1.050	10,500
Common Stock	80,000	1.000	80,000
Retained Earnings	20,000	Note G	20,000
Sales—Pome	80,000	1.030	82,400
Sales—Other	200,000	1.030	206,000
Gain on Sale of Depreciable Assets	2,000	Note H	2,760
Remeasurement Gain (to balance)			**930**
Total	443,000 BR		$456,140

Note A—Inventory:

The historical cost and fair value of the ending inventory must be remeasured into the functional currency before the rule of cost or market, whichever is lower, may be applied.

	FC Exchange Rate		U.S. Dollars
Historical cost	(10,000 × 1.045)	. . . .	$10,450
	(22,000 × 1.043)	. . . .	22,946
		. . . .	$33,396
Fair value	(30,000 × 1.05)	. . . .	$31,500

Because the fair value in functional currency is still less than the historical cost in functional currency, fair value will be the carrying basis.

Note B—Depreciable Assets:

	Balance in BR	Exchange Rate (Dollars/FC)	Remeasured Functional Currency (Dollars)
January 1, 20X0, acquisition	80,000 BR	1.00	$ 80,000
July 1, 20X1, acquisition	60,000	1.04	62,400
July 1, 20X1, disposition	(20,000)	1.00	(20,000)
	120,000 BR		$122,400

Note C—Accumulated Depreciation:

	Balance in BR	Exchange Rate (Dollars/FC)	Remeasured Functional Currency (Dollars)
January 1, 20X0, acquisition (60,000 BR ÷ 10 × 2)	12,000 BR	1.00	$12,000
July 1, 20X1, acquisition (60,000 BR ÷ 10 × ½) . . .	3,000	1.04	3,120
	15,000 BR		$15,120

Note D—Cost of sales is remeasured as follows:

	Balance in BR	Exchange Rate (Dollars/FC)	Remeasured Functional Currency (Dollars)
December 1, 20X0, acquisition	20,000 BR	1.000*	$ 20,000
March 1, 20X1	60,000	1.015	60,900
July 1, 20X1	80,000	1.040	83,200
October 1, 20X1	20,000	1.045	20,900
Total	180,000 BR		$185,000

*Note that the exchange rate on the parent's date of acquisition is used rather than any earlier historical exchange rates.

(continued)

Note E—Depreciation Expense:

	Balance in BR	Exchange Rate (Dollars/FC)	Remeasured Functional Currency (Dollars)
January 1, 20X0, acquisition (60,000 BR ÷ 10) ..	6,000 BR	1.00	$ 6,000
July 1, 20X1, disposal (20,000 BR ÷ 10 × ½) ...	1,000	1.00	1,000
July 1, 20X1, acquisition (60,000 BR ÷ 10 × ½) .	3,000	1.04	3,120
	10,000 BR		$10,120

Note F—Other expenses are remeasured as follows:

	Balance in BR	Exchange Rate (Dollars/FC)	Remeasured Functional Currency (Dollars)
Insurance expense......................	3,000 BR	1.045	$ 3,135
Balance of expense	20,000	1.030	20,600
			$23,735

Note G—Retained Earnings:

	Balance in BR	Exchange Rate (Dollars/FC)	Remeasured Functional Currency (Dollars)
January 1, 20X1, balance (date of investment)........................	20,000 BR	1.00	$20,000

The beginning balance of retained earnings normally is equal to the remeasured value of the previous period's ending retained earnings. However, since 20X1 is the first year Pome has owned Sori, the beginning balance is set equal to the January 1, 20X1 (acquisition date), balance of retained earnings in foreign currency remeasured at the January 1, 20X1, spot rate. The balance sheet for 20X1 would show a remeasured value for retained earnings equal to the remeasured beginning balance of retained earnings plus the remeasured value of net income less dividends remeasured at the rate existing on the declaration date.

Note H—Gain on Sale of Depreciable Assets:

	Balance in BR	Exchange Rate (Dollars/FC)	Remeasured Functional Currency (Dollars)
Cost..............................	20,000 BR		
Accumulated depreciation	(3,000)		
Book value........................	17,000 BR	1.00	$ 17,000
Selling price in U.S. dollars			(19,760)
Gain			$ 2,760

Worksheet 7-2: page 410

Worksheet 7-2, pages 410 and 411 shows the consolidated financial statements of the Pome and Sori corporations. The trial balance for Sori has been remeasured into dollars based on Illustration 7-7 (see page 396). Note that the remeasurement gain is included in the subsidiary income distribution schedule.

Remeasurement and Subsequent Translation when Functional Currency Is Not the Same as the Parent/Investor's Currency

Illustration 7-8 demonstrates the remeasurement of a subsidiary's trial balance into the functional currency and the subsequent translation into the parent's reporting currency. This might be the case if, by way of example, the subsidiary records in Japanese yen, functions in euros, and has a U.S. parent. Illustration 7-8 is based on the following information:

1. Chen Corporation began operations on January 1, 20X1, as a wholly owned foreign subsidiary of Drake Inc., a U.S. company. Chen maintains its financial statements in the books of record currency (BR), and its functional currency is the FC.

2. Inventory in the books of record currency (BR) is carried at fair value even though its historical cost is 16,000 BR. Inventory was acquired uniformly throughout the year. The weighted-average cost method is used to determine the cost of sales.

3. Depreciable assets were acquired (sold) on the following dates:

Date	Cost
January 1, 20X1	10,000 BR
	90,000
May 1, 20X1	30,000
July 1, 20X1	(10,000)

The asset sold was acquired on January 1, 20X1. The selling price of this asset was 11,000 BR.

4. Depreciation is based on the straight-line method and a 10-year useful life.

5. Relevant direct exchange rates are as follows:

Date	FC/BR	Dollars/FC
January 1, 20X1	1 BR = 2.0 FC	1 FC = $1.40
May 1, 20X1	1 BR = 2.1 FC	1 FC = 1.30
July 1, 20X1	1 BR = 2.4 FC	1 FC = 1.10
December 31, 20X1	1 BR = 2.8 FC	1 FC = 1.00
20X1 average	1 BR = 2.5 FC	1 FC = 1.25

Highly Inflationary Economies. When a foreign entity's financial statements are expressed in the functional currency, the statements are translated directly into the parent's reporting currency. However, this procedure is not followed for a foreign entity in a country that has a highly inflationary economy. The FASB defines such an economy as one that has a cumulative inflation rate of approximately 100% or more over a three-year period. Other factors, such as the trend of inflation, also may suggest a highly inflationary economy.[5]

If a foreign entity's currency has lost its utility as a measure of value and lacks stability, its use as a functional currency is likely to produce misleading results. The translation of non-current assets of a foreign company in a highly inflationary economy at current rates of exchange produces curious results. The translated amounts may not represent reasonable dollar-equivalent measures of those assets' historical costs.

Suppose a foreign company acquires a fixed asset for a cost of 100,000 FC when the exchange rate is 1 FC = $1.00. Since that time, the foreign country has experienced a three-year cumulative rate of inflation of 270%, and the current rate of exchange is 1 FC = $0.40. If the

---

fixed asset was translated using the current-rate method, the translated value of the asset would be $40,000 versus its original translated cost of $100,000. One proposed solution to this curious result would be to adjust the foreign financial statements for inflation rates since acquisition and then apply the current-rate method. The inflation-adjusted value of the fixed asset would be 270,000 FC (100,000 FC × 270%), and its translated value at current rates would be $108,000 (270,000 FC × $0.40). This translated amount is more meaningful than the $40,000 value previously determined. The FASB decided against adjusting foreign amounts for inflationary effects and instead decided that the domestic currency (dollars) should serve as the foreign entity's functional currency. Thus, the foreign entity's statements should be remeasured into the functional currency (U.S. dollars). Applying this to the fixed asset example would require the use of the original historical rate of exchange and result in a remeasured value of $100,000 (100,000 FC × $1.00). This value is more meaningful than the $40,000 value previously determined, and it does not commingle historical and inflation-adjusted values into the same set of financial statements. It is important to note that (1) this will result in the remeasurement of the statements into dollars, making any further translation unnecessary, and (2) the remeasurement gain or loss should be included in the net income for the period.

Illustration 7-8
Chen Corporation
Trial Balance Translation
December 31, 20X1

Account	Balance in BR	Relevant Exchange Rate (FC/BR)	Balance in FC	Relevant Exchange Rate (Dollars/FC)	Balance in Dollars
Cash	10,000 BR	2.80	28,000 FC	1.00	$ 28,000
Accounts Receivable	28,000	2.80	78,400	1.00	78,400
Inventory (at fair value)*	15,000	Note A	40,000	1.00	40,000
Prepaid Expenses	5,000	2.50	12,500	1.00	12,500
Depreciable Assets	120,000	Note B	243,000	1.00	243,000
Cost of Goods Sold	145,000	2.50	362,500	1.25	453,125
Depreciation Expense	11,500	Note C	23,200	1.25	29,000
Other Expenses	27,000	2.50	67,500	1.25	84,375
Income Tax Expense	16,500	2.50	41,250	1.25	51,562
Remeasurement Loss			**58,650**	**1.25**	**73,313**
Total Debits	378,000 BR		955,000 FC		$1,093,275
				1.00	$ 21,000
Accounts Payable	7,500 BR	2.80	21,000 FC		
Accrued Expenses	12,000	2.80	33,600	1.00	33,600
Notes Payable	84,000	2.80	235,200	1.00	235,200
Common Stock	40,000	2.00	80,000	1.40	112,000
Cumulative Transaction Adjustment	0		0		(33,075)
Retained Earnings	0	Note D	0		0
Sales	220,000	2.50	550,000	1.25	687,500
Gain on Sale of Depreciable Assets	1,500	Note E	7,400	1.25	9,250
Allowance for Doubtful Accounts	2,000	2.80	5,600	1.00	5,600
Accumulated Depreciation	11,000	Note F	22,200	1.00	22,200
Total Credits	378,000 BR		955,000 FC		$1,093,275

*In more complex instances, the remeasurement of ending inventory and cost of sales will depend on the inventory valuation method used. LIFO ending inventory will consist of the (1) beginning inventory multiplied by the applicable exchange rate(s) plus (2) unsold current purchases multiplied by the applicable exchange rate(s).

Note A—Inventory:

The historical cost and fair value of the ending inventory must be remeasured into the functional currency before the rule of cost or market, whichever is lower, may be applied.

	BR × Exchange Rate	FC
Historical cost (16,000 BR × 2.50)		40,000
Fair value (15,000 BR × 2.80)		42,000

Because the historical cost in functional currency is less than the fair value in functional currency, historical cost will be the carrying basis.

Note B—Depreciable Assets:

	Balance in BR	Exchange Rate (FC/BR)	Remeasured Functional Currency (FC)
January 1, 20X1, acquisition	90,000 BR	2.00	180,000 FC
January 1, 20X1, acquisition	10,000	2.00	20,000
May 1, 20X1, acquisition	30,000	2.10	63,000
July 1, 20X1, disposition	(10,000)	2.00	(20,000)
	120,000 BR		243,000 FC

Note C—Depreciation Expense:

	Balance in BR	Exchange Rate (FC/BR)	Remeasured Functional Currency (FC)
January 1, 20X1, acquisition (90,000 BR ÷ 10)	9,000 BR	2.00	18,000 FC
May 1, 20X1, acquisition (30,000 BR ÷ 10 × ⅔)	2,000	2.10	4,200
July 1, 20X1, disposal (10,000 BR ÷ 10 × ½)	500	2.00	1,000
	11,500 BR		23,200 FC

Note D—Retained Earnings:

The remeasured value of zero for retained earnings represents the beginning-of-period value. The balance sheet for 20X1 would show a remeasured value for retained earnings equal to the remeasured value of undistributed net income. This value also would represent the remeasured value for beginning retained earnings in the 20X2 trial balance.

Note E—Gain on Sale of Depreciable Assets:

The remeasured value of the gain must be inferred, based on the following entry to record the sale of the asset:

Cash (11,000 BR × 2.40)	26,400	
Accumulated Depreciation (500 BR × 2.00)	1,000	
Depreciable Assets (10,000 BR × 2.00)		20,000
Gain on Sale of Depreciable Assets		7,400

(continued)

	Balance in BR	Exchange Rate (FC/BR)	Remeasured Functional Currency (FC)
Cost (see Note B)	10,000 BR	2.00	20,000 FC
Accumulated depreciation (see Note F)	(500)	2.00	(1,000)
Book value	9,500 BR		19,000 FC
Selling price	11,000 BR	2.40	(26,400)
Gain			7,400 FC

Note F—Accumulated Depreciation:

	Balance in BR	Exchange Rate (FC/BR)	Remeasured Functional Currency (FC)
Annual expense	11,500 BR	see Note C	23,200 FC
Asset disposed	(500)	2.00	(1,000)
	11,000 BR		22,200 FC

Summary of Translation and Remeasurement Methodologies

This chapter has discussed the translation and/or remeasurement of foreign financial statements into the reporting currency (dollars) of the domestic parent/investor entity. The situations requiring the use of a particular translation and/or remeasurement methodology are summarized in Exhibit 7-2 and the flowchart in Exhibit 7-3.

Exhibit 7-2 compares the methodologies applicable to the remeasurement and translation processes. The following factors regarding Exhibit 7-2 should be noted:

1. When remeasuring, the exchange rates represent the relationship between the books of record currency and the functional currency. When translating, the exchange rates represent the relationship between the functional currency and the parent/investor currency.

2. Examples of accounts that should be remeasured (versus translated) at historical rates include the following:

   - Marketable securities carried at cost
   - Inventories carried at cost
   - Prepaid expenses such as insurance, advertising, and rent
   - Property, plant, and equipment
   - Accumulated depreciation on property, plant, and equipment
   - Patents, trademarks, licenses, and formulas
   - Goodwill
   - Other intangible assets
   - Deferred charges and credits except deferred income taxes and policy acquisition costs for life insurance companies
   - Deferred income
   - Common stock
   - Preferred stock carried at issuance price
   - Examples of revenues and expenses related to nonmonetary items:

     Cost of goods sold

     Depreciation of property, plant, and equipment

     Amortization of intangible items such as patents and licenses

     Amortization of deferred charges or credits except deferred income taxes and policy acquisition costs for life insurance companies[6]

---

6 *Ibid.,* par. 48.

3. If amounts to be remeasured at historical exchange rates are traceable to transactions occurring prior to the parent's date of acquisition, the historical exchange rate existing at the date of acquisition should be used.

4. The remeasurement gain or loss reflected in the remeasured functional currency trial balance is included as a component of net income. The translation adjustment only results from translating the remeasured trial balance into the parent/investor's (U.S. dollars) currency. The resulting translation adjustment reflected in the translated trial balance is not included as a component of net income but rather as a component of other comprehensive income.

Exhibit 7-2
Remeasurement and Translation Methodologies

	Remeasurement	Translation
	Investee's books of record remeasured into functional currency—**historical rate/temporal method**	Functional currency translated into parent/investor's reporting currency—**current rate/functional method**
When to use	When functional currency is not the books of record (local) currency or when functional currency is inflationary	when functional currency is highly of record (local) currency or when the functional currency is not highly inflationary
Assets and Liabilities:		
Monetary items* or measured at current values	Remeasure using current exchange rate	Translate using current exchange rate
Not monetary items or not measured at current values	Remeasure using historical exchange rates	Translate using current exchange rate
Equity Accounts:		
Equity accounts (excluding retained earnings)	Remeasure using historical exchange rates**	Translate using historical exchange rates**
Retained earnings	Beginning remeasured balance plus (minus) remeasured net income (loss) less dividends (remeasured using historical exchange rates)	Beginning translated balance plus (minus) translated net income (loss) less dividends (translated using historical exchange rates)
Revenues and Expenses:		
Representing amortization of historical amounts	Remeasure using historical exchange rates	Translate using weighted-average exchange rate for the period
Other income and expense items	Remeasure using weighted-average exchange rate for the period	Translate using weighted-average exchange rate for the period
Accounting for remeasurement gain or loss and transition adjustment	Remeasurement gain or loss recorded as a component of net income	Cumulative translation adjustment recorded as a component of other comprehensive income

*Monetary items represent rights to receive or pay an amount of money which is (1) fixed in amount or (2) determinable without reference to future prices of specific goods/services; that is, its value does not change according to changes in price levels.

**If amounts are to be remeasured or translated at historical exchange rates which are traceable to transactions occurring prior to the parent's date of acquisition, they should be remeasured/translated at the historical exchange rate existing at the parent's date of acquisition.

Exhibit 7-3
Translation/Remeasurement Flowchart

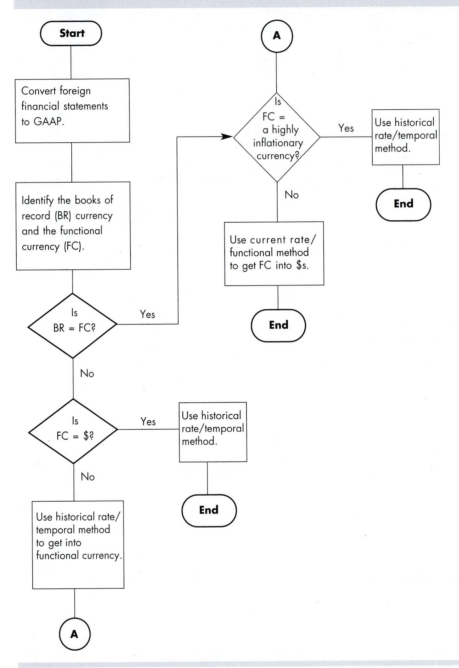

FASB Statement No. 52 requires that foreign currency transaction and hedging gains or losses included in the determination of net income be disclosed in the financial statements or the accompanying notes. An analysis of the separate component of other comprehensive income affected by certain foreign currency transactions and hedges and translation adjustments should be presented. The analysis may be in a separate statement, in a note to the financial statements, or as part of the statement of changes in equity. At a minimum, the analysis should disclose the following:

1. Beginning and ending amount of cumulative translation adjustments.
2. The aggregate adjustment for the period resulting from translation adjustments and gains and losses from certain hedges and intercompany balances.
3. The amount of income taxes for the period allocated to translation adjustments.

4. The amounts transferred from cumulative translation adjustments and included in determining net income for the period as a result of the sale or complete or substantially complete liquidation of an investment in a foreign entity.[7]

Although the various effects of rate changes subsequent to the end of the period normally are not disclosed, their effects on unsettled balances arising from foreign currency transactions should be disclosed if significant.

Exhibit 7-4 contains an example of an accounting policies note accompanying the financial statements of Ford Motor Company, which illustrates how both translation and remeasurement are applied to the foreign subsidiaries of a company.

Exhibit 7-4
Ford Motor Company

Foreign Currency Translation

The assets and liabilities of foreign subsidiaries using the local currency as their functional currency are translated to U.S. dollars based on current exchange rates and any resulting translation adjustments are included in *Accumulated other comprehensive income/(loss)*. The net translation adjustment for 2005 was a decrease of $3.4 billion (net of tax of $299 million). The net adjustment reflects amounts transferred to net income as a result of the sale or liquidation of an entity, resulting in $116 million gain (primarily from the sale of Hertz).

Also included in net income are the gains and losses arising from transactions denominated in a currency other than the functional currency of a location, the impact of remeasuring assets and liabilities of foreign subsidiaries using U.S. dollars as their functional currency, and the results of our foreign currency hedging activities; for additional discussion of hedging activities, see Note 20. The net after-tax income effects of these adjustments were gains of $609 million, $596 million and $454 million in 2005, 2004, and 2003 respectively.

Source: Ford Motor Company, 2005 Annual Report, Note 2. Summary of Accounting Policies.

REFLECTION

- If the foreign entity's functional currency is not its books of record (local) or reporting currency, the historical rate or temporal method is applied in order to remeasure the financial statements into the functional currency. This method is based on the premise that changes in the exchange rate between the books of record currency and the functional currency affect the cash flows and economic well-being of the foreign entity and parent/investor.

- The remeasurement process follows the historical rate/temporal method that remeasures foreign financial statements from their reporting currency into the functional currency. This method remeasures balances representing historical amounts using historical exchange rates.

- The remeasurement gain or loss is recognized as a component of current period earnings.

- If the foreign entity's functional currency is not the parent/investor's currency, the remeasured functional currency financial statements must be translated into the parent/investor's currency. The current-rate or functional method is used to translate the remeasured functional currency financial statements into the parent/investor's currency.

---

7 *Op. cit.*, par. 31.

Worksheet 7-1

Consolidating the Foreign Subsidiary
Pome Corporation and Subsidiary Sori Corporation
Worksheet for Consolidated Financial Statements (in dollars)
For Year Ended December 31, 20X1

| | (Credit balance amounts are in parentheses.) | Trial Balance | |
	In U.S. dollars	Pome Corporation	Sori Corporation
1	Cash	56,800	10,500
2	Accounts Receivable	112,000	22,050
3	Allowance for Doubtful Accounts	(5,600)	(1,050)
4	Due from Pome		14,700
5	Inventory, December 31, 20X1	154,700	31,500
6	Prepaid Insurance	9,050	3,150
7	Investment in Sori Corporation	141,153	
8			
9			
10	Land	125,000	18,900
11	Depreciable Assets and Patents	500,000	126,000
12	Accumulated Depreciation and Amortization	(100,000)	(15,750)
13	Accounts Payable	(112,000)	(21,000)
14	Taxes Payable	(150,000)	(31,500)
15	Accrued Interest Payable	(16,000)	(1,050)
16	Mortgage Payable—Land	(105,000)	(10,500)
17	Common Stock	(350,000)	(80,000)
18	Paid-In Capital in Excess of Par	(100,000)	
19	Retained Earnings, January 1, 20X1	(116,000)	(20,000)
20	**Cumulative Translation Adjustment—Sori**		(5,780)
21	**Cumulative Translation Adjustment—Pome**		
22			
23	Sales—Pome		(82,400)
24	Sales—Other	(908,600)	(206,000)
25	Gain on Sale of Depreciable Assets	(8,600)	(2,060)
26	Cost of Goods Sold	703,850	185,400
27	Depreciation and Amortization Expense	45,600	10,300
28	Income Tax Expense	108,000	30,900
29	Other Expenses (including interest)	51,800	23,690
30	Subsidiary Income	(36,153)	
31		0	0
32	Consolidated Net Income		
33	To Noncontrolling Interest		
34	Balance to Controlling Interest		
35	Total Noncontrolling Interest		
36	Retained Earnings, Controlling Interest, December 31, 20X1		
37			

Worksheet 7-1 (see page 388)

Eliminations & Adjustments				Consolidated Income Statement	Noncontrolling Interest (NCI)	Controlling Retained Earnings	Consolidated Balance Sheet	
Dr.		Cr.						
							67,300	1
							134,050	2
							(6,650)	3
		(IA)	14,700					4
							186,200	5
							12,200	6
		(CY1)	36,153					7
		(EL)	90,000					8
		(D)	15,000					9
							143,900	10
(D)	15,750						641,750	11
		(A)	1,575				(117,325)	12
(IA)	14,700						(118,300)	13
							(181,500)	14
							(17,050)	15
							(115,500)	16
(EL)	72,000				(8,000)		(350,000)	17
							(100,000)	18
(EL)	18,000				(2,000)	(116,000)		19
(CT)	5,202				(578)			20
		(CT)	5,202				(5,922)	21
(A)	30	(D)	750					22
(IS)	82,400							23
				(1,114,600)				24
				(10,660)				25
		(IS)	82,400	806,850				26
(A)	1,545			57,445				27
				138,900				28
				75,490				29
(CY1)	36,153							30
	245,780		245,780					31
				(46,575)				32
				4,017	(4,017)			33
				42,558		(42,558)		34
					(14,595)		(14,595)	35
						(158,558)	(158,558)	36
							0	37

Eliminations and Adjustments:

(CY1)   Eliminate the entries in the subsidiary income account against the investment in Sori account to record the parent's 90% controlling interest in the subsidiary.

(EL)   Eliminate 90% of the subsidiary's January 1, 20X1, equity balances against the balance of the investment account.

(CT)   Distribute the cumulative translation adjustment between controlling interest and NCI.

(D)   Distribute the excess of cost over book value of 15,000 FC to patent.

(A)   Record appropriate patent amortization.

(IA)   Eliminate the intercompany trade balances.

(IS)   Eliminate the intercompany sales assuming that none of the goods purchased from Sori remain in Pome's ending inventory.

Subsidiary Sori Corporation Income Distribution

Internally generated net income	$ 40,170
Adjusted income	$ 40,170
Noncontrolling share.	× 10%
NCI	$ 4,017

Parent Pome Corporation Income Distribution

Patent amortization . . . . **(A)** $1,500		
	Internally generated net income	$ 7,950
	Share of subsidiary income (90% × $40,170)	36,153
	Controlling interest	$42,558

Worksheet 7-2

Consolidating the Foreign Subsidiary
Pome Corporation and Subsidiary Sori Corporation
Worksheet for Consolidated Financial Statements (in dollars)
For Year Ended December 31, 20X1

	(Credit balance amounts are in parentheses.) In U.S. dollars	Trial Balance	
		Pome Corporation	Sori Corporation
1	Cash	56,800	10,500
2	Accounts Receivable	112,000	22,050
3	Allowance for Doubtful Accounts	(5,600)	(1,050)
4	Due from Pome		14,700
5	Inventory, December 31, 20X1	154,700	31,500
6	Prepaid Insurance	9,050	3,135
7	Investment in Sori Corporation	143,101	
8			
9			
10	Land	125,000	18,270
11	Depreciable Assets and Patents	500,000	122,400
12	Accumulated Depreciation and Amortization	(100,000)	(15,120)
13	Accounts Payable	(112,000)	(21,000)
14	Taxes Payable	(150,000)	(31,500)
15	Accrued Interest Payable	(16,000)	(1,050)
16	Mortgage Payable—Land	(105,000)	(10,500)
17	Common Stock	(350,000)	(80,000)
18	Paid-In Capital in Excess of Par	(100,000)	
19	Retained Earnings, January 1, 20X1	(116,000)	(20,000)
20	**Remeasurement Gain**		(930)
21			
22			
23	Sales—Pome		(82,400)
24	Sales—Other	(908,600)	(206,000)
25	Gain on Sale of Depreciable Assets	(8,600)	(2,760)
26	Cost of Goods Sold	703,850	185,000
27	Depreciation and Amortization Expense	45,600	10,120
28	Income Tax Expense	108,000	30,900
29	Other Expenses (including interest)	51,800	23,735
30	Subsidiary Income	(38,101)	
31		0	0
32	Consolidated Net Income		
33	To Noncontrolling Interest		
34	Balance to Controlling Interest		
35	Total Noncontrolling Interest		
36	Retained Earnings, Controlling Interest, December 31, 20X1		
37			

Worksheet 7-2 (see page 399)

Eliminations & Adjustments			Consolidated Income Statement	Noncontrolling Interest (NCI)	Controlling Retained Earnings	Consolidated Balance Sheet	
Dr.		Cr.					
							67,300	1
							134,050	2
							(6,650)	3
		(IA)	14,700					4
							186,200	5
							12,185	6
		(CY1)	38,101					7
		(EL)	90,000					8
		(D)	15,000					9
							143,270	10
(D)	15,000						637,400	11
		(A)	1,500				(116,620)	12
(IA)	14,700						(118,300)	13
							(181,500)	14
							(17,050)	15
							(115,500)	16
(EL)	72,000				(8,000)		(350,000)	17
							(100,000)	18
(EL)	18,000				(2,000)	(116,000)		19
				(930)				20
								21
								22
(IS)	82,400							23
				(1,114,600)				24
				(11,360)				25
		(IS)	82,400	806,450				26
(A)	1,500			57,220				27
				138,900				28
				75,535				29
(CY1)	38,101							30
	241,701		241,701					31
				(48,785)				32
				4,234	(4,234)			33
				44,551		(44,551)		34
					(14,234)		(14,234)	35
						(160,551)	(160,551)	36
							0	37

Eliminations and Adjustments:

(CY1) Eliminate the entries in the subsidiary income account against the investment in the Sori account to record the parent's 90% controlling interest in the subsidiary.

(EL) Eliminate 90% of the subsidiary's January 1, 20X1, equity balances against the balance of the investment account.

(D) Distribute the excess of cost over book value of 15,000 FC.

(A) Record appropriate amortization of patent.

(IA) Eliminate the intercompany trade balances.

(IS) Eliminate the intercompany sales assuming that none of the goods purchased from Sori remain in Pome's ending inventory.

Subsidiary Sori Corporation Income Distribution

Internally generated net income	$42,335*
Adjusted income	$42,335
Noncontrolling share	× 10%
NCI	$ 4,234

Parent Pome Corporation Income Distribution

Patent amortization . . . .(A)	$1,500	Internally generated net income	$ 7,950
		Share of subsidiary income (90% × $42,335)	38,101
		Controlling interest	$44,551

*This amount includes the remeasurement gain of $930.

UNDERSTANDING THE ISSUES

1. A foreign company maintains its books and records in its domestic currency. Identify several factors that might suggest that the domestic currency is not the entity's functional currency.

2. Assume that a U.S. company has a French subsidiary whose functional currency is the euro. Explain why the translation adjustment is not included as a component of net income on the consolidated income statement.

3. Explain how a German subsidiary's year-end balance in retained earnings is expressed in dollars assuming that the euro is the functional currency.

4. Assume that a U.S. company has a foreign subsidiary whose functional currency is the U.S. dollar. Explain how exchange rates between the foreign currency and the dollar would have to change in order to result in a current-year remeasurement loss and how the company could use a foreign currency loan receivable or payable to hedge against its net investment in the foreign subsidiary.

5. Explain why functional currency should be remeasured, rather than translated, when a foreign entity's functional currency is highly inflationary.

EXERCISES

Exercise 7-1 *(LO 3, 4)* **Direct calculation of a translation adjustment and hedging strategies.** At the beginning of 20X5, the rate of exchange between the foreign currency (FC) and the U.S. dollar was 1 FC = $1.20. A foreign company had net assets at the beginning of 20X5 in the amount of 150,000 FC and was wholly owned by a U.S. company. During 20X5, the foreign company had net income of 75,000 FC and sold additional common stock to the parent company. The common stock had a par value of 50,000 FC and was sold for 60,000 FC when the exchange rate was 1 FC = $1.15. The average exchange rate during 20X5 was 1 FC = $1.13, and at the end of 20X5, the rate was 1 FC = $1.10.

1. Calculate the amount of the translation adjustment which would be traceable to 20X5.
2. Explain how the company could hedge to reduce the effect of the reduction in other comprehensive income.
3. Discuss how to account for a hedge of the net investment in the above foreign operation.

Exercise 7-2 *(LO 2)* **The effect on a parent of alternative functional currencies.** Luxor Corporation has a 100% interest in a foreign subsidiary known as Luminaire. The foreign subsidiary was created for the primary purpose of distributing electronic components throughout a number of foreign countries. The parent initially invested 3,000,000 FC to finance equipment purchases, and it is anticipated that a dividend equivalent to $1,110,000 will be paid to the parent company at the end of each year. Luxor is trying to determine whether to structure the subsidiary with the foreign currency (FC) or the U.S. dollar ($) as Luminaire's functional currency. Projections for the subsidiary's first year of operations are as follows: sales of 10,000,000 FC; cost of sales (excluding depreciation) of 3,700,000 FC; and selling, general, and administrative expenses (excluding depreciation) of 1,200,000 FC. It is anticipated that the company will purchase 2,000,000 FC of equipment at the beginning of the year and another 1,000,000 FC of equipment at midyear. All equipment is depreciated over 10 years using the straight-line method.

It is anticipated that the exchange rate between the FC and the $ are as follows:

Beginning of year	1 FC = $1.00
Average for year	1 FC = 1.06
Midyear.	1 FC = 1.05
End of year	1 FC = 1.11

For the first year, prepare a schedule to determine the effect on the parent company's translated net income, balance sheet, and cash flows assuming the functional currency is: (a) the dollar and (b) the FC. (*Hint:* Assume that all sales revenues increase cash and that all cost of sales and selling, general, and administrative expenses decrease cash.)

Exercise 7-3 *(LO 5)* Net investment under the sophisticated equity method. On June 30, 20X5, Fabinet's, a foreign corporation, shareholders' equity was 10,500,000 FC. At that time, Newcore, a U.S. corporation, acquired 40% in Fabinet paying $3,120,000 when 1 FC was equal to $0.60. Equipment, with a fair market value that exceeded cost by $240,000, accounted for a portion of the cost in excess of book value. The equipment was expected to have a remaining useful life of 10 years and be depreciated using the straight-line method. The balance of the cost in excess of book value was traceable to goodwill.

During the balance of 20X5, Fabinet reported net income of 1,260,000 FC of which 126,000 FC was declared and paid as a dividend. At the end of 20X5, Newcore tested the goodwill for impairment and recognized an impairment loss of $100,000. Additional exchange rates are as follows:

Weighted average for last six months of 20X5	1 FC = $0.64
Date of dividend declaration	1 FC = 0.66
December 31, 20X5	1 FC = 0.68

Prepare all relevant entries to record Newcore's interest in Fabinet under the sophisticated equity method.

Exercise 7-4 *(LO 5)* Measurement of net investment under the sophisticated equity method. On June 1, 20X8, Auburn Company (a U.S. company) acquired a 30% interest in a foreign company which was formed on November 1, 20X7. Auburn accounted for the investment using the sophisticated equity method. At the date of acquisition, the net assets of the foreign company were 800,000 FC, and Auburn paid $600,000 for its interest. Appreciated land accounted for approximately 20% of the excess paid by Auburn, and the balance was traceable to depreciable assets. On average, depreciable assets have a remaining useful life of 12 years and are depreciated using the straight-line method of depreciation. The foreign company's net income for the last seven months of 20X8 was 140,000 FC. The functional currency is the FC, and the translation adjustment at year-end is a credit of $13,000. Selected exchange rates are as follows:

November 1, 20X7	1 FC = $2.10
Weighted-average (June 1 to December 31, 20X8)	1 FC = 2.24
June 1, 20X8	1 FC = 2.20
December 31, 20X8	1 FC = 2.27

Determine the U.S. dollar balance of Auburn's investment in the foreign company as of December 31, 20X8.

Exercise 7-5 *(LO 4)* Hedging a net investment in a foreign subsidiary. Crosswell Inc. has a 100% interest in a foreign subsidiary whose functional currency is the FC. The interest was acquired when 1 FC = $1.45. As of September 30, 20X4, the pre-closing trial balance as of December 31, 20X4, is forecasted to be as follows:

	Debit (Credit)
Cash	40,000 FC
Accounts Receivable	220,000
Inventory	320,000
Equipment (net of depreciation)	825,000
Accounts Payable	(360,000)

6% Note Payable	(400,000)
Accrued Interest Payable	(4,000)
Common Stock	(200,000)
Contributed Capital in Excess of Par Value	(200,000)
Beginning Retained Earnings	(140,000)
Sales	(600,000)
Cost of Sales	366,000
Selling Expenses	55,000
Administrative Expenses	48,000
Interest Expense	30,000
Total	0 FC

Actual exchange rates between the FC and the dollar are 1 FC = $1.40 as of January 1, 20X4, and $1.24 as of September 30, 20X4. It is estimated that the year-end 20X4 rate will be 1 FC = $1.20 and that the 20X4 weighted-average rate will be 1 FC = $1.28.

Crosswell is considering hedging its investment in the foreign subsidiary by borrowing or lending FC as of September 30, 20X4. The annual interest rate will be 6% with interest-only payments due at the end of each calendar quarter. At year-end 20X3, the cumulative translation adjustment was a $120,000 debit balance.

Determine the amount of the FC hedge that would be necessary to offset the 20X4 change in the translation adjustment. Assume that the translated value of retained earnings at December 31, 20X3, was $200,000.

Exercise 7-6 *(LO 6)* Remeasuring selected balances with various functional currencies.

For each of the following independent cases, determine the translated value of the relevant accounts:

Case A: A foreign subsidiary has inventory accounted for by the lower-of-cost-or-market rule. The 20X7 ending inventory, with a cost of 180,000 FC, was written down to a fair value of 176,000 FC. The cost of the inventory is traceable to an October 1, 20X7, purchase of 150,000 FC and a December 15, 20X7, purchase of 30,000 FC. The foreign company's functional currency is the U.S. dollar. Relevant exchange rates on October 1, 20X7, December 15, 20X7, and December 31, 20X7, are 1 FC = $1.76, 1 FC = $1.72, and 1 FC = $1.82, respectively. Calculate the translated value of the December 31, 20X7, ending inventory.

Case B: A foreign subsidiary purchased inventory for 380,000 FC from its U.S. parent on November 1, 20X7. The parent's cost of the inventory sold was $500,000. As of December 31, 20X7, the subsidiary has 60% of the inventory on hand. The subsidiary's functional currency is the FC. Relevant exchange rates on November 1, 20X7, and December 31, 20X7, are 1 FC = $2.00 and 1 FC = $2.10, respectively. Calculate the translated value of the subsidiary's December 31, 20X7, inventory after eliminating the intercompany profit.

Case C: A foreign subsidiary acquired depreciable assets measured in foreign currency A (FCA) over several years. The subsidiary's functional currency is foreign currency B (FCB). All assets are depreciable on a straight-line basis over a 10-year useful life. Relevant asset costs and exchange rates are as follows:

	Asset Cost	1 FCA =	1 FCB =
January 1, 20X6	380,000	2.10 FCB	$1.10
March 1, 20X6	710,000	1.98	1.08
July 1, 20X6	216,000	1.92	1.06
December 1, 20X6	30,000	2.01	1.04
20X6 average		2.03	1.05

Calculate the translated value of the 20X6 depreciation expense.

Exercise 7-7 *(LO 3)* **Translation of equity accounts and direct calculation of translation adjustment.** Paco Industries is a foreign corporation which was formed in 20X5. An analysis of activity affecting equity accounts reveals the following through December 31, 20X7:

Date	Activity/Event	Amount in Foreign Currency (FC)	Exchange Rate 1 FC =
Mar. 1, 20X5	Initial sale of common stock (1,400,000 par value)	2,000,000	$1.20
Mar. 1—Dec. 31, 20X5	Net income	200,000	1.25 weighted ave.
Mar. 1, 20X6	Dividend declared	30,000	1.27
Oct. 1, 20X6	Second offering of common stock (1,500,000 par value)	3,000,000	1.32
20X6	Net income	450,000	1.30 weighted ave.
Apr. 1, 20X7	Acquisition of treasury stock (210,000 par value)	300,000	1.28
July 1, 20X7	Dividend declared	90,000	1.25
20X7	Net income	550,000	1.22 weighted ave.

1. Assuming that the foreign currency is the functional currency, prepare the translated equity section for Paco as of December 31, 20X7, noting that the year-end exchange rates were as follows: 20X5, 1 FC = $1.29; 20X6, 1 FC = $1.32; 20X7, 1 FC = $1.21.
2. Calculate what amount of the December 31, 20X7, translation adjustment balance was traceable to 20X7.

PROBLEMS

Problem 7-1 *(LO 2, 3)* **Adjust to U.S. GAAP and translate trial balance.** On January 1, 20X8, Richter Corporation acquired an 80% interest in Morgan Company, a foreign company, for 9,000,000 FC. On the date of acquisition, Morgan's equity consisted of common stock of 3,000,000 FC and retained earnings of 5,500,000 FC. Any excess of cost over book value is attributable to additional depreciable assets, which have a useful life of 20 years. The unadjusted trial balances for Richter and Morgan as of December 31, 20X9, are as follows:

	Richter Corporation	Morgan Company
Cash	4,630,000	3,850,000 FC
Short-Term Investments	1,250,000	1,100,000
Accounts Receivable	3,790,000	4,620,000
Inventory	4,800,000	2,950,000
Investment in Morgan	6,930,000	
Depreciable Assets	27,400,000	17,700,000
Accumulated Depreciation	(12,120,000)	(7,250,000)
Depreciable Assets—Leased	4,540,000	
Accumulated Depreciation—Leased Assets	(1,900,000)	
Capitalized Research and Development		980,000
Accounts Payable	(2,860,000)	(1,200,000)
Interest Payable	(150,000)	

Obligation Under Capital Lease	(3,170,000)	
Common Stock	(10,000,000)	(3,000,000)
Retained Earnings, January 1, 20X9	(18,460,000)	(15,656,000)
Sales	(25,000,000)	(18,000,000)
Cost of Goods Sold	16,500,000	11,600,000
Depreciation Expense	2,875,000	1,550,000
Interest Expense	150,000	
Research and Development Expense	740,000	
Rent Expense		8,000
Other Expenses	955,000	748,000
OCI—Unrealized Holding Gain—AFS	(900,000)	
Total	0	0 FC

Morgan's trial balance is based, in part, on certain national accounting principles that are accepted in the country in which Morgan operates. However, these principles do not conform to U.S. GAAP. These differences include the following:

Short-Term Investments—All of these available-for-sale investments, acquired on January 1, 20X9, have been recorded at cost, without consideration of fair value. As of December 31, 20X9, fair value is 1,500,000 FC for these investments.

Research and Development—Research and development costs have been capitalized, although GAAP require these costs to be expensed in the period incurred. Morgan has no prior R&D costs. Therefore, all capitalized R&D costs were incurred uniformly during 20X9.

Leases—On January 1, 20X9, Morgan entered into a contract to lease machinery from an outside company. Morgan treated the lease as operating; however, GAAP require that it be capitalized. The lease contract requires an 8,000 FC payment at the start of each year for four years. At the end of the lease term, title to the asset is transferred to Morgan. The machinery has a fair value of 27,215 FC and is depreciated using the straight-line method over its remaining five-year life. The implicit interest rate is 12%.

Morgan employs the FIFO inventory method. The most recent purchases of inventory occurred on August 1, 20X9, and November 15, 20X9, in the amounts of 1,000,000 FC and 2,000,000 FC, respectively. Morgan acquired additional equipment costing 5,000,000 FC on July 1, 20X9. Equipment is depreciated over 10 years, using the straight-line method. No other equipment has been acquired or disposed of since January 1, 20X9.

The cost of sales is traceable to goods purchased during 20X9 as follows:

Acquired in the 4th quarter of 20X8	2,400,000 FC
Acquired uniformly over the first six months of 20X9	9,150,000 FC
Acquired August 1, 20X9	50,000 FC

No dividends are paid. Morgan's 20X8 remeasured income (excluding any remeasurement gain or loss) was $8,370,000.

Relevant exchange rates are as follows:

	1FC =		1FC =
January 1, 20X7	$0.78	1st Quarter, 20X9 Average	$0.81
20X7 Average	0.76	1st Six months, 20X9 Average	0.83
January 1, 20X8	0.77	July 1, 20X9	0.84

(continued)

	1FC =		1FC =
December 31, 20X8	0.80	August 1, 20X9	0.83
4th Quarter, 20X8 Average	0.78	November 15, 20X9	0.86
20X8 Average.	0.79	December 31, 20X9	0.89
January 1, 20X9	0.82	20X9 Average.	0.88

Required ▶ ▶ ▶ ▶ ▶

1. Prepare all relevant journal entries to adjust Morgan's trial balance to U.S. GAAP.
2. Assuming Morgan's functional currency is the U.S. dollar, prepare a consolidated worksheet through the "Eliminations and Adjustments" column.

Problem 7-2 *(LO 3, 5)* **Translate a trial balance and prepare a consolidation worksheet with amortization of patents.** Keltner Enterprises has acquired an 80% interest in Jacklandia (a foreign company). The acquisition was accounted for as a purchase and occurred on January 1, 20X6, as follows:

> Purchase price of 7,200,000 FC for net assets with a book
> value of $5,600,000 FC (7,000,000 FC × 80%)
> Allocation of excess paid:
> Patents (10-year remaining life, straight-line amortization) . . . .   1,600,000 FC

A condensed trial balance for both Keltner and Jacklandia as of December 31, 20X8, is as follows:

	Keltner (in dollars)	Jacklandia (in FC)
Working Capital	32,120,800	9,550,000
Due from Jacklandia	800,000	
Investment in Jacklandia	14,221,200	
Land.	5,120,000	1,000,000
Depreciable Assets	54,000,000	6,000,000
Accumulated Depreciation	(27,000,000)	(2,000,000)
Other Assets	5,978,800	1,500,000
Due to Keltner		(620,155)
Other Long-Term Debt	(31,320,800)	(4,679,845)
Common Stock (issued July 1, 20X5)	(30,000,000)	(5,000,000)
Paid-In Capital in Excess of Par	(6,000,000)	(1,000,000)
Retained Earnings	(15,000,000)	(3,450,000)
20X8 Net Income	(2,920,000)	(1,300,000)

Jacklandia had net income for 20X6 and 20X7 of 1,400,000 FC and 2,250,000 FC, respectively. Furthermore, Jacklandia declared a dividend of 1,200,000 FC on February 1, 20X8.

The FC is Jacklandia's functional currency, and various exchange rates are as follows:

July 1, 20X5	1 FC = $1.39	December 31, 20X7	1 FC = $1.32
January 1, 20X6	1 FC = 1.40	20X8 Average.	1 FC = 1.27
20X6 Average.	1 FC = 1.42	February 1, 20X8	1 FC = 1.25
20X7 Average.	1 FC = 1.35	December 31, 20X8	1 FC = 1.29

Required ▶ ▶ ▶ ▶ ▶

Prepare a columnar worksheet to present the combined income statement and balance sheet of Keltner and its foreign subsidiary, Jacklandia, with all amounts stated in U.S. dollars. Key and explain worksheet eliminations and adjustments, and show supporting computations in good form. Ignore income taxes, and assume use of the simple equity method. (You may want to prepare a translated trial balance for Jacklandia first and then prepare a consolidated worksheet.)

Problem 7-3 *(LO 3, 5)* **Translate a trial balance and prepare a consolidation worksheet with excess of cost over book value traceable to equipment.** Due to increasing pressures to expand globally, Pueblo Corporation acquired a 100% interest in Sorenson Company, a foreign company, on January 1, 20X6. Pueblo paid 12,000,000 FC, and Sorenson's equity consisted of the following:

Common stock.............................	3,000,000 FC
Paid-in capital in excess of par	2,000,000
Retained earnings	4,200,000
Total.....................................	9,200,000 FC

On the date of acquisition, equipment which has a 10-year life was undervalued by 500,000 FC. Any remaining excess of cost over book value is attributable to additional equipment, which has a 20-year life. The trial balances for Pueblo and Sorenson as of December 31, 20X8, are as follows:

	Pueblo Corporation	Sorenson Company
Cash	4,050,000	2,840,000 FC
Accounts Receivable	5,270,000	3,990,000
Inventory	5,540,000	5,800,000
Investment in Sorenson	20,969,000	
Fixed Assets................................	21,000,000	15,000,000
Accumulated Depreciation	(12,560,000)	(6,800,000)
Accounts Payable	(3,450,000)	(1,580,000)
Long-Term Debt	(10,000,000)	(5,000,000)
Common Stock	(4,000,000)	(3,000,000)
Paid-In Capital in Excess of Par	(6,500,000)	(2,000,000)
Retained Earnings, January 1, 20X8...........	(12,180,000)	(7,950,000)
Sales	(26,000,000)	(10,000,000)
Cost of Goods Sold	16,380,000	7,500,000
Operating Expenses	3,210,000	1,200,000
Subsidiary Income..........................	(1,729,000)	
Total.......................................	0	0 FC

The investment in Sorenson consists of the following:

Initial investment (12,000,000 FC × $1.20)	$14,400,000
20X6 Income (1,750,000 FC × $1.28)....................	2,240,000
20X7 Income (2,000,000 FC × $1.30)....................	2,600,000
20X8 Income.......................................	1,729,000
Total...	$20,969,000

Relevant exchange rates are as follows:

	1FC =
January 1, 20X6	$1.20
20X6 Average.....................	1.28
January 1, 20X7	1.25
20X7 Average.....................	1.30
December 31, 20X8	1.31
20X8 Average.....................	1.33

Assuming the FC is Sorenson's functional currency, prepare a consolidated worksheet. ◀ ◀ ◀ ◀ ◀ **Required**

Problem 7-4 *(LO 2, 5)* **Adjust to U.S. GAAP and translate trial balance.** Potter Corporation purchased a 100% interest in Stone Corporation, a foreign subsidiary, on January 1, 20X5, for 9,000,000 FC. On this date, Stone had common stock of 5,000,000 FC, paid-in capital in excess of par of 1,600,000 FC, and retained earnings of 2,000,000 FC. Bonds payable, which have a five-year life, were overvalued by 50,000 FC. Any remaining excess of cost over book value is attributable to goodwill. The December 31, 20X8, unadjusted trial balances for Stone and Potter are as follows:

	Stone Corporation	Potter Corporation
Cash	2,253,000 FC	4,862,000
Net Accounts Receivable	5,580,000	15,500,000
Inventory	6,400,000	11,138,000
Investment in Stone		14,664,900
Depreciable Assets	25,750,000	44,600,000
Accumulated Depreciation	(8,200,000)	(17,400,000)
Accounts Payable	(3,290,000)	(5,230,000)
Unearned Revenue	(2,437,000)	
Bonds Payable	(10,200,000)	(11,300,000)
Accrued Expenses	(2,180,000)	(3,961,100)
Common Stock	(5,000,000)	(20,000,000)
Paid-In Capital in Excess of Par	(1,600,000)	(4,750,000)
Retained Earnings, January 1, 20X8	(5,870,000)	(14,872,400)
Sales	(24,000,000)	(55,000,000)
Cost of Goods Sold	18,460,000	32,180,000
Operating Expenses	5,184,000	11,340,000
Interest Income		(146,000)
Subsidiary Income		(1,625,400)
Gain on Appreciation of Inventory	(650,000)	
Gain on Appreciation of Equipment	(200,000)	
Total	0 FC	0

Stone's trial balance contains amounts that reflect national accounting principles that are accepted in the country in which Stone operates, but do not conform to U.S. GAAP. These differences include the following:

Inventory—Stone records its inventory at fair value when goods are purchased and when they are sold. It has been determined that inventory would be valued at a lower amount had FIFO been used. Inventory is overvalued by 200,000 FC, and the related cost of goods sold is overvalued by 450,000 FC.

Depreciable Assets—Beginning in 20X7, appreciation was recognized on certain depreciable assets and included in net income. As of the beginning of 20X8, property, plant, and equipment and accumulated depreciation are overstated by 900,000 FC and 180,000 FC, respectively. During the current year, another 200,0000 FC of appreciation was recognized, and current-year depreciation expense was overstated by 55,000 FC.

Depreciable Assets—In 20X7, the company incurred 1,000,000 FC of research and development costs that were capitalized. These costs were amortized/depreciated over the life span of the resulting products. Annual amortization amounts were 400,000 FC and 300,000 FC for years 20X7 and 20X8, respectively.

The investment in Stone, expressed in dollars, consists of the following as measured by the simple equity method:

Initial investment (9,000,000 FC × $1.10)	$ 9,900,000
20X5 Income (1,000,000 FC × $1.15)	1,150,000
20X6 Income (1,200,000 FC × $1.27)	1,524,000
20X7 Income (350,000 FC × $1.33)	465,500
20X8 Income	1,625,400
Total	$14,664,900

Relevant exchange rates (dollars/FC) are as follows:

January 1, 20X5	$1.10
20X5 Average	1.15
20X6 Average	1.27
20X7 Average	1.33
December 31, 20X8	1.42
20X8 Average	1.40

Assuming the FC is Stone's functional currency, prepare all necessary adjustments to U.S. ◄ ◄ ◄ ◄ ◄ **Required** GAAP, and translate Stone's trial balance.

Problem 7-5 *(LO 3, 6, 7)* **Analyzing the effect of alternative functional currencies.**

Patterson Distributors, Inc. purchases various electronic components from a variety of manufacturers and then distributes the products to end users. In the past, both domestic and foreign manufacturers of the components shipped the product to Patterson's two U.S. distribution warehouses. In order to reduce costs and serve its customers on a more timely basis, Patterson is considering opening two international distribution centers. The company will form a 100%-owned foreign subsidiary to own the centers. The foreign subsidiary will need to secure financing and build and furnish a distribution warehouse in each location. Projections, in the respective country's foreign currency (FCA), for the first 12 months of operations are as follows:

	Company A (FCA)
Investment of parent company	1,000,000 FCA
Debt financing:	
Principal balance at beginning of year	4,000,000 FCA
Interest rate	6%
Repayment frequency	quarterly
Amortization period	20 quarters
Periodic payment	232,983 FCA
Year-end principal balance	3,292,344 FCA
Sales revenue	2,200,000 FCA
Inventory:	
Purchases	1,460,000 FCA
Frequency of purchases	equal amounts at end of each quarter
Ending inventory per LIFO	140,000 FCA
Other expenses (excluding interest and depreciation)	158,068 FCA
Cost of distribution center:	
Land	1,600,000 FCA
Building	2,200,000 FCA
Furnishings	720,000 FCA

(continued)

	Company A (FCA)
Useful life based on straight-line depreciation:	
Building	40 years
Furnishings.	12 years
End of year:	
Accounts receivable.	210,000 FCA
Accounts payable	130,000 FCA
Other current assets	50,000 FCA

Various projected exchange rates throughout the forecast period are as follows:

	1 FCA =
At beginning of year	$1.000
At end of first quarter	1.020
At end of second quarter	1.030
At end of third quarter	1.050
At end of fourth quarter	1.040
Average for the year	1.025

Although Patterson has prepared the projections in the respective foreign currencies, the company has the ability to structure transactions in such a way that either the foreign currency or the U.S. dollar is the functional currency.

Required ▶ ▶ ▶ ▶ ▶

1. Construct a year-end trial balance for the foreign subsidiary. Based on the information provided, calculate the translation adjustment and remeasurement gain or loss for the subsidiary assuming that the functional currency is the FCA and the dollar, respectively.
2. Discuss, in retrospect, whether the parent company would want to hedge its investment and, if so, how that might be accomplished.
3. Assume that the parent did hedge its investment in the subsidiary. This was accomplished by borrowing 600,000 FCA at the end of the first quarter. No principal payments were made during the year. How much of the gain or loss on this hedge would have been considered ineffective against the translation adjustment? The remeasurement gain?

Problem 7-6 *(LO 6)* **Prepare a remeasured trial balance and entries to eliminate excess of cost over book value.** On July 1, 20X6, Spencer International acquired an 80% interest in the net assets of Quatro Corporation, which is a foreign company, for $6,260,000. At that time, the net assets of Quatro in foreign currency (FC) were as follows:

Common stock.	8,000,000 FC
Paid-in capital in excess of par	1,000,000
Retained earnings	3,000,000

Any excess paid over book value was attributed to the fair value of certain licensing agreements which were held by Quatro. The agreements had an original useful life of 10 years, have a remaining life of five years, and are amortized using the straight-line method.

Spencer's investment in Quatro was designed to provide Spencer with additional manufacturing capacity for its product line and a distribution system which would allow for expanded sales in foreign markets. In order to implement these goals, Spencer loaned Quatro $5,940,000 in 20X6 for the purpose of improving the manufacturing capacity. For the next five years, only interest payments at the rate of 8% would be made on a monthly basis. The loan originated on October 1, 20X6, and the proceeds were disbursed at that time as follows:

Purchase of additional machinery.................	$3,410,000
Purchase of additional tooling....................	992,000
Purchase of additional inventory.................	1,538,000

On July 1, 20X6, depreciable asset balances were as follows:

Machinery and Equipment	17,450,000 FC
Accumulated Depreciation—Machinery and Equipment	2,617,500
Tooling	4,400,000
Accumulated Depreciation—Tooling	660,000

All depreciable assets are depreciated using the straight-line method, and salvage values are ignored. Machinery is depreciated over a 10-year useful life, and tooling is depreciated over 10 years. No other additions or dispositions of depreciable assets have occurred since Spencer's acquisition of Quatro.

The manufacturing lead time for Quatro's products is such that the inventory typically turns over approximately four times a year; however, production costs are incurred fairly uniformly throughout the year. Virtually all material costs are denominated in U.S. dollars, although labor costs are denominated in FCs. The company employs the FIFO inventory method, and 20X7 ending inventory and cost of sales details are as follows:

Ending Inventory

2,200,000 FC acquired in the last quarter of 20X7 when on average..............	1 FC = $0.55
1,500,000 FC acquired in the third quarter of 20X7 when on average.............	1 FC = 0.56

Cost of Sales

800,000 FC acquired in the third quarter of 20X6 when on average	1 FC = $0.61
1,200,000 FC acquired in the fourth quarter of 20X6 when on average............	1 FC = 0.62
3,200,000 FC acquired in the first quarter of 20X7 when on average.............	1 FC = 0.60
4,100,000 FC acquired in the second quarter of 20X7 when on average...........	1 FC = 0.57
3,400,000 FC acquired in the third quarter of 20X7 when on average.............	1 FC = 0.56

The December 31, 20X7, trial balance for Quatro is as follows:

	Debit	Credit
Cash and Receivables.....................................	2,200,000 FC	
Inventory	3,700,000	
Machinery and Equipment	22,950,000	
Accumulated Depreciation—Machinery and Equipment		5,922,500 FC
Tooling	6,000,000	
Accumulated Depreciation—Tooling		1,520,000
Licensing Agreements	500,000	
Accumulated Amortization—Licensing Agreements		325,000
Accounts and Notes Payable		2,000,000
Due to Spencer		11,000,000
Common Stock		8,000,000
Paid-In Capital in Excess of Par		1,000,000
Retained Earnings		3,700,000
Sales Revenue		20,527,500
Cost of Sales (excluding depreciation)	12,700,000	
Depreciation Expense	2,895,000	
Amortization Expense	50,000	
Other Expenses	3,000,000	
Total..	53,995,000 FC	53,995,000 FC

The retained earnings balance as of December 31, 20X7, reflects net income for the last half of 20X6 of 1,300,000 FC (which had a translated value of $806,000) and dividend declarations in the amount of 300,000 FC each on both August 1, 20X6, and August 1, 20X7.

Additional exchange rates are as follows:

July 1, 20X6	1 FC = $0.60	20X7 Average.	1 FC = $0.57
October 1, 20X6.	1 FC = 0.62	August 1, 20X7	1 FC = 0.55
August 1, 20X6	1 FC = 0.61	December 31, 20X7	1 FC = 0.54
Last half of 20X6 average	1 FC = 0.62		

Required ▶ ▶ ▶ ▶ ▶

1. Prepare a remeasured trial balance in dollars as of December 31, 20X7, assuming that Quatro's functional currency is the dollar.
2. Prepare all of the necessary elimination entries to account for the acquisition price being in excess of the book value of net assets.

Problem 7-7 *(LO 6)* Remeasurement: books of record (euro) and functional currency (FC) differ.

Husky Industries Inc. is a U.S. company that manufactures and distributes specialized emission control devices. In the past, approximately 5% of the company's sales came from export sales primarily in Western Europe. In 20X4, the company committed to an aggressive plan to expand export sales by acquiring a controlling interest in a British company that distributed specialized equipment throughout Western Europe and Asia. At the time of the acquisition, on September 1, 20X4, the British company's trial balance in euros was as follows:

	Debit (Credit)
Working Capital Excluding Inventory	(1,900,000) €
Inventory (per FIFO).	2,300,000
Licensing Agreements	840,000
Accumulated Amortization—Licensing Agreements	(400,000)
Equipment	840,000
Accumulated Depreciation—Equipment	(600,000)
Buildings	2,160,000
Accumulated Depreciation —Buildings.	(880,000)
Land.	500,000
Note Payable.	(1,000,000)
Common Stock	(400,000)
Paid-In Capital in Excess of Par	(860,000)
Retained Earnings	(600,000)
Total.	0 €

The British company's accounting policies regarding straight-line amortization and depreciation are as follows: licensing agreements, five-year useful life; equipment, 10-year useful life; and buildings, 40-year useful life.

Since September 1, 20X4, the British company reported the following transactions:

1. Earned net income from operations, excluding cost of inventory sold, amortization, and depreciation, of 650,000 euros in the last four months of 20X4 and 14,520,000 euros in 20X5.
2. Purchased inventory as follows: 3,000,000 euros evenly throughout the first quarter of 20X5, 4,000,000 euros on June 1, 20X5, and 5,400,000 euros on September 1, 20X5. Ending inventory on December 31 of 20X4 and 20X5 was 2,000,000 euros and 2,200,000 euros, respectively.
3. Made principal payments of 150,000 FC on the September 1, 20X4, note payable at the end of each calendar quarter. Borrowed 500,000 FC on October 31, 20X5, with principal and interest payments beginning in 20X6.
4. Acquired a licensing agreement of March 31, 20X5, for 286,000 FC.

5. Sold land on March 31, 20X5, with a book value on September 1, 20X4, of 100,000 euros for 200,000 euros. The gain on the sale was reported as other income, not operating income.
6. Declared and paid annual dividends of 143,000 FC on March 31, 20X5.

Although the British company records its transactions in euros, it has been determined that its functional currency is the FC. Various exchange rates are as follows:

	Direct Quote Euro to FC	Direct Quote FC to Dollar
September 1, 20X4........................	1.40	1.17
September 30, 20X4.......................	1.42	1.18
September 1–December 31, 20X4, average	1.44	1.19
December 31, 20X4	1.46	1.21
20X5 average............................	1.37	1.24
1st quarter, 20X5 average	1.45	1.24
March 31, 20X5	1.43	1.25
June 1, 20X5.............................	1.40	1.27
June 30, 20X5............................	1.39	1.26
September 1, 20X5........................	1.38	1.22
September 30, 20X5.......................	1.35	1.21
October 31, 20X5.........................	1.34	1.23
Last quarter, 20X5 average................	1.32	1.24
December 31, 20X5	1.30	1.25

1. Prepare a trial balance for the British company as of December 31, 20X5, expressed in its functional currency (FC). All supporting schedules should be in good form. ◄ ◄ ◄ ◄ ◄ **Required**
2. Compute the translated (in dollars) value of cost of sales for the four-month period ending December 31, 20X4, and the year ended December 31, 20X5.

Problem 7-8 *(LO 3, 5)* **Translate a trial balance and prepare a consolidation worksheet. Useful comparison with Problem 7-9.** Balfour Corporation acquired 100% of Tobac Inc., a foreign corporation, for 33,000,000 FC. The acquisition, which was accounted for as a purchase, occurred on July 1, 20X5, when Tobac's equity, in FC, was as follows:

Common stock...........................	19,000,000 FC
Paid-in capital in excess of par	8,480,000
Retained earnings	2,520,000

Any excess of cost over book value is traceable to equipment which is to be depreciated over 10 years. Balfour uses the simple equity method to account for its investment in Tobac.

On April 1, 20X7, Tobac acquired additional equipment costing 4,000,000 FC. Equipment is depreciated by the straight-line method over 10 years. No other equipment had been acquired or disposed of since 20X4. Tobac employs the LIFO inventory method. Ending inventory on December 31, 20X7, consists of the following:

Acquired in the 1st quarter of 20X4	1,000,000 FC
Acquired in the 1st quarter of 20X5	500,000
Acquired in the 1st quarter of 20X7	6,500,000

The cost of sales is traceable to goods purchased during 20X7 as follows:

Acquired uniformly over the last nine months	23,400,000 FC
Acquired in the 1st quarter	4,200,000

Other expenses were incurred evenly over the year.

On April 1, 20X7, Tobac borrowed $1,280,000 from the parent company in order to help finance the purchase of equipment. The note is due in one year and bears interest at the rate of 8%. Principal and interest amounts are due to the parent in dollars.

Various spot rates are as follows:

	1 FC =		1 FC =
1st Quarter, 20X4 Average........	$0.46	December 31, 20X6	$0.60
20X4 Average.................	0.49	1st Quarter, 20X7 Average........	0.62
January 1, 20X5	0.51	April 1, 20X7	0.64
1st Quarter, 20X5 Average.......	0.53	20X7 Average.................	0.67
July 1, 20X5	0.55	Last nine months, 20X7 Average.....	0.66
December 31, 20X5	0.58	December 31, 20X7	0.65
Last six months, 20X5 Average	0.57		
20X6 Average.................	0.58		

The December 31, 20X7, trial balances for Tobac and Balfour are as follows:

	Balfour Corporation	Tobac, Inc.
Cash	$ 4,463,200	3,087,385 FC
Net Accounts Receivable...............	15,350,000	12,000,000
Inventory	16,300,000	8,000,000
Due from Tobac......................	1,356,800	
Investment in Tobac—See Note A........	23,712,363	
Depreciable Assets	68,000,000	34,000,000
Accumulated Depreciation	(42,000,000)	(12,300,000)
Due to Balfour		(2,087,385)
Other Liabilities.....................	(27,000,000)	(3,700,000)
Common Stock	(35,000,000)	(19,000,000)
Paid-In Capital in Excess of Par	(2,000,000)	(8,480,000)
Retained Earnings, January 1, 20X7......	(4,500,000)	(7,520,000)
Sales	(98,000,000)	(40,000,000)
Cost of Sales	64,000,000	27,600,000
Depreciation Expense	8,076,800	3,300,000
Interest Expense on Balfour Loan (accrued on December 31, 20X7)—See Note B........		118,154
Exchange Gain on Balfour Loan—See Note B		(30,769)
Other Expenses.....................	10,000,000	5,012,615
Interest Income.....................	(76,800)	
Subsidiary Income...................	(2,682,363)	
Total.............................	$ 0	0 FC

Note A—Balfour's investment in Tobac consists of the following:

Initial investment (33,000,000 FC × $0.55)	$18,150,000
Last six months, 20X5 income (2,000,000 FC × $0.57)	1,140,000
20X6 income (3,000,000 FC × $0.58)...................	1,740,000
20X7 income......................................	2,682,363
Balance	$23,712,363

Note B—The original loan from Balfour was 2,000,000 FC, or $1,280,000 (2,000,000 FC × $0.64). On December 31, 20X7, it would require 1,969,231 FC ($1,280,000 ÷ $0.65) to settle the loan. This represents an exchange gain of 30,769 FC (2,000,000 FC − 1,969,231 FC).

The year-end balance due to Balfour is determined as follows:

Principal balance	1,969,231 FC
Accrued interest ($1,280,000 × 8% × 9/12 ÷ $0.65)	118,154
Balance	2,087,385 FC

The interest is accrued at year-end; therefore, interest expense should be translated at the year-end rate.

Assuming the FC is Tobac's functional currency, translate Tobac's trial balance, and prepare a consolidating worksheet. ◄ ◄ ◄ ◄ ◄ **Required**

Problem 7-9 *(LO 5, 6)* **Same facts as Problem 7-8 except involve remeasurement. Useful comparison with Problem 7-8.** Assume the same facts as Problem 7-8 with the following exceptions:

a. Tobac's functional currency is the U.S. dollar.
b. Balfour's investment in Tobac consists of the following:

Initial investment (33,000,000 FC × $0.55)	$18,150,000
Last six months, 20X5 income (including the remeasurement gain or loss)	1,610,000
20X6 income (including the remeasurement gain or loss)	1,860,000
20X7 income (excluding the remeasurement gain or loss)	3,495,363
Balance	$25,115,363

Note that the balance has not yet been adjusted for the 20X7 remeasurement gain or loss.

c. The trial balances for Tobac and Balfour are the same as in Problem 7-8 with the following exceptions:

Balfour

Investment in Tobac	$25,115,363
Retained earnings, January 1, 20X7	(5,090,000)
Subsidiary income	(3,495,363)

Remembering that Tobac's functional currency is the U.S. dollar, translate Tobac's trial balance and prepare a consolidating worksheet. ◄ ◄ ◄ ◄ ◄ **Required**

Remember that transactions traceable to pre-July 1, 20X5, should be remeasured at the rate in effect on July 1, 20X5. This is because on July 1, 20X5, Balfour acquired its interest in Tobac and established the dollar basis of net assets existing at that time.

Problem 7-10 *(LO 3, 5)* **Translation and consolidation with excess of cost over book value.** On July 1, 20X4, Troutman International acquired a 90% interest in Korbel Manufacturing when Korbel's shareholders' equity was 20,000,000 FC including retained earnings with a balance of 5,000,000 FC. Troutman paid 21,000,000 FC for its interest, when 1 FC equaled $1.10, and the excess of cost over book value was allocated as follows:

Licensing agreement	900,000 FC
Goodwill	2,100,000

The licensing agreement expired at the end of 20X8 and was to be amortized using a straight-line pattern. At year-end 20X5, Troutman recognized that the goodwill of 2,100,000 FC was impaired by 20%, or 420,000 FC.

Troutman records its investment in Korbel under the simple equity method, and Korbel's functional currency is the FC. Since the acquisition, Korbel has reported net income and dividends as follows:

	Last 6 Months of 20X4	20X5	20X6
Net income	900,000 FC	800,000 FC	1,100,000 FC
Dividends declared	240,000 FC	0 FC	200,000 FC
Average exchange rate (for 1 FC)......	$1.12	$1.20	$1.17
Exchange rate at year-end (for 1 FC)....	$1.14	$1.23	$1.15
Exchange rate when dividends were declared (for 1 FC)	$1.13		$1.20

A condensed trial balance for Troutman and Korbel as of December 31, 20X6, is as follows:

	Troutman (in dollars)	Korbel (in FC)
Working Capital	7,418,580	5,200,000
Depreciable Assets	34,000,000	22,500,000
Accumulated Depreciation	(11,560,000)	(6,740,000)
Due from Korbel......................................	92,000	
Investment in Korbel..................................	25,569,420	
Other Assets	2,070,000	3,080,000
Due to Troutman		(80,000)
Notes Payable.......................................	(4,000,000)	(1,600,000)
Common Stock at Par Value	(16,000,000)	(5,000,000)
Paid-In Capital in Excess of Par	(26,000,000)	(10,000,000)
Retained Earnings	(8,000,000)	(6,260,000)
20X6 Net Income	(3,590,000)	(1,100,000)
Total...	0	0

Required ▶ ▶ ▶ ▶ ▶   Prepare a columnar worksheet to present the 20X6 consolidated income statement and balance sheet for the parent company and its subsidiary with all amounts stated in U.S. dollars. Key and schedule worksheet eliminations and adjustments.

P A R T

Partnerships

3

Chapter 8: *Partnerships: Characteristics, Formation, and Accounting for Activities*

Chapter 9: *Partnerships: Ownership Changes and Liquidations*

A business may be organized in a variety of ways: as a sole proprietorship, a commercial corporation, a limited liability company, a limited liability partnership, or a regular partnership. Partnerships continue to be a common form of organization, and even the recent limited liability entities have many of the characteristics of a partnership. Assisting business owners in the proper selection of an organizational form is a necessary, yet complex, part of serving the needs of a business. A partnership is governed by a partnership agreement or, in some instances, by the Uniform Partnership Act. The partnership agreement must be carefully drafted to cover a variety of topics, including the purpose of the partnership, the responsibilities of

the partners, the allocation of profits and losses, the admission or withdrawal of a partner, and the valuation of the partnership given changes in the ownership structure. Changes in the ownership structure provide insight into some of the basic factors which must be considered in valuing a business, whether it be a partnership or not. In addition to special financial accounting principles governing partnerships, such entities are also required to follow different rules for determining income and basis for tax purposes. If a decision is made to terminate a partnership, several legal doctrines and special accounting procedures must be applied in order to produce an equitable distribution of partnership assets.

Partnerships: Characteristics, Formation, and Accounting for Activities

Learning Objectives

When you have completed this chapter, you should be able to

1. Explain the basic characteristics of a partnership.

2. Identify basic components that should be included in a partnership agreement.

3. Describe the relationship between a partner's drawing and capital accounts.

4. Demonstrate an understanding of the various bases that could be used to allocate profits or losses among partners.

A partnership is an association of two or more people for the purpose of carrying on a trade or business as co-owners. Partnerships continue to be a popular form of organization for many smaller businesses as well as certain larger businesses. Common examples of partnerships include professional services, such as the practice of accounting or law, real estate investment/development companies, and a variety of smaller manufacturing concerns. The magnitude of the partnership form of organization is suggested by the following statistics reported by the Internal Revenue Service for the year 2003:

	Domestic General Partnerships	Domestic Limited Partnerships	Domestic Limited Liability Companies
Number of partnerships	757,194	378,921	1,091,502
Number of partners	2,864,446	6,262,103	4,226,099
Total net income	$ 68 billion	$ 107 billion	$ 64 billion
Source: IRS, Statistics of Income Bulletin, Fall 2005, Publications 1136. (Rev. 12-05)			

In a majority of states, the legal nature and functioning of a partnership is governed by the *Uniform Partnership Act* (UPA). The UPA deals with such topics as the rights of partners, relations with persons dealing with the partnership, and the dissolution and termination of a partnership.

CHARACTERISTICS OF A PARTNERSHIP

1
OBJECTIVE

Explain the basic characteristics of a partnership.

Practicing accountants frequently are asked to advise clients regarding the formation of a business and the accounting for the business activities. Often, a choice must be made between a partnership and a corporate form of organization. Therefore, it is important for accounting students to understand the basic characteristics of a partnership and the related accounting implications.

Relationship of Partners

A partnership represents a voluntary association of individuals carrying out a business purpose. In this association, a *fiduciary relationship* exists among the partners, requiring them to exercise good faith, loyalty to the partnership, and sound business judgment in conducting the partnership's business. An individual partner is viewed as a co-owner of partnership property, creating a *tenancy in partnership*. When specific assets are contributed by a partner, they lose their identity as to source and become the shared property of the partnership. Without the consent of all partners, such property cannot be utilized by any partner for personal purposes.

The relationship between partners also is characterized as one of *mutual agency*, which means that each partner is an agent for the other partners and the partnership when transacting partnership business. Therefore, in carrying on the business of the partnership, the acts of every partner bind the partnership itself, even when a partner commits a wrongful act or a breach of trust. However, if a partner has no authority to act for the partnership and the party with whom the partner is dealing knows this, the partnership is not bound by the partner's actions.

Legal Liability of a Partnership

Partnerships are classified as either general or limited regarding liability of the partners. In a *general partnership*, the partners act publicly on behalf of the partnership and are personally liable, jointly and severally, for the unsatisfied obligations of the partnership. This unlimited liability is in sharp contrast to the limited liability of a corporation and its shareholders. Thus, if a partnership were insolvent, the unsatisfied creditors could seek to recover against the net personal assets of individual partners. Newly admitted partners, who are personally liable for partnership debts incurred subsequent to this admission, are liable for debts of the previous partnership only to the extent of their capital interest in the partnership.

In contrast, a *limited partnership* consists of one or more general partners and one or more limited partners who contribute capital but do not participate in the management of the company. The one or more general partners have unlimited liability as in the case of a general partnership. However, the limited partners' liability for partnership obligations is restricted to a stated amount, usually equal to their capital interest in the partnership.

The legal liability of partners is obviously a serious factor to consider when assessing whether a partnership is the appropriate form of organization. One could argue that unlimited liability, as a matter of social policy, is a good thing. Society has a right to be protected from the consequences of serious errors in judgment whether they be unintentional or intentional. However, without proper limits, such exposure to liability may also impair an entity's ability to provide useful goods or services. Virtually every product or service industry, from cigarette manufacturers to the medical profession, has been affected by liability issues. For example, the public accounting profession has had to operate in such a litigious environment that major initiatives have been undertaken in response to the legal liability crisis.

In response to this growing concern, two new forms of organization have been created, a *limited liability company* (LLC) and a *limited liability partnership* (LLP). The LLC is a hybrid form of organization which has many of the advantages of both a partnership and a corporation but few of the disadvantages of either. Similar to a corporation, shareholders of an LLC do not have personal legal liability for actions undertaken by the entity. This limited liability does not necessarily protect an individual shareholder from personal liability for his/her own wrongs. This is consistent with common law doctrine which views each individual as being responsible for the consequences of his/her own negligence and the ability of courts to "pierce the corporate veil" in order to seek recovery for wrongdoings.

An LLP is a subcategory of general partnerships. The LLP compares favorably to limited or general partnerships with respect to liability. All partners in an LLP may participate in management (unlike limited partners) and still have limited liability. Partners in an LLP are **not personally** jointly and/or severally liable for obligations of the partnership arising from the omissions, negligence, wrongful acts, misconduct, or malpractice of other partners. However, a partner does remain personally responsible for liabilities arising from his/her own actions and the actions of those who are acting under the partner's actual supervision and control in the specific activity in which the action occurred.

Underlying Equity Theories

Equity theories relate to how an entity is viewed from an accounting and legal viewpoint. These theories deal with the question of who is the entity. For example, an entity may be viewed as being providers of capital, individual owners (partners/shareholders), management, or a separate, distinct legal entity. Partnerships have been primarily affected by the *proprietary theory*, which looks at the entity through the eyes of the owners. Characteristics of a partnership that emphasize that the entity is viewed as the individual owners include the following:

◆ Salaries to partners are viewed as distribution of income rather than a component of income.
◆ Unlimited liability of general partners extends beyond the entity to the individual partners.
◆ Income of the partnership is not taxed at the partnership level but, rather, is included as part of the partners' individual taxable income.
◆ An original partnership is dissolved upon the admission or withdrawal of a partner.

Partnerships also have been influenced by the *entity theory* which views the business unit as a separate and distinct entity possessing its own existence apart from the individual partners. This theory is characteristic of corporations; yet, it is the basis for certain partnership characteristics. For example, a partnership may enter into contracts in its own name. Also, property contributed to a partnership by individual partners becomes the property of the partnership, and the contributing partner no longer retains a claim to the specific assets contributed.

Formation and Agreements

A partnership may come into existence without having to receive formal, legal, or state approval and may result simply from the actions of the parties involved. This lack of formality may be viewed as an advantage of a partnership. However, it is still necessary to carefully plan and evaluate various factors affecting the partnership. Forward and formal thinking when organizing a partnership will benefit both the business and its partners.

In order to properly capture the intent of the partners involved, it is advisable to develop a written partnership agreement. Critical issues that must be addressed include: admission of partners, withdrawal of partners, and the allocation of profits and losses. Such an agreement is referred to as the *articles of partnership* and, at minimum, should include the following provisions:

1. Partnership name and address.
2. Partners' names and addresses.
3. Effective date of partnership.
4. A description of the general business purpose and the limited duration of such purpose, if applicable.
5. Powers and duties of partners.
6. Procedures governing the valuation of assets invested.
7. Procedures governing the admission of a new partner(s).
8. Procedures governing the distribution of profits and losses.
9. Procedures governing the payment of receipt of interest on loans (versus capital contributions) among partners.
10. Salaries to be accrued to partners.
11. Withdrawals of capital to be allowed each partner and the determination of what constitutes excess withdrawals.
12. Procedures governing the voluntary withdrawal, disability, death, or divorce of a partner and the determination of the procedures for valuing the partner's interest in the partnership.
13. Matters requiring the consent of all partners.
14. The date when the profits and losses are divided and the partnership books are closed.
15. The basis of accounting (e.g., accrual or cash).

As the accounting for a partnership is developed more fully in this text, it will become apparent that the articles of partnership provide crucial guidance. Even though the UPA covers certain topics found in the articles of partnership, it is important to note that **many sections of the UPA are applicable only in the absence of a partnership agreement.** Legal and accounting issues affecting a partnership are often best resolved by evaluating the intent of the partners as set forth in a partnership agreement, rather than looking to the UPA.

2

OBJECTIVE

Identify basic components that should be included in a partnership agreement.

Acceptable Accounting Principles

There is a general presumption that an entity's financial position and results of operations should be accounted for in conformity with generally accepted accounting principles (GAAP). As GAAP have developed and become more complex, many have questioned the applicability of such principles to smaller business organizations, a large number of which are organized as partnerships. In response to this concern, it is recognized that, in some circumstances, a basis or method of accounting other than GAAP may be appropriate and may not adversely affect the fairness of the financial statements.

The Auditing Standards Board of the American Institute of Certified Public Accountants (AICPA) recognizes several *other comprehensive bases of accounting (OCBOA)* other than GAAP, including the following:

- The cash (receipts and disbursements) basis of accounting and modifications of the basis, such as a modified accrual basis.
- The tax basis of accounting based on taxation principles that are used to file an income tax return.

Tax-basis accounting generally consists of a cash-basis format or an accrual-basis format with certain exceptions primarily resulting from tax regulations differing from GAAP. The tax basis of accounting is a frequent choice of many partnerships. Depreciation accounting can be used to illustrate the focus of tax-basis accounting. Assume a depreciable asset has an economic useful life of six years and is consumed uniformly over its life. If accrual accounting were used, it would seem that the asset should be depreciated over six years using the straight-line method of depreciation. However, adoption of the tax basis of accounting could involve the use of a shorter life and an accelerated depreciation method. Furthermore, in some instances tax-basis accounting would allow the immediate expensing of depreciable assets even though such treatment would not be justified by accrual accounting.

The recognition of these other comprehensive bases provides many smaller and more specialized entities, many of which may be partnerships, with an acceptable alternative to GAAP. The use of OCBOA will not impair the fairness of their financial statements as evaluated by outside independent accountants. In practice, it is very common to find partnerships using a comprehensive basis of accounting other than GAAP. Due to the special tax aspects of a partnership, many such entities use the tax basis of accounting rather than GAAP.

Partnership Dissolution

Although a partnership is easily formed and does not need state approval, its life is limited and it may be dissolved much more easily than a corporation. *Dissolution* is defined in Section 29 of the UPA as "the change in the relation of the partners caused by any partner ceasing to be associated in the carrying on as distinguished from the winding up of the business." Generally, a partnership is dissolved upon the death, withdrawal, or bankruptcy of an individual partner (owner). The admission of a new partner also results in the dissolution of the former partnership. Thus, any change in the association of the individual partners is termed a dissolution.

Although dissolution occurs when there is a change in a partner's association with the other partners, it does not necessarily result in the termination of the basic business function. Therefore, a change in the ownership structure dissolves the former partnership, but often this change results in the formation of a new partnership to carry on the business purpose of the original partnership. The dissolution of a partnership resulting from the admission or withdrawal of a partner is more fully discussed in Chapter 9 of this text.

Tax Considerations

Unlike corporations, a partnership is not a separate taxable entity but a conduit through which taxable income or operating losses pass to the tax returns of the individual partners. The partnership must file an information return (Federal Form 1065) detailing the partnership revenues and expenses which pass through to the individual partners.

Even though a partnership is not a taxable entity, accounting for partnerships for tax-reporting purposes can become extremely complex. **The tax code does not view a partnership as a separate, distinct entity but focuses, rather, on the individual partners.** Therefore, activities of the partnership must be evaluated from a tax standpoint based on their impact on individual partners. This viewpoint results in special rules which must be understood by practicing accountants. Furthermore, the unique tax-related aspects of a partnership must be understood in order to advise clients as to whether the partnership form of organization is appropriate.

REFLECTION

- Partnerships have a number of characteristics of a legal, tax, and accounting nature that distinguish them from other forms of organization.

- A number of factors must be considered before forming a partnership, and a partnership agreement is a critical document that will help guide and manage the partnership.

ACCOUNTING FOR PARTNERSHIP ACTIVITIES

The activities of a partnership consist of several phases, including the initial contribution of capital to the partnership. This initial phase provides the capital necessary to begin operating activities. The remainder of this chapter discusses accounting for the partners' capital investments and the allocation of operating profits and losses among the partners. Although partners' capital investments may be subsequently influenced by partners entering or exiting the partnership and the liquidation of a partnership, these topics are discussed in the next chapter.

Contributions and Distributions of Capital

3

OBJECTIVE

Describe the relationship between a partner's drawing and capital accounts.

The capital contributed by shareholders to a corporation is accounted for in several accounts, including Capital Stock, Paid-In Capital in Excess of Par, and Retained Earnings. Unlike a corporation, the capital investment in a partnership generally is accounted for through two accounts for each partner, a temporary account referred to as the *drawing account* and a permanent account referred to as the *capital account.*

It is not unusual for a partner to withdraw available assets (typically cash) from a partnership throughout the year. Preferably, the amount and timing of a partner's withdrawal of assets should be addressed in the articles of partnership. Practically speaking, however, withdrawals are often informal and are not easily projected due to cash flow constraints. In some instances, withdrawals in excess of some amount are considered to be direct reductions of a partner's capital account rather than a withdrawal. Some partnerships view any withdrawal as a direct reduction of a capital account. However, in some partnerships, a separate account referred to as a drawing account is used to record a partner's withdrawal of capital. Withdrawals of assets, regardless of how accounted for, reduce the overall net capital of individual partners and the partnership.

A partner's withdrawals also include payments that are made by the partnership on behalf of an individual partner. For example, if a partnership pays off an individual partner's automobile loan, this is no different than if the partner had withdrawn the cash from the partnership and then paid off the loan personally.

The drawing account is a temporary account and is periodically closed to the partner's capital accounts. The balance sheet of a partnership, therefore, will present only the capital account balances of the partners. To summarize, the drawing account established for each partner is debited and credited for the following transactions:

Drawing Account

Debit	Credit
Periodic withdrawals of partnership assets up to a specified amount	Closing of balance to partner's capital account

Each partner's interest in the net assets of the partnership is measured at book value in the capital account established for that partner. This account indicates the destination of capital (claims to net assets) upon dissolution of the partnership. It is important to note that the capital balance does not normally reflect the fair value or tax basis of the partner's interest in the net assets of the partnership.

To summarize, the partner's capital account is debited and credited for the following transactions:

Capital Account

Debit	Credit
Withdrawals in excess of a specified amount	Initial and subsequent investments of capital
Closing of a net debit balance in the partner's drawing account	Partner's share of partnership profits
Partner's share of partnership losses	

As is the case with all entities, the investment of capital in a partnership should initially be measured at the fair value of all tangible and intangible assets contributed. An individual partner's liabilities that have been assumed by the partnership also should be recorded at fair value.

The exception to this would be in the case where a partnership has adopted the tax basis of accounting. The proper valuation of each partner's net investment of capital is extremely important. For example, if an asset invested by a partner is initially undervalued by the partnership and is sold immediately for a gain, all the partners share in the realized gain, which properly should have accrued to the original investing partner.

The post-closing balances in the capital accounts of the various partners represent each partner's interest in the net assets of the partnership at a point in time. A partner's interest in the partnership is different from the partner's interest in the profits and losses of the partnership. To illustrate, assume Partners A and B have capital balances of $8,000 and $32,000, respectively. Also assume that profits and losses are allocated to Partners A and B in the amount of 40% and 60%, respectively. These profit and loss ratios should not be confused with the partners' capital ratios which are 20% ($8,000 divided by $40,000) and 80% ($32,000 divided by $40,000) for A and B, respectively.

Occasionally, partners will loan assets to the partnership, or the partnership will loan assets to partners. It is important from a legal standpoint to differentiate between a loan and an additional investment of capital, especially when the liquidation of a partnership occurs. The nature of such transactions should be made clear by examining the intent of the individual partner or the partnership. If the contribution by a partner is really an additional investment of capital, it should be accounted for in the partner's capital account. However, if the transaction is truly a loan, it should be accounted for in a separate loan account for the partner, and provision for the payment of interest on the loan should be made.

Illustration 8-1 demonstrates the use of various partnership accounts in order to record partnership activity.

Illustration 8-1
Examples of Accounting for Partnership Activity

Event	Entry		
Partner A contributes cash to the partnership. Partner B contributes inventory and office equipment, and the partnership assumes the liability associated with the equipment. The equipment was recorded by B at a book value of $6,000. However, the equipment's fair value is $4,000.	Cash	10,000	
	Inventory	5,000	
	Office Equipment	4,000	
	Note Payable		2,000
	Partner A, Capital		10,000
	Partner B, Capital		7,000
Partner B loans the partnership $3,000 to be repaid in one year at a stated annual interest rate of 6%.	Cash	3,000	
	Partner B, Loan		3,000
A personal debt owed by Partner A is paid by the partnership.	Partner A, Drawing	500	
	Cash		500
Partners A and B withdraw cash of $500 and $1,200, respectively. Drawings in excess of $1,000 are viewed as excessive withdrawals and are charged against capital.	Partner A, Drawing	500	
	Partner B, Drawing	1,000	
	Partner B, Capital	200	
	Cash		1,700
The net income of the partnership is divided equally between the partners.	Income Summary	10,000	
	Partner A, Capital		5,000
	Partner B, Capital		5,000
The partners' drawing accounts are closed to their respective capital accounts.	Partner A, Capital	1,000	
	Partner B, Capital	1,000	
	Partner A, Drawing		1,000
	Partner B, Drawing		1,000

The Allocation or Division of Profits and Losses

4

OBJECTIVE

Demonstrate an understanding of the various bases that could be used to allocate profits or losses among partners.

An important process to be outlined in the articles of partnership is the manner in which profits and losses are to be divided among the partners. There are several alternative methods of allocating profits and losses. However, if the articles of partnership are silent on this point, Section 18 of the UPA states that profits and losses are to be divided equally among the partners. The division of partnership income should be based on an analysis of the correlation between the capital and labor committed to the firm by individual partners and the income that subsequently is generated. As a result, profits might be divided in one or more of the following ways:

1. According to a ratio.
2. According to the capital investments of the partners.
3. According to the labor (or service) rendered by the partners.

Profit and Loss Ratios. Partnership agreements frequently call for the allocation or division of profits and losses according to some ratio. Normally, the ratio set forth for the division of profits also is used for the division of losses, unless a specific provision to the contrary exists. This method obviously provides a simplified way of dividing profits and, if approached properly, may provide an equitable division as well. Theoretically, the ratio should attempt to combine into one base the capital and service contributions made by the respective partners. Again, it is important to note that a partner's interest in profits and losses is often different from the partner's interest in total partnership capital (net assets).

To illustrate this method, assume the articles of partnership state that partnership profits and losses should be divided between Partners A and B in the ratio of 60:40. Partnership income of $20,000 would be divided as follows:

	Partner A	Partner B
Income to partners:		
A: $20,000 × 60%.............	$12,000	
B: $20,000 × 40%.............		$8,000

Capital Investment of Partners. The capital investments of the partners, represented by the balances in their respective capital accounts, may be employed as a basis for dividing a portion of the profits. The division is accomplished by imputing interest on the invested capital at some specified rate. This interest is not viewed as a partnership expense but, rather, as a means of allocating profits and losses among the partners. Typically, the balance of profits not allocated on the basis of invested capital is allocated according to some profit and loss ratio.

When the partners' capital investments are to be used as the basis for allocating profits, the partnership agreement should specify the following:

1. Whether the respective partners' capital balances are to be determined before or after the partners' year-to-date withdrawals recorded in their drawing accounts are offset against their capital accounts.
2. Whether the amount of capital investment for allocation purposes is to be:
   a. Capital at the beginning of the accounting period,
   b. Capital at the end of the accounting period, or
   c. Weighted-average capital during the accounting period.
3. The rate of interest to be imputed on the invested capital.

With respect to the first point, it is important that the partnership agreement clearly establish how invested capital is to be determined. Since each partner's equity is really a combination of capital and drawing account balances, partners' drawings may be offset against the balances in their respective capital accounts for purposes of allocating income based on invested capital. However, a partnership agreement may state that only withdrawals above a certain limit are to be viewed as offsets against capital balances. It is possible for a partnership agreement to call for interest to be imputed only if the amount of invested capital exceeds some prescribed limit or average amount.

To illustrate the use of invested capital as a basis for allocating partnership profits, assume the following:

1. Partnership profit is $20,000.
2. Interest on invested capital is to be imputed at the rate of 10%. (Capital is determined before considering withdrawals.)
3. Profits not allocated on the basis of invested capital are to be allocated equally among the partners.
4. The capital accounts of Partners A and B, just prior to the closing of their drawing accounts, are as follows:

Partner A, Capital

Oct. 1, 20X1	30,000	Jan. 1, 20X1	100,000
		July 1, 20X1	10,000

Partner B, Capital

Apr. 1, 20X1	10,000	Jan. 1, 20X1	60,000

If interest is to be imputed on the partners' invested capital at the beginning of the period (January 1, 20X1), the partnership profit of $20,000 would be allocated as follows:

	Partner A	Partner B	Total
Interest on beginning capital:			
A: 10% × $100,000..........................	$10,000		$10,000
B: 10% × $60,000		$6,000	6,000
			$16,000
Balance per ratio (equally)	2,000	2,000	4,000
Allocation of profit.................................	$12,000	$8,000	$20,000

If interest is to be imputed on the partners' invested capital at the end of the period (December 31, 20X1), the partnership profit of $20,000 would be allocated as follows:

	Partner A	Partner B	Total
Interest on ending capital:			
A: 10% × $80,000............................	$ 8,000		$ 8,000
B: 10% × $50,000		$5,000	5,000
			$13,000
Balance per ratio (equally)	3,500	3,500	7,000
Allocation of profit.................................	$11,500	$8,500	$20,000

If interest is to be imputed on the partners' weighted-average invested capital during the period, the partnership profit of $20,000 would be allocated as follows:

	Partner A	Partner B	Total
Interest on weighted-average capital:			
A: 10% × $97,500 (Schedule A)	$ 9,750		$ 9,750
B: 10% × $52,500 (Schedule B)....................		$5,250	5,250
			$15,000
Balance per ratio (equally)	2,500	2,500	5,000
Allocation of profit.................................	$12,250	$7,750	$20,000

Schedule A
Weighted-Average Capital of Partner A

(1) Amount Invested	(2) Number of Months Invested	(1 × 2) Weighted Dollars
$100,000	6	$ 600,000
110,000	3	330,000
80,000	3	240,000
	12	$1,170,000

Weighted-average capital: $1,170,000 ÷ 12 = $ 97,500

Schedule B
Weighted-Average Capital of Partner B

(1) Amount Invested	(2) Number of Months Invested	(1 × 2) Weighted Dollars
$60,000	3	$180,000
50,000	9	450,000
	12	$630,000

Weighted-average capital: $630,000 ÷ 12 = $ 52,500

Services Rendered by Partners. A partner's labor or service to the partnership may be a primary force in the generation of revenue. Normally, the profit and loss agreement recognizes variations in effort by calling for a portion of income to be allocated to partners as salary. Such salaries, like interest on capital investments, are viewed as a means of allocating income rather than as an expense. It is important to note that this treatment of partners' salaries differs from the treatment of employee/shareholder salaries in a corporation, and the difference should be considered when the performance of a partnership is compared with that of a competing corporation.

When dealing with a profit and loss agreement that employs salaries as a means of allocating income, it is important not to confuse such salaries with partners' drawings. For example, a partner's withdrawal of $1,000 a month from the partnership may suggest that $12,000 of partnership income is being distributed to the partner as an annual salary or that these withdrawals may be ignored for purposes of dividing profits. Generally, a partner's drawing is not viewed as a salary but as a withdrawal of assets that reduces the partner's equity. For clarification purposes, the partnership agreement should state whether regular withdrawals of specific amounts should be viewed as salary for purposes of allocating income among the partners.

Bonuses to partners also may be used as a means of recognizing a partner's service to the partnership. Such bonuses are most often stated as a percentage of partnership income either before or after certain other components of the allocation process. Bonuses may be stated in reference to a variety of variables such as sales, gross profit, or a particular component of net income. In its most simple form, the bonus is a percentage of net income. However, if the bonus is to reward service beyond that already recognized by salaries and/or interest, the bonus may be expressed as a percentage of partnership net income after salaries and interest. In some instances, the bonus may be expressed as a percentage of net income after the bonus. To illustrate the calculation of a bonus, assume a partnership has net income of $120,000 of which $60,000 and $5,000 have already been allocated as salaries and interest, respectively. The bonus is defined in the partnership agreement as 10% of partnership net income after salaries and interest. The bonus is calculated as follows:

$$Bonus = X\% \ (Net \ Income - Salaries - Interest)$$
$$Bonus = 10\% \ (\$120,000 - \$60,000 - \$5,000)$$
$$Bonus = 10\% \ (\$55,000)$$
$$Bonus = \$5,500$$

If the agreement had stated that the bonus would be calculated based on net income after salaries, interest, and bonus, the calculation would be as follows:

$$Bonus = X\% \ (Net \ Income - Salaries - Interest - Bonus)$$
$$Bonus = 10\% \ (\$120,000 - \$60,000 - \$5,000 - Bonus)$$
$$110\% \ Bonus = 10\% \ (\$120,000 - \$60,000 - \$5,000)$$
$$110\% \ Bonus = 10\% \ (\$55,000)$$
$$110\% \ Bonus = \$5,500$$
$$Bonus = \$5,000$$

Multiple Bases of Allocation. In many cases, income is allocated to the respective partners by combining several allocation techniques. To illustrate, assume a profit and loss agreement of the ABC Partnership contains the following provisions:

1. Interest of 6% is to be allocated on that portion of a partner's ending capital balance in excess of $100,000.
2. Partner C is to be allocated a bonus equal to 10% of partnership income after the bonus.
3. Salaries of $13,000 and $12,000 are to be allocated to Partners A and C, respectively.
4. The balance of income is to be allocated in the ratio of 2:1:1 to A, B, and C, respectively.

Notice that these provisions govern the allocation of profit and not the actual distribution of assets.

Assuming a partnership income of $33,000 and ending capital balances of $80,000, $150,000, and $110,000 for Partners A, B, and C, respectively, income is allocated to the partners as shown in Illustration 8-2.

Illustration 8-2
Profit Allocation: Multiple Bases

	Partner A	Partner B	Partner C	Total
Interest on excess capital balance.....		$3,000	$ 600	$ 3,600
Bonus........................			3,000*	3,000
Salaries	$13,000		12,000	25,000
Subtotal	$13,000	$3,000	$15,600	$31,600
Remaining profit	700	350	350	1,400
Income allocation	$13,700	$3,350	$15,950	$33,000

$$*Bonus = 10\% \ (\text{Net Income} - \text{Bonus})$$
$$Bonus = 10\% \ (\$33,000 - \text{Bonus})$$
$$110\% \ \ Bonus = \$3,300$$
$$Bonus = \$3,000$$

Allocation of Profit Deficiencies and Losses. In the previous examples of profit allocations, the partnership income was large enough to satisfy all of the provisions of the profit and loss agreement. However, if the income is not sufficient or an operating loss exists, one of the two following alternatives may be employed assuming that the agreement governs both the allocation of profits or losses:

1. Completely satisfy all provisions of the profit and loss agreement and use the profit and loss ratios to absorb any deficiency or additional loss caused by such action.
2. Satisfy each of the provisions to whatever extent is possible. For example, the allocation of salaries would be satisfied to whatever extent possible before the allocation of interest is begun.

To illustrate these alternatives, assume the same information used in Illustration 8-2 for the ABC Partnership, except that the partnership income is $22,000. In Illustration 8-3, the income of $22,000 is divided by using the first alternative. When studying Illustration 8-3, it is important to note that the allocation of interest, bonus, and salaries results in an excessive allocation or deficiency of $8,600 (subtotal of $30,600 less the income of $22,000), which must be subtracted from the partners' previously allocated amounts. This deficiency is allocated among the partners according to their profit and loss ratios just like a remaining profit, except that the deficiency is subtracted rather than added.

Illustration 8-3
Profit Allocation: Deficiency Allocated in Profit and Loss Ratio

	Partner A	Partner B	Partner C	Total
Interest on excess capital balance		$ 3,000	$ 600	$ 3,600
Bonus			2,000*	2,000
Salaries	$13,000		12,000	25,000
Subtotal	$13,000	$ 3,000	$14,600	$30,600
Deficiency	(4,300)	(2,150)	(2,150)	(8,600)
Income allocation	$ 8,700	$ 850	$12,450	$22,000

$$*\text{Bonus} = 10\% \ (\text{Net Income} - \text{Bonus})$$
$$\text{Bonus} = 10\% \ (\$22,000 - \text{Bonus})$$
$$110\% \ \text{Bonus} = \$2,200$$
$$\text{Bonus} = \$2,000$$

Normally, the first method also is used when the partnership has an overall loss. For example, given a partnership loss of $2,400, the methodology in Illustration 8-3 would be employed, except that a bonus would not be recognized.

However, it is possible that a separate provision governs those situations in which a net loss exists. The allocation of the assumed loss of $2,400 is shown in Illustration 8-4. In this case, the allocation of the interest and salaries results in allocating $28,600 of income even though there is a loss of $2,400. This results in a deficiency of $31,000 (subtotal of $28,600 plus the loss of $2,400) which must be allocated among the partners according to their profit and loss ratios.

Illustration 8-4
Loss Allocation: Deficiency Allocated in Profit and Loss Ratio

	Partner A	Partner B	Partner C	Total
Interest on excess capital balance		$ 3,000	$ 600	$ 3,600
Bonus (not applicable)				
Salaries	$ 13,000		12,000	25,000
Subtotal	$ 13,000	$ 3,000	$12,600	$ 28,600
Deficiency	(15,500)	(7,750)	(7,750)	(31,000)
Loss allocation	$ (2,500)	$(4,750)	$ 4,850	$ (2,400)

The second alternative, which is used less frequently, requires that the provisions of the profit and loss agreement be ranked by order of priority. Assuming the components listed in Illustration 8-3 are already in order of priority, a partnership income of $22,000 would be distributed as shown in Illustration 8-5.

Illustration 8-5
Profit Allocation: Deficiency Allocated by Order of Priority

	Partner A	Partner B	Partner C	Total
Interest on excess capital balance		$3,000	$ 600	$ 3,600
Bonus.			2,000*	2,000
Salaries	$8,528		7,872	16,400
Income allocation	$8,528	$3,000	$10,472	$22,000

*Bonus = 10% (Net Income − Bonus)
    Bonus = 10% ($22,000 − Bonus)
110% Bonus = $2,200
     Bonus = $2,000

The salaries of $16,400 would be allocated to Partners A and C according to the ratio suggested by their normal salaries of $13,000 and $12,000, respectively. Therefore, A would receive 13/25 of the $16,400, or $8,528, while C would receive 12/25, or $7,872.

Special Allocation Procedures. A partnership profit and loss agreement may include special provisions for handling items that represent (1) corrections of prior years' income or (2) current-period, nonoperating gains or losses. Even though a correction of prior years' income may not satisfy the criteria for a prior-period adjustment, as defined by the Financial Accounting Standards Board, it may be more equitable to allocate the item among the partners according to the profit and loss agreement for the relevant prior period rather than the current period. For example, assume that Partners A, B, and C, who previously shared profits equally, currently share profits in the ratio of 2:2:1. Also assume that, in the current year, the partnership incurs a loss of $10,000 due to the settlement of litigation involving a matter arising in a prior period. Rather than allocating the loss according to the current profit ratios, it may be more equitable to base the allocation on the prior ratios.

A similar procedure may be adopted for the current-period recognition of nonoperating gains or losses. Rather than allocating a gain on the sale of a plant asset according to the partners' current profit-sharing ratios, it may be more equitable to use the ratios that existed during the period when unrealized appreciation actually took place.

To illustrate, assume that land with a basis of $40,000 has been held for three years and is sold for $60,000 in the current period. Based on the assumed profit-sharing ratios of prior periods and amounts of annual appreciation, the $20,000 gain would be allocated to Partners A, B, and C as follows:

Year	Profit Ratio	Appreciation	Profit Allocation		
			A	B	C
1	1:1:2	$ 4,000	$1,000	$1,000	$2,000
2	2:1:2	10,000	4,000	2,000	4,000
3	2:2:2	6,000	2,000	2,000	2,000
		$20,000	$7,000	$5,000	$8,000

If the partnership had not established special provisions for handling such items, the gain of $20,000 would have been allocated equally among the partners according to their current profit ratio of 2:2:2.

REFLECTION

- The balance in a partner's drawing account, along with the share of profits or losses, is closed out to the partner's capital account.

- The nature of the business a partnership is engaged in should suggest the various bases that might be appropriate for an allocation of profits or losses.

- The allocation of profits or losses may be based on salaries, bonuses, interest on invested capital, and/or a profit/loss percentage.

UNDERSTANDING THE ISSUES

1. A major issue faced by people who are starting their own business is the form of organization they should select. What are some major characteristics of a partnership that might influence their decision?

2. Under what circumstances might a salary or bonus be more appropriate than interest on capital balances as a means of allocating profits?

3. If the income of a partnership is not sufficient enough to satisfy all of the provisions of the partnership's profit-sharing agreement, how should this deficiency be handled?

4. Generally speaking, what events or activities would normally result in a partner's capital accounting being debited?

EXERCISES

Exercise 8-1 *(LO 1)* **Partnership versus corporate balance sheets and income statements.** In 20X1, a new partnership purchased land on the edge of the town of Otisville. The partners erected a building and opened a furniture and appliance store under the name of Otisville Furniture Fair. The partnership agreement specified that profits or losses should be shared equally after the allocation of partners' salary allowances and interest on average capital balances.

Otisville has grown considerably, and the store is now one of the most prominent stores in a fashionable suburban area. Good management, imaginative merchandising, and the general growth in the economy have made Otisville Furniture Fair the leading and most profitable company of its type in the Otisville trade area.

Now, the partners wish to admit another investor and incorporate the business. The original partners will purchase at par an amount of preferred stock equal to the book value of their interest in the partnership and common stock equal to that portion of fair value that exceeds their book value. The new investor will purchase, at a 10% premium over par value, common and preferred stock equal to one-third of the total number of shares purchased by the original partners. The corporation will then purchase the Otisville Furniture Fair partnership at its fair value from the partners. After the consummation of the partners' plan, the corporation will acquire the partnership assets, assume the liabilities, and employ the partners to manage the corporation.

1. List and explain the differences in terms and valuations that would be expected in comparing the assets that appear on the balance sheet of the proposed corporation and the assets that appear on the partnership balance sheet.
2. List and explain the differences that would be expected in a comparison of an income statement prepared for the proposed corporation and an income statement prepared for the partnership.

(AICPA adapted)

Exercise 8-2 *(LO 2)* **Partnership agreement.** Grandey, Feldman, and O'Connor (G, F, and O) have decided to form a partnership for the purpose of operating an environmental consulting firm. The partners will have to invest enough capital in order to acquire necessary working capital, diagnostic software, and a variety of other capital assets. Grandey and Feldman both have experience as environmental consultants and will be active in the firm. However, O'Connor has a marketing background and will not be active in the firm on a daily basis. O'Connor will be a major contributor of capital and provide advice as necessary.

The three partners have sketched out a preliminary agreement that contains the following components:

1. Normal income will be allocated among all three partners as follows: all partners will receive a salary, Feldman will receive a bonus equal to 10% of normal income, and all partners will receive interest on capital in excess of $50,000.
2. Nonnormal income will be allocated among all three partners according to their respective capital balances.
3. Upon withdrawal, a partner must first offer her or his partnership interest to the partnership for an amount equal to 120% of book value.
4. Capital balances will be measured according to generally accepted accounting principles.
5. No partner may withdraw more than 80% of his or her respective share of income.

The partners recognize that an independent party should review the preliminary agreement and provide appropriate advice. Identify potential problems and concerns with the agreement.

Exercise 8-3 *(LO 4)* **Evaluating a change to the partnership agreement.** Kennedy, Walker, and O'Brien are partners in an environmental engineering firm. The firm was originally started by Kennedy and Walker. O'Brien joined the firm in 20X4. The current partnership agreement calls for the allocation of profits as follows:

1. Salaries of $80,000, $80,000, and $60,000 for Kennedy, Walker, and O'Brien, respectively.
2. Interest on average capital of 5%. Measures of average capital exclude the first $30,000 of individual partner's annual withdrawals.
3. Annual allowance for charitable contributions of $4,000 per partner.
4. A bonus of 12% of net income after the bonus allocated equally between Kennedy and Walker.
5. All remaining profits are allocated 35%, 35%, and 30% to Kennedy, Walker, and O'Brien, respectively.

Net income for the year 20X6 was $420,000 after expensing charitable contributions of $63,000. The contributions made on behalf of Kennedy, Walker, and O'Brien were $30,000, $30,000, and $3,000, respectively. January 1, 20X6, capital balances and 20X6 withdrawals are as follows:

	Kennedy	Walker	O'Brien
January 1, 20X6, capital balances	$100,000	$120,000	$70,000
March 31 withdrawal	60,000	60,000	
July 1 withdrawal	20,000	20,000	30,000
November 30 withdrawal			30,000

During 20X6, O'Brien has become increasingly bothered by the profit-sharing agreement and feels that the partners have been especially harmed by the provisions related to interest on capital and charitable contributions. O'Brien is suggesting that the profit-sharing agreement be amended as follows: (a) net income excludes charitable contributions, (b) charitable contributions made by the partnership on behalf of partners are considered withdrawals, and (c) no amount of profit is allocated for a contribution allowance. All other previous profit allocation provisions are to remain the same. Furthermore, O'Brien is requesting that the three partners be allocated a one-time bonus of $30,000 in 20X7 representing a retroactive application of the proposal to the 20X6 net income.

O'Brien has been instrumental in securing a significant amount of new business and has indicated that he is considering leaving the partnership if things do not change. The possible loss of business is of concern to the senior partners, and they need to respond to O'Brien's concerns.

Kennedy and Walker are inclined to accept O'Brien's offer, except they think that the bonus in 20X7 is overstated.

Prepare a schedule that would provide Kennedy and Walker with a more reasonable measure of the effect of retroactively applying O'Brien's proposal.

Exercise 8-4 *(LO 4)* Approaches to the allocation of profits and losses.
Medina, Harris, and Anderson are partners in Entertainment Systems. The partnership earned a modest profit of $30,000 in 20X3. The partnership agreement includes the following regarding the allocation of profits or losses:

1. Interest of 8% is to be paid on the portion of a partner's ending capital balance in excess of $75,000.
2. Medina and Harris receive salaries of $20,000 and $30,000, respectively. Both individuals are actively involved with day-to-day operations.
3. The balance of income is to be distributed in the ratio of 2:1:1 to Medina, Harris, and Anderson, respectively.

Assume ending capital balances of $60,000, $80,000, and $100,000 for partners Medina, Harris, and Anderson, respectively.

1. Allocate the profit among the partners, assuming the following:
   a. The profit and loss ratios are used to absorb any deficiency or additional loss.
   b. Each of the provisions of the profit and loss agreement is satisfied to whatever extent possible. The priority order is interest, salaries, and then remaining amounts per the profit and loss ratios.
2. Discuss which method would be best suited for this partnership.

Exercise 8-5 *(LO 4)* Approaches to the allocation of profits and losses.
Collins, Baker, and Lebo are partners in a business that distributes various electronic components used to control machinery in the printing industry. The partners have a lucrative business and have allocated profits according to the following agreement:

1. Salaries of $50,000 to each of the partners.
2. A bonus to Baker of 5% of sales to International Printers Inc. in excess of $1,000,000.
3. A bonus to Collins of 10% of net income after this bonus.
4. Interest of 10% on each partner's average annual invested capital in excess of $100,000.
5. Remaining profits to be allocated in the ratio of 5:3:2 for Collins, Baker, and Lebo, respectively.

In a typical year, the above agreement is applied under the following conditions: net income of $880,000, sales to International Printers Inc. of $1,500,000, and average annual invested capital of $50,000, $120,000, and $250,000 for Collins, Baker, and Lebo, respectively.

Gordon, who is seeking to be admitted to the partnership, has approached the partners. Gordon has an exclusive licensing agreement with a manufacturer of control devices that can significantly reduce the amount of electricity used by machinery. Gordon is confident that these products will be extremely successful, but they lack an established customer base. Therefore, Gordon is most interested in pursuing discussions with the existing partnership. Gordon has proposed contributing $50,000 cash and the exclusive licensing agreement to the partnership in exchange for an interest in capital and profits. Furthermore, Gordon proposes that a new profit agreement be established with the following terms:

1. Salaries of $50,000 to each of the partners.
2. A bonus to Baker of 5% of sales to International Printers Inc. in excess of $1,000,000 traceable to products not covered by the exclusive licensing agreement.
3. A bonus to Gordon of 15% of sales in excess of $2,000,000 traceable to those products covered by the exclusive licensing agreement. Gordon estimates that total sales associated with these products will be approximately $4,200,000.
4. Interest of 10% on each partner's average annual invested capital in excess of $100,000.
5. Remaining profits to be allocated in the ratio of 3:3:2:2 for Collins, Baker, Lebo, and Gordon, respectively.

Collins is your personal tax client and comes to you for advice. Baker and Lebo are very excited about the Gordon proposal. However, Collins feels that Gordon may be unrealistic regarding the success of this new product line. Collins is concerned about giving Gordon a voice in the management of the partnership; but more importantly, she feels that her interest in profits may be less under the Gordon proposal. You understand your client's concern and try to be positive by saying that the Gordon proposal may be worth it. Collins responds by saying, "Maybe it is worth it if I can make another $60,000 before taxes." Prepare a quantitative analysis that your client Collins may use to better assess the implications associated with the Gordon proposal.

Exercise 8-6 *(LO 3)* **Assessing the impact of withdrawals on the allocation of profits.** Cramer, Larson, and Hughes have allocated profits of the partnership as follows:

1. Salaries of $80,000, $60,000, and $60,000 to Cramer, Larson, and Hughes, respectively.
2. All remaining profit is allocated equally among the partners.

In the past, the partners had not formalized policies regarding withdrawals of capital, and operating cash levels were adequate. Due to a changing business environment, the partnership has begun to experience liquidity problems and has had to increase its outside borrowings. The partners acknowledge that all partners bear the burden of increased interest expense and debt service. However, the partners do not equitably bear the impact of partner withdrawals.

As of January 1, 20X8, the partners have agreed to reallocate 20X6 and 20X7 profits among the partners. The reallocation of profits will follow the existing profit-sharing agreement with the addition of a provision that interest will be allocated to the partners based on 10% of the weighted-average capital balance including the withdrawals but excluding current-year profits. Net income for 20X6 and 20X7 was $500,000 and $410,000, respectively.

Capital balances and withdrawals are as follows:

	Cramer	Larson	Hughes
Capital balance as of December 31, 20X5	$180,000	$250,000	$ 60,000
March 31, 20X6, withdrawal	150,000	170,000	
September 30, 20X6, withdrawal....................	20,000	50,000	50,000
January 31, 20X7, withdrawal	170,000	190,000	150,000

Prepare the January 1, 20X8, entry to reallocate profits among the partners.

Exercise 8-7 *(LO 3, 4)* **Profit allocation based on several factors; weighted-average interest.** Gabriel and Hall are partners in a manufacturing business located in Portland, Oregon. Their profit and loss agreement contains the following provisions:

1. Salaries of $35,000 and $40,000 for Gabriel and Hall, respectively.
2. A bonus to Gabriel equal to 10% of net income after the bonus.
3. Interest on weighted-average capital at the rate of 8%. Annual drawings in excess of $20,000 are considered to be a reduction of capital for purposes of this calculation.
4. Profit and loss percentages of 40% and 60% for Gabriel and Hall, respectively.

Capital and drawing activity of the partners for the year 20X5 are as follows:

	Gabriel Capital	Gabriel Drawing	Hall Capital	Hall Drawing
Beginning balance	$120,000	$ 0	$ 60,000	$ 0
April 1	20,000			
June 1		15,000		20,000
September 1	30,000			
November 1		15,000	40,000	
Ending balance	$170,000	$30,000	$100,000	$20,000

Assuming net income for 20X5 of $132,000, determine how much profit should be allocated to each partner.

Exercise 8-8 *(LO 3, 4)* **Interest calculation; determination of capital account balances.** Xavier, Yates, and Zale are partners in a dry-cleaning business. Their partnership agreement provides that the partners shall receive interest on their respective average yearly capital balances at the rate of 8%. Any residual profits or losses shall be divided equally among the partners. The following information is available for the second year of operations:

a. Partners' capital balances as of January 1, 20X2:

Xavier	$24,000
Yates	17,500
Zale	13,000

b. Additional investments were made during the year as follows:

Xavier	$4,500 on April 1, 20X2
Zale	$2,000 on July 1, 20X2
	$15,000 on September 1, 20X2

c. The drawing accounts of the partners have the following debit balances at the end of 20X2:

Xavier	$1,000
Yates	1,000
Zale	500

d. Partnership income for the year is $21,100.

1. Discuss the advantages and disadvantages of using the weighted-average capital balance as the base for determining interest on capital contributed.
2. Determine the interest on weighted-average capital balances that partners Xavier, Yates, and Zale should receive for the year 20X2. Assume that the partners' withdrawals are not to influence the capital balances for purposes of computing interest.
3. Determine the capital account balances for Xavier, Yates, and Zale after all closing entries have been journalized and posted at the end of 20X2. Supporting schedules should be in good form.

Exercise 8-9 *(LO 4)* **Evaluating alternative profit-sharing arrangements.** Patton is considering joining Microtech Enterprises as a partner. The company provides data imaging for a variety of end users. Patton will have to contribute $100,000 of capital upon admission as a partner and will need to decide on a profit-sharing arrangement. Three alternatives are being proposed as follows:

Alternative A—Patton will be allocated a salary of $120,000, 10% of average capital after considering withdrawals, and 10% of net income. At the end of each calendar quarter, $30,000 will be distributed to Patton. No additional profits will be allocated to Patton.

Alternative B—Patton will be allocated a salary of $96,000, 10% of average capital after considering withdrawals in excess of $60,000, and a bonus of 10% of net income. At the end of the second, third, and fourth calendar quarters, Patton will receive a distribution of $24,000. At the end of the first quarter of the following year, Patton will receive a distribution of $60,000. No additional profits will be allocated to Patton.

Alternative C—Patton will be allocated a salary of $80,000 and 20% of net income. Patton will receive a distribution of $20,000 at the end of calendar quarters 1 through 3 and $80,000 at the end of quarter 4.

Patton has retained you to assist in evaluating the above alternatives and has asked you to assume that cash distributions could be reinvested at 6%. Furthermore, Patton believes that the probability of various levels of partnership income are as follows: a 30% probability of $500,000 of income, a 50% probability of $560,000 of income, and a 20% probability of $600,000 of income.

1. Prepare a schedule that evaluates the alternatives in terms of profitability and the present value of cash flows for the first year of the partnership.
2. Discuss which alternative you consider to be the most attractive.

PROBLEMS

Problem 8-1 *(LO 1)* **Characteristics of a partnership and proper organization form.** A client is seeking your advice on how to organize a new business. The client is proposing to acquire several single-story residences and convert them into group homes for the elderly. Each home would house eight elderly individuals, and the homes would be staffed 24 hours a day. Residents would receive housing, food, and daily-planned activities for a monthly fee. Group homes are licensed by the state and are closely monitored. Such homes do not provide any direct health care to the residents. The client plans to have an active role in the organization and management of the homes and is seeking another individual or two to provide necessary capital as passive investors. It is anticipated that the homes will operate at a loss for the first 12 to 18 months. The client hopes to open two group homes for each of the next four years and then sell his interest in the business. Your client is interested in organizing the company as a partnership and wants to know how that might affect him and other potential partners.

Identify and discuss some of the characteristics of a partnership of which your client should be aware. ◄ ◄ ◄ ◄ ◄ **Required**

Problem 8-2 *(LO 3, 4)* **Allocation of profits and determination of withdrawals.** Sandburg and Williams are the owners of a partnership that manufactures commercial lighting fixtures. Profits are allocated among the partners as follows:

	Sandburg	Williams
Salaries	$100,000	$125,000
Bonus as a percentage of net income after the bonus	10%	0%
Interest on weighted-average capital including withdrawals and excluding current-year profits	5%	5%

Sandburg was divorced as of the beginning of 20X5 and as part of the divorce stipulation agreed to the following:

1. The spouse is to receive annual distributions traceable to years 20X5 and 20X6. The annual distribution is to be the greater of $100,000 or 25% of base earnings.
2. Base earnings are defined as net income of the partnership less: (a) salaries traceable to Sandburg and Williams of $75,000 and $125,000, respectively, and (b) bonus to Sandburg as stated subject to the limitation that it not exceed $50,000.
3. Sandburg's spouse would receive a distribution from the partnership on August 31 of each current year and on February 28 of each subsequent year. The August 31 target distribution is $50,000. If the August distribution is less than $50,000, Sandburg's spouse will receive one-half year's interest on the deficiency at the rate of 10% per year. The following distribution on February 28 must be of an amount such that the two distributions equal the required distribution traceable to the calendar year just ended plus any interest associated with the August distribution.
4. All distributions to Sandburg's spouse are to be considered as a withdrawal of capital by Sandburg.
5. Aside from distributions to Sandburg's spouse, Sandburg's annual withdrawals cannot exceed $125,000.
6. Upon sale or dissolution of the partnership prior to February 28, 20X6, Sandburg's spouse would receive 50% of the net realizable value of Sandburg's partnership capital.
7. On February 28, 20X7, Sandburg's spouse will receive an additional final distribution equal to 50% of the sum of Sandburg's capital balance as of December 31, 20X6, less the amount of the February 20X7 distribution as called for by item (3) above.

Capital balances at the beginning of 20X5 were $180,000 and $125,000, respectively, for Sandburg and Williams. Activity related to the partnership during 20X5 and 20X6 is as follows:

	20X5	20X6
Partnership net income	$750,000	$700,000
Distribution to Sandburg's spouse:		
February 28	0	to be determined
August 31	40,000	50,000
Distributions to Sandburg:		
June 30.	60,000	125,000
September 30	65,000	0
Distributions to Williams:		
June 30.	30,000	300,000
September 30	90,000	20,000

Required ▶ ▶ ▶ ▶ ▶   Prepare a schedule to determine the total amount of the distributions due Sandburg's spouse as of February 28, 20X7. Note that the solution requires one to determine the amount of the February 20X6 distribution to Sandburg's wife.

Problem 8-3 *(LO 4)* **Decision to admit a new partner, profit allocation.** Thomas and Purnell are general partners in a partnership along with four limited partners. Ten percent of partnership profit is allocated to each of the limited partners, and the balance of the profits is allocated to Thomas and Purnell as follows:

1. Salaries of $40,000 and $60,000 to Thomas and Purnell, respectively.
2. A bonus to Thomas of 10% of sales in excess of $1,200,000.
3. A bonus to Purnell of 5% of net income after the bonus.
4. Remaining profits to be allocated 60% and 40%, respectively, to Thomas and Purnell.

The general partners have been approached by Wiggins, who has significant experience in the area of foreign sales and is seeking admission to the partnership. Wiggins is confident that she can generate significant increases in sales and that any capital needed to finance the expansion will be raised and guaranteed by her. Furthermore, Wiggins is proposing that the existing profit agreement be modified as follows:

1. Wiggins will be allocated a salary of $40,000.
2. A bonus to Wiggins of 15% of all international sales in excess of $500,000.
3. Thomas's bonus will be limited to domestic sales only.
4. Remaining profits to be allocated 40%, 40%, and 20% to Thomas, Purnell, and Wiggins, respectively.

The limited partners are in favor of admitting Wiggins, noting that their opportunities for increased profits would be improved. However, Thomas and Purnell are concerned that unless sales and profits grow significantly, they will receive a smaller allocation of profits than they did before Wiggins. Without Wiggins, the partnership is projecting domestic sales and profits of $1,450,000 and $280,000, respectively, for the next year. Thomas and Purnell feel that if their interest in profits increases by $16,000 and $24,000, respectively, they will be inclined to admit Wiggins as a partner.

Required ▶ ▶ ▶ ▶ ▶   Assume that Wiggins is able to generate $700,000 of additional foreign sales which include a 40% gross profit margin and that the general and administrative expenses associated with this increase are 15% of such sales. Prepare an analysis for Thomas and Purnell that summarizes their profit allocation with and without Wiggins.

Problem 8-4 *(LO 4)* **Expert witness, economic loss measurement.** A law firm that specializes in personal injury work has engaged you to assist in some litigation. The firm represents a Mr. Lawson, who was injured in an automobile accident and is alleging that he was totally disabled as a result of the accident. Lawson is seeking damages that in part reflect the loss of income from his interest in a partnership known as L & S Contractors (L & S). L & S is in the business of contracting to do residential remodeling jobs and has three partners: Lawson, Schmidt, and Jacobsen.

Sales and related income of the partnership have grown over the years although the residential construction industry is cyclical in nature. The law firm has provided you with copies of various partnership documents that may be relevant to this matter. A review of the partnership agreement reveals the following regarding the allocation of annual profits:

1. Salaries for Lawson, Schmidt, and Jacobsen of $60,000, $60,000, and $40,000, respectively.
2. Bonuses of 10% and 5% of net income after the bonuses for Lawson and Schmidt, respectively.
3. Profit and loss percentages of 30%, 30%, and 40% for Lawson, Schmidt, and Jacobsen, respectively.

Other relevant components of the partnership agreement are as follows:

1. Partners receive a draw on July 1 and December 1 of each year. Each partner's draw is equal to one-third of 40% of the net income from the preceding year. Partners will receive draws for all years in which they were active in the business.
2. Unless modified by a majority of the partners, no more than 80% of annual income may be distributed to the partners.
3. Upon total disability, death, or retirement of a partner (referred to as a triggering event), the partnership will acquire such partner's capital interest in the partnership. The amount paid will be equal to three times such partner's average share of annual partnership income for the two years prior to the year of the triggering event. The acquisition price will be paid out in four equal semiannual payments beginning six months after the triggering event.

The automobile accident involving Mr. Lawson occurred on December 31, 20X3. At his deposition, Mr. Lawson indicated the following:

1. He anticipated retiring at the end of 20X8.
2. Net income of the partnership for years 20X1, 20X2, and 20X3 was $161,000, $207,000, and $210,000, respectively.
3. Based on past and projected factors, he anticipated net income for years 20X4 through 20X8 to be $230,000 per year.

Prepare a tentative measure of the economic loss suffered by Mr. Lawson as a result of the alleged total disability. Your measure of loss should be expressed as of the date of the accident and include appropriate present-value considerations.   ◀ ◀ ◀ ◀ ◀ **Required**

Problem 8-5 *(LO 3, 4)* **Investment decision, capital retention decision.** Rodriquez
is one of your tax clients and has come to you seeking your input about a potential investment opportunity. Your client has the opportunity to acquire a 30% interest in the capital of a partnership. However, this would require him to give up his current job. The partnership will consist of Rodriquez, Monroe, and Zito, and the partners will allocate profits and losses as follows:

1. Salaries to Rodriquez and Monroe of $40,000 and $50,000, respectively.
2. Interest at the rate of 9% on weighted-average net capital in excess of $20,000. All partners are required to maintain $20,000 in their net capital accounts throughout the year. Net capital is defined in the partnership agreement as capital balances less drawing account balances. It is estimated that in all cases, Monroe and Zito will maintain weighted-average net capital balances of $40,000 and $150,000, respectively. Unless otherwise stated, it is assumed that Rodriquez will maintain the minimum balance of net capital.
3. Bonus to Monroe of 5% of sales in excess of $500,000. It is estimated that sales for the year will be $650,000.
4. Profit and loss percentages of 40%, 40%, and 20% for partners Rodriquez, Monroe, and Zito, respectively.

Rodriquez is very interested in the opportunities that the partnership presents. However, he is concerned that his allocation of profits may not justify changing jobs.

Required ▶ ▶ ▶ ▶ ▶

1. Determine how much partnership profit would have to be realized in order for Rodriquez's allocated portion to equal his current job salary of $60,000.
2. Determine whether Rodriquez is best advised to withdraw available capital in excess of the minimum balance or retain capital in the partnership.
3. Assume that annual sales were less than $500,000 and that Rodriquez maintained the minimum net capital balance during the year. The other partners are assumed to maintain capital balances as stated. Furthermore, assume that all allocated profits are withdrawn. What is the minimum amount of partnership income that would be necessary in order for Rodriquez not to have to make an additional investment of capital?

Problem 8-6 *(LO 3, 4)* **Correction of previously misstated capital and drawing accounts.** Lewis, Clark, and Jefferson are partners in a company that manufactures store fixtures. The partnership agreement calls for the following provisions regarding the allocation of profits:

1. Lewis and Clark will be allocated a quarterly salary of $20,000 each. Jefferson will be allocated a quarterly salary of $15,000.
2. Clark and Jefferson, both being responsible for sales, will share a bonus of 20% of net income after the bonus. Of the 20%, 40% is allocated to Clark, and the balance is allocated to Jefferson. Bonus amounts are to be determined semiannually.
3. Interest of 8% per year will be allocated to each partner's weighted-average annual capital balance.
4. Any remaining profits will be allocated to Lewis, Clark, and Jefferson in the amounts of 35%, 35%, and 30%, respectively.
5. In the case that net income is not adequate to satisfy the above requirements, any deficiency will be allocated to the partners in the percentages set forth in item (4) above.

The partnership agreement also contains the following provisions regarding capital and drawing balances:

1. For purposes of calculating interest on capital balances, drawing account balances and allocations of current-year profits are to be ignored. However, the beginning-of-year capital balance should include the effect of closing drawings and profits traceable to a given partner.
2. All partners are required to maintain a minimum capital balance of $50,000 at all times.
3. At the end of each quarter, the partners will receive a draw equal to 80% of their allocated quarterly salary.
4. Any draws beyond those provided by item (3) above must be approved by at least two of the partners and will be considered a direct reduction of capital for purposes of item (1) above.
5. Upon withdrawal of a partner, the existing partner will first offer their partnership interest to the partnership in exchange for consideration equal to 125% of their net capital and drawing account balances as of the end of the quarter prior to withdrawal.

The partnership began operations July 1, 20X5, with each partner contributing $50,000 of capital. The partnership has reported annual net income of $120,000, $300,000, and $420,000 for years 20X5 through 20X7, respectively. During this entire time, Jefferson assumed responsibility for overseeing the partnership's accounting function. Early in 20X7, Jefferson began to have some personal financial problems, and on March 31, 20X7, the partners unanimously approved an immediate draw by Jefferson of an additional $50,000. During the latter half of 20X7, Jefferson appeared to be extremely stressed out and began to miss a lot of work. Lewis and Clark became concerned; their concern was heightened in January of 20X8 when Jefferson indicated that he would be withdrawing immediately from the partnership. Furthermore, Jefferson became irate when the partners indicated that it would take at least a month to secure the $200,000 necessary to buy Jefferson out.

Due to the strange way in which Jefferson was acting, Lewis and Clark began to think that Jefferson might be involved in some type of impropriety. You have been retained to determine if the provisions of the partnership agreement relating to accounting and balances have been properly complied with. You have been provided with the post-closing capital account balances as of the end of 20X7 of $139,000, $176,000, and $185,000 for Lewis, Clark, and Jefferson, respectively, as determined by Jefferson. Upon further investigation, it appears that net income in 20X7 has been overstated by $90,000. The overstatement was achieved by a $65,000 overstatement of credit sales and a $25,000 overstatement in ending inventory.

Prepare a schedule to determine the proper equity balances of the partners as of December ◄ ◄ ◄ ◄ ◄ **Required** 31, 20X7, and also prepare the entry to correct the financial statements assuming 20X7 drawing account balances have been closed.

Problem 8-7 *(LO 3, 4)* **Error effect on capital balances.**
Carson, Dowman, and Evans own an office automation and consulting business organized as a partnership. Evans is considering retirement from the partnership. In order to more fairly measure Evans' interest in capital, an audit of the company's first two years of operations was performed in early 20X9. The original partnership agreement called for Carson to receive a 10% bonus on income after the bonus, with the remaining profits or losses to be divided as follows: Carson, 30%; Dowman, 30%; and Evans, 40%. Reported income for 20X7 was $44,000. In the second year of operations, the agreement was modified to reflect Evans' decision to become less involved in the business. The new agreement called for Carson still to receive a 10% bonus on income after the bonus, but it altered the allocation of remaining amounts as follows: Carson, 35%; Dowman, 35%; and Evans, 30%. Reported income for 20X8 was $42,000. The partners had always agreed that any adjustment to reported amounts would be allocated based on the profit and loss agreement in effect during the period to which the adjustment relates. The audit indicated that the following items were not properly accounted for:

1. 20X7:
   a. Failed to amortize the business name contributed by Carson. The fair value of the intangible was $50,000 and should have been amortized over a 10-year life using straight-line amortization.
   b. Failed to defer prepaid 20X8 insurance premiums of $3,000.
   c. A capital withdrawal of $5,000 made by Carson on July 1, 20X7, was classified incorrectly as a note receivable.
   d. Failed to accrue $2,000 of employee wages on December 31, 20X7.
   e. Failed to record consulting fees of $8,400 earned in 20X7 but billed in 20X8.
2. 20X8:
   a. Purchases of inventory included a computer invoiced on December 31, 20X8, for $4,000 but not yet received. Terms were f.o.b. destination. The item was not included in the year-end physical inventory.
   b. Failed to accrue $8,600 of rent expense on December 31, 20X8.
   c. Failed to reverse $3,000 of interest income properly accrued at the end of 20X7, resulting in income recognition in both years.

Assume the following unadjusted December 31, 20X8, capital account balances: Carson, ◄ ◄ ◄ ◄ ◄ **Required** $25,000; Dowman, $30,000; and Evans, $28,000. Prepare a schedule to reflect the adjusted capital balances as of December 31, 20X8. Supporting calculations should be in good form.

Problem 8-8 *(LO 3, 4)* **Determination of capital balances over time.**
At the beginning of 20X5, Harris, Piano, and Tyler each contributed $80,000 of assets to begin partnership. The partnership agreement provided for the following with respect to the allocation of profits and losses:

1. Salaries to Harris, Piano, and Tyler of $76,000, $76,000, and $48,000, respectively. Salaries are to be distributed to the individual partners in equal amounts at the end of each calendar quarter.
2. A bonus to Tyler of 5% of annual net sales.
3. Interest on average capital of 6%. During a given year, drawings, to the extent they exceed salaries, are to be offset against capital balances for purposes of this calculation. Beginning-of-year capital balances should reflect all appropriate closing entries.
4. Profit and loss percentages of 35%, 35%, and 30% for Harris, Piano, and Tyler, respectively.
5. Each of the provisions of the profit and loss agreement is satisfied to whatever extent possible. The priority order is salaries, bonus, interest, and then remaining amounts per the profit and loss percentages.

In addition to the distribution of salaries, withdrawals are as follows:

	Harris	Piano	Tyler
January 31, 20X6, withdrawal	$50,000		$ 30,000
February 28, 20X6, withdrawal	20,000	$48,000	
June 30, 20X7, withdrawal.	10,000	20,000	100,000

Early in April of 20X8, Piano was permanently disabled. The partnership agreement addresses the potential of a permanent disability of a partner and provides the following:

1. The affected partner will receive an immediate distribution equal to 20% of their annual salary.
2. The affected partner's capital balance will be credited for their profit and loss percentage of current partnership net income from the beginning of the current year to the end of the month preceding the determination of disability. This is in lieu of the normal agreement regarding the allocation of profits.
3. 125% of the affected partner's capital balance as of the end of the month preceding the determination of disability will be distributed to the partner in equal payments over each of the next six quarters including interest on the unpaid balance at the rate of 6%.

Income statement data for the partnership are as follows:

	20X5	20X6	20X7	Jan. 1– Mar. 31, 20X8
Sales	$800,000	$950,000	$1,400,000	$320,000
Sales returns and allowances	40,000	70,000	80,000	10,000
Net income	220,000	260,000	270,000	80,000

Required ▶ ▶ ▶ ▶ ▶

1. Prepare a schedule to Piano's capital balance as of March 31, 20X8.
2. Prepare a schedule that shows the payments to be received by Piano subsequent to the determination of their disability.

Partnerships: Ownership Changes and Liquidations

Learning Objectives

When you have completed this chapter, you should be able to

1. Define partnership dissolution, and explain what accounting issues should be addressed upon dissolution.

2. Account for the partners' capital balances under the bonus method.

3. Account for the partners' capital balances under the goodwill method.

4. Describe the conceptual differences between the bonus and goodwill methods.

5. Account for the admission of a new partner through direct contribution to an existing partner.

6. Explain the impact of a partner's withdrawal from the partnership.

7. Describe the order in which assets must be distributed upon liquidation of a partnership, and explain the right-of-offset concept.

8. Explain the doctrine of marshaling of assets.

9. Calculate the assets to be distributed to a given partner in a lump-sum or installment liquidation, and understand the concept of maximum loss absorbable.

10. Prepare an installment liquidation statement and a schedule of safe payments.

In theory, a partnership may be viewed as a conduit or entity through which individual partners carry on a common business purpose. It is natural that the circumstances surrounding the individual partners' lives may change and affect their involvement in the partnership. Individual partners may increase or decrease their interest in the partnership or withdraw entirely from the partnership. In turn, new partners may become involved in the partnership. Such ownership changes are common in a partnership just as they are in other forms of organizations, such as a corporation. However, unlike a corporation, which is recognized as a separate and distinct entity having an infinite life, changes in the ownership structure of a partnership result in the dissolution of the previous partnership.

The Uniform Partnership Act (UPA) defines *dissolution* as "the change in the relation of the partners caused by any partner ceasing to be associated in the carrying on as distinguished from the winding up of the business." Sections 31 and 32 of the UPA identify the various causes of dissolution and suggest that the admission or withdrawal of a partner results in dissolution. Although dissolution ends the association of partners for their original purpose, it does not result necessarily in the termination of the partnership's basic business function. The remaining partners may continue to operate the business, or they may decide to terminate, or *liquidate*, the business.

The previous chapter stressed the importance of a well-conceived partnership agreement. Changes in the ownership structure of a partnership are one of the most important areas that should be addressed. Often, the initial concerns of a new partnership are such that the partners overlook the certain reality that, someday, there will be a change in the ownership. Accountants can be of significant help to their clients in advising them in the structuring of buy/sell agreements for the partnership. Proper planning for such changes will help to ensure smooth and equitable transitions.

In certain instances, a partnership may elect not to continue but, rather, liquidate and distribute its net assets to the partners. For example, a partnership may be organized to develop and manage a real estate investment for a designated period of time. At the end of the designated period of time, the partnership will be liquidated. It is important to note that, unlike a dissolution where the partnership purpose continues, a liquidation results in the termination or winding up of the business purpose.

OWNERSHIP CHANGES

1

OBJECTIVE

Define partnership dissolution, and explain what accounting issues should be addressed upon dissolution.

Changes in the ownership structure of a corporation are everyday occurrences, as evidenced by the activity of security exchanges. These changes typically involve transactions between existing and prospective shareholders and, therefore, create no special accounting problems for the corporate entity other than updating its listings of stockholders. In the case of a partnership, however, changes in ownership structure are events that require special accounting treatment.

Accounting for changes in the ownership of a partnership is influenced heavily by the legal concept of dissolution. When there is a change in the ownership structure, the original partnership is dissolved and, most often, a new partnership is created. This dissolution and subsequent creation of a partnership indicate that a new legal entity has been created, and accounting should properly measure the initial contributions of capital being made to the new partnership.

Accounting for a partnership is influenced by the *propriety theory*, which views a partnership not as a distinct entity but, rather, as a group of individual investors. Measuring changes in the equity of the individual partners is a major aspect of partnership accounting. Because ownership changes result in the dissolution of the partnership, this provides an excellent opportunity for accounting to measure the current wealth or equity of the partners. Changes in the ownership structure of the partnership are presumed to be arm's-length transactions which reflect the current value of the partnership. Therefore, such changes may indicate that

1. Previously unrecorded intangible assets exist that are traceable to the original partnership; *and/or*
2. Intangible assets, such as goodwill, exist that are traceable to a new partner.

In practice, a change in ownership normally suggests the need to both revalue net assets and recognize intangible assets.

Admission of a New Partner

The admission of a new partner requires the approval of the existing partners, although a partner's interest may be assigned to someone outside the partnership without the consent of the other partners. However, **assigning an interest does not dissolve the partnership,** and it does not allow the assignee to participate in the management of the partnership or to review transactions and records of the partnership. The assignee receives only the agreed-upon portion of the assigning partner's profit or loss.

Assuming a new partner has been approved by the existing partners, the new partner, normally, will experience the same general risks and rights of ownership as do the other existing partners. However, creditors presenting claims against the partnership that were incurred prior to admission of the new partner cannot attach the personal assets of the new partner for settlement of their claims. Therefore, the level of liability of a new partner is less than that of an existing partner. Section 17 of the UPA states:

A person admitted as a partner into an existing partnership is liable for all the obligations of the partnership arising before his admission as though he had been a partner when such obligations were incurred, except that this liability shall be satisfied only out of partnership property.

Contribution of Assets to Existing Partnership. One method of gaining admission to an existing partnership involves contributing assets directly to the partnership entity itself. In this case, the exchange represents an arm's-length transaction between the entity and the incoming partner. If the book value of the original partnership's net assets approximates fair value, the incoming partner's contribution would be expected to be equal to his/her percentage interest in the capital of the new partnership. For example, if an incoming partner is to acquire a one-fourth interest in a partnership that has a book value and a fair value of $60,000, the original $60,000 would now represent a three-fourths interest in the new partnership. Therefore, the total partnership capital must be $80,000, of which $60,000 is traceable to the original partners and $20,000 is traceable to the assets contributed by the new partner.

An incoming partner may acquire an interest in the partnership for a price **in excess of** that indicated by the book value of the original partnership's net assets. This situation would suggest the existence of

1. Unrecognized appreciation on the recorded net assets of the original partnership, and/or
2. Unrecognized goodwill that also is traceable to the original partnership.

However, it is possible that an incoming partner may acquire an interest in the partnership at a price *less than* that indicated by the book value. This situation would suggest the existence of

1. Unrecognized depreciation or write-downs on the recorded net assets of the original partnership, and/or
2. A contribution by the incoming partner of some intangible asset (goodwill) in addition to a measured contribution.

When an incoming partner's contribution is different from that indicated by the book values of the original partnership, the admission of the partner, typically, is recorded by either the *bonus method* or *the goodwill method.* These two methods are mutually exclusive of each other. Both methods comprehend the possibility of adjusting the value of existing assets and/or the existence of goodwill. However, they differ in how these conditions are recognized.

Bonus Method. The bonus method generally follows a *book-value approach.* That is, existing book values should not be adjusted to current values unless such adjustments would have otherwise been allowed by generally accepted accounting principles (GAAP). More specifically, increases in the value of assets as suggested by the admission of a new partner should not be recognized until they are realized through an actual subsequent exchange transaction. However, following the principle of conservatism, decreases or write-downs in the value of assets, which are suggested by the admission of a new partner, may be recognized even though they are not realized. Recognition of unrealized losses is not unique to partnership accounting and is not in conflict with GAAP. Even if no new partner were being admitted, unrealized losses suggested by economic events should be recognized. For example, if inventory has a cost in excess of market, or if long-lived assets are impaired, these losses should be recognized regardless of whether a new partner is being admitted. Therefore, use of the bonus method should not preclude a partnership from recognizing losses which would otherwise be recognized through the application of GAAP. However, the bonus method does preclude the recognition of asset appreciation, which would otherwise not be allowed per GAAP.

Therefore, when a new partner is admitted to an existing partnership, the total capital of the new partnership consists of the following:

1. The book value of the previous partnership *less*
2. Any write-downs in the value of the previous partnership's assets as recognized by GAAP *plus*
3. The fair value of the consideration paid to the partnership by the incoming partner.

The book-value approach of the bonus method does not directly recognize increases in asset values suggested by the consideration that the incoming partner pays. However, the method does indirectly recognize such increases by reallocating or adjusting the capital

2

OBJECTIVE

Account for the partners' capital balances under the bonus method.

balances of the partners. For example, if increases in net asset values are suggested as being traceable to the original partners, this suggests that their equity or capital has increased. This increase in capital, or *bonus*, is accomplished by increasing their capital balances. If increases in asset values are not directly recognized, the indirect recognition through the capital balances of original partners must be offset by decreasing the capital of the incoming partner. Therefore, **the incoming partner's new capital balance is equal to the value of the consideration paid by the incoming partner less the bonus or increase in capital recorded for the original partners.** These adjustments result in the new incoming partner's capital balance always being equal to

1. The book value (BV) of the new partnership [book value of the previous partnership less asset write-downs plus the fair value (FV) of consideration received from the incoming partner] times
2. The interest in capital being acquired by the incoming partner.

$$\begin{bmatrix} \text{BV of Original} \\ \text{Partnership} - \text{Asset} \\ \text{Write-Downs} \\ + \\ \text{FV of New Partnership} \\ \text{Contribution} \end{bmatrix} \times \begin{array}{c} \text{New Partner's} \\ \text{Interest \%} \end{array} = \begin{array}{c} \text{New Partner's} \\ \text{Capital Balance} \end{array}$$

The difference between the value of the consideration received from the incoming partner and his/her capital balance represents the bonus traceable to the original partners. This bonus is allocated to the original partners according to their profit and loss ratios in existence prior to the new partner's admission.

It is important to note that the profit and loss ratios of the original partners are used for this allocation rather than their percentage interest in capital. If the increases in the value of assets, as suggested by the admission of a new partner(s), are traceable to the original partners, such increases could have been alternatively realized by a sale of appreciated assets to an outside party. If this were the case, the realized gains would have become a component of net income. This net income would have, in turn, been allocated to the original partners according to their profit and loss ratios.

If the gain on such appreciated assets were realized subsequent to the admission of a new partner(s), a portion of this gain would be allocated to the new partner based on his/her profit ratio. Keeping in mind that this original appreciation in value should not accrue to the benefit of the new partner, the reduction of his/her capital balance (equal to the bonus granted to the original partners) compensates for any subsequent allocation of gains resulting from the realization of such appreciated assets.

Bonus to the Original Partners. When an incoming partner's contribution indicates the existence of unrecorded asset appreciation and/or unrecorded goodwill, the bonus method does not record these previously unrecorded items but, rather, grants a "bonus" to the original partners. The bonus, which increases the capital accounts of the original partners and reduces the capital balance of the new partner(s), is made possible by recording in the new partner's capital account only a portion of the actual contribution to the partnership.

To illustrate this method, assume the following:

Existing Partners	Capital Balance	Percentage Interest in	
		Capital	Profit
Partner A	$30,000	40%	50%
Partner B	45,000	60	50

Then assume that C invests $27,000 in the partnership in exchange for a 20% interest in capital and a 20% interest in profits. The $27,000 of consideration invested by Partner C in exchange for a 20% interest in capital suggests that the total value of the new partnership is $135,000 ($27,000 ÷ 20%). The $135,000 of value is comprised of the following:

Book value of original partners	$ 75,000
Investment of new partner	27,000
	$102,000
Asset appreciation traceable to original partners	33,000
Total suggested value	$135,000

Partners A and B will each have a 40% interest in the profits of the new partnership. Since the total capital of the new partnership equals $102,000 ($30,000 + $45,000 + $27,000) and the new partner is acquiring a 20% interest in capital, it seems reasonable that the incoming partner's capital account initially should reflect 20% of the total capital, or $20,400. The $6,600 difference between C's contribution and the interest recorded for C indicates the existence of unrecorded intangibles (goodwill) or unrecorded appreciation on existing assets. Regardless of the identity of the $6,600, the value must be allocated to the appropriate parties. If the unrecorded value had been realized through a sale, the resulting profit would have been divided between the original partners in accordance with their profit and loss agreement. Therefore, assuming the $6,600 is identified as a bonus to the original partners and is divided between them according to their profit and loss ratio prior to admission of the new partner, the entry to record C's investment is as follows:

Assets.	27,000	
A, Capital		3,300
B, Capital.		3,300
C, Capital		20,400

If the suggested appreciation in value of $33,000 were subsequently realized, it would be allocated among Partners A, B, and C according to their profit and loss percentages of 40%, 40%, and 20%, respectively. Therefore, Partner C will be allocated $6,600 (20% × $33,000) of the gain. The $6,600 reduction in Partner C's initial capital balance, represented by the bonus to the original partners, compensates for or negates the subsequent allocation of the realized gain to Partner C. In substance, none of the $33,000 gain should accrue to the benefit of the new partner. The bonus of $6,600 to the original partners is, in substance, the reallocation to them of the subsequently realized gain that would be allocated to Partner C.

Bonus to the New Partner. When the new partner invests some intangible asset, such as business acumen or an established clientele, it is possible to have a bonus credited to the new partner. For example, given the same basic facts as in the previous illustration, assume that C invests $10,000 for a 20% interest in capital and a 20% interest in profits. Total capital of the partnership would be $85,000 ($30,000 + $45,000 + $10,000), and C's share of the total capital would be 20%, or $17,000. Partner C is acquiring a $17,000 interest in capital in exchange for an investment of $10,000, and the original partners are transferring $7,000 of their capital to C in exchange for unrecorded intangible assets invested by C. Partner C's admission is recorded by the following entry:

Assets.	10,000	
A, Capital	3,500	
B, Capital	3,500	
C, Capital		17,000

Partner C's bonus may be viewed as a cost incurred to acquire C's goodwill. Since all costs to acquire assets eventually affect income and are allocated among the partners, C's bonus is allocated to A and B according to their profit and loss ratio.

Overvaluation of the Original Partnership. The recording of a bonus traceable to the incoming partner was based on the assumption that the new partner was contributing an intangible asset in addition to other assets valued at $10,000. However, the substance of the transaction may indicate that no intangibles are being contributed and the existing assets of the old partnership are overvalued. For example, in the previous illustration, C invested $10,000 in return for a 20% interest in the new partnership's total capital. Therefore, the total capital of the new partnership may be interpreted from C's investment to be equal to $50,000 ($10,000 ÷ 20%). Of this total, $10,000 is traceable to the new partner, and the balance of $40,000 represents the fair value of the original partners' capital. Assuming this is a proper interpretation of the substance of the transaction between the new partner and the partnership, it suggests that the assets of the original partnership are overvalued by $35,000 ($75,000 less $40,000). C's admission to the partnership is recorded as follows:

A, Capital	17,500	
B, Capital	17,500	
Assets		35,000

To record the write-down of the original partners' capital from a book value of $75,000 ($30,000 + $45,000) to its implied fair value of $40,000.

Assets	10,000	
C, Capital		10,000

To record C's contribution of assets to the partnership.

After these entries are posted, the total capital of the new partnership is $50,000 ($30,000 + $45,000 − $35,000 + $10,000), of which C's share is $10,000 (20% × $50,000), as initially represented by the balance in C's capital account.

3

OBJECTIVE

Account for the partners' capital balances under the goodwill method.

Goodwill Method. The goodwill method emphasizes the legal significance of a change in the ownership structure of a partnership. From a legal viewpoint, the entrance of a new partner results in the dissolution of the previous partnership and the creation of a new legal entity. Since a new entity has resulted, the assets transferred to this entity should be recorded at their **current fair value.** After a complete analysis, both tangible and intangible assets acquired by the new entity, including goodwill created by the previous partnership, should be recorded. Therefore, the total capital of the new partnership will consist of the following values:

1. The book value of the net assets of the previous partnership *plus*
2. Unrecognized appreciation or less unrecognized depreciation on the recorded net assets of the previous partnership *plus*
3. Unrecognized goodwill (GW) traceable to the previous partnership *plus*
4. The fair value of the consideration, both tangible and intangible, received from the new incoming partner.

$$\text{BV of Original Partnership} + \text{Unrecognized Appreciation (or − Unrecognized Depreciation)} + \text{Unrecognized GW of Original Partnership} + \text{FV of New Partner's Contribution Including GW} = \text{Total Capital of New Partnership}$$

When the bonus method is used to account for the admission of a new partner, the total capital of the new entity equals the book value of the previous partners' capital adjusted for asset write-downs, if appropriate, plus the incoming partner's investment. When the goodwill method is employed, however, the total capital of the new partnership must approximate the fair value of the entity.

To illustrate the goodwill method, assume the following:

Existing Partners	Capital Balance	Percentage Interest in Capital	Profit
Partner A	$30,000	40%	50%
Partner B	45,000	60	50

If C invests $27,000 in the partnership in exchange for a 20% interest in capital and a 20% interest in profit, such an investment implies that the entity has a fair value of $135,000

($27,000 ÷ 20%). However, the book value of the new partnership equals only $102,000 when the former partners' capital balances of $75,000 are added to C's $27,000 investment. Thus, $33,000 must be added to the existing book value.

Another interpretation of the transaction would be that, given the $102,000 book value of the new partnership, a 20% interest should have cost $20,400 ($102,000 × 20%). The new partner paid an extra $6,600 ($27,000 − $20,400) for a 20% interest in the difference between the implied fair value and the book value of the new entity. Therefore, the total difference must be $33,000 ($6,600 ÷ 20%).

Asset Appreciation. The difference between the higher fair value and the book value of the new entity, as previously discussed, may be traceable to unrecognized appreciation and/or unrecognized goodwill. Each of these possible explanations should be thoroughly analyzed to properly account for a change in the ownership structure of a partnership. If differences between the fair value and the book value of recorded assets are identifiable, appropriate adjustments to asset balances should be considered. Since a change in ownership structure creates a new, distinct legal entity, every attempt should be made to identify differences between fair and book values, whether such differences represent appreciation or write-downs in value. However, the absence of objective and independent valuations often prevents such an analysis. For example, fair values are not readily available for certain specialized assets, and the alternative of engaging an independent appraiser could become an expensive option. Furthermore, estimating fair values with the use of specific price-level indexes is often difficult because of the absence of relevant indexes. Another reason for not recording changes in fair values is that the resulting differences between the bases for tax purposes and the bases for book purposes would require more complex records.

Assuming objective measures of unrecorded appreciation are available, the appreciation would be recognized and allocated to the previous partners according to their old profit and loss ratios. To illustrate, assume that the $33,000 difference in values from our previous example is entirely traceable to the unrecognized net appreciation of the recorded net assets of the previous partnership as follows:

Land appreciation	$ 43,000
Inventory write-down	(10,000)
Net appreciation	$ 33,000

This appreciation and the investment by C would be recorded as follows:

Assets (from C)	27,000	
Land	43,000	
Inventory		10,000
A, Capital		16,500
B, Capital		16,500
C, Capital		27,000

Goodwill Traceable to the Original Partners. Unrecorded goodwill also may be identifiable. In the previous example, assuming there are no differences between the fair value and book value of recorded assets, the new partner's willingness to pay more than the proportionate book value of the new entity indicates that goodwill existed prior to the new partner's admission. If this intangible asset could have been sold prior to the admission of the partner, the realized profit would have been allocated to the original partners. Therefore, the goodwill is recorded and allocated to the original partners according to their profit and loss ratio. The investment by C is recorded under the goodwill method as follows:

Assets (from C)	27,000	
Goodwill	33,000	
A, Capital		16,500
B, Capital		16,500
C, Capital		27,000

It is important to note that the new partner's capital account balance represents a 20% interest in the total capital of the new partnership, as verified by the following computation:

Original capital	$ 75,000
C's investment	27,000
Goodwill	33,000
	$135,000
C's interest	× 20%
C's capital balance	$ 27,000

In comparing the assumption that the $33,000 difference was traceable to net appreciation of assets versus goodwill, it should be noted that

1. In one case, the net appreciation is allocated to specific assets versus goodwill, yet the amount is the same.
2. Some combination of appreciated assets and goodwill could account for the $33,000 difference.
3. The adjusted capital balances of the partners are the same regardless of whether asset appreciation and/or goodwill is recognized.

The recognition of goodwill traceable to the previous partners is criticized by some accountants. If the concept of a new legal entity is cast aside, some would argue that the goodwill is self-created and, therefore, should not be recognized. APB Opinion No. 17, *Intangible Assets*, prohibits the recognition of goodwill unless it has been purchased from another entity. To argue that the new partnership is, in substance, a continuation of the previous partnership would prevent the recognition of goodwill traceable to the original partnership. Furthermore, viewing the new partnership as a continuation of the previous partnership would prevent the recognition of appreciation on other assets as well.

It also may be argued that the difficulties associated with the measurement of the fair value of existing assets unjustifiably forces the recognition of goodwill for lack of a more precise analysis. However, the argument that the fair value of a new partnership, as indicated by the new partner's investment, is not objectively or independently determined overlooks the basic nature of the transaction. Negotiations between previous partners and a new partner would be described as arm's length, since both parties involved are independently seeking a fair price.

Asset Write-Downs. Given the same basic facts as in the previous illustrations, assume that C invests $10,000 to acquire a 20% interest in the partnership of A and B. C's investment implies a fair value of the new entity equal to $50,000 ($10,000 ÷ 20%). However, the book value of the new partnership equals $85,000, consisting of the original partners' capital balances of $75,000 plus C's investment of $10,000. This difference between the fair value and the higher book value indicates the existence of unrecorded net write-downs and/or goodwill contributed by the incoming partner.

If objective evidence supports the write-down of existing assets, the previous partners' capital balances would be reduced accordingly in proportion to their profit and loss ratios. The amount of the suggested write-down is calculated by comparing the implied fair value of $50,000 to the $85,000 representing the book value of the previous partnership plus the new partner's investment. Therefore, the difference of $35,000 is equal to the necessary net write-down. Assuming the net write-down is represented by land appreciation of $20,000 and a write-down of $55,000 to inventory, the net write-down would be recorded as follows:

A, Capital	17,500	
B, Capital	17,500	
Land	20,000	
Inventory		55,000

This reduces the net assets of the previous partnership to $40,000, and the new partner's investment of $10,000 would then represent 20% of the new partnership's total capital of $50,000 ($40,000 + $10,000).

Goodwill Traceable to the New Partner. Assuming net assets of the original partnership are properly valued and should not be written down, it is possible that goodwill may be traceable to the incoming partner. The amount of this contributed goodwill may be computed as the difference between

1. The amount that should have been paid by the new partner, as indicated by the book value of the previous partnership (calculated by dividing the original book value of the partnership by the total percentage interest of the original partners in the new partnership, and subtracting the original book value),

$$\begin{bmatrix} \text{Book Value of} & \text{Original Partners'} \\ \text{Original} & \div & \text{Interest in \textbf{New}} \\ \text{Partnership} & \text{Partnership} \end{bmatrix} - \begin{matrix} \text{Book Value} \\ \text{of Original} \\ \text{Partnership} \end{matrix} = \begin{matrix} \text{New Partner's} \\ \text{Capital Balance} \end{matrix}$$

and

2. The amount of consideration, excluding any goodwill, contributed by the new partner.

Using the previous example, the $75,000 original book value would represent 80% of the new partnership capital, or $93,750 ($75,000 ÷ 80%). Therefore, it appears that the new partner should have paid $18,750 ($93,750 less the original $75,000 book value) for a 20% interest in the partnership; however, the partner actually paid only $10,000 cash. The difference between what should have been paid ($18,750) and the amount actually paid ($10,000) represents the goodwill traceable to the incoming partner. The investment by C would be recorded under the goodwill method as follows:

Assets.	10,000	
Goodwill	8,750	
C, Capital		18,750

Note that the new partner's capital account balance represents a 20% interest in the total capital of the new partnership, as shown by the following computation:

Original capital.	$75,000
C's investment of cash	10,000
Goodwill	8,750
	$93,750
C's interest.	× 20%
C's capital balance	$18,750

The fact that a new legal entity is created supports the recognition of goodwill and other contributed assets at their fair value. If the concept of a new entity is set aside, the goodwill may be viewed as being purchased by the previous partnership in exchange for partnership equity. Accounting theory and current practice support the recording of goodwill acquired or purchased from other entities.

Revaluation of Assets and Goodwill. The previous examples of accounting for a new partner's investment assumed that either asset revaluations or goodwill recognition were appropriate as mutually exclusive choices. In reality, some combination of the two may be appropriate. Continuing with the previous example, assume that the $75,000 book value of the previous partnership has a fair value of $64,000 and new partner C's investment remains at $10,000.

The first step to be taken is to recognize the write-down of the previous partnership's net assets as follows:

A, Capital	5,500	
B, Capital	5,500	
Assets.		11,000

The adjusted value of the previous partnership, then, is used to determine the goodwill traceable to the new partner. In this example, the $64,000 fair value of the previous partnership would represent 80% of the new partnership capital, or $80,000 ($64,000 ÷ 80%). Therefore, it appears that the new partner should have paid $16,000 ($80,000 less the fair value of the previous partnership) for a 20% interest in the partnership. The difference between what should have been paid ($16,000) and the amount actually paid ($10,000) represents the goodwill traceable to the incoming partner. The entry to record C's investment is as follows:

Assets.	10,000	
Goodwill	6,000	
C, Capital		16,000

Methodology for Determining Goodwill. An analysis of the previous examples reveals that goodwill may be traceable to either the original partners or the incoming partner. To properly apply the goodwill method, the following methodology may be helpful in identifying the origin of the goodwill and its amount:

1. Determine the entity's fair value, as indicated by the new partner's investment (new partner's investment divided by the percentage interest acquired in the partnership).
2. If the fair value determined is
   a. Greater than the book value of the new partnership adjusted for net appreciation or net write-downs, implied goodwill is traceable to the original partners and is allocated among them according to their original profit ratios. The amount of goodwill is equal to the difference between (1) the fair value indicated by the new partner's investment and (2) the adjusted book value of the new partnership.
   b. Less than the adjusted book value of the new partnership, implied goodwill is traceable to the new partner. The amount of goodwill is equal to the difference between (1) the amount that should have been paid by the new partner to acquire an interest in the adjusted book value of the previous partnership and (2) the actual amount paid.
3. The initial capital balance of the new partner always is equal to the new partner's interest in the total capital of the new partnership after goodwill is recognized.

Comparison of Bonus and Goodwill Methods. The bonus method adheres to the historical cost concept and is often used in accounting practice. It is objective in that it establishes total capital of the new partnership at an amount based on actual consideration received from the new partner. The bonus method indirectly acknowledges the existence of appreciation of assets and/or goodwill by giving a bonus to either original or new partners.

The goodwill method results in the recognition of an asset implied by a transaction rather than recognizing an asset actually purchased. Historically, goodwill has been recognized only when purchased so that a more objective measure of its value is established. Therefore, opponents of the goodwill method contend that goodwill is not determined objectively and other factors may have influenced the amount of investment required from the new partner. Also, certain recipients of partnership financial statements may question the valuation of goodwill, since increasing total assets may result in an understatement of the return on total assets or equity. However, in defense of the goodwill method, the current value of net assets, whether tangible or intangible, is reflected on the financial statements resulting in a more relevant measure of invested capital.

Use of the goodwill method could produce inequitable results if either of the following conditions exist:

1. The new partner's interest in profits does not equal the new partner's initial interest in capital.
2. After the formation of the new partnership, the former partners do not share profits and losses in the same relationship to each other as they did before the admission of a new partner.

The importance of these concepts can be illustrated using the following facts:

	Original Partners		New Partner
	A	B	C
Original capital..............................	$30,000	$45,000	
Original profit and loss percentage...............	50%	50%	
New partner's capital			$27,000
New profit and loss percentage	33 1/3%	33 1/3%	33 1/3%
New partner's interest in capital			20%

The new capital balances that result from using the goodwill method and the bonus method are as follows:

	Original Partners		New Partner
	A	B	C
Goodwill method:			
Goodwill allocation.........................	$16,500	$16,500	
New capital balances	46,500	61,500	$27,000
Bonus method:			
Bonus allocation	3,300	3,300	
New capital balances	33,300	48,300	20,400

Assuming the recorded goodwill proves to be worthless (or assuming that goodwill is amortized in total), the decline in asset value would reduce the partners' capital balances according to their profit and loss ratio as follows:

	Partners			
	A	B	C	Total
Capital balances if goodwill method is used.......................	$ 46,500	$ 61,500	$ 27,000	$135,000
Goodwill write-off (amortization)	(11,000)	(11,000)	(11,000)	(33,000)
Capital balances after write-off	$ 35,500	$ 50,500	$ 16,000	$102,000
Capital balances if bonus method is used.......................	33,300	48,300	20,400	102,000
Differences..........................	$ 2,200	$ 2,200	$ (4,400)	$ 0

The capital balances that result from using the two methods are different because the new partner's interest in profits and interest in capital are not equal. In this illustration, C acquired a 20% capital interest and a 33 1/3% interest in profits. Therefore, C paid for 20% of the implied goodwill but had to absorb 33 1/3% of the goodwill amortization.

To further illustrate these concepts, assume the same facts, except that the new profit and loss percentages are 50%, 30%, and 20% for Partners A, B, and C, respectively. If the recorded goodwill proves to be worthless, the decline in asset value would affect the partners' capital balances as follows:

	Partners			
	A	B	C	Total
Capital balances if goodwill method is used	$ 46,500	$61,500	$27,000	$135,000
Goodwill write-off (amortization)	(16,500)	(9,900)	(6,600)	(33,000)
Capital balances after write-off	$ 30,000	$51,600	$20,400	$102,000
Capital balances if bonus method is used	33,300	48,300	20,400	102,000
Differences.	$ (3,300)	$ 3,300	$ 0	$ 0

In this case, Partners A and B shared equally in the initial recording of goodwill but unequally in the subsequent amortization of goodwill.

Now, assume the same facts, except that the new profit and loss percentages are 40%, 40%, and 20% for Partners A, B, and C, respectively. After the amortization of goodwill, the capital balances would be identical to those achieved under the bonus method, as indicated in the following table:

	Partners			
	A	B	C	Total
Capital balances if goodwill method is used	$ 46,500	$ 61,500	$27,000	$135,000
Goodwill write-off (amortization)	(13,200)	(13,200)	(6,600)	(33,000)
Capital balances after write-off	$ 33,300	$ 48,300	$20,400	$102,000
Capital balances if bonus method is used	33,300	48,300	20,400	102,000
Differences.	$ 0	$ 0	$ 0	$ 0

The equality between the capital balances is achieved because neither of the two conditions that produce inequities exists. If these conditions do exist, preference is given, typically, to the bonus method because of the possible inequities that may result from the write-off of goodwill.

<table>
<tr><td>**5**</td></tr>
<tr><td>**OBJECTIVE**</td></tr>
</table>

Account for the admission of a new partner through direct contribution to an existing partner.

Contribution of Assets to Existing Partners. A new partner also may be admitted to the partnership by acquiring all or part of the capital interest of one or more existing partners in exchange for some consideration (assets). In this case, **the new partner deals directly with an existing partner or partners** rather than with the partnership entity. Therefore, the acquisition price is paid to the selling partner(s) and not to the partnership itself. The partnership records the redistribution of capital interests by transferring all or a portion of the seller's capital to the new partner's capital account but does not record the transfer of any assets.

To illustrate, assume the following facts:

		Percentage Interest in	
Existing Partners	Capital Balance	Capital	Profit
Partner A	$30,000	40%	50%
Partner B	45,000	60	50

Now, assume new Partner C purchased 50% of A's interest in capital and 50% of B's interest in capital in exchange for $50,000. This purchase resulted in C's having a 50% interest in the total partnership capital.

There are several alternative ways of recording the contribution of assets by C to the existing partners. If the consideration paid by the incoming partner is not used to impute the fair value of the partnership, the transaction would be recorded by the partnership entity as follows:

A, Capital (50% × $30,000)	15,000	
B, Capital (50% × $45,000)	22,500	
C, Capital		37,500

The $50,000 actually paid by C was not used as a basis for the entry because it represents consideration paid to the individual partners personally rather than to the partnership entity. This accounting treatment frequently is compared to that of a corporation when a stockholder sells shares or an interest in corporate capital to another investor in the corporation. The corporation does not record the transaction or use it as a basis for revaluing corporate assets but merely acknowledges the changing identity of its shareholders. The preceding entry would also be appropriate if the existing partners had sold their interests for less than book value. Even though depreciation of existing assets is suggested, such depreciation is not recorded because the transaction did not involve the partnership entity itself.

An alternative but less frequently used method of recording this transaction would be to impute the fair value of the partnership entity from the consideration paid by the new partner. For example, if C paid $50,000 to acquire a 50% interest in the capital of the partnership vis-à-vis the individual partners, the total implied current value of the original partnership would be $100,000 ($50,000 ÷ 50%). The difference between the imputed value of $100,000 and the partnership's previous book value of $75,000 ($30,000 + $45,000) is interpreted to represent undervalued existing assets and/or goodwill traceable to the original partnership. This alternative interpretation would result in recording the transaction as follows:

Assets and/or Goodwill	25,000	
A, Capital		12,500
B, Capital.		12,500
To record the previously unrecognized increase in value of the partnership.		
A, Capital [50% × ($30,000 + $12,500)]	21,250	
B, Capital [50% × ($45,000 + $12,500)]	28,750	
C, Capital		50,000
To record the transfer of the original partners' adjusted capital to incoming Partner C.		

Normally, this alternative method is not employed because (a) the transaction was not between the partnership and the incoming partner but, rather, between individual partners and (b) the consideration paid by the incoming partner may not provide a reliable indicator of the partnership entity's current value. However, the method may provide useful information for deciding how to allocate the acquisition price between the selling partners. The selling partners' original capital plus their share of any imputed value increments may indicate the current values for which the incoming partner was paying. For example, the purchase price of $50,000 may be allocated to Partners A and B as follows:

	Partners		
	A	B	Total
Original capital.	$30,000	$45,000	$ 75,000
Share of value increment.	12,500	12,500	25,000
Total imputed value	$42,500	$57,500	$100,000
Percentage acquired by new partner	× 50%	× 50%	× 50%
Total purchase price	$21,250	$28,750	$ 50,000

6

OBJECTIVE

Withdrawal of a Partner

When a partner withdraws, the partnership agreement should be consulted to determine whether any guidelines have been established that would influence the procedure.

Explain the impact of a partner's withdrawal from the partnership.

The withdrawal of a partner requires a determination of the fair value of the partnership entity and a measurement of partnership income to the date of withdrawal. Also, in many cases, the equity of the retiring partner may not be equal to the partner's capital balance as a result of (a) the existence of accounting errors, (b) differences between the fair value and the recorded book value of assets, and/or (c) unrecorded assets such as goodwill.

If accounting errors are discovered, they should be treated as prior-period adjustments and corrected by adjusting the capital balances of the partners. Theoretically, an error should be allocated to partners' capital balances according to the profit and loss ratio that existed when the error was committed. Therefore, it is necessary to identify the period to which the error is traceable. This practice can become complicated, and a well-designed partnership agreement should include procedures for dealing with the correction of errors.

Recognizing differences between book value and fair value may be as appropriate when an individual withdraws from the partnership as when an individual is admitted. If accounting recognition of such differences is not desired, however, these differences nevertheless should influence the amount to be paid to the withdrawing partner.

The Selling of an Interest to Existing Partners. As is the case with the admission of a partner, the withdrawal of a partner may involve (a) a transaction with existing partners or a new partner or (b) a transaction with the partnership entity itself. In the first case, the equity of the withdrawing partner will be purchased with the personal assets of existing or new partners rather than with the assets of the partnership.

To illustrate, assume the following:

	Partners		
	A	B	C
Capital balance.	$30,000	$50,000	$20,000
Profit and loss percentage	40%	40%	20%
Percentage interest in capital.	30%	50%	20%

Now assume Partner A withdraws from the partnership and C uses personal funds to purchase A's interest at its current value of $36,000. If the price paid by C is not used to impute the value of the entity, the transaction would be recorded as follows:

A, Capital	30,000	
C, Capital		30,000

The above entry also may be appropriate if the existing partners sold their interests for less than book value. Even though depreciation of existing assets is suggested, such depreciation is not recorded because the transaction did not involve the partnership entity itself. As previously discussed, an alternative treatment would be to recognize any suggested appreciation or write-downs indicated by the transaction and then transfer the adjusted capital balances.

The Selling of an Interest to the Partnership. When a withdrawing partner sells an interest to the partnership rather than to an individual partner, the bonus or goodwill methods may be employed. The bonus method is used most frequently, but the choice between methods should be based on a thorough analysis of the transaction. Using the same facts as in the previous illustration and assuming the use of the bonus method, the purchase of A's equity by the partnership would be recorded as follows:

A, Capital	30,000	
B, Capital	4,000	
C, Capital	2,000	
Cash		36,000

The entry indicates that the remaining partners granted a bonus to A, measured by the difference between the recorded capital and the fair value of A's equity. The bonus is charged to the remaining partners according to their proportionate profit and loss ratio.

The goodwill method focuses on the payment to the withdrawing partner as an indication of the fair value of the partnership. If the imputed goodwill or undervalued assets were disposed of, the partners would divide the gain according to their profit and loss ratio. Assuming existing assets are properly valued, the $36,000 payment to A consists of A's capital balance of $30,000 plus a $6,000 share of the unrecorded goodwill. Therefore, the $6,000 represents A's 40% interest in total goodwill of $15,000 ($6,000 ÷ 40%). Notice that the $6,000 represents A's interest in the gain, which would be realized if the unrecorded goodwill were sold. Therefore, A's profit percentage is used to suggest the total value of the goodwill.

Two alternatives are now available: (a) recognize only the goodwill that is traceable to the retiring partner or (b) recognize the amount of goodwill traceable to the entire entity. The first alternative stresses the importance of recognizing only the amount of goodwill that actually is purchased from the withdrawing partner. Using this alternative, A's withdrawal would be recorded as follows:

Goodwill	6,000	
A, Capital		6,000
A, Capital	36,000	
Cash		36,000

If the amount of goodwill traceable to the entire entity is recognized, the goodwill would be allocated to the partners according to their profit and loss ratio, as reflected in the following entries to record A's withdrawal:

Goodwill	15,000	
A, Capital		6,000
B, Capital.		6,000
C, Capital		3,000
A, Capital	36,000	
Cash		36,000

Whether part or all of the goodwill is recognized, opponents of this procedure contend that transactions between partners should not be viewed as arm's length; therefore, the measure of goodwill may not be determined objectively. Also, inequitable results may be produced if the remaining partners subsequently change their profit and loss ratio.

It is important to note that a withdrawing partner could sell his/her interest in a partnership for less than book value. If that interest is sold to the partnership, the following recognition would take place depending on whether the bonus or goodwill method is employed:

1. Bonus method: A bonus traceable to the remaining partners would be recognized. The bonus would be measured as the difference between the withdrawing partner's capital balance and the consideration paid for the partner's interest.

2. Goodwill method: Paying less than the withholding partner's capital balance (book value) would suggest that existing assets are overvalued. A write-down of existing assets would be recognized as the difference between the withdrawing partner's capital balance and the consideration paid for the partner's interest. As an alternative, the asset write-down traceable to the entire entity could be recognized based on the amount suggested by the transaction with the withholding partner. The write-down traceable to the withdrawing partner represents his/her percentage interest (based on profit and loss ratios) in the asset write-down traceable to the entire entity.

Effects of a Partner's Withdrawal. When the interest of a withdrawing partner is acquired by the remaining partners or the partnership, serious demands upon the liquidity of the partners and the partnership may result. If withdrawal is due to the death of the partner, funds may be provided from the proceeds of life insurance policies taken out by the partnership itself or by individual partners. For example, if Partner A takes out a life insurance policy on Partner B, and B subsequently dies, the proceeds payable to A may be used to acquire B's interest.

The UPA, in Section 42, states that a retiring or deceased partner's estate may receive interest as an ordinary creditor on that portion of the withdrawing partner's capital interest that remains in the partnership (i.e., has not yet been disbursed). In lieu of interest, the UPA states that the profits attributable to the use of the withdrawing partner's capital still retained in the partnership may be received. Once again, a partnership agreement that addresses the valuation of a withdrawing partner's interest and the means of payment is a valuable aid in properly accounting for the withdrawal of a partner.

REFLECTION

- A change in the ownership structure of a partnership results in the dissolution of the prior partnership and provides an opportunity to properly recognize and value the net assets of the partnership.

- The bonus and goodwill methods are alternative methods of accounting for the change in ownership of a partnership when a new partner acquires an interest from the partnership entity itself.

- The more conservative bonus method only recognizes declines in the value of net assets suggested by a change in ownership.

- The goodwill method recognizes both increases and decreases in the value of net assets.

- If a new partner acquires an interest in the partnership directly from a partner(s) as compared to from the partnership entity itself, neither the bonus nor goodwill methods are employed.

- When a partner withdraws by selling an interest to the partnership, a bonus or goodwill payment may be made to the exiting partner.

PARTNERSHIP LIQUIDATION

Unlike a dissolution where the partnership continues its business purpose, a liquidation results in the partnership's ending or terminating its business. The process of liquidation consists of the conversion of partnership assets into a distributable form and the distribution of these assets to creditors and owners. To achieve an orderly and legally sound liquidation, some fundamental guidelines need to be identified.

Liquidation Guidelines

7

OBJECTIVE

Describe the order in which assets must be distributed upon liquidation of a partnership, and explain the right-of-offset concept.

The underlying theme in accounting for partnership liquidation is the equitable distribution of the assets. To be equitable, a distribution should recognize the legal rights of the partnership creditors and individual partners. All liquidation expenses and gains or losses from conversion of partnership assets also must be allocated to the partners before assets actually are distributed to the individual partners. Failure to consider these factors may result in the premature or incorrect distribution of assets to a partner. If a premature or incorrect distribution of assets cannot be recovered, the partnership fiduciary who authorized the distribution may be held liable.

The Ranking of Partnership Liabilities. The UPA establishes rules governing the priority in which partnership assets are distributed to creditors and partners. Subject to any agreement to the contrary, the following sequence of payments should be observed:

1. Amounts owed to creditors other than partners.
2. Amounts owed to partners other than for capital and profits (i.e., partners' loans to the partnership).
3. Amounts owed to partners as capital.
4. Amounts owed to partners as profits not currently closed to partners' capital accounts.

Although loans from partners have a higher legal priority than amounts owed as capital and profits, the doctrine of *right of offset* sets aside this ranking in favor of procedural and economic considerations that facilitate the actual liquidation process. The effect of this doctrine is that loans due to partners, which have a credit balance, are combined with the respective partners' capital balances. Without the right of offset, it would be possible to distribute assets to a partner in payment of the loan balance while at the same time the partner has a debit capital account balance. In order to eliminate the debit capital balance, the partnership would have to recover personal assets from the partner. Therefore, it is possible for the partnership to distribute assets to the partner and then try to recover assets from the partner, hoping that such assets are still available. The doctrine of right of offset eliminates this problem by combining the loan and capital balances.

Amounts owed to partners as capital and profits are typically viewed as one element rather than two separate priority levels. Therefore, items (2), (3), and (4) may be combined without destroying the fairness of a distribution.

Liability for Debit Capital Balances. The UPA, in Section 40, states that partners should contribute assets to the partnership to the extent of their debit balances. However, if such a contribution is not possible because of special personal or legal considerations, the debit balance will be viewed as a realization loss and allocated according to the remaining partners' profit and loss ratio. For example, assume Partners A, B, and C share in profits and losses in the ratio of 1:2:1, respectively. If C is unable to contribute any asset to eliminate a debit capital balance, that balance would be allocated to A and B in the ratio of 1:2. Partners who absorb other partners' debit capital balances have a legal claim against the deficient partners. However, the collectibility of such a claim depends on the personal wealth of the deficient partners.

The Marshaling of Assets. The provisions that call for the contribution of personal assets to a liquidating partnership illustrate the characteristics of unlimited liability discussed in the previous chapter. However, such personal liability depends on the legal doctrine of *marshaling of assets*. This doctrine, which is applied when the partnership and/or one or more of the partners are insolvent, states that

<table>
<tr><td style="text-align:right">**8**</td></tr>
<tr><td>**OBJECTIVE**</td></tr>
<tr><td>Explain the doctrine of marshaling of assets.</td></tr>
</table>

1. Partnership assets are first available for the payment of partnership debts. Any excess assets are available for payment of the individual partner's debts, but only to the extent of the partner's interest in the capital of the partnership.
2. Personal assets of a partner are applied against personal debts, ranked in order of priority as follows:
   a. Amounts owed to personal creditors.
   b. Amounts owed to partnership creditors.
   c. Amounts owed to partners by way of contribution.

"Amounts owed to partners by way of contribution" refers to amounts owed the partnership as represented by the partner's debit capital balance. This amount is viewed by the UPA as separate from the amounts owed to personal creditors. For example, if a partner has personal assets of $12,000, personal liabilities of $8,000, and a debit capital balance of $16,000, personal assets would be distributed as follows:

Payable to personal creditors	$ 8,000
Payable to partnership for debit capital balance	4,000
Total personal assets	$12,000

Under common law and federal bankruptcy law, which may be applicable when the UPA has not been adopted, amounts owed to partners by way of contribution are on an equal basis (*pari passu*) with personal creditors of the partner. According to this rule, the $12,000 of personal assets would be distributed as follows:

Payable to personal liabilities [($8,000 ÷ $24,000) × $12,000]	$ 4,000
Payable to partnership for debit capital balance [($16,000 ÷ $24,000) × $12,000]	8,000
Total personal assets	$12,000

The legal doctrine of marshaling of assets is demonstrated by the following cases:

Case 1
Insolvent Partners

The partnership is solvent, with total assets of $16,000 and total liabilities of $9,000. Information relating to the individual partners is as follows:

	Partner A	Partner B
Total personal assets	$10,000	$15,000
Total personal liabilities	13,000	18,000
Partnership capital balances	5,000	2,000

Analysis: Unsatisfied personal creditors may attach a partner's interest in the solvent partnership but only to the extent of the partner's capital balance. Thus, unsatisfied personal creditors could seek recourse as follows:

	Partner A	Partner B
Unsatisfied personal creditors	$ 3,000	$ 3,000
Interest in partnership capital available to personal creditors	(3,000)	(2,000)
Personal liabilities not satisfied	$ 0	$ 1,000

Case 2
Insolvent Partnership

The partnership is insolvent, with total assets of $23,000 and total liabilities of $25,000. Information relating to individual partners is as follows:

	Partner A	Partner B
Total personal assets	$10,000	$ 8,000
Total personal liabilities	6,000	7,000
Partnership capital balances	500	(2,500)

Analysis: Unsatisfied partnership creditors may seek recourse from the individual partners in accordance with a proper marshaling of assets, as reflected in Illustration 9-1.

Illustration 9-1
Distribution of Assets—Insolvent Partnership

	Partner A		Partner B		AB Partnership			
	Assets	Liab.	Assets	Liab.	Assets	Liab.	A, Capital	B, Capital
Beginning balances[a]	$10,000	$6,000	$8,000	$7,000	$23,000	$25,000	$500	$(2,500)
Payment of liabilities	(6,000)	(6,000)	(7,000)	(7,000)	(23,000)	(23,000)		
	$4,000	$0	$1,000	$0	$0	$2,000	$500	$(2,500)
Payment toward debit capital balance[b]			(1,000)		1,000			1,000
	$4,000	$0	$0	$0	$1,000	$2,000	$500	$(1,500)
Payment of partnership creditors[c]	(1,000)				(1,000)	(2,000)	1,000	
Balances[d]	$3,000	$0	$0	$0	$0	$0	$1,500	$(1,500)

[a]Beginning asset balances represent realizable values.

[b]If the payment toward the debit capital balance had preceded B's payment of personal liabilities, a proper marshaling of assets would not have been achieved and B's personal creditors would not have been satisfied.

[c]Unsatisfied partnership creditors may claim the net personal assets of any solvent partner, regardless of the amount of the partner's interest in the capital of the partnership. A's capital interest is increased by the payment of partnership liabilities.

[d]If B later pays the debit capital balance, the funds would be distributed to A. However, if B cannot pay, the loss will be borne by A.

Case 3
Insolvent Partner and Partnership

The partnership is insolvent, with total assets of $20,000 and total liabilities of $25,000. Information relating to individual partners is as follows:

	Partner A	Partner B
Total personal assets	$13,000	$12,000
Total personal liabilities.	10,000	15,000
Partnership capital balances	(7,000)	2,000

Analysis: Partner B is insolvent, and the recourse B's personal creditors have against the partnership depends upon A's future contribution to the partnership. Illustration 9-2 reflects the distribution of assets in accordance with the marshaling concept.

Illustration 9-2
Distribution of Assets—Insolvent Partner and Partnership

	Partner A		Partner B		AB Partnership			
	Assets	Liab.	Assets	Liab.	Assets	Liab.	A, Capital	B, Capital
Beginning balances[a]	$13,000	$10,000	$12,000	$15,000	$20,000	$25,000	$(7,000)	$2,000
Payment of liabilities	(10,000)	(10,000)	(12,000)	(12,000)	(20,000)	(20,000)		
	$3,000	$0	$0	$3,000	$0	$5,000	$(7,000)	$2,000

(continued)

Payment of partnership								
creditors.............	(3,000)					(3,000)	3,000	
Balances[b]	$ 0	$ 0	$ 0	$ 3,000[c]	$ 0	$ 2,000	$(4,000)	$2,000

[a]Beginning asset balances represent realizable values.

[b]If A later pays $4,000 to the partnership to eliminate the debit capital balance, the payment will be allocated first to the partnership liabilities and then to B. However, if A is not able to make a payment, claims against the partnership by the creditors and B will be totally uncollectible.

[c]The unsatisfied personal creditors of B are unable to seek recovery against the credit capital balance of B because the partnership itself is not solvent.

9

Calculate the assets to be distributed to a given partner in a lump-sum or installment liquidation, and understand the concept of maximum loss absorbable.

Lump-Sum Liquidations

The guidelines discussed in the preceding section are important factors influencing the procedural and legal aspects of a partnership liquidation. Upon liquidation of a partnership, the amount of assets ultimately to be distributed to the individual partners is determined through the use of either a lump-sum liquidation schedule or an installment liquidation schedule. A *lump-sum liquidation* requires that all assets be realized before a distribution is made to partners, thus avoiding the possibility of a premature distribution. To illustrate a lump-sum liquidation, assume the following:

1. Asset, liability, loan, and capital balances are as shown in Illustration 9-3, after books for the final operational period are closed.
2. Profit and loss percentages for Partners A, B, and C are 40%, 40%, and 20%, respectively.
3. Personal assets and debts of the partners are as follows:

	A	B	C
Total personal assets	$30,000	$40,000	$20,000
Total personal liabilities............................	10,000	37,200	24,000

4. Sales of assets are as follows:

Date	Book Value	Selling Price	Gain (Loss)
February 15	$50,000	$60,000	$ 10,000
March 2	30,000	10,000	(20,000)
March 7	40,000	20,000	(20,000)

5. Total liquidation expenses of $2,000 are paid on March 4.

Illustration 9-3
Lump-Sum Liquidation Statement

					Capital Balances		
	Cash	Noncash Assets	Liabilities	Loan from A	A	B	C
Beginning balances.........	$ 10,000	$120,000	$ 80,000	$ 9,000	$ 25,000	$10,000	$ 6,000
February 15, sale of assets at a gain	60,000	(50,000)			4,000	4,000	2,000
March 2, sale of assets at a loss	10,000	(30,000)			(8,000)	(8,000)	(4,000)

Payment of liquidation expenses	(2,000)				(800)	(800)	(400)
March 7, sale of assets at a loss	20,000	(40,000)			(8,000)	(8,000)	(4,000)
Balances	$ 98,000	$ 0	$ 80,000	$ 9,000	$ 12,200	$ (2,800)	$ (400)
Payment of liabilities	(80,000)		(80,000)				
Balances	$ 18,000	$ 0	$ 0	$ 9,000	$ 12,200	$ (2,800)	$ (400)
B's contribution	2,800					2,800	
Balances	$ 20,800	$ 0	$ 0	$ 9,000	$ 12,200	$ 0	$ (400)
Absorption of C's balance. . . .					(400)		400
Balances	$ 20,800	$ 0	$ 0	$ 9,000	$ 11,800	$ 0	$ 0
Payment to A	(20,800)			(9,000)	(11,800)		
Final balances	$ 0	$ 0	$ 0	$ 0	$ 0	$ 0	$ 0

Illustration 9-3 presents the lump-sum distribution and demonstrates the following concepts that were discussed previously:

1. Gains and losses on realization are allocated according to the partners' profit and loss ratio.
2. Claims against the partnership are paid in the proper order.
3. The marshaling of assets doctrine is followed to determine the disposition of B's and C's debit balances in their capital accounts. That is, a partner's personal assets first are used to satisfy personal liabilities. Then, to the extent possible, remaining assets are contributed to the partnership to eliminate debit capital balances.
4. C's debit capital balance is charged against A, the only personally solvent partner.
5. Partner A will have a claim against C's future personal assets for the debit balance that was absorbed.

Installment Liquidations

The complete liquidation process might extend over several months or longer, and it may not be possible to postpone payments to creditors and partners until all assets have been realized. Therefore, payments may be made on an installment basis to creditors and partners during the liquidation process. To avoid the problem associated with premature or incorrect distributions to partners, installment payments may be made to partners only after anticipating all liabilities, possible losses, and liquidation expenses. To provide a proper solution to installment liquidations, generally a *schedule of safe payments,* showing appropriate distributions to partners, is prepared as amounts become available for distribution.

Schedule of Safe Payments. The possibility of premature payments to partners is reduced by using a schedule of safe payments, which reflects a conservative approach to liquidation. The schedule indicates how available funds should be distributed to partners. It is based on the anticipation of all possible liabilities and expenses, including those expected to be incurred in the process of liquidation. The effect of these items on partnership capital is allocated among the partners according to their profit and loss agreement.

In keeping with the conservative approach, the schedule also is based on the assumption that all noncash assets will be worthless; therefore, the assumed loss is allocated among the partners according to their profit and loss ratio. The allocation of the assumed loss could produce debit balances in partners' capital accounts, and these balances are treated as being uncollectible. Therefore, the assumed debit capital balances are allocated to those partners with credit balances according to their proportionate profit and loss ratio. When the allocation of estimated liabilities, expenses, liquidation losses, and debit balances is completed, assets may be distributed safely to the partners in amounts equal to the resulting credit capital balances.

10

OBJECTIVE

Prepare an installment liquidation statement and a schedule of safe payments.

A new schedule of safe payments is prepared each time a distribution to partners is scheduled. These schedules support an installment liquidation statement, which summarizes changes in real account balances as the liquidation proceeds. When the partners' combined capital and loan balances are in the profit and loss ratio, all partners will share in a given distribution. All future distributions to partners will be allocated automatically according to their profit ratio, thus eliminating the need for another schedule of safe payments.

To illustrate the use of schedules of safe payments in conjunction with an installment liquidation, assume the following:

1. Asset, liability, loan, and capital balances are shown, in Illustration 9-4, after books for the final operational period are closed.
2. Profit and loss percentages for Partners A, B, and C are 40%, 40%, and 20%, respectively.
3. Sales of assets are as follows:

Date	Book Value	Selling Price	Gain (Loss)
February 15	$ 60,000	$ 40,000	$ (20,000)
March 2	30,000	15,000	(15,000)
March 17	10,000	20,000	10,000
April 1	20,000	24,000	4,000

4. Liquidation expenses are estimated to be $10,000. Cash is to be restricted in that amount until expenses are paid.
5. Installment distributions of unrestricted cash are made on February 17, March 5, March 18, and April 2.
6. Total liquidation expenses of $8,000 are paid on March 4.

Illustration 9-4
Installment Liquidation Statement

	Cash	Noncash Assets	Liabilities	Loan from A	Capital Balances A	B	C
Beginning balances.........	$ 10,000	$120,000	$ 30,000	$ 5,000	$25,000	$ 55,000	$15,000
February 15, sale of assets ...	40,000	(60,000)			(8,000)	(8,000)	(4,000)
Balances	$ 50,000	$ 60,000	$ 30,000	$ 5,000	$17,000	$ 47,000	$11,000
Payment of liabilities	(30,000)		(30,000)				
February 17, distribution (Schedule A)	(10,000)					(10,000)	
Balances	$ 10,000	$ 60,000	$ 0	$ 5,000	$17,000	$ 37,000	$11,000
March 2, sale of assets	15,000	(30,000)			(6,000)	(6,000)	(3,000)
Payment of liquidation expenses	(8,000)				(3,200)	(3,200)	(1,600)
Balances	$ 17,000	$ 30,000	$ 0	$ 5,000	$ 7,800	$ 27,800	$ 6,400
March 5, distribution (Schedule A)	(17,000)			(800)		(15,800)	(400)
Balances*	$ 0	$ 30,000	$ 0	$ 4,200	$ 7,800	$ 12,000	$ 6,000
March 17, sale of assets	20,000	(10,000)			4,000	4,000	2,000
Balances	$ 20,000	$ 20,000	$ 0	$ 4,200	$11,800	$ 16,000	$ 8,000
March 18, distribution (per P&L ratios)..........	(20,000)			(4,200)	(3,800)	(8,000)	(4,000)
Balances	$ 0	$ 20,000	$ 0	$ 0	$ 8,000	$ 8,000	$ 4,000

April 1, sale of assets........	24,000	(20,000)	0	0	1,600	1,600	800
Balances	$ 24,000	$ 0	$ 0	$ 0	$ 9,600	$ 9,600	$ 4,800
Final distribution	(24,000)				(9,600)	(9,600)	(4,800)
Balances	$ 0	$ 0	$ 0	$ 0	$ 0	$ 0	$ 0

Schedule A—Schedule of Safe Payments

	A	B	C	Total
Profit and loss percentage	40%	40%	20%	100%
February 17 Distribution:				
Combined capital and loan balances before distribution	$ 22,000	$ 47,000	$ 11,000	$ 80,000
Estimated liquidation expenses	(4,000)	(4,000)	(2,000)	(10,000)
Balances	$ 18,000	$ 43,000	$ 9,000	$ 70,000
Maximum loss possible	(24,000)	(24,000)	(12,000)	(60,000)
Balances	$ (6,000)	$ 19,000	$ (3,000)	$ 10,000
Allocation of debit capital balances	6,000	(9,000)	3,000	0
Safe payment..	$ 0	$ 10,000	$ 0	$ 10,000
March 5 Distribution:				
Combined capital and loan balances before distribution	$ 12,800	$ 27,800	$ 6,400	$ 47,000
Maximum loss possible	(12,000)	(12,000)	(6,000)	(30,000)
Safe payments	$ 800	$ 15,800	$ 400	$ 17,000

*Note that the combined capital and loan balances for A, B, and C are $12,000, $12,000, and $6,000, respectively, and in total are $30,000. These balances are in the profit and loss ratios of 40%, 40%, and 20%, respectively. Therefore, subsequent to this point, all distributions will be allocated per the profit and loss ratio.

Illustration 9-4 is based on these facts and demonstrates the following concepts:

1. Gains and losses on realization are allocated according to the partners' profit and loss ratio.

2. Unsold noncash assets are assumed to be worthless for purposes of determining the safe payments to partners.

3. Loan balances are combined with capital balances according to the right-of-offset doctrine. This offset can result in partners receiving distributions of capital before other partners' loan accounts have been paid (as in the February 17 distribution in Illustration 9-4). However, such distributions may be placed in escrow until it is certain that debit balances will not develop in these partners' capital accounts.

4. Distributions are applied to a partner's loan balance before they are applied to the partner's capital balance.

5. Typically, the doctrine of marshaling of assets is ignored until all assets have been realized, at which time debit balances in partners' capital accounts may be satisfied through contributions of personal assets.

6. A schedule of safe payments is an iterative process that will cease when the schedule indicates that a given distribution will be shared among all partners. Further distributions will be allocated among the partners according to their profit and loss ratio. For example, when the March 5 distribution in Schedule A indicates that all partners will receive a portion of the distribution, the distribution on March 18 would be made in the profit and loss ratio, with results identical to those that would have been indicated by continuing the schedule of safe payments.

7. The partner with the greatest ability to absorb anticipated losses (i.e., to preserve a credit capital balance after allocating anticipated losses) will be the first to receive a safe payment.

It is important to further understand the significance of item (7) above. In a worst case scenario, during an installment liquidation anticipated losses could arise from liquidation expenses, losses on the sale of assets, and the assumption of another partner's deficit balance. Obviously, the stronger a given partner is in terms of absorbing these losses, the more likely it is that the partner will receive a distribution during the course of the liquidation. The strength of the partner is measured by the maximum loss that they could absorb.

In order to calculate a partner's initial maximum loss absorbable (MLA), all anticipated but unrecorded liabilities and liquidation expenses are allocated to the various partners' capital balances according to their profit and loss ratio. The resulting capital balances then are evaluated to determine the maximum loss from realization that could be absorbed by the partners before a debit balance is created in each of their capital accounts. As suggested by the schedule of safe payments, the partner who maintains a credit capital balance after assuming that all noncash assets are worthless is the partner with the greatest ability to absorb realization losses. Therefore, that partner will be the first to receive an actual distribution of assets.

The maximum loss a partner could absorb (maximum loss absorbable), before a debit balance in the partner's capital account is created, is determined by the following calculation:

$$\text{Maximum Loss Absorbable (MLA)} = \frac{\text{Partner's capital balance}}{\text{Partner's profit and loss percentage}}$$

Since the partner with the largest initial MLA will be the first to receive an actual distribution, the MLAs are used to indicate the order in which partners will receive distributions. However, it should be noted that the MLAs do not indicate the amounts of the distributions. To illustrate, assume a partnership consists of three partners (A, B, and C) who have capital balances, before the realization of noncash assets, of $70,000, $60,000, and $40,000, respectively, and profit and loss percentages of 35%, 25%, and 40%, respectively. The maximum losses absorbable by Partners A, B, and C are determined as follows:

Partner	(1) Capital Balance	(2) Profit and Loss Percentage	(1) ÷ (2) Maximum Loss Absorbable	Rank
A	$70,000	35%	$200,000	Second
B	60,000	25	240,000	First
C	40,000	40	100,000	Third

If all partners had identical MLAs, all partners would share in any given distribution. Therefore, the amount of any distribution to be paid to a particular partner can be determined by calculating the distributions needed ultimately to give all partners the same MLA. In the present example, Partner B should receive distributions first, until his/her MLA is equal to the next highest MLA of $200,000. If B's capital balance was reduced to $50,000 (next highest MLA multiplied by the partner's profit and loss percentage, $200,000 × 25%) as the result of an actual distribution of $10,000, B's new MLA would be equal to A's original MLA as follows:

Partner	(1) Capital Balance	(2) Profit and Loss Percentage	(1) ÷ (2) Maximum Loss Absorbable
A	$70,000	35%	$200,000
B	60,000	25	240,000
C	40,000	40	100,000

Therefore, the first $10,000, or any portion thereof, that is available for distribution to partners should be paid entirely to Partner B.

Partners A and B should now receive distributions until their MLAs of $200,000 are reduced to the next highest MLA of $100,000, traceable to Partner C. If A's capital balance was reduced to $35,000 ($100,000 × 35%) and B's capital balance was reduced to $25,000 ($100,000 × 25%) as the result of actual distributions of $35,000 and $25,000, respectively, to these partners, all partners would then have equivalent MLAs. This suggests that the next $60,000 ($35,000 + $25,000), or any portion thereof, that is available for distribution to partners should be paid to Partners A and B according to the profit ratio of 35:25 and all further distributions should be divided among all partners according to their respective profit ratio.

Knowledge of a partner's maximum loss absorbable is helpful in developing a general sense for which partners would be most likely to receive a distribution and to what extent during the course of an installment liquidation. Furthermore, this knowledge can also be used to develop a formal predistribution plan that would be followed during the course of the liquidation. However, if there should be any difference between the anticipated but unrecorded liabilities and liquidation expenses and the actual amounts, the predistribution plan would need to be revised. Therefore, a formal predistribution plan may have limited use in practice.

REFLECTION

- Upon liquidation of a partnership, the distribution of available assets must follow a prescribed order. The claims of outside creditors should always be satisfied before those of individual partners.

- The right-of-offset doctrine is important in a liquidation in order to make sure that partners with the potential for debit capital balances do not receive premature distributions of assets.

- The doctrine of marshaling of assets comes into play when either a partnership is insolvent and/or individual partners are personally insolvent.

- The actual liquidation of a partnership may follow several approaches, including a lump-sum liquidation or an installment liquidation supported by a schedule of safe payments. In all cases, the goal is to convert assets into a distributable form, respect the rights of those with claims against the partnership, and not make premature distributions. The calculation of partners' maximum loss absorbable provides insight regarding the order in which partners are likely to receive distributions.

UNDERSTANDING THE ISSUES

1. If consideration paid to acquire an interest in a partnership is based on the fair value of the net assets, why doesn't the bonus method recognize all of the suggested values?

2. If an individual were to acquire an interest in a partnership from the partnership entity itself, how would one calculate the suggested value of the acquired interest?

3. The liquidation of a partnership can be a complex and time-consuming process. What basic guidelines should be followed in order to ensure that the process is proper?

4. What does a partner's maximum loss absorbable (MLA) suggest in terms of the order in which liquidating distributions will be made available to partners?

EXERCISES

Exercise 9-1 *(LO 3, 4)* **Entry of a new partner under the goodwill method.** Pearson and Murphy have partner capital balances, at book value, of $45,000 and $65,000 as of December 31, 20X5. Pearson is allocated 60% of profits or losses, and Murphy is allocated the balance.

The partners believe that tangible net assets have a market value in excess of book value in the amount of $30,000 net. The $30,000 is allocated as follows:

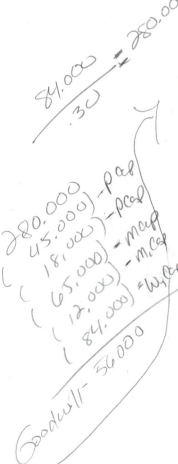

	Book Value	Market Value
Accounts receivable	$120,000	$102,000
Inventory	200,000	258,000
Warranty obligations	20,000	30,000

They are considering admitting Warner to the partnership in exchange for total consideration of $84,000 cash. In exchange for the consideration, Warner will receive a 30% interest in capital and a 35% interest in profits.

1. Prepare the entries associated with the admission of Warner to the partnership under the goodwill method.
2. If the goodwill suggested by the admission of Warner proved to be worthless, determine by how much Warner would be harmed.

Exercise 9-2 *(LO 2, 3)* **Entries for addition of new partner, bonus, goodwill.** Baxter and Murphy are partners whose profit and loss percentages are 60% and 40%, respectively. The book values of the partners' capital balances are $78,000 and $52,000 for Baxter and Murphy, respectively. The partners have agreed to admit Tuttle as a partner in exchange for a contribution to the partnership of cash, equipment, and land with fair values of $25,000, $30,000, and $35,000, respectively. In exchange for her investment, Tuttle will receive a 30% interest in capital and a 20% interest in profits and losses. Baxter and Murphy have agreed to revise their profit and loss percentages to 48% and 32%, respectively. An analysis of existing assets held by the original partnership indicates the following book values and current values:

	Book Value	Current Value
Accounts receivable	$120,000	$110,000
Inventory	200,000	240,000
Equipment	354,000	374,000

Prepare the entries to record the admission of Tuttle under both the bonus and goodwill methods.

Exercise 9-3 *(LO 4)* **Comparison of the bonus and goodwill methods.** Your client Kennedy is considering an investment in an existing partnership and is interested in knowing how her investment will be accounted for. You have explained to your client that an investment in a partnership may be accounted for by either the bonus method or the goodwill method. Your client has posed the following questions regarding these methods:

1. How do the methods differ with respect to how asset write-downs are accounted for?
2. How is goodwill traceable to the original partnership accounted for under the bonus method?
3. How is it possible that a new partner's initial capital balance may be more than the value of the net assets that the partner contributed to the partnership?
4. Which method would be most appropriate if the allocation of profits is based in part on interest on capital balances?
5. Assume that the goodwill method was used to recognize appreciated assets traceable to the original partners. If the value of these assets were erroneously overstated and subsequently restated, how would the end result differ from that which would have existed had the bonus method been used?

Provide a response to your client's questions.

Exercise 9-4 *(LO 2, 3, 5)* **Acquisition of a partnership interest from a partner versus the partnership.** Rainbow Properties is a partnership consisting of three partners: Ross, Gilmore, and Bates. The partnership's primary business is the acquisition and development of land into homesites. Projects require a significant amount of capital, which often is borrowed from area banks. The three partners share profits and losses equally and have the following capital balances: $160,000 for Ross, $120,000 for Gilmore, and $200,000 for Bates. Recently, Ross was approached to sell her personal interest in the partnership to William Lane for $210,000.

1. What advantages would there be to the partnership if Lane acquired an interest directly from the partnership rather than directly from Ross?
2. What amount would Lane have to contribute to the partnership in order to have the same interest in capital as would have been acquired had Lane purchased an interest directly from Ross?
3. Assume Lane purchased a one-fourth interest in the partnership by contributing $210,000 to the partnership. Prepare the entry to record the contribution noting that existing land has a fair value of $330,000 and a book value of $300,000 and goodwill is recognized.

Exercise 9-5 *(LO 3, 6)* **Withdrawal and admission of a partner using the goodwill method.** As of December 31, 20X5, Stegnitz, Hipki, and Ergos have capital balances of $70,000, $50,000, and $80,000, respectively. Profits and losses are shared equally among the partners. During the fourth quarter of 20X5, Ergos decided to withdraw from the partnership effective at the end of the year. The partnership agreed to distribute $105,000 to Ergos in exchange for his partnership interest. The amount paid to Ergos reflects the fact that accounts receivable are overstated by $21,000 and that unrecorded goodwill exists. Effective at the beginning of 20X6, Olsen will join the partnership with a 20% interest in capital and profits. In exchange for admission, Olsen will contribute $30,000 of cash plus intangibles.

Prepare the entries to record the withdrawal of Ergos and the admission of Olsen. The goodwill method is to be used to fully account for all goodwill suggested by the above transactions.

Exercise 9-6 *(LO 7)* **Liquidation, doctrine of right of offset.** The following information relates to Pfarr and Williams, who are partners in a business being liquidated:

	Pfarr	Williams
Partnership balances:		
Loan payable—Williams		$ 5,000
Capital balance (deficit)	$20,000	(14,000)
Personal assets (including partnership loan payable)	30,000	22,000
Personal liabilities	15,000	21,000
Profit and loss percentage	70%	30%

1. After applying the right-of-offset doctrine, indicate how each partner's personal assets would be distributed, assuming the Uniform Partnership Act is applicable.
2. Determine the effect on the calculations in item (1) if the right-of-offset doctrine were ignored.
3. After applying the right-of-offset doctrine, indicate how each partner's personal assets would be distributed assuming common law is applicable.

Exercise 9-7 *(LO 9)* **Adjustment of capital balances and lump-sum liquidation.** Palmyra Tooling is a partnership owned by Crawford, Meyer, and Jensen. Capital balances (deficits) and profit/loss percentages are as follows:

	Crawford	Meyer	Jensen
Capital balances at December 31, 20X5	$55,000	$115,000	$60,000
Profit and loss percentage	50%	30%	20%

The partnership agreement grants each of the partners a single vote and requires a majority vote to approve certain partnership actions including the liquidation of the partnership. Crawford and Meyer, as founders of Palmyra Tooling, have seen the company experience significant growth and then lose significant market share in the past five years due to local and foreign competition. Given the near term prospects of continuing difficulties and the further erosion of their capital balances, Crawford and Meyer have voted to liquidate the business. As of December 31, 20X5, book values differ from net realizable values as follows (all other assets/liabilities can be disposed of at book value):

	Book Value	Net Realizable Value
Accounts receivable	$130,000	$ 90,000
Inventory	35,000	15,000
Equipment (net)	725,000	645,000

Unlike his partners, Jensen feels that the company can restructure itself and that liquidation is not appropriate. Jensen is unable to persuade his partners and has offered to personally acquire Crawford's and Meyer's interests for $10,000 and $70,000, respectively. Unsure about the net personal assets of the individual partners, Meyer seeks your advice regarding whether it should accept Jensen's offer.

How would you advise Meyer?

Exercise 9-8 *(LO 1, 9)* **Admission of a new partner with determination of contribute vs. liquidation.** Arnold (A), Bower (B), and Chambers (C) are partners in a small manufacturing firm whose net assets are as follows:

	Book Value	Fair Value		Book Value	Fair Value
Current assets	$285,000	$210,000	Loan payable to Bower	$ 40,000	$ 40,000
Equipment (net of depreciation)	320,000	225,000	Other liabilities	430,000	434,000
			Arnold, capital	50,000	
Vacant land	60,000	85,000	Bower, capital	100,000	
Other assets	15,000	10,000	Chambers, capital	60,000	
Total assets	$680,000	$530,000	Total liabilities	$680,000	$474,000

The partnership agreement calls for the allocation of profits and losses as follows:

1. Salaries to A, B, and C of $30,000, $30,000, and $40,000, respectively.
2. Bonus to A of 10% of net income after the bonus.
3. Remaining amounts are allocated according to profit/loss percentages of 50%, 20%, and 30% for A, B, and C, respectively.

Unfortunately, the business finds itself in difficult times: Annual profits remain flat at approximately $132,000, additional capital is needed to finance equipment which is necessary to stay competitive, and all of the partners realize that they could make more money working for someone else, with a lot fewer headaches.

Chambers has identified Dawson (D) as an individual who might be willing to acquire an interest in the partnership. Dawson is proposing to acquire a 30% interest in the capital of the partnership and a revised partnership agreement, which calls for the allocation of profits as follows:

1. Salaries to A, B, C, and D of $30,000, $30,000, $40,000, and $30,000, respectively.
2. Bonus to D of $20,000 if net income exceeds $250,000.
3. Remaining amounts are allocated according to profit/loss percentages of 30%, 10%, 30%, and 30% for A, B, C, and D, respectively.

An alternative to admitting a new partner is to liquidate the partnership. Net personal assets of the partners are as follows:

	Arnold	Bower	Chambers
Personal assets	$240,000	$530,000	$300,000
Personal liabilities	228,000	150,000	200,000

Assuming that you are Bower's personal CPA, you have been asked to provide your client with your opinions regarding the alternatives facing the partnership.

1. Bower does not believe it would be worth it to him to admit a new partner unless his allocation of income increased by at least $10,000 over that which existed under the original partnership agreement. What would the average annual profit of the new partnership have to be in order for Bower to accept the idea of admitting a new partner?
2. Given the net assets of the original partnership, what is the suggested purchase price that Dawson should pay for a 30% interest in the partnership?
3. Assume that the original partnership was liquidated and Bower received a business vehicle, with a fair value of $15,000 and a net book value of $20,000, as part of his liquidation proceeds. How much additional cash would Bower receive if the partnership were liquidated?

Exercise 9-9 *(LO 8, 9)* **Installment liquidation with insolvent partners, the doctrine of marshaling of assets.** Coleman, Moore, and Ramsey are partners in a business being liquidated. The partnership has cash of $8,000, noncash assets with a book value of $96,000, and liabilities of $63,000. The following information relates to the individual partners as of June 1, 20X7:

	Coleman	Moore	Ramsey
Loan payable to partners.		$ 5,000	
Capital balance (deficit)	$47,000	(14,000)	$ 3,000
Personal assets.	10,000	15,000	25,000
Personal liabilities	5,000	6,000	15,000
Profit and loss percentage	60%	20%	20%

On June 15, 20X7, assets with a book value of $30,000 were sold for $20,000 cash. The proceeds were used to pay off liabilities of the partnership. During the balance of June, no additional assets were liquidated, and outside creditors began to pressure the partnership for payment. On July 1, the partners agreed to contribute personal assets, to whatever extent possible, in order to eliminate their respective capital deficits. Shortly thereafter, assets with a book value of $20,000 and a fair value of $23,000 were distributed to Coleman.

Assuming additional noncash assets with a book value of $40,000 are sold in July for $54,000, determine how available cash would be distributed.

Exercise 9-10 *(LO 9, 10)* **Installment liquidation, schedule of safe payments.** A real estate partnership had the following condensed balance sheet prior to liquidation:

Assets		Liabilities and Capital	
Cash	$ 12,000	Liabilities (to outsiders).	$ 35,000
Noncash assets	180,000	Loan payable to A	15,000
		A, capital (50%)	45,000
		B, capital (30%).	70,000
		C, capital (20%)	27,000
Total assets.	$192,000	Total liabilities and capital.	$192,000

The percentages in parentheses after the partners' capital balances represent their respective interests in profits and losses. The following situations are independent of each other unless otherwise stated:

1. If assets with a book value of $30,000 were sold for $20,000, how much of the available cash could be distributed to Partner A?
2. If assets with a book value of $60,000 were sold for $70,000, how much of the available cash could be distributed to Partner A?
3. Assume assets with a book value of $70,000 were sold for $50,000 and that all available cash was distributed. For what amount would the remaining assets have to be sold in order for Partner B to receive a total of $79,000 cash from all liquidation activities?

Exercise 9-11 *(LO 9)* **Calculate maximum loss absorbable.** Delaney, Gray, and Sullivan are considering the liquidation of their partnership, which has assets of $110,000 and liabilities, including a $10,000 loan from Sullivan, of $30,000. Delaney and Gray each have capital balances of $33,000. Profits and losses are shared 30%, 30%, and 40% for Delaney, Gray, and Sullivan, respectively.

Assuming liquidation expenses of $10,000, determine each partner's initial maximum loss absorbable (MLA) and indicate how distributions would be made until all partners have equal MLAs.

PROBLEMS

Problem 9-1 *(LO 2, 3, 5, 6)* **Admission and departure of partners under the goodwill method.** Carlton, Weber, and Stansbury share profits equally and have capital balances of $120,000, $70,000, and $80,000, respectively, as of December 31, 20X4. Effective January 1, 20X5, Stansbury has transferred his interest in the partnership to Laidlaw for total consideration of $100,000. As part of agreeing to admit Laidlaw to the partnership, the profit- and loss-sharing agreement was modified as follows:

1. Carlton, Weber, and Laidlaw would receive annual salaries of $120,000, $90,000, and $90,000, respectively, to be withdrawn in equal amounts at the end of each calendar quarter.
2. A bonus of 20% of net income after the bonus will be allocated between Weber and Laidlaw in the ratio of 1 to 3. The bonus would be distributed at the end of the first quarter subsequent to year-end.
3. Profit and loss percentages of 40%, 30%, and 30%, respectively, for Carlton, Weber, and Laidlaw.
4. If income is not sufficient or an operating loss exists, all provisions of the profit-sharing agreement are to be satisfied, and the profit and loss percentages are used to absorb any deficiency or additional losses.

The original partners were excited about the new arrangement because Laidlaw had indicated that they would be able to attract a number of customers from his previous place of employment. Weber was willing to shift some salary to a bonus status in order to capture more of the upside potential being presented by Laidlaw. As expected, over the first six months of 20X5, a number of Laidlaw's previous customers transferred their business to the partnership. However, the next 12 months were very disappointing. Not only did very few additional Laidlaw customers transfer their business, but it became clear that Laidlaw was not compatible with the other partners. Furthermore, a number of longstanding customers ceased doing business with the company due to issues with Laidlaw. Income for the year 20X5 was $300,000, and income for the first six months of 20X6 was only $120,000.

On July 1, 20X6, Carlton and Weber agreed to acquire Laidlaw's interest in the partnership. The transaction would be recorded as a purchase of Laidlaw's interest by the partnership under the bonus method. Laidlaw was paid $79,000 for their capital balance as of June 30, 20X6, and no other distributions were made to him.

After Laidlaw left the partnership, Carlton and Weber went back to sharing profits and losses equally with quarterly withdrawals of $10,000 per partner at the end of each calendar quarter. Weber agreed not to receive an additional distribution traceable to the bonus earned during the first six months of 20X6. Income in the second half of 20X6 was $73,000. However, the partners realized that they needed to expand operations if the company was to be saved. On January 1, 20X7, the partnership admitted Wilson. Wilson contributed tangible assets of $70,000 and intangibles to the partnership in exchange for a 40% interest in capital and one-third interest in profits. The admission of Wilson was recorded using the goodwill method. Carlton, Weber, and Wilson continued to share profits equally, and the partnership experienced net income of $420,000 in 20X7. Quarterly withdrawals of $30,000 were paid to each of the partners beginning in 20X7.

During the first six months of 20X8, the partnership had net income of $255,000 in spite of Carlton's reduced involvement due to health problems. On July 1, 20X8, Carlton sold his interest to the partnership for $160,000. The sale was recorded by recognizing the goodwill traceable to the entire partnership.

Prepare a schedule analyzing the changes in partners' capital accounts since December 31, ◄ ◄ ◄ ◄ ◄ **Required**
20X4. Supporting calculations should be in good form.

Problem 9-2 *(LO 1, 2, 3, 5)* **New partner, asset and capital balance determination, bonus, goodwill, tax basis.** Kravitz and Rowe are partners in an excavating business known as K & R Excavating. The partners are considering a number of options regarding the partnership, including the admission of a new partner and a potential sale of the partnership. The following information has been prepared as a basis for evaluating various alternatives:

Item	Book Value	Fair Value	Tax Basis
Cash and cash equivalents	$ 20,000	$ 20,000	$ 20,000
Accounts receivable	85,000	72,000	92,000
Inventory	42,000	30,000	50,000
Prepaid and other current assets	18,000	15,000	18,000
Property, plant, and equipment (net)	358,000	300,000	320,000
Total assets.	$523,000	$437,000	$500,000
Accounts payable	$ 54,000	$ 54,000	$ 54,000
Other current liabilities	29,000	35,000	29,000
Notes/loans payable	240,000	240,000	240,000
Kravitz, capital	120,000		
Rowe, capital.	80,000		
Total liabilities and capital.	$523,000		

The partners currently share profits and losses 60% and 40%, respectively, for Kravitz and Rowe.

Given the preceding information, respond to each of the following items: ◄ ◄ ◄ ◄ ◄ **Required**

1. Given the stated fair values, if Rowe were to sell one-half of her interest in capital to someone outside the partnership, what would be a suggested asking price?
2. Given the stated fair values, if a third party were to convey assets to the partnership in exchange for a 40% interest in the partnership, what would the value of those assets have to be?
3. Assume a new partner was admitted to the partnership with a 40% interest in capital in exchange for a cash contribution of $60,000. What would Rowe's capital balance be as a result of this transaction, assuming use of the bonus method?
4. Given the facts of (3) above, what would Rowe's capital balance be, assuming use of the goodwill method?
5. Assume a new partner was admitted to the partnership with a 30% interest in capital in exchange for a contribution of $55,000 of net tangible assets. What would the new partner's capital balance be as a result of this transaction, assuming use of the bonus method?
6. Assume a new partner was admitted to the partnership with a 30% interest in capital and a 40% interest in profits in exchange for net assets with the following tax bases: Inventory, $20,000; Equipment, $120,000; and Equipment Loan, $70,000. As a result of this transaction, what would be the tax basis in the partnership for the new partner?

Problem 9-3 *(LO 3)* **Determination of new partner contribution, evaluation of risks under the goodwill method.** Andrews and Block are partners in an engineering consulting company sharing profits and losses 40% and 60%, respectively, and their capital balances are $110,000 and $150,000, respectively. The recorded net assets of the company are as follows:

	Book Value	Fair Value
Working capital	$240,000	$220,000
Net property and equipment.	80,000	108,000
Noncurrent liabilities.	60,000	60,000

In addition to the recorded assets, the partners feel that the company has goodwill valued at $40,000 because the company enjoys a strong client base and has earnings that are consistently above industry averages.

Carver is interested in merging his environmental consulting company with Andrews and Block. Carver's net assets to be conveyed to the partnership include the following:

	Book Value	Fair Value
Working capital	$50,000	$40,000
Net equipment	60,000	50,000

In addition to the above recorded net assets, Carver feels that his business contacts and expertise will add value to the existing partnership. Carver has valued these intangibles at $20,000.

1. If Carver were to acquire a 30% interest in the new partnership, how much additional cash would Carver have to contribute to the partnership?
2. If Carver were admitted to the partnership, all partners would share equally in profits and losses. All parties are somewhat uncertain about the values placed on intangible assets. Andrews and Block favor using the goodwill method to record Carver's investment in the partnership. Calculate the amount of risk to all partners this method would entail should the intangible assets not have value.
3. Discuss how a profit and loss agreement might be used to reward a new partner for intangible assets while not recording the intangibles on the financial statements.

Problem 9-4 *(LO 2, 9)* **Exiting partners under the bonus method and liquidation.** Midway Construction was a partnership owned by Davis, Murray, and Clay with year-end 20X3 capital balances of $50,000, 80,000, and $70,000, respectively. Davis and Murray each received an annual salary of $100,000. Clay was primarily involved in sales and received a salary of $70,000 and a bonus of 20% of net income after salaries. All remaining profits were allocated equally among the partners. In the event of insufficient income or operating losses, each provision of the agreement would be satisfied to whatever extent possible given the order of salaries, interest, bonus, and percentages. Salaries are distributed at the end of each calendar quarter, and Clay's bonus is distributed at the end of the first month subsequent to year-end. Eighty percent of all other allocated income (income other than salary and bonus) is distributed to the partners at the end of the first quarter subsequent to year-end. During 20X3, the partnership had net income of $450,000 and proceeded to construct a number of spec homes during 20X4.

Unfortunately, during 20X4, interest rates increased, and the economy experienced a significant slowdown, resulting in partnership income of only $300,000. In order to improve cash flows, on January 1, 20X5, Rayburn would receive a profit allocation equal to interest of $5,900 in 20X5. In 20X6, Rayburn would receive interest of 10% on average capital, before allocation of 20X6 profits, and a 10% profit allocation. Rayburn would receive a profit allocation equal to interest on average capital of 10% and a 10% profit percentage. The previous partners' profit and loss agreement was modified to provide for salaries at one-half of previous levels, none of which were to be distributed, and profit percentages of 30% each. All other aspects of the previous profit-sharing agreement remained in effect. During the year 20X5, conditions worsened, and the partnership reported income of $142,000. At year-end 20X5, Davis sold its capital interest to the partnership in exchange for $49,400 and received no further distributions. At the beginning of 20X6, Murray loaned the partnership $50,000 with the necessary loan documents providing for interest at the rate of 6%. The profit-sharing agreement for 20X6 was completely changed to simply provide for interest on capital to Rayburn as previously set forth and all remaining profits to be allocated 40%, 40%, and 20% for Murray, Clay, and Rayburn, respectively. The only withdrawal to take place during 20X6 was the distribution of Clay's 20X5 bonus.

The partnership could no longer sustain the economic downturn, and the decision was made to liquidate the partnership after having reported net income of $110,000 during the first six months of 20X6. At the beginning of the liquidation process, the partnership had $15,000 in cash and liabilities, excluding loans from partners, of $84,000. Noncash assets of the partnership were liquidated as follows:

1. On August 1, 20X6, assets with a book value of $220,000 were sold for $180,000.
2. On September 1, 20X6, assets with a book value of $70,000 were sold for $82,000.

Prior to any further liquidation of assets, all available cash other than $10,000 held for future expenses was to be distributed to the partners on September 15, 20X6.

1. Prepare a schedule analyzing the partners' capital prior to liquidation of the partnership. Assume use of the bonus method to record all changes in the ownership structure of the partnership.   ◄ ◄ ◄ ◄ ◄ **Required**
2. Prepare a schedule of cash payments on September 15, 20X6, of the liquidation, showing how the available cash was distributed. Supporting calculations should be in good form.

Problem 9-5 *(LO 2, 3, 6)* Entries, new partner, old partner, alternative methods.
Buckner and Pressey are partners in a dry-cleaning business in which profits and losses are shared equally. Buckner and Pressey have capital balances of $40,000 and $60,000, respectively.

For each of the six situations presented, prepare the necessary journal entries for the partnership records.   ◄ ◄ ◄ ◄ ◄ **Required**

	Situations		
	(1)	(2)	(3)
Admission of new partner:			
Entering partner....................................	Nelson	Nelson	Nelson
Purchase price.....................................	$60,000	$30,000	$40,000
Interest in capital acquired	30%	20%	30%
Paid to	Partnership	Partnership	Pressey
Method used	Bonus	Goodwill	N/A

	Situations		
	(4)	(5)	(6)
Withdrawal of previous partner:			
Exiting partner....................................	Buckner	Buckner	Buckner
Selling price......................................	$48,000	$25,000	$39,000
Interest in capital sold	40%	20%	30%
Paid by	Partnership	Partnership	Partnership
Method used	Bonus	Goodwill traceable to exiting partner	Goodwill traceable to all partners

Problem 9-6 *(LO 9)* Installment liquidation, maximum loss absorbable, schedule of safe payments.
Part I: The partnership of Aikens, Barnes, and Clinton is winding up its affairs. The following information has been gathered:

a. The trial balance of the partnership at June 30, 20X7, is as follows:

	Debit	Credit
Cash	6,000	
Accounts Receivable..	22,000	
Inventory..	14,000	
Property, Plant, and Equipment (net)..............................	99,000	
Aikens, Loan..	12,000	
Clinton, Loan	7,500	
Accounts Payable		17,000
Aikens, Capital..		67,000

Barnes, Capital..		45,000
Clinton, Capital		31,500
Total	160,500	160,500

b. The partners share profits and losses as follows: Aikens, 50%; Barnes, 30%; and Clinton, 20%.

c. The partners are considering an offer of $100,000 for the accounts receivable, inventory, and plant assets as of June 30. Available cash would be paid to the partners in installments, but the number and amounts are to be negotiated.

Required ▶ ▶ ▶ ▶ ▶   Prepare a schedule as of June 30, 20X7, showing how the available cash would be distributed as it becomes available assuming that loans receivable from partners are offset against their capital balances.

Part II: Assume the same facts as in Part I, except that the partners have decided to liquidate their partnership instead of accepting the offer of $100,000. Cash is distributed to the partners at the end of each month. A summary of liquidation transactions follows:

July:

> $16,500—collected on accounts receivable; balance is uncollectible.
> $10,000—received from sale of entire inventory.
> $1,000—liquidation expenses paid.
> $8,000—cash retained in the business at the end of month.

August:

> $1,500—liquidation expenses paid. Clinton's capital was reduced when Clinton accepted a piece of special equipment that had a book value of $4,000. The partners agreed that a value of $10,000 should be placed on the machine for liquidation purposes.
> $2,500—cash retained in the business at the end of the month.

September:

> $75,000—received on sale of remaining plant assets.
> $1,000—liquidation expenses paid.
> No cash was retained in the business.

Required ▶ ▶ ▶ ▶ ▶   Prepare a schedule of cash payments as of September 30, 20X7, showing how the cash actually was distributed. Supporting calculations should be in good form.

(AICPA adapted)

Problem 9-7 *(LO 9)* **Liquidation.** In light of major downturns in the economy, Barker Manufacturing experienced declining profits and defaulted on several loans. In a recent meeting, the three partners in the business agreed to continue operations another six months if the partners would make personal loans to the company. These loans were made; yet no significant favorable changes occurred, and the partners agreed to liquidate the partnership. The trial balance prior to liquidation is as follows:

	Debit	Credit
Cash		2,000
Other Assets	141,000	
Loans from Barker		50,000
Loans from Dunton...		24,000
Other Liabilities		82,000
Capital, Barker		16,000
Capital, Dunton..	18,000	
Capital, Jacoby	15,000	
Total..	174,000	174,000

Following the decision to liquidate, the partners agreed that available funds will be distributed at the end of each month. Furthermore, if necessary, the partners will contribute available personal assets to satisfy capital deficits. However, they agreed that the right of offset, with respect to partnership loans, would be observed.

During the first month of liquidation, assets with a book value of $32,000 were sold for $26,000. Actual liquidation expenses of $4,000 occurred, and future liquidation expenses of $3,000 were estimated. Personal assets and liabilities were as follows:

	Barker	Dunton	Jacoby
Personal assets (including loans to partnership)	$160,000	$48,000	$50,000
Personal liabilities	100,000	30,000	21,000

During the second month of liquidation, assets with a book value of $68,000 were sold for $30,000. Actual liquidation expenses of $5,000 were incurred during the month, and no future liquidation expenses were anticipated. Personal assets and liabilities were as follows:

	Barker	Dunton	Jacoby
Personal assets (including loans to partnership)	$130,000	$40,000	$28,000
Personal liabilities	110,000	20,000	24,000

During the third and final month of liquidation, the balance of the other assets was sold for $11,000. Personal assets and liabilities were as follows:

	Barker	Dunton	Jacoby
Personal assets (including loans to partnership)	$108,000	$36,000	$20,000
Personal liabilities	90,000	18,000	26,000

Assume the profit and loss percentages are 50%, 30%, and 20% for Barker, Dunton, and Jacoby, respectively. Prepare a schedule that details monthly cash distributions for the liquidation.

 **Required**

Problem 9-8 *(LO 9)* **Installment liquidation, premature distributions, insolvent partners.** Green Acres Enterprises is a partnership that constructed and sold assisted living facilities for the elderly. The firm has been in existence for seven years, and the partners have decided that the market for such facilities has become saturated and that the partnership should be liquidated. The partners Dvorak, Kelsen, and Morgan share profits and losses 30%, 30%, and 40%, respectively. The following information, presented in chronological order, is relevant to the liquidation of the partnership.

1. The following balances existed prior to the commencement of the liquidation:

Assets		Liabilities and Capital	
Cash	$ 15,000	Accounts payable	$ 80,000
Accounts receivable	60,000	Note payable—mortgage	450,000
Inventory	90,000	Note payable—Kelsen	40,000
Prepaid assets	12,000	Contingent liability	83,000
Furniture and fixtures (net)	150,000	Dvorak, capital	20,000
Office equipment (net)	30,000	Kelsen, capital	47,000
Vehicles (net)	30,000	Morgan, capital	17,000
Assisted living home (net)	350,000		
Total assets	$737,000	Total liabilities and capital	$737,000

2. Accounts receivable with a book value of $40,000 were collected in the amount of $30,000. The inventory was sold for $60,000.
3. All the prepaid amounts were refunded to the company with the exception of $2,000 that was forfeited.
4. The partners agreed that any additional available cash should be used to pay off the accounts payable rather than the contingent liability.
5. Office equipment with a book value of $15,000 and a fair value of $12,000 was distributed to Morgan. A vehicle with a book value of $10,000 and a fair value of $8,000 was distributed to Dvorak.
6. The office equipment and vehicles were sold for 80% of their book value.
7. The contingent liability was settled for $43,000.
8. The partners agreed that 90% of any available cash should be distributed to the partners.
9. The furniture and fixtures were consigned to a broker who sold them for net proceeds of $120,000.
10. The balance of the accounts receivable had been turned over to a collection agency, and the partnership received $5,000 upon final settlement of all accounts.
11. The assisted living home proved difficult to dispose of and was finally sold for $400,000. Furthermore, legal fees and brokers' commissions totaling $25,000 were incurred in connection with the sale. The note payable—mortgage was paid off in full in addition to previously unrecorded interest in the amount of $5,000.
12. Prior to distributing the remaining cash, partners with deficit balances were required to make the necessary contribution from net personal assets. At that time, the net assets (liabilities) of the partners were as follows: Dvorak, ($8,000); Kelsen, $140,000; and Morgan, $10,000.
13. All available cash was distributed to the partners.

Required ▶ ▶ ▶ ▶ ▶
1. Prepare a liquidation schedule for the above partnership.
2. Determine whether the distributions of office equipment and vehicles to the individual partners were, in fact, "safe" distributions.
3. What is the nature of the claim solvent partners have against a partner who is not able to satisfy a deficit capital balance?

Problem 9-9 *(LO 9)* **Liquidate now or later.** Skeeba, Tank, and King are considering whether or not to liquidate their partnership due to worsening economic conditions. As of December 31, 20X4, the partnership had total assets and liabilities (excluding loans from partners) of $360,000 and $110,000, respectively. The following relates to the partners:

	Skeeba	Tank	King
Capital balance.	$80,000	$90,000	$40,000
Loan to partner balance.	$20,000		$20,000
Profit and loss percentage	40%	30%	30%

In 20X5, it is anticipated that the partnership could recognize $30,000 of normal operating income. Furthermore, if the partners were willing to contribute another $30,000, it appears that an additional $40,000 of nonrecurring income could be recognized. However, it is unlikely that the partnership could continue to operate beyond 20X5 without a significant change in its capital structure and the economic climate.

Each of the partners has been asked to contribute $10,000 of additional capital in order to continue operations into 20X5. However, King is not sure that this is a good decision. Alternatively, Tank has offered to purchase King's interest in the partnership as of year-end 20X4 for $60,000. It is also possible that King could convince the partnership to liquidate as of year-end 20X4. King is seriously considering selling its interest to Tank. However, it needs to consider whether liquidation at year-end 20X4 or 20X5 would be more advantageous.

Required ▶ ▶ ▶ ▶ ▶
Assuming you have been retained by King to evaluate its alternatives, prepare an analysis that would be useful to its decision process. Assume that net assets, excluding partnership loans,

could be liquidated for an amount equal to 80% and 85% of book value at the end of 20X4 and 20X5, respectively.

Problem 9-10 *(LO 6, 9)* **Decision to buy out other partners or to liquidate.** Partners Schmidt, Janis, and Glomski operate a fuel oil business serving both residential and commercial customers. Due to existing soil contamination and new federal environmental laws, the operation is being required to spend approximately $90,000 to correct present conditions and acquire new equipment. Rather than incur this expense, the partners are considering liquidating the company.

A summary of the net assets of the operation is as follows:

Net Assets	Book Value	Current Value
Cash	$ 25,000	$ 25,000
Receivables and prepaids	42,000	35,000
Inventory	27,000	22,000
Equipment	125,000	75,000
Real estate	210,000	140,000
Accounts payable	(40,000)	(40,000)
Mortgage payable	(54,000)	(54,000)
Note payable to previous partner	(100,000)	(90,000)
Equipment note	(80,000)	(80,000)
Total	$ 155,000	$ 33,000

It is estimated that, in order to realize the above current values, approximately $10,000 in expenses will have to be incurred for brokerage fees, commissions, and other liquidation costs.

Partnership and personal information relating to the partners is as follows:

	Schmidt	Janis	Glomski
Partnership capital balance	$ 85,000	$ 47,000	$ 23,000
Partnership profit and loss percentage	30%	35%	35%
Personal assets	225,000	167,000	140,000
Personal creditors	165,000	170,000	130,000

Schmidt had hoped to retire in three to five years and would welcome the opportunity to retire early. However, he is concerned that with the low liquidating values for the net assets of the company, it is possible that some of his net personal assets may have to be contributed to the partnership as part of the liquidation. Schmidt is also uncomfortable because he believes that his partners, especially Glomski, may not have adequate net personal assets to meet their partnership responsibilities. Schmidt's nephew has just returned from an extended stay in the Navy and had worked for the fuel company prior to his Navy career. The nephew has some net assets, is energetic, and is not adverse to working in the fuel business. Even though the cost to comply with the new federal standards is high, Schmidt feels that he could secure the necessary capital and persuade his nephew to join the business with an opportunity to ultimately own the company.

Schmidt has come to you seeking your advice. He is considering purchasing each of his partners' interests in the partnership rather than liquidating the company. Prepare an analysis which would suggest what Schmidt might offer to pay each of his partners, and summarize your findings in a memo to Schmidt.   ◄ ◄ ◄ ◄ ◄ **Required**

Problem 9-11 *(LO 8, 9, 10)* **Installment liquidation, schedule of safe payments, doctrine of marshaling of assets.** Ziegler, Nolan, and Petersen are partners in a residential construction business which has operated for the last 32 years in the Los Angeles area. The partners have decided to leave the business and focus on other pursuits. Initially, they had hoped to sell the business to an employee or other construction company. However, the weak housing market in the area has made liquidation of the company a more likely scenario.

You have been retained to account for the liquidation and to advise the partners as to how available assets of the company should be distributed. Events surrounding the liquidation during 20X8 are as follows:

1. On June 1, the company's balance sheet reflected the following: cash—$12,000; noncash assets—$228,000; liabilities to nonpartners—$120,000; loan payable to Nolan—$15,000; Ziegler, capital—$20,000; Nolan, capital—$35,000; and Petersen, capital—$50,000. Ziegler, Nolan, and Petersen share profits and losses of 30%, 30%, and 40%, respectively.
2. A review of the financial statements reveals that additional adjustments may be in order. The company has a contingent liability associated with a previous building contract dispute. It is probable that the company will incur $13,000 of cost in connection with this matter. Final wages and related payroll tax liabilities totaling $4,400 have not been accrued.
3. On June 15, vehicles with a current value of $23,000 and a book value of $14,000 were conveyed to Ziegler. Other assets with a book value of $90,000 were sold for $70,000 to a competing contractor. All available cash was distributed.
4. On June 30, inventory, tools, and other equipment were sold to various employees for a total of $92,000. The items had a book value of $80,000.
5. On July 10, a subcontractor was paid $15,000 to complete work on a final construction project which had not been finished prior to the liquidation. The customer was billed $20,000 for the work performed, and final payment was expected by late July.
6. On July 15, available cash was distributed. However, in addition to the $13,000 of cash retained to satisfy the contingent liability, another $5,000 of cash was retained as a precaution.
7. On July 25, title to a vehicle with a fair value of $12,000 and a book value of $8,000 was transferred to Petersen.
8. At the end of July, the contingent liability was settled for $10,000, and $20,000 was received from the last customer in payment for services performed in July.
9. On August 1, all available cash was distributed.
10. At mid-August, all the remaining assets were disposed of for $24,000. Associated attorney and accounting fees of $6,000 were paid. All available cash was distributed.

After all of the above events, the personal financial statements of the partners reveal the following:

	Ziegler	Nolan	Petersen
Personal assets.	$185,000	$187,000	$240,000
Personal creditors	165,000	140,000	120,000

Required ▶ ▶ ▶ ▶ ▶   Prepare an installment liquidation schedule with all necessary supporting schedules. The schedule should also reflect the marshaling-of-assets doctrine where appropriate.

Problem 9-12 *(LO 5, 8, 9)* **Decision to sell interest or liquidate a troubled partnership, doctrine of marshaling of assets.** Your client Baker is in a partnership that has encountered significant business difficulties. Baker has become increasingly disenchanted with the business and is suggesting that it be liquidated over the next six months. However, one of Baker's partners has offered to acquire Baker's interest in the partnership, including loans due Baker, for $200,000, payable in four equal semiannual payments. The first payment would be due upon transfer of the partnership interest. Your client is not convinced that this would be a more attractive alternative than liquidation. A detailed inventory of the partnership net assets is as follows:

Item	Book Value	Fair Value
Cash and cash equivalents	$ 10,000	$ 10,000
Accounts receivable	240,000	200,000
Inventory	320,000	280,000
Equipment (net)	480,000	400,000
Land	80,000	200,000
Goodwill	60,000	0
Total assets.	$1,190,000	$1,090,000

Accounts payable	$ 330,000	$ 330,000
Notes payable—bank	590,000	570,000
Notes payable—Baker	160,000	160,000
Baker, capital	60,000	
Meyer, capital	30,000	
Paulsen, capital	20,000	
Total liabilities and capital	$1,190,000	

If a partner has a deficit balance, the doctrine of marshaling of assets should be employed. It is estimated that the net assets of individual partners are as follows:

Partner	Assets	Liabilities
Baker	$400,000	$220,000
Meyer	180,000	140,000
Paulsen	122,000	107,000

Profits and losses are allocated among the partners as follows: Baker, 30%; Meyer, 50%; and Paulsen, 20%. It is estimated that liquidation/transaction costs associated with realizing the fair value of assets will be 8%.

Prepare a schedule that compares the options of selling or liquidating the partnership. ◄ ◄ ◄ ◄ ◄ **Required**

PART

Governmental and Not-for-Profit Accounting

4

Chapter 10: *Governmental Accounting: The General Fund and the Account Groups (including Other Governmental Funds, Proprietary Funds, and Fiduciary Funds)*

Chapter 11: *Financial Reporting Issues*

Chapter 12: *Accounting for Private Not-for-Profit Organizations (including Colleges and Universities and Health Care Organizations)*

Government and not-for-profit organizations are a major force in our society, comprising one-third of the United States expenditures and employing a substantial work force.

There are approximately 87,000 local governments in the United States. These include villages, towns, cities, counties, states, school districts, universities, public authorities, or special districts. There are over one million not-for-profits in the United States. These include schools; hospitals; social service, advocacy, cultural, and civic organizations; churches, synagogues, and mosques; and foundations.

The primary objective of external financial reporting for governmental units and not-for-profit organizations is accountability. However, there is no "bottom-line" amount or earnings per share figure to judge success. Instead, there is the elusive factor of service. To control activities and measure service, variations in the accounting and reporting process are introduced. Budgets have far greater power for control, particularly when they are entered formally into the accounting records in order to provide close comparisons with actual results. With financial resources being derived from many different sources, some with specific restrictions as to their consumption, fund accounting has traditionally been used to display proper use for intended purposes. More recently, standards setters have moved away from fund accounting for private not-for-profit organizations to an organization-wide reporting of unrestricted and donor-restricted assets and liabilities. Similarly, new government standards include entity-wide financial statements.

Governmental Accounting: The General Fund and the Account Groups (including Other Governmental Funds, Proprietary Funds, and Fiduciary Funds)

Learning Objectives

When you have completed this chapter, you should be able to

1. Explain the Governmental Accounting Standards Board's role in setting financial reporting standards for state and local governments.

2. Identify the types of funds and account groups in state and local governments.

3. Show how to account for transactions in governmental funds.

4. Explain the purpose of budgets and how governments account for appropriations.

5. Prepare journal entries for the general fund.

6. Demonstrate how to account for encumbrances.

7. Prepare fund financial statements for the general fund.

8. Complete schedules for general capital assets and long-term liabilities.

9. Tell why governments use special revenue, permanent, capital projects, and debt service funds, and demonstrate how transactions are accounted for and reported using those funds.

10. Account for and prepare financial statements of proprietary funds.

11. Explain the usefulness of and the accounting process for fiduciary funds and how these funds are reported.

12. Identify and account for transactions that affect different funds and/or account groups.

Accounting and financial reporting for governmental and not-for-profit (also called nonprofit) entities have become more important because an increasing portion of our national economy has been devoted to this sector. Decision makers, such as legislators, citizens, managers, and contributors, need better information about governmental and not-for-profit organizations if they are to make optimal resource allocations to those entities and manage them efficiently and effectively. In addition, many accounting students will hold governmental and not-for-profit accounting jobs, perform audits on such organizations, and take the CPA examination, which contains questions on governmental and not-for-profit accounting.

GASB Objectives of Financial Reporting

Differences in environments and purposes of financial reporting between business enterprises and governmental entities have led to the creation of separate financial reporting standard-setting boards for business enterprises and governments, and each board has examined and defined the objectives of financial reporting by its respective constituency. *Objectives of Financial Reporting by Business Enterprises*, Concept Statement No. 1, was issued by the Financial Accounting Standards Board (FASB) in 1978. *Objectives of Financial Reporting*, Concept Statement No. 1, was issued by the Governmental Accounting Standards Board (GASB) in 1987.

1

OBJECTIVE

Explain the Governmental Accounting Standards Board's role in setting financial reporting standards for state and local governments.

In its Concept Statement No. 1, the GASB stated that "**accountability** is the cornerstone of all financial reporting in government."[1] A closely related concept referred to by the GASB in the concept statement is **interperiod equity**. Both concepts are described below.

The GASB believes that financial reporting helps a government fulfill its duty to be publicly accountable to its citizenry. They believe that taxpayers have a "right to know;" that is, a right to receive information about government activities that may lead to public debates. At a minimum, *accountability* through financial reporting means "providing information to assist in evaluating whether the government was operated within the legal constraints imposed by the citizenry."[2]

A significant part of accountability is *interperiod equity*, which may be demonstrated by showing "whether current-year revenues are sufficient to pay for current-year services or whether future taxpayers will be required to assume burdens for services previously provided."[3] As with business financial reports, state and local government financial reports should possess the characteristics of understandability, reliability, relevance, timeliness, consistency, and comparability.

Measurement Focus and Basis of Accounting

Measurement focus refers to which resources are being measured. *Basis of accounting* refers to when the effects of transactions or events should be recognized for financial reporting purposes. The traditional measurement focus for state and local governments has been *financial resources*. In June 1999, the GASB issued Statement No. 34 after nearly 15 years of deliberation and dialogue with its constituents. Statement No. 34, *Basic Financial Statements—and Management's Discussion and Analysis—for State and Local Governments*, was a significant change in practice. Large governments implemented the standards in fiscal years beginning after June 15, 2001, and medium-size and smaller governments adopted the standard in fiscal years beginning after June 15, 2002, and 2003, respectively.[4]

Governments prepare two separate, but related, sets of financial statements. The first set, the fund financial statements, is similar to the former reporting model and focuses on reporting activity as a collection of separate funds. Governmental and business-type funds are reported on separate statements. And, rather than follow the reporting of traditional fund-types (as described in the following section), these statements report major funds and combine all the nonmajor funds into one column.

The second set of financial statements are government-wide statements that concentrate on the government as a whole. These statements adopt an *economic resources measurement focus* and consolidate all of a government's operations on *a full accrual basis* similar to that found in the business world.

The sections that follow present an overview of the main funds maintained by governments and describe the accounting for activities. A discussion of accounting for long-term assets and liabilities also follows. Chapter 11 describes the fund financial statements and the more recently required government-wide statements as well as the articulation from one to the other.

REFLECTION

- Governmental accounting and financial reporting standards for state and local governments are established by the GASB.

- Governments prepare both fund financial statements and government-wide statements.

---

1 GASB Concept Statement No. 1, Objectives of Financial Reporting (Norwalk, CT: Governmental Accounting Standards Board, 1987), par. 58.
2 *Ibid.*
3 *Ibid.*, par. 61.
4 GASB Statement No. 34, *Basic Financial Statements—and Management's Discussion and Analysis—for State and Local Governments* (Norwalk, CT: Governmental Accounting Standards Board, June 1999).

GOVERNMENTAL ACCOUNTING STRUCTURE OF FUNDS

2

OBJECTIVE

Identify the types of funds and account groups in state and local governments.

A variety of funds may be used to record events and to exhibit results for a specific area of responsibility. In a small town, there may not be enough activity to warrant more than a general fund, but the larger the governmental unit and the more diverse the activities with which it is involved, the greater the necessity to introduce special funds. Since too many funds will unnecessarily fragment financial reporting, a governmental unit should establish only the *mini-mum* number of funds consistent with legal and operating requirements.

Governmental units create individual funds to account for financial resources used for specific purposes. Each fund is an accounting entity containing a self-balancing set of accounts for which financial statements can be prepared. Business enterprises, on the other hand, report all of their profit-making activity on a single income statement and summarize their financial position on a single balance sheet.

Three fund types and two account groups are used in governments:

1. **Governmental funds** account for activities that provide citizens with services financed primarily by taxes and intergovernmental grants. These funds have a *working capital* focus and include only current assets and current liabilities.

2. **Proprietary funds** account for business-type activities that derive their revenue from charges to users for goods or services. They follow the commercial accounting model in measuring net income. An example would be a publicly owned utility.

3. **Fiduciary funds** account for resources for which the governmental unit acts as a trustee or agent.

4. **Account groups** account for and serve as a record of general capital assets and general long-term liabilities. Account groups are not required, but many governments continue to use them as a convenient means of keeping track of these items. Alternatively, some governments are changing their account systems to allow for the generation of lists of capital assets and long-term liabilities without using account groups.

Different methods of applying the accrual concept in accounting are used for governmental funds and proprietary funds. The *modified accrual basis*, a hybrid system that includes some aspects of both accrual and cash-basis accounting, is used for recognition of revenues and expenditures of governmental funds. The accrual basis is used to recognize revenues and expenses of proprietary funds and fiduciary funds as in business accounting. These methods are explained in the sections that follow.

Governmental Funds

All governments have a general fund and may have other governmental funds as well, depending on their types of activities. The five governmental funds are as follows:

1. The **general fund** accounts for resources that have no specific restrictions and are available for operational expenditures not relegated to one of the other governmental funds. Since it accounts for general operations, it is the most essential fund. Every governmental unit has a general fund.

2. **Special revenue funds** account for resources that legally are restricted to expenditures for specific operational purposes, such as a toll tax levied for road maintenance expenses.

3. **Capital projects funds** account for resources to be used for the construction or acquisition of major capital facilities.

4. **Debt service funds** account for resources to be used for payment of general long-term debt and interest.

5. **Permanent funds** account for resources that are legally restricted so that only their earnings, not the principal, may be used to finance operations.

3

OBJECTIVE

Show how to account for transactions in governmental funds.

Accounting for Transactions of Governmental Funds

The modified accrual method of accounting is used for governmental funds to measure the flow of working capital. Under modified accrual, revenue is recorded in the accounting period in which it is both measurable and available to finance expenditures made during the current fiscal period (this includes resources expected to be available shortly after year-end). Expenditures are recognized in the period in which the liabilities are both measurable and incurred.

Revenues. Increases in financial resources from transactions with external parties that do not have to be repaid are called **revenues.** Revenues may come from nonexchange or exchange transactions. Nonexchange transactions are those in which people and companies pay amounts to governments but governments give nothing directly to the payors in return. Exchange transactions are those in which the government provides goods or services for fees. Under modified accrual, some revenues are recognized on the accrual basis and some revenues are recognized on the cash basis. Revenue from property taxes, intergovernmental grants, entitlements, and shared revenues; interest on investments and delinquent taxes; and billed charges for services are normally recognized under the modified accrual basis if funds will be "collectible within the current period or soon enough thereafter to be used to pay liabilities of the current period."[5]

Property taxes, fines, and other *imposed* tax revenues are recorded as revenue at the time taxes are levied on property owners and others provided the taxes will be collected during the current period or soon enough after year-end to pay the liabilities of the current period. Taxes levied in one year but not available until the following year are recognized as deferred revenue. Governments are conservative in recognizing property tax revenue. Only the net amount estimated to be collected is recognized.

Resources to be received from federal, state, or local governmental units (intergovernmental grants, entitlements, and shared revenues for operational purposes) should be recognized as revenue in the year for which all eligibility requirements, including time restrictions, have been met and the resources are available to finance expenditures. If resources are received prior to the time period in which they may be used, or if the receivable is not expected to be collected soon enough to be used for the current fiscal period, Deferred Revenues is credited. Some grants to a governmental unit may carry strong restrictions on their use. For example, the federal government may be willing to give a locality a grant providing it builds a bridge over a river and connects its main road to the federal highway. In this case, the restricted grant should be recognized as revenue only to the extent that expenditures have been made, with the remainder of the grant recorded as deferred revenue. This type of restricted grant is sometimes called an *expenditure driven* grant.

Revenues from voluntary nonexchange transactions, such as donations and certain grants, should be recognized in governmental funds when the assets are received. Donations of capital assets are not recognized in governmental funds. Rather, donated capital assets are recorded in the general fixed assets account group discussed later in this chapter.

Revenue for service charges should be recognized when billed if it is expected to be received within the current period or soon enough thereafter to be used to pay liabilities of the current period. Such revenues may be from goods or services provided for fees, such as golf course fees, garbage removal fees, inspection fees, and sales of maps and other publications.

Interest and dividend revenue from investments should be recognized when earned. Investment gains and losses should be recognized when an investment is sold.

Revenues normally recognized under the cash-basis method include fees for licenses and permits, fines and forfeits, and parking meter receipts. These resources are recognized when received in cash because the amount is usually not known prior to collection. In addition, these items are often not an important source of a governmental unit's income.

Taxes levied directly on taxpayers are accounted for in the same modified accrual basis of accounting that already applies to most other revenue sources.[6] Examples are taxes on income, inheritance, gasoline, general sales, and tobacco. Revenue from these taxpayer-assessed or *derived* taxes, net of estimated refunds, is recognized in the accounting period in which they become susceptible to accrual [e.g., when the underlying transaction (sale or earning of income)

---

5 GASB Statement No. 33, *Accounting and Financial Reporting for Nonexchange Transactions* (Norwalk, CT: Governmental Accounting Standards Board, December 1998) identifies four classes of nonexchange transactions: *derived tax revenues,* such as income taxes and sales taxes; *imposed nonexchange revenues,* such as property taxes and fines; *government-mandated nonexchange transactions,* such as federal programs that state and local governments are required to perform; and *voluntary nonexchange transactions,* such as grants and private donations.

6 *Ibid.*

occurs and the amounts are measurable and will be collected within the current period or soon enough after year-end to finance expenditures for the period]. A lag often occurs from the time of the underlying transaction to the reporting of such events, so, in practice, revenue is recorded when either the merchant or the employer submits the required reports to the governmental unit.

Other Financing Sources. These inflows of financial resources arise from issuing general long-term debt, recording the present value of capital lease obligations, selling capital assets, and receiving interfund operating transfers from other governmental funds. Use of the **other financing sources** classification avoids multiple countings of inflows as revenues. Proceeds from issuing general long-term debt represent inflows of financial resources that must be repaid to lenders from later tax revenues. Tax revenue recorded in the general fund would be counted as revenue twice if amounts transferred to another governmental fund were recorded in the second fund as revenue rather than as other financing sources. The same is true for proceeds from the sale of a fixed asset. Financial resources raised by tax revenues are used to purchase fixed assets. Their later sale is a conversion of fixed assets into financial resources, not a raising of new financial resources from entities outside the governmental unit.

Expenditures. Most **expenditures** are decreases in financial resources as a result of transactions with external parties. Some expenditures, however, result from consumption of previously purchased financial resources, such as inventories and prepaid items. Expenditures are recognized in the period the fund liability is both measurable and incurred.[7] This usually means that an expenditure is recognized if the related liability is expected to be liquidated through the use of current-year expendable and available financial resources. Expenditures result from operating activities, acquiring capital assets, and payment of debt principal and interest. In many cases, expenditures will be recorded simultaneously with cash payments. Consider the following examples:

Expenditures	50,000	
Cash		50,000
The payment of current maintenance expenses.		
Expenditures	100,000	
Cash		100,000
Acquisition of a new capital asset for cash.		

Expenditures for interest and principal on general long-term debt are recorded on a cash basis when they are due to match them with the tax revenue raised for the interest and principal payment.

Expenditures	42,000	
Cash		42,000
Payment of $12,000 of interest and $30,000 principal on existing general obligation debt.		

Other expenditures will be recorded if the amount is to be paid with existing resources. Consider the following entries to record wages:

Expenditures	16,500	
Cash		10,500
Liability for State and Federal Withholdings		6,000

While the liability for withholdings is current, another common payroll liability for future payment of compensated absences (such as for vacations and holidays) is considered to be long term. Under the *modified accrual basis* of governmental accounting, such long-term liabilities

7 GASB Exposure Draft, *Recognition and Measurement of Certain Liabilities and Expenditures in Governmental Fund Financial Statements* (Norwalk, CT: Governmental Accounting Standards Board, June 1999).

would not be recorded in the general fund, but would appear in the government-wide statements. The traditional means of keeping track of long-term obligations has been through the use of account groups. The concept of using account groups for internal control and support for financial reporting will be described in detail later in this chapter. Long-term vacation and sick leave liabilities are recorded in the general long-term debt account group as follows:

Amount to Be Provided in Future Periods	1,500	
Liability for Compensated Absences		1,500

Only the expenditure and related current liability for compensated absences reasonably expected to be paid from the current governmental fund financial resources are included in the fund. All long-term liabilities are recorded separately.

Recording pension expenditures requires a calculation of the "actuarial required contribution" (ARC).[8] This calculation can be made using acceptable actuarial methods and assumptions. As in the preceding example for compensated absences, the portion of the ARC that will be paid from current resources will be recorded as an expenditure in the fund.

Expenditures	5,000	
Current Pension Liability		5,000

The portion to be funded from future resources is recorded as general long-term debt in the account group as follows:

Amount to Be Provided in Future Periods	2,000	
Unfunded Pension Liability		2,000

Governments are also required to measure and report on postretirement benefits such as health care and life insurance in a manner similar to the illustration for pension benefits above.[9]

A liability for claims and judgments outstanding is recognized if it is probable that the liability has been incurred and the amount can be reasonably estimated. During the year, the government will record the amounts paid or vouchered as payable as expenditures in the fund. The noncurrent liability for claims and judgments is recorded directly in the general long-term debt account group.

In many cases, cash will be paid or a liability recorded to purchase goods and services in advance of their use. These items are recorded in the fund as financial resources (assets) as follows:

Prepaid Rent	12,000	
Prepaid Insurance	18,000	
Supplies Inventory	40,000	
Cash		70,000
Acquiring goods and services to be consumed in the future.		

Expenditures are recorded in the fund as follows when the financial resources are consumed:

Expenditures	45,000	
Prepaid Rent		10,000
Prepaid Insurance		15,000
Supplies Inventory		20,000
Receiving services and consuming supplies acquired previously.		

---

8 GASB Statement No. 27, *Accounting for Pensions by State and Local Governmental Employers* (Norwalk, CT: Governmental Accounting Standards Board, November 1994).

9 GASB Statement No. 45, *Accounting and Financial Reporting by Employers for Postemployment Benefits Other than Pensions* (Norwalk, CT: Governmental Accounting Standards Board, June 2004).

Other Financing Uses. The greatest use of the **other financing uses** classification is for inter-fund operating transfers-out to other governmental funds. Using this classification for such fund outflows prevents double counting of expenditures. For example, if an amount transferred from the general fund to the debt service fund were debited to expenditures and then debited to expenditures again in the debt service fund when interest and long-term debt principal were liquidated, a double counting of expenditures would occur. Also classified as other financing uses are payments made from financial resources of refunding general long-term debt (using proceeds from issuing new debt to pay old debt).

Operating Debt. Governments may issue short- and long-term debt to finance their operating activities. Such financing is treated as **operating debt** when the debt is not incurred to acquire capital assets or other long-term economic benefits for the government. Examples of short-term operating debt include accounts payable to vendors and tax anticipation notes. Examples of long-term operating debt include certain bonds or notes payable and long-term vendor financing. Also recognized as long-term operating debt are those obligations described above that a government incurs but does not pay for in a particular year (e.g., liabilities for compensated absences, claims and judgments, and unfunded pensions).

Short-term debt is recorded in the fund as a liability if it is "normally expected to be liquidated with expendable available financial resources." Hence, governmental fund liabilities (and a corresponding expenditure) are recorded if they are normally paid in a timely manner from current financial resources. Examples are salaries, professional services, supplies, utilities, and travel. Long-term operating debt is reported as a liability in the general long-term debt account group. As this debt matures and becomes due and payable, it will become a fund liability.

Tax anticipation notes are an example of short-term operating debt. Cash inflows from property tax or income tax collections peak near the due dates for payment. Prior to their receipt, a governmental unit may have obligations that must be paid. Local banks usually provide short-term financing, using as security the taxing power of the government, which is required to sign an instrument referred to as a tax anticipation note. Receipt of cash from such notes would be recorded in the general fund with the following entry:

Cash	150,000	
Tax Anticipation Notes Payable		150,000

General Long-Term Capital Debt. Debt financing incurred to acquire capital assets or other long-term economic benefits through governmental funds is termed **general long-term capital debt.** The majority of the proceeds acquired from issuing this debt is accounted for in capital projects funds, as an other financing source. The face amount of capital debt is accounted for in the general long-term debt account group discussed later in this chapter. Debt service (principal and interest payments) expenditures on all general long-term debt are accounted for in the debt service funds.

Special and Extraordinary Items. Extraordinary items are those which are both unusual in nature and infrequent in occurrence. Special items arise from significant transactions or other events that are (1) within the control of management and (2) either unusual in nature or infrequent in occurrence. Special items are reported separately in the financial statements below nonoperating revenue and before extraordinary items. The recognition of special items and extraordinary items follows the revenue, expenditure, other financing source and use criteria described above. An example of an extraordinary item is a natural disaster. An example of a special item is the sale of a significant governmental asset or a loss incurred as a result of a civil riot. Separate reporting of such items serves to inform the citizens and other users of the financial statements when governments engage in unusual practices such as selling assets in order to balance the budget. Items that are either unusual or infrequent but not within the control of management should be disclosed in the notes to the financial statements.

REFLECTION

- Three fund types—governmental, proprietary, and fiduciary—are used to account for activities. Each fund type has a different measurement focus and basis of accounting.

- There are two types of account groups: general capital asset and general long-term liabilities.

- Governmental funds have a measurement focus of current financial resources and use a modified accrual basis of accounting.

- Revenues are recognized when they are measurable and available.

- Expenditures are recognized when current financial resources will be used.

4

OBJECTIVE

Explain the purpose of budgets and how governments account for appropriations.

USE OF BUDGETARY ACCOUNTING

Generally, finance personnel work with operating department personnel to develop a proposed expenditures budget for a fiscal year. The governmental unit's legislative body deliberates and acts on the budget which authorizes a certain level of expenditures for operating activities, capital acquisitions, and debt service. Authorized expenditures are termed **appropriations.** An authorization to raise revenue and, perhaps, long-term debt is approved. Estimates for other financing sources and other financing uses are also budgeted. An executive head, such as a governor or mayor, may be responsible for approving the budget or sending it back to the legislative body for further action. The budget, as finally approved, is recorded in the general ledger in summarized control accounts and in the subsidiary ledgers in detail accounts. Budgetary totals for appropriations (which are authorized expenditures), estimated revenues, other financing sources, and other financing uses are recorded in the general ledger.

REFLECTION

- Governments use budgets and funds because of the need to demonstrate accountability.

5

OBJECTIVE

Prepare journal entries for the general fund.

Accounting for the General Fund—An Expanded Example

To visualize the accounting process of the general fund and the flow of information that produces the financial reports, the activities of the city of Middletown are examined for the fiscal year ended September 30, 20X7. The general fund trial balance on September 30, 20X6, appears in Illustration 10-1.

The city has $271,000 in financial resources (cash, net receivables, and inventory). The liability Vouchers Payable offsets $170,000 of the resources with the fund balances offsetting the remaining $101,000. The fund balance may be *reserved* to show obligations of a fund or legal restrictions on financial resources. The fund balance also may be reserved if amounts are committed and not available as cash, such as outstanding purchase orders, petty cash, receivables that are long-term advances to other funds, or supplies inventory. The reserves are adjusted at year-end.

The second classification of fund balances is *unreserved,* which may be divided between *designated* and *undesignated.* The $16,000 designated for equipment may show the city council's intent to purchase a new police car. Only the $75,000 is unreserved and undesignated and, thus, available for unrestricted use in 20X7.

Uncollected property taxes may appear in three accounts. Taxes Receivable—Current is debited when property taxes are levied, and Revenue is credited. When uncollected property taxes are past due and interest revenue begins to accrue, the account balance is transferred to Taxes Receivable—Delinquent. When tax liens (a claim to take property for unpaid taxes) are

Illustration 10-1
City of Middletown
General Fund Trial Balance
September 30, 20X6

	Debit	Credit
Cash	82,000	
Investments	153,000	
Taxes Receivable—Delinquent	30,000	
Allowance for Uncollectible Delinquent Taxes		20,000
Tax Liens Receivable	24,000	
Allowance for Uncollectible Tax Liens		8,000
Supplies Inventory	10,000	
Vouchers Payable		170,000
Fund Balance—Reserved for Inventory		10,000
Fund Balance—Unreserved, Designated for Public Safety		16,000
Fund Balance—Unreserved, Undesignated		75,000
Total	299,000	299,000

placed on properties for uncollected taxes, the remaining amount of uncollected property taxes is transferred to Tax Liens Receivable. In the Middletown September 30, 20X6, general fund trial balance, all property taxes receivable are past due. An allowance account for estimated uncollectibles is established for each receivable.

Recording the Budget. The city council and the mayor have approved the budget for the following fiscal year, with estimated revenues of $1,350,000, appropriations of $1,300,000, and an estimated transfer of $30,000 to be made during the year to the debt service fund. Again, transfers to other funds are not expenditures and are segregated in the budgetary entry into a budgetary account labeled Estimated Other Financing Uses. The October 1, 20X6, entry to record Middletown's fiscal year 20X7 budget for its general fund is as follows:

		Debit	Credit
B1.	Estimated Revenues	1,350,000	
	Appropriations		1,300,000
	Estimated Other Financing Uses		30,000
	Budgetary Fund Balance—Unreserved		20,000

To support total estimated revenues of $1,350,000, a breakdown of sources should be provided in the explanation of the budget entry or in a separate schedule. In practice, there could be as many as 100 or more revenue items. As an example, however, the number of revenue items is condensed, as shown in the schedule of estimated revenues (Illustration 10-2).

Illustration 10-2
City of Middletown
General Fund Estimated Revenues
For Year Ended September 30, 20X7

General property taxes	$ 882,500
Fines	75,500
Licenses and permits	50,000
Revenue from federal grants	200,000
Other revenues	142,000
Total estimated revenues	$1,350,000

Illustration 10-3
City of Middletown
Department or Activity Appropriations
For Year Ended September 30, 20X7

General government: legislative, judicial, and executive	$ 129,000
Public safety	277,300
Education	591,450
Highways and streets	94,500
Sanitation and health	97,750
Welfare	51,000
Culture and recreation	59,000
Total appropriations	$1,300,000

Not only must the accounting system provide for control of revenues, but it also must accommodate expenditures. To provide a basis for comparison between expected and actual expenditures, budgetary as well as actual expenditures accounts are an integral part of the accounting system. In the entry to record Middletown's budget for its general fund, the credit to Appropriations represents the estimate of the expenditures of $1,300,000 for the coming year. In support of the appropriations total, a summary of approved estimated expenditures by departments or activities might appear as shown in Illustration 10-3.

Each of these departments or activities must submit detailed appropriation requests on the basis of subfunctions and object of expenditure.

Recording Actual Revenues and Transfers. Property taxes are a major source of revenue for Middletown's general fund and should be recognized in the fiscal period for which the taxes are levied. The property tax roll provides information about property owners, legal descriptions, and amounts of gross tax levies. The following journal entry shows that the total tax levy against property owners is debited to Taxes Receivable—Current in a general ledger entry. The amount of allowance for uncollectible taxes is credited in the same journal entry, and the net amount (the amount the government expects to receive) is credited to Revenues:

1.	Taxes Receivable—Current	919,000	
	Revenues		881,300
	Allowance for Uncollectible Current Taxes		37,700

During the year, the following additional events related to revenue are recorded in the general fund of Middletown:

Event	Entry in the General Fund		
2. Of the total delinquent taxes of $30,000 carried over from the prior period, $14,000 is collected. The balance is uncollectible.	Cash	14,000	
	Allowance for Uncollectible Delinquent Taxes	16,000	
	Taxes Receivable—Delinquent		30,000
3. The excess allowance for uncollectible delinquent taxes is transferred to Revenues. This transaction is viewed as a change in an accounting estimate made in a prior period.	Allowance for Uncollectible Delinquent Taxes	4,000	
	Revenues		4,000
4. Of $24,000 total tax liens carried over from the prior period, $11,000 is collected. The balance is uncollectible.	Cash	11,000	
	Allowance for Uncollectible Tax Liens	8,000	
	Tax Liens Receivable		19,000

Event	Entry in the General Fund		
5. The remaining Tax Liens Receivable are charged against Revenues. This transaction is viewed as a change in an accounting estimate made in a prior period.	Revenues .... Tax Liens Receivable	5,000	5,000
6. Of current taxes receivable (due on or before the end of the fiscal period), $850,000 is collected during the year and $12,700 is written off as uncollectible.	Cash .... Allowance for Uncollectible Current Taxes .... Taxes Receivable—Current	850,000 12,700	862,700
7. A 1% sales tax on restaurant food and beverages beginning on the first day of the last quarter is adopted by Middletown. The annual budget is amended to reflect the impact of this new legislation.	Estimated Revenues .... Budgetary Fund Balance—Unreserved	9,000	9,000
8. Restaurant food and beverage sales for the last quarter of the year are estimated at $950,000.	Sales Taxes Receivable .... Revenues	9,500	9,500
9. Police fines of $79,000 are imposed and collected during the year.	Cash .... Revenues	79,000	79,000
10. Pet licenses are sold for 2-year periods. Half of the pet license fees collected during the current year apply to the current year. The other half apply to next year. None of the fees are refundable.	Cash .... Revenues .... Deferred Revenues.........................	12,000	6,000 6,000
11. Revenues from other licenses and permits apply only to the current period and are not refundable.	Cash .... Revenues	35,000	35,000
12. Interest revenue earned on investment of idle cash during the year.	Cash .... Revenues	17,000	17,000
13. A contribution by a business to entice the city to extend a storm sewer to its property along a city street.	Cash .... Revenues	130,000	130,000
14. City council decided that the city's Fund Balance—Unreserved, Undesignated was too lean and rescinded its plan to buy a new police car.	Fund Balance—Unreserved, Designated for Public Safety .... Fund Balance—Unreserved, Undesignated....	16,000	16,000
15. At year-end, property taxes not collected are classified as delinquent, as are the estimated uncollectible allowances.	Taxes Receivable—Delinquent .... Taxes Receivable—Current ($919,000 − $862,700)	56,300	56,300
	Allowance for Uncollectible Current Taxes .... Allowance for Uncollectible Delinquent Taxes ($37,700 − $12,700)	25,000	25,000
16. Middletown receives a $150,000 check from the federal government for the current fiscal year to assist in the operation of its child-care program and documentation promising an additional $50,000, half of which is for the current fiscal year and half for the next fiscal year.	Cash .... Due from Federal Government .... Revenues .... Deferred Revenue	150,000 50,000	175,000 25,000

As indicated in the second and fourth entries, a revision of the estimated amount of uncollectible current and delinquent taxes and tax liens is treated as a change in accounting estimate through Revenues. Adjustments of confirmed errors of prior periods and adjustments from a change in accounting principle are recorded directly in the Fund Balance—Unreserved, Undesignated.

Recording Encumbrances and Actual Expenditures. To prevent overexpenditure, the Middletown general fund uses an encumbrance system. An encumbrance can be viewed as an *expected*

6

OBJECTIVE

Demonstrate how to account for encumbrances.

expenditure and assists the administration to avoid overspending and to plan for payment of the *expected liability* on a timely basis. It can also be viewed as a contra account to the fund balance to reflect the ultimate decrease that will occur. Under this system, whenever a purchase order or other commitment is approved, an entry is made to record the estimated cost of the commitment. For example, an approved purchase order for school supplies, estimated to cost $10,000, is recorded as follows:

17.	Encumbrances..	10,000	
	Fund Balance—Reserved for Encumbrances....................		10,000

When the invoice is received for the purchase of items or services, the encumbrance entry is reversed. The contra account to the fund balance is no longer needed since the expenditure recorded will directly reduce the fund balance in the closing procedure. Note that it is always the amount of the original estimate and not the actual cost that is used in the reversing entry. Assuming that the invoice for supplies amounts to $10,200, the two entries to record the receipt of the supplies invoice are as follows:

18.	Fund Balance—Reserved for Encumbrances....................	10,000	
	Encumbrances..		10,000
	To reverse entry for encumbrance at estimated cost.		
19.	Expenditures	10,200	
	Vouchers Payable		10,200
	To record invoice at actual cost.		

For expenditures such as salaries, which are subject to little variation and to additional internal controls, it is not customary to involve the encumbrance accounts. When salaries are paid, they are recorded directly as expenditures.

Encumbrances of a Prior Period.

When encumbrances are carried over from the prior year to the current year, the encumbrance closing entry of the prior year is reversed in order to reinstate the past commitments that will be honored in the current year.

Included in the current-year budgetary entry for appropriations should be an amount equal to that prior year-end encumbrance. The encumbrances will be disposed of in the manner described earlier. The unreserved fund balance will ultimately be reduced by the current year's actual expenditures.

The following events relate to Middletown's expenditures and transfers during the year.

	Event		Entry in the General Fund		
20.	Throughout the year, encumbrances totaling $738,000 were recorded; there were no prior-year encumbrances.		Encumbrances............................ Fund Balance—Reserved for Encumbrances..	738,000	738,000
21.	Vouchers were approved, liquidating $700,000 of encumbrances for:		Fund Balance—Reserved for Encumbrances.... Encumbrances.........................	700,000	700,000
	Supplies........................	$300,000			
	Building	200,000*	Inventory of Supplies......................	300,000	
	Other expenditures	272,000	Expenditures	472,000	
	Total........................	$772,000	Vouchers Payable		772,000

*This also requires an entry in the general fixed asset account group.

(continued)

Event	Entry in the General Fund		
22. Vouchers were approved for the following nonencumbered items:	Expenditures	518,000	
Salaries $490,000	Vouchers Payable		518,000
Other expenditures 28,000			
Total $518,000			
23. Vouchers totaling $1,300,000 were paid.	Vouchers Payable	1,300,000	
	Cash		1,300,000
24. Transfer of $30,000 is made to the debt service fund.	Other Financing Uses	30,000	
	Cash		30,000
25. Supplies totaling $260,000 were consumed.	Expenditures	260,000	
	Inventory of Supplies		260,000
26. Adjust Fund Balance—Reserved for Inventory of Supplies to equal inventory. (See following discussion.)	Fund Balance—Unreserved, Undesignated	40,000	
	Fund Balance—Reserved for Inventory of Supplies		40,000

Fund Balance Reserves. The amount of unreserved fund balance represents expendable, available financial resources. Any resources not available to finance expenditures of the current or future years must be removed from the unreserved fund balance. The reserve for encumbrances has already been discussed. An asset not available to finance expenditures for Middletown is the inventory of supplies, which will not be converted into cash and will not be available to meet future commitments. Therefore, the unreserved fund balance must be restricted by an amount equal to the inventory on the financial statement date. In this case, the amount of the inventory at year-end is $50,000 ($10,000 + $300,000 − $260,000). The account Fund Balance—Reserved for Inventory of Supplies is kept equal to the inventory amount by periodic adjustment through the unreserved fund balance account. Similarly, fund balance reserves may be established for petty cash and advances to other funds that will not be converted to cash in the current period.

Corrections of Prior Years' Errors. Corrections of previous years' errors are made directly through the account Fund Balance—Unreserved, Undesignated. For example, Middletown failed to record invoiced expenditures for last year of $30,600 that were not encumbered. Of this amount, $10,100 was paid this year and incorrectly debited to Expenditures. The unpaid portion of $20,500 is vouchered. The entry is as follows:

27. Fund Balance—Unreserved, Undesignated	30,600	
Expenditures		10,100
Vouchers Payable		20,500
To correct error for failure to record expenditures chargeable to last year.		

Reimbursement for Expenditure. When expenditures are made from the general fund on behalf of other funds, a transfer is made to reimburse the general fund. The reimbursement is recorded as an expenditure by the reimbursing fund and as a reduction in expenditures by the recipient (general) fund. For example, $3,000 is received from the special revenue fund to reimburse the general fund for payroll expenditures. The entry in the general fund is recorded as follows:

28. Cash	3,000	
Expenditures		3,000

Investments in Marketable Securities and Other Financial Instruments. Governmental entities frequently have cash available for short-, intermediate-, and long-term investment. For example, the general fund may have cash available for short periods of time pending disbursement for operating needs, the capital projects funds may have bond proceeds available for intermediate-term investment pending disbursement for construction costs, and fiduciary funds may have cash available for long-term investment. Investment pools used by several funds within a single government or by several governments may have cash available for investment for varying terms.

Governments usually make deposits with financial institutions (such as demand deposit accounts and certificates of deposit) and direct investments in U.S. government obligations. Governmental entities also invest in commercial paper, bankers' acceptances, mutual funds, pooled investment funds managed by a state treasurer, and repurchase agreements with broker-dealers. All investments, except for money market investments and participating interest-earning investment contracts with a remaining maturity of one year or less, are to be reported at fair value on the balance sheet. Fair value is defined as the amount at which an investment could be exchanged in a current transaction between willing parties, other than in a forced or liquidation sale.[10] The change in fair value of investments is reported as a *net increase (decrease) in the fair value of investments* and recognized as revenue in the operating statement. For example, if general fund investments increased in value during the period, the following entry would be made to reflect the change in fair value:

| 29. | Investments .... | 4,500 | |
| | Net Increase in the Fair Value of Investments .... | | 4,500 |

To meet cash flow requirements for operating or capital purposes, or to earn a higher return on investment, many governments enter into *reverse repurchase agreements* and/or *securities lending transactions*. In a reverse repurchase agreement, the government temporarily converts securities in their portfolios to cash by selling securities to a broker-dealer for cash, with a promise to repay cash plus interest in exchange for the return of the same securities.[11] In securities lending transactions, governments lend out their portfolio securities in return for collateral—which may be cash, securities, or letters of credit—and simultaneously agree to return the collateral for the same securities in the future.[12]

The investments must remain on the balance sheet of the government in both cases— whether selling securities with a promise to repurchase or lending them for a period of time. The agreements to repurchase (or return) are reported as fund liabilities. Any cash received (including cash received as collateral) is reported as an asset. Interest costs and broker fees are reported as expenditures and are not netted with any interest earned.

Extensive note disclosures on all investments and deposits with banks and other financial institutions are required. Governments must disclose their relevant accounting policies as to investments. They must also disclose credit risk, market risk, and legal risk for all investments, including derivatives.

The preclosing year-end trial balance for Middletown is presented in Illustration 10-4.

Closing the General Fund

The simplest closing process is, first, to reverse the budgetary entries and then to close the actual revenue and expenditure accounts, including the other financing sources and uses accounts, into the fund balance—unreserved, undesignated account. The outstanding balance in the encumbrances account is also temporarily closed. Budgetary closing entries for Middletown would appear as follows:

B2.	Appropriations	1,300,000	
	Estimated Other Financing Uses	30,000	
	Budgetary Fund Balance—Unreserved	29,000	
	Estimated Revenues		1,359,000
	To reverse entry recording budget (including amendment).		

---

10 GASB Statement No. 31, *Accounting and Financial Reporting for Certain Investments and for External Investment Pools* (Norwalk, CT: Governmental Accounting Standards Board, March 1997).

11 GASB Statement No. 3, *Deposits with Financial Institutions, Investments (including Repurchase Agreements, and Reverse Repurchase Agreements)* (Norwalk, CT: Governmental Accounting Standards Board, April 1986).

12 GASB Technical Bulletin No. 94-1, *Disclosure about Derivatives and Similar Debt and Investment Transactions* (Norwalk, CT: Governmental Accounting Standards Board, December 1994).

Illustration 10-4
City of Middletown
General Fund Trial Balance
September 30, 20X7

	Debit	Credit
Cash	50,000	
Investments	157,500	
Property Taxes Receivable—Delinquent	56,300	
Allowance for Uncollectible Delinquent Taxes		25,000
Deferred Revenue		31,000
Inventory of Supplies	50,000	
Vouchers Payable		190,700
Sales Taxes Receivable	9,500	
Due from Federal Government	50,000	
Fund Balance—Reserved for Inventory of Supplies		50,000
Fund Balance—Unreserved, Undesignated		20,400
Revenues		1,336,300
Expenditures	1,250,100	
Other Financing Uses	30,000	
Encumbrances	38,000	
Fund Balance—Reserved for Encumbrances		38,000
Estimated Revenues	1,359,000	
Appropriations		1,300,000
Estimated Other Financing Uses		30,000
Budgetary Fund Balance—Unreserved		29,000
Total	3,050,400	3,050,400

The actual closing entries are as follows:

30.	Revenues		1,336,300	
	Expenditures			1,250,100
	Other Financing Uses			30,000
	Fund Balance—Unreserved, Undesignated			56,200
	To close the actual accounts.			
31.	Fund Balance—Unreserved, Undesignated		38,000	
	Encumbrances			38,000
	To close outstanding encumbrances.			

REFLECTION

- The general ledger contains permanent balance sheet, budgetary, and operating accounts.

- Budgetary, operating, and closing entries are used in accounting for the general ledger accounts.

- Understanding the accounting and reporting procedures of the general fund will help in understanding accounting for other funds.

FINANCIAL REPORTS OF THE GENERAL FUND

Financial statements covering all funds of state and local governments are presented in Chapter 11. The required set of financial statements include fund-based and consolidated government-wide statements. The fund financial statements for Middletown's general fund are shown here, developed from the year-end trial balance shown on page 511. These reports consist of a balance sheet and a statement of revenues, expenditures, and changes in fund balances.

Balance Sheet

The general fund year-end balance sheet for the city of Middletown, shown in Illustration 10-5, differs substantially from its private business counterpart. First, it deals primarily with current assets and current liabilities, and the difference between these two amounts appears as the fund balance—either reserved (committed) or unreserved. Second, the long-term classifications of assets and liabilities are excluded, since the general fixed assets are included in the general fixed assets account group, and the general long-term debt is carried in the general long-term debt account group.

Statement of Revenues, Expenditures, and Changes in Fund Balances

The **statement of revenues, expenditures, and changes in fund balances** contains details on the major revenue sources and on expenditures by function or program. Other financing sources or uses and any corrections that altered the fund balance are also presented. The detailed source

---

Illustration 10-5
City of Middletown
General Fund Balance Sheet
September 30, 20X7

Assets

Cash		$ 50,000
Investments		157,500
Property taxes receivable—delinquent	$ 56,300	
Less allowance for uncollectible delinquent taxes	25,000	31,300
Sales taxes receivable		9,500
Due from federal government		50,000
Inventory of supplies		50,000
Total assets		$348,300

Liabilities and Fund Equity

Liabilities:		
Vouchers payable	$190,700	
Deferred revenue	31,000	
Total liabilities		$221,700
Fund balances:		
Reserved for encumbrances	$ 38,000	
Reserved for inventory of supplies	50,000	
Unreserved, undesignated	38,600	
Total fund balance		126,600
Total liabilities and fund balance		$348,300

of each revenue and purpose for each expenditure is obtained from the subsidiary ledger, not the control entries of the previous example.

For governmental funds for which an annual budget legally is adopted, a comparison of actual results to both the original and amended budget is required. The comparison can be accomplished either as a schedule provided as required supplementary information (RSI) immediately following the financial statements or as a separate statement. Both original and final budget amounts are compared with actual amounts, and a variance column showing the difference between budgeted and actual amounts is encouraged. In order for the comparisons to be meaningful, the actual amounts in the schedule are reported on a budgetary basis. A reconciliation from the budgetary basis to GAAP is required either on the face of the budgetary comparison statement or on a separate schedule.

The budgetary comparison schedule for the general fund of Middletown is shown in Illustration 10-6. Estimated and actual amounts of revenues, expenditures, and other changes are reported on a budgetary basis. The beginning and ending fund balances are reported. The final actual fund balances amount ($126,600) must agree with the total fund balance shown on the balance sheet.

Illustration 10-6
City of Middletown
Budgetary Comparison Schedule
General Fund
For Year Ended September 30, 20X7
(budgetary basis)

	Original Budget	Amended Budget	Actual Results	Variance Favorable (Unfavorable)
Revenues:				
General property taxes	$ 881,000	$ 882,500	$ 880,300	$ (2,200)
Fines	75,000	75,500	79,000	3,500
Licenses and permits	50,000	50,000	41,000	(9,000)
Intergovernmental revenues	200,000	200,000	175,000	(25,000)
Sales taxes	10,000	9,000	9,500	500
Other revenues	145,000	142,000	151,500	9,500
Total revenues	$1,361,000	$1,359,000	$1,336,300	$(22,700)
Expenditures:				
General government	$ 130,000	$ 129,000	$ 120,305	$ 8,695
Public safety	275,000	277,300	252,795	24,505
Highways and streets	95,000	94,500	86,100	8,400
Sanitation and health	98,000	97,750	87,750	10,000
Welfare	50,000	51,000	46,000	5,000
Culture and recreation	60,000	59,000	53,400	5,600
Education	590,000	591,450	603,750	(12,300)
Total expenditures	$1,298,000	$1,300,000	$1,250,100	$ 49,900
Excess of revenues over expenditures	$ 63,000	$ 59,000	$ 86,200	$ 27,200
Other financing sources (uses)	(30,000)	(30,000)	(30,000)	0
Excess of revenues and other sources over expenditures and other uses	$ 33,000	$ 29,000	$ 56,200	$ 27,200
Fund balances, October 1, 20X6	101,000	101,000	101,000	0
Correction of prior year's expenditures	0	0	(30,600)	(30,600)
Fund balances, September 30, 20X7	$ 134,000	$ 130,000	$ 126,600	$ (3,400)

REFLECTION

- The two year-end statements of the general fund are the balance sheet and the statement of revenues, expenditures, and changes in fund balances.

- Budgetary comparison schedules or statements are also required for the general fund and other funds for which a budget is adopted.

- Both annual statements differ significantly from those in the private sector.

8

OBJECTIVE

Complete schedules for general capital assets and long-term liabilities.

ACCOUNTING FOR GENERAL CAPITAL ASSETS AND GENERAL LONG-TERM OBLIGATIONS

Accounting control over general capital assets and general long-term obligations (including capital debt) has traditionally been maintained in the general fixed assets account group (GFAAG) and the general long-term debt account group (GLTDAG). The account groups are used only to keep accounting control of general capital assets and general long-term debt of the governmental unit. Account groups are not reported on the fund financial statements, but detailed information about general capital assets and long-term obligations is required in the notes and in the government-wide statements. The presentation in this text assumes that governments maintain account groups as convenient means of keeping track of such long-term items and for internal control. Some governments have found alternative types of records, including simple listings, to be more convenient or less costly.

Accounting and Financial Reporting for General Capital Assets

Fixed assets of a proprietary fund or a fiduciary fund are accounted for within those funds and often are referred to as **fund capital assets.** All other fixed assets are considered **general capital assets** and are accounted for in the general fixed assets account group. This account group, which was created to report capital assets that are not resources of any specific fund, may be thought of as an inventory record of fixed assets for the purpose of assigning responsibility for custody and proper use. Typical capital asset categories include: land, buildings, improvements other than buildings, machinery and equipment, and construction in progress. Major infrastructure assets, such as sidewalks, streets, curbs, and bridges acquired after 1980, must also be recorded.

The general fixed asset account group is little more than a list of government-owned assets in double-entry form. The acquisition of a general capital asset is recorded in the general fixed assets account group by a debit to one of the six specific asset accounts. The offsetting credit indicates the original funding source of the asset.

Fund or Group in which Entry Is Recorded	Entry		
32. General fund	Expenditures	200,000	
	Vouchers Payable		200,000
	(This entry is part of the entry on page 508, which records vouchers of $772,000.)		
33. General fixed assets account group	Buildings	200,000	
	Investment in General Fixed Assets—		
	General Fund Revenues		200,000
	To record the fixed asset.		

General capital assets are recorded at cost or, if the asset is donated, estimated fair value at time of receipt. Subsequent to the acquisition of a capital asset, capital outlay and maintenance expenditures must be accounted for separately, as they are in commercial accounting, since maintenance expenditures should not increase the book values of fixed assets.

Depreciation expense is reported in the government-wide statements. Depreciation expense, however, is not reported in the governmental funds.

> *To record depreciation expense in governmental funds would inappropriately mix two fundamentally different measurements, expenses and expenditures. General fixed asset acquisitions require the use of governmental fund financial resources and are recorded as expenditures. General fixed asset sale proceeds provide governmental fund financial resources. Depreciation expense is neither a source nor a use of governmental fund financial resources, and thus is not properly recorded in the accounts of such funds.*[13]

Governments must record accumulated depreciation of general capital assets in the government-wide statements. An entry is made in the general fixed assets account group by debiting the appropriate investment in the general fixed asset account and crediting the accumulated depreciation account.

When a governmental unit disposes of a general capital asset, the original cost (less accumulated depreciation) of the asset is removed from the general fixed assets account group. In the general fund, proceeds from the sale are recorded with a credit to Other Financing Sources. For example, if a governmental unit sells equipment for $90,000, carried in the general fixed assets account group at $100,000, the following entries would be made:

Fund or Group in which Entry Is Recorded	Entry		
34. General fund	Cash	90,000	
	Other Financing Sources		90,000
	To record the proceeds from the sale.		
35. General fixed assets account group	Investment in General Fixed Assets—		
	General Fund Revenues............................	100,000	
	Machinery and Equipment........................		100,000
	To remove the fixed asset.		

Instead of selling the equipment, assume the governmental unit traded it for a larger model costing $235,000, with an allowance of $90,000 for the smaller unit. The new asset is recorded at its total cost, with the trade-in value merely functioning as a reduction in the amount to be paid. The entries then would be as follows:

Fund or Group in which Entry Is Recorded	Entry		
36. General fund	Expenditures	145,000	
	Vouchers Payable		145,000
	To record the outflow of cash.		
37. General fixed assets account group	Investment in General Fixed Assets—		
	General Fund Revenues............................	100,000	
	Machinery and Equipment........................		100,000
	To remove the old asset.		
	Machinery and Equipment	235,000	
	Investment in General Fixed Assets—		
	General Fund Revenues............................		235,000
	To record the new fixed asset.		

Governments may avoid charging depreciation on infrastructure assets if they can demonstrate that they have incurred costs to preserve these assets at or above a conditional level established by the government. Under this *modified preservation approach*, all costs to maintain the

---

13 Statement 1, *Government Accounting and Financial Reporting Principles* (Chicago: Municipal Finance Officers Association of the United States and Canada, March 1979), p. 10.

Illustration 10-7
City of Middletown
Schedule of Capital Assets

	Beginning Balance	Additions	Retirements	Ending Balance
Governmental activities:				
Land..............................	$ 8,595,000	$4,000,000		$ 12,595,000
Buildings	28,555,000		$ (200,000)	28,355,000
Improvements other than buildings	10,367,500			10,367,500
Machinery and equipment..............	4,390,000	135,000		4,525,000
Construction in progress	17,222,500			17,222,500
Infrastructure	120,000,000		(2,000,000)	118,000,000
Totals (at historical cost)	$189,130,000	$4,135,000	$(2,200,000)	$191,065,000
Less accumulated depreciation:				
Buildings	$ (850,000)	$ (85,000)	$ 40,000	$ (895,000)
Improvements other than buildings	(150,000)	(20,000)		(170,000)
Machinery and equipment..............	(215,000)	(50,000)		(265,000)
Infrastructure	(15,000,000)	(350,000)	1,000,000	(14,350,000)
Total depreciation	$ (16,215,000)	$ (505,000)	$ 1,040,000	$ (15,680,000)
Governmental activities capital assets (net)...	$172,915,000	$3,630,000	$(1,160,000)	$175,385,000

assets are expensed, and no depreciation is recorded. If a government elects to follow the modified approach, it must assess periodically and disclose in the notes to the financial statements the condition of its infrastructure assets (usually an engineering report) and estimate the annual amount necessary to maintain and preserve the specified assets at or above the condition level. It must also disclose actual amounts spent compared to these estimates. A change from the depreciation method to the modified approach should be accounted for as a change in accounting estimate.

Governments are required to monitor and determine if impairment of a capital asset has occurred. A capital asset is considered impaired if *both* (a) the decline in service utility of the capital asset is large in magnitude *and* (b) the event or change in circumstance is outside the normal life cycle of the capital asset. Impaired capital assets that will no longer be used by the government should be reported at the lower of carrying value or fair value. Impairment losses on capital assets that will continue to be used by the government should be measured using a method that best reflects the diminished service utility of the capital asset, such as cost to restore, percentage of service units provided before and after the impairment, and deflated depreciated replacement cost.[14]

Disclosures about capital assets are required in the notes to the financial statements. Capital assets that are not being depreciated are disclosed separately from those assets that are being depreciated. In addition, beginning-of-year and end-of-year balances are shown along with capital acquisitions, sales, or other dispositions. A schedule of capital assets that will be included in the notes for Middletown is shown in Illustration 10-7.

Accounting and Financial Reporting for General Long-Term Debt

When long-term debt is related to and will be paid from proprietary or fiduciary funds, it is accounted for in those funds and is termed a specific fund liability. When long-term debt is

---

14 GASB Statement No. 42, *Accounting and Financial Reporting for Impairment of Capital Assets and for Insurance Recoveries* (Norwalk, CT: Governmental Accounting Standards Board, November 2003).

related to and will be paid from governmental funds, the liability is recorded in the general long-term debt account group.

The general long-term debt account group, which was designed to monitor long-term debt that is not the responsibility of any particular fund, furnishes a record of the unmatured principal of all general long-term obligations of the governmental unit. Referring to a long-term obligation as *general* indicates that the community can use its taxing power to pay debt principal and interest. The general long-term debt account group is not limited to liabilities arising from debt issuance and may include numerous types of unmatured general government liabilities; for example, claims and judgments, accumulated sick leave and other compensated absences, underfunded pension contributions, unfunded postretirement benefits other than pensions, and capital lease obligations, as well as unmatured bonds and notes. Interest is not accounted for in the general long-term debt account group. To maintain the self-balancing nature of the account group, the incurrence of long-term obligations is recorded by debiting Amount to Be Provided for Payment of (properly identified) Debt and crediting a liability account. As emphasized in the previous section, the use of account groups is a convenient mechanism for keeping track of long-term liabilities that may eventually be replaced by other means, such as simple ledgers.

To illustrate the entries for the general long-term debt account group, assume that a unit incurs a general long-term obligation in the form of term bonds of $1,000,000 to acquire property.[15] Regardless of whether the bonds are issued at a premium or discount, the bond issue is recorded at its face amount in the general long-term debt account group. As shown in the following entry, the bonds are recorded in the general long-term debt account group at the face value to be redeemed at maturity.

38.	Amount to Be Provided for Payment of Term Bonds	1,000,000	
	Term Bonds Payable		1,000,000

Payment of both principal and interest is handled by the debt service fund, where service is synonymous with *payment*, but the general long-term debt account group records only amounts that become available in the debt service fund for retirement of general long-term debt principal. Assuming the debt service fund receives an annual appropriation of $80,000 to provide for the eventual retirement of the term bonds, the following entry is recorded in the general long-term debt account group:

39.	Amount Available in Debt Service Funds—Term Bonds	80,000	
	Amount to Be Provided for Payment of Term Bonds		80,000

If sound actuarial practices have been employed, the debt service fund will retire the obligation at the appropriate time and the general long-term debt account group will make the following entry:

40.	Term Bonds Payable	1,000,000	
	Amount Available in Debt Service Funds—Term Bonds. . .		1,000,000

A schedule of general long-term liabilities for Middletown appears in Illustration 10-8. The schedule includes the example transactions in this section. Governments report long-term obligations on a full-accrued basis in the government-wide statements. A discussion of the adjusting entries needed to reflect amortization of premium or discount and interest accruals is found in Chapter 11.

Information about long-term debt, significant contingent liabilities, pension plan obligations, accumulated sick leave and other compensated absences, debt service requirements to maturity, commitments under noncapitalized leases, and changes in general long-term debt are required note disclosures.

Leasing of equipment has become common practice among governments. When leases qualify as operating, the rent expenditures are recorded in the fund, and no entry is made in the

---

15 A term bond is one in which the entire principal is due on one date; a serial bond issue is redeemed in periodic payments. Term bonds are rare, but they better illustrate entries in the general long-term debt account group.

Illustration 10-8
City of Middletown
Schedule of Long-Term Liabilities

	Beginning Balance	Additions	Retirements	Ending Balance
General long-term debt payable:				
General obligation debt	$21,962,000	$2,000,000	$999,950	$22,962,050
Special assessment debt	2,000,000			2,000,000
Unfunded pension costs.	139,000	2,123		141,123
Capital lease payable	99,950	35,944		135,894
Unfunded compensated absences.	160,325	3,433		163,758
Unfunded claims and judgment.	412,222	179,923		592,145
Total general long-term debt payable	$24,773,497	$2,221,423	$999,950	$25,994,970

account group. However, if a lease qualifies as a capital lease (using the criteria of FASB No. 13), then the substance of the transaction is similar to the purchase of a fixed asset with long-term debt proceeds. Therefore, entries are as follows:

	Event and Fund or Group in which Entry Is Recorded		Entry		
41.	At inception of the lease, the present value of the lease payments is recorded in the fund as expenditures and other financing sources.	General fund	Expenditures . . . . Other Financing Sources	50,000	50,000

42.	In the account group, the leased asset is recorded at its present value.	General fixed assets account group	Leased Asset . . . .
			    Investment in GFA—
			        General Funds . . . .
				50,000	50,000

43.	In the account group, the long-term lease obligation is recorded.	General long-term debt account group	Amount to Be Provided . . . . Lease Obligation	50,000	50,000

Subsequent lease payments are made from the Debt Service Fund as will be presented later in this chapter.

REFLECTION

- Account groups have traditionally been used to keep track of capital assets and long-term debt.

- Account groups will not be reported on the financial statements. Rather, schedules of capital assets and long-term liabilities will be presented in the notes to the financial statements. Capital assets and long-term debt will also be reported in the government-wide statements.

- Many governments continue to use the account groups as a convenient means of recording additions and deductions from capital assets and long-term debt.

- Governments are required to record infrastructure assets and depreciation.

OTHER GOVERNMENTAL FUNDS

Typical funds used by state and local governments include special revenue funds, permanent funds, capital project funds, and debt service funds. A special revenue fund would be used when revenues are collected for a specific purpose, such as road repair or education. Permanent funds are used to account for trusts that are set up to accomplish a specific, *public* purpose. The principal of a permanent fund must not be expended. When a major, general capital asset, such as a building, is being acquired, the governmental entity uses a capital project fund to account for related transactions. Once the government has borrowed money for a capital project or for other reasons, the debt principal is recorded and tracked in the long-term debt account group (see discussion earlier in chapter), and the accounting for the payment of principal and interest on that debt is recorded in a debt service fund.

Special Revenue Funds

When revenue obtained from specified sources is restricted by law or donor for a specified current operating purpose or to the acquisition of a relatively minor fixed asset, accounting is accomplished through a *special revenue fund*. Although the government will have only one general fund, it could have many special revenue funds, or none at all. Examples of activities that are accounted for in special revenue funds are nonexchange transactions, such as the hotel room taxes restricted for expenditures that promote tourism, federal and state grant proceeds restricted to financing community development expenditures, gasoline tax revenues for highway maintenance, specific federal and/or state funds for education, resources for food stamp programs administered by state governments, other pass-through grants and on-behalf payment programs for fringe benefits and salaries,[16] and exchange transactions such as golf fees charged at a city golf course to cover a portion of the cost of course maintenance.[17] Special revenue funds also account for activities of an expendable public-purpose trust fund; that is, both the principal and earnings can be spent for the benefit of the government's programs. These revenues are recognized under the modified accrual method of accounting. The following are examples of revenues recorded in the special revenue funds:

Event	Entry in the Special Revenue Funds		
1. During the year, local hotels/motels paid to the city a room tax totaling $98,000. The remittance included $6,000 payable from last year and $92,000 expected to be available in the current year.	Cash	98,000	
	Taxes Receivable		6,000
	Revenues		92,000
2. In addition, the city estimates a $9,000 receivable from December rentals. In this city, the hotels/motels are allowed a 1-month administrative lead time and are not required to pay the December tax until January 31 of the following year.	Taxes Receivable	9,000	
	Revenues		9,000
3. Federal food stamp coupons of $10,000 are received by the state government.	Food Stamp Coupons	10,000	
	Deferred Revenues		10,000
4. $9,000 of coupons are distributed.	Expenditures	9,000	
	Food Stamp Coupons		9,000
	Deferred Revenues	9,000	
	Revenues		9,000

(continued)

16 GASB Statement No. 24, *Accounting and Financial Reporting for Certain Grants and Other Financial Assistance* (Norwalk, CT: Governmental Accounting Standards Board, June 1994). Pass-through grants are defined in GASB No. 24 as grants received by a government to transfer to or spend on behalf of a secondary recipient. Generally, these transactions are to be accounted for in a special revenue fund or a general fund if the government has discretion over the distribution of these funds.
17 When revenue raised for activities is on a fee basis for goods or services provided and the operations are intended to be self-supporting, the flows of resources are accounted for in proprietary funds discussed later in this chapter.

Event	Entry in the Special Revenue Funds		
5. Charges for services from exchange transactions for the year are as follows:	Cash	370,000	
	Accounts Receivable	10,000	
	Revenues		360,000
	Deferred Revenues.................		20,000

	Earned	Collected
Golf fees (collected at time of use)	$ 35,000	$ 35,000
Garbage fees (collected in advance of providing service)	240,000	260,000
Snow removal fees (collected after service is provided)........	85,000	75,000
Total....................	$360,000	$370,000

Event	Entry in the Special Revenue Funds		
6. A $100,000 federal grant is received for economic development. An additional $50,000 is due prior to year-end. Revenue is recognized when expenditures are incurred for the grant program.	Cash	100,000	
	Due from Federal Government	50,000	
	Deferred Revenues.................		150,000

When a governmental unit has more than one special revenue fund, major funds are identified and nonmajor individual funds are presented in *combining* balance sheets and revenue and expenditure statements.

Permanent Funds

Permanent funds are established to account for public-purpose trusts for which the earnings are expendable for a specified purpose, but the principal amount is not expendable. These funds are often referred to as endowments. As described in the previous section, public-purpose trusts for which both principal and earnings can be spent for a specified purpose are accounted for in special revenue funds. Further, private-purpose trusts are accounted for in fiduciary funds as will be described later in this chapter. Permanent funds will capture much of the current trust activity in local governments. These trusts have been established to benefit a government program or function, or the citizens, rather than an external individual, organization, or government. For example, resources received to be invested of which only the income, not the principal, is expended to support a park, cemetery, library, or some other government program, are now accounted for in permanent funds.

The following are examples of transactions recorded in permanent funds:

Event	Entry in the Permanent Fund		
7. During the year, securities were received to initiate a trust fund to support the operations of the town cemetery. The donors stipulated that the earnings, not the principal, be spent. The fair value of the securities at the date of donation is $750,000.	Investment in Stocks..................	750,000	
	Revenues		750,000
8. Dividends are received on the investments, totaling $15,000.	Cash	15,000	
	Revenues		15,000
9. The earnings are transferred out to the Cemetery Operating Fund. Cemetery operations are accounted for in a Special Revenue Fund.	Other Financing Uses	15,000	
	Cash		15,000

The entry in the Special Revenue Fund to record the transfer-in is as follows:

Cash	15,000	
Other Financing Sources		15,000

When a governmental unit has more than one permanent fund, major funds are identified and nonmajor individual funds are presented in *combining* balance sheets and revenue and expenditure statements. Combining statements provide information on each permanent fund plus a total column of all the permanent funds.

Capital Projects Funds

Capital projects funds account for the purchase, construction, or capital lease of major, *general* capital assets, which excludes construction of capital facilities by proprietary funds that account for their own construction activities. Each project should be accounted for separately in subsidiary records to demonstrate compliance with legal and contractual provisions.

Resources for capital projects result from transfers received from the general fund or some other fund, proceeds of general obligation bonds, grants from another governmental unit, or special assessments levied against property owners who benefit from the project. Grants from another governmental unit and special assessments levied are recorded as revenues. Bond proceeds (because they must be repaid) and transfers from other funds (because they were previously recognized as revenue) are accounted for as other financing sources.

The full amount of the bond issue proceed is recorded as an other financing source in the fund that will use the resources. Bond premiums and discounts are recorded separately as other financing sources or uses, respectively. Bond issuance costs are recorded as expenditures. Since bond premiums and discounts arise because of adjustments to the interest rate, the premium and any payment received for accrued *interest* are transferred to the debt service fund to cover future *interest* payments. If bonds are sold at a discount, a project authorization must be reduced by the bond discount amount and/or issuance costs unless additional resources are transferred from the general fund or other funds.

Governments sometimes issue short-term *bond anticipation* notes after obtaining necessary voter and legislative authorization to issue long-term bonds. Since these short-term notes are expected to be replaced by long-term bonds, they are, in essence, long term and are accounted for in the General Long-Term Debt Account Group (GLTDAG). Proceeds of the bond anticipation notes are recorded in the governmental funds (often a Capital Project Fund) as other financing sources—proceeds from bond anticipation notes.[18]

Proceeds of bond issues not immediately needed for project expenditures are often temporarily invested to earn interest. These temporary investments are limited to securities whose yield does not exceed the interest rate of the tax-exempt borrowing. Interest earned on temporary investments is recognized as revenue in the capital projects fund. These earnings are often required to be transferred to the debt service fund to help finance bond interest expenditures.[19]

Capital projects funds have the authority through annually approved budgets to continue expenditures within prescribed limits until a project is completed. Although a project may not be completed at the end of a fiscal period, typical closing entries are recorded. Annual closing permits the actual activity to be compared with the legally adopted annual operating budget. Also, in the closing process, the credit to Expenditures provides the amount of capitalizable expenditures to be recorded in the general fixed assets account group as construction in progress.

The actual cost of a capital project probably will differ from its estimated cost. A deficiency usually is covered by a transfer from the general fund. If an excess of resources exists upon completion of the project, it generally is returned to the general fund or to the debt service fund. Such a transfer is reported as an other financing use on the statement of revenues, expenditures, and changes in fund balance. Upon completion of the project, it is customary to withhold part of the payment until final inspection and approval. The liability is recorded in contracts payable—retained percentage.

To illustrate accounting for capital projects funds, assume the city of Berryville plans to build a $300,000 addition to its municipal auditorium. The project will begin in 20X7 and is to be completed in 20X8. The following entries record the events that occur during construction:

---

18 The GASB states that a government may recognize bond anticipation notes as long-term obligations if, by the date the financial statements are issued, "all legal steps have been taken to refinance the bond anticipation notes and the intent is supported by an ability to consummate refinancing of the short-term note on a long-term basis." *Codification of Government Accounting and Reporting Standards* (Norwalk, CT: Governmental Accounting Standards Board, 1996, Section B50.101).

19 Governments are not required to capitalize construction-period interest for governmental activities.

Event	Entry in the Capital Projects Fund		

20X7

10. The project budget is $300,000, to be financed by a general bond issue. The 20X7 operating budget is based on one-third of the work being completed that year.

Estimated Other Financing Sources............	300,000	
Appropriations		100,000
Budgetary Fund Balance—Unreserved		200,000

11. A $300,000, 8% general obligation bond issue is floated at 101.

Cash	303,000	
Other Financing Sources..................		300,000
Other Financing Sources—Premium		3,000

An entry also is made in the general long-term debt account group as follows:

Amount to Be Provided	300,000	
Serial Bonds Payable.............		300,000

12. The bond premium is transferred to the debt service fund to be used for interest.

Other Financing Uses	3,000	
Cash		3,000

An entry also is made in the debt service fund as follows:

Cash	3,000	
Other Financing Sources		3,000

(*Note:* Since bond premium is assumed to be used for interest payments, no entry is made in the account group.)

13. A contract is signed for the auditorium construction at an estimated cost of $270,000.

Encumbrances............................	270,000	
Fund Balance—Reserved for		
Encumbrances		270,000

14. The architect's bill for $10,650 is received, of which $7,650 is paid. Upon final building approval, the balance is due. The item was not encumbered.

Expenditures	10,650	
Cash		7,650
Contracts Payable—Retained Percentage.....		3,000

15. A partial billing is received from the contractor for $60,000, equal to the amount encumbered for these items. The contracts payable account is credited for the liability to the principal contractor. (If the amount of equivalent encumbrance is not specified, the encumbrance entry is reversed for the amount of the billing.)

Fund Balance—Reserved for Encumbrances.....	60,000	
Encumbrances		60,000
Expenditures	60,000	
Contracts Payable		60,000

16. The contractor is paid $60,000.

Contracts Payable	60,000	
Cash		60,000

17. Books for 20X7 are closed.

Budgetary Fund Balance—Unreserved	200,000	
Appropriations	100,000	
Estimated Other Financing Sources..........		300,000

18.

The credit to Expenditures is the basis for the following entry in the general fixed assets account group:

Construction in Progress	70,650	
Investment in General Fixed		
Assets—Capital Project		
Funds		70,650

Other Financing Sources.....................	303,000	
Expenditures		70,650
Other Financing Uses		3,000
Fund Balance—Unreserved,		
Undesignated		229,350

(continued)

Event	Entry in the Capital Projects Fund		
19. Encumbrances are closed at year-end.	Fund Balance—Unreserved,		
	Undesignated	210,000	
	Encumbrances		210,000

20X8

Event	Entry in the Capital Projects Fund		
20. The operating budget for 20X8 is recorded; completion is estimated to cost an additional $215,000, including the amount encumbered in the previous year.	Budgetary Fund Balance—Unreserved . . . . Appropriations	215,000	215,000
21. The encumbrances are reinstated at the beginning of 20X8.	Encumbrances . . . . Fund Balance—Unreserved, Undesignated . . .	210,000	210,000
	Fund Balance—Reserved for Encumbrances . . . . . Encumbrances	210,000	210,000
22. The contract is completed in 20X8. Additional cost is $227,000, of which $10,000 is withheld in a separate account until final inspection and approval.	Expenditures . . . . Contracts Payable . . . . Contracts Payable—Retained Percentage	227,000	217,000 10,000
23. The construction is accepted, and the contractor and architect are paid.	Contracts Payable . . . . Contracts Payable—Retained Percentage . . . . Cash	217,000 13,000	230,000
24. Books for 20X8 are closed.	Appropriations . . . . Budgetary Fund Balance—Unreserved	215,000	215,000
	Fund Balance—Unreserved, Undesignated . . . . . Expenditures	227,000	227,000

25.

The credit to Expenditures is the basis for the following entry in the general fixed assets account group:		
Buildings	297,650	
Construction in Progress		70,650
Investment in General Fixed		
Assets—Capital Projects Funds . .		227,000

Event	Entry in the Capital Projects Fund		
26. The residual balance is transferred to the debt service fund.	Other Financing Uses . . . . Cash	2,350	2,350

An entry also is made in the debt service fund as follows:		
Cash	2,350	
Other Financing Sources		2,350
Other Financing Sources	2,350	
Fund Balance—Reserved for		
Debt Service		2,350

(*Note:* Since the project was financed with general obligation debt, an additional entry in the general long-term debt account group indicating availability of funds to repay the debt is required.)

Amount Available in the Debt		
Service Fund	2,350	
Amount to Be Provided		2,350

Event	Entry in the Capital Projects Fund		
27. The Municipal Auditorium Capital Project Fund is closed.	Fund Balance—Unreserved, Undesignated . . . . . Other Financing Uses	2,350	2,350

As with special revenue and permanent funds, when a governmental unit has more than one capital project, major funds are identified and nonmajor funds are presented in combining financial statements.

Debt Service Funds

The function of the general long-term debt account group is to provide a record of the unredeemed principal of long-term liabilities incurred to acquire general fixed assets. Closely related to this account group are *debt service funds*, whose primary function is to account for financial resources accumulated to cover the payment of principal and interest on general government obligations.

As in other governmental funds, the modified accrual basis is used for recognizing revenues, other financing sources, and expenditures in debt service funds. Interest and principal on general long-term debt are items for which the accrual basis is modified. For example, assume a governmental unit has a fiscal year ending June 30, with interest and principal on long-term debt to be paid on July 31. Since expenditures are authorized by appropriations, it is essential that expenditures be recorded in the same period as the appropriations. Thus, the interest and principal will not be accrued on June 30, because the appropriation to cover the principal and interest will not be provided until the budget for the next period is recorded on July 1. This method recognizes expenditures for interest and principal when they are *due*.

The most popular method of raising long-term resources is by the issuance of serial bonds, which are redeemed in a series of installments. Term bonds, whose total face value becomes due at one time, are now extremely rare. When serial bonds are issued, there is no substantial accumulation of cash in a sinking fund. Instead, the budget for the year of payment provides for interest and principal redemption. In debt service funds, an entry to record the budget is seldom used because expenditures for principal and interest are known and there is no need to compare them with budgetary amounts.

Resources to cover expenditures may come from several sources. A portion of a property tax levy may be authorized to be recorded directly into a debt service fund. The entries would be similar to those made in the general fund to record a tax levy. The net amount of taxes estimated to be collected is credited to Revenues since the resources are received from outsiders. Transfers received by the debt service fund from funds that have already recorded the resources as revenues are credited to Other Financing Sources. This procedure prevents revenues from being credited in two funds for the same resources—once in the originating fund (in this case, the general fund) and again in the recipient fund (in this case, debt service fund).

The following entries would be made in a debt service fund for the indicated events that relate to a serial bond issue. As demonstrated by these entries, the interaction between funds and groups is especially prevalent in accounting for general obligation bond issues.

Event	Entry in the Debt Service Fund		
28. An 8%, $300,000 general obligation serial bond issue for bridge construction is sold at 101. The premium is transferred from the capital projects fund to the debt service fund.	Cash .... Other Financing Sources	3,000	3,000

Entries are also made in the capital projects fund as follows:

Cash	303,000	
Other Financing Sources		300,000
Other Financing Sources—Premium		3,000
Other Financing Uses	3,000	
Cash		3,000

Entries are also made in the general long-term debt account group:

Amount to Be Provided	300,000	
Serial Bonds Payable............		300,000

Event	Entry in the Debt Service Fund		

29. Of the property taxes, $50,000 is levied specifically to cover debt service on these bonds; the levy, less 1% of the taxes estimated to be uncollectible, is recorded in the debt service fund.	Taxes Receivable—Current ....
	    Allowance for Uncollectible Current Taxes .
	    Revenues ....
		50,000	500
			 49,500

(continued)

Event	Entry in the Debt Service Fund		
30. All property taxes are collected except for $400 that is written off. The difference between estimated and actual uncollectible taxes is recorded in Revenues.	Cash	49,600	
	Allowance for Uncollectible Current Taxes ...	400	
	Taxes Receivable—Current		50,000
	Allowance for Uncollectible Current Taxes ...	100	
	Revenues		100

31. Assuming $30,000 is to be used toward the first installment on the principal payment, an additional entry is made in the general long-term debt account group as follows:
Amount Available in the Debt
   Service Fund 30,000
      Amount to Be Provided......... 30,000			

32. The fund receives $7,000 of its $9,000 share of state gasoline taxes. The city is not entitled to the balance until the next fiscal period.	Cash	7,000	
	Due from State	2,000	
	Revenues		7,000
	Deferred Revenues....................		2,000
33. A transfer of $30,000 is received from the general fund.	Cash	30,000	
	Other Financing Sources	30,000	

Since the $30,000 is for payment of principal, an additional entry is made in the general long-term account group debt:
 	
Amount Available in the Debt Service
   Fund........................ 30,000
      Amount to Be Provided......... 30,000			

34. Cash is transmitted to a fiscal agent for payment of the first $60,000 of maturing bonds and $24,000 of interest due on the last day of the fiscal period.	Cash with Fiscal Agent	84,000	
	Cash		84,000
35. The matured bonds and interest are recorded.	Expenditures	84,000	
	Matured Bonds Payable		60,000
	Matured Interest Payable..............		24,000

Principal of $60,000 is matured and no longer long term. The entry to reclassify the debt in the general long-term account group debt is as follows:
 	
Serial Bonds Payable.............. 60,000
   Amount Available in the Debt
     Service Fund................. 60,000			

36. The fiscal agent reports that all payments have been made except for $1,000 of interest.	Matured Bonds Payable	60,000	
	Matured Interest Payable.................	23,000	
	Cash with Fiscal Agent		83,000
37. Books are closed at year-end.	Revenues	56,600	
	Other Financing Sources.................	33,000	
	Expenditures		84,000
	Fund Balance—Reserved for Debt Service. .		5,600

Assets transferred to a debt service fund must be used to redeem bonds or to pay interest. There are no unreserved assets. Any excess of assets over liabilities is reserved for debt service. Therefore, at year-end, the accounts are closed to fund balance—reserved for debt service rather than to an unreserved fund balance.

In addition to term bonds and serial bonds, debt service funds may be used to service debt arising from notes or warrants having a maturity of more than one year after date of issue and to make periodic payments on capital leases. Although each issue of long-term debt is a separate obligation with unique legal restrictions and servicing requirements, GASB standards provide that, if legally permissible, a single debt service fund may be used to account for the service of all issues of tax-supported and special-assessment debt. If legal restrictions do not allow the servicing of all issues to be accounted for by a single debt service fund, the number of debt service funds should be held to a minimum.

Sometimes, governments will defease existing debt accounted for in the general long-term debt account group. Through advanced refunding, new debt is issued to provide resources to pay interest on old, outstanding debt as it becomes due and to pay the principal on the old debt either as it matures or for an earlier call date. As demonstrated by the following entries, when advanced refunding results in defeasance of debt (either legally or in substance), the proceeds of the new debt are reported as *other financing sources—proceeds of refunding bonds* in the debt service fund.[20] Subsequent payments from resources provided by the new debt to actually retire the old debt or to transfer funds to an escrow agent are other financing uses, not expenditures. In either case, the old debt is removed from the general long-term debt account group, and the new debt is reported as a long-term liability.

Event	Entry in the Debt Service Fund		
38. A $100,000 bond was issued, proceeds from which are to be used to pay principal and interest of an $85,000 old bond issue. The criteria for in-substance defeasance is met.	Cash .... Other Financing Sources—Proceeds of Refunding Bonds	100,000	100,000
39. Cash is transmitted to an escrow agent to administer the payment of principal and interest on the old debt. If the debt was actually retired, the debit would be to Other Financing Uses—Retirement of Old Bonds.	Other Financing Uses—Payment to Escrow Agent .... Cash	100,000	100,000

The entries in the general long-term debt account group to record the new debt are as follows:

Bonds Payable	85,000	
Amount to Be Provided.		85,000

The entries in the general long-term debt account group to record the new debt are as follows:

Amount to Be Provided.	100,000	
Bonds Payable.		100,000

If two or more debt service funds are used, major funds are identified and nonmajor funds are presented in combining statements.

Special Assessments. Local governments may provide capital improvements and services for the primary benefit of particular groups of property owners, which are paid partially or totally by the same property owners. Such arrangements are called *special assessment projects* and are accounted for through the local government.

Service-type special assessments cover operating activities, such as snow plowing, that do not result in increases in fixed assets. Payment for service special assessments seldom is arranged on an installment basis. A single charge is added to the property tax bill. Service assessments are accounted for in the fund type (usually the general fund, a special revenue fund, or an enterprise fund) that best reflects the nature of the transaction.

---

20 GASB Statement No. 7, *Advanced Refunding Resulting in Defeasance of Debt* (Norwalk, CT: Governmental Accounting Standards Board, March 1987).

Capital-improvement special assessments result in additions or improvements to a government's fixed assets. If an improvement provides capital assets that become part of an enterprise activity, such as water main construction for a utility, accounting would be done in an enterprise fund. If the improvement results in a general fixed asset, such as streets, gutters, or sidewalks, the asset would be recorded in the general fixed asset account group (if the government records infrastructure assets), in which case the accounting is divided into two phases.

When the capital improvements are financed by special-assessment-related debt for which the government is obligated in some manner, accounting procedures are the same as for other capital projects, assuming secondary liability in the event of default by property owners.[21] When the capital improvements are financed by debt for which the government is not obligated, proceeds from issuing the debt are credited by the governmental unit to contributions from property owners, in the capital projects fund.

When the government is not obligated to repay the debt, collection of the special assessment and debt service payments are accounted for in an agency fund (discussed on page 533) since the government is acting merely as an agent for the property owners and bondholders. In that case, the debt is not shown in the general long-term debt account group; it should appear, however, in the notes to the financial statements.

REFLECTION

- Accounting and financial reporting for other governmental funds follow the modified accrual basis of accounting.

- Commonly used are special revenue funds, capital project funds, and debt service funds.

- The permanent fund accounts for nonexpendable trust funds established for the sole purpose of supporting governmental activities or programs.

- When more than one fund of each type exists, major funds are identified and combining funds is necessary to total the amount of the nonmajor funds in each fund type. These totals are used on the financial statements.

PROPRIETARY FUNDS

10

OBJECTIVE

Account for and prepare financial statements of proprietary funds.

Governments account for their business-type activities in two types of proprietary funds. Enterprise funds account for operations in which goods or services are provided to the general public. Internal service funds account for operations in which goods or services are provided by one government department to other departments within the same government or to other governments.

Proprietary funds focus on capital maintenance to measure whether revenues are sufficient to cover expenses (including the amortization of noncurrent items) of the fiscal period. This is consistent with an economic resources measurement focus and the full accrual basis of accounting. Financial reporting for proprietary funds is similar to financial reporting for business enterprises in that income statements show revenues, expenses, and net income for a fiscal period, and balance sheets include both current and noncurrent assets and liabilities. The proprietary fund balance sheet residual is its net assets.

The GASB requires proprietary funds to follow all accounting standards set forth by the FASB prior to November 30, 1989, unless they have been specifically overridden by a GASB pronouncement. In addition, an enterprise fund (but not internal service funds) *may* apply all

---

21 GASB Statement No. 6, *Accounting and Financial Reporting for Special Assessments* (Norwalk, CT: Governmental Accounting Standards Board, January 1987), states that a government is obligated in some manner if (a) it is legally obligated to assume all or part of the debt in the event of default or (b) the government may take certain actions to assume secondary liability for all or part of the debt—and the government takes, or has given indications that it will take, these actions.

FASB pronouncements developed for business enterprises issued after that date unless they conflict with or contradict GASB standards.[22] Enterprise funds may also apply FASB standards and interpretations limited to not-for-profit organizations (such as FASB Statement Nos. 116, 117, 124, and 136 described in Chapter 12) to increase comparability between similar government enterprises and the private sector.

Enterprise Funds

Enterprise funds account for goods or services provided by a governmental unit to the general public. The user is charged for these goods or services, based on consumption. For example, the operations of utilities, public housing, public parking, municipal solid waste landfills, economic development corporations, cultural activities, and airports would be covered by enterprise funds. These funds continue indefinitely and are self-supporting, depending upon the amounts charged to cover part or all of the costs of operation, debt service, and maintenance of capital facilities.

Governments *may* account for any activity in an enterprise fund as long as it charges a fee to external users. Governments *must* use an enterprise fund if one of the following criteria is met: (1) the activity is financed solely with revenue debt secured merely by the revenues from a specific activity, (2) laws or regulations require that the activity's costs of providing services (including capital costs) be recovered by fees and charges rather than general taxes, or (3) the pricing policies of the activity establish fees and charges designed to recover its costs, including capital costs (such as depreciation or debt service).

When an enterprise fund (or internal service fund) is established, resources must be provided either by issuance of long-term debt or by transfer from some other source, such as a municipality's general fund. In the latter case, the contribution received is credited to an account labeled *interfund transfer in* from the general fund. These interfund transfers are reported below nonoperating revenues. Financing may also be provided from loans or advances by the municipality. In such cases, the loans or advances are recorded as interfund payables in the proprietary funds and as interfund receivables in the general fund.

Enterprise funds, in particular, receive contributions both from internal (other funds) and external (customers, developers, other governments) sources. Whatever the source, these contributions are recognized as revenues on a line below income from operations.

An enterprise fund's operational efficiency may be monitored in part by the net income or net loss figure. As in commercial operations, budgets are prepared. However, budgets are not recorded formally in the accounts, perhaps because the fund's self-supporting nature requires a high degree of operational freedom, but more likely because fixed budgetary amounts would be of much less value when there is a variable demand by the public for goods and services.

Control accounts for revenues and expenses commonly are used, with details in supporting records. In accounting for revenues, two control accounts are used: operating revenues for charges for services and nonoperating revenues for grants and interfund transfers received, interest and rent earned, or other miscellaneous financial revenues. A similar breakdown is used to account for expenses: operating expenses for expenses directly related to goods or services produced, such as salaries, depreciation, heat, light, materials, and taxes and nonoperating expenses for financial expenses, such as bond interest. Recording of revenues and expenses, including adjustments, is much the same as in private enterprise accounting.

One of the unusual features of accounting for enterprise funds is the introduction of restricted assets and the current liabilities to be paid with restricted assets. *Restricted assets* are assets (cash and investments) upon which some limitation has been imposed that makes them available only for designated purposes. Examples of restricted assets are amounts of customer deposits subject to refund, proceeds from long-term debt for construction, and monies set aside for bond interest or principal redemption. The existence of restricted assets and their related current liabilities is especially common when an enterprise fund is used to account for a public utility. A major source of funding for utilities is the sale of revenue

---

22 GASB Statement No. 20, *Accounting and Financial Reporting for Proprietary Funds and Other Governmental Entities that Use Proprietary Fund Accounting* (Norwalk, CT: Governmental Accounting Standards Board, September 1993).

bonds, which are issued to permit the construction of, or an addition to, a facility. Since payments for these bonds depend on the existence of operating income, the bond indenture usually includes several restrictions.

Most revenue bonds for enterprise funds are serial bonds that require the earmarking of monies for the payment of interest and for the establishment of a fund for principal redemption. These resources are labeled restricted assets. The current interest and serial installment payables are recorded as current liabilities payable from restricted assets. To further protect the bondholder, at least psychologically, many serial revenue bonds require that unreserved retained earnings be restricted in an amount equal to the excess of restricted assets related to debt service of the bond issue over the current liability for interest and principal.

GASB Statement No. 9, *Reporting Cash Flows of Proprietary and Nonexpendable Trust Funds and Governmental Entities that Use Proprietary Fund Accounting*, stipulates that a statement of cash flows for such funds shows movements of combined unrestricted and restricted cash and cash equivalents for the reported period, segregated into four categories:

1. Cash flows from *operating activities*, which would include cash received from sales of goods or services and cash paid to suppliers, employees, and providers of services.
2. Cash flows from *noncapital financing activities*, which would include proceeds from borrowings not related to capital asset acquisition and repayments thereon, as well as operating grants or transfers not related to capital asset acquisition.
3. Cash flows from *capital and related financing activities* to acquire or dispose of capital assets, which would include grants or transfers related to capital asset acquisition.
4. Cash flows from *investing activities*.

Government enterprises classify interest paid as financing activity and interest earned as investing activity rather than as operating activities. Whether interest paid is classified as capital or noncapital depends on the purpose of the underlying debt.

Many governments account for landfill operations in enterprise funds. Closure and post-closure costs are recognized in the years in which the landfill is in operation rather than when they are to be paid.[23] Therefore, in each year of the landfill's useful life, the government recognizes, as both an expense and an increase in a liability, a portion of the estimated costs for closure and post-closure care. The estimated total cost of landfill closure and post-closure care include:

1. The cost of equipment expected to be installed and facilities expected to be constructed (e.g., ground-water monitoring wells, storm-water management systems, gas monitoring systems, etc.) near or after the date that the landfill stops accepting waste.
2. The cost of final cover.
3. The cost of monitoring and maintaining the landfill during the post-closure period.

The current expense (and liability) is based on the percentage of the landfill actually used up during the current period multiplied by the total estimated cost of closure and post-closure care. For example, suppose a government uses 90,000 cubic feet of a landfill in one year. Total landfill capacity is estimated at 4.5 million cubic feet. If closure and post-closure care costs are estimated at $18,000,000, the entry to record the expense and liability for the year [based on $18,000,000 \times (90,000 \div 4,500,000)$] is as follows:

60. Landfill Expense...................................	360,000	
Liability for Landfill Costs		360,000

In year 2, closure and post-closure cost estimates are adjusted to $18,500,000. Landfill used during the year totaled 210,000 cubic feet. Landfill capacity has decreased to 4,250,000.

---

23 GASB Statement No. 18, *Accounting for Municipal Solid Waste Landfill Closure and Post-Closure Care Costs* (Norwalk, CT: Governmental Accounting Standards Board, August 1993). Landfills accounted for in governmental funds will calculate the accrued liability the same as in the given example. These landfills will recognize expenditures and fund liabilities using the modified accrual basis of accounting. The long-term portion of the liability will be reported in the general long-term debt account group.

The entry to record the expense and liability for year 2 [$18,500,000 × (210,000 ÷ 4,250,000)], less $360,000 already recognized in year 1, is as follows:

61. Landfill Expense...	554,118	
Liability for Landfill Costs		554,118

These standards allow for all expenses to be recognized by the date of the landfill closing. Any landfill capital assets excluded from the calculation of the estimated total cost of landfill closure and post-closure care should be fully depreciated by the date that the landfill stops accepting solid waste.

If a municipality operates more than one enterprise fund, combining statements are required in order to disclose the details of each nonmajor fund. *Different, identifiable activities* for major nonhomogeneous enterprise funds are presented separately to prevent misleading financial statements. Presentation of information about these activities in the notes to the financial statements is also required. An activity within an enterprise fund is *identifiable* if it has specific revenue stream and related expenses. An activity is *different* if the product, program, or services are generated from or provided by different activities. Examples of different, identifiable activities are natural gas, water, and electricity utility services that may be accounted for in one utility enterprise fund.

Internal Service Funds

Internal service funds are similar to enterprise funds in that they are self-sustaining, depend on amounts charged for services rendered, and receive start-up resources. The difference is that users of their services are other departments of the same governmental unit or other governmental units. A computer center, a printing department, a central purchasing department, a central garage, and risk financing and self-insurance activities are accounted for in internal service funds.

Governments establish internal service funds "to report any activity that provides goods or services to other funds, departments, or agencies of the primary government and its component units, or to other governments, on a cost-reimbursement basis."

Since internal service funds do not deal with the general public and usually do not issue bonds that result in restrictions, they do not have restricted assets. Their accounting procedures resemble those for a commercial business. Internal service funds must recover their costs, including depreciation, or be subsidized. Therefore, they maintain records of capital assets and use the accrual basis of accounting. Budgetary accounts are not used, although budget forecasts facilitate the calculation of overhead rates to be applied in determining charges. Billing rates of internal service funds have received much attention because of the impact on expenditures of other funds. Most experts agree that the amount of net income for any internal service fund should be sufficient to allow for replacement of capital assets or payment of risk-related losses but not so large as to accumulate large balances that could otherwise have stayed in the other funds.

As discussed for enterprise funds, the establishment of an internal service fund may result from a contribution or an advance from the municipality. Charges to customer departments are considered interfund services and appear as expenditures in the governmental funds, expenses in the other proprietary funds, and revenue to the internal service fund.[24]

The financial statements of internal service funds consist of the balance sheet, the statement of revenues, expenses, and changes in retained earnings, and the statement of cash flows. When more than one internal service fund exists, combining statements are prepared. Major internal services funds are not highlighted.

---

24 GASB Statement No. 10, *Accounting and Financial Reporting for Risk Financing and Related Insurance Issues* (Norwalk, CT: Governmental Accounting Standards Board, November 1989), allows governments to use either the general fund or internal service fund for all risk financing and self-insurance activities. Many governments choose an internal service fund to charge other funds of the government entity for claims liabilities, including future catastrophe losses based on actuarial estimates.

REFLECTION

- Proprietary funds have a measurement focus of economic resources and use full accrual basis accounting.

- The two proprietary funds are enterprise funds and internal service funds.

- Interfund activities between the proprietary funds and governmental funds are either reciprocal transactions for the provision of goods or services (accounted for as revenue and expenditures) or nonreciprocal (accounted for as interfund transfers).

FIDUCIARY FUNDS: TRUST AND AGENCY FUNDS

11

OBJECTIVE

Explain the usefulness of and the accounting process for fiduciary funds and how these funds are reported.

As mentioned earlier in this chapter, fiduciary funds account for resources for which a governmental unit is acting as a trustee or agent for an external individual, organization, or government. This category of funds includes private-purpose trust funds, investment trust funds, pension trust funds, and agency funds.

Private-Purpose Trust Funds

Private-purpose funds are established to hold performance deposits of licenses, scholarship funds to benefit external individuals, endowments to benefit needy employees or their families, Internal Revenue Code Section 457 deferred compensation plans,[25] and funds used to account for escheat property per GASB Statement No. 21. *Escheat property* is defined by the GASB as "the reversion of property to a government entity in the absence of legal claimants or heirs."[26] Since the rightful owner or heir can reclaim escheat property at any time, the receipt of escheat property is recorded in the governmental or proprietary fund in which the property ultimately will be used and is offset with a liability representing the best estimate of the amount ultimately expected to be reclaimed and paid. Revenue is recognized for the amount not expected to be reclaimed. Escheat property held for others is reported in a private-purpose trust or agency fund (depending on the length of time the assets are expected to be held). Agency funds are described later in this chapter.

Private-purpose trust funds are accounted for in much the same manner as proprietary funds. The establishment of these trusts results from the acceptance of assets that are invested to produce earnings for a designated external purpose. Depreciation on real property included in the principal of the trust would be recognized in order to protect that principal. It also would be essential to differentiate between principal items and revenue items. One common way to segregate the principal from revenues is to establish two funds—one to record principal items and another to account for the earnings. This procedure becomes especially useful if bonds are purchased at a premium as part of the trust fund. Cash flows and available revenue are not identical because of the amortization of the premium. The segregation process protects the principal. When donors establish a private-purpose trust, the assets donated are credited to Additions-Contributions in the endowment principal fund. Later, revenues earned are credited to Additions-Revenues. A liability to the endowment earnings fund for the period's interest earnings is established, and a debit is made to recognize the interfund operating transfer.

---

25 GASB Statement No. 32, *Accounting and Financial Reporting Internal Revenue Code Section 457, Deferred Compensation Plans* (Norwalk, CT: Governmental Accounting Standards Board, October 1997).

26 GASB Statement No. 21, *Accounting for Escheat Property* (Norwalk, CT: Governmental Accounting Standards Board, October 1993) as amended by GASB Statement No. 37, *Basic Financial Statements—and Management's Discussion and Analysis—for State and Local Governments: Omnibus* (Norwalk, CT: Governmental Accounting Standards Board, June 2001).

The only source of assets for the endowment earnings fund is the net earnings transferred from the private-purpose principal fund. These earnings are credited to Additions-Interfund Operating Transfers. Distributions of such revenues are recorded as deductions.

Investment Trust Funds

An *investment trust fund* is used to account for the assets, liabilities, net assets, and changes in net assets of external participants in an investment pool managed by the government for other governments and not-for-profit organizations. Because the accounting and financial reporting requirements are very similar to the private-purpose trust fund, already illustrated, no journal entries or financial statements are provided in this chapter. As in the examples of private-purpose trusts, proper accounting for gains and losses, whether realized through the sale of investments or unrealized through the appreciation or depreciation of fair value, is an important topic to the preservation of the trust. Thus, the economic measurement focus and full accrual basis of accounting are used in these funds.

Pension Trust Funds

Public employees retirement system funds are accounted for in *pension trust funds*. In no other area of accounting is actuarial assistance so vital. Abiding by the requirements of the retirement plan and considering the employee population as to age, gender, marital status, and the myriad of other variables that affect working lives and retirement, actuaries must estimate the amount of resources necessary as of a given date to meet retirement commitments. To protect the employees' interests, pension trust funds use a full accrual basis of accounting.

Contributions to a retirement plan may be from both the employer and employees (a contributory plan) or from the employer only (a noncontributory plan). Employees who resign usually have the option to withdraw their own contributions (but not the employer's contributions) or to leave them in the plan as vested amounts, providing certain requirements are met. The amounts belong to the employee, who will have access to them upon meeting prescribed retirement conditions.

Increases in the resources of pension trust funds result from employee and employer contributions, investment earnings, and net appreciation (depreciation) in plan assets. Decreases in resources result from payments to retired employees, refunds to contributors, and administrative costs.

All assets of a pension trust belong to the employees, and claims against these assets are reflected in either the liabilities or the restricted net asset balance.

The statement of plan net assets adheres to the all-inclusive approach, whereby the net increase (decrease) is added to the total of plan assets at the beginning of the period to yield their total at the end of the period. A statement of cash flows is not required. Governments must also include in the notes to the financial statements as Required Supplementary Information (1) a schedule of funding progress, (2) a schedule of employer contributions for at least six plan years, and (3) information on actuarial methods and assumptions.

Accounting and financial reporting for plans that provide other postemployment benefits (OPEB), such as health care benefits and life insurance are similar to pension reporting. The statement of postemployment plan net assets, statement of changes in postemployment plan net assets, and notes to the financial statements are all prepared in accordance with the pension plan reporting standards.[27]

Agency Funds

An *agency fund* is required when money collected or withheld, such as deductions from government employees' salaries for social security or for hospitalization premiums, must be forwarded

---

27 GASB Statement No. 43, *Financial Reporting for Postemployment Benefit Plans Other than Pension Plans* (Norwalk, CT: Governmental Accounting Standards Board, April 2004).

to the proper destination. Agency funds frequently have no end-of-period balances because money is transferred prior to the end of the period. When the money has not been forwarded, a liability to the ultimate recipient is shown. There is no fund equity, and the only financial statement would be a balance sheet listing the assets held and the related liabilities. A government may account for the proceeds and disbursement of "pass-through" grants, entitlements, or shared revenues from federal or state governments in an agency fund only when it serves as a cash conduit, e.g., merely transmitting funds to the secondary recipient without having any administrative or direct financial involvement in the grant.[28]

REFLECTION

- Fiduciary funds include private-purpose trust funds, investment trust funds, pension trust funds, and agency funds.

- Fiduciary funds use full accrual basis accounting.

- Financial statements of fiduciary funds include a statement of net assets and a statement of changes in net assets.

GOVERNMENTAL ACCOUNTING—INTERACTIONS AMONG FUNDS

12

OBJECTIVE

Identify and account for transactions that affect different funds and/or account groups.

In governmental accounting, each fund or group is a separate accounting entity, entrusted to record only a limited phase of an event. Complete recording often involves more than one fund or group. In addition, transactions among funds are frequent. Throughout this chapter, interfund transactions have been defined. They include:

1. interfund operating transfers between governmental funds for services provided and used—recorded as other financing sources/uses;
2. interfund operating transfers between governmental and proprietary funds for services provided and used—recorded as revenues and expenditures/expenses;
3. interfund nonreciprocal transfers (where no expectation or requirement of repayment exists as in the case of contributions and payments in lieu of taxes)—recorded as other financing sources/uses if between governmental funds, and as interfund transfers that appear after non-operating revenues if between governmental and proprietary funds; and
4. interfund loans—classified into two categories—as either due to/from other funds for short-term amounts or advances to/from other funds for amounts that will be repaid over several years.

A final interfund transaction is a reimbursement where one fund may reimburse another for supplies or other items paid on its behalf. For example, the general fund might pay the entire rental of a facility even though the facility is to be used for both the general government and activities of a special revenue fund. When the expenditure is made by the general fund, the entry is as follows:

Expenditures	XXX	
Cash		XXX

28 GASB Statement No. 24, *Accounting and Financial Reporting for Certain Grants and Other Financial Assistance* (Norwalk, CT: Governmental Accounting Standards Board, June 1994).

When the reimbursement is received from the special revenue fund for its share of the rent, the entries in each fund are as follows:

General fund:	Cash	XXX	
	Expenditures		XXX
Special revenue fund:	Expenditures	XXX	
	Cash		XXX

Illustration 10-9
Matrix of Selected Events Requiring Entry in More than One Fund or Account Group

Events to Be Recorded

1. Purchase of equipment with general fund resources for $40,000.
2. Issuance of $500,000 of general obligation serial bonds at an $8,000 premium for city hall construction.
3. Transfer by general fund to meet $100,000 matured serial bonds and $50,000 interest payments.
4. Payment of $50,000 bond interest and $100,000 matured serial bonds. Fiscal agent is used for payment.
5. Completion of special assessment construction project. $150,000 paid to date; $50,000 final payment.
6. Levy of $5,000 property taxes by general fund against city's utility (quasi-external).
7. Billing of general and special revenue funds for central computer service ($12,000 and $20,000) (quasi-external).
8. Contribution made by city to establish a nonexpendable trust fund of $98,500. Income will be used for library operations.
9. Remittance of the city's $16,000 share of self-insurance costs for current period to an internal service fund.
10. Reimbursement of $15,000 by the special revenue fund to the general fund for general government supplies expenditures initially made in the general fund properly charged to a community development project.
11. Recording of depreciation, $6,000 enterprise fund, $13,000 internal service fund.
12. Redemption of final $100,000 serial of general obligation bonds, with $3,000 deficiency covered by general fund. Fiscal agent is used for payment.
13. Closing entry for capital projects fund involving a partially completed project. Cost to date is $130,000; revenues during the period are $300,000.
14. Payroll expenditures totaled $5,000 and included $1,000 payroll withholdings for taxes and insurance plus employer's share of these costs. $1,000 is transferred to an agency fund for remittance as follows: Private insurance company, $200; federal government, $600; and state government, $150. The agency fund makes the remittances.
15. A 5-year lease agreement was signed for equipment. The present value of the lease payments is $50,000.
16. The actuarial required contribution for pensions was $4,500. Of this amount, $3,000 was transferred to the pension trust and $1,500 will be transferred in the future.
17. Claims and judgments against the city were estimated at $15,000. The city attorney determined that it was probable that the claims would be settled against the city. Of the $15,000, $3,000 was estimated to be paid out this fiscal year.
18. Closure and post-closure costs of local landfill were estimated at $600,000. Landfill used this period was estimated at 1,000 cubic yards, and total landfill is 100,000 cubic yards. Landfill operations are accounted for in enterprise funds.
19. Debt was refunded. The refunding met the criteria for in-substance defeasance. Proceeds of the new debt issue were placed in trust with an escrow agent.
20. Investments carried at $5,500 have a fair value of $5,750 in the general fund. Pension investments carried at $102,000 have a fair value of $101,000.

To serve as a reference and to review governmental accounting, Illustration 10-9 provides a matrix of selected events that are recorded in more than one fund or group. Used in the matrix are the five governmental funds (general, special revenue, debt service, capital projects, and permanent funds), the two types of proprietary funds (enterprise and internal service), trust and agency funds, and the two account groups for general fixed assets and general long-term debt.

Governmental Funds					Proprietary Funds		Fiduciary Fund	Account Groups		
General	Special Revenue	Debt Service	Capital Projects	Permanent	Enterprise	Internal Service	Trust and Agency	General Fixed Assets	General Long-Term Debt	
X	—	—	—	—	—	—	—	X	—	1.
—	—	X	X	—	—	—	—	—	X	2.
X	—	X	—	—	—	—	—	—	X	3.
—	—	X	—	—	—	—	—	—	X	4.
—	—	—	X	—	—	—	—	X	—	5.
X	—	—	—	—	X	—	—	—	—	6.
X	X	—	—	—	—	X	—	—	—	7.
X	—	—	—	X	—	—	—	—	—	8.
X	—	—	—	—	—	X	—	—	—	9.
X	X	—	—	—	—	—	—	—	—	10.
—	—	—	—	—	X	X	—	—	—	11.
X	—	X	—	—	—	—	—	—	X	12.
—	—	—	X	—	—	—	—	X	—	13.
X	—	—	—	—	—	—	X	—	—	14.
X	—	—	—	—	—	—	—	X	X	15.
X	—	—	—	—	—	—	X	—	X	16.
X	—	—	—	—	—	—	—	—	X	17.
—	—	—	—	—	X	—	—	—	—	18.
—	—	X	—	—	—	—	—	—	X	19.
X	—	—	—	—	—	—	X	—	—	20.

UNDERSTANDING THE ISSUES

1. Name three advantages gained by government reporting through the use of the three different fund types and the account groups.

2. Why are budgets crucial in accounting for governmental entities? If appropriations were not included in fund accounting, what impact would this exclusion have on the financial statements?

3. What advantage is gained by categorizing unreserved fund balances as designated and undesignated?

4. How does the use of an encumbrance system aid in accounting for governmental entities?

5. Why are fixed assets, acquired with proceeds from general obligation bond issues, not permanently accounted for in a capital projects fund?

6. When a debt service fund receives resources, it might credit Revenues or Other Financing Sources. Under what circumstances would each of these credits be used?

7. What characteristic determines whether an activity should be accounted for in a special revenue fund or in a permanent fund?

8. What is the difference between an enterprise fund and an internal service fund?

9. Describe the difference between accounting for governmental funds and proprietary funds.

10. What is the difference between a permanent fund and a private-purpose trust fund?

EXERCISES

Exercise 10-1 *(LO 1, 2, 3)* **Accounting for transactions.** Select the best answer for each of the following multiple-choice questions. (Nos. 3, 5, 8, and 9–11 are AICPA adapted.)

1. In a governmental fund, which one of the following constitutes revenue?

   a. Cash received from another fund of the same unit
   b. Bond proceeds
   c. Property taxes
   d. Refund on an invoice for fuel

2. In a governmental fund, which of the following is considered an expenditure?

   a. The purchase of a capital asset
   b. The consumption of supplies
   c. Salaries earned by employees
   d. All of the above

3. Fixed assets donated to a governmental unit should be recorded

   a. at estimated fair value when received.
   b. at the lower of donor's carrying amount or estimated fair value when received.
   c. at the donor's carrying amount.
   d. as a memorandum entry only.

4. In the recording of a city's budget, which one of the following accounts is debited?

   a. Appropriations
   b. Estimated Revenues
   c. Estimated Other Financing Uses
   d. Encumbrances

5. Which of the following accounts of a governmental unit is usually credited when taxpayers are billed for property taxes?

   a. Appropriations
   b. Taxes Receivable—Current
   c. Estimated Revenues
   d. Revenues

6. When a portion of property tax proceeds recorded in the general fund is transferred to another fund, the account to be debited in the general fund is

   a. Expenditures.
   b. Revenues.
   c. Estimated Revenues.
   d. Other Financing Uses.

7. The general long-term debt account group includes

   a. all long-term debt of a governmental unit.
   b. general long-term capital debt applicable to governmental funds.
   c. long-term capital debt and all long-term operating debt applicable to governmental funds.
   d. all general long-term capital debt plus accrued interest thereon.

8. When equipment was purchased with general fund resources, an appropriate entry was made in the general fixed asset account group. What account would have been debited in the general fund?

   a. Due from Other Funds
   b. Expenditures
   c. Appropriations
   d. No entry should be made in the general fund.

9. Which of the following accounts should Moon City close at the end of its fiscal year?

   a. Vouchers Payable
   b. Expenditures
   c. Fund Balance
   d. Fund Balance—Reserved for Encumbrances

10. Which of the following accounts of a governmental unit is debited when a purchase order is approved?

   a. Appropriations
   b. Vouchers Payable
   c. Fund Balance—Reserved for Encumbrances
   d. Encumbrances

Exercise 10-2 *(LO 3, 5, 7)* **Accounting and reporting.** Indicate the part of the general fund statement of revenues, expenditures, and changes in fund balance affected by the following transactions:

a. Revenues.
b. Expenditures.
c. Other financing sources and uses.
d. Residual equity transfers.
e. Statement of revenues, expenditures, and changes in fund balance is not affected.

1. An unrestricted state grant is received.
2. The general fund paid pension fund contributions that were recoverable (reimbursed) from an internal service fund.
3. The general fund paid $60,000 for electricity supplied by the electric utility enterprise fund.
4. General fund resources were used to subsidize the swimming pool enterprise fund.
5. $90,000 of general fund resources were loaned to an internal service fund.

6. A motor pool internal service fund was established by a transfer of $80,000 from the general fund. This amount will not be repaid unless the motor pool is disbanded.
7. General fund resources were used to pay amounts due on an operating lease.

(AICPA adapted)

Exercise 10-3 *(LO 3, 4)* **Budgetary accounting.** Given the following information, you have been asked to record the budget for the general fund of the city of Monroe.

1. Inflows for 20X4 are expected to total $552,000 and include property tax revenue of $355,000, fines of $7,000, state grants of $90,000, and bond issue proceeds of $100,000.
2. Expenditures for general operations and equipment purchases for the year are estimated to be $500,000.
3. Authorized transfers include $30,000 to the debt service fund to pay interest on bond indebtedness and $15,000 to the capital projects fund to pay for cost overruns on construction of a new civic center.
4. Additional estimated receipts include a $15,000 operating transfer from the special revenue fund and a $50,000 payment from the Electric Utility Enterprise Fund for property taxes.

Exercise 10-4 *(LO 1, 3, 5)* **Accounting for revenues.** The following information concerns tax revenues for the city of Cedar Crest. The balances concerning property taxes on January 1, 20X3, were as follows:

Delinquent property taxes receivable	$135,000
Allowance for uncollectible delinquent taxes	(40,000)
Tax liens receivable	45,000
Allowance for uncollectible tax liens	(23,000)

Prepare entries in the general fund for the following 20X3 events:

Jan.　Since current property taxes would not be collected for several months, $275,000 was borrowed using tax anticipation notes.

Feb.　Tax liens of $12,000 were collected; in addition, $2,000 of interest was collected that had not been accrued. The balance of tax liens was settled by receiving $16,000 for the property subject to the tax liens.

Apr.　Collections on delinquent property taxes were $100,000, and interest of $4,500 was collected. The interest had not been accrued. The balance of the account was converted into tax liens.

July　Current property taxes were levied for $422,000 with a 5% allowance for uncollectible amounts.

Sept.　Collection of current property taxes totaled $365,000. The tax anticipation notes were paid off with interest of $18,000.

Exercise 10-5 *(LO 1, 3, 5)* **Accounting for revenues and other inflows.** Prepare journal entries in the general fund for the following 20X4 transactions that represent inflows of financial resources to Bork City:

1. To pay the wages of part-time city maintenance employees, the Cemetery Expendable Trust Fund transfers $45,000 to the general fund.
2. A resident donates land worth $75,000 for a park.
3. The city is notified by the state that it will receive $30,000 in road assistance grants this year.
4. A fire truck with an original cost of $36,000 is sold for $9,000.
5. Sales of license stickers for park use total $5,000. The fees cover this year and next year. Patrolmen are paid from these fees to check for cars in the park without stickers.

Exercise 10-6 *(LO 1, 3, 5)* **Accounting for expenditures.** Prepare entries in the general fund for the following transactions that represent outflows of financial resources to the city of Greene in 20X4:

1. Vouchers are prepared for the following items and amounts:

Salaries	$120,000
Repairs and maintenance	60,000
Inventory of supplies	45,000
Capital equipment	125,000
Tax anticipation notes:	
Principal	200,000
Interest	13,000

2. A transfer of $57,000 is made to the debt service fund.
3. There was no inventory of supplies at the start of the year. The inventory of supplies at year-end is $2,500.

Exercise 10-7 *(LO 1, 5, 6, 7)* **Accounting for expenditures and encumbrances.** Laster City had the following balance sheet accounts and amounts as of January 1, 20X4:

Inventory of supplies	$ 31,000
Fund balance, reserved for inventory	(31,000)
Fund balance, reserved for encumbrances	(18,000)
Fund balance, unreserved, undesignated	(40,000)

Prepare general fund journal entries for the following 20X4 transactions:

1. Prior-period supplies encumbrances are reinstated in 20X4. These are included in the 20X4 budget.
2. Orders are placed for supplies inventory at an estimated cost of $70,000.
3. All inventory ordered (including amounts encumbered last year) is received; actual invoices are for $87,000.
4. The physical inventory of supplies at year-end is $35,000.

Exercise 10-8 *(LO 3, 5)* **Account for transactions.** Prepare the entries to record the following general fund transactions for the village of Spring Valley for the year ended September 30, 20X4:

a. Revenues are estimated at $520,000; expenditures are estimated at $515,000.
b. A tax levy is set at $378,788, of which 1% will likely be uncollectible.
c. Purchase orders amounting to $240,000 are authorized.
d. Tax receipts total $280,000.
e. Invoices totaling $225,000 are received and vouchered for orders originally estimated at $223,000.
f. Salaries amounting to $135,000 are approved for payment.
g. A state grant-in-aid of $100,000 is received.
h. Fines and penalties of $10,000 are collected.
i. Property for a village park is purchased, costing $120,000. No encumbrance had been made for this item.
j. Additional recreational property valued at $88,000 is donated.
k. Amounts of $12,000 due to other village funds are approved for payment. (*Note:* To establish the liability to other funds, credit Due to Other Funds.)
l. The village's share of sales tax due from the state is $30,000. Payment will be received in 30 days.
m. Vouchers totaling $175,000 are paid.
n. Accounts are closed at year-end.

Exercise 10-9 *(LO 2, 5, 8)* **Journal entries, capital assets.** For the following transactions, prepare the entries that would be recorded in the general fixed assets account group for the city of Evert.

a. The city purchased property costing $1,300,000, with three-fourths of the cost allocated to a building.

b. A mansion belonging to the great-granddaughter of the city's founder was donated to the city. The land cost the original owner $600, and the house was built for an additional $50,000. At the time of donation, the property had an estimated fair value of $550,000, of which $330,000 was allocable to the land. The property was accepted and is to be used as a park and a museum.

c. A central fire station, financed by general obligation bonds, was two-thirds complete at year-end with costs to date of $800,000 that were recorded in the capital project fund.

d. A new fire engine was purchased for $165,000. The city traded a used fire engine originally purchased for $100,000. The trade-in value was $25,000. Both engines were purchased from general property tax revenues.

e. A new street was completed at a cost of $250,000, which is to be charged, through the capital projects fund's special assessments, against property owners in the vicinity. The city follows GASB recommendations and records infrastructure assets.

Exercise 10-10 *(LO 2, 5)* **Journal entries, general long-term debt.** The following transactions directly affected Rose City's general fund and other governmental funds. Prepare journal entries to reflect their impact upon the general long-term debt account group.

1. Rose City employees earned $8.8 million in vacation pay during the year, of which they took only $6.6 million. They may take the balance in the following three years.

2. The employees took $0.4 million of vacation pay that they had earned in previous years.

3. Rose City settled a claim brought against it during the year by a building contractor. The city agreed to pay $7.5 million immediately and $11 million at the end of the following year.

4. Rose City issued $100 million in general obligation bonds at a price of $99.8 million—i.e., a discount of $0.2 million.

5. Rose City transferred $5 million from the general fund to the debt service fund. Of this, $4 million was for the first payment of interest; the balance was for repayment of principal.

6. Rose City earned $0.3 million in interest on investments held in the debt service fund. These investments have a fair value $4.5 million greater than at the end of last period. The funds are available for the repayment of debt principal.

Exercise 10-11 *(LO 9, 10)* **Other governmental funds, proprietary funds.** Select the best answer for each of the following multiple-choice items. (Numbers 1, 3, 5, 6, 8, and 9 are AICPA adapted.)

1. Revenues that are legally restricted to expenditures for specified purposes should be accounted for in special revenue funds, including

    a. accumulation of resources for payment of general long-term debt principal and interest.
    b. pension trust fund revenues.
    c. gasoline taxes to finance road repairs.
    d. proprietary fund revenues.

2. Bonds are issued at a premium by a capital projects fund. The premium should be

    a. retained in the capital projects fund.
    b. credited directly to the unreserved fund balance of the capital projects fund.
    c. transferred to the debt service funds.
    d. used to reduce the net cost of the project involved.

3. Which of the following funds of a governmental unit recognizes revenues in the accounting period in which they become available and measurable?

	General Fund	Enterprise Fund
a.	Yes	No
b.	No	Yes
c.	Yes	Yes
d.	No	No

4. At the beginning of a fiscal period, encumbrances that remained at the previous year-end relating to an incomplete project in the capital projects funds generally are reinstated by crediting

   a. Fund Balance—Unreserved, Undesignated.
   b. Fund Balance—Reserved for Encumbrances.
   c. Encumbrances.
   d. Expenditures.

5. Which of the following statements is *correct* concerning a governmental entity's statement of cash flows?

   a. Cash flows from capital financing activities and cash flows from noncapital financing activities are reported separately.
   b. The statement format is the same as that of a business enterprise's statement of cash flows.
   c. Cash flows from operating activities may not be reported using the indirect method.
   d. The statement format includes columns for the general, governmental, and proprietary fund types.

6. The billings for transportation services provided to other governmental units are recorded by the internal service fund as

   a. other financing sources.
   b. intergovernmental transfers.
   c. transportation appropriations.
   d. operating revenues.

7. Resources for a capital improvement are provided by special assessments. At the start of the second year of the project, a reclassification entry in the debt service fund that debits Deferred Revenues would credit

   a. Special Assessments Receivable—Deferred.
   b. Revenues.
   c. Unreserved Fund Balance.
   d. Fund Balance Reserved for Special Assessments.

8. Gaffney City's serial bonds are serviced through a debt service fund with cash provided by the general fund. In a debt service fund's statements, how are cash receipts and cash payments reported?

	Cash Receipts	Cash Payments
a.	Revenues	Expenditures
b.	Revenues	Operating transfers
c.	Operating transfers	Expenditures
d.	Operating transfers	Operating transfers

9. Eureka City should issue a statement of cash flows for which of the following funds?

	Eureka City Hall Capital Projects Fund	Eureka Water Enterprise Fund
a.	No	Yes
b.	No	No
c.	Yes	No
d.	Yes	Yes

10. If an internal service fund is intended to operate on a cost-reimbursement basis, then user charges should

   a. cover the full costs, both direct and indirect, of operating the fund.
   b. cover the full costs of operating the fund and provide for future expansion and replacement of capital assets.

   c. cover at a minimum the direct costs of operating the fund.
   d. do all of the above.

Exercise 10-12 *(LO 11, 12)* **Trust funds, various funds, and account groups.** Select the best answer for each of the following multiple-choice items. (Numbers 3, 6, and 8 are AICPA adapted.)

1. Accounting for permanent funds closely resembles the accounting for

   a. general funds.
   b. capital projects funds.
   c. enterprise funds.
   d. agency funds.

2. In which of the following fund types of a city government are revenues and expenditures recognized on the same basis of accounting as the general fund?

   a. Private-purpose trust funds
   b. Internal service
   c. Enterprise
   d. Debt service

3. On June 28, 20X1, Gus City's debt service fund received funds for the future repayment of bond principal. As a consequence, the general long-term debt account group reported

   a. an increase in the amount available in debt service funds and an increase in the fund balance.
   b. an increase in the amount available in debt service funds and an increase in the amount to be provided for bonds.
   c. an increase in the amount available in debt service funds and a decrease in the amount to be provided for bonds.
   d. no changes in any amount until the bond principal is actually paid.

4. A debt service fund should be used to account for the payment of interest and principal on

   a. debt recorded in the general long-term debt account group or similar list.
   b. debt secured by the revenues of an enterprise fund.
   c. debt recorded as a liability in the general fund.
   d. all of the above.

5. If a governmental unit makes no guarantees regarding repayment of a capital improvement special assessment bond issue, the liability for the bonds would

   a. not appear in the financial statements or in their notes.
   b. not appear in the financial statements but would appear in the notes to the financial statements.
   c. appear in the capital projects fund.
   d. appear in the general long-term debt account group.

6. Taxes collected and held by Dunne County for a school district would be accounted for in which of the following funds?

   a. Trust
   b. Agency
   c. Special revenue
   d. Internal service

7. The following is a correct entry:

   Construction in Progress   XXX
       Investment in General Fixed Assets—Capital Projects Funds.   XXX

The entry would be found in the

    a. capital projects fund.
    b. enterprise fund.
    c. general fund.
    d. general fixed assets account group.

8. In what fund type should the proceeds from special assessment bonds issued to finance construction of sidewalks in a new subdivision be reported?

    a. Agency fund
    b. Special revenue fund
    c. Enterprise fund
    d. Capital projects fund

9. When establishing an investment pool, Eureka City will account for all of the pooled investments in

    a. an investment trust fund at fair value at the date the pool is created.
    b. an agency fund at fair value as of the last balance sheet date.
    c. the general fund at fair value as of the last balance sheet date.
    d. the general fund at fair value at the date the pool is created.

10. Which of the following is not a fiduciary fund?

    a. Permanent fund
    b. Agency fund
    c. Investment trust fund
    d. Pension trust fund

Exercise 10-13 *(LO 9)* **General obligation bonds, fixed asset construction.** Prepare journal entries to record the following events. Identify every fund(s) or group of accounts in which an entry is made.

a. The city authorized the construction of a city hall to be financed by a $400,000 contribution of the general fund and the proceeds of a $2,000,000 general obligation serial bond issue. Both amounts are budgeted to be received in the current year. Expenditures during the current year are estimated to be $850,000. Budgetary accounts are used.
b. The general fund remits the $400,000.
c. The bonds are sold for 99; issue costs totaled $5,000.
d. A contract is signed with Rollins Construction Company for the construction of the city hall for an estimated contract cost of $2,300,000.
e. By year-end, $1,000,000 is paid against the contract with Rollins Construction Company.

Exercise 10-14 *(LO 9)* **Debt service fund, serial bonds.** Prepare journal entries required by a debt service fund to record the following transactions:

a. On January 2, a $5,000,000, 6%, 10-year general obligation serial bond issue is sold at 99. Interest is payable annually on December 31, along with one-tenth of the original principal.
b. At year-end, the first serial bond matures, along with interest on the bond issue.
c. The general fund transfers cash to meet the matured items.
d. A check for the matured items is sent to First Bank, the agent handling the payments.
e. Later, the bank reports that the first serial bond has been redeemed. One check for interest of $9,000 was returned by the post office because the bond owner had moved. The bank will search for the new address.

Exercise 10-15 *(LO 10)* **Enterprise fund.** Prepare journal entries to record the following events in the city of Rosewood's Water Commission enterprise fund:

a. From its general fund revenues, the city transferred $300,000, which is restricted for the drilling of additional wells.

b. Billings for water consumption for the month totaled $287,000, including $67,000 billed to other funds within the city.
c. The Water Commission collected $42,000 from other funds and $190,000 from other users on billings in item (b).
d. To raise additional funds, the utility issued $700,000 of 5%, 10-year revenue bonds at face value. Proceeds are restricted to the development of wells.
e. The contract with the well driller showed an estimated cost of $930,000.
f. The well driller bills its cost plus normal profit amount of $360,000 at year-end.
g. The utility pays a $300,000 bill from the well driller.

Exercise 10-16 *(LO 12)* **Impact of transactions on different funds.** Indicate into which fund a city would record each of the following transactions. (You need not make any entries.)

a. Fixed assets are purchased with general fund cash.
b. Long-term serial bonds are issued to finance the construction of a new art museum. The bonds are sold at a premium.
c. The general fund transfers a sufficient amount of money to cover principal and interest requirements of a debt issue.
d. The fund receiving the payment in item (c) makes the scheduled payment of principal and interest.
e. A special assessment project is one-half completed at year-end.
f. Income is earned by an endowment fund and is transferred to a recipient fund, which is restricted as to its expenditures by the trust agreement specified for a government program.
g. Possible depreciation entries on assets are recorded.
h. The government-owned water utility issues debt to purchase new equipment.
i. The new city prison is completed, and leftover funds are transferred to the fund responsible for repaying the debt used to finance the project.

Use the following symbols and funds for your responses:

GF	General Fund	PF	Permanent Fund
SRF	Special Revenue Fund	PPT	Private-Purpose Trust Fund
DSF	Debt Service Fund	GFAAG	General Fixed Assets Account Group
CPF	Capital Projects Fund	GLTDAG	General Long-Term Debt Account Group
ENT	Enterprise Fund		
INT	Internal Service Fund		

Exercise 10-17 *(LO 12)* **Selection of appropriate debit or credit entry, various funds.** Match the appropriate letter indicating the recording of the following transactions:

1. General obligation bonds were issued at par.
2. Approved purchase orders were issued for supplies.
3. The above-mentioned supplies were received, and the related invoices were approved.
4. General fund salaries and wages were incurred.
5. The internal service fund had interfund billings.
6. Revenues were earned from a previously awarded grant.
7. Property taxes were collected in advance.
8. Appropriations were recorded on adoption of the budget.
9. Short-term financing was received from a bank and secured by the city's taxing power.
10. There was an excess of estimated inflows over estimated outflows.

Recording of transactions:

a. Credit Appropriations.
b. Credit Budgetary Fund Balance—Unreserved.
c. Credit Expenditures.
d. Credit Deferred Revenues.
e. Credit Interfund Revenues.
f. Credit Tax Anticipation Notes Payable.

g. Credit Other Financing Sources.
h. Credit Other Financing Uses.
i. Debit Appropriations.
j. Debit Deferred Revenues.
k. Debit Encumbrances.
l. Debit Expenditures.

(AICPA adapted)

Exercise 10-18 *(LO 12)* **Identification of fund type.** Identify the letter that *best* describes the accounting and reporting by the following funds and account groups:

1. Enterprise fund fixed assets.
2. Capital projects fund.
3. General fixed assets.
4. Infrastructure fixed assets.
5. Enterprise fund cash.
6. General fund.
7. Agency fund cash.
8. General long-term debt.
9. Special revenue fund.
10. Debt service fund.

a. Accounted for in a fiduciary fund.
b. Accounted for in a proprietary fund.
c. Accounted for in a quasi-endowment fund.
d. Accounted for in a self-balancing account group and included in financial statements.
e. Accounted for in a special assessment fund.
f. Accounts for major construction activities.
g. Accounts for property tax revenues.
h. Accounts for payment of interest and principal on tax-supported debt.
i. Accounts for revenues from earmarked sources to finance designated activities.
j. Reporting is optional.

(AICPA adapted)

PROBLEMS

Problem 10-1 *(LO 1)* **Measurement focus and basis of accounting.** Select the best answer for each of the following multiple-choice questions. (Nos. 5 and 6 are AICPA adapted.)

1. The measurement focus for governmental funds is the

   a. flow of cash.
   b. flow of financial resources.
   c. amount of gross revenue.
   d. matching of revenues and expenditures.

2. Interperiod equity measurement for governmental funds determines whether

   a. there is a positive cash flow.
   b. there is a profit.
   c. current-year revenues are sufficient to pay for current-year services.
   d. actual amounts exceed budgeted amounts.

3. The proceeds of a long-term bond issue were used by a county to acquire general fixed assets. The long-term liability is recorded

   a. only in the general long-term debt account group.
   b. only in the general fund.

   c. both in the general fund and in the general long-term debt account group.

   d. in the appropriate governmental fund, depending on the nature of the asset involved.

4. What is the underlying reason a governmental unit uses separate funds to account for its transactions?

   a. Governmental units are so large that it would be unduly cumbersome to account for all transactions as a single unit.

   b. Because of the diverse nature of the services offered and legal provisions regarding activities of a governmental unit, it is necessary to segregate activities by functional nature.

   c. Generally accepted accounting principles require that not-for-profit entities report on a funds basis.

   d. Many activities carried on by governmental units are short lived, and their inclusion in a general set of accounts could cause undue probability of error and omission.

5. The primary authoritative body for determining the measurement focus and basis of accounting standards for governmental fund operating statements is the

   a. Governmental Accounting Standards Board (GASB).

   b. National Council on Governmental Accounting (NCGA).

   c. Government Accounting and Auditing Committee of the AICPA (GAAC).

   d. Financial Accounting Standards Board (FASB).

6. Encumbrances outstanding at year-end in a state's general fund should be reported as a

   a. liability in the general fund.

   b. fund balance reserve in the general fund.

   c. liability in the general long-term debt account group.

   d. fund balance designation in the general fund.

7. An expenditure for general obligation long-term debt is always recorded at year-end in the governmental funds for

   a. accrued interest and accrued principal.

   b. accrued principal but not accrued interest.

   c. accrued interest but not accrued principal.

   d. neither accrued interest nor accrued principal.

Problem 10-2 *(LO 1)* **Measurement focus and basis of accounting.** Select the best answer for each of the following multiple-choice questions. (Nos. 3 and 6–10 are AICPA adapted.)

1. Lacking sufficient cash for operations, a city borrows money from a bank, using as collateral the expected receipts from levied property taxes. Upon receipt of cash from the bank, the general fund would credit

   a. Revenues.

   b. Other Financing Sources.

   c. Tax Anticipation Notes Payable.

   d. Taxes Receivable—Delinquent.

2. The recorded amount for uncollectible taxes was overstated. To revise the estimate during the same fiscal period, the journal entry would credit

   a. Expenditures.

   b. Revenues.

   c. Allowance for Uncollectible Delinquent Taxes.

   d. Fund Balance—Unreserved, Undesignated.

3. The encumbrances control account of a governmental unit is increased when a voucher payable is

   a. not recorded and the budgetary accounts are not closed.

   b. not recorded but the budgetary accounts are closed.

    c. recorded and the budgetary accounts are closed.

    d. recorded but the budgetary accounts are not closed.

4. If not expenditure driven, a grant approved by the federal government to assist in a city's welfare program during the current year should be credited to

    a. Revenues.

    b. Fund Balance—Reserved for Welfare Programs.

    c. Fund Balance—Unreserved, Undesignated.

    d. Other Financing Sources.

5. Which one of the following equations will yield the available balance in an expenditure subsidiary ledger account?

    a. Appropriations − Expenditures Total

    b. Appropriations − Encumbrances Balance

    c. Appropriations − Expenditures Total − Encumbrances Balance

    d. Appropriations − Expenditures Total + Encumbrances Balance

6. Elm City issued a purchase order for supplies with an estimated cost of $5,000. When the supplies were received, the accompanying invoice indicated an actual price of $4,950. What amount should Elm debit (credit) to the reserve for encumbrances after the supplies and invoice were received?

    a. ($50)

    b. $50

    c. $4,950

    d. $5,000

7. Boa City had the following fixed assets:

Fixed assets used in proprietary fund activities	$1,000,000
Fixed assets used in general government activities	9,000,000

What aggregate amount should Boa account for in the general fixed assets account group?

    a. $9,000,000

    b. $10,000,000

    c. $10,800,000

    d. $11,800,000

8. Power City's year-end is June 30. Power levies property taxes in January of each year for the calendar year. One-half of the levy is due in May, and one-half is due in October. Property tax revenue is budgeted for the period in which payment is due. The following information pertains to Power's property taxes for the period from July 1, 20X0, to June 30, 20X1:

	Calendar Year	
	20X0	20X1
Levy	$2,000,000	$2,400,000
Collected in:		
May	950,000	1,100,000
July	50,000	60,000
October	920,000	
December	80,000	

The $40,000 balance due for the May 20X1 installments was expected to be collected in August 20X1. What amount should Power recognize for property tax revenue for the year ended June 30, 20X1?

    a. $2,160,000

    b. $2,200,000

c. $2,360,000
d. $2,400,000

9. Dodd Village received a gift of a new fire engine from a local civic group. The fair value of this fire engine was $400,000. Which of the following is the correct entry to be made in the general fixed assets account group for this gift?

		Debit	Credit
a.	Memorandum entry only		
b.	General Fund Assets	400,000	
	Private Gifts		400,000
c.	Investment in General Fixed Assets	400,000	
	Gift Revenue		400,000
d.	Machinery and Equipment	400,000	
	Investment in General Fixed Assets from Private Gifts		400,000

10. The following information pertains to Spruce City's liability for claims and judgments:

Current liability at January 1, 20X2	$100,000
Claims paid during 20X2	800,000
Current liability at December 31, 20X2	140,000
Noncurrent liability at December 31, 20X2	200,000

What amount should Spruce report for 20X2 claims and judgment expenditures?

a. $1,040,000
b. $940,000
c. $840,000
d. $800,000

Required ▶ ▶ ▶ ▶   **Problem 10-3** *(LO 5)* **Journal entries.** Omitting amounts, prepare journal entries in the general fund to record the following selected events:

a. The budget is approved. The city will float a bond issue to finance fixed assets. Inflows of resources are expected to exceed outflows.
b. Property taxes are levied, of which some percentage will be uncollectible.
c. Some of the delinquent property taxes from last year are collected. Others are written off as uncollectible, using the available allowance account.
d. Purchase orders are approved.
e. Payroll for the month is vouchered. Ignore payroll deductions.
f. An invoice is vouchered for an amount less than its encumbrance.
g. Bonds are sold at face value to finance the acquisition of new fixed assets.
h. Fixed assets are purchased.
i. Short-term tax anticipation notes are issued.

Problem 10-4 *(LO 2, 5)* **Journal entries, identify funds.** Sauk City leases a fleet of garbage trucks. The term of the lease is 10 years, approximately the useful life of the equipment. Based on a sales price of $800,000 and an interest rate of 6%, the city agrees to make annual payments of $108,694. Upon the expiration of the lease, the trucks will revert to the city.

Required ▶ ▶ ▶ ▶   1. Prepare appropriate journal entries in the general fund, the general fixed assets account group, and the general long-term debt account group to record the signing of the lease.
2. Prepare appropriate journal entries in the same funds and account groups to record the first payment on the lease. The city records depreciation on garbage trucks using the straight-line method.

Problem 10-5 *(LO 1, 3, 5)* **Journal entries, pensions.** Harth City maintains a defined benefit pension plan for its employees. In a recent year, the city contributed $4 million to its pension fund. However, its annual required contribution as calculated by its actuary was $6 million. The city accounts for the pension contributions in the general fund.

1. Record the pension expenditure and related liability in the general fund and account group. ◄ ◄ ◄ ◄ ◄ **Required**
2. Suppose that in the following year the city contributed $6 million to its pension fund, but its annual required contribution per its actuary was only $5 million. Prepare the appropriate journal entries.

Problem 10-6 *(LO 3, 5)* **Journal entries, leases.** Brock County has acquired equipment through a noncancelable lease-purchase agreement dated December 31, 20X7. This agreement requires no down payment and the following minimum lease payments:

December	Principal	Interest	Total
20X8	$50,000	$15,000	$65,000
20X9	50,000	10,000	60,000
20Y0	50,000	5,000	55,000

1. What account should be debited for $150,000 in the general fund at inception of the lease if ◄ ◄ ◄ ◄ ◄ **Required** the equipment is a general fixed asset and Brock does not use a capital projects fund?
2. What account should be credited for $150,000 in the general fixed assets account group at inception of the lease if the equipment is a general fixed asset?
3. What journal entry is required for $150,000 in the general long-term debt account group at inception of the lease if the lease payments are to be financed with general government resources?

(AICPA adapted)

Problem 10-7 *(LO 3, 5)* **Journal entries, capital assets.** Prepare journal entries to record ◄ ◄ ◄ ◄ ◄ **Required** the following events using the general fund and the general fixed assets account group:

a. The general fund vouchered the purchase of trucks for $75,000. The purchase had been encumbered earlier in the year at $70,000.
b. Several years ago, equipment costing $15,000 was acquired with general fund revenues. It was sold for $5,000, with proceeds belonging to the general fund.
c. Early in the year, a citizen donated to the city land appraised at $100,000. She submitted plans for a new library and agreed to cover the total cost of construction, paying the company directly as work proceeded. At year-end, the building was two-thirds finished, with costs to date of $300,000. The expenditures are recorded in a capital projects fund.
d. A snow plow was purchased with general fund cash for $68,000, which represented a cost of $80,000 less trade-in of $12,000 for an old snow plow originally purchased for $35,000 from special revenue funds. As an emergency purchase, the acquisition of the new snow plow had not been encumbered.

Problem 10-8 *(LO 2, 3, 5)* **Journal entries, general fund.** Prepare the necessary journal ◄ ◄ ◄ ◄ ◄ **Required** entries to record the following transaction for the city of Maineville during 20X7 in the general fund and account groups, and specify the account group used. Entries in the Debt Service Fund and Capital Projects Fund should be ignored.

a. General obligation term bonds with a face value of $2,700,000 were sold for $2,705,000. The proceeds from the bond issue were to be used to construct a new library and were received by the capital projects fund.
b. $200,000 was transferred from the general fund to the debt service fund to begin saving for the retirement of the bonds in transaction (a) at maturity.
c. $135,000 was transferred from the general fund to the debt service fund to retire a portion of a serial bond due in 20X9.
d. A police car was purchased for $22,000 plus the trade-in of an old police car with a fair value of $3,000, originally purchased for $15,000 from the general fund.
e. The serial bonds funded in transaction (c) were retired on their maturity date.
f. By year-end, $450,000 of the work had been completed on the new library.

Problem 10-9 *(LO 12)* **Various funds and account groups.** Select the *best* response for each of the following multiple-choice questions. (Numbers 1-8 are AICPA adapted.)

1. Maple Township issued the following bonds during the year ended June 30, 20X7:

Bonds issued for the Garbage Collection Enterprise Fund that will service the debt	$500,000
Revenue bonds to be repaid from admission fees collected by the Township Zoo Enterprise Fund	350,000

    What amount of these bonds should be accounted for in Maple's general long-term debt account group?

    a. $0
    b. $350,000
    c. $500,000
    d. $850,000

2. On December 31, 20X9, Elm Village paid a contractor $4,500,000 for the total cost of a new Village Hall built in 20X9 on Elm-owned land. Financing for the capital project was provided by a $3,000,000 general obligation bond issue sold at face amount on December 31, 20X9, with the remaining $1,500,000 transferred from the general fund. What account and amount should be reported in Elm's 20X9 fund financial statements for the general fund?

a. Other Financing Sources	$4,500,000
b. Expenditures	$4,500,000
c. Other Financing Sources	$3,000,000
d. Other Financing Uses	$1,500,000

3. During 20X9, Spruce City reported the following receipts from self-sustaining activities paid for by users of the services rendered:

Operation of water supply plant	$5,000,000
Operation of bus system	900,000

    What amount should be accounted for in Spruce's enterprise funds?

    a. $0
    b. $900,000
    c. $5,000,000
    d. $5,900,000

4. Through an internal service fund, Wood County operates a centralized data-processing center to provide services to Wood's other governmental units. In 20X9, this internal service fund billed Wood's Parks and Recreation Fund $75,000 for data-processing services. What account should Wood's internal service fund credit to record this $75,000 billing to the Parks and Recreation Fund?

    a. Operating Revenues
    b. Interfund Exchanges
    c. Intergovernmental Transfers
    d. Data-Processing Department Expenses

5. The following information pertains to Pine City's special revenue fund in 20X9:

Appropriations	$6,500,000
Expenditures	5,000,000
Other financing sources	1,500,000
Other financing uses	2,000,000
Revenues	8,000,000

After Pine's special revenue fund accounts were closed at the end of 20X9, the fund balance increased by

a. $3,000,000.
b. $2,500,000.
c. $1,500,000.
d. $1,000,000.

6. Kew City received a $15,000,000 federal grant to finance the construction of a center for rehabilitation of drug addicts. The proceeds of this grant should be accounted for in the

a. special revenue funds.
b. general fund.
c. capital projects funds.
d. trust funds.

7. Lisa County issued $5,000,000 of general obligation bonds at 101 to finance a capital project. The $50,000 premium was to be used for payment of interest. The transactions involving the premium should be accounted for in the

a. capital projects funds, debt service funds, and the general long-term debt account group.
b. capital projects funds and debt service funds only.
c. debt service funds and the general long-term debt account group only.
d. debt service funds only.

8. In 20X9, a state government collected income taxes of $8,000,000 for the benefit of one of its cities that imposes an income tax on its residents. The state periodically remitted these collections to the city. The state should account for the $8,000,000 in the

a. general fund.
b. agency funds.
c. internal service funds.
d. special assessment funds.

Problem 10-10 *(LO 10, 12)* **Internal service fund, effect on other funds/groups.**
Allioto County elects not to purchase commercial insurance. Instead, it sets aside resources for potential claims in an internal service "self-insurance" fund. During the year, the fund recognized $1.5 million for claims filed during the year. Of this amount, it paid $1.3 million. Based on the calculations of an independent actuary, the insurance fund billed and collected $2.0 million in premiums from the other county departments insured by the fund. Of this amount, $1.2 million was billed to the funds accounted for in the general fund and $0.8 million to the county utility fund. The total charge for premiums was based on historical experience and included a reasonable provision for future catastrophe losses.

1. Prepare the journal entries in the internal service fund to record the claims recognized and ◄ ◄ ◄ ◄ ◄ **Required**
   paid and the premiums billed and collected.
2. Prepare the journal entries in the other funds affected by the above.
3. If the county accounted for its self-insurance within its general fund, how would the above entries differ?

Problem 10-11 *(LO 12)* **Bonds, various funds/groups.** During 20X1, Krona City issued bonds for financing the construction of a civic center and bonds for financing improvements in the environmental controls for its water and sewer enterprise. The latter bonds require a sinking fund for their retirement. Items (1)–(4) represent items Krona should report in its 20X1 financial statements. Determine whether each item would be included in the following funds and account groups.

a. General fund. ◄ ◄ ◄ ◄ ◄ **Required**
b. Enterprise funds.
c. Capital projects funds.
d. Debt service funds.
e. General fixed assets account group.
f. General long-term debt account group.

1. Bonds payable.
2. Accumulated depreciation.
3. Amounts identified for the repayment of the two bond issues.
4. Reserved for encumbrances.

(AICPA adapted)

Problem 10-12 *(LO 12)* **Various funds and account groups.** Which fund or account group should be used to record the following?

1. A primary government's general fund equity interest in a joint venture.
2. Fixed assets of a governmental unit, other than those accounted for in a proprietary fund.
3. A governmental unit's unmatured general obligation bonds payable.
4. Cost of maintenance for a municipal motor pool that maintains all city-owned vehicles and charges the various departments for the cost of rendering those services.
5. General long-term debt of a governmental unit.
6. Deferred compensation plans, for other than proprietary fund employees, adopted under IRC457.
7. Debt service transactions of a special assessment issue for which the government is not obligated in any manner.
8. Taxes collected and held for a separate school district.
9. Investments donated to the city, income from which is to be used to acquire art for the city's museum.
10. Receipts from the federal government for the food stamp program.

Problem 10-13 *(LO 10)* **Internal service fund.** The city of Danbury operates a central computer center through an internal service fund. The Computer Internal Service Fund was established by a contribution of $1,000,000 from the general fund on July 1, 20X2, at which time a building was acquired at a cost of $300,000 cash. A used computer was purchased for $600,000. The post-closing trial balance of the fund at June 30, 20X3, was as follows:

	Debit	Credit
Cash	120,000	
Due from General Fund	140,000	
Inventory of Materials and Supplies	80,000	
Land	60,000	
Building	300,000	
Allowance for Depreciation—Building		15,000
Computer Equipment	660,000	
Allowance for Depreciation—Computer Equipment		264,000
Vouchers Payable (to outsiders)		41,000
Contributions from General Fund		1,000,000
Retained Earnings—Unreserved		40,000
Total	1,360,000	1,360,000

The following information applies to the year ended June 30, 20X4:

a. Materials and supplies were purchased on account for $72,000.
b. The inventory of materials and supplies at June 30, 20X4, was $65,000.
c. Salaries paid totaled $235,000, including related costs.
d. A billing from the Utility Enterprise Fund for $40,000 was received and paid.
e. Depreciation on the building and on the equipment was $6,500 and $133,000, respectively.
f. Billings to other departments for service were as follows:

General Fund	$392,000
Water and Sewer Fund	84,000
Special Revenue Fund	42,000

g. Unpaid interfund receivable balances at June 30, 20X4, were as follows:

General Fund. $136,000
Special Revenue Fund   16,000

h. Vouchers payable at June 30, 20X4, were $19,000.

1. For the period July 1, 20X3, through June 30, 20X4, prepare journal entries to record the ◄ ◄ ◄ ◄ ◄ **Required**
transactions in the Computer Internal Service Fund.
2. Prepare closing entries at June 30, 20X4.

Problem 10-14 *(LO 10, 12)* **Enterprise fund, general fund.** In 20X8, a city opens a
municipal landfill, which it will account for in an enterprise fund. It estimates capacity to be
6 million cubic feet and usable life to be 20 years. To close the landfill, the municipality expects
to incur labor, material, and equipment costs of $4 million. Thereafter, it expects to incur an
additional $6 million of cost to monitor and maintain the site.

1. In 20X8, the city uses 300,000 cubic feet of the landfill. Prepare the journal entry to record ◄ ◄ ◄ ◄ ◄ **Required**
the expense for closure and post-closure care.
2. In 20X9, it again uses 300,000 cubic feet of the landfill. It revises its estimate of available vol-
ume to 5.8 million cubic feet and closure and post-closure costs to $10.2 million. Prepare
the journal entry to record the expense for closure and post-closure care.
3. Suppose the city accounts for the landfill in the general fund. How would the above entries
for 20X8 and 20X9 differ?

Problem 10-15 *(LO 12)* **Various funds and account groups.** A selected list of transac-
tions for the city of Butler for the fiscal year ending June 30, 20X8, follows:

1. The city government authorized a budget with estimated revenues of $2,500,000 and
appropriations of $2,450,000.
2. The city's share of state gasoline taxes is estimated to be $264,500. These taxes are to be
used only for highway maintenance. Appropriations are authorized in the amount of
$250,000.
3. Property taxes of $1,400,000 are levied by the city. In the past, uncollectible taxes have
averaged 2% of the gross levy.
4. A $1,000,000 term bond issue for construction of a school is authorized and sold at 99.
Bond issue costs were $5,000.
5. Contracts are signed for the construction of the school at an estimated cost of $1,000,000.
6. The school is constructed at a cost of $990,000.
7. A transfer of $100,000 is made by the general fund to the debt service fund.
8. Land with a fair value of $100,000 is donated to the city.
9. The city received $205,000 in partial payment of its share of state gasoline taxes, with an
additional $60,000 due from the state government in 60 days.
10. Vouchers totaling $210,000, which represent highway labor maintenance costs, are
approved for payment by the special revenue fund.

For each event, prepare the journal entries for all of the funds and groups of accounts ◄ ◄ ◄ ◄ ◄ **Required**
involved.

Financial Reporting Issues

Learning Objectives

When you have completed this chapter, you should be able to

1. Identify the basic components of a comprehensive annual financial report (CAFR).

2. Explain which governmental entities are required to report financial information.

3. Demonstrate an understanding of the financial reporting model required by GASB.

4. Describe the requirements of the Single Audit Act.

This chapter is intended to provide a complete discussion of financial reporting for state and local governments. Required financial statements include (1) government-wide financial statements, (2) funds-based financial statements, and (3) a management's discussion and analysis (MD&A) report. In addition, certain information must be presented in the footnotes or in separate statements or schedules. This information is considered required supplementary information (RSI). The reporting model builds from the accounting standards described in Chapter 10. Information about the government as a whole is presented along with more detailed information about the funds.

ANNUAL FINANCIAL REPORTING

The principal role of financial reporting is to provide information. A *comprehensive annual financial report (CAFR)* should be prepared by every governmental unit in order to demonstrate that it has complied with the provisions of the law. The CAFR includes at least two sets of financial statements, along with their notes and any additional data that may be considered necessary. These two sets are (a) the general purpose financial statements (GPFS) and (b) combining statements for nonmajor funds by fund type.

A complete set of GPFS includes the following information:

1. Management's discussion and analysis statement (MD&A).
2. Separate fund financial statements for governmental, proprietary, and fiduciary funds.
3. Government-wide financial statements presenting the entire government.
4. Notes to the financial statements.
5. *Required supplementary information (RSI),* which includes a budgetary comparison statement or schedule, information about the condition of infrastructure assets, pension-related information, risk-financing and self-insurance activity.

The general purpose financial statements provide the minimum financial reporting necessary for a fair presentation according to generally accepted accounting principles. The GPFS are part of the *financial section* of a comprehensive annual financial report along with the auditor's report and combining and individual funds statements that provide more detailed financial information than the combined statements. Chapter 10 introduced combining statements for nonmajor special revenue, permanent, capital project, and debt service funds. Combining

1

OBJECTIVE

Identify the basic components of a comprehensive annual financial report (CAFR).

statements are used to add together funds of the same type in order to present summary data in the combined statements as follows:

Combined Fund Statements

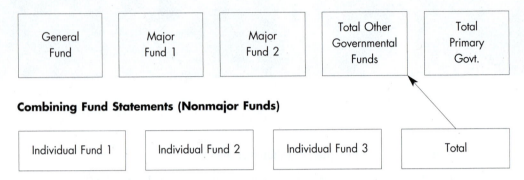

Combining Fund Statements (Nonmajor Funds)

Two additional sections of the CAFR, not part of the financial section, are the *introductory section* and the *statistical section*. The introductory section includes a table of contents, a letter of transmittal from the chief executive or finance officer to the mayor (or the mayor and legislative body), and other information. The letter of transmittal tells about the contents of the CAFR, management's view of the economic condition of the governmental unit, and the community and management's summary of governmental operating activity. The statistical section includes data, often in chart or graph form, about the governmental unit and the community such as general governmental expenditures by function and community demographic statistics.

REPORTING ENTITY

2

OBJECTIVE

Explain which governmental entities are required to report financial information.

GASB Statement No. 14, issued in June 1991, defines the criteria a government must use to determine whether its reporting entity should be limited to the primary government or whether one or more of the associated organizations (referred to as component units) are also part of the government's reporting entity. A primary government can be a state government, a general purpose local government such as a city or county, or a legally separate special purpose government that has a separately elected governing body and is fiscally independent of other state and local governments. A component unit is a legally separate organization for which the elected officials of the primary government are financially accountable or for which the nature and significance of the relationship with the primary government is such that exclusion would cause the financial statements of the primary government to be misleading or incomplete. Examples of component units are authorities, commissions, boards, pension plans, development corporations, hospitals, and school districts.

As indicated, the definition of the reporting entity is based primarily on the notion of *financial accountability*. Financial accountability is measured by (a) fiscal dependence or (b) the ability of a primary government to appoint a voting majority of an organization's governing body and either be able to impose its will on the potential component unit or have the potential to receive specific financial benefit or burden. Most component units should be included in the financial report by discrete presentation (i.e., in one or more columns that are separate from the financial data of the primary government) as shown below.

| Total | Total |
| Primary Government | Component Units |

Other component units are so intertwined with the primary government that they are blended or included with the primary government and only footnote disclosure can inform the reader of their existence. This usually happens either when the component unit is established to serve the primary government or the two boards are essentially the same. When a primary government blends one or more component units into its own financial statements, it reports the funds of the component unit as if they were its own funds. Thus, the primary government adds

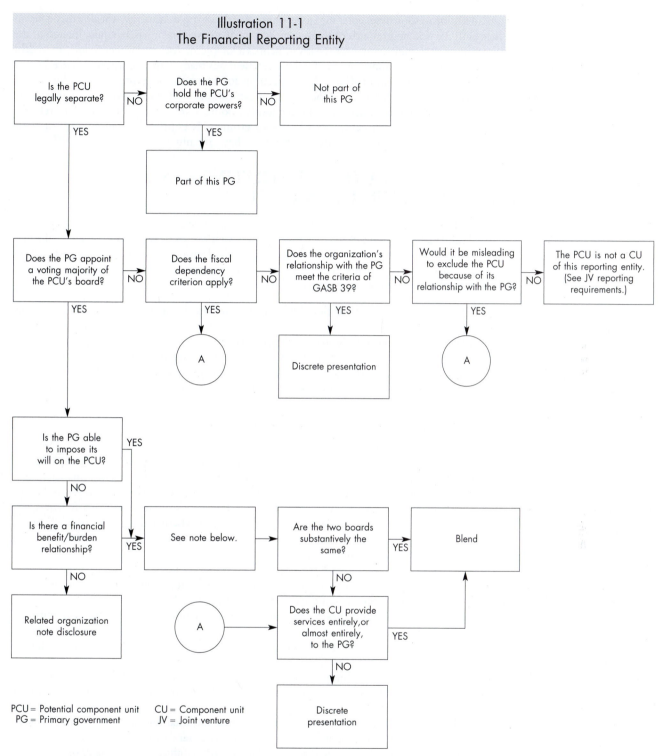

Illustration 11-1
The Financial Reporting Entity

Source: GASB Statement No. 39, *Determining Whether Certain Organizations Are Component Units*—an amendment to GASB 14, *The Financial Reporting Entity,* May 2002.

the component unit special revenue funds to its own. The only exception to this blending is that the general fund of a component unit should be blended into the primary government's special revenue fund. This is done so the primary government's very important general fund information is presented. The flowchart in Illustration 11-1 highlights the decision process for determining a component unit and its presentation in the financial statements.

Governments sometimes enter into joint ventures with other governments, whereby they agree to share both the risks and rewards of a common activity. If a government has an equity interest in the joint venture, it should account for the investment as a long-term asset in the general long-term debt account group (or in a proprietary fund if the investment was made with proprietary resources).

The GASB also requires affiliated organizations for which the government is not financially accountable, e.g., booster clubs, fund-raising organizations, and foundations, to be discretely presented as component units if (1) the economic resources are entirely, or almost entirely, for the benefit of the government, *and* (2) the government is entitled to the majority of these resources, *and* (3) these resources are significant to that government.[1]

3

OBJECTIVE

Demonstrate an understanding of the financial reporting model required by GASB.

HIGHLIGHTS AND ILLUSTRATIVE EXAMPLES OF THE REPORTING MODEL

Statement No. 34 resulted in a dramatic shift in the way state and local governments present financial information to the public. The statements have more and easier to understand information about the government. The reporting standard also reaffirms the importance of information that governments already include in their annual reports. Major innovations of Statement No. 34 can be summarized as follows:

- An introductory narrative section highlighting and analyzing the governments' financial performance.
- A refinement of the current funds-based information.
- An overall view of the government in new government-wide statements.
- Comprehensive information about the cost of delivering services to citizens.
- Information about infrastructure assets—such as bridges, roads, and storm sewers.

Management's Discussion and Analysis

The statement requires the inclusion of a management's discussion and analysis (MD&A) as supplementary information before the basic financial statements. The purpose of the MD&A is to give a concise overview and analysis of the information in the government's financial statements. This analysis is focused on the primary government and is based on currently known facts, decisions, or conditions. It is not a forecast. Its purpose is to help users (citizens, the media, bond raters, creditors, legislators, and others) assess whether the government's financial position has improved or deteriorated during the year. Governments must limit the topics discussed in the MD&A to the following:[2]

- A brief discussion of the basic financial statements, including how they relate to each other and the significant differences in the information they provide.
- Condensed current- and prior-year financial information from the government-wide financial statement.
- An analysis of the government's overall financial position and results of operations including impact of important economic factors.
- An analysis of individual fund financial information, including the reasons for significant changes in fund balances (or net assets) and whether limitations significantly affect the future use of the resources.
- An analysis of significant variations between original and final budget amounts and between final budget amounts and actual budget results for the general fund.
- A description of changes in capital assets and long-term liabilities during the year.
- A discussion of the condition of infrastructure assets.
- A description of currently known facts, decisions, or conditions that have, or are expected to have, a material effect on the financial position or results of operations.

---

1 GASB Statement No. 39, *Determining Whether Certain Organizations Are Component Units—an amendment to GASB 14,* (Norwalk, CT: Governmental Accounting Standards Board, May 2002).

2 GASB Statement No. 37, *Basic Financial Statements—and Management's Discussion and Analysis—for State and Local Governments: Omnibus* (Norwalk, CT: Governmental Accounting Standards Board, June 2001) requires governments to confine topics in the MD&A.

Funds-Based Statements

The focus in the funds-based statements is to provide detailed information about short-term spending and fiscal compliance by major funds. Separate funds-based statements for governmental, proprietary, and fiduciary funds are required. The statements highlight *major* funds and aggregate nonmajor funds into one column. The general fund is always considered a major fund. Other major funds are defined as those in which assets, liabilities, revenues, or expenditures/expenses are at least 10% of all funds in that category or type (i.e., all governmental *or* all enterprise funds, respectively), *and* the same element is also at least 5% of all government and enterprise funds combined. In addition, a government may designate as major any other governmental or enterprise fund it believes is important to the users of its financial statements. This gives government officials great latitude in deciding how data are presented in the statements to promote better understanding of its activities and financial health.

Illustrations 11-2 and 11-3 show examples of a governmental funds balance sheet and a governmental funds statement of revenues, expenditures, and changes in fund balances. Following a separate column for the general fund and each major fund, the remaining nonmajor funds are added together into one column, and the final column presents a total of all governmental funds. Note that the nonmajor funds are included in the column titled *Other Governmental Funds* and that the fund balance includes special revenue, debt service, capital project, and permanent fund information, after adjusting out the major fund balances.

Proprietary funds statements will include enterprise funds and internal service funds. Enterprise funds that meet the percentage test described previously will be presented individually. A column that summarizes all nonmajor enterprise funds is included, and a total for all enterprise funds is provided. The enterprise funds are labeled as *business-type activities*. Internal service funds are classified as proprietary funds in the funds-based statements reported as a separate column because their services usually are provided predominantly to general government activities. All internal service funds are labeled *governmental activities*.

Illustrations 11-4 and 11-5 present the proprietary funds balance sheet and the statement of revenues, expenses, and changes in fund net assets, respectively.

Note that in the net assets section of the balance sheet, there is a significant change in the classification of proprietary fund equity. Under the new standards, equity (or net assets) of a proprietary fund will be classified into three broad components:

1. *Invested in capital (fixed) assets, net of related debt*—This amount includes the fixed assets of the fund less all fixed asset-related debt (both current and long-term).
2. *Restricted*—This amount includes the difference between assets externally restricted by creditors, grantors, donors, or laws and regulations of other governments or internally restricted by constitutional provisions or enabling legislation and any liabilities payable from these restricted assets.
3. *Unrestricted*—This amount includes the difference between the remaining assets and liabilities in the fund as well as reclassified restricted assets when the government has satisfied the restriction.

In order to determine if the government's business-type activities have met their cash needs during the year and show how they have been met, a statement of cash flows is also required (see Illustration 11-6). All governments report their cash flows in four categories. *Operating cash flows* from basic operating purposes are reported first. Most of these cash flows are related to the provision of services and the production and sale of goods. *Cash flows from financing activities* are broken down into (a) *cash flows from noncapital financing*, which relate to borrowing for purposes other than buying or constructing capital assets and to certain grants and subsidies to and from other governments and (b) *capital and related financing cash flows* from borrowing and repaying funds for the purposes of purchasing, building, or reconstructing capital assets and selling capital assets and aid received from other levels of government to finance capital. Finally, *investing cash flows* relate to the acquisition and sale of investments, loan of money, and collection on loans. Almost all of the receipts in this category are interest and dividends from investments. All enterprise and internal service fund activities report cash flows. The *direct method* of presentation of cash

Illustration 11-2
City of Berryville
Balance Sheet
Governmental Funds
December 31, 20X2

	General Fund	Housing Program	Community Block Grants	Highway Fund	Other Governmental Funds	Total Governmental Funds
Assets:						
Cash and cash equivalents	$ 40,000	$12,400			$ 55,000	$107,400
Investments	—	—	$13,500	$ 75,000	35,000	123,500
Receivables, net.	37,400	29,500	35,500	51,000	1,500	154,900
Due from other funds	15,900		—	—		15,900
Receivables from other governments		12,000	—	—	16,000	28,000
Liens receivable	79,000	32,000	—	—	—	111,000
Inventories	18,500	—	—	—	—	18,500
Total assets.	$190,800	$85,900	$49,000	$126,000	$107,500	$559,200
Liabilities and fund balances:						
Liabilities:						
Accounts payable	$ 32,400	$13,000	$ 9,000	$ 11,000	$ 12,000	$ 77,400
Due to other funds	—	2,400	—	—	—	2,400
Payable to other governments . . .	9,400	—	—	—	—	9,400
Deferred revenue	41,000	6,300	15,000	51,000		113,300
Total liabilities	$ 82,800	$21,700	$24,000	$ 62,000	$ 12,000	$202,500
Fund balances:						
Reserved for:						
Inventories	$ 18,500		$ —	$ —	$ —	$ 18,500
Liens receivable	79,000		—	—	—	79,000
Encumbrances	4,100	$ 4,200	12,000	38,000	18,000	76,300
Debt services				—	38,000	38,000
Other purposes			—	—	14,000	14,000
Unreserved, reported in:			—	—	—	—
General fund	6,400		—	—	—	6,400
Special revenue funds		60,000	—	—	13,000	73,000
Capital projects funds	—	—	13,000	26,000	12,500	51,500
Total fund balances	$108,000	$64,200	$25,000	$ 64,000	$ 95,500	$356,700
Total liabilities and fund balances . .	$190,800	$85,900	$49,000	$126,000	$107,500	$559,200

Total fund balances—Governmental funds $ 356,700

Amounts reported for governmental funds in statement of net assets are different because:

Capital assets used in governmental activities are not financial resources and are not reported in the funds.   235,000

Other long-term assets not available to pay for current-period expenditures are deferred in the funds.   102,800

Internal service funds assets and liabilities are included in governmental activities in the statement of net assets.
(Illustrations 11-11 and 11-13)   10,100*

Long-term liabilities, including bonds payable, are not reported in the funds.   (135,600)

Net assets of governmental activities $ 569,000

*See Illustration 11-5 (Internal service funds, Total net assets—ending)
Source: Adapted from GASB 34, Appendix C.

Illustration 11-3
City of Berryville
Statement of Revenues, Expenditures, and Changes in Fund Balances
Governmental Funds
For Year Ended December 31, 20X2

	General Fund	Housing Program	Community Block Grants	Highway Fund	Other Governmental Funds	Total Governmental Funds
Revenues:						
Property taxes	$ 52,000	$ —	$ —	$ —	$ 47,000	$ 99,000
Franchise taxes	40,000	—	—	—		40,000
Public service taxes	90,000	—	—	—	—	90,000
Fees and fines	41,000	—	—	—	—	41,000
Licenses and permits	12,000	—	—	—	—	12,000
Intergovernmental	52,000	24,900			28,000	104,900
Charges for services	9,000	—	—	—	103,100	112,100
Investment earnings	55,000	37,000	35,000	27,200	36,500	190,700
Miscellaneous	88,000	52,000	—	3,000	100	143,100
Total revenues	$439,000	$113,900	$ 35,000	$30,200	$214,700	$ 832,800
Expenditures:						
Current:						
General government	$ 85,000	$ —	$ 22,500	$16,700	$ 11,500	$ 135,700
Public safety	42,000	—	—			42,000
Public works	49,000	—	—		37,500	86,500
Engineering services	13,000	—	—	—	—	13,000
Health and sanitation	61,000	—	—	—	—	61,000
Cemetery	70,000	—	—	—	—	70,000
Culture and recreation	11,000	—	—	—	—	11,000
Community development	—	29,500	—	—	—	29,500
Education—payment to school district	22,000	—	—	—	—	22,000
Debt service						
Principal	—	—	—	—	34,500	34,500
Interest and other charges	—	—	—	—	52,700	52,700
Capital outlay	—	—	22,500	11,500	32,000	66,000
Total expenditures	$353,000	$ 29,500	$ 45,000	$28,200	$168,200	$ 623,900
Excess (deficiency) of revenues over expenditure	$ 86,000	$ 84,400	$(10,000)	$ 2,000	$ 46,500	$ 208,900
Other financing sources (uses):						
Proceeds of refunding bonds	$ —	$ —	$ —	$ —	$ 38,000	$ 38,000
Proceeds of long-term capital-related debt	—	—	37,500	—	15,000	52,500
Payment to bond refunding escrow	—	—	—	—	(38,000)	(38,000)
Transfer-in	53,000	—	—	—	78,000	131,000
Transfer-out	(71,000)	(35,000)	(22,500)	—	(22,000)	(150,500)
Total other financing sources and uses	$ (18,000)	$ (35,000)	$ 15,000	$ —	$ 71,000	$ 33,000
Special item:						
Proceeds from sales in park	$ 34,750	$ —	$ —	$ —	$ —	$ 34,750
Net change in fund balances	$102,750	$ 49,400	$ 5,000	$ 2,000	$117,500	$ 276,650
Fund balances—beginning	5,250	14,800	20,000	62,000	(22,000)	80,050
Fund balances—ending	$108,000	$ 64,200	$ 25,000	$64,000	$ 95,500	$ 356,700

Source: Adapted from GASB 34, Appendix C.

(continued)

Illustration 11-3 *(continued)*
City of Berryville
Reconciliation of the Statement of Revenues, Expenditures, and
Changes in Fund Balances of Governmental Funds to the Statement of Activities
For Year Ended December 31, 20X2

Net change in fund balances—total governmental funds	$ 276,650
Amounts reported for governmental activities in the statement of activities are different because:	
In governmental funds, capital outlays are expenditures.	
However, in the statement of activities, depreciation expense is recorded. Necessary adjustment—the amount by which capital outlay exceeds depreciation.	36,000
In the statement of activities, only the gain on the sale of the park land is reported.	
In governmental funds, the proceeds from the sale increase financial resources. Necessary adjustment—the cost of the land sold.	7,750
Revenues in the statement of activities that do not provide current financial resources are not reported as revenues in the funds.	125,000
Bond proceeds provide current financial resources to governmental funds, but issuing debt increases long-term liabilities in the statement of net assets. Repayment of bond principal is an expenditure in the governmental funds, but the repayment reduces long-term liabilities in the statement of net assets. Necessary adjustment—amount of proceeds less repayments.	56,000
Some expenses reported in the statement of activities do not require the use of current financial resources and therefore are not reported as expenditures in governmental funds.	(116,300)
The net revenue (expense) of the internal service funds is reported with governmental activities.	(122,500)
Change in net assets of governmental activities (see Illustration 11-12).	$ 262,600

Source: Adapted from GASB 34, Appendix C.

Illustration 11-4
City of Berryville
Balance Sheet
Proprietary Funds
December 31, 20X2

	Business-Type Activities Enterprise Funds			Governmental Activities
	Electric Utility	City Bus	Totals	Internal Service Funds
Assets:				
Current assets:				
Cash	$ 94,000	$ 57,000	$151,000	$ 24,000
Investments.................................	—	—	—	15,000
Receivables, net.............................	46,000	2,500	48,500	16,000
Due from other governments	4,000	—	4,000	—
Inventories	13,000	—	13,000	14,000
Total current assets........................	$157,000	$ 59,500	$216,500	$ 69,000

(continued)

Illustration 11-4 *(continued)*

| | Business-Type Activities Enterprise Funds | | | Governmental Activities |
	Electric Utility	City Bus	Totals	Internal Service Funds
Assets (continued):				
Noncurrent assets:				
Restricted cash and cash equivalents.............	$ —	$ 25,000	$ 25,000	$ —
Capital assets:			—	
Land.....................................	81,000	100,000	181,000	—
Distribution and collection systems..............	49,500	—	49,500	—
Buildings and equipment	14,500	40,000	54,500	87,800
Less accumulated depreciation	(15,500)	(30,000)	(45,500)	(27,800)
Total noncurrent assets	$129,500	$135,000	$264,500	$ 60,000
Total assets	$286,500	$194,500	$481,000	$129,000
Liabilities:				
Current liabilities:				
Accounts payable	$ 35,000	$ 1,000	$ 36,000	$ 8,000
Due to other funds	17,500	—	17,500	—
Compensated absences	11,500	4,500	16,000	13,500
Claims and judgments.......................	—	—	—	8,000
Bonds, notes, and loans payable..................	39,000	16,000	55,000	25,000
Total current liabilities	$103,000	$ 21,500	$124,500	$ 54,500
Noncurrent liabilities:				
Compensated absences	$ 45,000	$ 15,000	$ 60,000	$ 10,000
Claims and judgments.......................	—	8,000	8,000	14,400
Bonds, notes, and loans payable..................	54,500	29,500	84,000	40,000
Total noncurrent liabilities	$ 99,500	$ 52,500	$152,000	$ 64,400
Total liabilities	$202,500	$ 74,000	$276,500	$118,900
Net assets:				
Invested in capital assets, net of related debt...........	$ 73,000	$ 95,000	$168,000	$ 47,000
Restricted for debt service	—	15,000	15,000	—
Unrestricted..................................	11,000	10,500	21,500	(36,900)
Total net assets................................	$ 84,000	$120,500	$204,500[a]	$ 10,100[b]
Total liabilities and net assets......................	$286,500	$194,500	$481,000	$129,000

[a]Although internal service funds are classified as proprietary funds, they account for governmental activities and are reported separately from the proprietary funds that account for business-type activities. Information in the Totals column on this statement flows directly to the Business-Type Activities column on the statement of net assets (see Illustration 11-11).
[b]Information in the Internal Service Funds column is combined with other governmental activities in Illustration 11-11.
Source: Adapted from GASB 34, Appendix C.

flows from operations is *required.* In addition, major enterprise funds are reported in separate columns.

The two required statements for the fiduciary funds, the statement of fiduciary net assets and the statement of changes in fiduciary net assets, are shown in Illustrations 11-7 and 11-8.

Illustration 11-5
City of Berryville
Statement of Revenues, Expenses, and Changes in Fund Net Assets
Proprietary Fund
For Year Ended December 31, 20X2

	Business-Type Activities Enterprise Funds			Governmental Activities
	Electric Utility	City Bus	Totals	Internal Service Funds
Operating revenues:				
Charges for services	$110,500	$ 53,000	$163,500	$ 15,000
Miscellaneous	—	3,800	3,800	11,000
Total operating revenues	$110,500	$ 56,800	$167,300	$ 26,000
Operating expenses:				
Personal services	$ 24,000	$ 7,500	$ 31,500	$ 42,000
Contractual services	25,000	9,500	34,500	58,000
Utilities	—	10,000	10,000	21,500
Repairs and maintenance	14,000	6,500	20,500	19,500
Other supplies and expenses	50,000	1,500	51,500	23,000
Insurance claims and expenses	—	—	—	8,000
Depreciation	11,500	5,400	16,900	17,000
Total operating expenses	$124,500	$ 40,400	$164,900	$ 189,000
Operating income (loss)	$ (14,000)	$ 16,400	$ 2,400	$(163,000)
Nonoperating revenues (expenses):				
Interest and investment revenue	$ 45,000	$ 15,000	$ 60,000	$ 13,500
Miscellaneous revenue	—	10,000	10,000	2,000
Interest expense	(16,000)	(11,000)	(27,000)	(4,000)
Miscellaneous expense	—	(8,500)	(8,500)	(17,500)
Total nonoperating revenue (expenses)	$ 29,000	$ 5,500	$ 34,500	$ (6,000)
Income (loss) before contributions and transfers	$ 15,000	$ 21,900	$ 36,900	$(169,000)
Capital contributions	$ 16,500	$ —	$ 16,500	$ 18,000
Transfers-out	(12,500)	(1,000)	(13,500)	(17,500)
Change in net assets	$ 19,000	$ 20,900	$ 39,900	$(168,500)
Total net assets—beginning	65,000	99,600	164,600	158,400
Total net assets—ending	$ 84,000	$120,500	$204,500	$ (10,100)

Source: Adapted from GASB 34, Appendix C.

Illustration 11-9 summarizes the measurement focus and basis of accounting and financial statement requirements for each fund type.

The most notable features of the funds statements are in the format (column titles) being given by major fund rather than by fund type; the use of separate statements for governmental, proprietary, and fiduciary funds; and the presentation of equity in the proprietary fund balance sheet. Other highlights include:

◆ As detailed in Chapter 10, permanent funds account for assets legally restricted so that the earnings, but not the principal, may be used to finance governmental programs.
◆ General fixed assets, including infrastructure assets, and general long-term debt are included only in the government-wide financial statements. A schedule is required for general fixed assets detailing the beginning balances—followed by additions, deductions, and

	Entry	
Reclassifications In—Unrestricted—Satisfaction of		
Time Restrictions	10,000	
Valley Air Project		132,000
Fish in the Lakes Program		184,450
Flood Control Program		251,000
Management and General Services		29,500
Fund-Raising Services		11,000
Membership Development		2,000
Cost of Special Events		2,000
Unrestricted Net Assets		**184,900**
Contributions—Temporarily Restricted	72,750	
Investment Revenue—Temporarily Restricted	7,000	
Temporarily Restricted Net Assets	**56,000**	
Reclassifications Out—Unrestricted—		
Satisfaction of Program Restrictions		103,750
Reclassifications Out—Unrestricted—		
Satisfaction of Equipment Acquisition		
Restrictions		22,000
Reclassifications Out—Unrestricted—		
Satisfaction of Time Restrictions		10,000
Legacies and Bequests—Endowment—		
Permanently Restricted	20,000	
Net Increase in Carrying Value of Endowment		
Investments—Permanently Restricted	29,000	
Gain on Sale of Endowment Investments—		
Permanently Restricted	2,000	
Permanently Restricted Net Assets . . .		**51,000**

The final entry at year-end closes the support and revenue accounts, as well as the program and supporting services expenses, into the appropriate net asset accounts. With expenses allocated to programs and supporting services, it is now possible to prepare the statement of activities (see Illustration 12-2). The sequence of items is suggested by the title. Inflows of resources from public support, revenues, and reclassification are listed first, followed by the expense totals for each program and supporting service, taken directly from the closing and allocation entries. The beginning net asset balance for each class is added, resulting in the net asset balance at the end of the period.

Since the investments account is carried at fair value, it is entirely possible that the carrying value may decrease. If this situation occurs, the account Net Decrease in Carrying Value of Investments is debited, and the investments account is credited. The closing entry would credit Net Decrease in Carrying Value of Investments and debit unrestricted or permanently restricted net assets depending on donor specifications or law.

The statement of activities of a VHWO provides valuable data on the total cost per period of each program and of supporting services. To provide the reader of its financial statements with additional information, a statement of functional expenses is included in the reports. This statement shows the allocation of each expense (salaries, rent, etc.) and reveals the cost by function of carrying on the organization's activities. The statement of functional expenses for PEP is shown in Illustration 12-3.

The statement of financial position for PEP on December 31, 20X7, is given in Illustration 12-4. The statement of cash flows shown in Illustration 12-5 includes, under *financing activities*, all cash inflows from contributions and investment income restricted by a donor for long-term investments (or endowments) or for acquisition of fixed assets.

As is true in reporting for-profit enterprises, financial statements of VHWOs would be prepared with comparative figures for the preceding year. The statements also should be accompanied by notes that would summarize significant accounting policies.

Illustration 12-2
People's Environmental Protection (PEP) Association
Statement of Activities
For Year Ended December 31, 20X7

	Unrestricted	Temporarily Restricted	Permanently Restricted	Total
Public support:				
Contributions	$ 397,100	$ 72,750		$ 469,850
Special events (net of $2,000 direct costs)	7,000			7,000
Legacies and bequests	100,000		$ 20,000	120,000
Received from federated and nonfederated campaigns	16,000			16,000
Total public support	$ 520,100	$ 72,750	$ 20,000	$ 612,850
Revenue:				
Membership dues	$ 118,000			$ 118,000
Investment revenue	21,000	$ 7,000		28,000
Net increase in carrying value of investments			$ 29,000	29,000
Realized gain on investments			2,000	2,000
Total revenue	$ 139,000	$ 7,000	$ 31,000	$ 177,000
Net assets released from restrictions:				
Satisfaction of program requirements	$ 103,750	$ (103,750)		
Satisfaction of equipment acquisition requirements	22,000	(22,000)		
Expiration of time restrictions	10,000	(10,000)		
Total net assets released from restrictions	$ 135,750	$ (135,750)		
Total public support and revenue	$ 794,850	$ (56,000)	$ 51,000	$ 789,850
Expenses:				
Valley Air Project	$ 132,000			$ 132,000
Fish in the Lakes program	184,450			184,450
Flood Control program	251,000			251,000
Management and general	29,500			29,500
Fund raising	11,000			11,000
Membership development	2,000			2,000
Total expenses	$ 609,950			$ 609,950
Change in net assets	**$184,900**	**$ (56,000)**	**$ 51,000**	**$ 179,900**
Net assets beginning of year	**289,000**	**687,000**	**253,000**	**1,229,000**
Net assets end of year	**$473,900**	**$631,000**	**$304,000**	**$1,408,900**

Illustration 12-3
People's Environmental Protection (PEP) Association
Statement of Functional Expenses
For Year Ended December 31, 20X7

	Total All Services	Program Services				Supporting Services			
		Valley Air Project	Fish in the Lakes	Flood Control	Total Programs	Management and General	Fund Raising	Membership Development	Total Supporting
Salaries	$200,000	$ 36,000	$ 60,000	$ 80,000	$176,000	$19,000	$ 4,500	$ 500	$24,000
Payroll taxes	30,000	5,400	9,000	12,000	26,400	3,000	500	100	3,600
Mailing and postage	50,000	10,000	20,000	19,700	49,700		200	100	300
Rent	28,000	8,000	5,000	11,600	24,600	2,000	400	1,000	3,400
Telephone	6,000	1,500	1,300	2,500	5,300		400	300	700
Research	215,000	35,000	80,000	100,000	215,000				
Professional: legal and audit	34,500	24,000	2,000	4,000	30,000	4,500			4,500
Supplies	14,450	10,100	1,450	2,900	14,450				
Provision for uncollectible contributions	5,000						5,000		5,000
Miscellaneous	5,000		2,700	2,300	5,000				
Total expenses before depreciation	$587,950	$130,000	$181,450	$235,000	$546,450	$28,500	$11,000	$2,000	$41,500
Depreciation of building and equipment	22,000	2,000	3,000	16,000	21,000	1,000			1,000
Total expenses	$609,950	$132,000	$184,450	$251,000	$567,450	$29,500	$11,000	$2,000	$42,500

Illustration 12-4
People's Environmental Protection (PEP) Association
Statement of Financial Position
As of December 31, 20X7

Assets:		
Cash and cash equivalents	$	268,000
Contributions receivable (net of $2,500 allowance)		21,000
Inventories		10,900
Short-term investments		152,000
Property, plant, and equipment (net of $38,700 accumulated depreciation)		800,000
Long-term endowment investments		304,000
Total assets		**$1,555,900**
Liabilities and net assets:		
Accounts payable	$	32,000
Refundable advances		5,000
Notes payable		110,000
Total liabilities	$	**147,000**
Net assets:		
Unrestricted	$	**473,900**
Temporarily restricted		**631,000**
Permanently restricted		**304,000**
Total net assets		**$1,408,900**
Total liabilities and net assets	$	1,555,900

Illustration 12-5
People's Environmental Protection (PEP) Association
Statement of Cash Flows
For Year Ended December 31, 20X7

Cash flows from operating activities:	
Cash received from members	$ 118,000
Cash received from contributions	402,500
Cash received from special events	7,000
Cash received from federated and nonfederated campaigns	16,000
Cash received from legacies and bequests	100,000
Cash received on a refundable advance	5,000
Interest and dividends received	21,000
Cash paid to employees and suppliers	(586,000)
Net cash provided by (used for) operating activities	**$ 83,500**
Cash flows from investing activities:	
Proceeds from sales and maturities of investments	$ 27,000
Purchases of investments	(46,000)
Purchase of land, building, and equipment	(146,000)
Net cash provided by (used for) investing activities	**$(165,000)**
Cash flow from financing activities:	
Proceeds from issuance of notes payable	$ 10,000
Receipts of interest and dividends restricted for reinvestment	7,000*
Contributions received restricted for long-term investment	20,000
Contributions received restricted for investment in plant	60,000
Net cash provided by (used for) financing activities	**$ 97,000**
Net increase (decrease) in cash and cash equivalents	**$ 15,500**
Cash and cash equivalents at beginning of year	**252,500**
Cash and cash equivalents at end of year	**$ 268,000**
Reconciliation of change in net assets to net cash provided by operating activities:	
Change in net assets	$ 179,900
Depreciation	22,000
Decrease in contributions receivable	500
Increase in inventories	(900)
Increase in notes payable	10,000
Increase in refundable advances	(5,000)
Decrease in accounts payable	(5,000)
Increase in net carrying value of investments	(29,000)
Gain on sale of investments	(2,000)
Interest restricted for long-term investment	(7,000)
Contributions restricted for long-term investment	(20,000)
Contributions restricted for plant	(60,000)
Net cash provided by operating activities	$ 83,500

*$4,000 of cash at beginning of year and $5,000 of cash at year-end are included in the classification "long-term endowment investments" on the statement of financial position.

REFLECTION

- Voluntary health and welfare organizations account for public support and revenues.

- Public support categories include contributions, special events, legacies and bequests, and federated and nonfederated campaigns.

- Expenditures are separated into program and supporting services. Joint cost allocation rules are followed for the allocation of fund-raising costs.

- A fourth financial statement is required of all VHWOs (but not of other not-for-profits)— the statement of functional expenses—which provides detailed information on the expenses for each program and support service.

The Budget

Budgets are also prepared in not-for-profit organizations. As in a commercial enterprise, the budgeting process involves the establishment of goals, the measurement of actual performance, and the comparison of actual with projected performance to evaluate results. This process requires the input of persons who can determine what resources will become available, what the organization desires to achieve with those resources, and how the resources should be applied to yield the greatest benefit. If the organization or program is well established, a useful starting point is the previous year's budget and its variances, adjusted for any changes in objectives. If the group or program is new, the preparation of an effective operating budget requires careful research to produce realistic estimates of both revenues and expenditures. Expenditures should be planned to maximize service output without producing either a surplus or a deficit. A sizable excess of revenues over expenditures implies that more or better service could be provided. A deficit may indicate the need to curtail future services, since future funds may have to be committed to cover past deficits.[9]

Summary

FASB Statement Nos. 116 and 117 serve to enhance the information provided to readers of the financial statements about financial viability, financial flexibility, liquidity, cash flows, and service efforts. Use of financial statements based on net asset classifications is a much different concept from traditional fund group reporting. While the detailed examples in this chapter focused on a VHWO, these same standards apply to all not-for-profits, including those in the arts, health care, and education.

ACCOUNTING FOR COLLEGES AND UNIVERSITIES

Funds

College and university funds include three broad categories: current funds, plant funds, and trust and agency funds. The day-to-day activities of a public university are recorded in its current funds, which consist of two self-balancing subfunds. The unrestricted current fund represents amounts that are available for any current activity commensurate with the university's budget.

11

OBJECTIVE

Demonstrate an understanding of the accounting for revenues and expenses for not-for-profit colleges and universities.

---

9 In accounting for not-for-profit organizations, it is not as common to find budgetary amounts formally entered into principal ledger accounts as it is in governmental accounting. If a budgetary entry is recorded, it would be similar to the one used in governmental accounting, and it would be reversed at year-end. Assuming estimated revenues exceed estimated expenditures and allocations, the budgetary journal entry for a governmental college or university would be as follows:

Estimated Revenues	XXX	
Estimated Expenditures (or Budget Allocations for Expenditures)		XXX
Unallocated Balance		XXX

Accounting for Revenues

Colleges and universities recognize revenues in all funds on the accrual basis. A university might establish one master control account for unrestricted revenues, with details as to major sources recorded in subsidiary records. More commonly, separate revenue accounts are established, using the following three major groups of revenues:

> *Educational and general revenues group*, with accounts for:
>> Student tuition and fees (recognized when due or billed, net of an appropriate allowance for uncollectibles)
>> Governmental appropriations (detailed as to federal, state, and local)
>> Governmental grants and contracts (detailed as to federal, state, and local)
>> Gifts and private grants
>> Endowment income
>> Other sources
> *Auxiliary enterprises revenues*
> *Expired term endowment revenues*

Operating revenues and nonoperating revenues are recorded in these accounts. Student tuition and fees, federal appropriations, and governmental grants are classified as operating revenues. All appropriations from the state government, gifts, investment income, endowment income, and interest are recorded as non-operating revenues. Auxiliary enterprises revenues are segregated to permit the evaluation of performance and the degree of self-support. Expired term endowment income represents dollar amounts of term endowments on which the restriction has lapsed, freeing them to become unrestricted resources.

Accounting for Expenses

Expenses are recognized in all funds on the accrual basis and may be classified on a natural basis or by function. The most common classification is by function for two major groupings, which are the same as the first two used to classify revenues.

> *Educational and general expenses group*, with accounts for:
>> Instruction (expenses for credit and noncredit courses)
>> Research (expenses to produce research results)
>> Public support (expenses for noninstructional services, including conferences, seminars, and consulting)
>> Academic support (expenses supporting instruction and public services, such as libraries, galleries, audiovisual services, and academic deans)
>> Student services (expenses for student admission and registration and cultural and athletic activities)
>> Institutional support (expenses for central administration)
>> Operation and maintenance of plant (expenses for capital repairs and depreciation)
>> Student aid (expenses for scholarships, fellowships, tuition remissions, and outright grants)
> *Auxiliary enterprises expenses*

Accounting for Contributions

Private colleges and universities recognize contributions and unconditional promises to give as revenues or gains in the period received and measured at their fair value. As with all not-for-profits, exceptions to the general recognition provision are made for contributions of services and works of art. Services are recognized only if they (a) create or enhance nonfinancial assets or (b) require specialized skills, are provided by individuals possessing those abilities, and typically would have to be purchased if not provided by donation. Private colleges and universities are not required to recognize contributions of works of art, historical treasures, and similar assets if the donated items are added to collections, held for public exhibition, and preserved, cared for, and protected.

Financial Statements

Private colleges and universities have the following required financial statements:

1. *Statement of Financial Position* (balance sheet) which will report organization-wide totals for assets, liabilities, net assets, and net assets identified as unrestricted, temporarily restricted, and permanently restricted (see Illustration 12-6).
2. *Statement of Activities* which reports revenues, expenses, gains, losses, and reclassifications (between classes of net assets). Minimum requirements are organization-wide totals, changes in net assets for each class of assets, and all expenses recognized only in the unrestricted classification. A display of a measure of operations in the statement of activities is permitted (see Illustration 12-7).
3. *Statement of Cash Flows* with categories (operating, financing, investing) similar to business organizations (see Illustration 12-8).

Most public colleges and universities report as special purpose governments engaged in business-type activities and, as such, will also prepare financial statements in conformance with the above format.

Illustration 12-6
Private University
Statement of Financial Position
For Period Ended June 30, 20X7

Assets:

Cash	$ 1,494,300
Short-term investments	673,000
Accounts receivable (net of $20,000 allowance)	130,000
Contributions receivable (net of $25,000 allowance)	335,481
Inventories of supplies	20,000
Prepaid expenses	28,000
Student loans receivable	55,500
Assets restricted to investment in land, buildings, and equipment	1,350,000
Land, buildings, and equipment (net of accumulated depreciation of $150,000)	41,450,000
Long-term investments	1,118,700
Endowment investments	954,000
Total assets	$47,608,981

Liabilities:

Accounts payable and accrued liabilities	$ 1,039,000
Other liabilities	1,500
Amounts held on behalf of others	110,000
U.S. government grants refundable	85,000
Annuities payable	237,481
Long-term debt	3,000,000
Total liabilities	$ 4,472,981

Net assets:

Unrestricted	**$40,168,500**
Temporarily restricted	**2,013,500**
Permanently restricted	**954,000**
Total net assets	**$43,136,000**
Total liabilities and net assets	**$47,608,981**

Illustration 12-7
Private University
Statement of Activities
For Year Ended June 30, 20X7

	Unrestricted	Temporarily Restricted	Permanently Restricted	Total
Changes in net assets:				
Revenues and gains:				
Tuition and fees	$ 1,700,000			$ 1,700,000
Contributions	575,000	$ 244,740	$ 120,000	939,740
Governmental appropriations, grants, and				
contracts.	795,000			795,000
Investment income on endowment	70,000	28,000		98,000
Other investment income	251,000	45,000		296,000
Sales and services of auxiliary enterprises.	400,000			400,000
Investment income on life income and annuity				
agreements		30,000		30,000
Net realized gains on other investments.		10,000		10,000
Net realized gains on endowment.	60,000			60,000
Total revenues and gains	$ 3,851,000	$ 357,740	$ 120,000	$ 4,328,740
Net assets released from restrictions:				
Satisfaction of program restrictions	$ 102,000	$ (102,000)		$ 0
Satisfaction of plant acquisitions restrictions	250,000	(250,000)		0
Satisfaction of time restrictions	20,000	(20,000)		0
Total net assets released from restriction.	$ 372,000	$ (372,000)		$ 0
Total revenues and gains and other support. . . .	$ 4,223,000	$ (14,260)	$ 120,000	$ 4,328,740
Expenses and losses:				
Educational and general:				
Instruction.	$ 1,353,000			$ 1,353,000
Research	145,000			145,000
Academic support	217,000			217,000
Student services	222,000			222,000
Institutional support	245,500			245,500
Operation and maintenance of plant.	600,000			600,000
Student aid.	221,000			221,000
Total educational and general expenses	$ 3,003,500			$ 3,003,500
Auxiliary enterprises	350,000			350,000
Total expenses	$ 3,353,500	$ 0	$ 0	$ 3,353,500
Actuarial adjustment on annuity obligations		3,221		3,221
Payments to life income beneficiaries		12,000		12,000
Total expenses and losses	$ 3,353,500	$ 15,221	$ 0	$ 3,368,721
Increase (decrease) in net assets	**$ 869,500**	**$ (29,481)**	**$120,000**	**$ 960,019**
Net assets at beginning of year	**39,299,000**	**2,042,981**	**834,000**	**42,175,981**
Net assets at end of year	**$40,168,500**	**$2,013,500**	**$954,000**	**$43,136,000**

REFLECTION

- Private colleges and universities follow FASB standards.

- Public colleges and universities will report as special purpose governments engaged in business-type activities and, as such, follow FASB standards per GASB Statement No. 35.

- Universities use fund accounting for internal control and decision making, but funds are not required in the external financial reports.

Illustration 12-8
Private University
Statement of Cash Flows
For Period Ended June 30, 20X7

Cash flows from operating activities:	
Student tuition and auxiliary fees	$ 2,030,000
Governmental appropriations	650,000
Research activities receipts	100,000
Interest and dividends received	308,000
Contributions received	395,000
Other receipts	75,000
Salaries and wages paid to faculty and staff	(1,935,000)
Payments to vendors for goods and services	(958,000)
Disbursements to students for financial aid	(81,000)
Payments to life income beneficiaries	(12,000)
Net cash provided by (used for) operating activities	**$ 572,000**
Cash flows from investing activities:	
Proceeds from sales and maturities of investments	$ 325,000
Purchases of investments	(360,000)
Purchases of land, buildings, and equipment	(840,000)
Disbursements of loans to students and faculty	(24,000)
Repayments of loans from students and faculty	20,000
Net cash provided by (used for) investing activities	**$ (879,000)**
Cash flows from financing activities:	
Proceeds from issuance of notes payable	$ 800,000
Payments on long-term debt	(100,000)
Receipts of interest and dividends restricted for reinvestment	75,000
Contributions received restricted for long-term investment	200,000
Payments to annuitants	(6,000)
Receipts of refundable government loans funds	30,000
Net cash provided by (used for) financing activities	**$ 999,000**
Net increase (decrease) in cash and cash equivalents	**$ 692,000**
Cash and cash equivalents at beginning of year	**802,300**
Cash and cash equivalents at end of year	**$1,494,300**

ACCOUNTING FOR PROVIDERS OF HEALTH CARE SERVICES—GOVERNMENTAL AND PRIVATE

Advancement in medical practice and increased demand for access to health care services have led to significant growth in the health care industry. Expenditures for medical care now equal more than 10% of the gross national product. Health care entities include hospitals, clinics, continuing care retirement communities, health maintenance organizations, home health agencies, and nursing homes. Classified by sponsorship or equity structure, health care units fall into three categories:

1. Investor-owned health care entities (or proprietary entities), which are privately owned and operated for a profit.
2. Governmental health care entities (or public entities), which are operated by a governmental unit and accounted for as an enterprise fund, such as a veterans' hospital.
3. Voluntary not-for-profit health care entities, including those with a religious affiliation, which are organized and sustained by members of a community.

A modern health care provider may be a complex entity with medical, surgical, research, teaching, and public service aspects. One very unusual element about health care operations is the manner of payment for services. A significant portion of the fees for health care service is paid by a third party, such as Medicare, Medicaid, Blue Cross, or some other insurance provider. Health care entities are reimbursed not on the basis of listed prices but on the basis of the cost of providing services, as that cost is defined by the third-party payor. A cost determination must be made according to formulas agreed upon in the law (Medicare and Medicaid) or in the contract (other insurance providers). Cost determination requires allocation of overhead, including depreciation. Thus, not-for-profit health care organizations follow the accrual basis of accounting, permitting comparison of results with profit-oriented health care units.

Generally Accepted Accounting Principles

Generally accepted accounting principles (GAAP) for hospitals and other health care organizations have evolved through the efforts of two industry professional associations, the American Hospital Association (AHA) and the Health Care Financial Management Association (HFMA), and the American Institute of Certified Public Accountants (AICPA). Governmental hospitals or health care providers are considered special purpose governments engaged in business-type activities. As such, *health care entities will report as enterprise funds* and adopt the same financial statement format as their private counterparts.

Funds

With the many restrictions resulting from donations, endowments, insurance company contracts, and government regulations for reimbursement, the activities of a health care provider have traditionally been accounted for using fund accounting.[10] Health care entities employ two classes of funds:

1. *General funds*, which account for resources available for general operations, with no restrictions placed upon those resources by an outsider, and other exchange transactions including resources from government grants and subsidies, tax support, and reimbursements from insurance contracts.
2. *Donor-restricted funds*, which account for temporarily and permanently restricted resources. This class is subdivided into:

   a. *Specific purpose funds*, which account for donor-restricted resources temporarily restricted for current but specified operations.

---

10 Most hospitals have traditionally used the fund structure described in this chapter. However, other health care entities, such as health maintenance organizations, nursing homes, and home health care agencies may find it unnecessary to use fund accounting.

    b. *Plant replacement and expansion funds*, which account for resources temporarily restricted by the donor for the acquisition, construction, or improvement of property, plant, and equipment.

    c. *Endowment funds*, which account for resources that are received to create permanently restricted endowments (whose income only may be expended) and temporarily restricted term endowments (whose principal eventually will become available for expenditure).

    d. Other donor-restricted funds such as annuities, life income funds, or loan funds.

Each fund consists of a set of self-balancing accounts designed to reflect activities within its domain.

Classification of Assets and Liabilities

Assets of a health care provider comprise three distinct segments: current assets, assets whose use is limited, and property and equipment. Assets and liabilities are sequenced by liquidity and are classified as current or noncurrent according to GAAP.

Assets whose use is limited include assets set aside by the governing board for a specific purpose, sometimes referred to as board-designated assets. For example, the board may authorize that $10,000 be set aside for capital improvements, which would be recorded as follows:

Cash—Limited in Use for Capital Expansion	10,000	
Cash		10,000

Since the limitation on these assets is internal, they remain unrestricted since "restrictions" can only be created by outside sources. This segment also includes assets resulting from an operational agreement entered into by the board, such as the proceeds of a bond issue limited in use as stipulated by the bond indenture. Assets set aside to provide for self-insurance or to meet depreciation fund requirements with third-party payors belong to this segment as well.

Property and equipment include the physical properties used in operations, along with their accumulated depreciation. Current liabilities may include accounts and notes payable, deposits from patients, and advances from and amounts payable to third-party payors. Long-term liabilities may include notes, mortgages, capital leases, bond payables, and estimated malpractice costs. The net assets of the entire health care organization (which represents the difference between assets and liabilities) are divided into three classes—permanently restricted net assets, temporarily restricted net assets, and unrestricted net assets—based on the existence or absence of donor-imposed restrictions.

Classification of Revenues, Expenses, Gains, and Losses

Revenues, expenses, gains, and losses increase or decrease the net assets of a health care entity. Other events, such as expirations of donor-imposed restrictions, that simultaneously increase one class of net assets and decrease another (reclassifications) are reported as separate items. Revenues and gains may increase unrestricted net assets, temporarily restricted net assets, or permanently restricted net assets. Expenses reduce unrestricted net assets.

Revenues and expenses are considered operating if they relate to the principal activity of providing health care services. Revenues, expenses, gains, or losses from activities that are incidental to the providing of health care services or from events beyond the entity's control are classified as nonoperating.

Hospital payment systems have changed significantly in recent years. The systems include fees based on *diagnosis-related groups (DRGs), capitation premiums* (paid per member, per month), *fees based on negotiated bids,* and *cost-reimbursement methods.* Some payments are established prospectively (in advance of service delivery) at fixed amounts. Other payment rates may be based on interim billing amounts, subject to retrospective (after the accounting period ends) adjustment. Medicare generally pays hospitals prospectively, based on DRGs. Under the DRG system, all potential diagnoses are classified into a number of medically meaningful groups, each of which has a different value. Each hospital in a specific geographical region receives the same amount for each DRG, depending on whether the hospital is classified as urban or rural, and teaching or nonteaching. The thinking behind the DRG system is that a hospital that is more efficient will benefit because it may keep any reimbursement in excess of cost.

13

OBJECTIVE

Demonstrate an understanding of how revenues and expenses are calculated and accounted for by governmental and private health care service providers.

Under capitation agreements with HMOs, hospitals generally receive agreed-upon monthly premiums based on the number of participants in the HMO. In exchange, the hospitals agree to provide all medical services to the HMO's subscribers. The hospitals will receive the capitation payment regardless of the actual services they perform. The hospitals may also receive fees from the HMO for certain services. Other payment methods include prospectively determined rates per discharge, prospectively determined daily rates, and discounts from established charges. When rates are determined retrospectively, the hospital is generally required to submit audited cost reports with detail on allowable costs. Retrospective adjustment can result in either an increase or decrease to the rates allowed for interim billing purposes.

The following operating revenue classifications are used in health care:

1. *Patient Service Revenue*, the major revenue account for a hospital, in which the gross revenues earned are recorded on an accrual basis at established rates for:

   a. Routine services (room and board, general nursing, and home health care).
   b. Other nursing services (in operating, recovery, and delivery rooms).
   c. Professional services (physician's care, lab work, pharmacy, blood bank, radiology, dialysis, and physical therapy).

2. *Premium Revenue*, based on fees from agreements under which a hospital or HMO has agreed to provide any necessary patient services for a specific fee, e.g., a capitation agreement whereby the HMO receives an agreed-upon payment from another HMO for a specific number of members per month regardless of actual services.

3. *Resident Service Revenue*, the major revenue account for a nursing home or continuing care retirement community. It records rental fees earned from residents or amortization of their advance payment of fees.

4. *Other Operating Revenue*, which records revenue from services other than health care provided to patients and residents. Also recorded is revenue from sales or services to persons other than patients. Thus, Other Operating Revenue would include:

   a. Revenue from educational programs, such as nursing school tuition.
   b. Revenue from specific-purpose contributions.
   c. Revenue from government grants to the extent that the related expenditures are included in operations. Grants that may be refundable if provisions that are not met are recorded as a liability. As expenses are incurred, a matching portion of the grant is recorded from liabilities and recognized as current-period revenue.
   d. Revenue from sales of medical or pharmacy supplies to employees or physicians.
   e. Revenue from the sale of cafeteria meals to employees, medical staff, and visitors.
   f. Revenue from snack bars, gift shops, parking lots, and other service facilities.

The control account Nonoperating Revenue records revenue not related directly to an entity's principal operations. These items are primarily financial in nature and include unrestricted and donor-restricted pledges, gifts, or grants, unrestricted income from endowment funds, maturing of term endowment funds, income and gains from investments, and gains on sales of hospital property. Investments are reported at fair value with both realized and unrealized gains included as part of nonoperating revenue.

Patient Service Revenue is initially recorded at the hospital's gross (established) rates. A third-party payor, such as Blue Cross, HMOs, Medicare, or Medicaid, may reimburse a hospital on the basis of predetermined amounts that are less than the original gross charges for described services. The difference between the gross revenue and the amount expected to be collected from the third-party payors is referred to as the *contractual adjustment*. It is deducted from the gross patient service revenue prior to preparing the financial statements. A credit is made to an allowance account in order to reduce the receivables to net expected. Also deducted from gross revenue are adjustments for services provided as courtesy allowances granted to hospital employees. Not-for-profit hospitals also provide care without charge (charitable services) to persons who have demonstrated an inability to pay. Each hospital is required to establish criteria for charity care consistent with its mission statement and financial ability. Charity services are not reported as revenues or as receivables in the financial statements. Hospitals may, however, initially record the patient services charges because of an initial lack of knowledge that an account qualifies as charity service and the need to disclose the level of charity service. Under these circumstances, the charity care amount is recorded as contra revenue with a credit to an allowance account to reduce the receivable similar to the contractual adjustment. Since charity care represents health care services that are provided but are never expected to result in cash flows, it is distinguished from bad debts. Other uncollectible amounts are reported as bad debt expense. The objective of grouping these items is to be able to show accurate net patient service revenue, an expense for uncollectibles, and net receivables on the financial statements. Illustrative entries are as follows:

Patient Accounts Receivable	XXX	
Patient Service Revenues		XXX
Contractual Adjustments	XXX	
Allowance for Uncollectible Third-Party Contracts and Charity		XXX
Provision for Bad Debts	XXX	
Allowance for Uncollectible Third-Party Contracts and Charity		XXX
Charity Services	XXX	
Accounts Receivable		XXX

Payments made to a health care unit by third parties include reimbursement for depreciation. Often this portion of the payment is limited in use to replacing or adding to property, plant, or equipment. Total billings are included in revenue of the general funds to permit matching of total revenues and expenses. When collected, the specified portion is transferred to a special account with the following entry:

Cash—Assets Whose Use Is Limited by Agreement with		
Third-Party Payors for Funded Depreciation	XXX	
Cash		XXX

Titles given to operating expenses of a health care facility may differ, depending upon the nature of the facility's activities. Expenses may be reported on the face of the financial statements using either a natural classification or a functional presentation. Functional allocations are to be based on full cost allocations. The following functional expense categories are common to many health care organizations:

1. Nursing Services Expense, for the cost of nursing services directly related to the patient or resident.
2. Other Professional Services Expense, for professional services indirectly related to the patient or resident, such as lab fees or pharmacy costs. Note that some hospitals combine the two accounts Nursing Services Expense and Other Professional Services Expense into one account labeled Professional Care of Patients Expense.
3. General Services Expense, for costs of the cafeteria, food service, and housekeeping. Where food services constitute a major cost, some hospitals prefer to segregate them into the account Dietary Services Expense.
4. Fiscal Services Expense, for admitting, data processing, billing, and accounting costs.
5. Administrative Services Expense, for purchasing, public relations, insurance, taxes, and personnel costs.
6. Other Services.
7. Malpractice Insurance Expense, if not already allocated.
8. Depreciation Expense, if not already allocated.
9. Interest Expense, if not already allocated.
10. Provision for Bad Debts, if not already allocated.

For example, salaries expense is often recorded and allocated to the first six functional expense accounts at year-end. The statement of activities (operating statement) would show the total for each service, such as Nursing Services Expense, but not the nature of that total (salaries, supplies, etc.). The footnotes to the financial statements provide detail on the natural classifications of the expense, such as salaries, supplies, etc.

14

OBJECTIVE

Demonstrate an understanding of the accounting for unrestricted and restricted contributions to governmental and private health care service providers.

Accounting for Donations/Contributions Received

Health care entities may receive gifts or donations that meet the definition of an unconditional contribution. These contributions may be unrestricted as to use or may be limited to a specific use. Unrestricted contributions are recognized at fair value with a credit to Other Operating Revenue—Unrestricted, or Nonoperating Revenue—Unrestricted, depending on whether these contributions are deemed to be ongoing major or central activities, or peripheral or incidental transactions.

Bequests and gifts restricted by the donor to be used for (1) specific operating purposes, (2) additions to plant, (3) endowments, or (4) annuities or life incomes are recorded when received at their fair value with a credit to Revenues (other operating or nonoperating)—Temporarily Restricted or Revenues (other operating or nonoperating)—Permanently Restricted. When expenditures are made consistent with the donor's stipulation, or when term endowments become available, a reclassification is made from the temporarily restricted net asset category to an unrestricted net asset category. Should resources from expired term endowments be restricted further, for example, to purchase equipment, they will remain in the temporarily restricted net asset category. Resources temporarily restricted for the purchase or construction of property, plant, and equipment may be released from restriction either in the period the asset is placed into service or over its useful life. Donor-restricted contributions in which the restriction will be met in the current period may be classified as unrestricted revenues. Some promises to give are conditional and will not be recognized until the condition is met.

Activities of health care providers are enhanced by volunteers who donate their time and abilities. Donated services must be recognized if the services received (1) create or enhance nonfinancial assets or (2) require specialized skills, are provided by individuals possessing those skills who are scheduled and supervised in much the same way as employees, and would typically need to be purchased if not contributed. Services provided by doctors, nurses, and other professionals in a health care entity may meet the above criteria. Incidental services provided by other volunteers for such things as fund raising or other activities that would not otherwise be staffed by employees would not meet the criteria. For example, most voluntary service by senior citizens, candy stripers, and others is not recorded. When an institution is operated by a religious group whose members receive token payment or no payment at all, the value of donated services should be charged to the proper expense account and credited to other operating revenue or nonoperating revenue depending on the nature of the donated services.

Professional Care of Patients Expense	XXX	
Other Revenue—Donated Services		XXX

Donated items may also be unrestricted or restricted. Examples of donated items in a health care entity are laboratory and pharmaceutical supplies donated by drug companies or associations of doctors; donated property, plant, and equipment; and contributed use of facilities. Donated items are recognized at fair value with a credit to Other Operating Revenue—Unrestricted or Nonoperating Revenue—Unrestricted, depending on whether the donations constitute the entity's ongoing major or central operations or are peripheral or incidental transactions. If donated items have a donor-specified use, they may be temporarily restricted until they are used for their intended purpose. Unrestricted donations of property are recognized as Nonoperating Revenue—Unrestricted. If donations of property are donor restricted, the same entry is made but with a credit to temporarily or permanently restricted revenues.

15

OBJECTIVE

Explain the financial impact of medical malpractice claims on governmental and private health care service providers.

Medical Malpractice Claims

Settlements and judgments on medical malpractice claims constitute a potential major expense for hospitals. The current environment in relation to medical malpractice claims has caused insurance companies to raise premiums to health care providers dramatically or to limit the amount of risk they are willing to insure. To find a health care provider that is fully insured against medical malpractice losses is a rarity. Many have dropped their malpractice insurance or have adopted other approaches for protection. Some pay losses as they occur. Others establish trust funds with a trustee.

Whether expenses and liabilities need to be recognized on malpractice claims depends on whether risk has been transferred by the hospital to the third-party insurance company or to public entity risk pools. An AICPA statement stipulates that:

> *The ultimate costs of malpractice claims, which include costs associated with litigating or settling claims, should be accrued when the incidents occur that give rise to the claims, if it can be determined that it is probable that liabilities have been incurred and if the amounts of the losses can be reasonably estimated.*[11]

The basic rule applies whether or not claims for incidents occurring before the balance sheet date [incurred but not reported (IBNR)] have been asserted. An estimate must be made for losses on IBNR claims if it is probable that incidents have occurred and that losses will result. Historical experience of both the hospital and the health care industry are often used in estimating the probability of IBNR claims. If the health care provider is covered by insurance, the premiums applicable to the reporting period are expensed. The entry to record payment of insurance premums is as follows:

Medical Malpractice Costs (or administrative services expense)	XXX	
Cash		XXX

The entry to record an amount for estimated claim costs for the reporting period not covered by the insurance arrangement is as follows:

Medical Malpractice Costs (or administrative services expense)	XXX	
Estimated Additional Malpractice Liability		XXX

Although hospitals report expenses on a functional basis by major program area, the medical malpractice costs are sometimes segregated from the other administrative services costs to emphasize their critical nature.

As a result of the large settlements granted in malpractice cases, some health care organizations became self-insured, establishing a trust account with an outside trustee who determines funding requirements. Two entries are necessary. The first establishes the estimated claim costs and liability as follows:

Medical Malpractice Costs (or administrative services expense)	XXX	
Estimated Malpractice Liability		XXX

The second entry records the contribution to the trustee:

Cash—Limited in Use Under Malpractice Funding Arrangement	XXX	
Cash		XXX

The amount in the trust account is reported in the balance sheet as an asset whose use is limited. Claims expected to be paid during the next operating cycle are classified as current liabilities, while the remainder of the liability balance is shown as noncurrent.

---

11 Statement of Position 87-1, *Accounting for Asserted and Unasserted Medical Malpractice Claims of Health Care Providers and Related Issues* (New York: American Institute of Certified Public Accountants, March 16, 1987), par. 21.

Whether the health care provider is covered by insurance, pays losses as they occur, or has a trust fund arrangement, the amount of the expense should reflect the best estimate of ultimate costs of malpractice claims related to incidents that occurred during the reporting period.

Financial Statements of a Private Health Care Provider

16

OBJECTIVE

Prepare financial statements for governmental and private health care service providers.

The financial statements of a private health care provider include a statement of activities which presents organization-wide totals for changes in unrestricted net assets, temporarily restricted net assets, and permanently restricted net assets. The form is straightforward, showing operating revenues minus operating expenses as an increase (decrease) in net assets from operations. The nonoperating revenue is added to this amount. Expenses are reported using functional classifications. Further information on natural classifications of expenses is a suggested footnote disclosure. The results of only one year's activities are shown in Illustration 12-9.

In addition to the statement of activities, a private health care organization provides a statement of financial position and a statement of cash flows. The statement of financial position, shown in Illustration 12-10, includes assets and liabilities of all funds. The sequence begins with current assets, assets whose use is limited, property and equipment, and possibly other assets. Also shown are the current and other liabilities of the organization and the three classes of net assets, which represent the equity of the hospital.

The statement of cash flows, shown in Illustration 12-11, follows FASB Statement No. 95 that encourages the use of the direct method to present cash flows, although it does accept the indirect method.

Illustration 12-9
Columbia Hospital
Statement of Activities
For Year Ended December 31, 20X5

	Unrestricted	Temporarily Restricted	Permanently Restricted	Total
Revenues, gains, and other support:				
Patient service revenue (net of adjustments)	$ 4,420,000			$ 4,420,000
Other operating revenue	222,000	$ 750,000		972,000
Net assets released from restrictions:				
Satisfaction of program restrictions	50,000	(50,000)		0
Satisfaction of equipment acquisitions restrictions ...	200,000	(200,000)		0
Expiration of time restrictions	150,000	(150,000)		0
Total operating revenues and other support......	$ 5,042,000	$ 350,000		$ 5,392,000
Expenses and losses:				
Nursing services	$ 1,774,000			$ 1,774,000
Other professional services	1,240,000			1,240,000
General services	995,000			995,000
Fiscal services	283,000			283,000
Administrative services	791,000			791,000
Total expenses and losses	$ 5,083,000			$ 5,083,000
Increase (decrease) in net assets from operations ...	$ (41,000)	$ 350,000		$ 309,000
Nonoperating revenue	$ 720,606	$ 75,000	$ 500,000	$ 1,295,606
Increase (decrease) in net assets	**$ 679,606**	**$ 425,000**	**$ 500,000**	**$ 1,604,606**
Net assets at beginning of year	**4,538,000**	**879,000**	**3,560,000**	**8,977,000**
Net assets at end of year	**$5,217,606**	**$1,304,000**	**$4,060,000**	**$10,581,606**

Illustration 12-10
Columbia Hospital
Statement of Financial Position
As of December 31, 20X5

Assets:		
Cash and cash equivalents	$	735,000
Accounts and interest receivable		908,000
Inventories		81,000
Contributions receivable		265,606
Short-term investments		400,000
Assets restricted to investment in land, buildings, and equipment		445,000
Assets limited in use under malpractice funding agreement		440,000
Property, plant, and equipment (net of depreciation)		5,250,000
Long-term investments		540,000
Endowment investments		4,060,000
Total assets		**$13,124,606**
Liabilities and net assets:		
Accounts payable	$	53,000
Current installments of long-term debts		80,000
Accrued expenses		100,000
Notes payable		500,000
Estimated malpractice costs		640,000
Long-term debt		1,170,000
Total liabilities		**$ 2,543,000**
Net assets:		
Unrestricted		**$ 5,217,606**
Temporarily restricted		**1,304,000**
Permanently restricted		**4,060,000**
Total net assets		**$10,581,606**
Total liabilities and net assets		**$13,124,606**

Governmental Health Care Organizations

Governmental health care organizations are classified as special purpose governments engaged only in business-type activities. As such, they will present the financial statements required for organizations that use proprietary fund accounting. Many government health care organizations are also component units of another government, e.g., a university hospital, county health care organization or hospital, and state hospitals.

REFLECTION

- Private health care organizations follow FASB standards.

- Governmental health care organizations will report as special purpose governments engaged in business-type activities and, as such, follow FASB standards.

- Contractual agreements, courtesy care, and charity care are reductions from patient services revenue. The provision for bad debts is recorded as an expense.

- Many health care organizations use fund accounting for internal control and decision making, but funds are not required in the external financial reports.

Illustration 12-11
Columbia Hospital
Statement of Cash Flows
For Year Ended December 31, 20X5

Cash flows from operating activities:	
Cash received from patients and third-party payors	$ 3,800,000
Cash received from contributions	450,000
Interest and dividends received	615,000
Cash paid to employees and suppliers	(3,990,000)
Interest paid	(66,000)
Net cash provided by (used for) operating activities	**$ 809,000**
Cash flows from investing activities:	
Purchases of investments	$ (500,000)
Purchases of land, buildings, and equipment	(310,000)
Net cash provided by (used for) investing activities	**$ (810,000)**
Cash flows from financing activities:	
Payments on notes payable	$ (200,000)
Payments on long-term debt	(80,000)
Contributions received restricted for endowment	500,000
Contributions received restricted for property, plant, and equipment	200,000
Net cash provided by (used for) financing activities	**$ 420,000**
Net increase (decrease) in cash and cash equivalents	**$ 419,000**
Cash and cash equivalents at beginning of year	**316,000**
Cash and cash equivalents at end of year	**$ 735,000**
Reconciliation of change in net assets to net cash provided by (used for) operating activities:	
Change in net assets	$ 1,604,606
Adjustments to reconcile change in net assets to net cash provided by (used for) operating activities:	
Depreciation	440,000
Increase in accounts receivable	(798,000)
Increase in contributions receivable	(265,606)
Decrease in inventories	18,000
Increase in accounts payable and accrued liabilities	60,000
Contributions received restricted for endowment	(500,000)
Contributions received restricted for property, plant, and equipment	(200,000)
Increase in liability for estimated malpractice costs	450,000
Net cash provided by (used for operating activities)	**$ 809,000**

UNDERSTANDING THE ISSUES

1. How is it helpful for a private not-for-profit organization to account for current funds as restricted or unrestricted?

2. The FASB requires for-profit entities to classify their investments as trading, available-for-sale, or held-to-maturity. However, it does not require not-for-profit entities to do the same. What might be the reasoning for this difference in requirements? Which approach is more beneficial to the readers of the financial statements of a not-for-profit organization? Why?

3. Differentiate between public support and revenues as sources of assets for private not-for-profit organizations. What benefit is there in accounting for these differently?

4. Explain the accounting for funds received by an organization acting as an agent, trustee, or intermediary, rather than as a donor or donee. What might be the reasoning for the differences?

5. A voluntary health and welfare organization is required to present an additional financial statement that is not required of other private not-for-profit entities. Why is this an important statement?

6. Explain how restricted gifts and grants are accounted for by colleges and universities.

7. Distinguish assets limited as to use from restricted assets.

8. Explain a hospital's rigid adherence to gross revenue determination.

9. What is the special concern over accounting for medical malpractice claims? How does accounting for such claims compare to accounting for contingencies in a for-profit business environment?

EXERCISES

Exercise 12-1 *(LO 1, 2, 6)* **Understanding not-for-profit financial statements.** Go to the Web site of a not-for-profit organization. Are audited financial statements provided on the Web site? Is other financial information made available? Assuming you are a potential donor, evaluate its performance compared with similar organizations. What benchmarks (or industry averages) for this type of not-for-profit did you use in your evaluation? Were they financial or nonfinancial indicators of performance? [*Hint:* Goodwill Industries is a not-for-profit organization (http://www.goodwill.org). The National Charities Information Bureau (http://www.give.org) and the Council of Better Business Bureau (CBBB) Philanthropic Advisory Service (http://www.bbb.org) have comparison data on not-for-profit organizations.]

Exercise 12-2 *(LO 4, 6)* **Contributions, statement of activities.** Early in 20X8, a not-for-profit organization received a $4,000,000 gift from a wealthy benefactor. This benefactor specified that the gift be invested in perpetuity with income restricted to provide speaker fees for a lecture series named for the benefactor. The not-for-profit is permitted to choose suitable investments and is responsible for all other costs associated with initiating and administering this series. Neither the donor's stipulation nor the law addresses gains and losses on this permanent endowment. In 20X8, the investments purchased with the gift earned $100,000 in dividend income. The fair value of the investments increased by $240,000.

Three presentations in the lecture series were held in 20X8. The speaker fees for the three presentations amounted to $140,000. The not-for-profit organization used the $100,000 dividend income to cover part of the total fees. Because the board of directors did not wish to sell part of the investments, the organization used $40,000 in unrestricted resources to pay the remainder of the speaker fees.

For items (1) through (5), determine whether the transaction should be recorded in the 20X8 statement of activities as an increase in:

A. Unrestricted net assets.
B. Temporarily restricted net assets.
C. Permanently restricted net assets.
D. Either unrestricted or temporarily restricted net assets.

1. The receipt of the $4,000,000 gift
2. The $100,000 in dividend income assuming the not-for-profit's accounting policy is to record increases in net assets, for which a donor-imposed restriction is met in the same

accounting period as gains and investment income are recognized, as increases in unrestricted net assets

3. The $240,000 unrealized gain
4. The $100,000 in dividend income, assuming the lecture series is not to begin until 20X9
5. The $240,000 unrealized gain, assuming the lecture series is not to begin until 20X9

Exercise 12-3 *(LO 1, 3, 8, 9)* **Comparison of accounting for VHWO and governmental organizations.** Distinguish between accounting and financial reporting for state and local governments and VHWOs for the following issues:

a. Measurement focus and basis of accounting
b. Revenue recognition
c. Expenses or expenditures
d. Capital assets

Exercise 12-4 *(LO 9)* **VHWO, statement of activities.** The Better Life Clinic is a VHWO that has three main programs:

    Drug rehabilitation
    Alcohol recovery
    Weight control

Unrestricted public support received during the period was $35,000; revenues from membership services were $12,000. The following expenses and allocations to program and supporting services are shown for 20X0. Better Life elects to release donor restrictions for property, plant, and equipment over the useful life of the asset.

Item	Amount	Drug Rehab.	Alcohol Recovery	Weight Control	Fund Raising	Gen. & Adm.
			Distribution			
Secretarial salary................	$ 5,000					100%
Office supplies..................	6,000	20%	10%	10%	10%	50
Printing	8,000	10	10	20	50	10
Depreciation (All depreciation is on assets acquired with donor-restricted contributions.) . . .	4,000	20	20	20		40
Instruction	9,000	30	25	35	10	
Rent..........................	10,000	30	20	30		20

Temporarily restricted net assets totaled $30,000 on January 1; the unrestricted net asset balance was $12,000. Prepare a statement of activities for the year.

Exercise 12-5 *(LO 10)* **VHWO, journal entries.** Record the following events of the Chemical Dependency Clinic, a VHWO:

1. Membership dues of $9,000 were collected.
2. Cash contributions of $22,000 and pledges for $32,000 were received.
3. It is estimated that 10% of the above pledges will prove uncollectible.
4. A fund-raising dinner grossed $12,000 from the sale of 480 tickets. The catered dinner cost $15 each for the 420 people who attended, plus $200 for the rental of the dining room. Payment for these costs was made.
5. A classic car was donated to the organization. The car has an estimated fair value of $75,000. It will be the main attraction of an auction to be held in the next accounting period. The proceeds of the auction are part of the budget for activities in the next period.
6. To expand the services of the clinic, a professional fund-raising group was hired to undertake a six-month campaign. At the end of the six months, the group submitted the following report:

Cash collected.	$ 70,000
Pledges (estimated to be 95% collectible)	30,000
Total proceeds.	$100,000
Less 20% fund-raising fee (regardless of collections).	20,000
Net proceeds from drive	$ 80,000

Exercise 12-6 *(LO 10)* **VHWO, journal entries.** Record the following events of the Mental Health Clinic, a VHWO:

1. A contribution of $10,000 was received and is to be used for the purchase of equipment, but not until an addition to the building is constructed. Construction has begun on the building.
2. Equipment costing $17,000, with a book value of $8,000, was sold for $10,000. The gain is unrestricted.
3. Depreciation of $9,000 is recorded on various plant items.
4. Equipment was purchased for $12,000, with payment due in 30 days from donor-restricted resources. Mental Health Clinic elects to release the donor restriction upon acquisition of the equipment.
5. The liability for the equipment purchased in item (4) was paid.

Exercise 12-7 *(LO 10)* **VHWO, journal entries.** Record the following events of Mercy Health Clinic, a VHWO:

1. In her will, a leading citizen left a bequest of $200,000 to the clinic. Stipulations were that the amount was to become the corpus of a permanent endowment. Any income received would be used first to cover any loss of principal, with the remaining revenue to be used for an educational program on mental problems. The total amount was received and invested in 8% municipal bonds purchased at face value on an interest date.
2. Three months later, half of the bond investment was sold at 101, plus $2,500 of accrued interest.
3. The remaining endowment bond investments earned $6,000. The amount is not subject to any limitations.
4. At year-end, the remaining endowment bond investments have a fair value of $ 103,500.

Exercise 12-8 *(LO X)* **Private university, contributions.** Indicate (with choices a–f) how the following events are recorded in a private university:

a. Credit Contributions—Unrestricted
b. Credit Contributions—Temporarily Restricted
c. Credit Contributions—Permanently Restricted
d. Credit Refundable Deposits
e. Credit Fund Balance
f. No entry

1. Receipt of an unconditional promise to give. _____
2. Receipt of a fixed asset with donor-specified use for an outreach program. _____
3. Receipt of an unconditional cash contribution. _____
4. Receipt of cash to be used for a specific purpose. _____
5. Receipt of free accounting services. _____
6. Receipt of time of volunteers who helped with fund-raising mailings. _____
7. Receipt of an unconditional promise to give over a five-year period. _____
8. Receipt of investments that are to be used to set up an endowment with earnings available for operations. _____

9. Receipt of a conditional promise to give.   _____

10. Receipt of a fixed asset with no donor restriction.   _____

11. Receipt of a cash contribution to be used next year for a
    research project.   _____

12. Receipt of a cash contribution to be used next year for
    general operations at the discretion of management.   _____

13. Receipt of cash as part of a government grant funding a
    cancer research project. A report with research results will
    be prepared for the government funding agency.   _____

14. Receipt of a cash contribution to be used for acquisition
    of fixed assets.   _____

15. Receipt of a permanent collection of geography maps that
    will be displayed to the public.   _____

Exercise 12-9 *(LO 12, 13)* **Health care, revenues.** A hospital has three revenue-controlling accounts: Patient Service Revenue, Other Operating Revenue, and Nonoperating Revenue.

a. State in general terms the type of revenue found in each controlling account.
b. Indicate into which of the three controlling accounts each of the following would be placed by using the symbols PS for Patient Service Revenue, OO for Other Operating Revenue, N for Nonoperating Revenue, and N/A if not a revenue item:

1. Tuition for entry to the nursing school.   _____

2. An unrestricted gift of cash.   _____

3. General nursing fees charged to patients.   _____

4. Charges for physicians' care.   _____

5. A restricted gift used for research on genes.   _____

6. Dividends from the hospital's investments.   _____

7. Revenue from gift shop sales.   _____

8. Patient room and board charges.   _____

9. Proceeds from sales of cafeteria meals.   _____

10. Recovery room fees.   _____

11. Contributions for plant replacement and expansion.   _____

Exercise 12-10 *(LO 12, 13, 14)* **Health care, revenues, expenses, contributions.** Record the following events of Elmwood Hospital.

a. Patients were billed for the following gross charges:

Room and board..........	$680,000
Physicians' care...........	220,000
Laboratory and radiology...	110,000

b. A donation of drugs with a fair value of $12,000 was received from a doctor. The drugs are normally purchased.
c. Revenues were reported from:

Newsstand and snack bar ...	$15,800
Parking lot charges	3,200
Vending machines	9,800

d. A charity allowance of $13,000 was granted to indigent patients.
e. Contractual adjustments granted to patients for Medicare charges totaled $68,000.
f. The hospital recorded an increase in the provision of $26,000 for uncollectible receivables.

Exercise 12-11 *(LO 16)* **Health care, statement of activities.** The Pure Air Rehabilitation Hospital has the following balances that are extracted from its December 31, 20X7, trial balance:

Account	Debit	Credit
Nursing Services Expense	230,000	
Professional Fees Expense	340,000	
General and Administrative Expense	150,000	
Depreciation Expense	90,000	
Interest Expense	13,000	
Asset Whose Use Is Limited	55,000	
Repairs and Maintenance Expense	110,000	
Provision for Uncollectible Accounts	14,000	
Contractual Adjustments	26,000	
Patient Service Revenue		740,000
Income, Seminars		23,000
Child Day Care Revenue		15,000
Parking Fees		4,500
Endowment Income—Temporarily Restricted		120,000
Interest Income—Unrestricted		3,000
Donations—Temporarily Restricted		18,000
Gains (Distributable) on Sale of Endowments—Temporarily Restricted		56,000
Net Assets—Unrestricted (January 1, 20X7)		800,000
Net Assets—Temporarily Restricted (January 1, 20X7)		755,000
Net Assets—Permanently Restricted (January 1, 20X7)		750,000

From the above information, prepare a statement of activities for the year ended December 31, 20X7.

Exercise 12-12 *(LO 12, 13, 14)* **Health care, financial statement impact of transactions.** Alpha Hospital, a nongovernmental not-for-profit organization, has adopted an accounting policy that does not imply a time restriction on gifts of long-lived assets. For items (1) through (6), indicate the manner in which the transaction affects Alpha's financial statements.

A. Increase in unrestricted revenues, gains, and other support.
B. Decrease in an expense.
C. Increase in temporarily restricted net assets.
D. Increase in permanently restricted net assets.
E. No required reportable event.

1. Alpha's board designates $1,000,000 to purchase investments whose income will be used for capital improvements.
2. Income from investments in item (1) above, which was not previously accrued, is received.
3. A benefactor provided funds for building expansion.
4. The funds in item (3) above are used to purchase a building in the fiscal period following the period the funds were received.
5. An accounting firm prepared Alpha's annual financial statements without charge to Alpha.
6. Alpha received investments subject to the donor's requirement that investment income be used to pay for outpatient services.

(AICPA adapted)

PROBLEMS

Problem 12-1 *(LO 3, 4, 6)* **FASB Nos. 116 and 117, contributions.** Select the best answer for each of the following multiple-choice items dealing with not-for-profit organizations.

1. Under FASB No. 117, which of the following statements is *true?*
   a. All not-for-profit organizations must include a statement of functional expenses.
   b. Donor-restricted contributions whose restrictions have been met in the reporting period may be reported as unrestricted support.
   c. Statements should focus on the individual unrestricted and restricted funds of the organization.
   d. FASB No. 117 contains requirements that are generally more stringent than those relating to for-profit organizations.

2. Which of the following factors, if present, would indicate that a transaction is *not* a contribution under FASB No. 116?
   a. The resource provider entered into the transaction voluntarily.
   b. The resource provider received value in exchange.
   c. The transfer of assets was unconditional.
   d. The organization has discretion in the use of the assets received.

3. Securities donated to voluntary health and welfare organizations should be recorded
   a. at the donor's recorded amount.
   b. at fair value at the date of the gift.
   c. at fair value at the date of the gift or the donor's recorded amount, whichever is lower.
   d. at fair value at the date of the gift or the donor's recorded amount, whichever is higher.

4. Which of the following is *not* a criterion that must be met under FASB No. 116 for contributed services?
   a. They are provided by persons possessing required skills.
   b. They are provided by licensed professionals.
   c. They create or enhance nonfinancial assets.
   d. They would typically have to be purchased if not provided by the donors/volunteers.

5. Which of the following criteria would suggest that a not-for-profit capitalize its works of art, historical treasures, or similar assets?
   a. They are held for public inspection, education, or research in furtherance of public service rather than financial gain.
   b. They are protected, kept unencumbered, cared for, and preserved.
   c. They are subject to be used in the acquisition of other items for the collection.
   d. They are held primarily to be resold for financial gain.

Problem 12-2 *(LO 8, 9)* **VHWO, accounting and reporting.** Select the best answer for each of the following multiple-choice items. Items (1) through (3) are based on the following:

    The Bay Ridge Humane Society, a VHWO caring for lost animals, had the following financial inflows and outflows for the year ended December 31, 20X5:

Inflows:

Cash received from federated campaign	$680,000
Cash received that is designated for 20X6 operations	30,000
Contributions pledged for 20X5, not yet received	90,000
Contributions pledged for 20X6, not yet received	25,000
Sales of pet supplies	10,000
Pet adoption fees	50,000

Outflows:

Kennel operations	$350,000
Pet health care	100,000
Advertising pets for adoption	50,000
Fund raising	70,000
Administrative and general	200,000

1. In the humane society's statement of activities for the year ended December 31, 20X5, what amount should be reported under the classification of public support—unrestricted?

   a. $740,000
   b. $762,000
   c. $770,000
   d. $825,000

2. In the humane society's statement of activities for the year ended December 31, 20X5, what amount should be reported under the classification of program services expense?

   a. $770,000
   b. $450,000
   c. $550,000
   d. $500,000

3. In the humane society's balance sheet as of December 31, 20X5, what amount should be reported under the classification of public support—temporarily restricted?

   a. $55,000
   b. $30,000
   c. $25,000
   d. $0

4. Arbor Haven, a voluntary welfare organization funded by contributions from the general public, received unrestricted pledges of $500,000 during 20X6. It was estimated that 12% of these pledges would be uncollectible. By the end of 20X6, $400,000 of the pledges had been collected, and it was expected that $40,000 more would be collected in 20X7, with the balance of $60,000 to be written off as uncollectible. Donors did not specify any periods during which the donations were to be used. What amount should Arbor Haven include under public support in 20X6 for contributions?

   a. $500,000
   b. $452,000
   c. $440,000
   d. $400,000

5. The following expenditures were among those incurred by a voluntary welfare organization during 20X7:

Printing of annual report	$10,000
Unsolicited merchandise sent to encourage contributions.	20,000

   What amount should be classified as fund-raising costs in the society's statement of activities?

   a. $0
   b. $10,000
   c. $20,000
   d. $30,000

6. Apex Inc. donated a computer to Bird Shelter, a voluntary welfare organization. The computer cost Apex $40,000. On the date of donation, it had a book value of $25,000 and a fair value of $20,000. Bird Shelter's depreciation expense should be based on

   a. $40,000.
   b. $25,000.
   c. $20,000.
   d. $15,000.

Problem 12-3 *(LO 5, 7, 8, 9)* **Expenses.** Select the best answer for each of the following multiple-choice items. (No. 1 is AICPA adapted.)

1. In the statement of activities of a not-for-profit, depreciation expense should

   a. be included as an element of expense.
   b. be included as an element of other changes in fund balances.
   c. be included as an element of support.
   d. not be included.

2. Environs, a community foundation, incurred $10,000 in management and general expenses during 20X1. In Environs' statement of activities for the year ended December 31, 20X1, the $10,000 should be reported as

   a. a direct reduction of unrestricted net assets.
   b. part of supporting services expense.
   c. part of program services expense.
   d. a contra account to offset revenue and support.

3. Super Seniors is a not-for-profit organization that provides services to senior citizens. Super employs a full-time staff of 10 people at an annual cost of $150,000. In addition, two volunteers work as part-time secretaries replacing last year's full-time secretary who earned $10,000. Services performed by other volunteers for special events had an estimated value of $15,000. These volunteers were employees of local businesses, and they received small-value items for their participation. What amount should Super report for salary and wage expenses related to the above items?

   a. $150,000
   b. $160,000
   c. $165,000
   d. $175,000

4. The League, a not-for-profit organization, received the following pledges:

Unrestricted	$200,000
Restricted for capital additions	150,000

   All pledges are legally enforceable; however, the League's experience indicates that 10% of all pledges prove to be uncollectible. What amount should the League report as pledges receivable net of any required allowance account?

   a. $135,000
   b. $180,000
   c. $315,000
   d. $350,000

5. When a nonprofit organization combines fund-raising efforts with bona fide educational efforts or program services, the total combined costs incurred are

   a. reported as program services expenses.
   b. allocated between fund-raising and program services expenses using an appropriate allocation basis.
   c. reported as fund-raising costs.
   d. reported as management and general expenses.

Problem 12-4 *(LO 3, 4, 7, 8, 9)* **Assets.** Select the best answer for each of the following multiple-choice questions.

1. A VHWO receives a donation that is restricted to its endowment and another donation that is restricted to use in acquiring a child care center. How should these donations be reported in the year received, assuming neither donation is expended in that year?

	Donation for Endowment	Donation for Child Care Center
a.	Contributions—Temporarily Restricted	Contributions—Temporarily Restricted
b.	Deferred Capital Additions	Capital Additions
c.	Contributions—Unrestricted	Contributions—Unrestricted
d.	Capital Additions Deferred	Capital Additions
e.	Contributions—Permanently Restricted	Contributions—Temporarily Restricted

2. Donor-restricted contributions that have been given to a VHWO for the purpose of purchasing fixed assets should be recorded as increases to

   a. Unrestricted Net Assets.
   b. Temporarily Restricted Net Assets.
   c. Permanently Restricted Net Assets.
   d. Fund Balance—Restricted.

3. The following correct entry is found on the books of a VHWO:

Unrestricted Net Assets—Undesignated	XXX	
Unrestricted Net Assets—Designated for AIDS Research		XXX

   From the entry, one should conclude that the board of directors has

   a. designated a portion of the unrestricted net assets for a future AIDS research program.
   b. designated a portion of the restricted net assets for a future AIDS research program.
   c. transferred resources to an AIDS research program.
   d. directed that unused resources previously assigned to an AIDS research program be returned to unrestricted net asset classification.

4. Friends of the Forest received a donation of marketable equity securities from a member. The securities had appreciated in value after they were purchased by the donor, and they continued to appreciate through the end of Friends of the Forest's fiscal year. At what amount should Friends of the Forest report its investment in marketable equity securities in its year-end balance sheet?

   a. Donor's cost
   b. Fair value at the date of receipt
   c. Fair value at the balance sheet date
   d. Fair value at either the date of receipt or the balance sheet date

5. The investments of a VHWO are carried at fair value. At the end of the period, there is a decrease in total fair value. The fair value decrease should

   a. not be recorded until the loss is realized.
   b. be debited to Realized Loss on Pooled Investments.
   c. be debited to Endowment Fund Balance.
   d. be debited to Net Decrease in Carrying Value of Investments.

(AICPA adapted)

Problem 12-5 *(LO 9, 10)* Journal entries, statement of activities.

The following selected events relate to the 20X7 activities of Aires Nursing Home, Inc., a not-for-profit agency:

a. Gross patient service revenue totaled $2,200,000. The provision for uncollectible accounts was estimated at $92,000. The allowance for contractual adjustments was increased by $120,000.
b. After a conference with representatives of Gold Star Insurance Company, differences between the amounts accrued and subsequent settlements reduced receivables by $60,000.
c. A grateful patient donated securities with a cost of $20,000 and a fair value at date of donation of $75,000. The donation was restricted to expenditure for modernization of equipment. The donation was accepted.
d. Cash of $37,000 that had been restricted by a donor for the purchase of furniture was used this year. Aires chose to release the donor restriction over the useful life of the asset.

e. The board voluntarily transferred $50,000 of cash to add to the resources held for capital improvements.
f. Pledges of $60,000 and cash of $20,000 were received to defer operating expenses. Of the pledges, 10% are considered uncollectible. Term endowments of $10,000 matured and were released to cover operations.
g. Equipment costing $250,000 was purchased on account. Restricted resources held for that purpose will be released from restriction over the useful life of the asset.
h. The nursing home uses functional operating expense control accounts. Expenses for the year were as follows:

Nursing services	$1,120,000
Dietary services	230,000
Maintenance services	115,000
Administrative services	285,000
Interest	160,000
Subtotal (of which $253,000 is unpaid)	$1,910,000
Depreciation [$20,000 from assets purchased with resources in items (d) and (g) above]	60,000
Total	$1,970,000

Required ▶ ▶ ▶ ▶ ▶
1. Omitting explanations, prepare journal entries for the foregoing events.
2. Prepare a statement of activities for the year ended December 31, 20X7.

Problem 12-6 *(LO 10)* **Journal entries.** The Super Senior Agency is a VHWO. The following events occurred during the year. The agency uses one control account for its fixed assets, with supporting subsidiary records.

a. Property was purchased for $200,000. A down payment of $40,000 was made from unrestricted cash, and a 14% mortgage was signed for the remainder.
b. Office furniture was purchased for $9,000 on open account.
c. A local corporation donated and installed room partitions. The value of the donated items and services was $4,000. Super Senior's policy is to release donor restrictions over the useful life of the assets to match depreciation expense.
d. At year-end, a payment was made covering mortgage interest for one year, plus a $10,000 payment on the principal.
e. Office equipment costing $3,000, with a book value of $1,000, was sold for $1,800 cash. The gain is unrestricted.
f. Fully depreciated equipment costing $7,000 was written off. There was no scrap value.
g. A depreciation schedule was prepared, showing annual depreciation expense of $46,000, which was recorded. Depreciation of $20,000 was for equipment donated or purchased with donated cash.
h. Two years ago, the will of an agency volunteer granted $50,000 for the acquisition and installation of theater equipment, providing the organization acquired a new building. The amount now was expended in accordance with the stipulations of the will, and payment of $50,000 was made.

Required ▶ ▶ ▶ ▶ ▶ Prepare journal entries to record the preceding events.

Problem 12-7 *(LO 10)* **Journal entries.** Carleton Agency, a VHWO, conducts two programs: Medical Services and Community Information Services. It had the following transactions during the year ended June 30, 20X9:

1. Received the following contributions:

Unrestricted pledges	$800,000
Restricted cash	95,000

Building fund pledges	....	50,000
Endowment fund cash	....	1,000

2. Collected the following pledges:

Unrestricted	....	$450,000
Building fund	....	20,000

3. Received the following unrestricted cash flows from:

Theater party (net of direct costs)	....	$12,000
Bequests	....	10,000
Membership dues	....	8,000
Interest and dividends	....	5,000

4. Program expenses incurred (processed through vouchers payable):

Medical services	....	$60,000
Community information services	....	15,000

5. Services expenses incurred (processed through vouchers payable):

General administration	....	$150,000
Fund raising	....	200,000

6. Purchased fixed assets:

Fixed assets purchased with donor-restricted cash	....	$18,000

Carleton's policy is to release donor restrictions when assets are placed in service.

7. Depreciation of all buildings and equipment in the land, buildings, and equipment fund was allocated as follows:

Medical services program	....	$4,000
Community information services program	....	3,000
General administration	....	6,000
Fund raising	....	2,000

8. Vouchers paid:

Paid vouchers payable	....	$330,000

(AICPA adapted)

Record journal entries for the preceding transactions. Number your journal entries to coincide with the preceding transaction numbers. ◄ ◄ ◄ ◄ ◄ **Required**

Problem 12-8 *(LO 8, 9, 10)* **Allocation of expenses, journal entries.** The Caring Clinic, a VHWO, conducts two programs: Alcohol and Drug Abuse and Outreach to Teens. It has the typical supporting services of management and fund raising. Expense accounts from the preallocation trial balances as of December 31, 20X7, are as follows:

	Funded by Unrestricted Resources	Funded by Donor-Restricted Resources	Total
Salaries and Payroll Taxes	63,000	23,000	86,000
Telephone and Miscellaneous Expenses	10,000	2,000	12,000
Nursing and Medical Fees	70,000	50,000	120,000
			(continued)

	Funded by Unrestricted Resources	Funded by Donor-Restricted Resources	Total
Educational Seminars Expense	46,000	20,000	66,000
Research Expense	137,000	16,000	153,000
Medical Supplies Expense.	65,000	22,000	87,000
Rent Expense		10,000	10,000
Interest Expense on Equipment Mortgage	4,000		4,000
Depreciation Expense		20,000	20,000
Provision for Uncollectible Pledges	26,000		26,000
Totals	421,000	163,000	584,000

In preparation for the allocation of expenses to programs and supporting services, a study was conducted to determine an equitable manner for assigning each expense. The study resulted in the following table for percentage allocations:

Percentage of Allocations

	Programs		Supporting Services	
	Alcohol and	Outreach to		
Expenses to Be Allocated	Drug Abuse	Teens	Management	Fund Raising
All expenses (other than depreciation) financed by				
donor-restricted contributions	60%	40%		
Expenses financed by unrestricted resources:				
Salaries and payroll taxes	30	20	30%	20%
Telephone and miscellaneous	20	20	15	45
Nursing and medical fees	70	30		
Educational seminars.	30	60		10
Research	60	40		
Medical supplies	90	10		
Equipment-related expenses:				
Interest.	50	10	30	10
Depreciation	50	10	30	10

Required ▶ ▶ ▶ ▶ ▶

1. Using a total of allocable expenses financed by donor-restricted resources, prepare a journal entry to assign those expenses to the programs.

2. With the following format, prepare a schedule to show the assignment of the allocable expenses financed by unrestricted resources to the various programs and supporting services, using the percentages provided by the problem.

Caring Clinic Allocation of Expenses Financed by Unrestricted Resources
For Year Ended December 31, 20X7

		Programs		Supporting Services	
Expense Allocated	Total Amount	Alcohol and Drug Abuse	Outreach to Teens	Management	Fund Raising

3. Using the schedule from requirement (2), prepare a journal entry to record the allocation and closing of expenses financed by unrestricted resources.
4. Prepare a journal entry to assign plant-related expenses to programs and support services.

 Problem 12-9 *(LO 9)* **Statement of functional expenses.** From the expense accounts information and allocation schedule shown in Problem 12-8, prepare a statement of functional expenses for the Caring Clinic for the year ended December 31, 20X7.

Problem 12-10 *(LO 11)* **Public and private universities, multiple-choice.** Select the best answer for each of the following multiple-choice items dealing with universities:

1. For the 20X7 fall semester, Brook Public University assessed its students $4,000,000 (net of refunds), covering tuition and fees for educational and general purposes. However, only $3,700,000 was expected to be realized because tuition remissions of $80,000 were allowed to faculty members' children attending Brook, and scholarships totaling $220,000 were granted to students. What amount should Brook include in educational and general current funds revenues from student tuition and fees?

    a. $4,000,000
    b. $3,920,000
    c. $3,780,000
    d. $3,700,000

2. Private College is sponsored by a religious group. Volunteers from this religious group regularly contribute their skilled services to Private and are paid nominal amounts to cover their commuting costs. If Private did not receive these volunteer services, it would have to purchase similar services. During 20X6, the total amount paid to these volunteers was $12,000. The gross value of services performed by them, as determined by reference to lay-equivalent salaries, amounted to $300,000. What amount should Private record as expenses in 20X6 for these volunteers' services?

    a. $312,000
    b. $300,000
    c. $12,000
    d. $0

3. Abbott Public University's unrestricted current fund comprised the following:

Assets.	$5,000,000
Liabilities (including deferred revenues of $100,000)	3,000,000

    The fund balance of Abbott's unrestricted current fund was

    a. $1,900,000.
    b. $2,000,000.
    c. $2,100,000.
    d. $5,000,000.

4. The following receipts are among those recorded by Curry Private College during 20X9:

Unrestricted gifts	$500,000
Restricted gifts (expended for current operating purposes)	200,000
Restricted gifts (not yet expended)	100,000

    The amount that should be included in revenues is

    a. $800,000.
    b. $700,000.
    c. $600,000.
    d. $500,000.

5. In 20X7, the board of trustees of Burr Private University designated $100,000 from its current funds for college scholarships. Also in 20X7, the university received a bequest of $200,000 from an estate of a benefactor who specified that the bequest was to be used for hiring teachers to tutor handicapped students. None of the bequest has been spent. What amount should be accounted for as restricted net assets?

    a. $0
    b. $100,000
    c. $200,000
    d. $300,000

6. The following information pertains to interest received by Beech Public University from endowment fund investments for the year ended June 30, 20X8:

	Received	Expended for Current Operations
Unrestricted	$300,000	$100,000
Restricted	500,000	75,000

What amount should be credited to endowment income for the year ended June 30, 20X8?

a. $800,000
b. $375,000
c. $175,000
d. $100,000

7. On July 31, 20X8, Sabio Public College showed the following amounts to be used for:

Renewal and replacement of college properties	$200,000
Retirement of indebtedness on college properties	300,000
Purchase of physical properties for college purposes, but unexpended at July 31, 20X8	400,000

What total amount should be included in Sabio's plant funds at July 31, 20X8?

a. $900,000
b. $600,000
c. $400,000
d. $200,000

8. The following expenditures were among those incurred by Cheviot Public University during 20X7:

Administrative data processing	$ 50,000
Scholarships and fellowships	100,000
Operation and maintenance of physical plant	200,000

The amount to be included in the functional classification "Institutional Support" expenditures account is

a. $50,000.
b. $150,000.
c. $250,000.
d. $350,000.

9. Assets that the governing board of a public university, rather than a donor or outside agency, has determined are to be retained and invested for purposes other than loan or plant would be accounted for as

a. an endowment.
b. unrestricted net assets.
c. deposits held in custody for others.
d. restricted net assets.

10. Which of the following statements usually will not be included in the annual financial report of a public university engaged only in business-type activities?

a. Statement of activities
b. Statement of net assets
c. Statement of cash flows
d. Statement of revenues, expenses, and changes in net assets

(AICPA adapted)

Problem 12-11 *(LO 11)* **Public and private universities, multiple-choice.** Select the best answer for each of the following multiple-choice items. (Nos. 1–11 are AICPA adapted.)

1. An alumnus donates securities to Rex Private College and stipulates that the principal be held in perpetuity and revenues be used for faculty travel. Dividends received from the securities should be recognized as revenues in

    a. endowment funds.
    b. quasi-endowment funds.
    c. restricted current funds.
    d. unrestricted current funds.

2. A private college's plant funds group includes which of the following subgroups?

    (1) Renewals and replacement funds
    (2) Retirement of indebtedness funds
    (3) Restricted current funds

    a. 1 and 2
    b. 1 and 3
    c. 2 and 3
    d. None of the above

3. Funds received by a private college from donors who have stipulated that the principal is nonexpendable but the income generated may be expended for current operating needs would be accounted for as

    a. contributions—permanently restricted.
    b. contributions—temporarily restricted.
    c. contributions—unrestricted.
    d. fund balance increases.

4. The following funds were among those held by State College at December 31, 20X1:

Principal specified by the donor as nonexpendable	$500,000
Principal expendable after the year 20X9	300,000
Principal designated from unrestricted net assets	100,000

    What amount should State College classify as permanently restricted endowments?

    a. $100,000
    b. $300,000
    c. $500,000
    d. $900,000

5. In 20X2, State University's board of trustees established a $100,000 fund to be retained and invested for scholarship grants. In 20X2, the fund earned $6,000, which had not been disbursed at December 31, 20X2. What amount should State report as unrestricted investment earnings at December 31, 20X2?

    a. $0
    b. $6,000
    c. $100,000
    d. $106,000

6. On January 2, 20X2, a graduate of Oak Private College established a permanent trust fund and appointed Security Bank as the trustee. The income from the trust fund is to be paid to Oak and used only by the School of Business to support student scholarships. What entry is required on Oak's books to record the receipt of cash from the interest on the trust fund?

    a. Debit Cash and credit Deferred Revenues
    b. Debit Cash and credit Temporarily Restricted Endowment Revenue
    c. Debit Cash and credit Temporarily Restricted Contributions
    d. Debit Cash and credit Unrestricted Endowment Revenue

7. At the end of the year, Cramer Private University's balance sheet comprised $15,000,000 of assets and $9,000,000 of liabilities (including deferred revenues of $300,000). What is the balance of Cramer's net assets?

    a. $5,700,000
    b. $6,000,000
    c. $6,300,000
    d. $15,000,000

8. Financial resources of a college or university that are currently expendable at the discretion of the governing board and that have not been restricted externally nondesignated by the board for a specific purpose should be reported in the balance sheet as

    a. board-designated current funds.
    b. permanently restricted net assets.
    c. unrestricted net assets.
    d. temporarily restricted net assets.

9. Which of the following accounts would appear in the plant fund of a not-for-profit private college?

	Fuel Inventory for Power Plant	Equipment
a.	Yes	Yes
b.	No	Yes
c.	No	No
d.	Yes	No

10. Which of the following is required as part of the complete set of financial statements for a private college or university?

    a. Statement of changes in financial position
    b. Statement of activities
    c. Statement of revenues, expenses, and changes in net assets
    d. None of the above

Problem 12-12 *(LO 12, 13, 14)* **Health care, multiple-choice.** Select the best answer for each of the following multiple-choice items dealing with hospitals.

1. On March 1, 20X8, A. C. Rowe established a $100,000 endowment fund, the income from which is to be paid to Elm Hospital for general operating purposes. Elm does not control the fund's principal. Rowe appointed West National Bank as trustee of this fund. What journal entry is required by Elm to record the establishment of the endowment?

    a. Cash 100,000
           Nonexpendable Endowment Fund 100,000

    b. Cash 100,000
           Nonoperating Revenue 100,000

    c. Nonexpendable Endowment Fund 100,000
           Endowment Fund Balance 100,000

    d. A memorandum entry only.

2. In 20X8, Wells Hospital received an unrestricted bequest of common stock with a fair value of $50,000 on the date of receipt of the stock. The testator had paid $20,000 for this stock in 20X6. Wells should record this bequest as

    a. nonoperating revenue of $50,000.
    b. nonoperating revenue of $30,000.

   c. nonoperating revenue of $20,000.

   d. a memorandum entry only.

3. Cedar Hospital has a marketable equity securities portfolio that is included appropriately in noncurrent assets in unrestricted funds. The portfolio has an aggregate cost of $300,000. It had an aggregate fair value of $250,000 at the end of 20X7 and $290,000 at the end of 20X6. If the portfolio was reported properly in the balance sheet at the end of 20X6, the change in the valuation allowance at the end of 20X7 should be

   a. $0.

   b. a decrease of $40,000.

   c. an increase of $40,000.

   d. an increase of $50,000.

4. Ross Hospital's accounting records disclosed the following information:

Net resources invested in plant assets (hospital policy is to release donor restrictions when assets are placed in service)	$10,000,000
Board-designated funds.	2,000,000

  What amount should be included as unrestricted net assets?

   a. $12,000,000

   b. $10,000,000

   c. $2,000,000

   d. $0

5. Under Cura Hospital's established rate structure, patient service revenues of $9,000,000 would have been earned for the year ended December 31, 20X7. However, only $6,750,000 was collected because of charity allowances of $1,500,000 and discounts of $750,000 to third-party payors. For the year ended December 31, 20X7, what amount should Cura record as net patient service revenues?

   a. $6,750,000

   b. $7,500,000

   c. $8,250,000

   d. $9,000,000

6. An organization of high school seniors performs services for patients at Leer Hospital. These students are volunteers and perform services that the hospital would not otherwise provide, such as wheeling patients in the park and reading to patients. These volunteers donated 5,000 hours of service to Leer in 20X7. At the minimum wage rate, these services would amount to $22,500, while it is estimated that the fair value of these services was $27,000. In Leer's 20X7 statement of revenues and expenses, what amount should be reported as nonoperating revenue?

   a. $27,000

   b. $22,500

   c. $6,250

   d. $0

7. In June 20X8, Park Hospital purchased medicines from Jove Pharmaceutical Company at a cost of $2,000. However, Jove notified Park that the invoice was being cancelled and the medicines were being donated to Park. Park should record this donation of medicines as

   a. a memorandum entry only.

   b. other operating revenue of $2,000.

   c. a $2,000 credit to operating expenses.

   d. a $2,000 credit to nonoperating expenses.

8. Palma Hospital's patient service revenues for services provided in 20X8, at established rates, amounted to $8,000,000 on the accrual basis. For internal reporting, Palma uses the discharge method. Under this method, patient service revenues are recognized only when

patients are discharged, with no recognition given to revenues accruing for services to patients not yet discharged. Patient service revenues at established rates using the discharge method amounted to $7,000,000 for 20X8. According to GAAP, Palma should report patient service revenues for 20X8 of

- a. either $8,000,000 or $7,000,000, at the option of the hospital.
- b. $8,000,000.
- c. $7,500,000.
- d. $7,000,000.

9. In 20X6, Pyle Hospital received a $250,000 pure endowment grant. Also in 20X6, Pyle's governing board designated, for special uses, $300,000 which had originated from unrestricted gifts. What amount of these resources should be accounted for as part of the unrestricted net asset class?

- a. $0
- b. $250,000
- c. $300,000
- d. $550,000

10. Cura Hospital's property, plant, and equipment, net of depreciation, amounted to $10,000,000, with related mortgage liabilities of $1,000,000. What amount should be included in the permanently restricted net asset class?

- a. $0
- b. $1,000,000
- c. $9,000,000
- d. $10,000,000

(AICPA adapted)

Problem 12-13 *(LO 13, 14)* **Health care, multiple-choice.** Select the best answer for each of the following multiple-choice items dealing with health care organizations.

1. Inventory donated for use in a hospital should be reported as
   - a. other operating revenue.
   - b. nonoperating revenue.
   - c. an addition to the unrestricted net assets.
   - d. an addition to the restricted net assets.

2. Dee City's community hospital, which uses enterprise fund reporting and chooses to follow FASB guidelines, normally includes proceeds from sale of cafeteria meals in
   - a. patient service revenues.
   - b. other operating revenues.
   - c. ancillary service revenues.
   - d. deductions from dietary service expenses.

3. During 20X1, Trained Hospital received $90,000 in third-party reimbursements for depreciation. These reimbursements were restricted as follows:

For replacement of fully depreciated equipment	$25,000
For additions to property	65,000

   What amount of these reimbursements should Trained include in revenue for the year ended December 31, 20X1?

   - a. $0
   - b. $25,000
   - c. $65,000
   - d. $90,000

4. A hospital should report earnings from endowment funds that are restricted to a specific operating purpose as

 a. temporarily restricted revenues.
 b. permanently restricted revenues.
 c. unrestricted revenues.
 d. unrestricted revenues when expended.

5. Hospital financial resources are required by a bond indenture to be set aside to finance construction of a new pediatrics facility. In which of the following hospital net asset classes should these resources be reported?

 a. Permanently restricted
 b. Temporarily restricted
 c. Unrestricted
 d. Refundable deposits

6. Which of the following sets of financial statements is required for private not-for-profit health care organizations?

 a. Balance sheet, statement of revenues, expenses, and changes in fund balances
 b. Balance sheet, statement of revenues and expenses, and statement of cash flows
 c. Balance sheet, statement of changes in fund balances, and statement of cash flows
 d. Balance sheet, statement of operations, and statement of cash flows

7. Land valued at $400,000 and subject to a $150,000 mortgage was donated to Beaty Hospital without restriction as to use. Which of the following entries should Beaty make to record this donation?

a. Land..	400,000	
Mortgage Payable...................................		150,000
Endowment Fund Balance		250,000
b. Land..	400,000	
Mortgage Payable...................................		150,000
Contributions—Unrestricted		250,000
c. Land..	400,000	
Debt Fund Balance.................................		150,000
Endowment Fund Balance		250,000
d. Land..	400,000	
Mortgage Payable...................................		150,000
Unrestricted Fund Balance...........................		250,000

8. In hospital accounting, restricted net assets are

 a. not available unless the board of directors removes the restrictions.
 b. restricted as to use only for board-designated purposes.
 c. not available for current operating use; however, the income generated by the funds is available for current operating use.
 d. restricted as to use by the donor, grantor, or other source of the resources.

9. A not-for-profit hospital that follows FASB standards should report investment income from an endowment that is restricted to a specific operating purpose as
 a. general fund revenue.
 b. endowment fund revenue.
 c. unrestricted revenue.
 d. temporarily restricted revenue.

10. Restricted funds are
 a. not available unless the board of directors removes the restrictions.
 b. restricted as to use of the donor, grantor, or other source of the resources.

c. not available for current operating use; however, the income earned on the funds is available.

d. restricted as to use only for board-designated purposes.

(AICPA adapted)

Problem 12-14 *(LO 12, 13, 14, 16)* **Health care, statement of activities.** The June 30, 20X7, adjusted trial balances of the Bayfield Community Health Care Association follow.

Bayfield Community Health Care Association
Adjusted Current Funds Trial Balances
June 30, 20X7

	Unrestricted		Restricted	
Cash	11,000		29,000	
Bequest Receivable			5,000	
Pledges Receivable	12,000			
Accrued Interest Receivable	1,000			
Investments (at cost, which approximates market)	140,000			
Endowment Investments			250,000	
Accounts Payable and Accrued Expenses		50,000		1,000
Refundable Deposits		2,000		
Allowance for Uncollectible Pledges		3,000		
Net Assets, July 1, 20X6:				
Designated, Unrestricted		12,000		
Undesignated, Unrestricted		26,000		
Temporarily Restricted				3,000
Permanently Restricted				250,000
Endowment Revenue—Temporarily Restricted				20,000
Contributions		300,000		15,000
Membership Dues		25,000		
Program Service Fees		30,000		
Investment Income		10,000		
Auction Proceeds		42,000		
Auction Expenses	11,000			
Deaf Children's Program	120,000			
Blind Children's Program	150,000			
Management and General Services	49,000			
Fund-Raising Services	9,000			
Provision for Uncollectible Pledges	2,000			
Reclassifications In—Satisfaction of Program Restrictions		5,000		
Reclassifications Out—Satisfaction of Program Restrictions			5,000	
	505,000	505,000	289,000	289,000

Required ▶ ▶ ▶ ▶ ▶

1. Prepare a statement of activities for the year ended June 30, 20X7.
2. Prepare a statement of financial position as of June 30, 20X7.

Index of APB and FASB Pronouncements

The following list of pronouncements by the Accounting Principles Board and the Financial Accounting Standards Board (as of June 30, 2005) is provided as an overview of the standards issued since 1962. Some of the pronouncements by the Committee on Accounting Procedure are still authoritative; most of these are summarized in *Accounting Research Bulletin No. 43* issued in June 1953. A number of the APB and FASB pronouncements have been superseded.

FASB Statement No.	Statement Title	Issue Date
1	*Disclosure of Foreign Currency Translation Information*	
2	*Accounting for Research and Development Costs*	10/74
3	*Reporting Accounting Changes in Interim Financial Statements—an amendment of APB Opinion No. 28*	12/74
4	*Reporting Gains and Losses from Extinguishment of Debt—an amendment of APB Opinion No. 30*	3/75
5	*Accounting for Contingencies*	3/75
6	*Classification of Short-Term Obligations Expected to Be Refinanced—an amendment of ARB No. 43, Chapter 3A*	5/75
7	*Accounting and Reporting by Development Stage Enterprises*	6/75
8	*Accounting for the Translation of Foreign Currency Transactions and Foreign Currency Financial Statements*	10/75
9	*Accounting for Income Taxes: Oil and Gas Producing Companies—an amendment of APB Opinions No. 11 and 23*	10/75
10	*Extension of "Grandfather" Provisions for Business Combinations—an amendment of APB Opinion No. 16*	10/75
11	*Accounting for Contingencies: Transition Method—an amendment of FASB Statement No. 5*	12/75
12	*Accounting for Certain Marketable Securities*	12/75
13	*Accounting for Leases*	11/76
14	*Financial Reporting for Segments of a Business Enterprise*	12/76
15	*Accounting by Debtors and Creditors for Troubled Debt Restructurings*	6/77
16	*Prior Period Adjustments*	6/77
17	*Accounting for Leases: Initial Direct Costs—an amendment of FASB Statement No. 13*	11/77
18	*Financial Reporting for Segments of a Business Enterprise: Interim Financial Statements—an amendment of FASB Statement No. 14*	11/77
19	*Financial Accounting and Reporting by Oil and Gas Producing Companies*	12/77
20	*Accounting for Forward Exchange Contracts—an amendment of FASB Statement No. 8*	12/77

FASB Statement No.	Statement Title	Issue Date
21	Suspension of the Reporting of Earnings per Share and Segment Information by Nonpublic Enterprises—an amendment of APB Opinion No. 15 and FASB Statement No. 14	4/78
22	Changes in the Provisions of Lease Agreements Resulting from Refundings of Tax-Exempt Debt—an amendment of FASB Statement No. 13	6/78
23	Inception of the Lease—an amendment of FASB Statement No. 13	8/78
24	Reporting Segment Information in Financial Statements That Are Presented in Another Enterprise's Financial Report—an amendment of FASB Statement No. 14	12/78
25	Suspension of Certain Accounting Requirements for Oil and Gas Producing Companies—an amendment of FASB Statement No. 19	2/79
26	Profit Recognition on Sales-Type Leases of Real Estate—an amendment of FASB Statement No. 13	4/79
27	Classification of Renewals or Extensions of Existing Sales-Type or Direct Financing Leases—an amendment of FASB Statement No. 13	5/79
28	Accounting for Sales with Leasebacks—an amendment of FASB Statement No. 13	5/79
29	Determining Contingent Rentals—an amendment of FASB Statement No. 13	6/79
30	Disclosure of Information about Major Customers—an amendment of FASB Statement No. 14	8/79
31	Accounting for Tax Benefits Related to U.K. Tax Legislation Concerning Stock Relief	9/79
32	Specialized Accounting and Reporting Principles and Practices in AICPA Statements of Position and Guides on Accounting and Auditing Matters—an amendment of APB Opinion No. 20	9/79
33	Financial Reporting and Changing Prices	9/79
34	Capitalization of Interest Cost	10/79
35	Accounting and Reporting by Defined Benefit Pension Plans	3/80
36	Disclosure of Pension Information—an amendment of APB Opinion No. 8	5/80
37	Balance Sheet Classification of Deferred Income Taxes—an amendment of APB Opinion No. 11	7/80
38	Accounting for Preacquisition Contingencies of Purchased Enterprises—an amendment of APB Opinion No. 16	9/80
39	Financial Reporting and Changing Prices: Specialized Assets-Mining and Oil and Gas—a supplement to FASB Statement No. 33	10/80
40	Financial Reporting and Changing Prices: Specialized Assets-Timberlands and Growing Timber—a supplement to FASB Statement No. 33	11/80

FASB Statement

No.	Statement Title	Issue Date
41	*Financial Reporting and Changing Prices: Specialized Assets-Income-Producing Real Estate—a supplement to FASB Statement No. 33*	11/80
42	*Determining Materiality for Capitalization of Interest Cost—an amendment of FASB Statement No. 34*	11/80
43	*Accounting for Compensated Absences*	11/80
44	*Accounting for Intangible Assets of Motor Carriers—an amendment of Chapter 5 of ARB No. 43 and an interpretation of APB Opinions 17 and 30*	12/80
45	*Accounting for Franchise Fee Revenue*	3/81
46	*Financial Reporting and Changing Prices: Motion Picture Films*	3/81
47	*Disclosure of Long-Term Obligations*	3/81
48	*Revenue Recognition When Right of Return Exists*	6/81
49	*Accounting for Product Financing Arrangements*	6/81
50	*Financial Reporting in the Record and Music Industry*	11/81
51	*Financial Reporting by Cable Television Companies*	11/81
52	*Foreign Currency Translation*	12/81
53	*Financial Reporting by Producers and Distributors of Motion Picture Films*	12/81
54	*Financial Reporting and Changing Prices: Investment Companies—an amendment of FASB Statement No. 33*	1/81
55	*Determining whether a Convertible Security is a Common Stock Equivalent—an amendment of APB Opinion No. 15*	2/82
56	*Designation of AICPA Guide and Statement of Position (SOP) 81-1 on Contractor Accounting and SOP 81-2 concerning Hospital-Related Organizations as Preferable for Purposes of Applying APB Opinion 20—an amendment of FASB Statement No. 32*	2/82
57	*Related Party Disclosures*	3/82
58	*Capitalization of Interest Cost in Financial Statements That Include Investments Accounted for by the Equity Method—an amendment of FASB Statement No. 34*	4/82
59	*Deferral of the Effective Date of Certain Accounting Requirements for Pension Plans of State and Local Governmental Units—an amendment of FASB Statement No. 35*	4/82
60	*Accounting and Reporting by Insurance Enterprises*	6/82
61	*Accounting for Title Plant*	6/82
62	*Capitalization of Interest Cost in Situations Involving Certain Tax-Exempt Borrowings and Certain Gifts and Grants—an amendment of FASB Statement No. 34*	6/82
63	*Financial Reporting by Broadcasters*	6/82
64	*Extinguishments of Debt Made to Satisfy Sinking-Fund Requirements—an amendment of FASB Statement No. 4*	9/82
65	*Accounting for Certain Mortgage Banking Activities*	9/82

FASB Statement No.	Statement Title	Issue Date
66	*Accounting for Sales of Real Estate*	10/82
67	*Accounting for Costs and Initial Rental Operations of Real Estate Projects*	10/82
68	*Research and Development Arrangements*	10/82
69	*Disclosures about Oil and Gas Producing Activities—an amendment of FASB Statements 19, 25, 33, and 39*	11/82
70	*Financial Reporting and Changing Prices: Foreign Currency Translation—an amendment of FASB Statement No. 33*	12/82
71	*Accounting for the Effects of Certain Types of Regulation*	12/82
72	*Accounting for Certain Acquisitions of Banking or Thrift Institutions—an amendment of APB Opinion No. 17, an interpretation of APB Opinions 16 and 17, and an amendment of FASB Interpretation No. 9*	2/83
73	*Reporting a Change in Accounting for Railroad Track Structures—an amendment of APB Opinion No. 20*	8/83
74	*Accounting for Special Termination Benefits Paid to Employees*	8/83
75	*Deferral of the Effective Date of Certain Accounting Requirements for Pension Plans of State and Local Governmental Units—an amendment of FASB Statement No. 35*	11/83
76	*Extinguishment of Debt—an amendment of APB Opinion No. 26*	11/83
77	*Reporting by Transferors for Transfers of Receivables with Recourse*	12/83
78	*Classification of Obligations That Are Callable by the Creditor—an amendment of ARB No. 43, Chapter 3A*	12/83
79	*Elimination of Certain Disclosures for Business Combinations by Nonpublic Enterprises—an amendment of APB Opinion No. 16*	2/84
80	*Accounting for Futures Contracts*	8/84
81	*Disclosure of Postretirement Health Care and Life Insurance Benefits*	11/84
82	*Financial Reporting and Changing Prices: Elimination of Certain Disclosures—an amendment of FASB Statement No. 33*	11/84
83	*Designation of AICPA Guides and Statement of Position on Accounting by Brokers and Dealers in Securities, by Employee Benefit Plans, and by Banks as Preferable for Purposes of Applying APB Opinion 20—an amendment FASB Statement No. 32 and APB Opinion No. 30 and a rescission of FASB Interpretation No. 10*	3/85
84	*Induced Conversions of Convertible Debt—an amendment of APB Opinion No. 26*	3/85
85	*Yield Test for Determining whether a Convertible Security is a Common Stock Equivalent—an amendment of APB Opinion No. 15*	3/85

FASB Statement
No.

Statement Title

Issue Date

No.	Statement Title	Issue Date
86	*Accounting for the Costs of Computer Software to Be Sold, Leased, or Otherwise Marketed*	8/85
87	*Employers' Accounting for Pensions*	12/85
88	*Employers' Accounting for Settlements and Curtailments of Defined Benefit Pension Plans and for Termination Benefits*	12/85
89	*Financial Reporting and Changing Prices*	12/86
90	*Regulated Enterprises-Accounting for Abandonments and Disallowances of Plant Costs—an amendment of FASB Statement No. 71*	12/86
91	*Accounting for Nonrefundable Fees and Costs Associated with Originating or Acquiring Loans and Initial Direct Costs of Leases—an amendment of FASB Statements No. 13, 60, and 65 and a rescission of FASB Statement No. 17*	12/86
92	*Regulated Enterprises-Accounting for Phase-in Plans—an amendment of FASB Statement No. 71*	8/87
93	*Recognition of Depreciation by Not-for-Profit Organizations*	8/87
94	*Consolidation of All Majority-owned Subsidiaries—an amendment of ARB No. 51, with related amendments of APB Opinion No. 18 and ARB No. 43, Chapter 12*	10/87
95	*Statement of Cash Flows*	11/87
96	*Accounting for Income Taxes*	12/87
97	*Accounting and Reporting by Insurance Enterprises for Certain Long-Duration Contracts and for Realized Gains and Losses from the Sale of Investments*	12/87
98	*Accounting for Leases: Sale-Leaseback Transactions Involving Real Estate, Sales-Type Leases of Real Estate, Definition of the Lease Term, and Initial Direct Costs of Direct Financing Leases—an amendment of FASB Statements No. 13, 66, and 91 and a rescission of FASB Statement No. 26 and Technical Bulletin No. 79-11*	5/88
99	*Deferral of the Effective Date of Recognition of Depreciation by Not-for-Profit Organizations—an amendment of FASB Statement No. 93*	9/88
100	*Accounting for Income Taxes-Deferral of the Effective Date of FASB Statement No. 96—an amendment of FASB Statement No. 96*	12/88
101	*Regulated Enterprises-Accounting for the Discontinuation of Application of FASB Statement No. 71*	12/88
102	*Statement of Cash Flows-Exemption of Certain Enterprises and Classification of Cash Flows from Certain Securities Acquired for Resale—an amendment of FASB Statement No. 95*	2/89
103	*Accounting for Income Taxes-Deferral of the Effective Date of FASB Statement No. 96—an amendment of FASB Statement No. 96*	12/89

FASB Statement No.	Statement Title	Issue Date
104	*Statement of Cash Flows-Net Reporting of Certain Cash Receipts and Cash Payments and Classification of Cash Flows from Hedging Transactions—an amendment of FASB Statement No. 95*	12/89
105	*Disclosure of Information about Financial Instruments with Off-Balance-Sheet Risk and Financial Instruments with Concentrations of Credit Risk*	3/90
106	*Employers' Accounting for Postretirement Benefits Other Than Pensions*	12/90
107	*Disclosures about Fair Value of Financial Instruments*	12/91
108	*Accounting for Income Taxes-Deferral of the Effective Date of FASB Statement No. 96—an amendment of FASB Statement No. 96*	12/91
109	*Accounting for Income Taxes*	2/92
110	*Reporting by Defined Benefit Pension Plans of Investment Contracts—an amendment of FASB Statement No. 35*	8/92
111	*Rescission of FASB Statement No. 32 and Technical Corrections*	11/92
112	*Employers' Accounting for Postemployment Benefits—an amendment of FASB Statements No. 5 and 43*	11/92
113	*Accounting and Reporting for Reinsurance of Short-Duration and Long-Duration Contracts*	12/92
114	*Accounting by Creditors for Impairment of a Loan—an amendment of FASB Statements No. 5 and 15*	5/93
115	*Accounting for Certain Investments in Debt and Equity Securities*	5/93
116	*Accounting for Contributions Received and Contributions Made*	6/93
117	*Financial Statements of Not-for-Profit Organizations*	6/93
118	*Accounting by Creditors for Impairment of a Loan-Income Recognition and Disclosures—an amendment of FASB Statement No. 114*	10/94
119	*Disclosure about Derivative Financial Instruments and Fair Value of Financial Instruments*	10/94
120	*Accounting and Reporting by Mutual Life Insurance Enterprises and by Insurance Enterprises for Certain Long-Duration Participating Contracts—an amendment of FASB Statements 60, 97, and 113 and Interpretation No. 40*	1/95
121	*Accounting for the Impairment of Long-Lived Assets and for Long-Lived Assets to Be Disposed Of*	3/95
122	*Accounting for Mortgage Servicing Rights—an amendment of FASB Statement No. 65*	5/95
123	*Accounting for Stock-Based Compensation*	10/95
123 (revised 2004)	*Share-Based Payment*	12/04
124	*Accounting for Certain Investments Held by Not-for-Profit Organizations*	11/95

FASB Statement No.	Statement Title	Issue Date
125	*Accounting for Transfers and Servicing of Financial Assets and Extinguishments of Liabilities*	6/96
126	*Exemption from Certain Required Disclosures about Financial Instruments for Certain Nonpublic Entities—an amendment to FASB Statement No. 107*	12/96
127	*Deferral of the Effective Date of Certain Provisions of FASB Statement No. 125—an amendment to FASB Statement No. 125*	12/96
128	*Earnings per Share*	2/97
129	*Disclosure of Information about Capital Structure*	2/97
130	*Reporting Comprehensive Income*	6/97
131	*Disclosures about Segments of an Enterprise and Related Information*	6/97
132	*Employers' Disclosures about Pensions and Other Postretirement Benefits—an amendment of FASB Statements No. 87, 88, and 106*	2/98
132 (revised 2003)	*Employers' Disclosures about Pensions and Other Postretirement Benefits—an amendment of FASB Statements No. 87, 88, and 106*	12/03
133	*Accounting for Derivative Instruments and Hedging Activities*	6/98
134	*Accounting for Mortgage-Backed Securities Retained after the Securitization of Mortgage Loans Held for Sale by a Mortgage Banking Enterprise—an amendment of FASB Statement No. 65*	10/98
135	*Rescission of FASB Statement No. 75 and Technical Corrections*	2/99
136	*Transfers of Assets to a Not-for-Profit Organization or Charitable Trust That Raises or Holds Contributions for Others*	6/99
137	*Accounting for Derivative Instruments and Hedging Activities—Deferral of the Effective Date of FASB Statement No. 133—an amendment of FASB Statement No. 133*	6/99
138	*Accounting for Certain Derivative Instruments and Certain Hedging Activities—an amendment of FASB Statement No. 133*	6/00
139	*Rescission of FASB Statement No. 53 and amendments to FASB Statements No. 63, 89, and 121*	6/00
140	*Accounting for Transfers and Servicing of Financial Assets and Extinguishments of Liabilities—a replacement of FASB Statement No. 125*	9/00
141	*Business Combinations*	6/01
142	*Goodwill and Other Intangible Assets*	6/01
143	*Accounting for Asset Retirement Obligations*	6/01
144	*Accounting for the Impairment or Disposal of Long-Lived Assets*	8/01
145	*Rescission of FASB Statements No. 4, 44, and 64, Amendment of FASB Statement No. 13, and Technical Corrections*	4/02

FASB Statement No.	Statement Title	Issue Date
146	*Accounting for Costs Associated with Exit or Disposal Activities*	6/02
147	*Acquisitions of Certain Financial Institutions—an amendment of FASB Statements No. 72 and 144 and FASB Interpretation No. 9*	10/02
148	*Accounting for Stock-Based Compensation-Transition and Disclosure—an amendment of FASB Statement No. 123*	12/02
149	*Amendment of Statement 133 on Derivative Instruments and Hedging Activities*	4/03
150	*Accounting for Certain Financial Instruments with Characteristics of both Liabilities and Equity*	5/03
151	*Inventory Costs—an amendment of ARB No. 43, Chapter 4*	11/04
152	*Accounting for Real Estate Time-Sharing Transactions—an amendment of FASB Statements No. 66 and 67*	12/04
153	*Exchanges of Nonmonetary Assets—an amendment of APB Opinion No. 29*	12/04
154	*Accounting Changes and Error Corrections—a replacement of APB Opinion No. 20 and FASB Statement No. 3*	5/05

CITY OF MILWAUKEE, WISCONSIN
COMPREHENSIVE ANNUAL FINANCIAL REPORT
FOR THE YEAR ENDED DECEMBER 31, 2004

Source: City of Milwaukee Web site. For the full report, go to http://isdweb1.ci.mil.wi.us/citygov/cms/comptroller/2004FinancialReportWEB.pdf.

CITY OF MILWAUKEE
STATEMENT OF NET ASSETS
December 31, 2004
(Thousands of Dollars)

Exhibit 1

| | Primary Government | | | Component Units |
	Governmental Activities	Business-type Activities	Total	
Assets				
Cash and cash equivalents	$ 259,928	$ 50,538	$ 310,466	$ 53,517
Investments	55,736	24,361	80,097	1,885
Receivables (net):				
Taxes	159,997	-	159,997	-
Accounts	16,333	23,811	40,144	4,605
Unbilled accounts	485	14,084	14,569	-
Special assessments	15,520	-	15,520	-
Notes and loans	44,952	-	44,952	80,015
Accrued interest	1,031	85	1,116	1,377
Due from component units	18,061	-	18,061	-
Due from primary government	-	-	-	3,597
Due from other governmental agencies	197,654	-	197,654	13,321
Inventory of materials and supplies	5,920	2,597	8,517	-
Inventory of property for resale	26	-	26	12,934
Prepaid items	562	13	575	1,501
Deferred charges	1,971	657	2,628	147
Other assets	-	336	336	697
Total non-capital assets	778,176	116,482	894,658	173,596
Capital assets:				
Capital assets not being depreciated:				
Land	163,552	18,388	181,940	55,788
Construction in progress	59,902	45,909	105,811	21,787
Capital assets being depreciated:				
Buildings	140,186	84,395	224,581	337,789
Infrastructure	1,263,394	576,906	1,840,300	-
Improvements other than buildings	8,733	24,457	33,190	258
Machinery and equipment	121,327	203,243	324,570	3,893
Furniture and furnishings	-	70	70	-
Nonutility property	-	540	540	-
Accumulated depreciation	(915,371)	(293,244)	(1,208,615)	(181,483)
Total Capital Assets	841,723	660,664	1,502,387	238,032
Total Assets	1,619,899	777,146	2,397,045	411,628

CITY OF MILWAUKEE
STATEMENT OF NET ASSETS
December 31, 2004
(Thousands of Dollars)

Exhibit 1 (Continued)

| | Primary Government | | | Component Units |
	Governmental Activities	Business-type Activities	Total	
LIABILITIES				
Accounts payable	$ 41,902	$ 15,342	$ 57,244	$ 7,848
Accrued expenses	23,053	2,008	25,061	8,014
Accrued interest payable	8,506	939	9,445	-
Internal balances	554	(554)	-	-
Due to component units	3,597	-	3,597	-
Due to other governmental agencies	4,852	-	4,852	6,871
Deferred revenue	267,189	160	267,349	1,922
Revenue anticipation notes payable	172,000	-	172,000	-
Other liabilities	-	-	-	6,919
Due to primary government:				
Due within one year	-	-	-	1,959
Due in more than one year	-	-	-	16,102
Long-term obligations:				
Due within one year	89,958	13,281	103,239	7,251
Due in more than one year	612,505	119,557	732,062	52,582
Total Liabilities	1,224,116	150,733	1,374,849	109,468
NET ASSETS				
Invested in capital assets, net of related debt	444,873	529,213	974,086	189,903
Restricted for:				
Debt Service	110,135	8,123	118,258	-
Other purposes	282	-	282	52,011
Unrestricted	(159,507)	89,077	(70,430)	60,246
Total Net Assets	$ 395,783	$ 626,413	$ 1,022,196	$ 302,160

The notes to the financial statements are an integral part of this statement.

CITY OF MILWAUKEE
STATEMENT OF ACTIVITIES
FOR THE YEAR ENDED DECEMBER 31, 2004
(Thousands of Dollars)

Exhibit 2

Functions/Programs	Expenses	Charges for Services	Operating Grants and Contributions	Capital Grants and Contributions
Primary government:				
Governmental Activities:				
General government	$ 177,761	$ 10,460	$ 2,171	$ -
Public safety	241,027	13,153	9,728	-
Public works	150,591	33,305	3,485	-
Health	27,251	911	16,625	-
Culture and recreation	29,014	2,412	1,910	-
Conservation and development	57,967	584	26,509	-
Capital contribution to Milwaukee Public Schools	15,686	-	-	-
Contributions	20,582	-	22,236	-
Interest on long-term debt	24,159	-	-	-
Total Governmental Activities	744,038	60,825	82,664	-
Business-type Activities:				
Water	54,030	71,579	-	2,093
Sewer Maintenance	24,361	30,959	-	-
Parking	22,283	41,470	-	-
Port of Milwaukee	2,981	3,943	-	143
Metropolitan Sewerage District User Charges	31,233	29,688	-	-
Total Business-type Activities	134,888	177,639	-	2,236
Total Primary Government	$ 878,926	$ 238,464	$ 82,664	$ 2,236
Component units:				
Housing Authority	$ 87,306	$ 16,684	$ 54,250	$ 8,142
Redevelopment Authority	11,113	2,236	9,774	-
Milwaukee Economic Development Authority	1,744	2,364	25	-
Neighborhood Improvement Development Corporation	4,018	1,486	3,768	-
Total Component Units	$ 104,181	$ 22,770	$ 67,817	$ 8,142

General revenues:
    Property taxes and other taxes ....
    State aids for General Fund ....
    Grants and contributions not restricted to specific programs ....
    Miscellaneous ....
Transfers ....
    Total General Revenues and Transfers ....

Change in Net Assets ....

Net Assets - Beginning, as Restated ....

Net Assets - Ending ....

The notes to the financial statements are an integral part of this statement.

Exhibit 2 (Continued)

| | Net (Expenses) Revenue and Changes in Net Assets | | | |
| | Primary Government | | | |
	Governmental Activities	Business-type Activities	Total	Component Units
	$ (165,130)		$ (165,130)	
	(218,146)		(218,146)	
	(113,801)		(113,801)	
	(9,715)		(9,715)	
	(24,692)		(24,692)	
	(30,874)		(30,874)	
	(15,686)		(15,686)	
	1,654		1,654	
	(24,159)		(24,159)	
	(600,549)		(600,549)	
	-	19,642	19,642	
	-	6,598	6,598	
	-	19,187	19,187	
	-	1,105	1,105	
	-			
	-	(1,545)	(1,545)	
	-	44,987	44,987	
	(600,549)	44,987	(555,562)	
				$ (8,230)
				897
				645
				1,236
				(5,452)
	217,762	-	217,762	-
	273,865	-	273,865	-
	-	-	-	
	56,321	797	57,118	2,576
	22,622	(22,622)	-	-
	570,570	(21,825)	548,745	2,576
	(29,979)	23,162	(6,817)	(2,876)
	425,762	603,251	1,029,013	305,036
	$ 395,783	$ 626,413	$ 1,022,196	$ 302,160

CITY OF MILWAUKEE
BALANCE SHEET
GOVERNMENTAL FUNDS
DECEMBER 31, 2004
(Thousands of Dollars)

Exhibit A-1

	General
ASSETS	
Assets:	
Cash and cash equivalents	$ 118,556
Investments	282
Receivables (net):	
Taxes	102,499
Accounts	10,901
Unbilled accounts	485
Special assessments	-
Notes and loans	299
Accrued interest	840
Due from other funds	27,583
Due from component units	2,026
Due from other governmental agencies	668
Advances to other funds	13,431
Inventory of materials and supplies	5,658
Inventory of property for resale	26
Prepaid items	271
Total Assets	**$ 283,525**
LIABILITIES AND FUND BALANCES	
Liabilities:	
Accounts payable	$ 25,457
Accrued expenses	23,053
Due to other funds	1,566
Due to component units	6
Due to other governmental agencies	1
Deferred revenue	146,406
Revenue anticipation notes payable	-
Advances from other funds	-
Total Liabilities	196,489
Fund Balances:	
Reserved for debt service	-
Reserved for delinquent taxes receivable	-
Reserved for economic development	-
Reserved for encumbrances, prepaids, and carryovers	30,288
Reserved for inventory	5,684
Reserved for mortgage trust	282
Reserved for environmental remediation	303
Reserved for tax stabilization - 2005	16,621
Reserved for tax stabilization - 2006 and subsequent years' budgets and advances to other funds	33,858
Unreserved:	
Undesignated	-
Special assessment (deficit)	-
Total Fund Balances	87,036
Total Liabilities and Fund Balances	**$ 283,525**

The notes to the financial statements are an integral part of this statement.

Exhibit A-1 (Continued)

	General Obligation Debt Service	Public Debt Amortization	Capital Projects	Nonmajor Governmental Funds	Total
	$ 80,337	$ 19,328	$ 28,272	$ 13,435	$ 259,928
	-	55,454	-	-	55,736
	40,420	-	7,627	9,451	159,997
	-	-	3,019	2,413	16,333
	-	-	-	-	485
	-	-	15,520	-	15,520
	36,681	-	-	7,972	44,952
	138	52	-	1	1,031
	291	-	-	-	27,874
	15,641	-	-	394	18,061
	172,000	-	13,820	11,166	197,654
	-	-	-	-	13,431
	-	-	262	-	5,920
	-	-	-	-	26
	-	291	-	-	562
	$ 345,508	$ 75,125	$ 68,520	$ 44,832	$ 817,510
	$ -	$ -	$ 9,990	$ 6,455	$ 41,902
	-	-	-	-	23,053
	8,768	291	12,562	5,241	28,428
	-	-	2,661	930	3,597
	-	-	3,900	951	4,852
	120,933	-	38,254	19,134	324,727
	172,000	-	-	-	172,000
	-	-	13,431	-	13,431
	301,701	291	80,798	32,711	611,990
	43,807	74,834	-	8,960	127,601
	-	-	-	7,335	7,335
	-	-	-	3	3
	-	-	576	-	30,864
	-	-	262	-	5,946
	-	-	-	-	282
	-	-	-	-	303
	-	-	-	-	16,621
	-	-	-	-	33,858
	-	-	-	(4,177)	(4,177)
	-	-	(13,116)	-	(13,116)
	43,807	74,834	(12,278)	12,121	205,520
	$ 345,508	$ 75,125	$ 68,520	$ 44,832	$ 817,510

This page left blank intentionally.

CITY OF MILWAUKEE
RECONCILIATION OF THE GOVERNMENTAL FUNDS BALANCE SHEET
TO THE STATEMENT OF NET ASSETS
DECEMBER 31, 2004
(Thousands of Dollars)

Exhibit A-2

Fund balances - total governmental funds		$ 205,520
Amounts reported for governmental activities in the statement of net assets (Exhibit A-1) are different because:		
Capital assets used in governmental activities are not financial resources and therefore are not reported in the funds. Those assets consist of:		
Land	$ 163,552	
Buildings, net of $62,116 accumulated depreciation	78,070	
Infrastructure, net of $768,943 accumulated depreciation	494,451	
Improvements Other than buildings, net of $6,750 accumulated depreciation	1,983	
Machinery and equipment, net of $77,562 accumulated depreciation	43,765	
Construction in progress	59,902	
		841,723
Deferred charges for debt issuance costs are not available to pay for current-period expenditures and therefore are deferred in the funds.		1,971
Some revenues are deferred in the funds because they are not available to pay current period's expenditures.		
Taxes to be collected after year end	6,387	
Special assessments to be collected after year end	14,470	
Notes and loans receivable to repay long-term bonds and notes	36,681	
		57,538
Long-term liabilities are not due and payable in the current period and therefore are not reported in the funds. Interest on long-term debt is not accrued in governmental funds, but rather is recognized as an expenditure when due. All liabilities - both current and long-term - are reported in the statement of net assets.		
Accrued interest payable	(8,506)	
Bonds and Notes Payable	(618,988)	
Deferred amount on refunding	8,372	
Unamortized premiums	(25,559)	
Compensated absences	(37,003)	
Claims and judgments	(28,936)	
Capitalized lease	(349)	
		(710,969)
Total net assets of governmental activities (Exhibit 1)		**$ 395,783**

The notes to the financial statements are an integral part of this reconciliation.

CITY OF MILWAUKEE   Exhibit A-3
STATEMENT OF REVENUES, EXPENDITURES AND CHANGES IN FUND BALANCES
GOVERNMENTAL FUNDS
FOR THE YEAR ENDED DECEMBER 31, 2004
(Thousands of Dollars)

	General
Revenues:	
Property taxes	$ 129,120
Other taxes	3,563
Special assessments	-
Licenses and permits	11,530
Intergovernmental	273,865
Charges for services	60,825
Fines and forfeits	5,647
Contributions received	22,236
Other	8,108
Total Revenues	514,894
Expenditures:	
Current:	
General government	200,124
Public safety	231,371
Public works	89,562
Health	10,724
Culture and recreation	17,822
Conservation and development	3,495
Capital outlay	-
Debt Service:	
Principal retirement	-
Interest	-
Bond issuance costs	-
Total Expenditures	553,098
Excess (deficiency) of Revenues over Expenditures	(38,204)
Other Financing Sources (Uses):	
General obligation bonds and notes issued	2,000
Issuance premium	-
Transfers in	33,269
Transfers out	(10)
Total Other Financing Sources and Uses	35,259
Net Change in Fund Balances	(2,945)
Fund Balances - Beginning	89,981
Fund Balances - Ending	**$ 87,036**

The notes to the financial statements are an integral part of this statement.

	General Obligation Debt Service	Public Debt Amortization	Capital Projects	Nonmajor Governmental Funds	Total
	$ 53,995	$ -	$ 12,077	$ 3,746	$ 198,938
	13,948	1,773	-	-	19,284
	-	-	4,665	-	4,665
	-	-	-	-	11,530
	1,482	-	5,418	56,293	337,058
	5,584	-	-	-	66,409
	-	-	-	-	5,647
	-	-	-	-	22,236
	3,218	3,611	3,392	6,482	24,811
	78,227	5,384	25,552	66,521	690,578
	-	3	-	3,204	203,331
	-	-	-	9,729	241,100
	-	-	-	3,485	93,047
	-	-	-	16,641	27,365
	-	-	-	1,914	19,736
	-	-	-	31,134	34,629
	-	-	104,842	-	104,842
	68,618	-	-	-	68,618
	28,620	-	-	-	28,620
	411	-	-	-	411
	97,649	3	104,842	66,107	821,699
	(19,422)	5,381	(79,290)	414	(131,121)
	-	-	72,331	15,000	89,331
	10,467	-	-	-	10,467
	24,043	-	-	-	57,312
	(6,646)	(7,183)	(2,795)	(18,056)	(34,690)
	27,864	(7,183)	69,536	(3,056)	122,420
	8,442	(1,802)	(9,754)	(2,642)	(8,701)
	35,365	76,636	(2,524)	14,763	214,221
	$ 43,807	$ 74,834	$ (12,278)	$ 12,121	$ 205,520

CITY OF MILWAUKEE   Exhibit A-4
RECONCILIATION OF THE STATEMENT OF REVENUES,
EXPENDITURES, AND CHANGES IN FUND BALANCES OF GOVERNMENTAL FUNDS
TO THE STATEMENT OF ACTIVITIES
FOR THE YEAR ENDED DECEMBER 31, 2004
(Thousands of Dollars)

Net change in fund balances - total governmental funds (Exhibit A-3)		$ (8,701)
Amounts reported for governmental activities in the statement of activities are different because:		
Governmental funds report capital outlays as expenditures. However, in the statement of activities the cost of those assets is allocated over their estimated useful lives and reported as depreciation expense. This is the amount by which capital outlay ($44,246) exceeded depreciation expense ($42,361) in the current period less loss on disposals ($528)		1,357
Notes and loans receivable to repay long-term bonds and notes		(3,346)
Revenues in the statement of activities that do not provide current financial resources are reported as deferred revenue in the funds.		
Taxes accrued in prior years	$ (460)	
Special assessments deferred revenue beginning of the year $12,623 less deferred at end of the year $14,470	1,847	
		1,387
The issuance of long-term debt (e.g., bonds, leases) provides current financial resources to governmental funds, while the repayment of the principal of long-term debt consumes the current financial resources of governmental funds. Neither transaction, however, has any effect on net assets. Also, governmental funds report the effect of issuance costs, premiums and similar items when debt is first issued, whereas these amounts are deferred and amortized in the statement of activities. This amount is the net effect of these differences in the treatment of long-term debt and related items.		
Debt issued:		
Bonds and notes issued	(89,331)	
Issuance premiums	(10,467)	
Repayments:		
Principal retirement	68,618	
Bond issuance costs	679	
Capital lease current payment	174	
Amortization:		
Issuance costs	(445)	
Premiums	6,820	
Deferred amount on refunding	(1,530)	
		(25,482)
Under the modified accrual basis of accounting used in the governmental funds, expenditures are not recognized for transactions that are not normal paid with expendable available financial resources. In the statement of activities, however, which is presented on the accrual basis, expenses and liabilities are reported regardless of when financial resources are available. In addition, interest on long-term debt is not recognized under the modified accrual basis of accounting until due, rather as it accrues. The adjustment combines the net changes of the following balances.		
Compensated absences	767	
Claims and judgments	4,868	
Accrued interest on bonds and notes	(829)	
		4,806
Changes in net assets of governmental activities (Exhibit 2)		**$ (29,979)**

The notes to the financial statements are an integral part of this reconciliation.

CITY OF MILW...
STATEMENT OF REVENUES, EXPENSES A...
ENTERPRISE...
FOR THE YEAR ENDED D...
(Thousands o...)

	W... W...
Operating Revenues:	
Charges for Services:	
Water sales	$ 57
Statutory sewer user fee	
Sewer maintenance fee	
Rent	
Fire protection service	
Parking meters	
Parking permits	
Vehicle towing	
Parking forfeitures	
Other	
Total Operating Revenues	7
Operating Expenses:	
Milwaukee Metropolitan Sewerage District charges	
Employee services	
Administrative and general	
Depreciation	1
Transmission and distribution	1
Services, supplies and materials	
Water treatment	
Water pumping	
Billing and collection	
Total Operating Expenses	5
Operating Income (Loss)	1
Nonoperating Revenues (Expenses):	
Investment income	
Interest expense	(
Gain (loss) on disposal of fixed assets	
Other	
Total Nonoperating Revenues (Expenses)	(
Income (Loss) before Contributions and Transfers..	1
Capital contributions	
Transfers in	
Transfers out	
Change in Net Assets	
Total Net Assets - Beginning	3
Total Net Assets - Ending	$ 3

The notes to the financial statements are an integral part of this...

CITY OF MILWAUKEE
STATEMENT OF NET ASSETS
ENTERPRISE FUNDS
DECEMBER 31, 2004
(Thousands of Dollars)

Exhibit B-1

ASSETS	Water Works	Sewer Maintenance	Parking	Nonmajor Enterprise Funds	Total
Current Assets:					
Cash and cash equivalents	$ 5,225	$ 13,097	$ 24,092	$ 1	$ 42,415
Restricted cash and cash equivalents	610	-	-	-	610
Investments	24,361	-	-	-	24,361
Receivables (net):					
Accounts	10,149	7,003	-	6,659	23,811
Unbilled accounts	9,585	2,397	-	2,102	14,084
Accrued interest	70	15	-	-	85
Due from other funds	8,030	981	-	836	9,847
Inventory of materials and supplies	2,597	-	-	-	2,597
Prepaid items	13	-	-	-	13
Deferred charges	-	657	-	-	657
Other assets	336	-	-	-	336
Total Current Assets	60,976	24,150	24,092	9,598	118,816
Noncurrent assets:					
Restricted cash and cash equivalents	-	7,513	-	-	7,513
Capital assets:					
Capital assets not being depreciated:					
Land	1,568	-	8,913	7,907	18,388
Construction in progress	20,251	23,938	1,548	172	45,909
Capital assets being depreciated:					
Buildings	22,987	-	49,076	12,332	84,395
Infrastructure	275,709	301,197			576,906
Improvements other than buildings	-		5,630	18,827	24,457
Machinery and equipment	195,798	1,887	1,011	4,547	203,243
Furniture and furnishings	-	22	-	48	70
Nonutility property	540	-	-	-	540
Accumulated depreciation	(157,731)	(90,203)	(23,390)	(21,920)	(293,244)
Total Noncurrent Assets	359,122	244,354	42,788	21,913	668,177
Total Assets	420,098	268,504	66,880	31,511	786,993

CITY OF MILW
STATEMENT OF
ENTERPRISE
DECEMBER
(Thousands o

Wate
Works

LIABILITIES

Current Liabilities:
Accounts payable .... $ 4,63(
Accrued expenses 1,01:
Accrued interest payable .... 44!
Compensated absences 94
Due to other funds 3,19
Deferred revenue ....
General obligation debt payable - current 4,85
Revenue bonds payable - current 82
Total Current Liabilities 15,90

Current Liabilities Payable from Restricted Assets:
Revenue bonds payable ....
Accrued interest payable ....
Total Current Liabilities Payable from
Restricted Assets ....

Noncurrent Liabilities:
General obligation debt 28,37
Revenue bonds payable 12,92
Total Noncurrent Liabilities 41,30

Total Liabilities 57,20

Net Assets:

Invested in capital assets, net of related debt 312,14
Restricted for Debt Service .... 6!
Unrestricted 50,13

Total Net Assets .... $ 362,8!

The notes to the financial statements are an integral part of this

---

Governmental accounting *(Continued)*
  financial reports of general fund, 512–514
  highlights and illustrative examples of reporting model, 558–576
  interactions among funds, 533–535
  other governmental funds, 519–527
  proprietary funds, 527–531
  reporting and auditing implementation and issues, 576–580
  reporting entity, 556–558
  structure of funds, 499–504
  use of budgetary accounting, 504–511
Governmental Accounting Standards Board. *See* GASB
Governmental activities, 559
Governmental funds, 499
  accounting for transactions of, 499–504
  other, 519–527
  See also Capital projects funds; Debt service funds; General fund; Governmental accounting; Permanent funds; Special revenue funds
Governmental health care organizations, 621–622
Government-wide financial statements, 567–569
  converting funds-based statement to, 574–576

H

Health Care Financial Management Association (HFMA), 590, 614
Health care services providers
  accounting for governmental and private, 614–622
  See also Not-for-profit organizations; Voluntary health and welfare organizations
Hedge of a net investment, 334
Hedges
  accounting for derivatives that are designated as, 338–340
  of foreign currency exposure, disclosures regarding, 360
Hedging
  existing foreign currency denominated asset or liability, 340–345
  forecasted transaction with a forward contract, 355–358
  forecasted transaction with an option, 352–355
  foreign currency forecasted transaction, 351–358
  identifiable foreign currency firm commitment, 346–350
  special complications, 345–346
  transactions, summary of, 358–359
  with a foreign currency option, 344–345
  with a forward contract, 341–344
Hedging instrument
  expires after settlement date, 346
  expires before settlement date, 346
  notional amount different from transaction amount, 346
Historical rate method, 383
Holder, 335
Horizontal combinations, 3

Horizontal worksheet format, 251
Human service organizations, 590

I

Impairment loss calculation, 25
Impairment test, 25
  FASB Statement No. 121, 19, 20
Income distribution schedules (IDS), 114
Income, gains and losses excluded from, 389–391
Indirect method, calculating statement of cash flows, 240
Indirect quotes, exchange rates, 327
Influence, gain or loss of, 251
Influential investments, unconsolidated investments, 246
Intangible assets
  APB Opinion No. 17, 462
  examples of, 9
  separately identified, 20
Intercompany bonds, purchase of, 238
Intercompany debt, 194–195
Intercompany foreign currency transactions of a long-term nature, 391
Intercompany investment in bonds, 227–234
Intercompany merchandise sales, 181–190
Intercompany plant asset sales, 190–194
Intercompany sale
  losses on, 189–190
  of a depreciable asset, 192–194
  of a nondepreciable asset, 190–192
Intercompany transactions
  by investee, 247–248
  by investor, 250
  debt, 194–195
  merchandise sales, 181–190
  plant asset sales, 190–194
Interest
  bargain purchases—100%, 70–72
  cash acquisition of controlling, 235–236
  complicated purchase—less than 100%, 75–81
  complicated purchases—100%, 65–69
  consolidating a less than 100%, 75–81
  extraordinary gain—100%, 72–75
  noncash acquisition of controlling, 236–237
Internal Revenue Code Section 457 deferred compensation plans, 531
Internal service funds, 530
Internally generated net income, 114
International Monetary Fund (IMF), 326
International monetary system, 326–330
  alternative, 326–327
  See also Foreign currency transactions
Interperiod equity, 498
Intraperiod purchase
  under cost method, 131
  under simple equity method, 128–131
Inventories
  after purchase accounting, 19
  eliminations for periodic, 188–189

intercompany goods in purchasing company's beginning and ending, 187–188
intercompany goods in purchasing company's ending, 185–186
no intercompany goods in purchasing company's, 183–185
Inventory profit, effect of lower-of-cost-market method on, 189
Invested in capital (fixed) assets, net of related debt, classification of proprietary fund equity, 559
Investee
    intercompany transactions by, 247–248
    stock transactions, 249
    with preferred stock, 249
Investing activities, 235, 529
Investing cash flows, 559
Investment trust funds, fiduciary funds, 532
Investments
    equity method for unconsolidated, 246–251
    in a foreign subsidiary, 334
    in marketable securities and other financial instruments, 509–510
    in subsidiary, accounting for, 109–112
    levels of, 58–59
    net increase (decrease) in the fair value of, 510
    nonconsolidated, 238
    private not-for-profit organizations, 593
Investor, intercompany transactions by, 250

L

Lease agreements, 30
Legacies and bequests, VHWO, 597
Liabilities
    after purchase accounting for acquired, 19–26
    assigning value to, 8
    health care service providers classification of, 615
    ranking, liquidation of partnership, 470–471
Liability for debit capital balances, partnership liquidation, 471
Limited liability company (LLC), 432
Limited liability partnership (LLP), 432
Limited partnership, 432
Liquidate, 455
Liquidation
    guidelines, 470–474
    lump-sum, 474–475
    partnerships, 470–479
Long position, 335
Long-term liabilities, revaluation of, 29–30
Loss
    goodwill impairment, 25–26
    health care service providers classification of, 615–618
    intercompany sales, 189–190
    partnership allocation or division of, 437–443
    retirement, 228
Lump-sum liquidation, 474–475

M

Management's discussion and analysis (MD&A), 558
Marketable securities, investments in, 509–510
Marshaling of assets, 471–474
Measurement currency, 326
Measurement focus, 498
Medical malpractice claims, health care service providers, 618–620
Merchandise sales, intercompany, 181–190
Merger, 1
    completion record 1996–2005, 2
    See also Business combinations
Modified accrual basis of governmental accounting, 501
Modified approach, 571
Modified preservation approach, 515
Mutual agency, 432

N

National Association of College and University Business Officers (NACUBO), 590
Net assets
    purchase of, 7
    statement of, 569–571
Net investment
    hedge of, 334
    in a foreign entity, foreign currency transactions as hedges of, 389–391
Net settlement, 335
Noncapital financing activities, 529
Noncash acquisition of controlling interest, 236–237
Nonconsolidated investments, 238
Noncontrolling interest (NCI), 75
Nonpriority accounts, 26
Nontaxable exchanges, 31–32
Notes to consolidated financial statements, 14–18
Not-for-profit organizations, 590
    colleges and universities, 609–613
    private, 591–595
    providers of health care services, 614–622
    VHWO, 595–609
Notional amount, 335

O

Operating activities, 238, 529
Operating cash flows, 559
Operating debt, 503
Operating information, 577
Operating revenue, other, 616
Option, illustration of hedging a forecasted transaction with, 352–355
Other comprehensive bases of accounting (OCBOA), 434
Other comprehensive income (OCI), 340
Other financing sources, 501
Other financing uses, 503

P

Parent, 4, 57
Pari passu, 472
Partner(s)
    admission of a new, 456–467
    capital investment of, 438–440
    maximum loss absorbable (MLA), 478
    relationships of, 431–432
    selling of an interest to existing, 468
    services rendered by, 440
    withdrawal of, 467–470
Partner's interest
    selling of to existing partners, 468
    selling of to the partnership, 468–469
Partnership dissolution, 434
Partnership liquidation, 470–479
    liability for debit capital balances, 471
    marshaling of assets, 471–474
    ranking of liabilities, 470–471
Partnership(s)
    acceptable accounting principles, 434
    accounting for activities, 435–443
    admission of a new partner, 456–467
    allocation or division of profits and losses, 437–443
    articles of, 433
    characteristics of, 431–435
    contribution of assets to existing, 457
    dissolution, 455
    effects of a partner's withdrawal, 469–470
    Form 1065, 434
    formation and agreements, 433
    installment liquidation, 475–479
    legal liability of, 432
    lump-sum liquidation, 474–475
    multiple bases of allocation, 441
    overvaluation of original, 459–460
    ownership changes, 456–470
    partner withdrawal, 467–470
    selling of an interest to, 468–469
    special allocation procedures, 443
    tax considerations, 434–435
    underlying equity theories, 432–433
Patient service revenue, 616
Pension trust funds, fiduciary funds, 532
Performance audits, 576
Permanent funds, 499, 520–521
    See also Governmental funds
Plant asset sales, intercompany 190–194
Plant replacement and expansion funds, health care service providers, 615
Pledges, unconditional and conditional, 592
Pooling of interests method, 35
    versus purchase method, 6–7
Postemployment benefits (OPEB), 532
Preferred stock, investee with, 249
Premium, 329
    option contract, 337
    price, 27, 67, 76–78

revenue, 616
Price analysis, 67–68
    schedule, 68
Priorities, applying, 26–28
Priority accounts, 26
Private not-for-profit organizations, accounting for, 591–595
Private-purpose trust funds, 531–532
Pro forma income disclosures, 13
Profit and loss ratios, 437–438
Profit deficiencies, partnership allocation of, 441–443
Profits, partnership allocation or division of, 437–443
Program costs, VHWO, 598–599
Program-specific operating and capital grants, 571
Proprietary funds, 499, 527–531
    See also Governmental accounting
Proprietary theory, 433
Propriety theory, 456
Public purpose, governmental funds, 519
Public support, VHWO, 596–598
Purchase accounting, added considerations, 29–35
Purchase agreement, contingent consideration included in, 32–35
Purchase (80%)
    alternative prices, 309
    at less than fair value of net identifiable assets, elimination entries only, 310
    equity method worksheet, several adjustments, 320–321
    goodwill, 309, 310–311
Purchase method
    valuation under, 7–10
    versus pooling method, 6–7
Purchase of net assets, 7
Purchases
    analysis of complicated—100% interest, 65–69
    analysis of complicated—less than 100% interest, 75–81
    complicated, several distributions of excess, 121–128
    recording of, 295–297
Push-down accounting, 84
Put option, 337

R

Ratios, profit and loss, 437–438
Receivables, after purchase accounting, 19
Remeasured financial statements, 392–405
Remeasurement
    and translation methodologies, 403
    gain or loss, 393
    methodologies, summary of, 402–405
    or temporal method, 383
    when functional currency not the same as parent/investor's currency, 399–402
    when functional currency same as parent/investor's currency, 394–399
Reporting and auditing implementation and issues, 576–580
Reporting entity, 556–558

Reporting model, highlights and illustrative examples of, 558–576
Required supplementary information (RSI), 555
Reserved fund balance, 504
Resident service revenue, 616
Restricted
     assets, 528
     classification of proprietary fund equity, 559
Revaluations, 327
Revenue capacity information, 577
Revenues, 500–501
     accounting for private not-for-profit organizations, 591–593
     health care service providers classification of, 615–618
     universities/colleges accounting for, 610
     VHWO, 598
Reverse repurchase agreements, 510
Right of offset, 471

S

Schedule of safe payments, installment liquidation, 475–479
Securities lending transactions, 510
Service costs, VHWO, 598–599
Services
     charges for, 571
     rendered by partners, 440
Service-type special assessment, 526
Short position, 335
Simple equity method
     effect of on consolidation, 112–117
     intraperiod purchase under, 128–131
Single Audit Act, 576
Smithsonian Agreement, 327
Sophisticated equity method, effect of on consolidation, 119–120
Special assessments, 526–527
Special events support, VHWO, 597
Special items, 503, 566
Special revenue funds, 499, 519–520
     See also Governmental funds
Specific purpose funds, health care service providers, 614
Spot rate, 328
Statement of activities, 571–574
     private not-for-profit organizations, 594
     universities/colleges, 611
Statement of cash flows
     private not-for-profit organizations, 594
     universities/colleges, 611
Statement of Financial Accounting Standards (SFAS) No. 133, 389
Statement of financial position
     private not-for-profit organizations, 594
     universities/colleges, 611
Statement of functional expenses, private not-for-profit organizations, 594
Statement of net assets, 569–571

Statement of revenues, expenditures, and changes in fund balances, governmental accounting, 512–514
Statistical section
     governmental accounting, 577
     of the CAFR, 556
Statutory consolidation, 4
Statutory merger, 4
Stock acquisition, 4, 61
     consolidating, 63
Stock, investee with preferred, 249
Stock transactions, investee, 249
Strike price, 336
Subsidiary, 4, 57
     accounting for investment in, 109–112
     gain on purchase of, 303–305
Subsidiary accounts
     adjustment of, 64–75
     analysis of complicated purchases—100% interest, 65–69
     bargain purchases—100% interest, 70–72
     extraordinary gain—100% interest, 72–75
Subsidiary books
     closed, 128–129
     not closed, 129–131
Subsidiary dividends, 238
Subsidiary shares, purchase of additional, 238
Symmetric return profile, 336

T

Tangible assets, after purchase accounting, 19
Tax advantages of business combinations, 3–4
Tax anticipation notes, 503
Tax considerations of partnerships, 434–435
Tax-free exchange, 134
Tax-related adjustments, 134–135
Temporal or remeasurement method, 383
Tenancy in partnership, 432
Tender offer, 5
Time value, 329
Transactions, VHWO, 601–609
Transition issues, business combinations, 35–36
Translation
     accomplishing the objectives of, 386
     for the cost or equity method, unconsolidated investments, 391–392
     methodologies, summary of, 402–405
     or functional method, 382
     when functional currency not the same as parent/investor's currency, 399–402
Translation adjustment
     accounting for the cumulative, 385
     direct calculation of the current period, 385–386
     subsequent recognition of, 386
Translation process
     basic, 382–392
     objectives of, 374–382
Translation/remeasurement flowchart, 404

Trust funds, fiduciary funds, 531–533
Two-transactions method, foreign currency
        transactions, 331

U

U.S. General Accounting Office (GAO), 576
Unconditional pledges, 592
Unconsolidated investments
        equity method for, 246–251
        translation for the cost or equity method, 391–392
Unconsolidated subsidiaries, unconsolidated
        investments, 246
Underlying, 335
Undesignated fund balance, 504
Uniform Partnership Act (UPA), 431, 455
Universities and colleges
        accounting for, 609–613
        See also Not-for-profit organizations
Unreserved fund balance, 504
Unrestricted, classification of proprietary fund equity, 559

V

Valuation schedule strategy, 305–306
Vertical combinations, 3
Vertical worksheet, 251–253
Voluntary health and welfare organizations
        (VHWO), 590, 595
        accounting for, 595–609
        illustrative transactions for, 601–609
        See also Health care service providers; Not-for-profit
                organizations

W

Wall Street Journal, The, 327
Williams Act of 1968, 5
Working capital focus, 499
Worksheet
        consolidating the foreign subsidiary, 406–407, 410–411
        cost method, 140–141, 142–143

80% bargain purchase, 91
intercompany notes, 208–209
intercompany sale of depreciable asset, 204–205,
        206–207
intercompany sales; no intercompany goods in
        inventories, 196–197
simple equity method, 136–137, 138–139, 144–145,
        148–149, 316–317
technique, consolidated statements, 132
vertical format, simple equity method, 262–263
vertical worksheet alternative, 264–265
Worksheet, 80% interest
        price exceeds fair value of priority accounts, 90
        price exceeds fair value of net identifiable assets, 307
        price is less than fair value of net identifiable assets, 308
Worksheet, intercompany bonds
        interest method of amortization, 260–261
        subsequent period, straight-line method of
                amortization, 258–259
Worksheet, intercompany goods
        in beginning and ending inventories, 200–201, 202–203
        in ending inventory, 198–199
Worksheet, intercompany investment in bonds
        year of acquisition, straight-line method of
                amortization, 254–255
        year subsequent to acquisition, straight-line method of
                amortization, 256–257
Worksheet, intraperiod purchases
        subsidiary books closed on purchase date, 152–153
        subsidiary books not closed on purchase date, 154–155
Worksheet, 100% interest
        price equals book value, 85
        price exceeds book value, 86
        price exceeds fair value of priority accounts, 88
        price exceeds market value of identifiable net assets, 87
        price is less than fair value of priority accounts, 89
Write-down to market value, unusual equity adjustment,
        249
Writer, 335

Z

Zero investment balance, unusual equity
        adjustment, 249–250
Zone analysis, 26, 67

PRESENT VALUE TABLES

Present Value of $1 Due in n Periods

$$PV = A\left[\frac{1}{(1+i)^n}\right] = A(PVF_{\overline{n}|})$$

n	2%	3%	4%	5%	6%	8%	10%	12%	16%	20%
1	0.9804	0.9709	0.9615	0.9524	0.9434	0.9259	0.9091	0.8929	0.8621	0.8333
2	0.9612	0.9426	0.9246	0.9070	0.8900	0.8573	0.8264	0.7972	0.7432	0.6944
3	0.9423	0.9151	0.8890	0.8638	0.8396	0.7938	0.7513	0.7118	0.6407	0.5787
4	0.9238	0.8885	0.8548	0.8227	0.7921	0.7350	0.6830	0.6355	0.5523	0.4823
5	0.9057	0.8626	0.8219	0.7835	0.7473	0.6806	0.6209	0.5674	0.4761	0.4019
6	0.8880	0.8375	0.7903	0.7462	0.7050	0.6302	0.5645	0.5066	0.4104	0.3349
7	0.8706	0.8131	0.7599	0.7170	0.6651	0.5835	0.5132	0.4523	0.3538	0.2791
8	0.8535	0.7894	0.7307	0.6768	0.6274	0.5403	0.4665	0.4039	0.3050	0.2326
9	0.8368	0.7664	0.7026	0.6446	0.5919	0.5002	0.4241	0.3606	0.2630	0.1938
10	0.8203	0.7441	0.6756	0.6139	0.5584	0.4632	0.3855	0.3220	0.2267	0.1615
11	0.8043	0.7224	0.6496	0.5847	0.5268	0.4289	0.3505	0.2875	0.1954	0.1346
12	0.7885	0.7014	0.6246	0.5568	0.4970	0.3971	0.3186	0.2567	0.1685	0.1122
13	0.7730	0.6810	0.6006	0.5303	0.4688	0.3677	0.2897	0.2292	0.1452	0.0935
14	0.7579	0.6611	0.5775	0.5051	0.4423	0.3405	0.2633	0.2046	0.1252	0.0779
15	0.7430	0.6419	0.5553	0.4810	0.4173	0.3152	0.2394	0.1827	0.1079	0.0649
16	0.7284	0.6232	0.5339	0.4581	0.3936	0.2919	0.2176	0.1631	0.0930	0.0541
17	0.7142	0.6050	0.5134	0.4363	0.3714	0.2703	0.1978	0.1456	0.0802	0.0451
18	0.7002	0.5874	0.4936	0.4155	0.3503	0.2502	0.1799	0.1300	0.0691	0.0376
19	0.6864	0.5703	0.4746	0.3957	0.3305	0.2317	0.1635	0.1161	0.0596	0.0313
20	0.6730	0.5537	0.4564	0.3769	0.3118	0.2145	0.1486	0.1037	0.0514	0.0261
25	0.6095	0.4776	0.3751	0.2953	0.2330	0.1460	0.0923	0.0588	0.0245	0.0105
30	0.5521	0.4120	0.3083	0.2314	0.1741	0.0994	0.0573	0.0334	0.0116	0.0042
40	0.4529	0.3066	0.2083	0.1420	0.0972	0.0460	0.0221	0.0107	0.0026	0.0007
50	0.3715	0.2281	0.1407	0.0872	0.0543	0.0213	0.0085	0.0035	0.0006	0.0001